INTERNATIONAL NARCOTICS CONTROL E
ORGANE INTERNATIONAL DE CONTRÔLE DES STUPEFIAN
JUNTA INTERNACIONAL DE FISCALIZACIÓN DE ESTUPEFACIENTES

Psychotropic Substances
Substances psychotropes
Sustancias sicotrópicas

Statistics for 2005
Assessments of Annual
Medical and Scientific Requirements
for Substances in Schedules II, III and IV
of the Convention on Psychotropic Substances of 1971

Statistiques pour 2005
Prévisions des besoins annuels
médicaux et scientifiques concernant
les substances des Tableaux II, III et IV
de la Convention de 1971 sur les substances psychotropes

Estadísticas de 2005
Previsiones de las necesidades anuales
para fines médicos y científicos
de las sustancias de las Listas II, III y IV
del Convenio de 1971 sobre Sustancias Sicotrópicas

UNITED NATIONS
NATIONS UNIES
NACIONES UNIDAS
New York, 2007

E/INCB/2006/3

UNITED NATIONS PUBLICATION
Sales No.: E/F/S.07.XI.14
ISBN-10: 92-1-048114-3
ISBN-13: 978-92-1-048114-4
ISSN: 0253-9403

CONTENTS

TABLE DES MATIÈRES

ÍNDICE

Introduction

1.   In addition to its annual report, the International Narcotics Control Board (INCB) publishes technical information in accordance with the following provisions of the Convention on Psychotropic Substances of 1971:

"Article 18

"Reports of the Board

"1.   The Board shall prepare annual reports on its work containing an analysis of the statistical information at its disposal, and, in appropriate cases, an account of the explanations, if any, given by or required of Governments, together with any observations and recommendations which the Board desires to make. The Board may make such additional reports as it considers necessary. The reports shall be submitted to the Council through the Commission, which may make such comments as it sees fit.

"2.   The reports of the Board shall be communicated to the Parties and subsequently published by the Secretary-General. The Parties shall permit their unrestricted distribution."

2.   The technical data are published for control purposes and to meet the needs of researchers, enterprises and the general public. Pursuant to the provisions of article 16 , paragraph 4, parties are required to furnish to the Board annual statistical reports relating to the substances listed in Schedules I-IV of the 1971 Convention. The statistical data that parties to the 1971 Convention are required to furnish to the Board differ according to the Schedule in which a given substance is included. The individual tables of the present technical report are based on those data.

3.   Data reported later than 1 November 2006 could not be taken into consideration in preparing this technical report.

4.   In 2004 and 2005, the Board carried out a survey of needs of users of its technical reports on narcotic drugs and psychotropic substances. Information from users was obtained, inter alia, by means of a questionnaire that was sent to the competent authorities of all countries and territories, selected pharmaceutical companies and other users, including international organizations and associations of professionals.

5.   Based on the information received during the survey, the Board decided to make some modifications to the technical report on psychotropic substances. Introductory notes have been added before each statistical table to provide more detailed explanations on the information contained in the publication. Table IV, which presents the comparative analysis of the levels of calculated consumption for psychotropic substances, has been expanded to include relevant information on two substances, namely buprenorphine and methylphenidate.

Introduction

1.   Outre son rapport annuel, l'Organe international de contrôle des stupéfiants (OICS) publie des informations techniques conformément aux dispositions ci-après de la Convention de 1971 sur les substances psychotropes.

"Article 18

Rapports de l'Organe

1.   L'Organe établit sur ses travaux des rapports annuels dans lesquels figurent une analyse des renseignements statistiques dont il dispose et, dans les cas appropriés, un exposé des explications que les gouvernements ont pu fournir ou ont été requis de fournir, ainsi que toute observation et recommandation que l'Organe peut vouloir formuler. L'Organe peut également faire tous rapports supplémentaires qu'il peut juger nécessaires. Les rapports sont présentés au Conseil par l'intermédiaire de la Commission, qui peut formuler les observations qu'elle juge opportunes.

2.   Les rapports de l'Organe sont communiqués aux Parties et publiés ultérieurement par le Secrétaire général. Les Parties autorisent la libre distribution de ces rapports."

2.   Les renseignements techniques sont publiés à des fins de contrôle et à l'intention des chercheurs, des entreprises et du public. Conformément aux dispositions du paragraphe 4 de l'article 16, les Parties sont tenues de fournir à l'Organe des rapports statistiques annuels sur les substances des Tableaux I à IV de la Convention de 1971. Les informations statistiques que les Parties à la Convention de 1971 ont l'obligation de fournir à l'Organe varient selon le tableau auquel appartient une substance donnée. Les différents tableaux du présent rapport technique sont basés sur ces données.

3.   Les données communiquées après le 1er novembre 2006 n'ont pas été prises en compte pour la préparation du présent rapport technique.

4.   En 2004 et 2005, l'Organe a réalisé une enquête sur les besoins des utilisateurs de ses rapports techniques sur les stupéfiants et les substances psychotropes. Des renseignements ont été recueillis auprès des utilisateurs au moyen notamment d'un questionnaire qui a été adressé aux autorités compétentes de tous les pays et territoires, à certaines sociétés pharmaceutiques ainsi qu'à d'autres utilisateurs, dont des organisations internationales et des associations professionnelles.

5.   Compte tenu des renseignements reçus dans le cadre de cette enquête, l'Organe a décidé d'apporter quelques modifications au rapport technique sur les substances psychotropes. Des notes liminaires ont été ajoutées à chaque tableau statistique pour fournir des explications plus détaillées sur les informations contenues dans cette publication. Le tableau IV, qui présente l'analyse comparative des niveaux de consommation calculée des substances psychotropes, a été étoffé pour inclure des informations pertinentes sur deux substances, à savoir la buprénorphine et le méthylphénidate.

Introducción

1. La Junta Internacional de Fiscalización de Estupefacientes (JIFE) publica, además de su informe anual, información técnica de conformidad con las siguientes disposiciones del Convenio de 1971 sobre sustancias sicotrópicas:

"Artículo 18

Informes de la Junta

1. La Junta preparará informes anuales sobre su labor; dichos informes contendrán un análisis de los datos estadísticos de que disponga la Junta y, cuando proceda, una reseña de las declaraciones hechas por los gobiernos o que se les hayan pedido, si las hubiere, junto con las observaciones y recomendaciones que la Junta desee hacer. La Junta podrá preparar los informes complementarios que considere necesarios. Los informes serán sometidos al Consejo [Económico y Social] por intermedio de la Comisión, que formulará las observaciones que estime oportunas.

2. Los informes de la Junta serán comunicados a las Partes y publicados posteriormente por el Secretario General. Las Partes permitirán que se distribuyan sin restricciones."

2. Los datos técnicos se publican para fines de control y para satisfacer las necesidades de los investigadores, las empresas y el público en general. En cumplimiento de lo dispuesto en el párrafo 4 del artículo 16, se pide a las Partes que faciliten a la Junta informes estadísticos anuales en relación con las sustancias incluidas en las Listas I a IV del Convenio de 1971. Los datos estadísticos que las Partes en el Convenio de 1971 deben suministrar a la Junta varían según la Lista en la cual esté incluida la sustancia de que se trate. En los diferentes cuadros del presente informe técnico se resumen esos datos.

3. Los datos comunicados después del 1.º de noviembre de 2006 no se pudieron tener en cuenta al preparar este informe técnico.

4. En 2004 y 2005 la Junta realizó un estudio de las necesidades de los usuarios de sus informes técnicos sobre estupefacientes y sustancias sicotrópicas. La información proporcionada por los usuarios se obtuvo mediante, entre otras cosas, un cuestionario que se envió a las autoridades competentes de todos los países y territorios, determinadas empresas farmacéuticas y otros usuarios, incluso organizaciones internacionales y asociaciones de profesionales.

5. Sobre la base de la información recibida en el marco del estudio, la Junta decidió introducir algunas modificaciones en los informes técnicos sobre sustancias sicotrópicas. Se han agregado notas introductorias delante de cada cuadro estadístico para explicar más detalladamente la información presentada en la publicación. Se ha ampliado el cuadro IV, que contiene un análisis comparativo de los niveles calculados de consumo de sustancias sicotrópicas, a fin de incluir información pertinente sobre dos sustancias, a saber, la buprenorfina y el metilfenidato.

Table I.   Parties and non-parties to the Convention on Psychotropic Substances of 1971, by continent

Tableau I.   Parties et non-parties à la Convention de 1971 sur les substances psychotropes, par continent

Cuadro I.   Partes y no partes en el Convenio de 1971 sobre las Sustancias Sicotrópicas, por continente

Continent Continente	Party to the 1971 Convention[a] Partie à la Convention de 1971[a] Parte en el Convenio de 1971[a]		Non-party to the 1971 Convention Non-partie à la Convention de 1971 No parte en el Convenio de 1971
Africa **Afrique** **África** *Number of States:* *Nombre d'États:* *Número de Estados:* 53 *Parties:* *Parties:* *Partes:* 51 *Non-parties:* *Non-parties:* *No partes:* 2	Algeria (14.7.1978) Algérie Argelia Angola (26.10.2005) Benin (6.11.1973) Bénin Botswana (27.12.1984) Burkina Faso (20.1.1987) Burundi (18.2.1993) Cameroon (15.5.1981) Cameroun Camerún Cape Verde (24.5.1990) Cap-Vert Cabo Verde Central African Republic (15.10.2001) République centrafricaine República Centroafricana Chad (9.6.1995) Tchad Comoros (1.3.2000) Comores Comoras Congo (3.3.2004) Côte d'Ivoire* (11.4.1984)	Dem. Rep. of the Congo (12.10.1977) Rép. dém. du Congo Rep. Dem. del Congo Djibouti (22.2.2001) Egypt (14.6.1972) Égypte Egipto Eritrea (30.1.2002) Érythrée Ethiopia (23.6.1980) Éthiopie Etiopía Gabon (14.10.1981) Gabón Gambia (23.4.1996) Gambie Ghana (10.4.1990) Guinea (27.12.1990) Guinée Guinea-Bissau (27.10.1995) Guinée-Bissau Kenya (19.10.2000) Lesotho (23.4.1975) Libyan Arab Jamahiriya (24.4.1979) Jamah. arabe libyenne Jamahiriya Árabe Libia	Equatorial Guinea Guinée équatoriale Guinea Ecuatorial Liberia Libéria

Table I.   Parties and non-parties to the 1971 Convention *(continued)*
Tableau I.   Parties et non-parties à la Convention de 1971 *(suite)*
Cuadro I.   Partes y no partes en el Convenio de 1971 *(continuación)*

Continent Continente	Party to the 1971 Convention[a] Partie à la Convention de 1971[a] Parte en el Convenio de 1971[a]		Non-party to the 1971 Convention Non-partie à la Convention de 1971 No parte en el Convenio de 1971
Africa **Afrique** **África**	Madagascar (20.6.1974)	Seychelles (27.2.1992)	
	Malawi (9.4.1980)	Sierra Leone (6.6.1994) Sierra Leona	
	Mali (31.10.1995) Malí	Somalia (2.9.1986) Somalie	
	Mauritania (20.10.1989) Mauritanie	South Africa (27.11.1972) Afrique du Sud Sudáfrica	
	Mauritius (8.5.1973) Maurice Mauricio	Sudan (26.7.1993) Soudan Sudán	
	Morocco (11.2.1980) Maroc Marruecos	Swaziland (3.10.1995) Swazilandia	
	Mozambique (8.6.1998)	Togo (17.5.1976)	
	Namibia (31.3.1998) Namibie	Tunisia (23.7.1979) Tunisie Túnez	
	Niger (10.11.1992) Níger	Uganda (15.4.1988) Ouganda	
	Nigeria (23.5.1981) Nigéria	United Republic of Tanzania (7.12.2000) République-Unie de Tanzanie República Unida de Tanzanía	
	Rwanda (15.7.1981)		
	Sao Tome and Principe (20.6.1996) Sao Tomé-et-Principe Santo Tomé y Príncipe	Zambia (28.5.1993) Zambie	
	Senegal (10.6.1977) Sénégal	Zimbabwe (30.7.1993)	

Table I.   Parties and non-parties to the 1971 Convention *(continued)*
Tableau I.   Parties et non-parties à la Convention de 1971 *(suite)*
Cuadro I.   Partes y no partes en el Convenio de 1971 *(continuación)*

Continent Continente	Party to the 1971 Convention[a] Partie à la Convention de 1971[a] Parte en el Convenio de 1971[a]		Non-party to the 1971 Convention Non-partie à la Convention de 1971 No parte en el Convenio de 1971

The Americas
Les Amériques
Las Américas
 	
Number of States:
Nombre d'États:
Número de Estados:
35
 	
Parties:
Parties:
Partes:
34
 	
Non-parties:
Non-parties:
No partes:
1
	Antigua and Barbuda
	    (5.4.1993)
	Antigua-et-Barbuda
	Antigua y Barbuda
	
	Argentina (16.2.1978)
	Argentine
	
	Bahamas (31.8.1987)
	
	Barbados (28.1.1975)
	Barbade
	
	Belize (18.12.2001)
	Belice
	
	Bolivia (18.3.1985)
	Bolivie
	
	Brazil (14.2.1973)
	Brésil
	Brasil
	
	Canada (18.6.1987)
	Canadá
	
	Chile (8.5.1972)
	Chili
	
	Colombia (12.6.1981)
	Colombie
	
	Costa Rica (16.2.1977)
	
	Cuba (26.4.1976)
	
	Dominica (24.9.1993)
	Dominique
	
	Dominican Republic
	    (19.11.1975)
	République dominicaine
	República Dominicana
	
	Ecuador (7.9.1973)
	Équateur
	
	El Salvador (11.6.1998)
		Grenada (25.4.1980)
		Grenade
		Granada
		
		Guatemala (13.8.1979)
		
		Guyana (4.5.1977)
		
		Honduras (23.5.2005)
		
		Jamaica (6.10.1989)
		Jamaïque
		
		Mexico (20.2.1975)
		Mexique
		México
		
		Nicaragua (24.10.1973)
		
		Panama (18.2.1972)
		Panamá
		
		Paraguay (3.2.1972)
		
		Peru (21.2.1979)
		Pérou
		Perú
		
		Saint Kitts and Nevis
		    (9.5.1994)
		Saint-Kitts-et-Nevis
		Saint Kitts y Nevis
		
		Saint Lucia (16.1.2003)
		Sainte-Lucie
		Santa Lucía
		
		Saint Vincent and
		    the Grenadines (3.12.2001)
		Saint-Vincent-et-les-
		    Grenadines
		San Vicente y las Granadinas
		
		Suriname (29.3.1990)
		
		Trinidad and Tobago
		    (14.3.1979)
		Trinité-et-Tobago
		Trinidad y Tabago
			Haiti
			Haïti
			Haití

Table I. Parties and non-parties to the 1971 Convention *(continued)*
Tableau I. Parties et non-parties à la Convention de 1971 *(suite)*
Cuadro I. Partes y no partes en el Convenio de 1971 *(continuación)*

Continent Continente	Party to the 1971 Convention[a] Partie à la Convention de 1971[a] Parte en el Convenio de 1971[a]		Non-party to the 1971 Convention Non-partie à la Convention de 1971 No parte en el Convenio de 1971
The Americas **Les Amériques** **Las Américas**	United States (16.4.1980) États-Unis Estados Unidos Uruguay (16.3.1976)	Venezuela (Bolivarian Rep. of) (23.5.1972) Venezuela (Rép. bolivarienne du) Venezuela (Rep. Bolivariana de)	
Asia **Asie** *Number of States: Nombre d'États: Número de Estados:* 46 *Parties: Parties: Partes:* 43 *Non-parties: Non-parties: No partes:* 3	Afghanistan (21.5.1985) Afganistán Armenia (13.9.1993) Arménie Azerbaijan (11.1.1999) Azerbaïdjan Azerbaiyán Bahrain (7.2.1990) Bahreïn Bahrein Bangladesh (11.10.1990) Bhutan (18.8.2005) Bhoutan Bhután Brunei Darussalam (24.11.1987) Brunéi Darussalam Cambodia (7.7.2005) Cambodge Camboya China (23.8.1985) Chine Georgia (8.1.1998) Géorgie India (23.4.1975) Inde Indonesia (19.12.1996) Indonésie Iran (Islamic Rep. of) (9.8.2000) Iran (Rép. islamique d') Irán (Rep. Islámica del)	Iraq (18.5.1976) Israel (10.6.1993) Israël Japan (31.8.1990) Japon Japón Jordan (8.8.1975) Jordanie Jordania Kazakhstan (29.4.1997) Kazajstán Kuwait (13.7.1979) Koweït Kyrgyzstan (7.10.1994) Kirghizistan Kirguistán Lao People's Democratic Republic (22.9.1997) République démocratique populaire lao República Democrática Popular Lao Lebanon (15.12.1994) Liban Líbano Malaysia (22.7.1986) Malaisie Malasia	Democratic People's Republic of Korea République populaire démocratique de Corée República Popular Democrática de Corea Nepal Népal Timor-Leste

8

Table I.   Parties and non-parties to the 1971 Convention *(continued)*
Tableau I.   Parties et non-parties à la Convention de 1971 *(suite)*
Cuadro I.   Partes y no partes en el Convenio de 1971 *(continuación)*

Continent Continente	Party to the 1971 Convention[a] Partie à la Convention de 1971[a] Parte en el Convenio de 1971[a]		Non-party to the 1971 Convention Non-partie à la Convention de 1971 No parte en el Convenio de 1971
Asia **Asie**	Maldives (7.9.2000) Maldivas Mongolia (22.12.1999) Mongolie Myanmar (20.6.1994) Oman (3.7.1997) Omán Pakistan (9.6.1977) Pakistán Philippines (7.6.1974) Filipinas Qatar (18.12.1986) Rep. of Korea (12.1.1978) République de Corée República de Corea Saudi Arabia (29.1.1975) Arabie saoudite Arabia Saudita Singapore (17.9.1990) Singapour Singapur Sri Lanka (15.3.1993)	Syrian Arab Rep. (8.3.1976) République arabe syrienne República Árabe Siria Tajikistan (26.3.1997) Tadjikistan Tayikistán Thailand (21.11.1975) Thaïlande Tailandia Turkey (1.4.1981) Turquie Turquía Turkmenistan (21.2.1996) Turkménistan Turkmenistán United Arab Emirates (21.11.1975) Émirats arabes unis Emiratos Árabes Unidos Uzbekistan (12.7.1995) Ouzbékistan Uzbekistán Viet Nam (4.11.1997) Yemen (23.6.1996) Yémen	
Europe **Europa** *Number of States:* *Nombre d'États:* *Número de Estados:* 45 *Parties:* *Parties:* *Partes:* 44 *Non-parties:* *Non-parties:* *No partes:* 1	Albania (24.1.2003) Albanie Austria (23.6.1997) Autriche Belarus (15.12.1978) Bélarus Belarús Belgium (25.10.1995) Belgique Bélgica Bosnia and Herzegovina (1.9.1993) Bosnie-Herzégovine Bosnia y Herzegovina	Bulgaria (18.5.1972) Bulgarie Croatia (26.7.1993) Croatie Croacia Cyprus (26.11.1973) Chypre Chipre Czech Rep. (30.12.1993) République tchèque República Checa Denmark (18.4.1975) Danemark Dinamarca	Andorra Andorre

9

Table I.   Parties and non-parties to the 1971 Convention *(continued)*
Tableau I.   Parties et non-parties à la Convention de 1971 *(suite)*
Cuadro I.   Partes y no partes en el Convenio de 1971 *(continuación)*

Continent Continente	Party to the 1971 Convention[a] Partie à la Convention de 1971[a] Parte en el Convenio de 1971[a]		Non-party to the 1971 Convention Non-partie à la Convention de 1971 No parte en el Convenio de 1971
Europe **Europa**	Estonia (5.7.1996) Estonie	Luxembourg (7.2.1991) Luxemburgo	
	Finland (20.11.1972) Finlande Finlandia	Malta (22.2.1990) Malte	
		Moldova[b] (16.5.1995)	
	France (28.1.1975) Francia	Monaco (6.7.1977) Mónaco	
	Germany (8.11.1976) Allemagne Alemania	Montenegro[c] (23.10.2006) Monténégro	
	Greece (10.2.1977) Grèce Grecia	Netherlands (8.9.1993) Pays-Bas Países Bajos	
	Holy See (7.1.1976) Saint-Siège Santa Sede	Norway (18.7.1975) Norvège Noruega	
	Hungary (19.7.1979) Hongrie Hungría	Poland (3.1.1975) Pologne Polonia	
	Iceland (18.12.1974) Islande Islandia	Portugal (20.4.1979)	
	Ireland (7.8.1992) Irlande Irlanda	Romania (21.1.1993) Roumanie Rumania	
	Italy (27.11.1981) Italie Italia	Russian Federation (3.11.1978) Fédération de Russie Federación de Rusia	
	Latvia (16.7.1993) Lettonie Letonia	San Marino (10.10.2000) Saint-Marin	
	Liechtenstein (24.11.1999)	Serbia[d] (12.3.2001) Serbie Serbia	
	Lithuania (28.2.1994) Lituanie Lituania	Slovakia (28.5.1993) Slovaquie Eslovaquia	

Table I.   Parties and non-parties to the 1971 Convention *(concluded)*
Tableau I.   Parties et non-parties à la Convention de 1971 *(fin)*
Cuadro I.   Partes y no partes en el Convenio de 1971 *(conclusión)*

Continent Continente	Party to the 1971 Convention[a] Partie à la Convention de 1971[a] Parte en el Convenio de 1971[a]		Non-party to the 1971 Convention Non-partie à la Convention de 1971 No parte en el Convenio de 1971
Europe **Europa**	Slovenia (6.7.1992) Slovénie Eslovenia Spain (20.7.1973) Espagne España Sweden (5.12.1972) Suède Suecia Switzerland (22.4.1996) Suisse Suiza	The former Yugoslav Republic of Macedonia (13.10.1993) L'ex-République yougoslave de Macédoine La ex República Yugoslava de Macedonia Ukraine (20.11.1978) Ucrania United Kingdom (24.3.1986) Royaume-Uni Reino Unido	
Oceania **Océanie** **Oceanía** *Number of States:* *Nombre d'États:* *Número de Estados:* 15 *Parties:* *Parties:* *Partes:* 8 *Non-parties:* *Non-parties:* *No partes:* 7	Australia (19.5.1982) Australie Fiji (25.3.1993) Fidji Marshall Islands (9.8.1991) Îles Marshall Islas Marshall Micronesia (Federated States of) (29.4.1991) Micronésie (États fédérés de) Micronesia (Estados Federados de)	New Zealand (7.6.1990) Nouvelle-Zélande Nueva Zelandia Palau (19.8.1998) Palaos Papua New Guinea (28.10.1980) Papouasie-Nouvelle-Guinée Papua Nueva Guinea Tonga (24.10.1975)	Cook Islands Îles Cook Islas Cook Kiribati Nauru Samoa Solomon Islands Îles Salomon Islas Salomón Tuvalu Vanuatu

World total	*Number of States — Nombre d'États — Número de Estados*	194
Total mondial	*Parties — Parties — Partes*	179
Total mundial	*Non-parties — Non-parties — No partes*	15

[a]For parties, the dates on which the instruments of ratification or accession were deposited are indicated in parentheses. — Pour les parties, la date du dépôt des instruments de ratification ou d'adhésion est indiquée entre parenthèses. — Para los países que son partes en el Convenio, se indican entre paréntesis las fechas en que se depositaron los instrumentos de ratificación o adhesión.

[b] Since 16 October 2006, "Moldova" has replaced "Republic of Moldova" as the short name that is used in the United Nations.— Depuis le 16 octobre 2006, "Moldova" est la forme courte utilisée dans l'Organisation des Nations Unies à la place de "Republique de Moldova". — A partir del 16 de octubre de 2006, "Moldova" reemplaza a "República de Moldova" como nombre abreviado en las Naciones Unidas.

[c] By its resolution 60/264 of 28 June 2006, the General Assembly decided to admit Montenegro to membership in the United Nations. — Par sa résolution 60/264 du 28 juin 2006, l'Assemblée générale a décidé d'admettre le Monténégro comme membre des Nations Unies. — En su resolución 60/264, de 28 de junio de 2006, la Asamblea General decidió admitir a Montenegro como Estado Miembro de las Naciones Unidas.

[d] Since 3 June 2006, the membership of Serbia and Montenegro in the United Nations has been continued by Serbia. — Depuis le 3 juin 2006, la Serbie a succédé à la Serbie-et-Monténégro comme membre des Nations Unies. — A partir del 3 de junio de 2006, Serbia ha sucedido a Serbia y Montenegro como Estado Miembro de las Naciones Unidas.

Table II.   Receipt of statistics for 2005

Table II below reflects the extent of compliance by Governments with the provisions of article 16 of the 1971 Convention in submitting to INCB annual statistical information for 2005. The table also shows to what extent Governments have voluntarily submitted additional information to INCB, pursuant to recommendations of the Board endorsed by the Economic and Social Council, that is, quarterly statistics on international trade in substances in Schedule II and information on countries of destination of exports and countries of origin of imports of substances in Schedules III and IV (Council resolutions 1981/7, 1985/15 and 1987/30). The following symbols are used in table II:

Footnote (^{b}) indicates that the State is not a party to the 1971 Convention;

A question mark (?) indicates that the statistical report for 2005 had not been received by 1 November 2006;

The etter "×" indicates that the substances listed in the relevant Schedule are under national control and that the competent administration has furnished for 2005 at least part of the required statistical information;

A dash (—) indicates that the substances listed in the relevant Schedule are under national control but no movement of the substances has been reported by the competent administration;

The letter "o" indicates that substances in Schedule II are neither imported into nor exported from the country or territory and therefore the Government was not requested by INCB to provide quarterly trade statistics;

Two dots (. .) indicate that the competent administration was not able to furnish data on the substances in the relevant Schedule for 2005, mostly due to a lack of legislative and/or administrative measures enabling the data to be collected. If, however, a competent administration has supplied information on some of the substances listed in the respective Schedule, such cases are mentioned in a footnote.

Countries and non-metropolitan territories are listed in English alphabetical order; the names of territories are shown in italics. The names of countries and territories are those that were in official use at the time the data were collected (in 2005).

Tableau II. Réception des statistiques pour 2005

Le Tableau II indique quels gouvernements se sont conformés aux dispositions de l'article 16 de la Convention de 1971 en soumettant à l'OICS des statistiques annuelles pour 2005. Ce Tableau indique aussi dans quelle mesure les gouvernements ont volontairement soumis à l'OICS des informations supplémentaires, conformément aux recommandations de l'Organe approuvées par le Conseil économique et social, c'est-à-dire des statistiques trimestrielles sur le commerce international des substances du Tableau II et des renseignements sur les pays de destination des exportations et les pays d'origine des importations de substances inscrites aux Tableaux III et IV (résolutions 1981/7, 1985/15 et 1987/30 du Conseil économique et social). Dans ce Tableau, les symboles suivants ont été utilisés:

L'appel de note (^{b}) indique que cet État est non partie à la Convention de 1971;

Un point d'interrogation (?) indique que le rapport statistique pour 2005 n'avait pas encore été reçu au 1er novembre 2006;

La lettre "×" indique que les substances inscrites à un tableau donné sont sous contrôle national et que l'administration compétente a fourni au moins une partie des données statistiques pour 2005;

Un tiret (—) indique que les substances inscrites à un tableau donné sont sous contrôle national, mais que l'administration compétente n'a enregistré aucun mouvement des substances en question;

La lettre "o" indique que des substances du Tableau II ne sont ni importées dans le pays ou le territoire, ni exportées de ce pays ou de ce territoire et que, par conséquent, l'OICS n'a pas demandé au gouvernement de fournir des statistiques trimestrielles sur le commerce de ces substances;

Deux points (. .) indiquent que l'administration compétente n'a pas été en mesure de fournir pour 2005 les statistiques relatives aux substances inscrites au Tableau en question du fait, le plus souvent, de l'insuffisance des mesures législatives ou administratives permettant de recueillir les informations requises. Au cas où les administrations compétentes ont fourni des informations sur certaines des substances inscrites à ce Tableau, mention en est faite dans une note.

Les pays et territoires figurent dans l'ordre alphabétique anglais. Les noms des territoires apparaissent en italique. Les noms des pays et territoires sont ceux qui étaient officiellement en usage au moment où les données ont été recueillies (en 2005).

Cuadro II.   Recepción de las estadísticas de 2005

En el cuadro II se refleja la medida en que los gobiernos cumplen con las disposiciones del artículo 16 del Convenio de 1971 en lo que respecta a la presentación a la JIFE de la información estadística anual correspondiente a 2005. En el cuadro también se indica en qué medida los gobiernos han presentado voluntariamente a la JIFE, en cumplimiento de las recomendaciones de la Junta, que hizo suyas el Consejo Económico y Social, información adicional, como, por ejemplo, estadísticas trimestrales sobre comercio internacional de sustancias incluidas en la Lista II e información sobre los países de destino de las exportaciones y los países de origen de las importaciones de sustancias incluidas en las Listas III y IV (resoluciones 1981/7, 1985/15 y 1987/30 del Consejo Económico y Social). En dicho cuadro se utilizan los símbolos siguientes:

La nota de pie de página (*b*) indica que el Estado es no parte en el Convenio de 1971;

El signo de interrogación (?) indica que al 1.º de noviembre de 2006 no se había recibido el informe estadístico correspondiente a 2005;

La letra "×" indica que las sustancias incluidas en la Lista correspondiente están sometidas a fiscalización nacional y que la administración competente ha facilitado por lo menos una parte de la información estadística requerida correspondiente a 2005;

El guión largo (—) indica que las sustancias incluidas en la Lista correspondiente están sometidas a fiscalización, pero que la administración competente no registró ningún movimiento;

La letra "o" indica que las sustancias incluidas en la Lista II no se importan ni se exportan de este país o región y que, por consiguiente, la JIFE no pidió al gobierno que suministrara estadísticas de comercio trimestrales;

Los dos puntos suspensivos (..) indican que la administración del país de que se trate no pudo facilitar datos correspondientes a 2005 acerca de las sustancias incluidas en la Lista pertinente debido a que todavía no se han adoptado medidas legislativas y administrativas que permitan reunir los datos. No obstante, si las administraciones competentes han suministrado información sobre algunas sustancias incluidas en la Lista respectiva, esos casos se mencionan en notas de pie de página.

Los países y territorios se enumeran en orden alfabético inglés. Los nombres de los territorios aparecen en letra cursiva. Los nombres de los países y territorios son los que se utilizaban oficialmente en el momento en que se obtuvo la información (en 2005).

Table II.   Receipt of statistics for 2005
Tableau II.   Réception des statistiques pour 2005
Cuadro II.   Recepción de las estadísticas de 2005

Country or territory / Pays ou territoire / País o territorio	Annual statistics, by Schedule / Statistiques annuelles, par Tableau / Estadísticas anuales, por Lista				Imports and exports / Importations et exportations / Importaciones y exportaciones					
					Annual[a] / Annuelles[a] / Anuales[a]		Quarterly / Trimestrielles / Trimestrales			
					Schedule III / Tableau III / Lista III	Schedule IV / Tableau IV / Lista IV	Schedule II / Tableau II / Lista II			
	I	II	III	IV			1	2	3	4
Afghanistan — Afganistán	?	?	?	?	?	?	?	?	?	?
Albania — Albanie	—	—	—	×	—	×	—	—	—	—
Algeria — Algérie — Argelia	—	—	—	×	—	×	—	—	—	—
Andorra — Andorre[b]	—	×	—	×		×	×	×	×	×
Angola	?	?	?	?	?	?	×	—	—	—
Anguilla — Anguila	?	?	?	?	?	?	?	?	?	?
Antigua and Barbuda — Antigua-et-Barbuda — Antigua y Barbuda	?	?	?	?	?	?	?	?	?	?
Argentina — Argentine	—	×	×	×	×	×	×	×	—	—
Armenia — Arménie	?	?	?	?	?	?	?	?	?	?
Aruba	?	?	?	?	?	?	?	?	?	?
Ascension Island — Île de l'Ascension — Isla de la Ascensión	—	—	—	—	—		?	?	?	?
Australia — Australie	×	×	×	×	×	×	×	×	×	×
Austria — Autriche	—	×	×	×	×	×	×	×	×	×
Azerbaijan — Azerbaïdjan — Azerbaiyán	—	—	—	×	—	×	?	?	?	?
Bahamas	—	×	—	—	—	—	×	×	×	—
Bahrain — Bahreïn — Bahrein	—	×	—	×	—	×	×	—	×	×
Bangladesh	—	—	—	×	—	×	—	—	—	—
Barbados — Barbade	—	×	×	×	×	×	×	×	—	—
Belarus — Bélarus — Belarús	—	—	×	×	×	×	—	—	—	—
Belgium — Belgique — Bélgica	—	×	×	×	×	×	×	×	×	×
Belize — Belice	?	?	?	?	?	?	—	—	—	—
Benin — Bénin	—	—	—	×	—	×	—	—	—	—
Bermuda — Bermudes — Bermudas	?	?	?	?	?	?	?	?	?	?
Bhutan — Bhoutan — Bhután	—	—	—	—	—	—	?	?	?	?
Bolivia — Bolivie	—	×	×	×	—	—	—	×	×	×
Bosnia and Herzegovina — Bosnie-Herzégovine — Bosnia y Herzegovina	?	?	?	?	?	?	?	?	?	?
Botswana	—	×	×	×	×	×	—	×	×	×
Brazil — Brésil — Brasil	—	×	×	×	×	×	×	×	×	×

Table II.   Receipt of statistics for 2005 *(continued)*
Tableau II.   Réception des statistiques pour 2005 *(suite)*
Cuadro II.   Recepción de las estadísticas de 2005 *(continuación)*

Country or territory Pays ou territoire País o territorio	Annual statistics, by Schedule Statistiques annuelles, par Tableau Estadísticas anuales, por Lista				Imports and exports — Importations et exportations — Importaciones y exportaciones					
					Annual[a] Annuelles[a] Anuales[a]		Quarterly Trimestrielles Trimestrales			
					Schedule III Tableau III Lista III	Schedule IV Tableau IV Lista IV	Schedule II — Tableau II — Lista II			
	I	II	III	IV			1	2	3	4
British Virgin Islands — Îles Vierges britanniques — Islas Vírgenes Británicas	?	?	?	?	?	?	—	×	—	—
Brunei Darussalam — Brunéi Darussalam	—	×	×	×	×	×	—	×	×	×
Bulgaria — Bulgarie	—	×	×	×	×	×	—	—	—	×
Burkina Faso	—	—	—	×	—	×	—	—	—	—
Burundi	—	—	—	×	—	×	×	—	—	—
Cambodia — Cambodge — Camboya	—	—	—	×	—	×	—	—	—	—
Cameroon — Cameroun — Camerún	?	?	?	?	?	?	—	—	—	—
Canada — Canadá	—	×	×	×	×	×	—	×	×	×
Cape Verde — Cap-Vert — Cabo Verde	—	—	—	×	—	×	?	?	?	?
Cayman Islands — Îles Caïmanes — Islas Caimanes	?	?	?	?	?	?	?	?	?	?
Central African Republic — République centrafricaine — República Centroafricana	?	?	?	?	?	?	?	?	?	?
Chad — Tchad	?	?	?	?	?	?	—	—	—	—
Chile — Chili	—	×	×	×	×	×	×	×	×	×
China — Chine	×	×	×	×	×	×	—	×	—	—
Hong Kong SAR of China — RAS de Hong Kong (Chine) — RAE de Hong Kong de China										
Macao SAR of China — RAS de Macao (Chine) — RAE de Macao de China	—	×	×	×	×	×	×	×	×	—
Christmas Island — Île Christmas — Isla Christmas	—	×	—	—	—	—	×	—	×	×
Cocos (Keeling) Islands — Îles Cocos (Keeling) — Islas Cocos (Keeling)	—	—	—	—	—	—	—	—	—	—
Cook Islands — Îles Cook — Islas Cook[b]	×	×	×	×	×	×	×	×	×	×
Colombia — Colombie	—	×	×	×	×	×	×	×	×	—
Comoros — Comores — Comoras	?	?	?	?	?	?	—	—	—	—
Congo	?	?	?	?	?	?	?	?	?	?
Costa Rica	—	×	—	×	—	×	×	—	×	×
Côte d'Ivoire	—	—	—	×	—	×	—	—	—	—
Croatia — Croatie — Croacia	×	—	×	×	×	×	—	—	×	—

Table II. Receipt of statistics for 2005 (continued)
Tableau II. Réception des statistiques pour 2005 (suite)
Cuadro II. Recepción de las estadísticas de 2005 (continuación)

Country or territory / Pays ou territoire / País o territorio	Annual statistics, by Schedule / Statistiques annuelles, par Tableau / Estadísticas anuales, por Lista				Imports and exports / Importations et exportations / Importaciones y exportaciones					
					Annual[a] / Annuelles[a] / Anuales[a]		Quarterly / Trimestrielles / Trimestrales			
					Schedule III / Tableau III / Lista III	Schedule IV / Tableau IV / Lista IV	Schedule II / Tableau II / Lista II			
	I	II	III	IV			1	2	3	4
Cuba	—	×	—	×	—	×	×	×	×	—
Cyprus — Chypre — Chipre	—	×	—	×	—	×	×	×	×	×
Czech Republic — République tchèque — República Checa	×	×	×	×	×	×	×	—	×	×
Dem. People's Republic of Korea — République populaire dém. de Corée — República Popular Dem. de Corea[b]	—	—	—	×	—	×	?	?	?	?
Democratic Republic of the Congo — Républiqe démocratique du Congo — República Democrática del Congo	—	—	×	×	×	×	?	?	?	?
Denmark — Danemark — Dinamarca	×	×	×	×	×	×	×	×	×	×
Djibouti	—	—	—	×	—	×	?	?	?	?
Dominica — Dominique	—	×	—	×	—	×	—	—	—	×
Dominican Republic — République dominicaine — República Dominicana	—	×	—	×	—	×	×	×	—	—
Ecuador — Équateur	—	×	×	×	×	×	×	×	—	×
Egypt — Égypte — Egipto	—	×	×	×	×	×	×	—	×	—
El Salvador	—	×	×	×	×	×	×	×	×	—
Equatorial Guinea — Guinée équatoriale — Guinea Ecuatorial[b]	?	?	?	?	?	?	?	?	?	?
Eritrea — Érythrée	—	—	—	×	—	×	—	—	—	—
Estonia — Estonie	—	×	×	×	×	×	×	×	×	×
Ethiopia — Éthiopie — Etiopía	—	—	—	×	—	×	?	?	?	?
Falkland Islands (Malvinas) — Îles Falkland (Malvinas) — Islas Malvinas (Falkland Islands)	—	×	×	—	×	—	×	—	×	—
Fiji — Fidji	?	?	?	?	?	?	?	?	?	?
Finland — Finlande — Finlandia	—	×	×	×	×	×	×	×	×	×
France — Francia	×	×	×	×	×	×	×	×	×	×
French Polynesia — Polynésie française — Polinesia Francesa	?	?	?	?	?	?	×	—	—	—
Gabon — Gabón	—	—	—	×	—	×	—	—	—	—
Gambia — Gambie	—	—	—	—	—	—	—	—	—	—
Georgia — Géorgie	—	—	×	×	×	×	—	—	—	—

Table II. Receipt of statistics for 2005 (continued)
Tableau II. Réception des statistiques pour 2005 (suite)
Cuadro II. Recepción de las estadísticas de 2005 (continuación)

Country or territory / Pays ou territoire / País o territorio	Annual statistics, by Schedule / Statistiques annuelles, par Tableau / Estadísticas anuales, por Lista				Imports and exports / Importations et exportations / Importaciones y exportaciones					
					Annual[a] / Annuelles[a] / Anuales[a]		Quarterly / Trimestrielles / Trimestrales			
					Schedule III / Tableau III / Lista III	Schedule IV / Tableau IV / Lista IV	Schedule II / Tableau II / Lista II			
	I	II	III	IV			1	2	3	4
Germany — Allemagne — Alemania	×	×	×	×	×	×	×	×	×	×
Ghana	—	—	—	×	—	×	—	—	—	—
Gibraltar	—	×	—	—	—	—	—	×	—	×
Greece — Grèce — Grecia	—	×	×	×	×	×	—	×	×	—
Grenada — Grenade — Granada	—	—	—	—	—	—	—	—	×	×
Guatemala	?	?	?	?	?	?	×	×	×	—
Guinea — Guinée	—	—	—	×	—	×	?	?	?	?
Guinea-Bissau — Guinée-Bissau	?	?	?	?	?	?	?	?	?	?
Guyana	—	—	—	×	—	—	—	—	—	—
Haiti — Haïti — Haití[b]	—	—	—	×	—	×	—	—	—	—
Holy See — Saint-Siège — Santa Sede	?	?	?	?	?	?	?	?	?	?
Honduras	?	?	?	?	?	?	—	—	×	×
Hungary — Hongrie — Hungría	×	×	×	×	×	×	—	×	×	—
Iceland — Islande — Islandia	—	×	×	×	×	×	×	×	×	×
India — Inde	—	×	×	×	×	×	—	×	×	×
Indonesia — Indonésie	×	×	×	×	×	×	×	×	×	×
Iran (Islamic Republic of) — Iran (République islamique d') — Irán (República Islámica del)	—	×	×	×	×	×	?	?	?	?
Iraq	?	?	?	?	?	?	?	?	?	?
Ireland — Irlande — Irlanda	×	×	×	×	×	×	×	×	×	×
Israel — Israël	×	×	×	×	×	×	×	×	—	×
Italy — Italie — Italia	—	×	×	×	×	×	×	—	×	—
Jamaica — Jamaïque	—	×	—	×	—	×	×	×	×	×
Japan — Japon — Japón	—	×	×	×	×	×	×	×	×	×
Jordan — Jordanie — Jordania	—	×	×	×	×	×	×	—	×	×
Kazakhstan — Kazajstán	—	—	—	×	—	×	?	?	?	?
Kenya	?	?	?	?	?	?	—	×	—	—
Kiribati[b]	?	?	?	?	?	?	—	—	—	—
Kuwait — Koweït	—	×	—	×	—	×	—	—	—	—
Kyrgyzstan — Kirghizistan — Kirguistán	—	—	—	×	—	×	—	—	—	—
Lao People's Democratic Republic — République dém. populaire lao — República dem. Popular Lao	—	—	—	×	—	×	—	×	×	—

19

Table II.   Receipt of statistics for 2005 *(continued)*
Tableau II.   Réception des statistiques pour 2005 *(suite)*
Cuadro II.   Recepción de las estadísticas de 2005 *(continuación)*

Country or territory / Pays ou territoire / País o territorio	Annual statistics, by Schedule / Statistiques annuelles, par Tableau / Estadísticas anuales, por Lista				Imports and exports / Importations et exportations / Importaciones y exportaciones					
					Annual[a] / Annuelles[a] / Anuales[a]		Quarterly / Trimestrielles / Trimestrales			
					Schedule III / Tableau III / Lista III	Schedule IV / Tableau IV / Lista IV	Schedule II / Tableau II / Lista II			
	I	II	III	IV			1	2	3	4
Latvia — Lettonie — Letonia	—	×	×	×	×	×	—	—	—	—
Lebanon — Liban — Líbano	—	×	—	×	—	×	×	×	×	×
Lesotho	—	×	—	×	—	×	?	?	?	?
Liberia — Libéria[b]	?	?	?	?	?	?	?	?	?	?
Libyan Arab Jamahiriya — Jamahiriya arabe libyenne — Jamahiriya Árabe Libia	—	—	—	×	—	×	—	—	—	—
Liechtenstein	c	c	c	c	c	c	c	c	c	c
Lithuania — Lituanie — Lituania	—	×	×	×	×	×	×	×	×	×
Luxembourg — Luxemburgo	—	×	×	×	—	—	×	×	×	×
Madagascar	—	—	—	—	—	—	—	—	—	—
Malawi	?	?	?	?	?	?	—	—	×	—
Malaysia — Malaisie — Malasia	×	×	×	×	×	×	×	×	×	×
Maldives — Maldivas	—	—	—	×	—	×	?	?	?	?
Mali — Malí	—	—	×	×	—	—	—	—	—	—
Malta — Malte	—	×	×	×	×	×	×	—	—	—
Marshall Islands — Îles Marshall — Islas Marshall	—	—	—	—	—	—	—	—	—	—
Mauritania — Mauritanie	?	?	?	?	?	?	—	—	—	—
Mauritius — Maurice — Mauricio	—	×	×	×	×	×	×	—	×	—
Mexico — Mexique — México	?	?	?	?	?	?	×	×	×	×
Micronesia (Federated States of) — Micronésie (États fédérés de) — Micronesia (Estados Federados de)	—	—	—	×	—	×	—	—	—	—
Monaco — Mónaco	d	d	d	d	d	d	d	d	d	d
Mongolia — Mongolie	?	?	?	?	?	?	×	—	×	—
Montserrat	?	?	?	?	?	?	—	—	—	—
Morocco — Maroc — Marruecos	—	—	×	×	×	×	×	×	—	—
Mozambique	?	?	?	?	?	?	—	—	—	—
Myanmar	—	—	—	—	—	—	—	—	—	—
Namibia — Namibie	—	×	×	×	×	×	?	?	?	?
Nauru[b]	?	?	?	?	?	?	—	—	—	—
Nepal — Népal[b]	?	?	?	?	?	?	—	—	—	—
Netherlands — Pays-Bas — Países Bajos	×	×	×	×	×	×	?	?	?	?

Table II.   Receipt of statistics for 2005 *(continued)*
Tableau II.   Réception des statistiques pour 2005 *(suite)*
Cuadro II.   Recepción de las estadísticas de 2005 *(continuación)*

Country or territory / Pays ou territoire / País o territorio	Annual statistics, by Schedule / Statistiques annuelles, par Tableau / Estadísticas anuales, por Lista				Imports and exports / Importations et exportations / Importaciones y exportaciones					
					Annual[a] / Annuelles[a] / Anuales[a]		Quarterly / Trimestrielles / Trimestrales — Schedule II / Tableau II / Lista II			
	I	II	III	IV	Schedule III / Tableau III / Lista III	Schedule IV / Tableau IV / Lista IV	1	2	3	4
Netherlands Antilles — Antilles néerlandaises — Antillas Neerlandesas	—	×	×	×	×	×	—	×	×	×
New Caledonia — Nouvelle-Calédonie — Nueva Caledonia	—	×	—	×		×	—	—	—	×
New Zealand — Nouvelle-Zélande — Nueva Zelandia	×	×	×	×	×	×	×	×	×	×
Nicaragua	—	×	—	×	—	×	×	×	×	×
Niger — Níger	—	—	—	×		×	?	?	?	?
Nigeria — Nigéria	—	—	×	×	×	×	—	—	—	—
Niue — Nioué	?	?	?	?	?	?	?	?	?	?
Norfolk Island — Île Norfolk — Isla Norfolk	—	×	—	—	—	—	—	×	×	×
Norway — Norvège — Noruega	—	×	×	×	×	×	×	×	×	×
Oman — Omán	—	×	—	×	—	×	×	—	—	×
Pakistan — Pakistán	—	×	×	×	×	×	—	—	—	×
Palau — Palaos	—	×	—	×		×	—	×	×	—
Panama — Panamá	—	×	×	×	×	×	—	×	×	×
Papua New Guinea — Papouasie-Nouvelle-Guinée — Papua Nueva Guinea	?	?	?	?	?	?	?	?	?	?
Paraguay	?	?	?	?	?	?	×	—	×	×
Philippines — Filipinas	?	?	?	?	?	?	×	—	×	—
Poland — Pologne — Polonia	×	×	×	×	×	×	×	×	×	×
Portugal	—	×	×	×	×	×	—	×	×	×
Qatar	—	×	—	×	—	×	×	×	×	×
Republic of Korea — République de Corée — República de Corea	—	—	×	×	×	×	—	×	×	×
Republic of Moldova — République de Moldova — República de Moldova	?	?	?	?	?	?	?	?	?	?
Romania — Roumanie — Rumania	—	—	×	×	—	—	—	—	×	—
Russian Federation — Fédération de Russie — Federación de Rusia	—	×	×	×	×	—	—	—	—	—
Rwanda	—	—	—	×		×	—	—	—	—

Table II.   Receipt of statistics for 2005 *(continued)*
Tableau II.   Réception des statistiques pour 2005 *(suite)*
Cuadro II.   Recepción de las estadísticas de 2005 *(continuación)*

Country or territory / Pays ou territoire / País o territorio	Annual statistics, by Schedule / Statistiques annuelles, par Tableau / Estadísticas anuales, por Lista				Imports and exports / Importations et exportations / Importaciones y exportaciones					
					Annual[a] / Annuelles[a] / Anuales[a]		Quarterly / Trimestrielles / Trimestrales			
					Schedule III / Tableau III / Lista III	Schedule IV / Tableau IV / Lista IV	Schedule II / Tableau II / Lista II			
	I	II	III	IV			1	2	3	4
Saint Helena — Sainte-Hélène — Santa Elena	—	×	—	—	—	—	—	×	—	—
Saint Kitts and Nevis — Saint-Kitts-et-Nevis — Saint Kitts y Nevis	?	?	?	?	?	?	?	?	?	?
Saint Lucia — Sainte-Lucie — Santa Lucía	—	×	—	—	—	—	×	×	—	—
Saint Vincent and the Grenadines — Saint-Vincent-et-les-Grenadines — San Vicente y las Granadinas	—	×	×	×	×	×	×	×	—	×
Samoa[b]	—	—	—	×	—	×	?	?	?	?
San Marino — Saint-Marin	e	e	e	e	e	e	e	e	e	e
Sao Tome and Principe — Sao Tomé-et-Principe — Santo Tomé y Príncipe	—	—	—	×	—	×	—	—	—	—
Saudi Arabia — Arabie saoudite — Arabia Saudita	—	×	—	×	—	×	—	×	×	×
Senegal — Sénégal	—	—	—	×	—	×	?	?	?	?
Serbia and Montenegro — Serbie-et-Monténégro — Serbia y Montenegro	?	?	?	?	?	?	?	?	?	?
Seychelles	?	?	?	?	?	?	?	?	?	?
Sierra Leone — Sierra Leona	—	×	—	×	—	×	—	—	—	×
Singapore — Singapour — Singapur	×	×	×	×	×	×	×	×	×	×
Slovakia — Slovaquie — Eslovaquia	—	—	×	×	×	×	—	—	—	—
Slovenia — Slovénie — Eslovenia	—	×	×	×	×	×	×	×	×	×
Solomon Islands — Îles Salomon — Islas Salomón[b]	?	?	?	?	?	?	?	?	?	?
Somalia — Somalie	?	?	?	?	?	?	?	?	?	?
South Africa — Afrique du Sud — Sudáfrica	—	×	×	×	×	×	×	×	×	×
Spain — Espagne — España	×	×	×	×	×	×	×	×	×	×
Sri Lanka	—	×	—	×	—	×	×	—	×	×
Sudan — Soudan — Sudán	?	?	?	?	?	?	—	—	—	—
Suriname	—	—	—	×	—	×	×	—	×	—
Swaziland — Swazilandia	?	?	?	?	?	?	—	—	—	—
Sweden — Suède — Suecia	×	×	×	×	×	×	×	×	×	×

Table II.   Receipt of statistics for 2005 *(continued)*
Tableau II.   Réception des statistiques pour 2005 *(suite)*
Cuadro II.   Recepción de las estadísticas de 2005 *(continuación)*

Country or territory / Pays ou territoire / País o territorio	Annual statistics, by Schedule / Statistiques annuelles, par Tableau / Estadísticas anuales, por Lista				Imports and exports / Importations et exportations / Importaciones y exportaciones					
					Annual[a] / Annuelles[a] / Anuales[a]		Quarterly / Trimestrielles / Trimestrales			
	I	II	III	IV	Schedule III / Tableau III / Lista III	Schedule IV / Tableau IV / Lista IV	Schedule II / Tableau II / Lista II			
							1	2	3	4
Switzerland — Suisse — Suiza	×	×	×	×	×	×	×	×	×	×
Syrian Arab Republic — République arabe syrienne — República Árabe Siria	—	×	—	×	—	×	—	×	×	—
Tajikistan — Tadjikistan — Tayikistán	?	?	?	?	?	?	o	o	o	o
Thailand — Thaïlande — Tailandia	—	×	×	×	×	×	×	×	×	—
The form. Yug. Rep. of Macedonia — L'ex-Rép. yougosl. de Macédoine — La ex Rep. Yug. de Macedonia	—	—	—	×	—	×	?	?	?	?
Timor-Leste[b]	?	?	?	?	?	?	?	?	?	?
Togo	—	—	—	×	—	×	—	—	—	—
Tonga	—	×	—	×	—	×	—	—	—	—
Trinidad and Tobago — Trinité-et-Tobago — Trinidad y Tabago	—	×	×	×	×	×	×	×	—	—
Tristan da Cunha — Tristán da Cunha	?	?	?	?	?	?	?	?	?	?
Tunisia — Tunisie — Túnez	—	×	—	×	—	×	—	—	×	—
Turkey — Turquie — Turquía	—	×	—	×	—	×	—	×	×	×
Turkmenistan — Turkménistan — Turkmenistán	?	?	?	?	?	?	o	o	o	o
Turks and Caicos Islands — Îles Turques et Caïques — Islas Turcas y Caicos	—	×	—	—	—	—	—	×	—	—
Tuvalu[b]	?	?	?	?	?	?	?	?	?	?
Uganda — Ouganda	?	?	?	?	?	?	—	—	—	—
Ukraine — Ucrania	—	—	×	×	×	×	—	—	—	—
United Arab Emirates — Émirats arabes unis — Emiratos Árabes Unidos	—	×	—	×	—	×	×	—	×	×
United Kingdom — Royaume-Uni — Reino Unido	×	×	×	×	×	×	×	×	×	—
United Republic of Tanzania — République-Unie de Tanzanie — República Unida de Tanzanía	—	—	×	×	—	×	—	—	—	—
United States of America — États-Unis d'Amérique — Estados Unidos de América	×	×	×	×	×	×	×	×	×	—
Uruguay	?	?	?	?	?	?	×	×	×	×

Table II. Receipt of statistics for 2005 (concluded)
Tableau II. Réception des statistiques pour 2005 (fin)
Cuadro II. Recepción de las estadísticas de 2005 (conclusión)

Country or territory Pays ou territoire País o territorio	Annual statistics, by Schedule Statistiques annuelles, par Tableau Estadísticas anuales, por Lista				Imports and exports Importations et exportations Importaciones y exportaciones					
					Annual[c] Annuelles[a] Anuales[a]		Quarterly Trimestrielles Trimestrales			
					Schedule III Tableau III Lista III	Schedule IV Tableau IV Lista IV	Schedule II Tableau II Lista II			
	I	II	III	IV			1	2	3	4
Uzbekistan — Ouzbékistan — Uzbekistán	—	—	—	×	—	×	?	?	?	?
Vanuatu[b]	?	?	?	?	?	?	—	—	—	—
Venezuela (Bolivarian Rep. of) Venezuela (Rép. bolivarienne du) Venezuela (Rep. Bolivariana de)	—	×	—	×	—	×	—	—	×	×
Viet Nam	—	—	—	×	—	×	?	?	?	?
Wallis and Futuna Islands — Îles Wallis-et-Futuna — Islas Wallis y Futuna	—	—	—	×	—	—	—	—	—	—
Yemen — Yémen	—	—	—	×	—	×	o	o	o	o
Zambia — Zambie	—	×	—	×	—	×	o	o	o	o
Zimbabwe	—	×	—	×	—	×	?	?	?	?

[a]Including information on origin of imports and destination of exports. — Information sur l'origine des importations et la destination des exportations incluse. — Incluida información sobre el origen de las importaciones y el destino de las exportaciones.

[b]Non-party to the 1971 Convention. — Non-partie à la Convention de 1971. — No parte en el Convenio de 1971.

[c]Statistics included in the report of Switzerland. — Statistiques incluses dans celles de la Suisse. — Las estadísticas han sido incluidas en el informe de Suiza.

[d]Statistics included in the report of France. — Statistiques incluses dans celles de la France. — Las estadísticas han sido incluidas en el informe de Francia.

[e]Statistics included in the report of Italy. — Statistiques incluses dans celles de l'Italie. — Las estadísticas han sido incluidas en el informe de Italia.

Table III.   Defined daily doses for statistical purposes (S-DDD) for psychotropic substances

The term "defined daily doses for statistical purposes (S-DDD)" replaces the term "defined daily doses (DDD)" previously used by INCB. The S-DDD is a technical unit of measurement for the purpose of statistical analysis and is not a recommended prescription dose. Its definition is not free of a certain degree of arbitrariness. Certain psychotropic substances may be used in certain countries for different treatments or in accordance with different medical practices, and therefore a different daily dose could be more appropriate. The S-DDD indicated should be considered approximate and subject to modifications if more precise information becomes available. The basis for the grouping of the substances was, as far as possible, the anatomical therapeutic chemical (ATC) classification system used in the Nordic Statistics on Medicines and recommended by the World Health Organization (WHO) for drug utilization studies. In addition, the grouping reflects the Schedules of the 1971 Convention.

Tableau III.   Doses quotidiennes déterminées à des fins statistiques (S-DDD) pour les substances psychotropes

Les termes "doses quotidiennes déterminées à des fins statistiques (S-DDD)" remplaces les termes "doses quotidiennes déterminées" utilisé précédemment par l'OICS. La S-DDD est une unité de mesure technique utilisée aux fins de l'analyse statistique et non une recommandation posologique. Sa définition n'est pas dépourvue d'un certain caractère arbitraire. Certaines substances psychotropes pouvant être utilisées pour différents traitements ou conformément à des pratiques médicales différentes dans certains pays, une autre dose quotidienne pourrait être mieux adaptée. Les S-DDD indiquées devraient être considérées comme approximatives et sujettes à modification si des indications plus précises venaient à être disponibles. Pour le regroupement des substances, on s'est fondé, dans la mesure du possible, sur le système de classification anatomique, thérapeutique et chimique (ATC) utilisé dans les statistiques nordiques des médicaments et recommandé par l'Organisation mondiale de la santé (OMS) pour les études sur l'utilisation des médicaments. En outre, ce regroupement correspond aux tableaux de la Convention de 1971.

Cuadro III.   Dosis diarias definidas con fines estadísticos (S-DDD) para las sustancias sicotrópicas

La expresión "dosis diarias definidas" utilizada anteriormente por la JIFE fue sustituida por la expresión "dosis diarias definidas con fines estadísticos (S-DDD)". La S-DDD es una unidad técnica de medida que se utiliza a efectos del análisis estadístico, y no una dosis de prescripción recomendada. Su definición no está exenta de cierto grado de arbitrariedad. Es posible que determinadas sustancias se utilicen en determinados países para tratamientos diferentes o conforme a prácticas médicas diferentes y que, por lo tanto, resulte más apropiada otra dosis diaria. Las S-DDD que se indican deben considerarse aproximadas y podrían modificarse si se contara con información más precisa. En la medida de lo posible, las sustancias se agruparon con arreglo al sistema de clasificación anatómica, terapéutica y química (ATQ) utilizado en las estadísticas nórdicas sobre medicamentos y recomendado por la Organización Mundial de la Salud (OMS) para los estudios sobre utilización de medicamentos. Además, es la forma en que están agrupadas en las listas del Convenio de 1971.

Table III.1. Defined daily doses for statistical purposes (S-DDD) for psychotropic substances, by Schedule

Tableau III.1. Doses quotidiennes déterminées à des fins statistiques (S-DDD) pour les substances psychotropes, par tableau

Cuadro III.1. Dosis diarias definidas con fines estadísticos (S-DDD) para las sustancias sicotrópicas, por lista

	S-DDD (mg)
Substances listed in Schedule II	
Substances inscrites au Tableau II	
Sustancias incluidas en la Lista II	
Amfetamine — Amfétamine — Anfetamina	15.00
Amineptine — Amineptina	—
2 C-B	—
Delta-9-tetrahydrocannabinol and its stereochemical variants — *Delta*-9-tétrahydrocannabinol et ses variantes stéréochimiques — *Delta*-9-tetrahidrocannabinol y sus variantes estereoquímicas	30.00
Dexamfetamine — Dexamfétamine — Dexanfetamina	15.00
Fenetylline — Fénétylline — Fenetilina	50.00
Levamfetamine — Lévamfétamine — Levanfetamina	15.00
Levomethamphetamine — Lévométhamphétamine — Levometanfetamina	15.00
Mecloqualone — Mécloqualone — Meclocualona	200.00
Metamfetamine — Métamfétamine — Metanfetamina	15.00
Metamfetamine racemate — Racémate de métamfétamine — Racemato de metanfetamina	15.00
Methaqualone — Méthaqualone — Metacualona	200.00
Methylphenidate — Méthylphénidate — Metilfenidato	30.00
Phencyclidine — Fenciclidina	—
Phenmetrazine — Phenmétrazine — Fenmetracina	50.00
Secobarbital — Sécobarbital	100.00
Zipeprol — Zipéprol	200.00
Substances listed in Schedule III	
Substances inscrites au Tableau III	
Sustancias incluidas en la Lista III	
Amobarbital	100.00
Buprenorphine — Buprénorphine — Buprenorfina	1.20
Butalbital	75.00
Cathine — Catina	20.00
Cyclobarbital — Ciclobarbital	200.00
Flunitrazepam — Flunitrazépam	1.00
Glutethimide — Glutéthimide — Glutetimida	250.00
Pentazocine — Pentazocina	200.00
Pentobarbital	100.00
Substances listed in Schedule IV	
Substances inscrites au Tableau IV	
Sustancias incluidas en la Lista IV	
Allobarbital — Alobarbital	100.00
Alprazolam	1.00
Amfepramone — Amfépramone — Anfepramona	75.00
Aminorex	—
Barbital	500.00
Benzfetamine — Benzfétamine — Benzfetamina	75.00
Bromazepam — Bromazépam	10.00
Brotizolam	0.25
Butobarbital	150.00
Camazepam — Camazépam	30.00
Chlordiazepoxide — Chlordiazépoxide — Clordiazepóxido	30.00
Clobazam	20.00

	S-DDD (mg)
Clonazepam — Clonazépam	8.00
Clorazepate — Clorazépate — Clorazepato	20.00
Clotiazepam — Clotiazépam	15.00
Cloxazolam	9.00
Delorazepam — Délorazépam	3.00
Diazepam — Diazépam	10.00
Estazolam	3.00
Ethchlorvynol — Etclorvinol	500.00
Ethinamate — Éthinamate — Etinamato	500.00
Ethyl loflazepate — Loflazépate d'éthyle — Loflazepato de etilo	2.00
Etilamfetamine — Étilamfétamine — Etilanfetamina	30.00
Fencamfamin — Fencamfamine — Fencanfamina	80.00
Fenproporex	20.00
Fludiazepam — Fludiazépam	0.75
Flurazepam — Flurazépam	30.00
Gamma-hydroxybutyric acid (GHB) — Acide *gamma*-hydroxybutirique (GHB) — Ácido *gamma*-hidroxibutírico (GHB)	—
Halazepam — Halazépam	100.00
Haloxazolam	7.50
Ketazolam — Kétazolam	30.00
Lefetamine (SPA) — Léfétamine (SPA) — Lefetamina (SPA)	75.00
Loprazolam	1.00
Lorazepam — Lorazépam	2.50
Lormetazepam — Lormétazépam	1.00
Mazindol	1.00
Medazepam — Médazépam	20.00
Mefenorex — Méfénorex	60.00
Meprobamate — Méprobamate — Meprobamato	1 200.00
Mesocarb — Mésocarbe — Mesocarbo	25.00
Methylphenobarbital — Méthylphénobarbital — Metilfenobarbital	100.00
Methyprylon — Méthyprylone — Metiprilona	200.00
Midazolam	20.00
Nimetazepam — Nimétazépam	5.00
Nitrazepam — Nitrazépam	5.00
Nordazepam — Nordazépam	15.00
Oxazepam — Oxazépam	50.00
Oxazolam	40.00
Pemoline — Pémoline — Pemolina	40.00
Phendimetrazine — Phendimétrazine — Fendimetracina	70.00
Phenobarbital — Phénobarbital — Fenobarbital	100.00
Phentermine — Fentermina	15.00
Pinazepam — Pinazépam	15.00
Pipradrol	30.00
Prazepam — Prazépam	30.00
Pyrovalerone — Pyrovalérone — Pirovalerona	40.00
Secbutabarbital	75.00
Temazepam — Témazépam	20.00
Tetrazepam — Tétrazépam	100.00
Triazolam	0.25
Vinylbital — Vinilbital	150.00
Zolpidem	10.00

Table III.2.   Defined daily doses for statistical purposes (S-DDD) for psychotropic substances, by substance group

Tableau III.2.   Doses quotidiennes déterminées à des fins statistiques (S-DDD) pour les substances psychotropes, par groupe de substance

Cuadro III.2.   Dosis diarias definidas con fines estadísticos (S-DDD) para las sustancias sicotrópicas, por grupos de sustancias

	S-DDD (mg)		S-DDD (mg)
Stimulants **Estimulantes**		**Sedative-hypnotics and anxiolytics** **Sédatifs-hypnotiques et anxiolytiques** **Sedantes-hipnóticos y ansiolíticos**	
A. Amphetamines in Schedule II *Amfétamines au Tableau II* *Anfetaminas de la Lista II*		**Sedative-hypnotics** **Sédatifs-hypnotiques** **Sedantes-hipnóticos**	
Amfetamine — Amfétamine — Anfetamina	15.00		
Dexamfetamine — Dexamfétamine — Dexanfetamina	15.00	*E. Barbiturates in Schedule III and secobarbital (Schedule II)* *Barbituriques au Tableau III et sécobarbital (Tableau II)* *Barbitúricos de la Lista III y secobarbital (Lista II)*	
Levamfetamine — Lévamfétamine — Levanfetamina	15.00		
Levomethamphetamine — Lévométhamphétamine — Levometanfetamina	15.00		
Metamfetamine — Métamfétamine — Metanfetamina	15.00	Amobarbital	100.00
Metamfetamine racemate — Racémate de métamfétamine — Racemato de metanfetamina	15.00	Butalbital	75.00
		Cyclobarbital — Ciclobarbital	200.00
B. Other stimulants in Schedule II *Autres stimulants au Tableau II* *Otros estimulantes de la Lista II*		Pentobarbital	100.00
		Secobarbital — Sécobarbital	100.00
2 C-B	—		
Fenetylline — Fénétylline — Fenetilina	50.00	*F. Barbiturates in Schedule IV* *Barbituriques au Tableau IV* *Barbitúricos de la Lista IV*	
Methylphenidate — Méthylphénidate — Metilfenidato	30.00		
Phencyclidine — Fenciclidina	—		
Phenmetrazine — Phenmétrazine — Fenmetracina	50.00	Allobarbital — Alobarbital	100.00
		Barbital	500.00
C. Stimulants in Schedule III *Stimulants au Tableau III* *Estimulantes de la Lista III*		Butobarbital	150.00
		Secbutabarbital	75.00
		Vinylbital — Vinilbital	150.00
Cathine — Catina	20.00		
		G. Benzodiazepines *Benzodiazépines* *Benzodiazepinas*	
D. Stimulants in Schedule IV *Stimulants au Tableau IV* *Estimulantes de la Lista IV*			
		Brotizolam	0.25
		Estazolam	3.00
Amfepramone — Amfépramone — Anfepramona	75.00	Flunitrazepam — Flunitrazépam	1.00
Aminorex	—	Flurazepam — Flurazépam	30.00
Benzfetamine — Benzfétamine — Benzfetamina	75.00	Haloxazolam	7.50
Etilamfetamine — Étilamfétamine — Etilanfetamina	30.00	Loprazolam	1.00
		Lormetazepam — Lormétazépam	1.00
Fencamfamin — Fencamfamine — Fencanfamina	80.00	Midazolam	20.00
Fenproporex	20.00	Nimetazepam — Nimétazépam	5.00
Mazindol	1.00	Nitrazepam — Nitrazépam	5.00
Mefenorex — Méfénorex	60.00	Temazepam — Témazépam	20.00
Mesocarb — Mésocarbe — Mesocarbo	25.00	Triazolam	0.25
Pemoline — Pémoline — Pemolina	40.00		
Phendimetrazine — Phendimétrazine — Fendimetracina	70.00	*H. Other sedative-hypnotics in Schedule III* *Autres sédatifs-hypnotiques au Tableau III* *Otros sedantes-hipnóticos de la Lista III*	
Phentermine — Fentermina	15.00		
Pipradrol	30.00		
Pyrovalerone — Pyrovalérone — Pirovalerona	40.00	Glutethimide — Glutéthimide — Glutetimida	250.00

Table III.2. Defined daily doses for statistical purposes (S-DDD) for psychotropic substances, by substance group *(concluded)*

Tableau III.2. Doses quotidiennes déterminées à des fins statistiques (S-DDD) pour les substances psychotropes, par groupe de substance *(fin)*

Cuadro III.2. Dosis diarias definidas con fines estadísticos (S-DDD) para las sustancias sicotrópicas, por grupo de sustancias *(conclusión)*

	S-DDD (mg)
I. Other sedative-hypnotics in Schedule IV	
Autres sédatifs-hypnotiques au Tableau IV	
Otros sedantes-hipnóticos de la Lista IV	
Ethchlorvynol — Etclorvinol	500.00
Ethinamate — Éthinamate — Etinamato	500.00
Gamma-hydroxybutyric acid (GHB) —	
Acide *gamma*-hydroxybutirique (GHB) —	
Ácido *gamma*-hidroxibutírico (GHB)	—
Methyprylon — Méthyprylone — Metiprilona	200.00
Zolpidem	10.00
J. Other sedative-hypnotics in Schedule II	
except secobarbital	
Autres sédatifs-hypnotiques au Tableau II	
à l'exception du sécobarbital	
Otros sedantes-hipnóticos de la Lista II	
con excepción del secobarbital	
Mecloqualone — Mécloqualone — Meclocualona	200.00
Methaqualone — Méthaqualone — Metacualona	200.00

Anxiolytics. Anxiolytiques. Ansiolíticos

	S-DDD (mg)
K. Benzodiazepines	
Benzodiazépines	
Benzodiazepinas	
Alprazolam	1.00
Bromazepam — Bromazépam	10.00
Camazepam — Camazépam	30.00
Chlordiazepoxide — Chlordiazépoxide — Clordiazepóxido	30.00
Clobazam	20.00
Clorazepate — Clorazépate — Clorazepato	20.00
Clotiazepam — Clotiazépam	15.00
Cloxazolam	9.00
Delorazepam — Délorazépam	3.00
Diazepam — Diazépam	10.00
Ethyl loflazepate — Loflazépate d'éthyle —	
Loflazepato de etilo	2.00
Fludiazepam — Fludiazépam	0.75
Halazepam— Halazépam	100.00
Ketazolam — Kétazolam	30.00
Lorazepam — Lorazépam	2.50
Medazepam — Médazépam	20.00
Nordazepam — Nordazépam	15.00
Oxazepam — Oxazépam	50.00
Oxazolam	40.00
Pinazepam — Pinazépam	15.00
Prazepam — Prazépam	30.00
Tetrazepam — Tétrazépam	100.00

	S-DDD (mg)
L. Other anxiolytics	
Autres anxiolytiques	
Otros ansiolíticos	
Meprobamate — Méprobamate — Meprobamato	1 200.00

Anti-epileptics. Antiépileptiques. Antiepilépticos

	S-DDD (mg)
M. Barbiturates	
Barbituriques	
Barbitúricos	
Methylphenobarbital — Méthylphénobarbital —	
Metilfenobarbital	100.00
Phenobarbital — Phénobarbital — Fenobarbital	100.00
N. Benzodiazepines	
Benzodiazépines	
Benzodiazepinas	
Clonazepam — Clonazépam	8.00

Analgesics. Analgésiques. Analgésicos

	S-DDD (mg)
O. Analgesics	
Analgésiques	
Analgésicos	
Buprenorphine — Buprénorphine — Buprenorfina	1.20
Pentazocine — Pentazocina	200.00
Lefetamine (SPA) — Léfétamine (SPA) — Lefetamina (SPA)	75.00

Anti-emetics. Antiémétiques. Antieméticos

	S-DDD (mg)
P. Anti-emetics	
Antiémétiques	
Antieméticos	
Delta-9-tetrahydrocannabinol and its stereochemical variants —	
Delta-9-tétrahydrocannabinol et ses variantes stéréochimiques —	
Delta-9-tetrahidrocannabinol y sus variantes estereoquímicas	30.00

Antitussives. Antitussifs. Antitusígenos

	S-DDD (mg)
Q. Antitussives	
Antitussifs	
Antitusígenos	
Zipeprol — Zipéprol	200.00

Antidepressants. Antidépresseurs. Antidepresivos

	S-DDD (mg)
R. Antidepressants	
Antidépresseurs	
Antidepresivos	
Amineptine — Amineptina	—

Comments on reported statistics

Commentaires sur les statistiques communiquées

Comentarios sobre las estadísticas comunicadas

COMMENTS ON THE REPORTED STATISTICS ON PSYCHOTROPIC SUBSTANCES

Summary

Use of substances included in Schedule I of the Convention on Psychotropic Substances of 1971 is very limited; it is restricted to scientific research and the exceptional manufacture of psychotropic substances listed in other schedules. That is also the case with *delta*-8-tetrahydrocannabinol, whose manufacture has increased markedly over the past years in order to obtain dronabinol, one of the stereochemical variants of *delta*-9-tetrahydrocannabinol (*delta*-9-THC) listed in Schedule II. Preparations containing dronabinol are used in a few countries as an anti-emetic for the relief of nausea. The manufacture and stock levels of *delta*-9-THC, which were stable in past years, have recently increased. Dronabinol is consumed mainly in the United States of America, as well as in a number of other countries, including Canada and Germany.

Amphetamines (central nervous system stimulants listed in Schedule II) are widely used, predominantly for the manufacture of other psychotropic substances and substances not under international control but also for medical purposes such as the treatment of attention-deficit disorder (ADD) and narcolepsy. Mainly manufactured by France and the United States, global output of amphetamines peaked at 45 tons in 2005 as a result of increased consumption in the United States. That country, which is by far the largest consumer, accounted for 80 per cent of calculated global consumption of amphetamines in 2005. A growing number of countries are using amphetamines (mainly methylphenidate), notably Canada, Germany and Spain.

Consumption of buprenorphine, an opioid analgesic listed in Schedule III of the 1971 Convention, has increased significantly in recent years as a result of its use for detoxification and substitution treatment of heroin addicts since the early 1990s. More than 40 countries are currently importing buprenorphine for that purpose, the largest importers being France and Germany.

Currently, 35 benzodiazepines are under international control. In medical practice, benzodiazepines are used for the short-term management of insomnia and for premedication and induction of general anaesthesia. Benzodiazepines are classified as anxiolytics and sedative-hypnotics. Consumption of benzodiazepine-type anxiolytics, notably diazepam, is higher in Europe than in any other region of the world. In contrast, total reported manufacture and consumption of benzodiazepine-type sedative-hypnotics, including flunitrazepam, have fluctuated significantly. In recent years, global reported consumption of flunitrazepam has shown a downward trend, while consumption of brotizolam has been on the increase. International trade in flunitrazepam has fluctuated at about 1 ton per year. Japan continues to be the leading importer of flunitrazepam, accounting for more than half of annual global imports.

Of the 12 barbiturates listed in the 1971 Convention, phenobarbital is the most widely used, particularly for the treatment of epilepsy. The substance accounts for 71 per cent of the combined manufacture of all barbiturates in 2005. Other important barbiturates are barbital, pentobarbital, butalbital and amobarbital, together accounting for about 28 per cent of total reported manufacture. China is the largest manufacturer, accounting for about 60 per cent of global output; it is followed by the Russian Federation and India. The bulk of the barbiturates is consumed in the Americas, Asia and Europe, each with an average consumption of about 1.7 billion defined daily doses for statistical purposes (S-DDD) per year.

The stimulants listed in Schedule IV of the 1971 Convention are essentially used as anorectics or for the treatment of ADD. Following strong fluctuations in the 1990s, total reported manufacture of this group of substances stabilized at an annual average of about 1.8 billion S-DDD during the period 2001-2005. In 2005, the main substances manufactured were phentermine (45 per cent), fenproporex (23 per cent) and amfepramone (18 per cent). Phentermine has been the most widely used substance in that group. The highest per capita consumption of stimulants listed in Schedule IV has traditionally been in the Americas. While the consumption of those stimulants in the Americas has continued to increase, the rates of consumption of those stimulants in Asia, Europe and Oceania have decreased markedly since 2000.

---

1.   The purpose of these comments is to facilitate the study of the statistical information on licitly manufactured psychotropic substances that is presented in the tables of reported statistics (see pages 109-256 below). The tables contain information submitted by Governments to the International Narcotics Control Board (INCB) pursuant to the provisions of article 16 of the Convention on Psychotropic Substances of 1971.

2.   There are currently 116 substances listed in the four schedules of the 1971 Convention. Comments are provided on substances reported to have been used for medical and scientific purposes. Since only a few Governments have reported manufacture of substances in Schedule I and since

international trade in those substances has been very limited, a table summarizing the movement of substances listed in Schedule I in 2005 is included in the section containing tables of reported statistics. With respect to substances in Schedules II and III of the 1971 Convention, the information on the five-year period 2001-2005 is presented in the statistical tables. With respect to substances in Schedule IV, information on the three-year period 2003-2005 is included in the statistical tables. Statistics relating to a few substances, namely, mecloqualone and phencyclidine, both included in Schedule II, and amineptine and lefetamine, included in Schedule IV, are not included in the statistical tables but are reflected in the comments.

3. There are currently 28 substances listed in Schedule I. Pursuant to the provisions of article 7 of the 1971 Convention, the use of those substances should be prohibited except for scientific and very limited medical purposes by duly authorized persons in medical or scientific establishments that are directly under the control of or specifically approved by their Governments. This restriction results from the fact that all substances in Schedule I are hallucinogens and/or central nervous system stimulants with very limited or no medical use. The manufacture and stocks of and trade in those substances have, therefore, been very limited. Exceptions are noted below.

4. The 1971 Convention does not envisage any use of psychotropic substances in Schedule I in industry for the manufacture of non-psychotropic substances or products. The substance 2,5-dimethoxyamphetamine (DMA), however, has been used for that purpose in the United States of America, the sole manufacturer of the substance, where it is utilized in the manufacture of special photographic films. The manufacture of DMA in that country was stable, averaging 8 tons annually until 2001, when manufacture decreased by around 50 per cent. The reported manufacture of DMA by the United States in 2005 was 520 kg. In the past five years, manufacture of DMA in the United States has amounted to 1,603 kg on average. Stocks of DMA held in the United States at the end of 2005 amounted to 236 kg. There is reportedly no substitute for DMA in the above-mentioned manufacturing process. Although the use of DMA in the United States has substantially decreased, it seems that the industrial use of the substance in the manufacture of a photographic film dye has not yet been discontinued.[1]

5. Eight countries reported the manufacture of 3,4-methylenedioxymetamfetamine (MDMA) in the last five years: Australia, Denmark, Hungary, Ireland, Israel, Poland, Switzerland and United States. Global stocks of MDMA at the end of 2005 amounted to less than 500 grams, partly held by Australia, Switzerland and the United States. In the period 2001-2005, four countries, namely, Australia, Israel, Switzerland and the United States, reported having manufactured a few grams of tenamfetamine (MDA). Stocks of this substance are mainly held in Switzerland and the United States. In 2005, Denmark reported for the first time the manufacture of almost 25 kg of PMA (p-methoxy-alpha-methylphenethylamine) and held nearly 40 kg in stock at the end of the year.

6. Parties to the 1971 Convention may authorize limited use of substances listed in Schedule I for the manufacture of psychotropic substances in other schedules. The isomers of tetrahydrocannabinol (THC) included in Schedule I, mainly *delta*-8-tetrahydrocannabinol, have been manufactured in the United States and used in the manufacture of *delta*-9-tetrahydrocannabinol (*delta*-9-THC), a psychotropic substance listed in Schedule II since 1991. Only one stereochemical variant of *delta*-9-THC, dronabinol, is used in the manufacture of pharmaceutical preparations for therapeutic purposes. The United States is the only manufacturer of the isomers of THC included in Schedule I. The manufacture of those isomers of THC increased by nearly 140 per cent in 1998 and 1999. The manufacture of isomers of THC in the past five years has continued to increase by about 16 per cent per year on average. Total manufacture in the United States in 2005 was 308 kg. By the end of 2005, only the United States held stocks, amounting to 445 kg.

7. The manufacture in 2005 of a few grams of other substances in Schedule I for scientific purposes, not commented on above, was reported by only four countries: Germany (methcathinone), Ireland (cathinone, *N*-ethyl-MDA and tenamfetamine), Switzerland (mescaline, *N*-ethyl-MDA and psilocybin) and the United States (*N*-ethyl-MDA, psilocine and tenamfetamine).

8. Quantities of substances in Schedule I, ranging from a few grams to several hundred grams, were held in stocks at the end of 2005, mainly in the United States. Stocks of most of those substances have been relatively stable in recent years. Other countries reporting stocks of a few grams of substances in Schedule I at the end of 2005 were Australia, Switzerland and the United Kingdom of Great Britain and Northern Ireland. Stocks of DMA and THC are referred to in paragraphs 4 and 6 above.

9. International trade in substances in Schedule I has always been restricted to occasional transactions of no more than a few grams. In the period 2001-2005, small imports or exports of some of those substances were reported by Australia, Canada, China, Denmark, France, Germany, Ireland, Israel, New Zealand, Switzerland, the United Kingdom and the United States.

Substances listed in Schedule II

10. Seventeen substances are listed in Schedule II whose liability to abuse constitutes a substantial risk to public health and which have little to moderate therapeutic usefulness. The substances belong to the following groups: central nervous system stimulants; anti-emetics; hallucinogens; sedative-hypnotics; antitussives and antidepressants. In addition to their various applications in human and/or veterinary medicine, some of these substances are used in industry for the manufacture of other psychotropic substances or for conversion into non-psychotropic substances.

Central nervous system stimulants

Amphetamines

11. Both optical isomers of amfetamine (levamfetamine and dexamfetamine) and their racemic mixture (amfetamine), as well as both optical isomers of metamfetamine (levomethamphetamine and metamfetamine) and their racemic mixture (metamfetamine racemate), are listed in Schedule II. Statistical reports on amfetamine, dexamfetamine and metamfetamine have been received by INCB from Governments since the 1970s. Statistics for

---

[1] See *Report of the International Narcotics Control Board for 1994* (United Nations publication, Sales No. E.95.XI.4), para. 75.

levamfetamine and levomethamphetamine have been available since 1986, and statistics for metamfetamine racemate since 1988, owing to the different dates on which those substances were brought under the control of the 1971 Convention.

12. Amphetamines in Schedule II are used not only directly for medical purposes, but also in industry as intermediary products for the manufacture of other substances. Those new substances may be divided into two groups: other psychotropic substances, including those which are optical isomers of the original substance; and substances not controlled under the 1971 Convention. In recent years, amphetamines have mainly been converted to substances used as anorectics (benzfetamine, clobenzorex, fenproporex and levopropylhexedrine) and antiparkinsonian drugs (selegiline). Occasionally, small quantities of amphetamines are also converted into other substances, such as famprofazone (an analgesic) and amfetaminil (a psychostimulant). Benzfetamine and fenproporex are included in Schedule IV of the 1971 Convention, whereas amfetaminil, clobenzorex, famprofazone, levopropylhexedrine and selegiline are not under international control.

Use as intermediate substances

13. In the United States, imported precursors (phenylacetone and norephedrine) and metamfetamine racemate are utilized for the manufacture of amfetamine and dexamfetamine, which are subsequently processed to make pharmaceutical preparations. In 2005, a total of 6.7 tons of amfetamine and 6.2 tons of dexamfetamine were manufactured in that country. In 2005, the United States imported 2.4 tons of metamfetamine racemate (from France), of which 1.9 tons were converted into 1.2 tons of metamfetamine and 580 kg of levomethamphetamine. About 542 kg of the obtained metamfetamine was then used to manufacture 719 kg of benzfetamine, while levomethamphetamine was used for the manufacture of over-the-counter nasal inhalers. As a result, in the United States 6.7 tons of amfetamine, 6.2 tons of dexamfetamine, 452 kg of metamfetamine racemate and 612 kg of metamfetamine were available for direct medical use.

14. In 2005, France manufactured 10.9 tons of amfetamine, of which 2.9 tons were utilized for the manufacture of about 2.2 tons of dexamfetamine, 7.5 tons were used to manufacture 6.5 tons of levamfetamine and the rest was added to the stocks. A total of 4.9 tons of levamfetamine was converted back into 4.7 tons of amfetamine. Of the 2.9 tons of metamfetamine racemate manufactured in France in 2005, about 2.4 tons were exported to the United States and the remaining 533 kg were converted into 500 kg of metamfetamine, which was added to stocks.

Direct medical use

15. For direct medical purposes, amphetamines are used mainly for the treatment of attention-deficit disorder (ADD, called attention-deficit/hyperactivity disorder (ADHD) in the United States), narcolepsy and obesity, although the widespread use of those substances as anorectics for the treatment of obesity has been discontinued or considerably reduced in most countries.

16. In 2005, the quantity of amphetamines listed in Schedule II that were manufactured worldwide totalled 45.1 tons (over 3 billion defined daily doses for statistical purposes (S-DDD)), which represents an increase of 636 kg over the previous year. The manufacture of amfetamine (41.4 per cent), dexamfetamine (25.3 per cent) and levamfetamine (14.3 per cent) accounted for 81 per cent of the global output of this group of substances (see figure 1). Almost all of this output was manufactured by France (58 per cent) and the United States (33 per cent), while Germany contributed 977 kg of amfetamine and 3.1 tons of levomethamphetamine that were used for the manufacture of non-psychotropic substances.

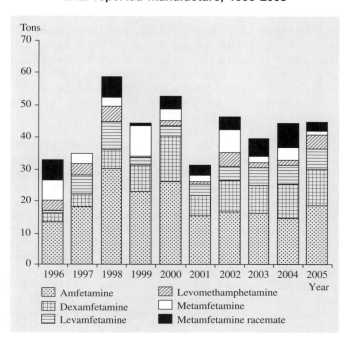

Figure 1. Schedule II stimulants: total reported manufacture, 1996-2005

17. The growth in the manufacture of amphetamines in recent years can be attributed to the rapid increase in the medical use of amfetamine and dexamfetamine in the United States since 1998, when products combining both amfetamine and dexamfetamine started to be used mostly for the treatment of ADD. In 2005, 6.7 tons of amfetamine and 6.2 tons of dexamfetamine were manufactured for such use in the United States. France is another traditional major manufacturer of the amphetamines, contributing on average 52.6 per cent of amfetamine, 44 per cent of dexamfetamine and almost 100 per cent of levamfetamine in global output during the period 2001-2005.

18. The manufacture of amfetamine gradually increased and then peaked at over 30 tons in 1998. In the past five years, the global output of this substance has been substantially lower, although the total reported manufacture of amfetamine increased from 14.6 tons in 2004 to 18.7 tons in 2005. Global stocks also increased, reaching 6 tons in 2005, 71 per cent of which were held by the United States. In 2005, 63 kg of amfetamine were traded internationally, the

main importers being Chile (35 per cent), Canada (30 per cent), Sweden (12 per cent), Belgium (9 per cent) and the Russian Federation (7 per cent).

19. While the manufacture of dexamfetamine during the 1980s was stable, at a level of approximately 350 kg annually, it began to rise sharply after 1991, totalling almost 1.7 tons in 1995. Since then, the manufacture of that substance has steadily increased, peaking at 14.3 tons in 2000 and dropping to 6.6 tons in 2001, prior to stabilizing at an annual average of 10.2 tons during the period 2002-2005. France and the United States are major users of dexamfetamine, where it is prescribed for the treatment of ADD, obesity and narcolepsy, but significant medical use of that substance has also been reported in a number of other countries, including Australia, Canada, Chile, Germany and the United Kingdom. Global stocks of dexamfetamine increased from 1 ton in 1995 to 7.3 tons in 2003 and fell to 5.9 tons in 2005. With 16.4 and 4.3 S-DDD per 1,000 inhabitants per day respectively, France and the United States had the highest calculated rate of use of dexamfetamine. While 25 countries reported imports of this substance in 2005, over 91 per cent of the 492 kg of global dexamfetamine imports was accounted for by Canada (54.6 per cent), Australia (26.8 per cent) and the United Kingdom (10.3 per cent).

20. In addition to its direct medical use, metamfetamine is also used for the manufacture of benzfetamine, prescribed for obesity disorders. In 1999, the total reported manufacture of metamfetamine stood at 9.5 tons. Since then, the global output fluctuated significantly, falling, in 2005, to 1.4 tons, 80 per cent of which was manufactured in the United States. France is another regular manufacturer of metamfetamine, although it reported a decrease in output from 642 kg in 2004 to 289 kg in 2005. The manufacture of metamfetamine in Germany is highly irregular, fluctuating between 5.2 tons in 2002 and 2 grams in 2005, which is reflected in the global trends. The United States is the main regular user of metamfetamine. In 2005 its calculated rate of consumption increased from 0.26 to 0.42 S-DDD per 1,000 inhabitants per day. Eleven countries reported imports of metamfetamine in 2005, the main importers being Chile and Switzerland. In the past, Ireland and the United Kingdom have also reported large quantities of metamfetamine imports.

21. In the United States, levomethamphetamine is used for the manufacture of over-the-counter nasal inhalers, which are exempted in that country from certain control measures in accordance with article 3 of the 1971 Convention. In the past 10 years, the total reported manufacture of levomethamphetamine was highly irregular, fluctuating significantly between 433 kg and 5.1 tons. In 2005, the total manufacture once again sharply increased, growing by threefold to reach 4.3 tons. Germany, the United States, France and the Czech Republic are the main manufacturers and users of the substance. Levomethamphetamine is also used in Ireland and Italy, which are the main importers of the substance.

22. France and Hungary are the main manufacturers of metamfetamine racemate. The substance has mainly been exported (a total of 20.1 tons since 1996) or converted into levomethamphetamine and metamfetamine. In the past five years, the total manufacture reported by those two countries gradually increased from 3.3 tons in 2001 to 7.5 tons in 2004. In 2005, however, the quantity manufactured fell to 2.8 ton—a 62 per cent decrease—due to a sharp drop in the

level of manufacture of Hungary, which reported a decrease from more than 4 tons in 2004 to less than 2 kg in 2005. The global stocks followed a similar trend, falling from an average of 3.7 tons during 2001-2004 to 1.9 tons in 2005. The level of manufacture of metamfetamine racemate in France has remained stable in recent years, averaging 3 tons annually in the period 2001-2005, which represents 64 per cent of global output in that period. The United States is the sole importer of the substance, importing 2.5-3 tons of metamfetamine racemate annually in the past five years.

23. The countries with the highest levels of medical and industrial use of amphetamines as a group, calculated on the basis of statistics provided for the years 2001, 2003 and 2005[2] and expressed in S-DDD per 1,000 inhabitants per day,[3] are listed in table 1 according to their rate of calculated use for the year 2005.

Table 1. **Calculated rate of use of stimulants in Schedule II, excluding methylphenidate, 2001, 2003 and 2005**

Country[a]	S-DDD per 1,000 inhabitants per day		
	2001	2003	2005
United States	6.07	6.86	10.22
Canada	0.42	0.81	1.95
Australia	1.54	1.76	1.24
Belgium	0.08	0.03	0.26
Chile	0.28	0.18	0.25
Switzerland	4.04	0.04	0.23
Sweden	0.20	0.22	0.20
Norway	0.07	0.14	0.19
United Kingdom	0.23	0.14	0.15
New Zealand	0.14	0.14	0.11

[a] Countries are listed according to their level of use of stimulants in Schedule II in 2005.

Fenetylline

24. Fenetylline was brought under international control in 1986. Manufacture of the substance was last reported in 1987. Worldwide stocks of fenetylline, which amounted to nearly 4 tons in 1987, were significantly reduced as a result of the voluntary destruction of all stocks of the substance in Switzerland in 1991 and of 50 per cent of the stocks in Germany in 1992. Those stocks were destroyed in order to put an end to attempts by drug traffickers to divert fenetylline into illicit channels by using falsified import authorizations.[4] By 2000, the remaining half of the German stocks had gradually been exported to the Netherlands. The Netherlands remains the only country holding significant stocks of fenetylline (212 kg at the end of 2005) and is the main exporter of the substance, accounting for 90 per cent of global exports. The main importer in 2005 was Belgium (68 kg), re-exporting a small part of its imports (7.6 kg) to Germany and France. No other country has reported the use of fenetylline for medical purposes since 2003.

[2] The method of calculating levels of consumption of psychotropic substances is explained in the explanatory note to table III of the present publication.

[3] The list of defined daily doses for statistical purposes (S-DDD) used in these calculations is presented in table IV of the present publication.

[4] See Report of the International Narcotics Control Board for 1999 (United Nations publication, Sales No. E.00.XI.1), para. 85.

Methylphenidate

25. The use of methylphenidate[5] for medical purposes increased significantly in the 1990s. That large increase was mainly a result of developments in the United States, where the substance is heavily advertised, including direct advertisement to potential consumers. It is frequently prescribed for the treatment of ADD, primarily in children. However, since the late 1990s, the use of methylphenidate for the treatment of ADD has risen sharply in many other countries. The global calculated consumption of the substance increased from 18.5 tons in 2001 to 30.4 tons in 2005. In addition to its primary use in the treatment of ADD, methylphenidate is also prescribed for the treatment of narcolepsy.

26. The global manufacture of methylphenidate rose very rapidly in the first half of the 1990s, from 2.8 tons in 1990 to 19.1 tons in 1999. As a result of the increasing use of amphetamines for the treatment of ADD, methylphenidate manufacture dropped to 16 tons in 2000 (see figure 2). Since then, total reported manufacture of the substance fluctuated while following an overall increasing trend, peaking at 33.5 tons in 2004 before falling to 28.8 tons in 2005. The United States has been the leading manufacturer of methylphenidate, increasing its output from 1.8 tons in 1990 to 28.3 tons in 2005. While almost all of the methylphenidate manufactured in the United States had been for domestic use, exports gradually increased from 33 kg in 1996 to 2.7 tons in 2005. Global stocks of methylphenidate followed the trend in manufacture, increasing from 15.5 tons in 2001 to 23.4 tons in 2005. The United States accounted for 83 per cent of global stocks in 2005, increasing them significantly, from 500 kg in 1992 to 19.5 tons in 2005. Serious concern has been raised in the United States about the possible overdiagnosing of ADD and the overprescribing of methylphenidate.

27. The medical requirements for methylphenidate outside the United States are mainly covered by imports, and the number of countries reporting imports of the substance increased from 70 in 1996 to 88 in 2005. International trade in methylphenidate decreased from an annual average of 11.5 tons during the period 2003-2004 to 9.2 tons in 2005. Australia, Canada, Germany, the Netherlands, South Africa, Spain, Switzerland and the United Kingdom are the main importers of methylphenidate, mostly for re-export, their combined total accounting for 84 per cent of global imports. Spain, Switzerland, the United Kingdom and the United States are the main suppliers of that substance on the world market. In the 1980s, methylphenidate exports from Switzerland were stable at a level of less than 400 kg annually. After 1991, Swiss exports of methylphenidate gradually increased to 1.4 tons in 1996 and reached an average of 4 tons annually during the period 2003-2005. Until 1996, exports of the substance from Switzerland were drawn from local manufacture of the raw material. Since 1997, imports of methylphenidate, mainly from Spain and the United Kingdom, have supplied the raw material for the manufacture of preparations.

28. The number of countries and territories importing methylphenidate for domestic consumption has been growing. Since 1995, 121 Governments have reported such imports. In 2005, 33 Governments reported imports of methylphenidate in amounts exceeding 10 kg. Consumption of methylphenidate in the United States, by far the largest consumer of the substance, accounting for 80 per cent of the calculated worldwide use of the substance in 2005, has been characterized by a strong and steady increase since the beginning of the 1990s. Use of the substance further increased from 317 million S-DDD in 1996 to 808 million S-DDD in 2005 (see figure 3).

Figure 2. Manufacture of methylphenidate, 1996-2005

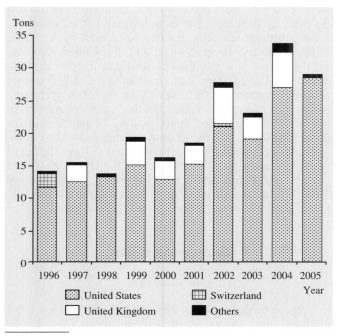

Figure 3. Calculated medical consumption of methylphenidate, 1996-2005

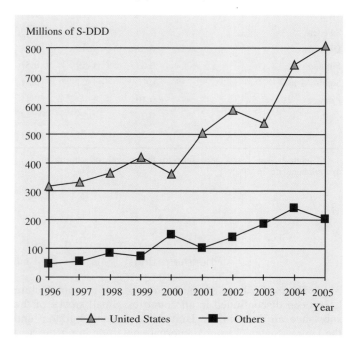

---

[5] See table IV for details.

29. The level of methylphenidate use in the rest of the world averaged about 200 million S-DDD per year in the past three years. Recent changes include a decrease of consumption in Canada, where use of this substance fell from 48 million S-DDD per year during the period 2003-2004 to 29 million S-DDD in 2005, and an increase of consumption in Germany, from 33 million S-DDD in 2004 to 44 million S-DDD in 2005. The other main consumer countries are the United Kingdom and Spain. Methylphenidate use increased in recent years in those two countries, reaching 27 and 17 million S-DDD, respectively, in 2005.

30. The countries with the highest level of medical use of methylphenidate, calculated on the basis of statistics provided for the years 2001, 2003 and 2005 and expressed in S-DDD per 1,000 inhabitants per day, are listed in table 2 according to their level of consumption in the year 2005.

Table 2. Calculated medical consumption of methylphenidate, 2001, 2003 and 2005

Country[a]	S-DDD per 1,000 inhabitants per day		
	2001	2003	2005
United States	5.11	5.21	7.61
Israel	0.72	5.27	2.69
Norway	0.78	2.13	2.61
Canada	0.29	4.24	2.55
Netherlands	1.11	1.38	1.81
Germany	0.67	0.99	1.47
Australia	0.89	1.34	1.44
Switzerland	2.82	2.23	1.36
Belgium	0.51	1.12	1.24
New Zealand	1.29	1.35	1.23
United Kingdom	1.04	0.95	1.23
Spain	0.66	0.78	1.11
Sweden	0.16	0.35	0.89
Denmark	0.22	0.40	0.88
Finland	0.07	0.29	0.57
South Africa	0.16	0.27	0.51
Panama	0.10	—	0.45
Chile	0.24	0.35	0.44
Iceland	2.35	5.21	0.01

[a] Countries are listed according to their level of consumption of methylphenidate in 2005.

Phenmetrazine

31. The medical use of phenmetrazine and its manufacture have been discontinued in all countries. Small stocks of the substance are held in the United Kingdom (14 grams) and the United States (1 gram). International trade in phenmetrazine is limited to rare transactions of a few grams.

Anti-emetics

Delta-9-tetrahydrocannabinol and its stereochemical variants

32. The substance *delta*-9-THC, together with its stereochemical variants, was originally included in Schedule I but was transferred to Schedule II in 1991 in view of the use of one of its stereochemical variants (dronabinol) for the relief of nausea. The United States is the only country that has reported the manufacture of *delta*-9-THC in significant quantities. The manufacture of *delta*-9-THC in that country was relatively stable, with an annual average of 66 kg at the end of the 1990s. However, the quantity manufactured has increased considerably since 2000, averaging 170 kg in the past five years (180 kg in 2005). The other two countries that reported manufacture of the substance in the past five years, but in much smaller quantities, are Germany (averaging 7 kg) and the United Kingdom (averaging 2 kg). In 2005, Canada and Switzerland reported for the first time the manufacture of *delta*-9-THC, also in small amounts: 3 kg and 13 kg, respectively.

33. Almost all the *delta*-9-THC manufactured in Canada, Germany and the United States was used domestically. Switzerland and the United Kingdom reported little or no use of the substance but both increased their stocks. Total reported stocks of the substance in 2005 (385 kg) were held almost entirely by the United States and the United Kingdom; that represents an increase of 65 per cent compared with stocks held in 2004. Several countries reported imports of the substance in 2005, the most significant quantities being reported by Germany (2,461 g) and Canada (2,187 g), which, together with the United States, have been the main users of *delta* 9-THC.

Hallucinogens

Phencyclidine

34. Phencyclidine is primarily used as an anaesthetic agent in veterinary medicine. The manufacture of small quantities of the substance has been reported in the past by Australia, France, Hungary, Israel, Switzerland, the United Kingdom and the United States (a total of 4.5 kg in the period 1996-2005). The United States and Israel were the only countries reporting manufacture in 2005 (2 kg and 146 g, respectively). Ten countries reported holding stocks of phencyclidine in 2005, the United States holding 84 per cent of the global total (3.1 kg). Other countries holding stocks of phencyclidine were France (210 g) and Israel (146 g), followed by, in decreasing order of stock levels, the United Kingdom, Switzerland, Denmark, Canada, Hungary, Australia and Finland. International trade in phencyclidine has been limited to occasional transactions of only a few grams.

Sedative-hypnotics

Mecloqualone

35. Mecloqualone has not been manufactured since 1980, although some stocks are being maintained. The United Kingdom reported stocks of 152 grams of mecloqualone in

2001. Since then, the United States is the only country to report stocks of that substance, remaining at 35 grams in 2005.

Methaqualone

36. In recent years, the manufacture of methaqualone has decreased dramatically from its peak level of over 50 tons annually in the 1980s. The last significant manufacture of the substance was reported in 1997 by Switzerland (340 kg) and the Czech Republic (43 kg). Since then, a further decrease in global manufacture has been observed, as smaller quantities (4 g in 2003 and 3 g in 2004) of methaqualone have been manufactured only in the United States, and no manufacture was reported in 2005. During the period 1997-2005, global stocks of methaqualone, held almost entirely by Switzerland, decreased from 2.4 tons in 1997 to 257 kg in 2005, as a result of the continued global medical use of methaqualone. In recent years, global use of the substance has fluctuated significantly, falling from an annual average of 1.1 million S-DDD in the period 1999-2000 to less than 6,000 S-DDD in 2005. Methaqualone continues to be consumed, although not in significant quantities, practically only in Switzerland.

Secobarbital

37. The manufacture of secobarbital, a substance that in the past was frequently diverted from licit manufacture and trade into the illicit traffic, has declined substantially since its transfer from Schedule III to Schedule II in 1988. More than 11 tons were reported to have been manufactured worldwide in 1988. That total dropped to 2.6 tons in 1990 and declined further to an annual average of 1.8 tons during the period 1997-2001. In 2001, the manufacture of secobarbital reached its highest level since 1989, 4.2 tons (see figure 4) attributed to only two countries: Germany (2.3 tons) and the United States (1.9 tons). The total manufacture of secobarbital increased slightly, from 811 kg in 2004 to 817 kg in 2005. Global stocks of secobarbital decreased from 1.4 tons in 2004 to 736 kg in 2005, 65 per cent being held by Germany and 30 per cent by the United States.

38. The manufacture of secobarbital was reported at least once during the period 2001-2005 by five countries (listed in decreasing order of the amounts manufactured): Germany (for domestic use and export), the United States (mainly for domestic use), Denmark (almost exclusively for export), Japan and China (for domestic use). In 2005, only two countries, Germany (817 kg) and Ireland (79 kg), reported the manufacture of secobarbital. There was a marked decrease in the stocks of the United States from 2001 (1.7 tons) to 2005

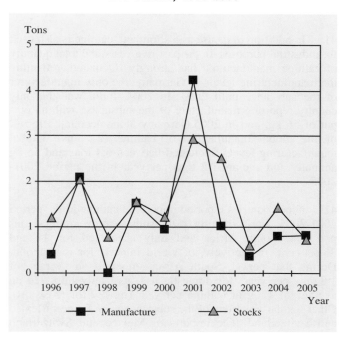

Figure 4. Secobarbital: total reported manufacture and stocks, 1996-2005

(220 kg). Global average annual imports of secobarbital were 670 kg for the period 2003-2005, after a peak of 1.7 tons in 2001. The main traders of the substance in recent years have been Germany (the main exporter) and the United Kingdom (the main importer). Other importers of secobarbital include Belgium, Canada, Denmark, Ireland, the Netherlands and Sweden.

Antitussives

Zipeprol

39. Zipeprol, an antitussive with bronchospasmolytic and mucolytic activities, was brought under international control in 1995. Statistics on the substance have been available only since that year. The manufacture of zipeprol was last reported in 2001, the sole manufacturer being France (666 kg). Stocks of zipeprol in 2005 were held mainly by Switzerland (588 kg), followed by Chile (10 kg). In 2005, exports of the substance were reported only by Switzerland (168 kg). Chile, Mexico and the Republic of Korea are the only countries that have reported use of the substance in recent years.

Substances listed in Schedule III

40. Nine substances are listed in Schedule III. According to the scheduling criteria adopted by the World Health Organization (WHO) Expert Committee on Drug Dependence, substances in Schedule III are those whose liability to abuse constitutes a substantial risk to public health and which have moderate to great therapeutic usefulness. One substance, cathine, belongs to the group of central nervous system stimulants; six substances belong to the group of sedative-hypnotics, four barbiturates (amobarbital, butalbital, cyclobarbital and pentobarbital), glutethimide and flunitrazepam; and the two remaining substances, buprenorphine and pentazocine, belong to the group of analgesics.

Central nervous system stimulants

Cathine

41.   In addition to its use as a stimulant, cathine is also used for industrial purposes. In the past five years, the total quantity of cathine manufactured has strongly fluctuated, reflecting the manufacturing levels of Germany, the only manufacturer of the substance until 2003. In 2004, India was the only country reporting manufacture of the substance, with an output of 56 kg, and in 2005 Germany alone accounted for all of the global manufacture of cathine (2.2 tons). Global manufacturing levels fluctuated between 6.4 tons and 56 kg annually and averaged 2 tons per year in the period 2001-2005.

42.   Nine countries reported imports of cathine in the period 2001-2005, world imports of the substance averaging 4 tons per year. South Africa and Italy accounted for 44 and 26 per cent, respectively, of world imports for that period. During that period, South Africa imported an average of 1.8 tons per year (for domestic use) and Italy imported an average of 1 ton of cathine per year (mostly for re-export). Other regular importers of the substance were France, Mexico and Switzerland. The imports of Mexico and Switzerland decreased in 2004, compared with the levels in the period 1997-2001, to about 850 kg and 40 kg, respectively, and they reported no imports in 2005. Cathine imports by France averaged over 300 kg annually in the period 2001-2005. Of the seven countries that reported exports of cathine in recent years, Germany remained the leading exporter, exporting an average of 2.4 tons annually in the period 2001-2005.

Sedative-hypnotics

43.   Barbiturates are a group of central nervous system depressants that are closely related in their chemical structure. Classified as sedatives-hypnotics, they used to be prescribed for the treatment of insomnia, anxiety, stress and epilepsy. Some barbiturates were also used as anaesthetics for short surgery interventions (ultra-short-acting substances) while others have selective anticonvulsant activity. Individual barbiturates differ in speed of onset, duration of action and potency. A low dose of 50 mg can relieve anxiety and tension, while a higher dose of 100-200 mg usually leads to sleep. Like benzodiazepines, barbiturates encountered on the illicit market have usually been diverted from licit circuits rather than synthesized in clandestine laboratories. The potential for abuse is great, and the long-term effects include the development of tolerance and strong physical and psychological dependence.

Amobarbital, butalbital, cyclobarbital and pentobarbital

44.   The substances amobarbital, cyclobarbital and pentobarbital were scheduled in 1971 when the 1971 Convention was adopted, while butalbital was added in 1987 to Schedule III of the Convention. Three of these barbiturates, amobarbital, butalbital and cyclobarbital, are mainly used as hypnotics (to induce sleep) and therefore have a place today in the treatment of intractable insomnia. Pentobarbital has also been used for pre-medication in anaesthesia. In per capita terms, during the period 2001-2005, Denmark, the United States and Canada had the highest calculated usage rates of these

four substances, with 17.2, 6.7 and 2.8 S-DDD per 1,000 inhabitants per day, respectively. Total reported manufacture of those substances fluctuated around 1.4 billion S-DDD during the period 2000-2003 and then gradually fell to 881 million S-DDD in 2005 (see figure 5). Figure 6 shows the distribution of total output during the period 2001-2005 by the manufacturing countries.

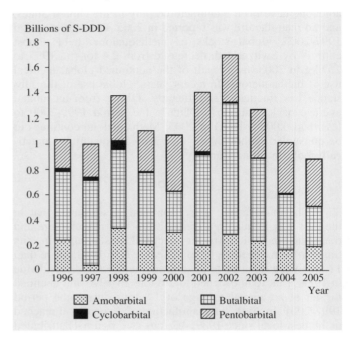

Figure 5.   Barbiturates listed in Schedule III: total reported manufacture, 1996-2005

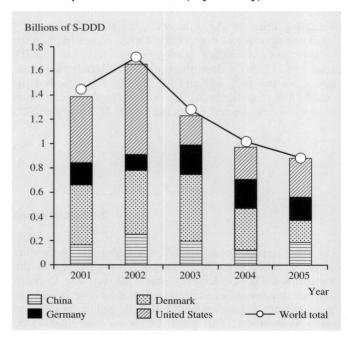

Figure 6.   Barbiturates listed in Schedule III: total reported manufacture, by country, 2001-2005

45. Traditionally, the United States has been the main manufacturer of butalbital, accounting for up to three quarters of the total output. Global manufacture of the substance decreased gradually from 76 tons in 2002 to 24 tons in 2005 (see figure 7). In addition to the United States, the only regular manufacturers of butalbital in the past decade were Denmark and Germany. Butalbital has been used for the manufacture of a number of preparations exempted in the United States from certain control measures in accordance with article 3 of the 1971 Convention. In recent years, the manufacture of butalbital in the United States has fluctuated, falling sharply from 40 tons in 2002 to an average of 7.4 tons in the period 2003-2005. The quantities manufactured in Denmark decreased steadily from 38.7 tons in 2003 to 12.8 tons in 2005, returning to almost the same level of average annual production as during the period 1996-2000 (14 tons). In 2005, the United States and Denmark accounted for 38 and 53 per cent, respectively, of global output, and Germany manufactured slightly more than 2 tons of the substance.

46. Ten countries reported exports of butalbital during the five-year period 2001-2005. Denmark accounted for as much as 96 per cent of global exports of the substance in 2001 and remained the biggest exporter in 2005, supplying 86 per cent of the 22.1 tons exported globally. Exports of butalbital by the United States were highly irregular, fluctuating between zero and 2 tons in the 10-year period 1996-2005. Italy and Switzerland were among the smaller exporters of the substance during the period 2001-2005, supplying an average of 179.4 and 103 kg of butalbital, respectively, per year. The United States, Italy and Canada have remained the main importers of butalbital. In recent years, Denmark, the United States, Italy and Canada have been the countries with the highest rates of use of the substance.

47. The total reported manufacture of pentobarbital decreased in recent years, falling from 45 tons in 2001 to an average of 37.7 tons in the period 2002-2005 (see figure 8). The United States, Germany, Denmark and Switzerland have been the leading manufacturers of the substance in the past 10 years, the first three countries producing 52.5, 44.5 and 2.8 per cent of global output, respectively, in 2005. Australia, Denmark, Ireland and New Zealand had the highest average rates of use of the substance over the past five years, ranging from 2.5 to 3.8 S-DDD per 1,000 inhabitants per day.

48. An annual average of about 26 tons of pentobarbital were traded internationally during the five-year period 2001-2005. The biggest exporters of the substance during that period were (listed in decreasing order by export volume), Germany, the United States, Canada, Denmark and France; together, they accounted for over 92 per cent of global exports of the substance during that period. During the period 2001-2005, German exports stabilized at an annual average of 11 tons, while exports by the United States of pentobarbital fluctuated between 3.5 tons and 6 tons. According to the reported statistics, 67 countries imported pentobarbital during that period. China (45.5 tons), Canada (6.7 tons), France (4.5 tons), Australia (2.6 tons) and the United Kingdom (2.1 tons) were the biggest importers of the substance in 2005, accounting for 86 per cent of global imports.

49. During the period 2001-2004, the main countries manufacturing amobarbital were China, Denmark and Japan, while in 2005, only China reported having manufactured the substance (18 tons) (see figure 9). Global stocks of amobarbital, after falling gradually from over 2 tons in 2001 to 1.7 tons in 2003, increased once again, to 3.2 tons in 2004

Figure 7. Butalbital: total reported manufacture, 1996-2005

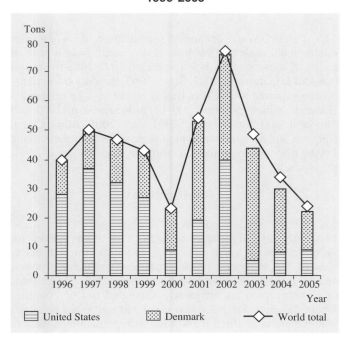

Figure 8. Pentobarbital: total reported manufacture, 1996-2005

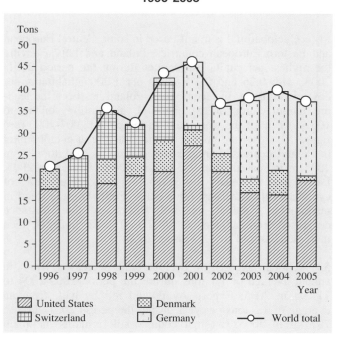

Figure 9. Amobarbital: total reported manufacture, 1996-2005

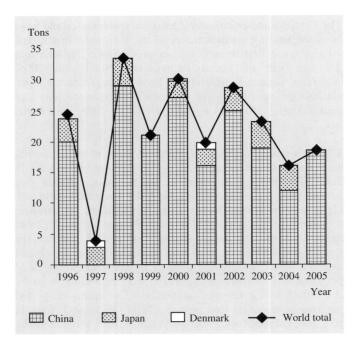

Figure 10. Cyclobarbital: total reported manufacture, 1996-2005

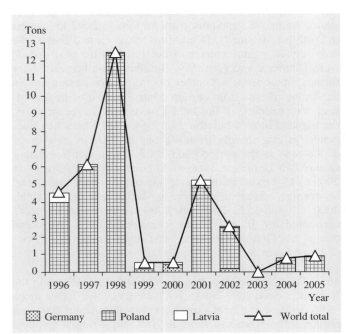

and to 7.3 tons in 2005. Global calculated use of the substance fluctuated around an average of 21.7 tons during the period 2001-2005, Romania, Japan and China having the highest calculated rates of amobarbital consumption during that period.

50. Global exports of amobarbital fluctuated with an increasing trend, with an annual average of 5.6 tons, during the period 2001-2005. Global annual imports of the substance peaked at 10.2 tons in 2005, Romania, the Netherlands (for re-export), Ireland and Hungary, in decreasing order, being the world's largest importers of amobarbital in recent years. In the Netherlands, imports of amobarbital showed a notable decrease from an annual average of 2.3 tons during the period 2002-2003 to 52 kg in 2005. The imports of Romania also decreased from 7.1 tons in 2002 to 2 tons in 2004, only to rise again to 9.7 tons in 2005.

51. Cyclobarbital is mainly used in some Central European and Eastern European countries, Poland and Latvia having the highest per capita usage rates during the period 2001-2005, with 0.26 and 0.3 S-DDD per 1,000 inhabitants per day, respectively. In recent years, Poland has been the leading manufacturer of cyclobarbital, accounting for up to 100 per cent of the world total in the period 2004-2005 (see figure 10). After the volume of manufacture of cyclobarbital in Poland decreased from about 5 tons in 2001 to zero in 2003, it increased from 755 kg in 2004 to 914 kg in 2005. Latvia and Germany have reported no manufacture of cyclobarbital in the past three years. Following the trend in manufacture, global reported stocks of the substance decreased from 2.6 tons in 2002 to 110 kg in 2004, then increased 10-fold to 1.1 tons in 2005.

52. Global exports of cyclobarbital decreased from an annual average of 1.1 tons during the period 2003-2004 to 711 kg in 2005. Exports by Poland fell by half, from an average of 1.5 tons per year during the period 2001-2004 to 707 kg in 2005, but that country still remains the main

exporter of the substance. Belarus, Georgia, Latvia, Lithuania and Switzerland were the other leading importers of cyclobarbital in the period 2003-2005.

Glutethimide

53. As in the previous few years, no manufacture of glutethimide was reported to INCB for 2005. During the early 1980s, several dozen tons of that substance were manufactured annually, mainly for conversion into amino glutethimide, a non-psychotropic substance used as an antineoplastic agent. Global manufacture declined steadily during the 1990s and came to a standstill in 1998. Since then, manufacture of that substance has been reported only by Hungary, which manufactured about 700 kg of glutethimide in 2001, and China, which manufactured 240 kg in 2005.

54. Parallel to the decline in manufacture, the volume of international trade in glutethimide decreased, from a peak of about 15 tons per annum in the period 1997-1998 to several hundred kilograms in 2002. Since 2003, the only trade transactions reported to INCB in quantities above 1 kg concerned Hungary, which exported 300 kg to Romania in 2003 and imported 200 kg in both 2004 and 2005 from China. Bulgaria and Switzerland, which were major importers in the 1990s, have not imported glutethimide since 2002 and 2001, respectively.

Flunitrazepam

55. Flunitrazepam continues to be one of the most frequently abused benzodiazepines. The illicit market for flunitrazepam appears to be supplied mainly through diversion of the substance from domestic distribution channels and not through diversion from international trade. Preparations of flunitrazepam are frequently smuggled out of countries where the diversion has taken place and into other countries where there is an illicit market for such preparations. Due to

frequent diversions and abuse, flunitrazepam was transferred from Schedule IV to Schedule III in 1995. Several countries, including major manufacturers and importers of the substance, have adopted strict control policies for flunitrazepam, in close cooperation with the pharmaceutical industry.

56. In medical practice, flunitrazepam is used, like diazepam, for the short-term management of insomnia and, in some countries, for pre-medication and for induction of general anaesthesia. Up to 1996, manufacture of flunitrazepam was reported by a number of countries, including Argentina, Brazil, the Czech Republic, Denmark, Italy, Japan, Spain and Turkey. Since then, only Italy and Switzerland, which started manufacture in 1997, continue to manufacture flunitrazepam. While in 2004, manufacture by those two countries combined totalled more than 1.5 tons, which is the largest amount of flunitrazepam ever reported, global manufacture dropped to a record low of 84 kg in 2005. That decrease occurred because Switzerland did not manufacture flunitrazepam in 2005, owing to the high stocks it still held (see figures 22 and 23 and para. 105 below).

57. International trade in flunitrazepam was relatively stable during the period 1990-2003, fluctuating at about 1.1 tons per year. In 2004, trade began to decline, and decreased further to 700 kg in 2005. Switzerland, which has been the leading exporter of the substance since 1997, and Italy together accounted for 96 per cent of global exports in 2005. In addition, some countries re-exported flunitrazepam during that year, notably, Brazil, the Czech Republic, France, Germany and Ireland.

58. Global imports of flunitrazepam, which reached a peak of over 1.4 tons in 1995, have declined steadily since then, most probably due to strict national control measures and the transfer, in 1995, of the substance to Schedule III of the 1971 Convention. Japan continues to be the leading importer of flunitrazepam, accounting for more than half of annual global imports (421 kg in 2005). In addition, some 25 countries reported imports of flunitrazepam in quantities exceeding 1 kg in 2005, including Australia, Austria, Belgium, Brazil, France, Germany, Greece, the Republic of Korea and Sweden, in amounts between 10 kg and 40 kg.

Analgesics

Buprenorphine

59. Buprenorphine,[6] listed in Schedule III since 1989, belongs to the family of opioids used mainly as analgesics. In several countries, buprenorphine is also used in the detoxification and substitution treatment of opioid dependence. The total manufacture of the substance, which increased steadily from 1993 onwards, reached an average of nearly 2 tons in the period 2003-2005, which is double the amount manufactured in the late 1990s, when the substance started to be used in higher doses for the treatment for opioid addiction. The United Kingdom continued to be the main manufacturer of buprenorphine, accounting for 75 per cent of the world total on average during the period 2001-2005; its manufacture of the substance increased significantly from 274 kg in 1996 to 1,542 kg in 2005. The second-largest manufacturer of buprenorphine in the past five years was Australia, which manufactured 383 kg in 2005, mainly destined for export.

That country's manufacture has increased since 1999, when it first reported manufacture. India has also been a regular manufacturer of buprenorphine, with an annual average manufacture of 15 kg during the period 2001-2005. Other manufacturers of buprenorphine in 2005 included the Netherlands (30 kg), Belgium (12 kg), the Czech Republic (10 kg) and China (9.5 kg). As expected, total stocks of the substance also increased markedly from 115 kg in 1996 to 1,614 kg in 2005. In 2005, stocks of buprenorphine were held mainly by the United Kingdom (728 kg), Germany (246 kg), France (192 kg), Australia (108 kg) and the Netherlands (49 kg).

60. Total exports of buprenorphine rose significantly from 100 kg in 1996 to 1,236 kg in 2005. That trend was driven by the rise in buprenorphine exports from Australia, Germany and the United Kingdom, the main exporters of the substance. Belgium, Denmark, France, India and the Netherlands have also reported exports of buprenorphine in recent years.

61. Germany and France were the largest importers (accounting for 60 per cent of total imports) among the 43 countries that reported annual imports of more than 1 kg of buprenorphine in the period 2001-2005. Other major importers of buprenorphine in 2005 were the United States (176 kg), Spain (70 kg), Italy (57 kg), Belgium (24 kg), Portugal (13 kg), Switzerland (12 kg) and Malaysia (11 kg), all for domestic consumption. Increased use of the substance is reflected in statistical reports from Australia, Austria, Belgium, the Czech Republic, France, Germany, Italy, Malaysia, Portugal, Spain, Sweden, Switzerland, the United Kingdom and the United States, while small-scale use for that purpose has also been reported by a number of countries, including China, Denmark, Estonia, Finland, Greece, Iceland, India, Indonesia, Ireland, Israel, Latvia, Mexico, Norway, Pakistan and Singapore.

Pentazocine

62. Pentazocine is an opioid analgesic with actions and uses similar to those of morphine. It was included in Schedule III in 1984. The total reported manufacture of pentazocine showed marked fluctuations in the period 1996-2005, with an annual average of more than 4.5 tons. In 2005, manufacture was led by India (3,027 kg) and Italy (1,446 kg). While practically all of the pentazocine manufactured by India was for domestic consumption, all of the pentazocine manufactured in Italy was destined for export. Italy accounted for more than 50 per cent of global exports of pentazocine in 2005. Three other countries, Hungary (136 kg in 2001), the United Kingdom (258 kg in 2002) and the United States (171 kg in 2001 and 316 kg in 2002), have also manufactured the substance in recent years, although in much smaller quantities. Total stocks of pentazocine also fluctuated during the period 2001-2005, averaging 3.4 tons. In addition to the main manufacturers, India and Italy, a few countries reported holding large stocks of the substance at the end of 2005: United States (762 kg), Pakistan (357 kg) and Slovenia (173 kg).

63. The major importers of pentazocine in 2005 were the United States (1,357 kg), Pakistan (598 kg), Japan (450 kg), Canada (177 kg) and Nigeria (120 kg). Significant quantities were also imported in 2005 by Switzerland (451 kg) and Portugal (229 kg), mainly for re-export. The main consumers of pentazocine included Canada, India, Japan, Nigeria, Pakistan and the United States.

---

[6] See table IV for details.

64. According to WHO scheduling criteria for the inclusion of substances in Schedule IV of the 1971 Convention, substances for inclusion in that Schedule are those whose liability to abuse constitutes a smaller but still significant risk to public health than substances included in Schedule III and which have a therapeutic usefulness from little to great. Sixty-three substances with various applications in medicine are listed in Schedule IV. Substances included in that Schedule belong to the following groups: central nervous system stimulants (14 substances); benzodiazepine-type anxiolytics (22 substances); other anxiolytics (1 substance); benzodiazepine-type sedative-hypnotics (11 substances); benzodiazepine-type anti-epileptics (1 substance); barbiturate-type sedative-hypnotics and anti-epileptics (7 substances); other sedative-hypnotics (5 substances); analgesics (1 substance); and anti-depressants (1 substance).

Central nervous system stimulants

65. Fourteen stimulants are listed in Schedule IV: amfepramone, aminorex, benzfetamine, etilamfetamine, fencamfamin, fenproporex, mazindol, mefenorex, mesocarb, pemoline, phendimetrazine, phentermine, pipradrol and pyrovalerone. Both amfepramone and pipradrol were originally included in Schedule IV, while all the other stimulants were added at later stages. The stimulants in Schedule IV are essentially used as anorectics or for the treatment of ADD.

66. The total reported manufacture of central nervous system stimulants listed in Schedule IV showed extreme fluctuations during the late 1990s and stabilized at an annual average of about 1.8 billion S-DDD during the period 2000-2005 (see figure 11). In 1996, a record level of manufacture (3.9 billion S-DDD) was reached. It started to decrease in 1997 and reached a record low in 1998 (356 million S-DDD). After 1998, total reported manufacture gradually increased, reaching a global total of 2.2 billion S-DDD in 2001. Global manufacture decreased slightly, to 1.6 billion S-DDD in 2003, but gradually increased to 2 billion S-DDD in 2005.

67. In 2005, of the total reported manufacture of the 14 stimulants in Schedule IV, the manufacture of phentermine (923 million S-DDD) comprised 45 per cent, fenproporex (474 million S-DDD) accounted for 23 per cent and amfepramone (371 million S-DDD) accounted for 18 per cent (see figure 12). Mazindol (175 million S-DDD) and phendimetrazine (100 million S-DDD) accounted for 9 and 4 per cent, respectively, while benzfetamine (10 million S-DDD) accounted for 0.5 per cent. No manufacture of pemoline or any other central nervous system stimulant listed in Schedule IV was reported in 2005.

68. The fluctuations in total reported manufacture and use of central nervous system stimulants listed in Schedule IV are mainly a reflection of developments in the use of phentermine in the United States (see figure 13). The sharp increase in the consumption of phentermine in the United States in 1996 and 1997 was due to its prescription for the treatment of obesity in combination with another anorectic (fenfluramine). After the withdrawal in September 1997 of fenfluramine from the market of the United States because of the serious adverse effects of that substance, the use of phentermine also dropped noticeably. Since 2000, manufacture and consumption have picked up again, and phentermine has once again become the most used anorectic in the United States. Of the 1.9 billion S-DDD of substances

Figure 11. Central nervous system stimulants listed in Schedule IV: total reported manufacture, 1996-2005

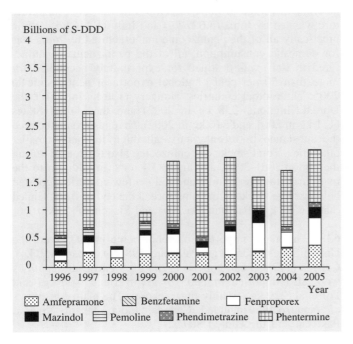

Figure 12. Central nervous system stimulants listed in Schedule IV: total reported manufacture of individual substances, 2005

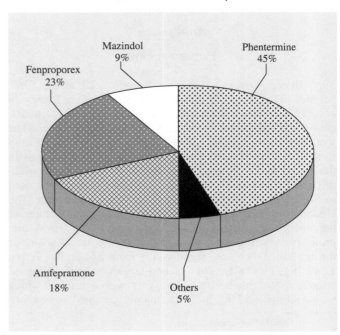

in this group used globally in 2005, the most used substance was phentermine (795 million S-DDD), followed by fenproporex (456 million S-DDD), amfepramone (378 million S-DDD) and phendimetrazine (87 million S-DDD).

69.   The highest per capita consumption of stimulants in Schedule IV during the 1990s took place in the Americas. The temporary decline in the use of phentermine in the United States and measures against the inappropriate use of some stimulants in a number of countries in South America (most notably Argentina and Chile) had led to a decrease in consumption levels. However, since 2000, consumption of phentermine in the United States has been rising again. At the same time, the consumption of Schedule IV stimulants continued to increase significantly in some countries of the Americas, such as Argentina, Brazil and the United States. Overall, an average of 10.4 S-DDD per 1,000 inhabitants per day were consumed in the Americas during 2003-2005 (see figure 14).

70.   The rest of the world experienced a decrease in consumption of these stimulants. In Asia, the rate of consumption increased slightly between the late 1990s and the period 2000-2002, in particular in the Republic of Korea, Malaysia, and Singapore. However the annual average rate of consumption was 32 per cent lower during the period 2003-2005: 1.7 S-DDD per 1,000 inhabitants per day. Similarly, in Europe, after relatively stable consumption rates during the period 1997-2002, the average rate fell from 4 S-DDD to 1.6 S-DDD per 1,000 inhabitants per day in the period 2003-2005. That change was mainly attributable to a sharp decline in the consumption of phentermine in Belgium and the

United Kingdom, as well as lower consumption of fenproporex and amfepramone in Belgium, Denmark, Germany and Switzerland. The decrease in the calculated rate of consumption was even more dramatic in Oceania, where it fell from 7.5 to 2.3 S-DDD during that same period. That decrease was due to a decline of 72 and 76 per cent in consumption of phentermine in Australia and New Zealand, respectively.

71.   Worldwide, in 2005, Brazil (12.5 S-DDD per 1,000 inhabitants per day), Argentina (11.8 S-DDD), the Republic of Korea (9.8 S-DDD) and the United States (4.9 S-DDD) had the highest calculated rate of use of the central nervous system stimulants listed in Schedule IV.

72.   Phentermine has been the major substance in the group of stimulants in Schedule IV, its share of total stimulant manufacture fluctuating widely between zero and 76 per cent in recent years. Total reported manufacture of this substance increased from an average of 9.5 tons annually during the period 1991-1995 to 50 tons in 1996, the highest level ever reported. Since then, global reported manufacture has fluctuated between 2.6 tons and 30 tons, averaging 14.2 tons in the period 2004-2005, the main manufacturers being Germany, Italy and the United States.

73.   Ten countries have reported the export of at least 100 kg of phentermine at least once during the period 2001-2005. Germany was the largest exporter of the substance again in 2005 (4.4 tons), followed by Italy (3.5 tons), the United States (3 tons), Australia, Switzerland and the Netherlands, the first three countries accounting for 84 per cent of global

Figure 13.   Central nervous system stimulants listed in Schedule IV: calculated global consumption,[a] **1996-2005**

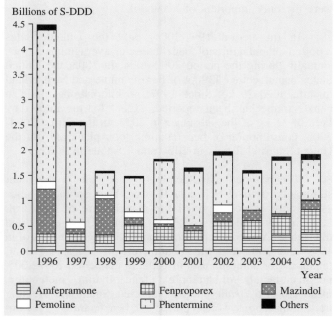

[a] Statistical data submitted by Governments are used to calculate the approximate global consumption in a given year. These consumption figures are expressed in defined daily doses for statistical purposes (S-DDD).

Figure 14. Central nervous system stimulants listed in Schedule IV: average national consumption by region,[a] **1997-1999, 2000-2002 and 2003-2005**

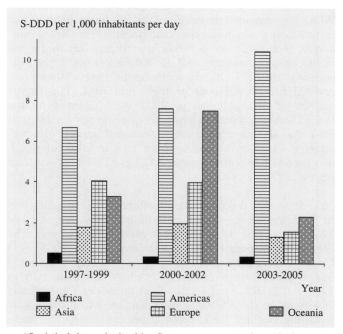

[a] Statistical data submitted by Governments are used to calculate average annual consumption for a three-year period.

exports. Forty-six countries reported imports of phentermine at least once during the five-year period 2001-2005. The United States was the main importer of the substance in 2005 (5.3 tons), accounting for 47 per cent of global imports, and re-exported over half of it. The other main importers of phentermine in 2005 were the Republic of Korea (2.2 tons) and Australia (1.1 tons), their combined total increasing by 23 per cent over the previous year.

74. Fenproporex, which was brought under international control in 1986, is mainly used as an appetite suppressant. Since 1986, only Brazil, France, Switzerland and, more recently, Germany and India have reported its manufacture. After a steady growth from 3 tons in 1998 to 10 tons in 2003, total reported manufacture of fenproporex fell to 5 tons in 2004. However, in 2005 global output increased by 82 per cent, reaching 9.5 tons. Brazil and Germany were the only manufacturers of the substance in 2005, Brazil accounting for 87 per cent of the total. In the period 1995-1999, the manufacture of fenproporex in France varied greatly, averaging about 1.3 tons annually, a significant drop from the annual average of nearly 3 tons in that country in the period 1992-1994. France last reported manufacture of fenproporex in 2003 (2.6 tons), and Switzerland last reported manufacture of the substance in 2000 (4.9 tons). The fenproporex manufactured in Brazil was for domestic consumption, and that country was also the leading importer of the substance in 2005 (1.6 tons), accounting for 98 per cent of global imports.

75. In 2005, total reported manufacture of amfepramone, a substance mainly used as an anorectic, amounted to about 28 tons. Three countries reported the manufacture of amfepramone in 2005: Brazil (27.6 tons), Italy (251 kg) and Switzerland (22 kg). The level of manufacture of Switzerland has decreased significantly from 2004, when it manufactured 3.9 tons of amfepramone. However, Switzerland remains by far the main exporter of the substance, with exports increasing from an annual average of 2.8 tons during the period 2002-2004 to 5.8 tons in 2005. Germany, Italy and Brazil were the other main exporters of amfepramone. While Italy exported almost all of the substance that it manufactured, the amfepramone manufactured in Brazil was almost exclusively for domestic use. Brazil was by far the main consumer country (5.3 S-DDD per 1,000 inhabitants per day); in 2005, its consumption of the substance accounted for 90 per cent of the world total. The largest imports of amfepramone in 2005 were reported by the United States (1.4 tons), Germany (1.2 tons) and Switzerland (913 kg). Sixteen other countries reported imports of amfepramone in quantities greater than 1 kg in 2005, of which two reported imports of over 200 kg: Chile (297 kg) and Australia (255 kg).

76. Italy was the main manufacturer of phendimetrazine. In 2005, the global manufacture of that substance stood at 7 tons, an increase of 44 per cent over the previous year. The only other manufacturers of the substance in 2005 were China (700 kg for export) and Germany (5 kg). The United States reported the manufacture of phendimetrazine only in 1999 and 2001, in relatively small quantities (560 kg and 274 kg, respectively). Phendimetrazine manufactured in Italy is mainly destined for export (80 per cent in 2005). Traditionally, the main importer of the substance has been the United States (3.1 tons in 2005), followed by the Republic of Korea (1.7 tons annually in the period 2004-2005, a 20-fold

increase since 2001). Since 2000, five other countries have reported imports of phendimetrazine in quantities of more than 1 kg: Colombia, Denmark, Italy, Malaysia and South Africa. Of the countries that reported use of phendimetrazine in 2005, by far the greatest consumer of the substance was the Republic of Korea (1.4 S-DDD per 1,000 inhabitants per day), followed by Italy (0.7 S-DDD), Malaysia (0.6 S-DDD), the United States (0.4 S DDD) and three other countries.

77. Global manufacture of pemoline, a substance under international control since 1989, fluctuated significantly during the period 1996-2005. Global output totalled 8.7 tons in 1995 and then declined sharply to 4.6 tons in 1997. There was no reported manufacture of the substance in 1998 and 2005. In 2001, only the United States reported manufacture of the substance (35 kg). In both 2002 and 2004, Switzerland reported manufacture of about 1.1 tons of pemoline. The only other manufacturers of the substance in the period 2001-2005 were the United States (465 kg in 2002) and China (6 kg in 2003). Switzerland (312 kg) and the Netherlands (128 kg) were the only exporters of the substance in 2005. The main importers of pemoline in 2005 were the United States (300 kg), Germany (45 kg), Switzerland (23 kg), the Netherlands (21 kg) and Chile (15 kg). In addition to its use as a stimulant, pemoline is used for the treatment of ADD.

78. In the past, mazindol was manufactured almost exclusively in Brazil: an average of 75 kg during the period 1999-2003, about half of which was for domestic consumption and the rest for export. Two other countries reported the manufacture of mazindol in the period 1996-2005: Poland in 1998 (25 kg) and 1999 (1 kg) and Argentina in 2002 (22 kg), 2003 (165 kg) and 2005 (175 kg). No manufacture of the substance was reported in 2004. Global use of the substance fell sharply from 702 kg in 1998 to an annual average of 150 kg during the period 2001-2005. During the same period, 17 countries reported having imported mazindol in quantities of at least 1 kg, the main importers of the substance being Mexico (49 per cent of global imports) and Switzerland (28 per cent). In 2005, Japan (3 kg) and Switzerland (1 kg) were the only importers of mazindol.

79. In the period 1997-2004, only the United States reported manufacture of benzfetamine, averaging 1.1 tons annually during the period 2000-2004. In 2005, the United States manufactured 729 kg of benzfetamine and Switzerland manufactured 29 kg. Since 1997, no international trade in benzfetamine has been reported, except for the import by Peru of 31 kg of the substance in 2003. In the period 2004-2005, consumption of benzfetamine took place only in the United States: 1.2 tons in 2004 and 1.8 tons in 2005.

80. The reported manufacture of and trade in the other stimulants listed in Schedule IV have been sporadic. Since 1995, only France reported the manufacture of pipradrol: 20 kg in 1999 and 8 kg in 2004, of which 2 kg were exported to Canada. Australia reported imports of 2 kg of pipradrol in 1999 and 2002 and the manufacture of 3 kg of etilamfetamine (for domestic use) in 2002. In the period 2001-2005, no manufacture of aminorex, fencamfamin, mefenorex, mesocarb or pyrovalerone was reported. Small and irregular trade transactions were reported for benzfetamine, fencamfamine, mefenorex and pipradrol, while no international trade was reported for aminorex, etilamfetamine, mesocarb and pyrovalerone.

Benzodiazepines

81. Thirty-three benzodiazepines were included in Schedule IV in 1984. Midazolam was added to Schedule IV in 1990, and brotizolam was added in 1995. Flunitrazepam was transferred from Schedule IV to Schedule III in 1995.

82. The number of countries and territories reporting benzodiazepine manufacture and/or trade has increased considerably. Since 1990, about 200 countries and territories have reported at least once the manufacture of or trade in benzodiazepines in quantities of more than 1 kg. Global reporting on the manufacture of and trade in benzodiazepines was not complete until recently, when a number of important manufacturing and trading countries established national control measures for those substances. Data on benzodiazepines have been made available by Switzerland only since 1997, by Austria since 1998, by Belgium in 1999 and by Canada in 2001.

Benzodiazepine-type anxiolytics

83. Twenty-two benzodiazepines are generally classified as anxiolytics. The total reported manufacture of this group of substances rose steadily from 1996 to 2001, when it reached a peak of 29 billion S-DDD. Global manufacture then decreased slightly, totalling 22 billion S-DDD in 2005 (see figure 15). Fluctuations in the level of manufacture of benzodiazepine-type anxiolytics are usually a reflection of fluctuations in the manufacture of diazepam, the main substance of this group, accounting for 31 per cent (or 6.9 billion S-DDD) of the total in 2005. In that year, the share of alprazolam (6.6 billion S-DDD) increased to 30 per cent, while the manufacture of lorazepam (4.2 billion S-DDD) accounted for 19 per cent of total output. Bromazepam, chlordiazepoxide and oxazepam each accounted for

3 per cent, clorazepate for 2 per cent and nordazepam for 1 per cent of the total reported manufacture of benzodiazepine-type anxiolytics in 2005 (see figure 16). The remaining 12 substances in that group (clobazam, clotiazepam, cloxazolam, delorazepam, ethyl loflazepate, fludiazepam, halazepam, ketazolam, medazepam, pinazepam, prazepam and tetrazepam) each accounted for less than 1 per cent of the total reported manufacture calculated in S-DDD. No manufacture of camazepam or oxazolam was reported in 2005. As shown in figures 17 and 18, China and Italy were

Figure 16. Benzodiazepine-type anxiolytics: share of total reported manufacture, 2005

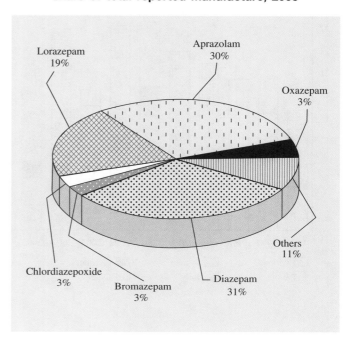

Figure 15. Benzodiazepine-type anxiolytics: total reported manufacture, 1996-2005

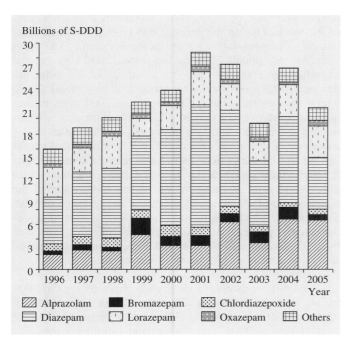

Figure 17. Benzodiazepine-type anxiolytics: countries' shares of total reported manufacture, 2005

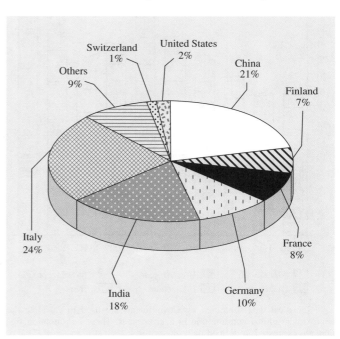

the leading manufacturers of benzodiazepine-type anxiolytics in the 10-year period 1995-2004 and, together with India and Germany, accounted for 73 per cent of total manufacture in 2005.

84. While approximate consumption levels, calculated by INCB, usually follow the trend in manufacture, in 2005 total consumption of this group of substances reached 27.7 billion S-DDD (see figure 19), which was considerably more than the quantity manufactured in 2005. The calculated average national consumption of benzodiazepine-type anxiolytics is higher in Europe than in other regions (see figure 20).

Figure 18. Benzodiazepine-type anxiolytics: manufacture reported by selected countries, 1996-2005

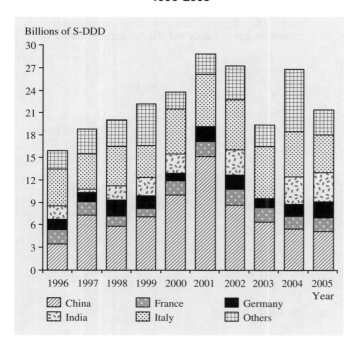

Figure 20. Benzodiazepine-type anxiolytics: average national consumption,[a] by region, 1997-1999, 2000-2002 and 2003-2005

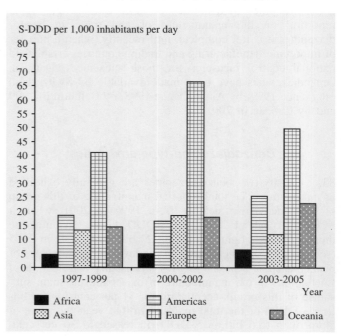

[a] Statistical data submitted by Governments are used to calculate the average annual consumption for a three-year period. Data from the five countries with the highest consumption were included in the calculation for each region.

Figure 19. Benzodiazepine-type anxiolytics: calculated global consumption, 1996-2005[a]

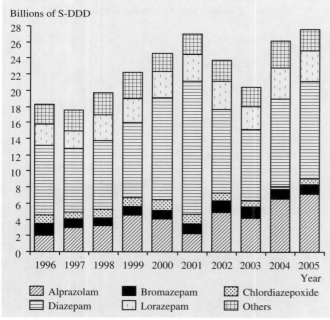

[a] Statistical data submitted by Governments are used to calculate the approximate global consumption in a given year. These consumption figures are expressed in defined daily doses for statistical purposes (S-DDD).

Diazepam

85. Diazepam, the most traded substance in the group of benzodiazepine-type anxiolytics, is consumed in all regions of the world. During the period 1990-1999, global manufacture of diazepam followed an increasing trend, averaging over 76 tons annually. During the period 2000-2004, global manufacture averaged 123 tons. In 2005, manufacture dropped to 69 tons, mainly on account of the United States, which did not manufacture diazepam in 2005 after having manufactured over 29 tons in 2004. China, which has traditionally been the major manufacturer and exporter of the substance, accounting for about 70 per cent of global manufacture during the period 2000-2004, manufactured 45 tons in 2005. Italy reported the second largest manufacture in 2005, at 12 tons. In addition, Brazil and India reported the manufacture of quantities of diazepam in the range of tons. Switzerland, which had manufactured several tons of diazepam annually since 1997, did not manufacture that substance in 2005. Poland and the Russian Federation manufactured several hundreds of kilograms of diazepam.

86. Export levels decreased slightly, from 61 tons in 2004 to 60 tons in 2005. At 21 tons, China accounted for 35 per cent of that amount. Italy's exports remained stable, at over 16 tons in 2005, and Switzerland exported 7 tons.

87. Diazepam is widely used, with about 120 countries and territories reporting imports in quantities of more than 1 kg every year. In 2005, the largest importers were Denmark (6.7 tons), Germany (4.2 tons), the United States (3.6 tons), Switzerland (2.8 tons) and Spain (2 tons), together accounting for over 40 per cent of global imports. Amounts between 1 and 2 tons were imported by Pakistan, Ghana, Ireland, Canada, the Islamic Republic of Iran, Thailand and Nigeria, in that order. Spain, formerly the main importer of diazepam, reduced its imports of the substance from 29 tons (used mainly for veterinary purposes) in 1989 to 10 tons in 1997 and to 2 tons in 2005. Global consumption of diazepam remained stable, standing at 12 billion S-DDD in 2005. According to calculated consumption figures, the United Kingdom (5.2 billion S-DDD), China (2.5 billion S-DDD), the United States (664 million S-DDD) and Brazil (611 million S-DDD) are the world's main consumers of the substance.

Alprazolam

88. Total reported manufacture of alprazolam grew steadily from about 1 ton per year in 1986 to 6.7 tons in 2005. After 2002, global output remained at more than 6 tons every year, with the exception of 2003, when global manufacture fell to 3.6 tons because of non-manufacture by the United States. Fluctuations in the level of global manufacture reflect, to a large extent, manufacturing levels in India and the United States, which are the major manufacturers of alprazolam. In 2005, India manufactured 2.3 tons, the largest amount ever manufactured by that country, whereas the output of the United States fell from 1.7 tons in 2004 to 302 kg in 2005. In 2005, Italy manufactured 1.5 tons; Finland, 1.2 tons; and France, nearly 1 ton. Those countries together accounted for 94 per cent of global manufacture of alprazolam in 2005. They were also the main exporters of the substance, together accounting for more than 74 per cent of total exports in 2005.

89. In 2005, over 70 countries and territories in all regions of the world reported imports of alprazolam in quantities exceeding 1 kg. Total imports increased from 1.6 tons in 1998 to an annual average of 5.7 tons in the period 1999-2004 and reached a new record in 2004 (6.8 tons); that was followed by a slightly lower output in 2005, at 6.7 tons. In 2005, the main importers of alprazolam were the United States (2 tons), Belgium (970 kg) and Spain (628 kg), which together accounted for over 53 per cent of the total import volume. Global consumption during the period 2000-2005 averaged 4.8 billion S-DDD, the United States remaining the highest consumer (1.8 billion S-DDD in 2005).

Lorazepam

90. Total reported manufacture of lorazepam dropped from 11.1 tons in 2001 to 6.5 tons in 2003, a level comparable to the average level during the period 1999-2000. In 2004, manufacturing levels rose again, reaching over 10 tons in both 2004 and 2005. Such fluctuations are attributable to significant changes in the levels of manufacture of Italy and Germany, the two main manufacturers of lorazepam. In 2005, Italy and Germany manufactured over 5 tons and 3 tons, respectively. Combined with India (1.6 tons), they accounted for about 97 per cent of total manufacture. Other countries that reported manufacture of lorazepam in 2005 were Brazil and Poland (105 kg each).

91. Exports of lorazepam averaged 10 tons annually in the period 2000-2004 and rose to 11.7 tons in 2005. Italy and Germany were the main exporters of the substance. Those countries, together with Ireland, a major re-exporter, accounted for more than 80 per cent of total exports of the substance in 2005. Approximately 100 countries imported more than 1 kg of lorazepam at least once in the period 2001-2005. Of those countries, Ireland and the United States imported the most, together accounting for about 40 per cent of total imports of the substance during 2005. The other main importers of lorazepam in 2005 included Spain (924 kg), France (758 kg) and Germany (742 kg). Global calculated consumption averaged 3.5 billion S-DDD in the period 2001-2005, Germany (987 million S-DDD) being the main consumer in 2005.

Bromazepam

92. Total reported manufacture of bromazepam fluctuated significantly in the period 1999-2005. After having increased sharply from an annual average of 6 tons during the period 1997-1998, global output of the substance peaked at over 21 tons in 1999 and declined to an average of 13.5 tons in the years thereafter. In 2005, global output dropped to 7.3 tons. This decline was due to Switzerland, the leading manufacturer since 1998 (averaging 7.8 tons per year), which did not manufacture bromazepam in 2005, because of its high level of stocks. Thus, the largest manufacturer in 2005 was Italy (4.8 tons), followed by Brazil (1.6 tons) and India (554 kg).

93. In 2005, global exports of bromazepam, at 15.0 tons, remained slightly below the average of 15.4 tons per year in the period 1997-2004. As in previous years, the main exporters were Switzerland (6.8 tons) and Italy (5.2 tons), which together accounted for 80 per cent of total exports of the substance. Of the 84 countries that reported imports of bromazepam in quantities of more than 1 kg in 2005, five of them accounted for 51 per cent of global imports, namely, France, Switzerland, Brazil, Germany and Italy, in that order. During the period 2000-2005, all of the bromazepam imported by Switzerland and Italy was re-exported; during the same period, France and Brazil imported bromazepam mainly for domestic use, but also re-exported several hundred kilograms per year. Calculated global consumption of bromazepam, which had fluctuated at about 1.3 billion S-DDD annually during the period 2000-2004, decreased slightly to 1.2 billion S-DDD in 2005.

Chlordiazepoxide

94. Total reported manufacture of chlordiazepoxide decreased steadily from 43 tons in 2000 to 21 tons in 2005. That decrease reflects the reductions in quantities of chlordiazepoxide manufactured in China, India and Italy, the main manufacturing countries. In 2005, China manufactured 11 tons, accounting for 52 per cent of global output of chlordiazepoxide, and India reported the manufacture of 6.3 tons (30 per cent). Most of the chlordiazepoxide manufactured in China and Italy was for re-export, while the larger part of the output of India was for domestic consumption.

95. Global imports of chlordiazepoxide decreased from 24 tons in 2000 to 13 tons in 2005; after 1997, over 100 countries reported at least once imports of the substance in quantities exceeding 1 kg. The main importers of chlordiazepoxide

in 2005 were Switzerland (1.7 tons, entirely for re-export) and Cuba, the United States and Egypt (1.3 tons, 1.2 tons and 1 ton, respectively, for domestic use). In the period 2001-2005, global consumption of the substance decreased from 1.2 billion S-DDD to 678 million S-DDD.

Oxazepam

96. The total manufacture of oxazepam was fairly stable in the period 1998-2002, averaging nearly 30 tons per year. In 2003, it rose to 34 tons, fell to 22 tons the following year and reached 27 tons in 2005. The main manufacturers of oxazepam in 2005 were Italy (14.3 tons) and France (10.4 tons), which together accounted for 91 per cent of global output. The volume of trade in oxazepam averaged about 40 tons annually during the five-year period 2001-2005. Ireland and France were the main importers of oxazepam. While Ireland imported the substance mainly for re-export, France also used large quantities for domestic consumption, accounting for 25 per cent of global calculated consumption in the period 2001-2005.

Clorazepate

97. Total reported manufacture of clorazepate remained stable, averaging 8.4 tons during the period 2001-2005. France (5.8 tons) and Italy (1.1 tons) accounted for 86 per cent of total output of clorazepate in 2005. Fifty-four countries imported a total of 8.8 tons of clorazepate. The main importers were Spain (re-exporting about half of its imports) and France (re-exporting all of its imports).

Clobazam

98. Total reported manufacture of clobazam decreased from 5.5 tons in 2004 to 3.5 tons in 2005, the main manufacturers being Germany (1.2 tons) and France (1.4 tons). International trade amounted to approximately 5 tons, with 58 countries reporting imports of more than 1 kg.

Others

99. In 2005, combined total reported manufacture of fludiazepam, halazepam, nordazepam, pinazepam and prazepam increased from 435 million S-DDD in 2004 to 478 million S-DDD in 2005. The combined manufacture of camazepam, clotiazepam, cloxazolam, delorazepam, ethyl loflazepate, ketazolam, medazepam and tetrazepam increased from 680 million S-DDD in 2004 to 778 million S-DDD in 2005.

Other anxiolytics

Meprobamate

100. Due to its gradual replacement by benzodiazepines, the manufacture of meprobamate, the only non-benzodiazepine- type substance in Schedule IV used as an anxiolytic, decreased continuously, from a record level of nearly 1,000 tons in the late 1970s to an annual average of

Figure 21. Meprobamate: reported manufacture, 1996-2005

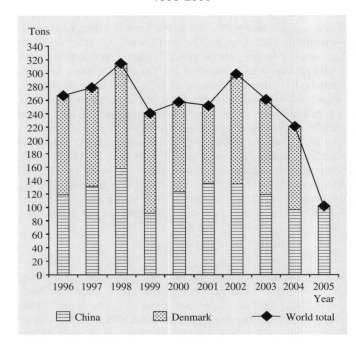

a little more than one quarter of that amount in the 10-year period 1993-2003 (see figure 21). Global manufacture fell from 260 tons in 2003 to 103 tons in 2005. That decline can be attributed to China, which had manufactured almost half the global supply in previous years but did not manufacture that substance in 2005. Denmark, the other major supplier, accounted for almost all of global output that year. In addition, India and Spain resumed manufacture of meprobamate after more than a decade, manufacturing 400 kg and 107 kg, respectively, in 2005. Most of the meprobamate manufactured by Denmark was exported to over 20 countries. During the period 2001-2005, France and Denmark held the highest level of stocks of meprobamate (averaging 53 tons and 48 tons, respectively, per year). Hungary was third, with an average of 17 tons. China has never reported data on stocks of meprobamate.

101. The level of imports of meprobamate averaged about 250 tons annually in the five-year period 2001-2005; about 80 countries reported imports of the substance at least once during that period. France was the main importer of meprobamate, purchasing an average of 90 tons annually during the period 2001-2005, almost all of it for domestic use. The other main importers of the substance in 2005 were Cuba (25 tons), Hungary (15 tons), South Africa (14 tons), Romania and the United States (6 tons each) and Turkey (5 tons).

Benzodiazepine-type sedative-hypnotics

102. Twelve benzodiazepines are generally used as sedative-hypnotics: brotizolam, estazolam, flunitrazepam (the only benzodiazepine included in Schedule III), flurazepam, haloxazolam, loprazolam, lormetazepam, midazolam, nimetazepam, nitrazepam, temazepam and triazolam.

Figure 22. Benzodiazepine-type sedative hypnotics, total reported manufacture, by substance, 1996-2005

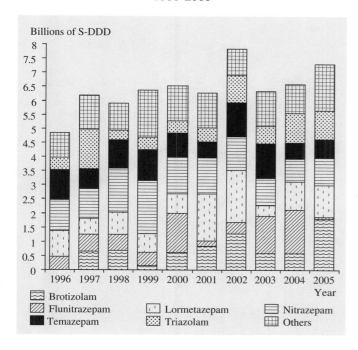

Figure 23. Benzodiazepine-type sedative hypnotics: calculated global consumption,[a] 1996-2005

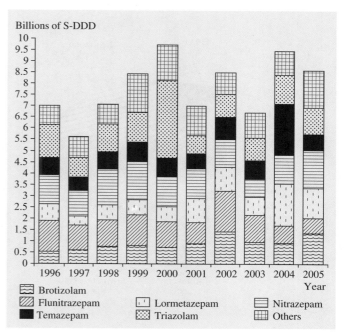

[a] Statistical data submitted by Governments are used to calculate the approximate global consumption in a given year. These consumption figures are expressed in defined daily doses for statistical purposes (S-DDD).

Comments on flunitrazepam, a substance that was transferred from Schedule IV to Schedule III in 1995, are included in paragraphs 55-58 above.

103. After an increase of total reported manufacture of the 12 substances in the group from an average of 6.3 billion S-DDD per year during the period 1997-2001 to 7.8 billion S-DDD in 2002, manufacturing levels reverted to their former level in 2003-2004, averaging 6.4 billion S-DDD per year. In 2005, global manufacture rose again, to 7.3 billion S-DDD, the second highest amount ever reported. During the period 1998-2002, Belgium, Canada and Switzerland started reporting to INCB on their manufacture of benzo-diazepines, which brought the calculated levels of annual consumption closer to the levels of total manufacture (see figures 22 and 23).

104. The calculated average national consumption of benzodiazepine-type sedative-hypnotics, expressed in S-DDD per 1,000 inhabitants per day, is higher in Europe than in the other regions (see figure 24).

105. Since 2000, the share of flunitrazepam in the combined manufacture of those 12 benzodiazepines has fluctuated considerably. Falling from 21 per cent (1.4 billion S-DDD) of the total in that year to 3 per cent (207 million S-DDD) in 2001, manufacture of flunitrazepam recovered in 2003, reaching, in 2004, the highest share of this group, at 23 per cent (1.5 billion S-DDD), but plummeted again in 2005, falling to its lowest level ever, 1 per cent (84 million S-DDD). That decline was caused by Switzerland, a major manufacturer of flunitrazepam, which did not manufacture the substance in 2005 (see also paras. 57-58 above). In contrast, as global manufacture of brotizolam more than tripled between 2004 and 2005, from 580 million S-DDD to 1.8 billion S-DDD (see para. 113 below), that substance accounted

Figure 24. Benzodiazepine-type hypnotics: average national consumption,[a] by region, 1997-1999, 2000-2002 and 2003-2005

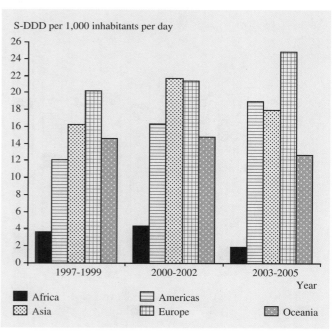

[a] Statistical data submitted by Governments are used to calculate the average annual consumption for a three-year period.

for the largest share (25 per cent) of total manufacture of benzodiazepine-type sedative-hypnotics in 2005. Lormetazepam was second at 15 per cent (1.1 billion S-DDD);

Figure 25. Benzodiazepine-type sedative-hypnotics: share in total reported manufacture, 2005

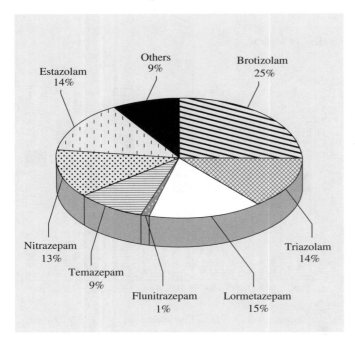

Figure 27. Benzodiazepine-type sedative-hypnotics: countries' shares of total reported manufacture, 2005

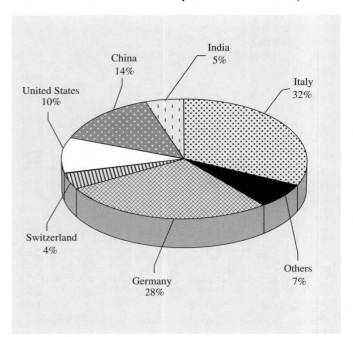

Figure 26. Benzodiazepine-type sedative-hypnotics: reported total manufacture, selected countries, 1996-2005

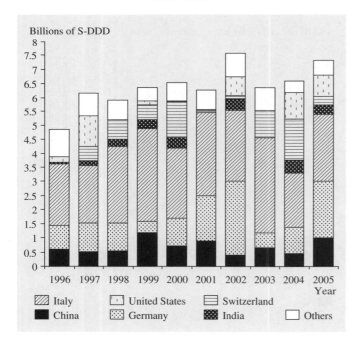

it was followed by estazolam and triazolam at 14 per cent (1 billion S-DDD each), nitrazepam at 13 per cent (946 million S-DDD) and temazepam at 9 per cent (664 million S-DDD). Midazolam (435 million S-DDD), flurazepam (138 million S-DDD) and loprazolam (72 million S-DDD)

together accounted for 9 per cent of the total (see figure 25). Manufacture of haloxazolam and nimetazepam accounted for less than 1 per cent of global manufacture of benzodiazepine-type sedative-hypnotics.

106. Figure 26 shows the main manufacturers during the period 1996-2005. In 2005, Italy continued to be the main manufacturer of that group of substances (2.4 billion S-DDD), accounting for 32 per cent of global manufacture (see figure 27).

Triazolam

107. Triazolam is a potent hypnotic, having, together with brotizolam, the lowest S-DDD of all psychotropic substances (0.25 mg). The substance is manufactured in amounts of several hundred kilograms per year. In 2005, 245 kg (980 million S-DDD) were reported as manufactured. The major manufacturer is the United States, which reported manufacture of 190 kg in 2005. Triazolam is also manufactured by China and Italy. France, Japan and Spain, which manufactured triazolam in the past, have not reported any manufacture of that substance in recent years.

108. The major exporters of triazolam were the United States and Italy, in that order. In addition, Australia, Switzerland and the United Kingdom regularly import and re-export triazolam. Japan was the largest importer and user, accounting for nearly half of world imports. The United States, which used 94 kg (376 million S-DDD) in 2005, was the largest user during that year; it was followed by Japan, with 88 kg (352 million S-DDD)

Lormetazepam

109. The manufacture of lormetazepam increased steadily after 1991, reaching a peak of 1.9 tons in 2002. After a brief drop in 2003 to 380 kg, manufacture picked up again in 2004 and totalled 1.1 tons in 2005. Those totals reflected fluctuations in manufacturing by Germany and Italy, the two main manufacturers of lormetazepam. Germany and Italy are also the main exporters of that substance. In addition, France, Ireland, the Netherlands and Spain are significant re-exporters of lormetazepam, importing and exporting quantities of approximately 200 kg per year. Calculated global consumption increased from 415 kg in 1997 to 1.3 tons in 2005. Spain, Italy, Belgium, France and Germany, in that order, were the largest users.

Nitrazepam

110. Global manufacture of nitrazepam, which had slowly decreased in recent years, from 6.5 tons in 2000 to 4 tons in 2004, increased again in 2005, to 4.7 tons. The substance was manufactured by Italy (2.4 tons in 2005), India (1.7 tons) and China (0.7 tons). Exports of nitrazepam, which had averaged about 6 tons annually during the period 1998-2002, continued to decrease, totalling 3.9 tons in 2005. As in previous years, Italy remained the main exporter of the substance, accounting for 65 per cent of total exports in 2005. Many countries are importing nitrazepam. Since 1998, about 80 countries have reported, at least once, nitrazepam imports in excess of 1 kg. Japan remained the single largest importer, reporting imports of 1.6 tons in 2005; it was followed by Cuba (550 kg) and the United Kingdom (317 kg).

Temazepam

111. Temazepam is manufactured by Italy, Poland and the United States in amounts totalling between 10 and 25 tons per year. In 2005, global manufacture of temazepam amounted to slightly over 13 tons. Italy, the single largest supplier of the world market, accounted for, on average, 91 per cent of global manufacture in the period 1996-2005. The United States intermittently manufactures amounts of 2-3 tons per year, and Poland manufactures several hundred kilograms every year, mainly for domestic use.

112. The largest importer was the United States, which imported over 7 tons in 2005; it was followed by Australia, Canada, Finland, Germany, Ireland, the Netherlands and the United Kingdom; each imported over 1 ton per year. About 30 countries report imported of over 1 kg per year. As in previous years, the United States was the major user in 2005, accounting for 60 per cent of global calculated consumption (682 million S-DDD).

Brotizolam

113. In 1995, brotizolam, a potent hypnotic with the same S-DDD as triazolam (S-DDD of 0.25 mg), was included in Schedule IV of the 1971 Convention. The manufacture of that substance was reported for the first time in 1997, by Germany. Brotizolam is manufactured by Germany in amounts of several hundred kilograms per year and by Italy and Japan in amounts of several dozen kilograms per year. In 2005, total manufacture was 451 kg. Japan is the largest importer. Switzerland also imports significant quantities for re-export. In 2005, 12 countries reported imports of more than 1 kg of brotizolam, totalling 477 kg. Global calculated consumption amounted to 1.4 billion S-DDD, with Japan (532 million S-DDD), Germany (324 million S-DDD) and Colombia (324 million S-DDD) accounting for 84 per cent of global consumption of the substance in 2005.

Estazolam

114. During the period 1995-2004, global manufacture of estazolam fluctuated between 1.5 tons and 2.6 tons per year, mainly accounted for by China, Japan and the United States. In 2005, manufacture rose to a record 3 tons, of which China accounted for 2.4 tons. Japan manufactured 341 kg, and Poland and Italy combined manufactured 261 kg. The United States did not manufacture estazolam in 2005. Of the 10 countries importing the substance in quantities of more than 1 kg, Brazil, France, the Netherlands, Portugal and the United States accounted for 60 per cent of total imports in 2005.

Midazolam

115. Total reported manufacture of midazolam, which had been stable at about 2.6 tons per year during the period 2000-2004, jumped to 8.7 tons in 2005, the second highest amount ever recorded. The increase was attributable to the sharp increase in manufacture by Switzerland, from 2.8 tons in 2004 to 6.3 tons in 2005. Israel was second, at 1.4 tons; it was followed by Brazil, India and Italy, in that order. In contrast, the level of international trade in midazolam fell to 3.5 tons in 2005, the lowest level since 1998, resulting in a record increase in global manufacturers' stocks, to 6.8 tons. Midazolam is widely used, with about 80 countries reporting imports of that substance in 2005. The major importers in 2005 were Brazil, Germany, the Republic of Korea and the United States, which together accounted for 40 per cent of global imports.

Flurazepam

116. Having gradually declined from 10.6 tons in 1997 to 3.6 tons in 2004, global manufacture of flurazepam rose again slightly, to 4.1 tons, in 2005. Flurazepam is currently manufactured by only Brazil, China and Italy. Italy is the single largest manufacturer and exporter, supplying almost 90 per cent of global demand for that substance. In 2005, 25 countries reported imports of flurazepam in quantities over 1 kg. Major importers were Switzerland (1.7 tons) and Spain (1.5 tons), which together accounted for 50 per cent of global imports in 2005. Significant quantities were also imported by the United States and Canada, which each imported approximately 750 kg during that year.

Loprazolam

117. Total reported manufacture of loprazolam amounted to 72 kg in 2005, France being the only manufacturer and the leading exporter of the substance. The United Kingdom (25 kg in 2000) and Spain (202 kg in 1993) are the only other countries that have ever reported manufacture of loprazolam. In 2005, imports of loprazolam were reported by nine countries, each importing quantities of 1-10 kg.

Benzodiazepine-type anti-epileptics

Clonazepam

118. Clonazepam is a benzodiazepine mainly used as an anti-epileptic. Total reported manufacture of clonazepam, which had remained at an annual average of about 4 tons during the period 1998-2003, started to rise in 2004 and reached 6.4 tons in 2005, the highest level ever recorded. That increase reflected the increase in manufacture by Switzerland, the world's leading manufacturer of clonazepam, from 1.9 tons in 2004 to almost 3 tons in 2005. India (1.8 tons) remained the second largest manufacturer of clonazepam that year; it was followed by Italy (500 kg). Significant quantities of the substance were manufactured also by Brazil, China, Israel and Poland in 2005.

119. Global trade in clonazepam steadily increased from about 0.5 ton in 1995 to 6.8 tons in 2005. Clonazepam is widely traded, with some 100 countries reporting imports of the substance in amounts exceeding 1 kg. In 2005, the United States was again the world's largest importer of clonazepam (1.2 tons); it was followed by Brazil (934 kg) and Canada (707 kg). In addition, amounts of the substance greater than 100 kg were also imported by, in decreasing order, Argentina, Switzerland, France, Italy, Japan, the Islamic Republic of Iran, Spain and Chile. Global calculated consumption has shown an upward trend as well since the mid-1990s, increasing steadily from 273 million S-DDD in 1996 to a new record of 720 million S-DDD in 2005. The United States remained the largest user of clonazepam (131 million S-DDD); it was followed by Brazil, Argentina and Canada.

Barbiturate-type sedative-hypnotics and anti-epileptics

Allobarbital, barbital, butobarbital, methylphenobarbital, phenobarbital, secbutabarbital and vinylbital

120. The seven barbiturates listed in Schedule IV are pharmacologically related to those included in Schedule III. Five of those substances, namely, allobarbital, barbital, butobarbital, secbutabarbital and vinylbital, are intermediate-acting barbiturates and are mainly used as hypnotics (to induce sleep) in the treatment of intractable insomnia. They are no longer used as daytime sedatives. The two other sub-

stances, methylphenobarbital and phenobarbital,[7] have additional properties and are also used as anti-epileptics (long-acting barbiturates). Barbital, methylphenobarbital and phenobarbital were listed under Schedule IV when the 1971 Convention was adopted, while the other four substances were included in that Schedule in 1987.

121. The most widely used substance in the group of barbiturates remains phenobarbital, which has been described as a drug of choice for the treatment of epilepsy. Total reported manufacture of those barbiturates (for both direct medical use and the manufacture of non-psychotropic substances) has been gradually increasing, reaching 653 tons in 1998 (5.4 billion S-DDD). It briefly fell below 4 billion S-DDD in the period 1999-2000, then gradually rose to an average of 5 billion S-DDD in the period 2004-2005. During the period 2001-2005, phenobarbital accounted, on average, for over 95 per cent of total manufacture of the barbiturates included in Schedule IV (in S-DDD). Barbital was second, accounting for 4 per cent of total manufacture; it was followed by methylphenobarbital and allobarbital. No manufacture of vinylbital has been reported since 1996, and no manufacture of butobarbital has been reported since 1999.

122. In recent years, Poland, followed by China and Japan, had the highest calculated rates of use of barbiturate-type sedative-hypnotics, averaging between 0.3 and 0.45 S-DDD per 1,000 inhabitants per day. With respect to the barbiturate-type anti-epileptics listed in Schedule IV, Brazil, Bulgaria, Croatia, Kazakhstan, Romania, the Russian Federation and Ukraine were the countries with the highest rates of use during the period 2001-2005, consuming on average between 6 and 15.7 S-DDD per 1,000 inhabitants per day.

Figure 28. Phenobarbital: total reported manufacture, 1996-2005

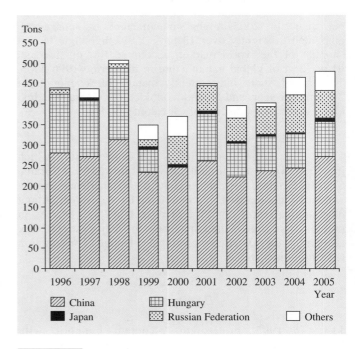

---

[7] See table IV for details.

123. Total reported manufacture of phenobarbital averaged 438 tons annually in the period 2001-2005, having declined from its peak of 508 tons in 1998. In 2005, 56.8 per cent of the total volume of phenobarbital was manufactured in China. Other countries among the main manufacturers of phenobarbital in 2005 were Hungary (84 tons), the Russian Federation (66 tons), India (35 tons) and Brazil (10 tons). In the period 2001-2005, phenobarbital was reported to have been manufactured also in Hungary (mostly for export), Germany, Iraq, Japan, Kazakhstan, Switzerland and the United States (see figure 28).

124. Phenobarbital continues to be one of the most widely traded psychotropic substances. During the period 2001-2005, 163 countries and territories reported having imported the substance at least once. Total reported imports amounted to 270 tons in 2005, the main importers being Brazil (36 tons), Switzerland (34 tons), Ukraine (29 tons), Denmark (25 tons), Germany (20 tons), Japan (10 tons) and the United States (18 tons), together accounting for 60 per cent of the total.

126. In addition to its medical use as a sedative-hypnotic, barbital is also used in industry for the manufacture of non-psychotropic substances. The calculated global use of barbital, including both medical and industrial use, increased from an average of 95 tons annually during the period 2001-2002 to 106 tons in the period 2003-2005. Total reported manufacture of barbital declined steeply in the period 1993-2001, losing two thirds of its volume. Total output of barbital then increased somewhat, from 87 tons in 2001 to 111 tons in 2005. China remained the main manufacturer of the substance, accounting for 96 per cent of global manufacture on average during the period 2000-2005. Aside from China, Japan (2.7 tons) was the only country reporting manufacture of barbital in 2005.

127. After 1997, the volume of trade in barbital gradually fell, from 72 tons in 1998 to 11 tons in 2002, and in the following three years, total imports of the substance averaged 16 tons per year. In 2005, 92.6 per cent of global exports were accounted for by China and Germany. Fifty-two countries imported barbital at least once during the period 2001-2005. Germany (mainly for re-export), India and Japan were the leading importers of the substance in that period.

128. Germany manufactured almost 8 tons of methyl-phenobarbital in 1990. Since 1990, Switzerland has been the main manufacturer of the substance. Its output fluctuated around an average of 2.7 tons per year during the four-year period 1999-2002, while it reported no manufacture in 2003. Total reported manufacture of methylphenobarbital decreased sharply from 3.8 tons in 2004 (75 per cent of which was manufactured in Switzerland) to 884 kg in 2005 (two thirds of which was manufactured in Switzerland and the rest in the United States). Croatia, Italy, Switzerland and the United States were the main users of methylpheno-barbital in 2005.

129. International trade in methylphenobarbital fluctuated between 1.7 tons and 5.2 tons per year, averaging

3.2 tons annually during the period 2001-2005. Of the seven countries that reported exports of methylphenobarbital during the period 2001-2005, Switzerland supplied, on average, 49 per cent of global exports, the other main exporter of methylphenobarbital in 2005 being Germany (702 kg). Sixteen countries imported the substance at least once during the period 2001-2005. Germany was the main regular importer of methylphenobarbital (its imports being entirely for re-export), with about 44 per cent of total imports going to Croatia in 2005.

130. Only Germany has reported the manufacture of allobarbital since Denmark and Poland discontinued manufacture of that substance in the period 1994-1995. Manufacture of allobarbital by Germany increased significantly, from 393 kg in 1998, when the country resumed its manufacture of that substance, to about 4 tons in 2000. Subsequently, German manufacture of allobarbital gradually fell to about 1.6 tons in 2002. While no manufacture was reported in 2003, Germany manufactured an average of 1 ton annually in the period 2004-2005. Consequently, total stocks of the substance decreased from an average of 2.5 tons in the period 2001-2002 to just over 1 ton in 2004, before decreasing even further to 509 kg in 2005.

131. Total exports of allobarbital fluctuated between 2.4 tons in 2001 and 1.5 tons in 2005, averaging 2.3 tons per year in that five-year period. Germany was the largest exporter, accounting for about 67 per cent of the global total during that period. Seventeen countries imported the substance at least once during the period 2001-2005. In 2005, the major importers of the substance were Sri Lanka (701 kg), Switzerland (202 kg, for re-export), Poland (200 kg), Turkey (200 kg) and Hungary (60 kg). Global consumption of allobarbital decreased by almost half, from 21.4 million S-DDD in 2001 to 11 million S-DDD in 2005. The reduction is attributable to significantly lower rates of use in the Czech Republic, Hungary and Poland. In Poland, for example, the calculated use of allobarbital decreased from 2.3 S-DDD per 1,000 inhabitants per day in 2000 to 1 S-DDD per 1,000 inhabitants per day in 2005.

132. Total manufacture of secbutabarbital decreased sharply, from 653 kg in 2002 (of which 78 per cent was manufactured in the United States) to 128 kg in 2003, and no manufacture of the substance was reported in the period 2004-2005. Germany had reported the manufacture of an average of 136 kg of secbutabarbital during the period 2002-2003. Germany, Lebanon, Switzerland, the United Kingdom and the United States are the only countries that have reported trade in that substance in the past five years.

133. Only two countries reported manufacture of buto-barbital in the period 1996 2005: Denmark (1.3 tons in 1998) and Germany (304 kg in 1997). After that, no manufacture of butobarbital was reported. Consequently, global stocks of the substance continued to decrease, gradually falling from 1.7 tons in 1998 to 311 kg in 2005. The volume of international trade in butobarbital also fell, by some 96 per cent, from 3.7 tons in 1998 to 53 kg in 2005. Butobarbital consumption decreased eight-fold between 2004 and 2005.

Figure 29. Barbiturates listed in Schedules II, III and IV: total reported manufacture, by substance, 2005

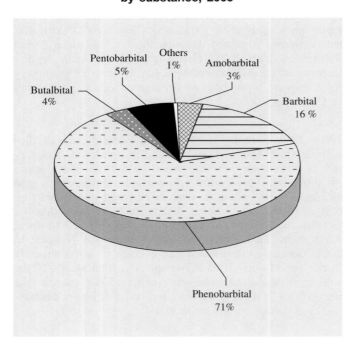

Figure 30. Barbiturates listed in Schedules II, III and IV: total reported manufacture in selected countries, 2005

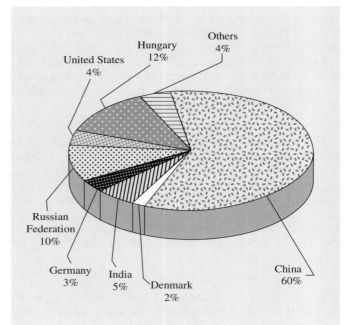

134. Of the 12 barbiturates listed in Schedules II, III and IV of the 1971 Convention, five substances accounted for 98 per cent of total reported manufacture in the five-year period 2001-2005: phenobarbital (67 per cent), barbital (15 per cent), butalbital (7 per cent), pentobarbital (6 per cent) and amobarbital (3 per cent). The distribution of the barbiturates manufactured in 2005 is presented in figure 29. In 2005, China (60 per cent), Hungary (12 per cent), the Russian Federation (10 per cent), India (5 per cent), the United States (4 per cent), Germany (3 per cent) and Denmark (2 per cent) together accounted for 96 per cent of the total manufacture of the entire group of barbiturates (see figure 30). The notable change here is that the share of China increased from 54 per cent of total reported manufacture in 2004 to 60 per cent in 2005.

Other sedative-hypnotics

135. Five substances from the group of sedative-hypnotics in Schedule IV are neither barbiturates nor benzodiazepines. While ethchlorvynol, ethinamate and methyprylon have been listed in Schedule IV since the adoption of the 1971 Convention, the other two substances, *gamma*-hydroxybutyric acid (GHB) and zolpidem, were added to the group of sedative-hypnotics in Schedule IV in 2001.

136. The manufacture of ethchlorvynol was last reported, by the United States, in 1999 (1.3 tons), and use of the substance was discontinued in 2001. The manufacture of ethinamate was last reported, by Germany, in 1988 (500 kg), and the manufacture of methyprylon was last reported, by the United States, in 1990 (2.1 tons). There have been no reports of

manufacture of or international trade in either ethinamate or methyprylon since 1991.

137. Very limited data are available for GHB for 2001, when the substance was put under international control. With the introduction of national control measures, the number of countries able to report on manufacture of and trade in GHB has increased. In 2005, Germany (5.7 tons) and Latvia (3.6 tons) were the main manufacturers of GHB, together accounting for 86 per cent of global manufacture. The other main manufacturers in the period 2001-2005 were the United States (3.9 tons on average) and Ukraine (3.8 tons on average), followed, with much lesser amounts, by China, France and Azerbaijan. The main exporters in 2005 were Germany, Latvia and the United States, and the main importers were Italy (4.6 tons) and the United Kingdom (1.8 tons). In the period 2003-2005, 25 countries reported the import of more than 1 kg of GHB at least once.

138. Data on zolpidem are available for the period 2001-2005 for a number of countries. The main manufacturer was France, which accounted for 86 per cent of global output (32 tons); it was followed by the Czech Republic (3.5 tons) and India (709 kg). Argentina, China, Germany, Israel, Slovakia, Spain and the United States also reported manufacture of zolpidem in recent years. The main exporter of zolpidem was France, which accounted for 55 per cent of global exports (19 tons). Zolpidem is a widely used substance, France, the United States, Japan and the Czech Republic being the main users. During the five-year period 2001-2005, more than

100 countries reported the import of more than 1 kg of zolpidem at least once.

Analgesics

139.   Lefetamine is the only analgesic included in Schedule IV. No manufacture of or trade in the substance has been reported since 1996. One kilogram of the substance is currently held in stock by Italy.

Antidepressants

140.   The only substance representative of this group is amineptine. It was included in Schedule II of the 1971 Convention in 2003. Not much information has been reported on this substance. Brazil is the only country that has reported holding small quantities of stocks in the past two years.

COMMENTAIRES SUR LES STATISTIQUES COMMUNIQUÉES AU SUJET DES SUBSTANCES PSYCHOTROPES

Résumé

L'utilisation de substances inscrites au Tableau I de la Convention de 1971 sur les substances psychotropes est très restreinte: elle se limite à la recherche scientifique et à la fabrication exceptionnelle de substances psychotropes inscrites aux autres tableaux. C'est également le cas du *delta*-8-tétrahydrocannabinol, dont la fabrication a fortement augmenté ces dernières années pour la production de dronabinol, l'une des variantes stéréochimiques du *delta*-9-tétrahydrocannabinol (*delta*-9-THC) inscrites au Tableau II. Les préparations contenant du dronabinol sont utilisées dans certains pays comme antiémétiques pour le traitement de la nausée. Le niveau de fabrication et de stocks du *delta*-9-THC, stable ces dernières années, a récemment augmenté. Le dronabinol est consommé principalement aux États-Unis d'Amérique, ainsi que dans plusieurs autres pays, dont l'Allemagne et le Canada.

Les amphétamines (stimulants du système nerveux central inscrits au Tableau II) sont largement utilisées, surtout pour la fabrication d'autres substances psychotropes et de substances qui ne sont pas soumises à un contrôle international, mais aussi à des fins médicales comme le traitement du trouble déficitaire de l'attention et de la narcolepsie. Essentiellement fabriquées aux États-Unis et en France, la production mondiale d'amphétamines a atteint le chiffre maximal de 45 tonnes en 2005 sous l'effet de l'accroissement de la consommation aux États-Unis. Ce pays, qui est le plus gros consommateur mondial de ces substances, et de loin, a représenté 80 % de l'utilisation calculée d'amphétamines dans le monde en 2005. Un nombre croissant d'autres pays utilisent également des amphétamines (principalement du méthylphénidate), en particulier l'Allemagne, le Canada et l'Espagne.

La consommation de buprénorphine, analgésique opiacé inscrit au Tableau III de la Convention de 1971, a beaucoup augmenté ces dernières années, ce produit étant utilisé pour la désintoxication et le traitement de substitution des héroïnomanes depuis le début des années 90. Plus de 40 pays importent actuellement de la buprénorphine à cette fin, les plus gros importateurs étant l'Allemagne et la France.

À l'heure actuelle, 35 benzodiazépines sont soumises à un contrôle international. En médecine, les benzodiazépines sont utilisées pour la gestion ponctuelle de l'insomnie ainsi que pour la prémédication et l'induction de l'anesthésie générale. Les benzodiazépines font partie de la catégorie des anxiolytiques et des sédatifs-hypnotiques. La consommation globale d'anxiolytiques de type benzodiazépine, en particulier de diazépam, est plus élevée en Europe que dans toutes autres régions du monde. En revanche, les quantités totales déclarées concernant la fabrication et la consommation de sédatifs-hypnotiques de type benzodiazépine, dont le flunitrazépam, ont beaucoup varié. Ces quelques dernières années, la consommation totale déclarée de flunitrazépam a fait apparaître une tendance à la baisse, tandis que celle de brotizolam a été en hausse. Le commerce international de flunitrazépam a tourné autour de 1 tonne par an. Le Japon demeure le principal importateur de flunitrazépam, avec plus de la moitié des importations mondiales annuelles.

Parmi les 12 barbituriques inscrits aux Tableaux de la Convention de 1971, le phénobarbital est le plus largement utilisé, surtout pour le traitement de l'épilepsie. Cette substance représente 71 % de la fabrication totale de tous les barbituriques en 2005. Les autres principaux barbituriques sont le barbital, le pentobarbital, le butalbital et l'amobarbital, qui représentent ensemble environ 28 % du total de la fabrication déclarée. La Chine, principal producteur, fabrique environ 60 % du total mondial, suivie par la Fédération de Russie et l'Inde. La majeure partie des barbituriques est consommée dans les Amériques, en Asie et en Europe, régions qui représentent chacune en moyenne 1,7 milliard de doses quotidiennes déterminées à des fins statistiques (S-DDD) par an.

Les stimulants inscrits au Tableau IV de la Convention de 1971 sont essentiellement utilisés comme anoxérigènes ou pour le traitement des troubles de l'attention. Après des fluctuations marquées pendant les années 90, la fabrication totale déclarée de ces deux substances s'est stabilisée à une moyenne annuelle d'environ 1,8 milliard de S-DDD pendant la période 2001-2005. En 2005, les principales substances fabriquées étaient la phentermine (45 %), le fenproporex (23 %) et l'amfépramone (18 %). La phentermine est la substance de ce groupe la plus largement utilisée. La consommation par habitant la plus élevée de stimulants inscrits au Tableau IV a toujours été observée dans les Amériques. La consommation continue d'avoir tendance à augmenter dans ces régions, mais les taux de consommation en Asie, en Europe et en Océanie ont beaucoup diminué depuis 2000.

---

1. Les présents commentaires ont pour but de faciliter l'étude des informations statistiques sur les substances psychotropes fabriquées de manière licite qui figurent dans les tableaux (voir pages 109-256 ci-dessous) établis à partir des données que les gouvernements ont présentées à l'Organe international de contrôle des stupéfiants (OICS) conformément aux dispositions de l'article 16 de la Convention de 1971 sur les substances psychotropes.

2. Actuellement, 116 substances sont inscrites aux quatre Tableaux de la Convention de 1971. Les commentaires portent sur les substances déclarées comme ayant été utilisées à des fins médicales et scientifiques. Étant donné que quelques pays seulement ont fait état de la fabrication de substances du Tableau I et que le commerce international de ces substances a été très limité, les données concernant leur mouvement en 2005 sont récapitulées dans l'un des tableaux statistiques figurant à la fin du présent document. En ce qui concerne les substances inscrites aux Tableaux II et III de la Convention de 1971, les renseignements fournis dans les tableaux statistiques couvrent une période de cinq ans (2001-2005). En ce qui concerne les substances du Tableau IV,

ils couvrent une période de trois ans (2003-2005). Les statistiques concernant un petit nombre de substances, à savoir la mécloqualone et la phencyclidine, toutes deux inscrites au Tableau II, ainsi que l'amineptine et la léfétamine, inscrites au Tableau IV, ne sont pas incluses dans les tableaux statistiques mais sont reflétées dans les commentaires.

Substances inscrites au Tableau I

3. À l'heure actuelle, 28 substances figurent au Tableau I. Conformément aux dispositions de l'article 7 de la Convention de 1971, il faudrait interdire toute utilisation de ces substances, sauf à des fins scientifiques ou à des fins médicales très limitées par des personnes dûment autorisées qui travaillent dans des établissements médicaux ou scientifiques relevant directement des pouvoirs publics ou expressément autorisés par eux. Cette restriction est due au fait que toutes les substances du Tableau I sont des hallucinogènes et/ou des stimulants du système nerveux central dont l'utilisation médicale est extrêmement limitée, voire inexistante. Leur fabrication, leur stockage et leur commerce sont par conséquent très peu développés. Des exceptions sont signalées ci-dessous.

4. La Convention de 1971 ne prévoit aucune utilisation industrielle des substances psychotropes du Tableau I pour la fabrication de substances ou produits non psychotropes. Aux États-Unis d'Amérique, toutefois, seul fabricant de cette substance, la 2,5-diméthoxyamphétamine (DMA) est utilisée dans la fabrication de pellicules photographiques spéciales. La fabrication de DMA dans ce pays a été stable, s'établissant en moyenne à 8 tonnes par an jusqu'en 2001, année où elle a diminué d'environ 50 %. En 2005, les États-Unis ont déclaré avoir fabriqué 520 kg de cette substance. En moyenne, les États-Unis ont fabriqué 1 603 kg de DMA au cours des cinq dernières années. Les stocks de DMA détenus aux États-Unis à la fin de 2005 étaient de 236 kg. Il n'existe apparemment pas de produit pour remplacer la DMA dans le procédé de fabrication de ces pellicules. Bien que l'utilisation de DMA aux États-Unis ait nettement diminué, il semble que cette substance continue d'être utilisée par l'industrie pour la fabrication d'une teinture pour pellicules photographiques[1].

5. Les pays ayant signalé la fabrication de 3,4-méthylènedioxyméthamphétamine (MDMA) au cours des cinq dernières années sont au nombre de huit, à savoir l'Australie, le Danemark, les États-Unis, la Hongrie, l'Irlande, Israël, la Pologne et la Suisse. À la fin de 2005, les stocks de MDMA étaient inférieurs à 500 grammes, et étaient détenus notamment par l'Australie, les États-Unis et la Suisse. Entre 2001 et 2005, quatre pays, l'Australie, les États-Unis, Israël et la Suisse, ont indiqué avoir fabriqué quelques grammes de ténamphétamine (MDA). Des stocks de cette substance sont surtout détenus aux États-Unis et en Suisse. En 2005, le Danemark a pour la première fois déclaré avoir fabriqué environ 25 kg de PMA (p-méthoxy-alphaméthylphentyhylamine), et ce pays en détenait en fin d'année des stocks de près de 40 kg.

6. Les Parties à la Convention de 1971 peuvent autoriser une utilisation limitée des substances du Tableau I pour la fabrication de substances psychotropes inscrites à d'autres Tableaux. Les États-Unis fabriquent des isomères du tétrahydrocannabinol (THC) inscrits au Tableau I — principalement du *delta*-8-tétrahydrocannabinol — qui servent à fabriquer du *delta*-9-tétrahydrocannabinol (*delta*-9-THC), substance psychotrope inscrite au Tableau II depuis 1991. Une seule des variantes stéréochimiques du *delta*-9-THC, le dronabinol, est utilisée pour la fabrication de préparations pharmaceutiques à des fins thérapeutiques. Les États-Unis sont le seul pays qui fabrique des isomères du THC inscrits au Tableau I. La fabrication de ces isomères du THC a augmenté de près de 140 % en 1998 et 1999. Au cours des cinq dernières années, la fabrication d'isomères du THC a continué de faire apparaître une tendance à la hausse d'environ 16 % par an en moyenne. Les quantités totales fabriquées en 2005 aux États-Unis ont été de 308 kg et seul ce pays en détenait en stock à la fin de 2005 (445 kg).

7. En 2005, la fabrication à des fins scientifiques de quelques grammes d'autres substances inscrites au Tableau I, qui n'ont pas été mentionnées plus haut, n'a été signalée que par quatre pays: l'Allemagne (méthcathinone), les États-Unis (*N*-éthyl-MDA, psilocine et ténamphétamine), l'Irlande (cathinone, *N*-éthyl-MDA et ténamphétamine) et la Suisse (mescaline, *N*-éthyl-MDA et psilocybine).

8. À la fin de 2005, les quantités de substances du Tableau I en stock, principalement aux États-Unis, allaient de quelques grammes à plusieurs centaines de grammes. Les stocks de la plupart de ces substances sont restés relativement stables ces dernières années. Les autres pays ayant déclaré détenir en stock quelques grammes de substances inscrites au Tableau I à la fin de 2005 étaient l'Australie, le Royaume-Uni et la Suisse. Pour ce qui est des stocks de DMA et de THC, voir les paragraphes 4 à 6 ci-dessus.

9. Le commerce international des substances du Tableau I s'est toujours limité à des transactions occasionnelles portant au maximum sur quelques grammes. Entre 2001 et 2005, l'Allemagne, l'Australie, le Canada, la Chine, le Danemark, les États-Unis, la France, l'Irlande, Israël, la Nouvelle-Zélande, le Royaume-Uni et la Suisse ont signalé avoir importé ou exporté de petites quantités de certaines de ces substances.

Substances inscrites au Tableau II

10. Dix-sept substances, qui risquent de donner lieu à des abus, constituent un gros risque pour la santé publique et ont une utilité thérapeutique faible ou moyenne, figurent au Tableau II. Elles appartiennent aux groupes suivants: stimulants du système nerveux central; antiémétiques; hallucinogènes; sédatifs-hypnotiques; antitussifs et antidépresseurs. Outre leurs diverses applications en médecine humaine et/ou vétérinaire, certaines sont utilisées dans l'industrie pour fabriquer d'autres substances psychotropes ou être transformées en substances non psychotropes.

---

[1]Voir *Rapport de l'Organe international de contrôle des stupéfiants pour 1994* (publication des Nations Unies, numéro de vente: F.95.XI.4), par. 75.

Stimulants du système nerveux central

Amphétamines

11. Les deux isomères optiques de l'amphétamine (lévamphétamine et dexamphétamine) et leur mélange racémique (amphétamine), ainsi que les deux isomères optiques de la méthamphétamine (lévométhamphétamine et méthamphétamine) et leur mélange racémique (racémate de méthamphétamine) figurent au Tableau II. Étant donné les différentes dates auxquelles ces substances ont été placées sous contrôle en vertu de la Convention de 1971, l'Organe reçoit depuis les années 70 des informations statistiques sur l'amphétamine, la dexamphétamine et la méthamphétamine alors que les statistiques ne sont disponibles que depuis 1986 pour la lévamphétamine et la lévométhamphétamine et depuis 1988 pour le racémate de méthamphétamine.

12. Les amphétamines du Tableau II sont utilisées non seulement à des fins médicales directes, mais aussi dans l'industrie comme produits intermédiaires pour fabriquer d'autres substances. Ces dernières peuvent être divisées en deux groupes: autres substances psychotropes, dont les isomères optiques de la substance d'origine; et substances n'entrant pas dans le champ d'application de la Convention de 1971. Ces dernières années, les amphétamines ont été surtout converties en substances utilisées comme anoxérigènes (benzphétamine, clobenzorex, fenproporex et lévopropylhexédrine) et pour le traitement de la maladie de Parkinson (sélégiline). Parfois, de petites quantités d'amphétamines sont également converties en d'autres substances, comme la famprofazone (utilisée comme analgésique) et l'amfétaminil (psychostimulant). La benzphétamine et le fenproporex sont inscrits au Tableau IV de la Convention de 1971, tandis que l'amfétaminil, le clobenzorex, la famprofazone, la lévopropylhexédrine et la sélégiline ne font l'objet d'aucun contrôle international.

Utilisation en tant que substances intermédiaires

13. Aux États-Unis, les précurseurs importés (phénylacétone et noréphédrine) et le racémate de méthamphétamine sont utilisés pour la fabrication d'amphétamine et de dexamphétamine, qui servent ensuite à la fabrication de préparations pharmaceutiques. En 2005, ce pays a fabriqué au total 6,7 tonnes d'amphétamine et 6,2 tonnes de dexamphétamine. En 2005, les États-Unis ont importé 2,4 tonnes de racémate de méthamphétamine (en provenance de France), dont 1,9 tonne a été transformée en 1,2 tonne de méthamphétamine et 580 kg de lévométhamphétamine. Environ 542 kg de la méthamphétamine ainsi obtenue a ensuite été utilisée pour fabriquer 719 kg de benzphétamine, tandis que la lévométhamphétamine sert à la fabrication de produits d'inhalation par voie nasale vendus sans ordonnance. Ainsi, les quantités de ces substances disponibles pour des utilisations médicales directes aux États-Unis ont été de 6,7 tonnes d'amphétamine, de 6,2 tonnes de dexamphétamine, de 452 kg de racémate de méthamphétamine et de 612 kg de méthamphétamine.

14. En 2005, la France a fabriqué 10,9 tonnes d'amphétamine, dont 2,9 tonnes ont été utilisées pour la fabrication de quelque 2,2 tonnes de dexamphétamine et 7,5 tonnes pour la fabrication de 6,5 tonnes de lévamphétamine, le reste venant s'ajouter aux stocks. En tout, 4,9 tonnes de lévamphétamine ont été reconverties en 4,7 tonnes d'amphétamine. Sur les 2,9 tonnes de racémate de méthamphétamine fabriquées en France en 2005, environ 2,4 tonnes ont été exportées aux États-Unis et les 533 kg restants ont été convertis en 500 kg de méthamphétamine qui ont été ajoutés aux stocks.

Utilisation médicale directe

15. En médecine, les amphétamines sont utilisées principalement pour le traitement des troubles déficitaires de l'attention (également connu sous le nom de "trouble déficitaire de l'attention/hyperactivité" aux États-Unis), de la narcolepsie et de l'obésité, bien que la plupart des pays aient cessé d'utiliser ces substances comme anoxérigènes pour le traitement de l'obésité ou en utilisent beaucoup moins.

16. En 2005, les quantités d'amphétamines inscrites au Tableau II qui ont été fabriquées dans le monde ont atteint au total 45,1 tonnes (plus de 3 milliards de doses quotidiennes définies à des fins statistiques (S-DDD), soit 636 kg de plus que l'année précédente. La fabrication d'amphétamine (41,4 %), de dexamphétamine (25,3 %) et de lévamphétamine (14,3 %) a représenté 81 % de la production totale de ce groupe de substances (voir la figure 1). La quasi-totalité de cette production a été imputable à la France (58 %) et aux États-Unis (33 %), tandis que l'Allemagne a, pour sa part, fabriqué 977 kg d'amphétamine et 3,1 tonnes de lévométhamphétamine qui ont été transformées en substances non psychotropes.

17. La progression de la fabrication d'amphétamines ces dernières années peut être presque exclusivement attribuée à l'augmentation rapide des quantités d'amphétamine et de dexamphétamine utilisées en médecine aux États-Unis depuis 1998, lorsqu'on a commencé à recourir à des produits contenant ces deux substances surtout pour traiter le trouble déficitaire de l'attention. En 2005, les États-Unis ont fabriqué à cette fin environ 6,7 tonnes d'amphétamine et 6,2 tonnes de dexamphétamine. La France a aussi toujours été un important fabricant d'amphétamine et, pendant la période 2001-2005, a été à l'origine en moyenne de 52,6 % de la

Figure 1.   Fabrication totale déclarée de stimulants du Tableau II, 1996-2005

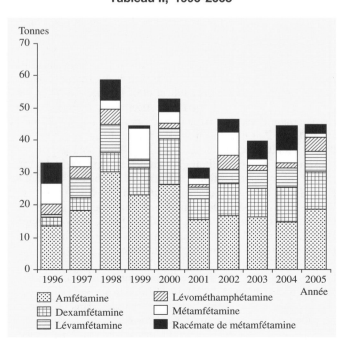

59

production mondiale d'amphétamine, de 44 % de la production de dexamphétamine et de près de 100 % de celle de lévamphétamine.

18. La fabrication d'amphétamine a augmenté peu à peu et a même dépassé 30 tonnes en 1998. Au cours des cinq dernières années, la production mondiale de cette substance a nettement baissé, bien que le total de la fabrication déclarée d'amphétamine soit passé de 14,6 tonnes en 2004 à 18,7 tonnes en 2005. Les stocks mondiaux ont eux aussi augmenté pour se situer à 6 tonnes en 2005, dont 71 % étaient détenus par les États-Unis. En 2005, 63 kg d'amphétamine ont été exportés, les principaux importateurs étant le Chili (35 %), le Canada (30 %), la Suède (12 %), la Belgique (9 %) et la Fédération de Russie (7 %).

19. La fabrication de dexamphétamine a été stable pendant les années 80 (environ 350 kg par an) mais a commencé à augmenter dans des proportions significatives après 1991 pour atteindre presque 1,7 tonne en 1995. Depuis lors, la fabrication de cette substance a continué d'augmenter peu à peu pour se monter à 14,3 tonnes en 2000 avant de chuter à 6,6 tonnes en 2001 et de se stabiliser à 102 tonnes par an en moyenne pendant la période 2002-2005. Les États-Unis et la France sont les principaux consommateurs de dexamphétamine, qui est prescrite pour le traitement du trouble déficitaire de l'attention, de l'obésité et de la narcolepsie, mais un usage important de cette substance en médecine a également été signalé dans divers autres pays, dont l'Allemagne, l'Australie, le Canada, le Chili et le Royaume-Uni. Les stocks mondiaux de dexamphétamine sont passés de 1 tonne en 1995 à 7,3 tonnes en 2003 avant de retomber à 5,9 tonnes en 2005. Le taux calculé d'utilisation de dexamphétamine a été le plus élevé en France et aux États-Unis, avec 16,4 et 4,3 S-DDD pour 1 000 habitants et par jour respectivement. Si 25 pays ont déclaré avoir importé cette substance en 2005, plus de 91 % des 492 kg des importations mondiales de dexamphétamine ont été imputables au Canada (54,6 %), à l'Australie (26,8 %) et au Royaume-Uni (10,3 %).

20. Indépendamment de ses utilisations médicales directes, la méthamphétamine sert également à la fabrication de benzphétamine, prescrite pour les troubles de l'obésité. En 1999, la fabrication totale déclarée de méthamphétamine a été de 9,5 tonnes et, depuis lors, la production mondiale a beaucoup fluctué et est tombée à 1,4 tonne en 2005, dont 80 % fabriquées aux États-Unis. La France est un autre des pays qui fabriquent habituellement de la méthamphétamine mais a déclaré que sa production était tombée de 642 kg en 2004 à 289 kg en 2005. La fabrication de méthamphétamine en Allemagne est très irrégulière, fluctuant entre 5,2 tonnes en 2002 et 2 grammes en 2005, variation qui s'est reflétée dans les tendances mondiales. Les États-Unis sont le principal consommateur de méthamphétamine et, en 2005, le taux calculé de consommation est passé de 0,26 à 0,42 S-DDD pour 1 000 habitants et par jour. En 2005, 11 pays ont signalé avoir importé de la méthamphétamine, les principaux importateurs étant le Chili et la Suisse. Par le passé, l'Irlande et le Royaume-Uni ont également déclaré avoir importé de grandes quantités de méthamphétamine.

21. Aux États-Unis, la lévométhamphétamine est utilisée pour la fabrication de produits d'inhalation par voie nasale vendus sans ordonnance, qui sont exemptés dans ce pays de certaines mesures de contrôle conformément à l'article 3 de la Convention de 1971. Au cours des dix dernières années,

la fabrication totale déclarée de lévométhamphétamine a été très irrégulière et a beaucoup varié, allant de 433 kg à 5,1 tonnes. En 2005, la production totale a de nouveau beaucoup augmenté: elle a triplé pour se situer à 4,3 tonnes. Les principaux fabricants et consommateurs de cette substance sont l'Allemagne, les États-Unis, la France et la République tchèque. La lévométhamphétamine est utilisée également en Irlande et en Italie, qui sont les principaux pays importateurs de cette substance.

22. Les principaux fabricants de racémate de méthamphétamine sont la France et la Hongrie. La majeure partie de cette substance a été exportée (20,1 tonnes au total depuis 1996) ou transformée en lévométhamphétamine et en méthamphétamine. Au cours des cinq dernières années, la fabrication totale déclarée par ces deux pays a augmenté régulièrement pour passer de 3,3 tonnes en 2001 à 7,5 tonnes en 2004. En 2005, cependant, les quantités fabriquées sont tombées à 2,8 tonnes, soit une diminution de 62 % due au fléchissement marqué de la production en Hongrie, qui a signalé que celle-ci était tombée de plus de 4 tonnes en 2004 à moins de 2 kg en 2005. Les stocks mondiaux ont subi une tendance semblable, tombant de 3,7 tonnes par an en moyenne pendant la période 2001-2004 à 1,9 tonne en 2005. Les quantités de racémate de méthamphétamine fabriquées en France sont restées stables ces dernières années et ont représenté en moyenne 3 tonnes par an pendant la période 2001-2005, soit 64 % de la production mondiale enregistrée pendant cette période. Les États-Unis, seul importateur de cette substance, en ont importé de 2,5 à 3 tonnes par an au cours des cinq dernières années.

23. Le tableau 1 indique les dix plus gros consommateurs d'amphétamines à des fins médicales et industrielles, classés en fonction de leur consommation calculée pour 2005, selon les statistiques communiquées pour les années 2001, 2003 et 2005[2]. Les quantités sont exprimées en S-DDD pour 1 000 habitants et par jour[3].

Tableau 1. Consommation calculée de stimulants inscrits au Tableau II, à l'exception du méthylphénidate, 2001, 2003 et 2005

Pays[a]	S-DDD pour 1 000 habitants et par jour		
	2001	2003	2005
États-Unis	5,42	6,25	7,73
États-Unis	6,07	6,86	10,22
Canada	0,42	0,81	1,95
Australie	1,54	1,76	1,24
Belgique	0,08	0,03	0,26
Chili	0,28	0,18	0,25
Suisse	4,04	0,04	0,23
Suède	0,20	0,22	0,20
Norvège	0,07	0,14	0,19
Royaume-Uni	0,23	0,14	0,15
Nouvelle-Zélande	0,14	0,14	0,11

[a]Les pays sont rangés selon leur consommation de stimulants inscrits au Tableau II en 2005.

[2]La méthode utilisée pour calculer la consommation de substances psychotropes est exposée dans la note explicative du tableau III de la présente publication.

[3]La liste des doses quotidiennes déterminées à des fins statistiques (S-DDD) qui sont utilisées pour ces calculs figure au tableau IV de la présente publication.

Fénétylline

24. La fénétylline est placée sous contrôle international depuis 1986 et la fabrication de cette substance a été signalée la dernière fois en 1987. Les stocks mondiaux, qui s'élevaient à près de 4 tonnes en 1987, ont fortement diminué à la suite de la destruction volontaire, en 1991, de tous les stocks suisses et, en 1992, de la moitié des stocks allemands, afin de mettre fin aux tentatives des trafiquants qui essayaient de détourner la fénétylline au moyen d'autorisations d'importation falsifiées[4]. En 2000, la seconde moitié des stocks allemands avait été peu à peu exportée vers les Pays-Bas. Ce dernier pays est le seul qui détient encore d'importants stocks de fénétylline (212 kg à la fin de 2005) et est le premier exportateur de cette substance, représentant 90 % des exportations mondiales. En 2005, le plus gros importateur était la Belgique (68 kg), qui réexportait une petite partie des quantités importées (7,6 kg) vers l'Allemagne et la France. Aucun autre pays n'a indiqué avoir utilisé de la fénétylline à des fins médicales depuis 2003.

Méthylphénidate

25. L'utilisation de méthylphénidate[5] à des fins médicales s'est sensiblement développée au cours des années 90, principalement parce qu'aux États-Unis cette substance fait l'objet de campagnes publicitaires intenses, qui s'adressent directement aux consommateurs potentiels. Le méthylphénidate est fréquemment prescrit pour le traitement du trouble déficitaire de l'attention, surtout chez l'enfant. Cet emploi s'est également développé dans de nombreux autres pays depuis la fin des années 90. La consommation totale calculée de cette substance est passée de 18,5 tonnes en 2001 à 30,4 tonnes en 2005. À côté de son utilisation principale pour le traitement du trouble déficitaire de l'attention, le méthylphénidate est également prescrit pour le traitement de la narcolepsie.

26. Les quantités totales de méthylphénidate fabriquées dans le monde ont très rapidement augmenté au cours de la première moitié des années 90, passant de 2,8 tonnes en 1990 à 19,1 tonnes en 1999, avant de revenir à 16 tonnes en 2000 (voir la figure 2), du fait de l'utilisation croissante d'amphétamines pour le traitement du trouble déficitaire de l'attention. Depuis lors, la production totale déclarée de cette substance a varié mais a suivi une tendance à la hausse pour atteindre 33,5 tonnes en 2004, chiffre inégalé jusque-là, avant de retomber à 28,8 tonnes en 2005. Les États-Unis sont le plus gros fabricant, avec une production qui est passée de 1,8 tonne en 1990 à 28,3 tonnes en 2005. La quasi-totalité des quantités fabriquées dans le pays est destinée à la consommation intérieure, mais les États-Unis ont peu à peu accru leurs exportations de cette substance, qui sont passées de 33 kg en 1996 à 2,7 tonnes en 2005. Les stocks mondiaux de méthylphénidate ont suivi la même tendance à la hausse que la fabrication et sont passés de 15,5 tonnes en 2001 à 23,4 tonnes en 2005, dont 83 % étaient détenus aux États-Unis (soit une hausse significative, ces stocks étant passés de 500 kg en 1992 à 19,5 tonnes en 2005). Dans ce pays, de

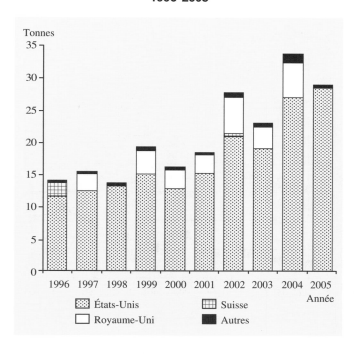

Figure 2. Fabrication de méthylphénidate, 1996-2005

vives inquiétudes ont été exprimées quant à l'éventuel surdiagnostic du trouble déficitaire de l'attention et à la prescription excessive de méthylphénidate.

27. Les pays autres que les États-Unis couvrent leurs besoins médicaux en méthylphénidate principalement par des importations, et le nombre de pays ayant déclaré avoir importé cette substance est passé de 70 en 1996 à 88 en 2005. Le commerce international de méthylphénidate a diminué, tombant de 11,5 tonnes par an en moyenne en 2003-2004 à 9,2 tonnes en 2005. L'Afrique du Sud, l'Allemagne, l'Australie, le Canada, l'Espagne, les Pays-Bas, le Royaume-Uni et la Suisse sont les principaux importateurs de méthylphénidate, essentiellement à des fins de réexportation, représentant ensemble 84 % des importations mondiales. Les principaux pays exportateurs sont l'Espagne, les États-Unis, le Royaume-Uni et la Suisse. Pendant les années 80, les exportations suisses de méthylphénidate ont été stables (moins de 400 kg par an), mais depuis 1991 elles ont progressivement augmenté pour atteindre 1,4 tonne en 1996 puis 4 tonnes en moyenne pendant la période 2003-2005. Jusqu'en 1996, les exportations suisses de cette substance provenaient d'une fabrication locale de la matière première. Depuis 1997, la matière première nécessaire à la fabrication de préparations est venue d'importations de méthylphénidate, principalement en provenance de l'Espagne et du Royaume-Uni.

28. Le nombre de pays et territoires qui importent du méthylphénidate pour la consommation intérieure est en augmentation. Depuis 1995, 121 pays ont signalé de telles importations. En 2005, 33 pays ont signalé avoir importé plus de 10 kg de méthylphénidate. L'utilisation de méthylphénidate aux États-Unis, qui sont de loin le principal consommateur (80 % de la consommation mondiale calculée en 2005), a été caractérisée par une progression forte et régulière depuis le début des années 90. La consommation de cette substance a continué d'augmenter, passant de 317 millions de S-DDD en 1996 à 808 millions de S-DDD en 2005 (voir la figure 3).

---

[4]Voir *Rapport de l'Organe international de contrôle des stupéfiants pour 1999* (publication des Nations Unies, numéro de vente: F.00.XI.1), par. 85.

[5]Voir le Tableau IV pour plus de détails.

Figure 3. Consommation médicale calculée de méthylphénidate, 1996-2005

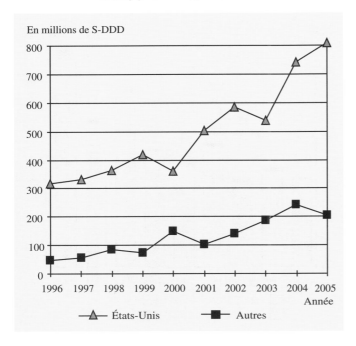

En millions de S-DDD

—▲— États-Unis   —■— Autres

Tableau 2. Consommation médicale calculée de méthylphénidate, 2001, 2003 et 2005

Pays[a]	S-DDD pour 1 000 habitants et par jour		
	2001	2003	2005
États-Unis	5,11	5,21	7,61
Israël	0,72	5,27	2,69
Norvège	0,78	2,13	2,61
Canada	0,29	4,24	2,55
Pays-Bas	1,11	1,38	1,81
Allemagne	0,67	0,99	1,47
Australie	0,89	1,34	1,44
Suisse	2,82	2,23	1,36
Belgique	0,51	1,12	1,24
Nouvelle-Zélande	1,29	1,35	1,23
Royaume-Uni	1,04	0,95	1,23
Espagne	0,66	0,78	1,11
Suède	0,16	0,35	0,89
Danemark	0,22	0,40	0,88
Finlande	0,07	0,29	0,57
Afrique du Sud	0,16	0,27	0,51
Panama	0,10	—	0,45
Chili	0,24	0,35	0,44
Islande	2,35	5,21	0,01

[a] Les pays sont rangés selon leur consommation de méthylphénidate en 2005.

29. La consommation de méthylphénidate dans le reste du monde a représenté en moyenne quelque 200 millions de S-DDD par an au cours des trois dernières années. L'évolution récente est imputable à la diminution de la consommation au Canada, qui est tombée de 48 millions de S-DDD par an en 2003-2004 à 29 millions en 2005, ainsi qu'à un accroissement de la consommation en Allemagne, où elle est passée de 33 millions de S-DDD en 2004 à 44 millions de S-DDD

en 2005. Les autres principaux pays consommateurs sont le Royaume-Uni et l'Espagne, où la consommation de méthylphénidate a augmenté ces dernières années, atteignant en 2005 27 et 17 millions de S-DDD respectivement.

30. Le tableau 2 indique, dans l'ordre décroissant, les plus gros consommateurs de méthylphénidate à des fins médicales en 2005, cette consommation étant calculée à partir de statistiques communiquées pour 2001, 2003 et 2005. Les quantités sont exprimées en S-DDD pour 1 000 habitants et par jour.

Phenmétrazine

31. La phenmétrazine n'est plus utilisée dans aucun pays à des fins médicales. De modestes stocks de la substance sont détenus au Royaume-Uni (14 grammes) et aux États-Unis (1 gramme). Le commerce international de phenmétrazine se limite à des transactions occasionnelles portant sur quelques grammes seulement.

Antiémétiques

Delta-9-tétrahydrocannabinol et ses variantes stéréochimiques

32. Le *delta*-9-THC avait initialement été inscrit au Tableau I, avec ses variantes stéréochimiques, mais il a été transféré en 1991 au Tableau II en raison de l'utilisation d'une de ses variantes stéréochimiques (le dronabinol) pour soulager les nausées. Les États-Unis sont le seul pays à avoir déclaré la fabrication de quantités importantes de *delta*-9-THC à un niveau qui est demeuré relativement stable (66 kg par an en moyenne) à la fin des années 90. Toutefois, les quantités fabriquées ont considérablement augmenté depuis 2000, s'établissant en moyenne à 170 kg par an au cours des cinq dernières années (180 kg en 2005). Deux autres pays ont déclaré avoir fabriqué cette substance au cours des cinq dernières années, mais en quantités bien moindres: l'Allemagne (7 kg en moyenne) et le Royaume-Uni (2 kg en moyenne). En 2005, le Canada et la Suisse ont déclaré pour la première fois avoir fabriqué de petites quantités de *delta*-9-THC, à savoir 3 kg et 13 kg respectivement.

33. Les quantités de *delta*-9-THC fabriquées en Allemagne, au Canada et aux États-Unis ont été dans leur quasi-totalité utilisées sur place. Le Royaume-Uni et la Suisse n'ont pas signalé avoir fabriqué ni utilisé cette substance en 2005 mais ont accru leurs stocks. Le total des stocks déclarés en 2005 (385 kg), qui se trouvaient en majeure partie aux États-Unis et au Royaume-Uni, reflète une augmentation de 65 % par rapport à 2004. Plusieurs pays ont déclaré avoir importé cette substance en 2005, les quantités les plus importantes ayant été signalées par l'Allemagne (2 461 g) et le Canada (2 187 g), pays qui, avec les États-Unis, sont les principaux consommateurs de *delta*-9-THC.

Hallucinogènes

Phencyclidine

34. La phencyclidine est principalement utilisée comme anesthésique en médecine vétérinaire. Par le passé, la fabrication de petites quantités de cette substance a été signalée

par l'Australie, les États-Unis, la France, la Hongrie, Israël, le Royaume-Uni et la Suisse (4,5 kg au total pour la période 1996-2005). Les États-Unis et Israël ont été les seuls pays à avoir signalé une fabrication de cette substance en 2005 (2 kg et 146 g respectivement). Dix pays ont signalé détenir des stocks de phencyclidine en 2005, les États-Unis représentant 84 % du total mondial (3,1 kg). Les autres pays détenant des stocks de phencyclidine étaient la France (210 g) et Israël (146 g) suivis par (dans l'ordre décroissant) le Royaume-Uni, la Suisse, le Danemark, le Canada, la Hongrie, l'Australie et la Finlande. Le commerce international de phencyclidine se limite à des transactions occasionnelles portant sur quelques grammes seulement.

Sédatifs-hypnotiques

Mécloqualone

35.   La mécloqualone n'est pas fabriquée depuis 1980, bien que certaines quantités en soient conservées en stock. Le Royaume-Uni a déclaré en détenir 152 g en 2001. Depuis lors, les États-Unis sont le seul pays à déclarer des stocks de la substance (35 g en 2005).

Méthaqualone

36.   Ces dernières années, la fabrication de méthaqualone a considérablement diminué par rapport aux quantités record atteintes dans les années 80 (plus de 50 tonnes par an). C'est en 1997 que la fabrication de quantités importantes de cette substance a été déclarée pour la dernière fois par la Suisse (340 kg) et la République tchèque (43 kg). Depuis lors, la production mondiale a continué de baisser, les États-Unis en ayant fabriqué en petites quantités (4 g en 2003 et 3 g en 2004), mais il n'a été déclaré aucune fabrication en 2005. Pendant la période 1997-2005, les stocks mondiaux, détenus presque uniquement par la Suisse, sont tombés de 2,4 tonnes en 1997 à 257 kg en 2005, la méthaqualone continuant d'être utilisée à des fins médicales. Au cours des dernières années, la consommation mondiale a accusé de fortes variations, passant de 1,1 million de S-DDD en moyenne pour la période 1999-2000 à moins de 6 000 S-DDD en 2005. C'est essentiellement en Suisse seulement que cette substance continue d'être consommée, mais pas en quantités significatives.

Sécobarbital

37.   La fabrication de sécobarbital a sensiblement diminué depuis que cette substance, souvent détournée de la fabrication et du commerce licites vers le trafic illicite par le passé, a été transférée du Tableau III au Tableau II en 1988. Cette année-là, la fabrication mondiale déclarée avait dépassé les 11 tonnes. Elle est tombée à 2,6 tonnes en 1990 puis à 1,8 tonne en moyenne par an entre 1997 et 2001. En 2001, elle a atteint son niveau le plus élevé depuis 1989, à savoir 4,2 tonnes (voir la figure 4), fabriquées par deux pays seulement: l'Allemagne (2,3 tonnes) et les États-Unis (1,9 tonne). Ces deux dernières années, les quantités totales fabriquées ont légèrement augmenté, passant de 811 kg en 2004 à 817 kg en 2005. Les stocks mondiaux de sécobarbital, qui sont tombés de 1,4 tonne en 2004 à 736 kg en 2005, sont détenus à concurrence de 65 % par l'Allemagne et de 30 % par les États-Unis.

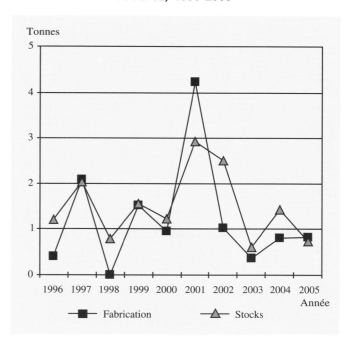

Figure 4.   Sécobarbital: fabrication et stocks totaux déclarés, 1996-2005

38.   Pendant la période 2001-2005, cinq pays ont déclaré avoir fabriqué au moins une fois du sécobarbital, à savoir, dans l'ordre décroissant, l'Allemagne (pour la consommation nationale et l'exportation), les États-Unis (principalement pour la consommation nationale), le Danemark (presque exclusivement pour l'exportation), le Japon et la Chine (pour la consommation nationale). En 2005, l'Allemagne (817 kg) et l'Irlande (79 kg) ont été les seuls pays à avoir signalé une fabrication de sécobarbital. Ces dernières années, les stocks des États-Unis ont nettement baissé, tombant de 1,7 tonne en 2001 à 220 kg en 2005. Les importations annuelles mondiales de sécobarbital ont été en moyenne de 670 kg pendant la période 2003-2005 après avoir atteint le chiffre record de 1,7 tonne en 2001. Les principaux pays à faire le commerce de cette substance ces dernières années ont été l'Allemagne (principal exportateur) et le Royaume-Uni (principal importateur). Les autres pays ayant importé du sécobarbital ont notamment été la Belgique, le Canada, le Danemark, l'Irlande, les Pays-Bas et la Suède.

Antitussifs

Zipéprol

39.   Le zipéprol, antitussif à propriétés bronchospasmolytiques et mucolytiques, a été placé sous contrôle international en 1995, année à partir de laquelle des statistiques sont donc disponibles. Seule la France a déclaré pour la dernière fois, en 2001, avoir fabriqué du zipéprol (666 kg). En 2005, les stocks de zipéprol étaient détenus principalement par la Suisse (588 kg), suivie par le Chili (10 kg). En 2005, seule la Suisse a signalé avoir exporté cette substance (168 kg). Les seuls pays ayant déclaré utiliser cette substance ces dernières années ont été le Chili, le Mexique et la République de Corée.

40. Neuf substances sont inscrites au Tableau III. Selon les critères d'inscription aux Tableaux adoptés par le Comité d'experts sur la toxicodépendance de l'Organisation mondiale de la santé (OMS), les substances du Tableau III sont celles dont les risques d'abus constituent un danger majeur pour la santé publique mais qui ont une utilité thérapeutique modérée ou considérable. Une de ces substances, la cathine, appartient au groupe des stimulants du système nerveux central, six autres au groupe des sédatifs-hypnotiques — à savoir quatre barbituriques (amobarbital, butalbital, cyclobarbital et pentobarbital) ainsi que le gluthétimide et le flunitrazépam — et les deux dernières, la buprénorphine et la pentazocine, au groupe des analgésiques.

Stimulants du système nerveux central

Cathine

41. La cathine, indépendamment de son utilisation comme stimulant, est également employée dans l'industrie. Au cours des cinq dernières années, la quantité de cathine fabriquée dans le monde a connu de fortes variations en fonction de la quantité produite par l'Allemagne, seul pays à en fabriquer jusqu'en 2003. En 2004, l'Inde a été le seul pays ayant déclaré avoir fabriqué cette substance (56 kg), mais, en 2005, c'est l'Allemagne qui a fabriqué l'intégralité des 2,2 tonnes de cathine produites dans le monde. Les niveaux de la production mondiale ont varié entre 6,4 tonnes et 56 kg par an et ont représenté une moyenne de 2 tonnes par an pendant la période 2001-2005.

42. Au cours de la période 2001-2005, neuf pays ont déclaré avoir importé de la cathine et les importations totales de cette substance ont été en moyenne de 4 tonnes par an. Pendant cette période, l'Afrique du Sud et l'Italie ont représenté respectivement 44 et 26 % des importations mondiales. En moyenne, l'Afrique du Sud a importé pendant cette période 1,8 tonne de cathine (pour la consommation nationale) et l'Italie 1 tonne (principalement pour la réexportation). Les autres pays ayant régulièrement importé cette substance ont été la France, le Mexique et la Suisse. Les importations du Mexique et de la Suisse ont baissé par rapport à leur niveau de 1997-2001 pour tomber à environ 850 kg et 40 kg respectivement en 2004, même si ces deux pays n'ont pas déclaré d'importations en 2005. Les importations de cathine par la France ont été en moyenne de plus de 300 kg par an pour la période 2001-2005. L'Allemagne, qui est l'un des sept pays ayant déclaré avoir exporté de la cathine ces dernières années, demeure le principal exportateur, avec en moyenne 2,4 tonnes par an pendant la période 2001-2005.

Sédatifs-hypnotiques

43. Les barbituriques sont un groupe de dépresseurs du système nerveux central qui sont étroitement liés par leur structure chimique. Rangés dans la catégorie des sédatifs-hypnotiques, ils étaient jadis prescrits surtout pour le traitement de l'insomnie, de l'anxiété, du stress et de l'épilepsie. Quelques-uns étaient utilisés aussi comme anesthésiques pour les brèves interventions chirurgicales (substances à action ultracourte), tandis que d'autres ont des propriétés anticonvulsives sélectives. Les divers barbituriques se distinguent par la rapidité, la durée et la puissance de leur action. Une faible dose de 50 mg peut atténuer l'anxiété et la tension, mais une dose plus forte, de 100 à 200 mg, entraîne habituellement le sommeil. Comme les benzodiazépines, les barbituriques que l'on trouve sur le marché illicite n'ont habituellement pas été fabriqués par synthèse dans des laboratoires clandestins mais détournés des circuits licites. Les possibilités d'abus sont considérables et les effets à long terme de leur usage sont notamment l'apparition d'une tolérance et d'une forte dépendance physique et psychologique.

Amobarbital, butalbital, cyclobarbital et pentobarbital

44. L'amobarbital, le cyclobarbital et le pentobarbital sont placés sous contrôle depuis l'adoption de la Convention de 1971, et le butalbital a été inscrit en 1987 au Tableau III de cette convention. Les trois barbituriques, l'amobarbital, le butalbital et le cyclobarbital, sont utilisés principalement comme hypnotiques (pour induire le sommeil) et ont donc aujourd'hui leur place pour le traitement de l'insomnie chronique. Le pentobarbital, barbiturique à action courte, a été également utilisé en prémédication avant une anesthésie. Au cours de la période 2001-2005, le Danemark, les États-Unis et le Canada sont les pays pour lesquels on a calculé la consommation la plus élevée de ces quatre substances par rapport au chiffre de la population: 17,2, 6,7 et 2,8 S-DDD pour 1 000 habitants et par jour respectivement. La fabrication totale déclarée de ces substances, après avoir été de 1,4 milliard de S-DDD en moyenne pendant la période 2000-2003, est progressivement tombée à 881 millions de S-DDD en 2005 (voir la figure 5). La figure 6 montre, pour la période 2001-2005, la répartition de la production totale entre les pays fabricants.

45. Traditionnellement, les États-Unis ont été le principal fabricant de butalbital, entrant en moyenne jusqu'à 75 % dans la production mondiale. Ces dernières années, la fabrication mondiale de cette substance a diminué progressivement pour tomber de 76 tonnes en 2002 à 24 tonnes en 2005 (voir la figure 7). Au cours des dix dernières années, seuls l'Allemagne, le Danemark et les États-Unis ont régulièrement fabriqué du butalbital. Le butalbital a été utilisé dans la fabrication de préparations qui, aux États-Unis, sont exemptées de certaines mesures de contrôle, conformément à l'article 3 de la Convention de 1971. Ces dernières années, les quantités fabriquées y ont fluctué, tombant brusquement de 40 tonnes en 2002 à 7,4 tonnes en moyenne au cours de la période 2003-2005. Les quantités fabriquées au Danemark ont diminué régulièrement pour tomber de 38,7 tonnes en 2003 à 12,8 tonnes en 2005, soit à peu près le même niveau que la production annuelle moyenne pendant la période 1996-2000 (14 tonnes). En 2005, le Danemark et les États-Unis ont fabriqué respectivement 53 % et 38 % de la production mondiale et l'Allemagne un peu plus de 2 tonnes de cette substance.

46. Parmi les 10 pays ayant déclaré des exportations de butalbital au cours de la période de cinq ans 2001-2005, le Danemark, dont les exportations représentaient 96 % du total mondial en 2001, est demeuré le premier exportateur en

Figure 5. Barbituriques inscrits au Tableau III: fabrication totale déclarée, 1996-2005

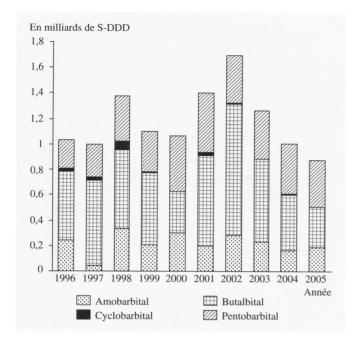

Figure 7. Butalbital: fabrication totale déclarée, 1996-2005

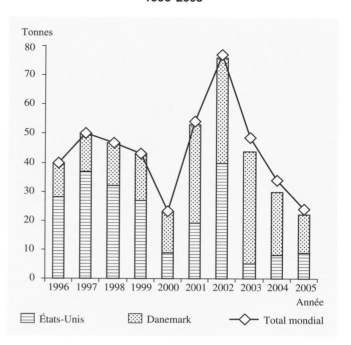

Figure 6. Barbituriques inscrits au Tableau III: fabrication totale déclarée, par pays, 2001-2005

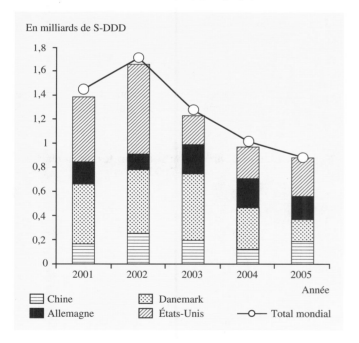

Figure 8. Pentobarbital: fabrication totale déclarée, 1996-2005

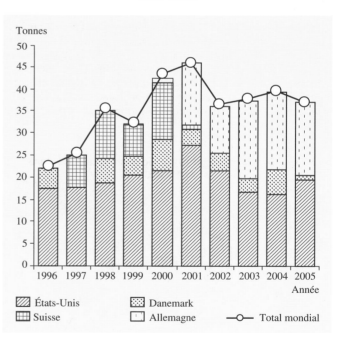

2005, fournissant 86 % des 22,1 tonnes exportées dans le monde. Les exportations de butalbital en provenance des États-Unis ont été très irrégulières, variant entre zéro et 2 tonnes au cours des 10 dernières années (1996-2005). Pendant la période 2001-2005, l'Italie et la Suisse figuraient parmi les petits exportateurs, avec une moyenne annuelle de 179,4 kg et de 103 kg respectivement. Les États-Unis, l'Italie et le Canada demeurent les principaux importateurs de butalbital. Ces dernières années, le Danemark, les États-Unis, l'Italie et le Canada ont été les pays où la consommation de cette substance a été la plus élevée.

47. La fabrication mondiale déclarée de pentobarbital a diminué ces dernières années, tombant de 45 tonnes en 2001 à 37,7 tonnes en moyenne pendant la période 2002-2005 (voir la figure 8). Les États-Unis, l'Allemagne, le Danemark et la Suisse ont été les principaux fabricants au cours des 10 dernières années, les trois premiers de ces pays ayant représenté 52,5 %, 44,5 % et 2,8 % de la production mondiale en 2005, respectivement. Ces cinq dernières années, l'Australie, le Danemark, l'Irlande et la Nouvelle-Zélande ont enregistré la consommation relative la plus élevée, allant de 2,5 à 3,8 S-DDD pour 1 000 habitants et par jour.

48. Au cours de la période 2001-2005, les quantités de pentobarbital entrant dans le commerce international ont fluctué autour d'une moyenne annuelle de 26 tonnes. L'Allemagne, les États-Unis, le Canada, le Danemark et la France, dans l'ordre descendant, sont restés au cours de cette période les plus gros exportateurs: mises ensemble, leurs exportations représentaient plus de 92 % des exportations mondiales. Pendant la période 2001-2005, les exportations allemandes ont été stables (11 tonnes en moyenne), alors que les exportations de pentobarbital des États-Unis ont fluctué entre 3,5 tonnes et 6 tonnes. Selon les statistiques communiquées, 67 pays ont importé du pentobarbital pendant la période 2001-2005. En 2005, la Chine (45,5 tonnes), le Canada (6,7 tonnes), la France (4,5 tonnes), l'Australie (2,6 tonnes) et le Royaume-Uni (2,1 tonnes) en ont été les plus gros importateurs, comptant pour 86 % des importations totales.

49. Pendant la période 2001-2004, la Chine, le Danemark et le Japon ont été les principaux pays fabriquant de l'amobarbital. En 2005, seule la Chine a déclaré avoir fabriqué cette substance (18 tonnes) (voir la figure 9). Les stocks mondiaux d'amobarbital, qui avaient diminué progressivement pour tomber de plus de 2 tonnes en 2000 à 1,7 tonne en 2003, sont remontés à 3,2 tonnes en 2004 puis à nouveau à 7,3 tonnes en 2005. La consommation mondiale calculée de cette substance a fluctué autour d'une moyenne de 21,7 tonnes au cours de la période 2001-2005, la Roumanie, le Japon et la Chine étant les plus gros consommateurs.

50. Les exportations mondiales d'amobarbital, tout en faisant apparaître une tendance à la hausse, ont fluctué autour d'une moyenne annuelle de 5,6 tonnes pendant la période 2001-2005. Les importations annuelles mondiales de cette substance ont atteint le chiffre record de 10,2 tonnes en 2005, les plus gros importateurs mondiaux ces dernières années étant, dans l'ordre descendant, la Roumanie, les Pays-Bas (pour la réexportation), l'Irlande et la Hongrie. Aux Pays-Bas, les importations d'amobarbital ont nettement

baissé pour tomber d'une moyenne annuelle de 2,3 tonnes pendant la période 2002-2003 à 52 kg en 2005. Les importations roumaines ont elles aussi chuté de 7,1 tonnes en 2002 à 2 tonnes en 2004, mais ont de nouveau augmenté pour se situer à 9,7 tonnes en 2005.

51. Le cyclobarbital est essentiellement employé dans certains pays d'Europe centrale et orientale, la plus forte consommation par habitant ayant été enregistrée en Pologne et en Lettonie au cours de la période 2001-2005 (0,26 et 0,3 S-DDD pour 1 000 habitants et par jour respectivement). Ces dernières années, la Pologne a été le principal fabricant, sa part représentant jusqu'à 100 % du total mondial pendant la période 2004-2005 (voir la figure 10). La fabrication de cyclobarbital en Pologne, après avoir baissé pour tomber de 5 tonnes environ en 2001 à zéro en 2003, a recommencé à augmenter, passant de 755 kg en 2004 à 914 kg en 2005. La Lettonie et l'Allemagne n'ont pas déclaré de fabrication de cyclobarbital les trois dernières années. Suivant les variations de la fabrication, les stocks mondiaux de la substance ont également diminué, tombant de 2,6 tonnes en 2002 à 110 kg en 2004, avant de décupler pour atteindre 1,1 tonne en 2005.

52. Les exportations mondiales de cyclobarbital ont diminué, reculant d'une moyenne annuelle de 1,1 tonne pendant la période 2003-2004 à 711 kg en 2005. La Pologne demeure le principal exportateur de la substance, bien que ses exportations aient diminué de moitié, tombant de 1,5 tonne en moyenne par an au cours de la période 2001-2004 à 707 kg en 2005. Le Bélarus, la Géorgie, la Lettonie, la Lituanie et la Suisse en ont aussi importé de grandes quantités pendant la période 2003-2005.

Glutéthimide

53. Comme au cours des quelques années précédentes, il n'a pas été déclaré de fabrication de glutéthimide à l'OICS

Figure 9. Amobarbital: fabrication totale déclarée, 1996-2005

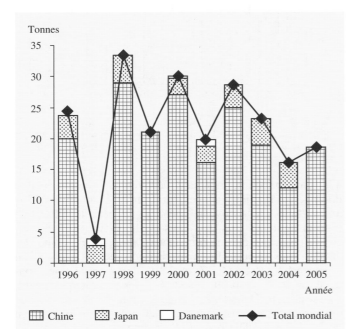

Figure 10. Cyclobarbital: fabrication totale déclarée, 1996-2005

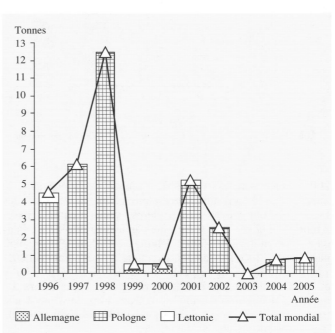

en 2005. Au début des années 80, il a été fabriqué plusieurs dizaines de tonnes par an de cette substance, principalement en vue de sa transformation en aminoglutéthimide, substance non psychotrope utilisée comme agent antinéoplastique. La fabrication mondiale de glutéthimide n'a cessé de diminuer pendant les années 90 pour disparaître totalement en 1998. Depuis lors, aucun pays n'a déclaré avoir fabriqué cette substance, à l'exception de la Hongrie, qui a signalé en avoir fabriqué environ 700 kg en 2001 et de la Chine, avec 240 kg en 2005.

54. Parallèlement à la chute de la fabrication, le volume des échanges internationaux de glutéthimide a baissé lui aussi tombant d'un niveau maximal d'environ 15 tonnes par an pendant la période 1997-1998 à quelques centaines de kilogrammes en 2002. Depuis 2003, les seules transactions commerciales signalées à l'OICS en quantités supérieures à 1 kg ont été imputables à la Hongrie, qui en a exporté 300 kg en Roumanie en 2003 et qui en a importé 200 kg en 2004 puis à nouveau en 2005 en provenance de la Chine. La Bulgarie et la Suisse, qui étaient de gros importateurs de cette substance pendant les années 90, n'ont pas importé de glutéthimide depuis 2002 et 2001 respectivement.

Flunitrazépam

55. Le flunitrazépam demeure l'une des benzodiazépines dont l'abus est le plus fréquent. Visiblement, le marché illicite de flunitrazépam est surtout alimenté par les détournements de cette substance des circuits nationaux de distribution et non du commerce international. Les préparations à base de flunitrazépam sont souvent exportées clandestinement des pays où elles ont été détournées et introduites dans d'autres pays où il existe un marché illicite. En raison de la fréquence des détournements et de l'abus, le flunitrazépam a été transféré en 1995 du Tableau IV au Tableau III. Plusieurs pays, dont les principaux fabricants et importateurs de cette substance, agissant en étroite coopération avec l'industrie pharmaceutique, ont adopté une politique rigoureuse de contrôle.

56. Dans la pratique médicale, le flunitrazépam est, comme le diazépam, utilisé pour le traitement à court terme de l'insomnie et, dans certains pays, pour la prémédication et l'induction de l'anesthésie générale. Jusqu'en 1996, plusieurs pays, dont l'Argentine, le Brésil, le Danemark, l'Espagne, l'Italie, le Japon, la République tchèque et la Turquie, avaient déclaré fabriquer du flunitrazépam. Depuis lors, seules l'Italie et la Suisse, qui ont commencé à en fabriquer en 1997, continuent de produire du flunitrazépam. Si, en 2004, la production de ces deux pays ensemble représentait plus de 1,5 tonne, c'est-à-dire la plus grande quantité de flunitrazépam jamais déclarée, la fabrication mondiale est tombée à 84 kg, chiffre le plus faible jamais enregistré, en 2005. Cette diminution est imputable au fait que la Suisse n'a pas fabriqué de flunitrazépam en 2005 en raison des stocks considérables qu'elle détenait encore (voir les figures 22 et 23 et le paragraphe 105 ci-dessous).

57. Les échanges internationaux de flunitrazépam ont été relativement stables pendant la période 1990-2003, s'établissant autour de 1,1 tonne en moyenne par an. En 2004, ils ont commencé à baisser et ont continué à diminuer en 2005 pour tomber à 700 kg. La Suisse, principal exportateur de cette substance depuis 1997, et l'Italie représentaient ensemble

96 % des exportations mondiales en 2005. En outre, cette dernière année, plusieurs pays ont réexporté du flunitrazépam, en particulier l'Allemagne, le Brésil, la France, l'Irlande et la République tchèque.

58. Les importations mondiales de flunitrazépam, qui avaient atteint le chiffre record de plus de 1,4 tonne en 1995, ont diminué régulièrement depuis lors, très probablement par suite de l'application de rigoureuses mesures nationales de contrôle et du transfert de cette substance, en 1995, au Tableau III de la Convention de 1971. Le Japon demeure le plus gros importateur de flunitrazépam, avec plus de la moitié des importations mondiales annuelles (421 kg en 2005). En outre, environ 25 pays ont signalé avoir importé du flunitrazépam en quantités supérieures à 1 kg en 2005, dont l'Allemagne, l'Australie, l'Autriche, la Belgique, le Brésil, la France, la Grèce, la République de Corée et la Suède, qui en ont importé entre 10 et 40 kg.

Analgésiques

Buprénorphine

59. Inscrite au Tableau III depuis 1989, la buprénorphine[6] appartient à la famille des opioïdes utilisés principalement comme analgésiques. Dans plusieurs pays, la buprénorphine est aussi utilisée pour la désintoxication des héroïnomanes et les traitements de substitution de la dépendance aux opiacés. La fabrication totale de la substance a augmenté régulièrement depuis 1993 et a atteint près de 2 tonnes en moyenne pendant la période 2003-2005, soit deux fois plus que pendant la fin des années 90, lorsque cette substance a commencé d'être utilisée à plus fortes doses pour le traitement de la dépendance à l'égard des opiacés. Le Royaume-Uni est demeuré le plus gros fabricant de buprénorphine, avec 75 % du total mondial en moyenne pendant la période 2001-2005, les quantités fabriquées augmentant considérablement au cours des dix dernières années pour passer de 274 kg en 1996 à 1 542 kg en 2005. Au cours des cinq dernières années, le deuxième fabricant mondial a été l'Australie (383 kg en 2005), principalement pour l'exportation, avec également une tendance à la hausse depuis 1999, année pendant laquelle la fabrication de buprénorphine a été signalée pour la première fois. L'Inde aussi a fabriqué régulièrement de la buprénorphine, avec une production annuelle moyenne de 15 kg, pendant la période 2001-2005. Cette dernière année, les autres fabricants de buprénorphine ont été les Pays-Bas (30 kg), la Belgique (12 kg), la République tchèque (10 kg) et la Chine (9,5 kg). Logiquement, les stocks totaux de cette substance ont eux aussi beaucoup augmenté (115 kg en 1996 mais 1 641 kg en 2005). En 2005, les stocks de buprénorphine étaient détenus principalement par le Royaume-Uni (728 kg), l'Allemagne (246 kg), la France (192 kg), l'Australie (110 kg) et les Pays-Bas (49 kg).

60. Les exportations totales de buprénorphine ont sensiblement augmenté, passant de 100 kg en 1996 à 1 236 kg en 2005. Cette évolution a été due à la progression des exportations de buprénorphine de l'Allemagne, de l'Australie et du Royaume-Uni, qui en sont les principaux exportateurs. La Belgique, le Danemark, la France, l'Inde et les Pays-Bas ont également déclaré avoir exporté de la buprénorphine ces dernières années.

---

[6]Voir le Tableau IV pour plus de détails.

61. L'Allemagne et la France ont été les plus gros importateurs (avec 60 % des importations totales) des 43 pays qui ont signalé avoir importé chaque année plus de 1 kg de buprénorphine pendant la période 2001-2005. Les autres principaux importateurs de cette substance en 2005 ont été les États-Unis (176 kg), l'Espagne (70 kg), l'Italie (57 kg), la Belgique (24 kg), le Portugal (13 kg), la Suisse (12 kg) et la Malaisie (11 kg), dans tous les cas pour la consommation nationale. L'emploi accru de cette substance se reflète dans les statistiques communiquées par l'Allemagne, l'Australie, l'Autriche, la Belgique, l'Espagne, les États-Unis, la France, l'Italie, la Malaisie, le Portugal, la République tchèque, le Royaume-Uni, la Suède et la Suisse alors que l'utilisation de petites quantités à ces mêmes fins a également été déclarée par la Chine, le Danemark, l'Estonie, la Finlande, la Grèce, l'Inde, l'Indonésie, l'Irlande, l'Islande, Israël, la Lettonie, le Mexique, la Norvège, le Pakistan et Singapour.

Pentazocine

62. La pentazocine est un analgésique opioïde dont l'effet et les utilisations sont semblables à ceux de la morphine. Elle a été inscrite au Tableau III en 1984. La fabrication mondiale totale déclarée de pentazocine a continué de beaucoup fluctuer pendant la période 1996-2005 et a dépassé 4,5 tonnes par an en moyenne. En 2005, presque toute la production a été imputable à l'Inde — le plus gros fabricant mondial — avec 3 027 kg, et à l'Italie, avec 1 446 kg. Presque toute la pentazocine fabriquée en Inde a été destinée à la consommation nationale mais toute la production italienne a été destinée à l'exportation. En 2005, l'Italie a été à l'origine de plus de 50 % des exportations mondiales de pentazocine. Trois autres pays, à savoir les États-Unis (171 kg en 2001 et 316 kg en 2002), la Hongrie (136 kg en 2001) et le Royaume-Uni (258 kg en 2002), ont également fabriqué cette substance ces dernières années, mais en quantités beaucoup plus modestes. Les stocks totaux de pentazocine ont eux aussi fluctué pendant la période 2001-2005 et se sont situés à 3,4 tonnes en moyenne. Indépendamment des principaux fabricants, l'Inde et l'Italie, plusieurs pays ont signalé détenir d'importants stocks de cette substance à la fin de 2005, à savoir les États-Unis (762 kg), le Pakistan (357 kg) et la Slovénie (173 kg).

63. Les principaux importateurs de pentazocine en 2005 ont été les États-Unis (1 357 kg), suivis du Pakistan (598 kg), du Japon (450 kg), du Canada (177 kg) et du Nigéria (120 kg). La Suisse (451 kg) et le Portugal (229 kg) ont également importé d'importantes quantités de cette substance en 2005, destinées surtout à la réexportation. Le Canada, les États-Unis, l'Inde, le Japon, le Nigéria et le Pakistan ont été parmi les principaux pays consommateurs de pentazocine.

Substances inscrites au Tableau IV

64. Selon les critères de l'OMS concernant l'inscription de substances au Tableau IV de la Convention de 1971, les substances à inscrire à ce Tableau sont celles dont l'abus représente pour la santé publique un risque encore important mais moindre que celui lié aux substances inscrites au Tableau III, et qui ont une utilité thérapeutique variant entre modérée et considérable. Sont inscrites au Tableau IV 63 substances ayant diverses applications en médecine et appartenant aux groupes suivants: stimulants du système nerveux central (14 substances); anxiolytiques de type benzodiazépine (22 substances); autres anxiolytiques (1 substance); sédatifs-hypnotiques de type benzodiazépine (11 substances); antiépileptiques de type benzodiazépine (1 substance); sédatifs hypnotiques et antiépileptiques de type barbiturique (7 substances); autres sédatifs-hypnotiques (5 substances); analgésiques (1 substance) et antidépresseurs (1 substance).

Stimulants du système nerveux central

65. Quatorze stimulants sont inscrits au Tableau IV: l'amfépramone, l'aminorex, la benzphétamine, l'éthylamphétamine, la fencamfamine, le fenproporex, le mazindol, le méfénorex, le mésocarbe, la pémoline, la phendimétrazine, la phentermine, le pipradrol et la pyrovalérone. Seuls l'amfépramone et le pipradrol figuraient dès l'origine au Tableau IV, tous les autres stimulants ayant été inscrits par la suite. Ces substances sont utilisées essentiellement comme anorexigènes ou pour le traitement des troubles de l'attention.

66. La fabrication totale déclarée des stimulants du système nerveux central inscrits au Tableau IV a beaucoup fluctué pendant la fin des années 90 et s'est stabilisée à une moyenne annuelle d'environ 1,8 milliard de S-DDD pendant la période 2000-2005 (voir la figure 11). En 1996, un niveau record de 3,9 milliards de S-DDD a été atteint. La production a commencé à diminuer en 1997 pour atteindre un plancher en 1998 (356 millions de S-DDD). Après 1998, elle est de nouveau remontée jusqu'à un volume total de 2,2 milliards de S-DDD en 2001. Depuis lors, la production mondiale a légèrement diminué pour tomber à 1,6 milliard de S-DDD en 2003 avant de remonter progressivement pour atteindre 2 milliards de S-DDD en 2005.

67. En 2005, sur la fabrication totale déclarée des 14 stimulants inscrits au Tableau IV, la fabrication de phentermine (923 millions de S-DDD) avait représenté 45 %, celle de fenproporex (474 millions de S-DDD) 23 % et celle d'amfépramone (371 millions de S-DDD) 18 % (voir la figure 12). La production de mazindol (175 millions de S-DDD) et de phendimétrazine (100 millions de S-DDD) ont représenté 9 % et 4 % du total respectivement, et celle de benzphétamine (10 millions de S-DDD) 0,5 %. En 2005, il n'a pas été déclaré de fabrication de pémoline ou d'autres stimulants du système nerveux central inscrits au Tableau IV.

68. Les fluctuations de la fabrication totale déclarée et de l'utilisation des stimulants du système nerveux central inscrits au Tableau IV s'expliquent principalement par l'évolution de l'utilisation de la phentermine aux États-Unis (voir la figure 13). La forte hausse de la consommation de cette substance aux États-Unis observée en 1996 et en 1997 était due à sa prescription pour le traitement de l'obésité en association avec un autre anorexigène, la fenfluramine. Après le

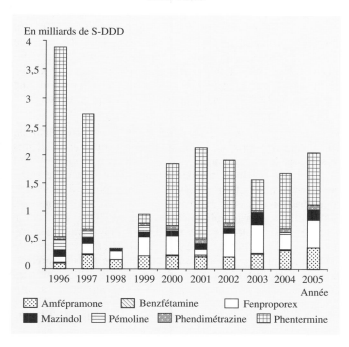

Figure 11. Stimulants du système nerveux central inscrits au Tableau IV: fabrication totale déclarée, 1996-2005

En milliards de S-DDD

Année

Amfépramone   Benzfétamine   Fenproporex
Mazindol   Pémoline   Phendimétrazine   Phentermine

Figure 12. Stimulants du système nerveux central inscrits au Tableau IV: part des diverses substances dans la fabrication totale déclarée, 2005

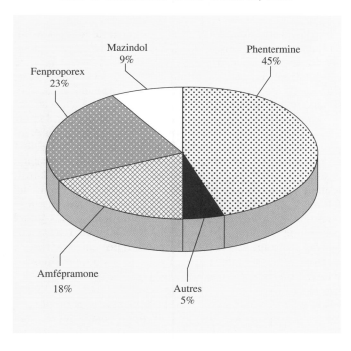

Mazindol 9%
Phentermine 45%
Fenproporex 23%
Amfépramone 18%
Autres 5%

retrait de la fenfluramine dans ce pays en 1997 en raison de ses graves effets secondaires, la phentermine a été nettement moins utilisée. Depuis 2000, la fabrication et la consommation ont repris et la phentermine est de nouveau l'anorexigène le plus consommé aux États-Unis. Sur les 1,9 milliard de S-DDD de substances de ce groupe qui ont été consommées dans le monde en 2005, la phentermine a été la substance la plus largement utilisée (795 millions de S-DDD),

Figure 13. Stimulants du système nerveux central inscrits au Tableau IV: consommation mondiale calculée[a], 1996-2005

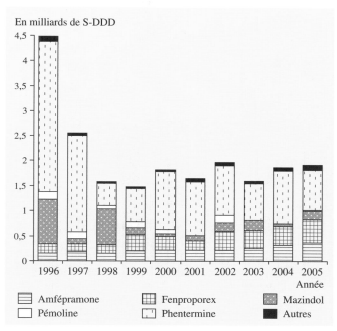

En milliards de S-DDD

Année

Amfépramone   Fenproporex   Mazindol
Pémoline   Phentermine   Autres

[a]Calculée sur la base des données statistiques communiquées par les États, la moyenne des consommations annuelles porte sur une période de trois ans.

suivie par le fenproporex (456 millions de S-DDD), l'amfépramone (378 millions de S-DDD) et la phendimétrazine (87 millions de S-DDD).

69. Pendant les années 90, c'est sur le continent américain que la consommation par habitant de stimulants inscrits au Tableau IV a été la plus importante. La baisse temporaire de la consommation de phentermine aux États-Unis et les mesures prises par certains pays d'Amérique du Sud (surtout l'Argentine et le Chili) contre l'utilisation inappropriée de plusieurs stimulants ont entraîné une baisse de la consommation. Depuis 2000, la consommation de phentermine a remonté toutefois de nouveau aux États-Unis. En même temps, la consommation de stimulants inscrits au Tableau IV a continué d'augmenter nettement dans certains pays des Amériques, par exemple en Argentine, au Brésil et aux États-Unis, la consommation dans cette région étant en moyenne de 10,4 S-DDD pour 1 000 habitants et par jour pendant la période 2003-2005 (voir la figure 14).

70. Dans le reste du monde, la consommation de ces stimulants a diminué. En Asie, la consommation a légèrement progressé entre la fin des années 90 et la période 2000-2002, surtout en Malaisie, en République de Corée et à Singapour. Toutefois, la consommation annuelle moyenne a reculé de 32 % pendant la période 2003-2005 pour se situer à 1,7 S-DDD pour 1 000 habitants et par jour. De même, en Europe, après avoir été relativement stable pendant la période 1997-2002, la consommation moyenne est tombée de 4 S-DDD à 1,6 S-DDD pour 1 000 habitants et par jour pendant la période 2003-2005. Cette diminution a été imputable principalement à la baisse marquée de la consommation de la phentermine en Belgique et au Royaume-Uni ainsi qu'à

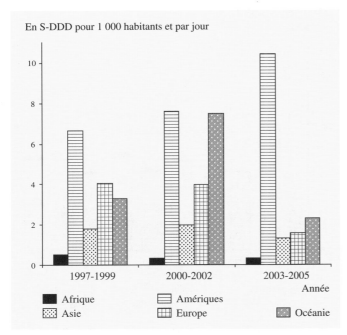

Figure 14. Stimulants du système nerveux central inscrits au Tableau IV: consommation nationale moyenne par région[a], 1997-1999, 2000-2002 et 2003-2005

En S-DDD pour 1 000 habitants et par jour

Année

- ■ Afrique
- ▤ Amériques
- ▦ Asie
- ▥ Europe
- ▨ Océanie

[a]Calculée sur la base des données statistiques communiquées par les États, la moyenne des consommations annuelles porte sur une période de trois ans.

la diminution de la consommation de fenproporex et d'amfépramone en Allemagne, en Belgique, au Danemark et en Suisse. Le recul de la consommation calculée a été encore plus marqué en Océanie, où elle est tombée de 7,5 à 2,3 S-DDD pendant cette période, ce qui a été imputable à une diminution de 72 % et de 76 % de la consommation de phentermine en Australie et en Nouvelle-Zélande respectivement.

71. Au plan mondial, ce sont le Brésil (avec 12,5 S-DDD pour 1 000 habitants et par jour), l'Argentine (11,8 S-DDD), la République de Corée (9,8 S-DDD) et les États-Unis (4,9 S-DDD) où la consommation calculée de stimulants du système nerveux central inscrits au Tableau IV a été la plus élevée en 2005.

72. La phentermine est la principale substance du groupe des stimulants inscrits au Tableau IV, et sa part dans la fabrication totale de stimulants a beaucoup fluctué ces dernières années (entre zéro et 76 %). Au cours de la période 1991-1995, les quantités de phentermine fabriquées étaient en moyenne de 9,5 tonnes par an, mais en 1996 elles se sont élevées à 50 tonnes, le maximum jamais déclaré. Depuis lors, la production totale déclarée a fluctué entre 2,6 et 30 tonnes et a représenté en moyenne 14,2 tonnes pendant la période 2004-2005, les principaux fabricants étant l'Allemagne, les États-Unis et l'Italie.

73. Dix pays ont déclaré avoir exporté de la phentermine en quantités supérieures à 100 kg au moins une fois pendant la période 2001-2005. En 2005, l'Allemagne a de nouveau été le principal exportateur de cette substance (4,4 tonnes),

suivie par l'Italie (3,5 tonnes), les États-Unis (3 tonnes), l'Australie, la Suisse et les Pays-Bas, les trois premiers pays représentant 84 % des exportations mondiales. Quarante-six pays ont déclaré avoir importé de la phentermine au moins une fois au cours de la période de cinq ans 2001-2005. En 2005, le principal importateur a été les États-Unis (avec 5,3 tonnes ou 47 % du total des importations mondiales), qui en ont réexporté la moitié, suivis par la République de Corée (2,2 tonnes) et par l'Australie (1,1 tonne), leur total combiné augmentant de 23 % par rapport à l'année précédente.

74. Le fenproporex, placé sous contrôle international en 1986, est principalement utilisé comme coupe-faim. Depuis lors, seuls le Brésil, la France et la Suisse, et récemment l'Allemagne et l'Inde, ont déclaré avoir fabriqué cette substance. Si la production mondiale de fenproporex a augmenté régulièrement, passant de 3 tonnes en 1998 à 10 tonnes en 2003, elle a considérablement baissé en 2004, tombant à 5 tonnes, mais elle a repris en 2005 et augmenté de 82 % pour atteindre 9,5 tonnes. Le Brésil et l'Allemagne ont été le seul fabricant de cette substance en 2005, le Brésil représentant 87 % du total. Au cours de la période 1995-1999, les quantités fabriquées en France ont beaucoup varié, autour d'une moyenne de 1,3 tonne par an, ce qui constitue une forte baisse par rapport à la moyenne annuelle de près de 3 tonnes enregistrée dans ce pays entre 1992 et 1994. La France a déclaré avoir fabriqué du fenproporex pour la dernière fois en 2003 (2,6 tonnes) et la Suisse en 2000 (4,9 tonnes). Le fenproporex fabriqué au Brésil est destiné à la consommation intérieure et ce pays a été aussi le premier importateur de cette substance (1,6 tonne) en 2005, comptant pour 98 % des importations mondiales.

75. En 2005, la fabrication totale déclarée d'amfépramone, substance principalement utilisée comme anorexigène, a été d'environ 28 tonnes. Trois pays ont signalé avoir fabriqué cette substance cette même année: le Brésil (27,6 tonnes), l'Italie (251 kg) et la Suisse (22 kg). La production suisse a beaucoup baissé par rapport à 2004, lorsqu'elle avait atteint 3,9 tonnes. La Suisse demeure néanmoins, et de loin, le plus gros exportateur de cette substance, ses exportations étant passées d'une moyenne annuelle de 2,8 tonnes en 2002-2004 à 5,8 tonnes en 2005. Les autres principaux exportateurs d'amfépramone sont l'Allemagne, l'Italie et le Brésil. L'Italie exporte presque toute sa production. L'amfépramone fabriquée au Brésil est presque exclusivement destinée à la consommation intérieure. Ce pays est de loin le plus grand consommateur d'amfépramone (5,3 S-DDD pour 1 000 habitants et par jour) et, en 2005, sa part a représenté 90 % de la consommation mondiale. En 2005 aussi, les importations les plus importantes de cette substance ont été déclarées par les États-Unis (1,4 tonne), l'Allemagne (1,2 tonne) et la Suisse (913 kg). Seize autres pays ont déclaré avoir importé plus de 1 kg d'amfépramone en 2005 et deux seulement en ont importé plus de 200 kg: le Chili (297 kg) et l'Australie (255 kg).

76. L'Italie était le principal fabricant de phendimétrazine. En 2005, la fabrication mondiale de cette substance a été de 7 tonnes, soit 44 % de plus que l'année précédente. Les seuls autres producteurs de cette substance en 2005 ont été la Chine (700 kg pour l'exportation) et l'Allemagne (5 kg). Les États-Unis n'ont déclaré avoir fabriqué de la phendimétrazine qu'en 1999 et 2001, dans les deux cas en quantités relativement réduites (560 kg et 274 kg respectivement). La

phendimétrazine fabriquée en Italie est destinée principalement à l'exportation (80 % en 2005). Traditionnellement, le plus gros importateur de cette substance était les États-Unis (3,1 tonnes en 2005), suivis par la République de Corée (1,7 tonne par an pour la période 2004-2005, soit 20 fois plus que les quantités importées par ce pays en 2001). Depuis 2000, cinq autres pays ont déclaré avoir importé de la phendimétrazine en quantités supérieures à 1 kg, à savoir l'Afrique du Sud, la Colombie, le Danemark, l'Italie et la Malaisie. Parmi les pays ayant déclaré avoir consommé de la phendimétrazine en 2005, la République de Corée a été, et de loin, le plus gros consommateur avec 1,4 S-DDD pour 1 000 habitants et par jour, suivie par l'Italie (0,7 S-DDD), la Malaisie (0,6 S-DDD), les États-Unis (0,4 S-DDD) et trois autres pays.

77. La fabrication totale de pémoline, substance placée sous contrôle international depuis 1989, a beaucoup fluctué pendant la période 1996-2005. De 8,7 tonnes en 1995, elle a fortement baissé en 1997, tombant à 4,6 tonnes. En 1998 et en 2005, il n'y a pas eu de fabrication déclarée de la substance. Seuls les États-Unis ont déclaré en avoir fabriqué en 2001 (35 kg). En 2002 et en 2004, la Suisse a déclaré avoir fabriqué environ 1,1 tonne de pémoline chacune de ces deux années. Pendant la période 2001-2005, les seuls autres producteurs de cette substance ont été les États-Unis (465 kg) en 2002 et la Chine (6 kg en 2003). En 2005, les seuls exportateurs ont été la Suisse (312 kg) et les Pays-Bas (128 kg). La même année, les principaux importateurs ont été les États-Unis (300 kg), l'Allemagne (45 kg), la Suisse (23 kg), les Pays-Bas (21 kg) et le Chili (15 kg). Outre son emploi comme stimulant, la pémoline est aussi utilisée dans le traitement du trouble déficitaire de l'attention.

78. Par le passé, le mazindol était fabriqué presque exclusivement au Brésil (75 kg en moyenne pour la période 1999-2003), la moitié environ étant destinée à la consommation intérieure et le reste à l'exportation. Deux autres pays ont déclaré une fabrication de mazindol pendant la période 1996-2005: la Pologne (25 kg en 1998 et 1 kg en 1999) et l'Argentine (22 kg en 2002, 165 kg en 2003 et 175 kg en 2005). Aucune fabrication de cette substance n'a été signalée en 2004. La consommation mondiale a beaucoup diminué, tombant de 702 kg en 1998 à une moyenne annuelle de 150 kg pendant la période 2001-2005. Pendant la même période, 17 pays ont déclaré avoir importé au moins 1 kg de mazindol, les principaux importateurs étant le Mexique (49 % des importations mondiales) et la Suisse (28 %). En 2005, le Japon (3 kg) et la Suisse (1 kg) ont été les seuls importateurs de mazindol.

79. Pendant la période 1997-2004, seuls les États-Unis ont déclaré fabriquer de la benzphétamine (1,1 tonne par an en moyenne pendant la période 2000-2004). En 2005, les États-Unis en ont fabriqué 729 kg et la Suisse 29 kg. Depuis 1997, il n'y a pas eu d'échanges internationaux de cette substance, à l'exception du Pérou, qui en a importé 31 kg en 2003. Pendant la période 2004-2005, seuls les États-Unis ont consommé de la benzphétamine: 1,2 tonne en 2004 et 1,8 tonne en 2005.

80. La fabrication et le commerce des autres stimulants inscrits au Tableau IV ont été signalés sporadiquement. Depuis 1995, seule la France a signalé une fabrication de pipradrol: 20 kg en 1999 et 8 kg en 2004, dont 2 kg ont ensuite été exportés au Canada. L'Australie a déclaré avoir importé 2 kg de pipradrol en 1999 et en 2002 et avoir fabriqué 3 kg d'éthylamphétamine (pour la consommation intérieure) en 2002. Aucune fabrication d'aminorex, de fencamfamine, de méfénorex, de mésocarbe ou de pyrovalérone n'a été signalée durant la période 2001-2005. Des transactions commerciales occasionnelles ont été déclarées en ce qui concerne la benzphétamine, la fencamfamine, le méfénorex et le pipradrol, mais l'aminorex, l'éthylamphétamine, le mésocarbe et la pyrovalérone n'ont pas fait l'objet d'échanges internationaux.

Benzodiazépines

81. En 1984, 33 benzodiazépines ont été inscrites au Tableau IV. Le midazolam y a été ajouté en 1990 et le brotizolam en 1995. Le flunitrazépam a été transféré du Tableau IV au Tableau III en 1995.

82. Le nombre de pays et de territoires déclarant la fabrication et/ou le commerce de benzodiazépines a très fortement augmenté. Depuis 1990, environ 200 pays et territoires ont fait état au moins une fois de la fabrication ou du commerce de ces substances en quantités supérieures à 1 kilogramme. Ce n'est que récemment que des données complètes concernant la fabrication et le commerce de benzodiazépines sont devenues disponibles, lorsque plusieurs grands pays producteurs et exportateurs ont établi des mesures nationales de contrôle pour ces groupes de substances. Des données concernant les benzodiazépines ne sont communiquées par la Suisse que depuis 1997, par l'Autriche depuis 1998, par la Belgique depuis 1999 et par le Canada depuis 2001.

Anxiolytiques de type benzodiazépine

83. Vingt-deux benzodiazépines sont généralement classées parmi les anxiolytiques. La fabrication totale déclarée de ce groupe de substances, exprimée en S-DDD, a constamment augmenté entre 1996 et 2001, pour atteindre un niveau record de 29 milliards de S-DDD. Depuis lors, la production mondiale a légèrement diminué et elle s'est située à 22 milliards de S-DDD en 2005 (voir la figure 15). La fabrication d'anxiolytiques de type benzodiazépine varie généralement en fonction de celle du diazépam, qui est la principale substance de ce groupe et qui représentait 31 % (soit 6,9 milliards de S-DDD) de la fabrication totale en 2005. La même année, la part de l'alprazolam (6,6 milliards de S-DDD) a augmenté, atteignant 30 %, tandis que celle du lorazépam (4,2 milliards de S-DDD) représentait 19 % de la production totale. En 2005, le bromazépam, le chlordiazépoxide et l'oxazépam représentaient chacun 3 %, le clorazépate 2 % et le nordazépam 1 % de la fabrication totale déclarée d'anxiolytiques de type benzodiazépine (voir la figure 16). Les 12 autres substances de ce groupe (clobazam, clotiazépam, cloxazolam, délorazépam, loflazépate d'éthyle, fludiazépam, halazépam, kétazolam, médazépam, pinazépam, prazépam et tétrazépam) représentaient chacune moins de 1 % de la fabrication totale déclarée calculée en S-DDD. Aucune fabrication de camazépam ou d'oxazolam n'a été déclarée en 2005. Comme le montrent les figures 17 et 18, la Chine et l'Italie ont été les principaux fabricants d'anxiolytiques de type benzodiazépine au cours de la période 1995-2004 assurant en 2005, avec l'Inde et l'Allemagne, 73 % de la fabrication mondiale.

Figure 15. Anxiolytiques de type benzodiazépine: fabrication totale déclarée, 1996-2005

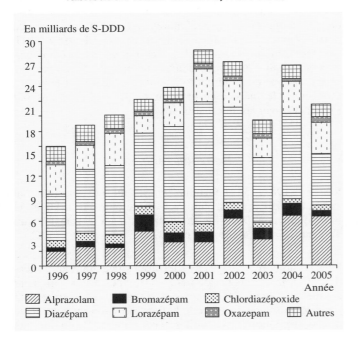

Figure 17. Anxiolytiques de type benzodiazépine: part des pays dans la fabrication totale déclarée, 2005

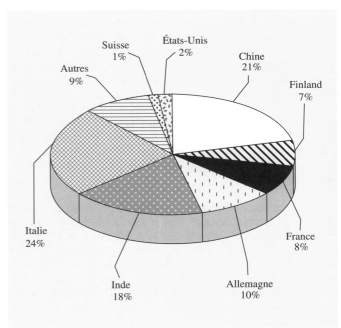

Figure 16. Anxiolytiques de type benzodiazépine: ventilation de la fabrication totale déclarée, 2005

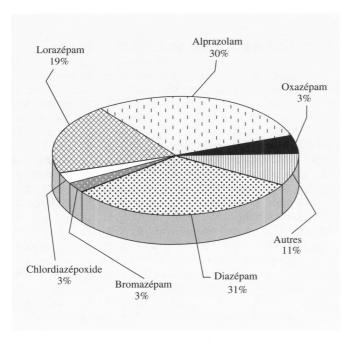

Figure 18. Anxiolytiques de type benzodiazépine: fabrication déclarée de quelques pays, 1996-2005

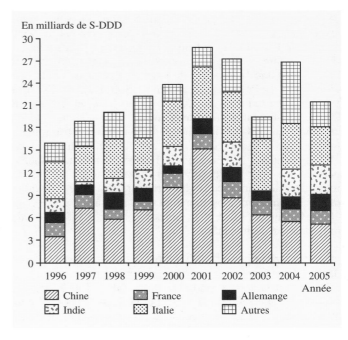

84. La consommation approximative, telle que calculée par l'Organe, a généralement suivi les orientations de la fabrication (voir la figure 19), mais, en 2005, la consommation totale de ce groupe de substances a été de 27,7 milliards de S-DDD, c'est-à-dire beaucoup plus importante que la quantité fabriquée. La consommation nationale moyenne calculée d'anxiolytiques de type benzodiazépine est plus élevée en Europe que dans les autres régions (voir la figure 20).

Figure 19. Anxiolytiques de type benzodiazépine: consommation mondiale calculée, 1996-2005[a]

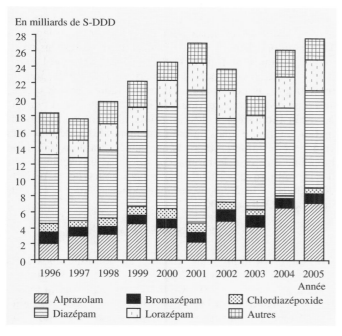

[a]La consommation mondiale approximative pour une année donnée est calculée sur la base des statistiques communiquées par les États. Elle est exprimée en doses quotidiennes déterminées à des fins statistiques (S-DDD).

Figure 20. Anxiolytiques de type benzodiazépine: consommation nationale moyenne[a], par région, 1997-1999, 2000-2002 et 2003-2005

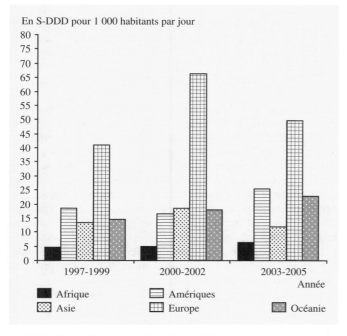

[a]Calculée sur la base des données statistiques communiquées par les États, la moyenne des consommations annuelles porte sur une période de trois ans. Les données sur les cinq pays ayant la consommation la plus élevée ont été prises en compte dans le calcul pour chaque région.

Diazépam

85. Le diazépam, qui est la substance du groupe des anxiolytiques de type benzodiazépine faisant l'objet des échanges les plus importants, est consommé partout dans le monde. Pendant la période 1990-1999, la fabrication mondiale de diazépam a suivi une tendance à la hausse, représentant plus de 76 tonnes par an et, pendant la période 2000-2004, 123 tonnes en moyenne. En 2005, la fabrication est tombée à 69 tonnes, essentiellement du fait que les États-Unis n'ont pas fabriqué de diazépam en 2005 après en avoir fabriqué plus de 29 tonnes en 2004. La Chine, qui a traditionnellement été le plus gros fabricant et exportateur de cette substance, représentant environ 70 % de la fabrication mondiale pendant la période 2000-2004, en a fabriqué 45 tonnes en 2005. Est venue ensuite l'Italie, avec 12 tonnes en 2005. En outre, le Brésil et l'Inde ont signalé avoir fabriqué plusieurs tonnes de diazépam. La Suisse, qui a également fabriqué plusieurs tonnes de diazépam chaque année depuis 1997, n'en a pas produit en 2005. La Pologne et la Fédération de Russie ont également fabriqué quelques centaines de kilogrammes de diazépam.

86. Les exportations ont légèrement reculé, tombant de 61 tonnes en 2004 à 60 tonnes en 2005. La Chine, avec 21 tonnes, a représenté 35 % du total. Les exportations italiennes sont restées stables (plus de 16 tonnes en 2005), tandis que la Suisse a exporté 7 tonnes de diazépam.

87. Le diazépam est largement utilisé, et environ 120 pays et territoires déclarent chaque année en importer plus de 1 kg. En 2005, les plus gros importateurs ont été le Danemark (6,7 tonnes), l'Allemagne (4,2 tonnes), les États-Unis (3,6 tonnes), la Suisse (2,8 tonnes) et l'Espagne (2 tonnes), représentant ensemble plus de 40 % des importations mondiales. Des quantités de diazépam comprises entre 1 et 2 tonnes ont également été importées, dans l'ordre, par le Pakistan, le Ghana, l'Irlande, le Canada, la République islamique d'Iran, la Thaïlande et le Nigéria. L'Espagne, qui était jadis le plus gros importateur de diazépam, a ramené ses importations de 29 tonnes (principalement à usage vétérinaire) en 1989 à 10 tonnes en 1997 et à 2 tonnes en 2005. La consommation mondiale de diazépam est restée stable (12 milliards de S-DDD en 2005). Selon la consommation calculée, les principaux consommateurs de cette substance sont le Royaume-Uni (5,2 milliards de S-DDD), la Chine (2,5 milliards de S-DDD), les États-Unis (664 millions de S-DDD) et le Brésil (611 millions de S-DDD).

Alprazolam

88. La fabrication totale déclarée d'alprazolam a régulièrement augmenté, passant d'environ 1 tonne par an en 1986 à 6,7 tonnes en 2005. Depuis 2002, la production mondiale a dépassé 6 tonnes par an, sauf en 2003, année pendant laquelle elle est retombée à 3,6 tonnes, les États-Unis n'ayant pas fabriqué d'alprazolam cette année-là. Les fluctuations de la production mondiale sont dues dans une large mesure à la variation des quantités fabriquées en Inde et aux États-Unis, qui sont les plus gros fabricants. En 2005, l'Inde a produit 2,3 tonnes d'alprazolam, soit plus que jamais, tandis que la production des États-Unis est tombée de 1,7 tonne en 2004 à 302 kg en 2005. En 2005, l'Italie en a fabriqué 1,5 tonne, la Finlande 1,2 tonne et la France près de 1 tonne. Ces pays ont représenté ensemble 94 % de la production mondiale

d'alprazolam en 2005. Ils ont également été les principaux exportateurs de cette substance, représentant ensemble plus de 74 % des exportations mondiales en 2005.

89. En 2005, plus de 70 pays et territoires de toutes les régions du monde ont déclaré avoir importé des quantités d'alprazolam supérieures à 1 kg. Les importations totales sont passées de 1,6 tonne en 1998 à une moyenne annuelle de 5,7 tonnes pendant la période 1999-2004 et ont atteint le nouveau chiffre record de 6,8 tonnes en 2004 avant de diminuer légèrement en 2005 pour se situer à 6,7 tonnes. En 2005, les États-Unis (2 tonnes), la Belgique (970 kg) et l'Espagne (628 kg) ont été les principaux importateurs d'alprazolam, représentant ensemble plus de 53 % du volume total. La consommation mondiale pendant la période 2000-2005 a été en moyenne de 4,8 milliards de S-DDD, la consommation la plus forte étant celle des États-Unis (1,8 milliard de S-DDD en 2005).

Lorazépam

90. La fabrication totale déclarée de lorazépam est tombée de 11,1 tonnes en 2001 à 6,5 tonnes en 2003, soit un chiffre comparable à la moyenne de la période 1999-2000. En 2004, la production s'est accrue de nouveau et a dépassé 10 tonnes aussi bien en 2004 qu'en 2005. Ces fluctuations sont imputables aux importantes variations de la production de l'Allemagne et de l'Italie, qui sont les deux principaux fabricants. En 2005, ces deux pays en ont fabriqué 3 tonnes et plus de 5 tonnes respectivement, représentant, avec l'Inde (1,6 tonne), environ 97 % de la production totale. Les autres pays qui ont signalé avoir fabriqué du lorazépam en 2005 ont été le Brésil et la Pologne (105 kg chacun).

91. Les exportations de lorazépam ont été en moyenne de 10 tonnes par an au cours de la période 2000-2004 et ont atteint 11,7 tonnes en 2005. L'Italie et l'Allemagne ont été les principaux exportateurs de cette substance représentant, avec l'Irlande — important réexportateur — plus de 80 % des exportations totales en 2005. Parmi la centaine de pays qui ont importé plus de 1 kg de lorazépam au moins une fois pendant la période 2001-2005, les États-Unis et l'Irlande figurent au premier rang, ayant contribué à eux deux pour 40 % environ aux importations totales de cette substance en 2005. L'Espagne (924 kg), la France (758 kg) et l'Allemagne (742 kg) ont été d'autres importateurs importants en 2005. La consommation mondiale calculée a été en moyenne de 3,5 milliards de S-DDD pendant la période 2001-2005, le principal consommateur ayant été l'Allemagne (987 millions de S-DDD) en 2005.

Bromazépam

92. La fabrication totale déclarée de bromazépam a beaucoup fluctué pendant la période 1999-2005. Après avoir fortement augmenté par rapport à la moyenne annuelle de 6 tonnes enregistrée en 1997-1998, elle a culminé à plus de 21 tonnes en 1999 pour tomber à 13,5 tonnes en moyenne les années suivantes. En 2005, la production mondiale est tombée à 7,3 tonnes du fait que la Suisse, plus gros fabricant depuis 1998 (avec une moyenne de 7,8 tonnes par an), n'a pas produit de bromazépam en 2005, ses stocks étant élevés. En 2005, le premier fabricant mondial est ainsi devenu l'Italie (4,8 tonnes) suivie par le Brésil (1,6 tonne) et l'Inde (554 kg).

93. Les exportations mondiales de bromazépam ont atteint 15 tonnes en 2005, soit un peu moins que la moyenne de

15,4 tonnes par an enregistrée pendant la période 1997-2004, les principaux exportateurs étant, comme les années précédentes, la Suisse (6,8 tonnes) et l'Italie (5,2 tonnes), qui ont ensemble assuré 80 % des exportations totales de la substance. Cette même année, sur les 84 pays qui ont déclaré avoir importé du bromazépam en quantités supérieures à 1 kg, cinq ont compté pour 51 % dans les importations mondiales: la France, la Suisse, le Brésil, l'Allemagne et l'Italie, dans cet ordre. Au cours de la période 2000-2005, tout le bromazépam importé par la Suisse et l'Italie a été réexporté; au cours de la même période, la France et le Brésil ont importé du bromazépam destiné principalement à la consommation intérieure, mais en ont également réexporté plusieurs centaines de kilogrammes chaque année. La consommation mondiale calculée de bromazépam, qui avait oscillé autour de 1,3 milliard de S-DDD par an au cours de la période 2000-2004, a légèrement diminué pour se situer à 1,2 milliard de S-DDD en 2005.

Chlordiazépoxide

94. La fabrication totale déclarée de chlordiazépoxide a fortement et régulièrement diminué, tombant de 43 tonnes en 2000 à 21 tonnes en 2005. Ce recul s'explique par la réduction des quantités fabriquées en Chine, en Inde et en Italie, qui étaient auparavant les principaux fabricants de cette substance. En 2005, la Chine a fabriqué 11 tonnes de chlordiazépoxide, soit 52 % de la production mondiale, et l'Inde a déclaré en avoir produit 6,3 tonnes (30 %). La majeure partie de la production de la Chine et de l'Italie a été réexportée, mais le gros de la production indienne a été destiné à la consommation intérieure.

95. Les échanges internationaux de chlordiazépoxide sont tombés de 24 tonnes en 2000 à 13 tonnes en 2005. Depuis 1997, plus de 100 pays ont déclaré avoir importé au moins une fois plus de 1 kg de cette substance. En 2005, les principaux importateurs ont été la Suisse (1,7 tonne destinée entièrement à la réexportation), Cuba, les États-Unis et l'Égypte (1,3 tonne, 1,2 tonne et 1 tonne respectivement, pour la consommation intérieure). Au cours de la période 2001-2005, la consommation mondiale a baissé, tombant de 1,2 milliard de S-DDD à 678 millions de S-DDD par an.

Oxazépam

96. La fabrication totale d'oxazépam est restée relativement stable, de l'ordre de 30 tonnes par an, sur la période 1998-2002. En 2003, elle a atteint 34 tonnes pour retomber à 22 tonnes en 2004 avant de remonter pour atteindre 27 tonnes en 2005. Cette même année, les principaux fabricants ont été l'Italie (14,3 tonnes) et la France (10,4 tonnes), qui ont contribué ensemble pour 91 % à la production mondiale. Les échanges internationaux ont porté en moyenne sur quelque 40 tonnes par an pendant la période 2001-2005. L'Irlande et la France ont été les principaux importateurs d'oxazépam. L'Irlande réexporte la majeure partie des quantités importées, mais la France en utilise également de grandes quantités pour la consommation intérieure, représentant 25 % de la consommation totale calculée pendant la période 2000-2005.

Clorazépate

97. La fabrication totale déclarée de clorazépate est restée stable (8,4 tonnes en moyenne) pendant la période 2001-2005. En 2005, la France (5,8 tonnes) et l'Italie

(1,1 tonne) ont représenté 86 % de la production totale. Cinquante-quatre pays ont importé 8,8 tonnes de clorazépate. Les principaux importateurs ont été l'Espagne (dont la moitié environ pour la réexportation) et la France (intégralement pour la réexportation).

Clobazam

98. La fabrication totale déclarée de clobazam est tombée de 5,5 tonnes en 2004 à 3,5 tonnes en 2005, les principaux fabricants étant l'Allemagne et la France (1,2 tonne et 1,4 tonne respectivement). Les échanges internationaux se sont montés approximativement à 5 tonnes, et 58 pays ont déclaré avoir importé plus de 1 kg de clobazam.

Autres substances

99. En 2005, la fabrication totale combinée déclarée de fludiazépam, d'halazépam, de nordazépam, de pinazépam et de prazépam a atteint 478 millions de S-DDD, contre 435 millions de S-DDD en 2004. La fabrication combinée de camazépam, de clotiazépam, de cloxazolam, de délorazépam, d'éthyle de loflazépate, de kétazolam, de médazépam et de tétrazépam a presque doublé pour passer de 680 millions de S-DDD en 2004 à 778 millions de S-DDD en 2005.

Autres anxiolytiques

Méprobamate

100. Du fait du remplacement progressif de cette substance par les benzodiazépines, la fabrication de méprobamate, seul anxiolytique inscrit au Tableau IV qui ne soit pas de type benzodiazépine, n'a cessé de reculer depuis la fin des années 70, chutant d'un niveau record de près de 1 000 tonnes à une moyenne annuelle égale à un peu plus d'un quart de ce volume au cours de la décennie 1993-2003 (voir la figure 21). La fabrication totale est tombée de 260 tonnes en 2003 à 103 tonnes en 2005. Cette baisse est imputable à la Chine, qui avait fabriqué près de la moitié de la production mondiale les années précédentes mais n'en a pas produit en 2005. Le Danemark, autre gros fournisseur, a été à l'origine de presque toute la production mondiale cette année-là. En outre, l'Espagne et l'Inde ont recommencé à fabriquer du méprobamate après plus de dix ans d'interruption, avec 107 kg et 400 kg respectivement en 2005. La majeure partie du méprobamate fabriqué par le Danemark a été exportée vers plus de 20 pays. Pendant la période 2001-2005, ce sont la France et le Danemark qui ont détenu les plus importants stocks de méprobamate (53 tonnes et 48 tonnes en moyenne respectivement par an), la Hongrie venant en troisième position avec 17 tonnes en moyenne. La Chine n'a jamais communiqué de données concernant ses stocks de méprobamate.

101. Les importations de méprobamate se sont établies en moyenne à plus de 250 tonnes par an durant la période 2001-2005, environ 80 pays ayant déclaré en avoir importé au moins une fois. Au cours de cette même période, la France en a été le principal importateur, achetant en moyenne 90 tonnes par an, destinées presque exclusivement à la consommation intérieure. En 2005, les autres gros importateurs ont été Cuba (25 tonnes), la Hongrie (15 tonnes), l'Afrique du Sud (14 tonnes), la Roumanie et les États-Unis (6 tonnes chacun) et la Turquie (5 tonnes).

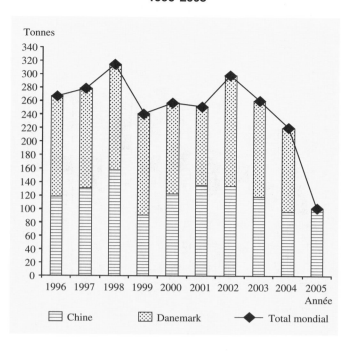

Figure 21. Méprobamate: fabrication déclarée, 1996-2005

Sédatifs-hypnotiques de type benzodiazépine

102. Douze benzodiazépines sont généralement utilisées comme sédatifs-hypnotiques, à savoir le brotizolam, l'estazolam, le flunitrazépam (seule benzodiazépine inscrite au Tableau III), le flurazépam, l'haloxazolam, le loprazolam, le lormétazépam, le midazolam, le nimétazépam, le nitrazépam, le témazépam et le triazolam. On trouvera des observations concernant le flunitrazépam, substance qui a été transférée du Tableau IV au Tableau III en 1995, aux paragraphes 55 à 58 ci-dessus.

103. Après avoir progressé d'une moyenne de 6,3 milliards de S-DDD par an au cours de la période 1997-2001 à 7,8 milliards de S-DDD en 2002, la fabrication totale déclarée de ces douze substances est revenue en 2003-2004 à son niveau antérieur, à savoir en moyenne 6,4 milliards de S-DDD par an. En 2005, la production mondiale a de nouveau augmenté pour se situer à 7,3 milliards de S-DDD, chiffre qui n'a précédemment été dépassé qu'une seule fois. Entre 1998 et 2002, la Belgique, le Canada et la Suisse ont commencé à faire rapport à l'Organe sur la fabrication de benzodiazépines, ce qui a permis de mieux faire concorder les chiffres de la consommation annuelle calculée avec ceux de la fabrication totale (voir les figures 22 et 23).

104. La consommation nationale moyenne calculée de sédatifs-hypnotiques de type benzodiazépine, exprimée en S-DDD pour 1 000 habitants et par jour, est plus élevée en Europe que dans les autres régions (voir la figure 24).

105. Depuis 2000, la part du flunitrazépam dans la fabrication globale de ces 12 benzodiazépines a beaucoup varié, tombant de 21 % (1,4 milliard de S-DDD) à 3 % du total en 2001 (207 millions de S-DDD) avant de reprendre en 2003 pour représenter en 2004 la plus forte proportion de ce groupe (23 %), avec 1,5 milliard de S-DDD, et de chuter en 2005 pour retomber à un niveau jamais atteint précédemment (1 %) avec 84 millions de S-DDD. Ce recul est imputable à

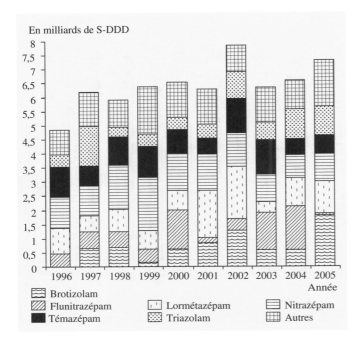

Figure 22. Sédatifs-hypnotiques de type benzodiazépine: fabrication totale déclarée par substance, 1996-2005

En milliards de S-DDD

Légende: Brotizolam, Flunitrazépam, Témazépam, Lormétazépam, Triazolam, Nitrazépam, Autres

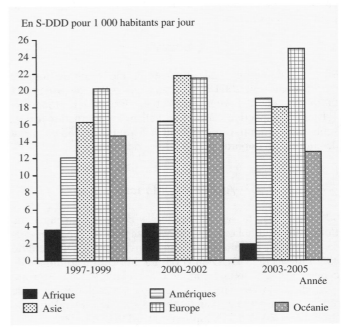

Figure 24. Sédatifs-hypnotiques de type benzodiazépine: consommation nationale moyenne[a], par région, 1997-1999, 2000-2002 et 2003-2005

En S-DDD pour 1 000 habitants par jour

Légende: Afrique, Asie, Amériques, Europe, Océanie

[a]Calculée sur la base des données statistiques communiquées par les États, la moyenne des consommations annuelles porte sur une période de trois ans.

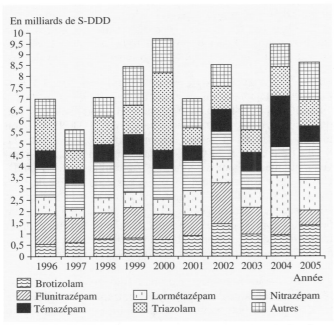

Figure 23. Sédatifs-hypnotiques de type benzodiazépine: consommation mondiale calculée[a], 1996-2005

En milliards de S-DDD

Légende: Brotizolam, Flunitrazépam, Témazépam, Lormétazépam, Triazolam, Nitrazépam, Autres

[a]La consommation mondiale approximative pour une année donnée est calculée sur la base des statistiques communiquées par les États. La consommation est exprimée en doses quotidiennes déterminées à des fins statistiques (S-DDD).

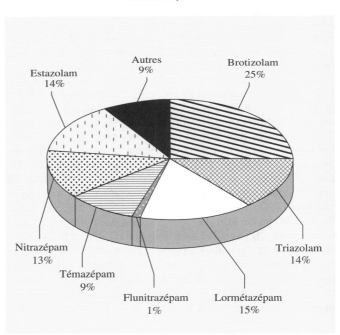

Figure 25. Sédatifs-hypnotiques de type benzodiazépine: ventilation de la fabrication totale déclarée, 2005

Estazolam 14%
Autres 9%
Brotizolam 25%
Triazolam 14%
Lormétazépam 15%
Flunitrazépam 1%
Témazépam 9%
Nitrazépam 13%

la Suisse, gros fabricant de flunitrazépam, qui n'en a pas fabriqué en 2005 (voir également les paragraphes 57 et 58 ci-dessus). En revanche, la fabrication mondiale de brotizolam a plus que triplé entre 2004 et 2005, passant de 580 millions de S-DDD à 1,8 milliard de S-DDD (voir le paragraphe 113 ci-dessous), cette substance représentant la plus forte proportion (25 %) de la production totale de sédatifs-hypnotiques de type benzodiazépine en 2005. Sont ensuite venus le lormétazépam avec 15 % (1,1 milliard de S-DDD), et ensuite l'estazolam et le triazolam avec 14 % (1 milliard de S-DDD chacun), le nitrazépam avec 13 % (946 millions de S-DDD)

Figure 26. Sédatifs-hypnotiques de type benzodiazépine: fabrication totale déclarée, pays sélectionnés, 1996-2005

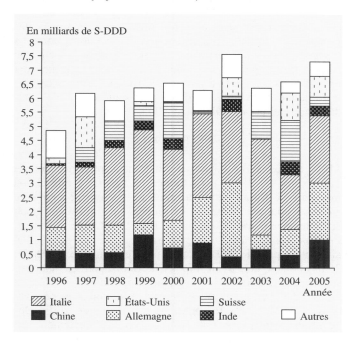

106. La figure 26 illustre l'évolution de la production des principaux fabricants pendant la période 1996-2005. En 2005, l'Italie est demeurée le plus gros fabricant de ce groupe de substances, avec 2,4 milliards de S-DDD, soit 32 % de la production totale (voir la figure 27).

Triazolam

107. Le triazolam est un hypnotique puissant qui est, avec le brotizolam, la substance psychotrope dont la S-DDD est la plus faible (0,25 mg). Plusieurs centaines de kilogrammes en sont fabriqués chaque année. En 2005, la fabrication déclarée a été de 245 kg (980 millions de S-DDD). Le plus gros fabricant est les États-Unis d'Amérique avec 190 kg en 2005. Le triazolam est également fabriqué par la Chine et l'Italie. L'Espagne, la France et le Japon, qui en avaient fabriqué par le passé, n'ont pas déclaré de production ces dernières années.

108. Les principaux exportateurs sont les États-Unis, suivis par l'Italie. En outre, l'Australie, le Royaume-Uni et la Suisse en exportent et réexportent régulièrement une certaine quantité. Le principal importateur et consommateur est le Japon, avec près de la moitié des importations mondiales. Les États-Unis, qui ont consommé 94 kg (soit 376 millions de S-DDD) en 2005, étaient le premier consommateur cette année-là. Ils étaient suivis par le Japon, avec 88 kg (soit 352 millions de S-DDD).

Figure 27. Sédatifs-hypnotiques de type benzodiazépine: part des pays dans la fabrication totale déclarée, 2005

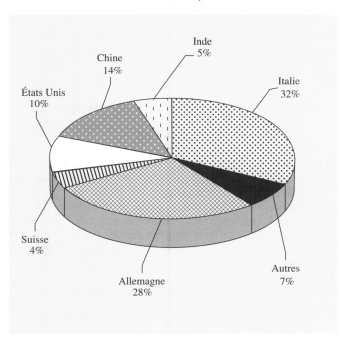

Lormétazépam

109. La fabrication de lormétazépam a régulièrement augmenté depuis 1991, atteignant un niveau record de 1,9 tonne en 2002. Après avoir brièvement reculé en 2003 pour tomber à 380 kg, niveau le plus bas jamais enregistré, elle a repris en 2004 et a atteint 1,1 tonne en 2005. Ces fluctuations s'expliquent par l'évolution de la production de l'Allemagne et de l'Italie, les deux principaux fabricants de lormétazépam, qui en sont également les plus gros exportateurs. En outre, l'Espagne, la France, l'Irlande et les Pays-Bas réexportent des quantités significatives de lormétazépam, en important et en exportant chaque année environ 200 kg. La consommation mondiale calculée est passée de 415 kg en 1997 à 1,3 tonne en 2005. Les principaux pays consommateurs sont l'Espagne, l'Italie, la Belgique, la France et l'Allemagne, dans cet ordre.

Nitrazépam

110. La fabrication mondiale de nitrazépam, qui avait lentement diminué depuis plusieurs années, tombant de 6,5 tonnes en 2000 à 4 tonnes en 2004, a repris en 2005 pour se situer à 4,7 tonnes. Cette substance est fabriquée par l'Italie, qui en a produit 2,4 tonnes en 2005, l'Inde (1,7 tonne) et la Chine (0,7 tonne). Les exportations de nitrazépam, qui avaient été en moyenne de quelque 6 tonnes pendant la période 1998-2002, ont continué de diminuer et n'ont été que de 3,9 tonnes en 2005. Comme les années précédentes, le plus gros exportateur de cette substance est resté l'Italie, avec 65 % du total mondial en 2005. Beaucoup de pays importent du nitrazépam. Ainsi, depuis 1998, environ 80 pays ont déclaré avoir importé au moins une fois plus de 1 kg de nitrazépam. Le Japon est demeuré le plus gros importateur, ayant déclaré avoir importé 1,6 tonne de nitrazépam en 2005. Il était suivi par Cuba (550 kg) et le Royaume-Uni (317 kg).

et le témazépam avec 9 % (664 millions de S-DDD). Le midazolam (435 millions de S-DDD), le flurazépam (138 millions de S-DDD) et le loprazolam (72 millions de S-DDD) ont représenté ensemble 9 % du total (voir la figure 25). La fabrication d'haloxazolam et de nimétazépam a représenté moins de 1 % de la fabrication mondiale de sédatifs-hypnotiques de type benzodiazépine.

Témazépam

111. Le témazépam est fabriqué par les États-Unis, l'Italie et la Pologne, en quantités qui atteignent au total entre 10 et 25 tonnes par an. En 2005, la production mondiale a légèrement dépassé 13 tonnes. L'Italie, premier fournisseur mondial, a représenté en moyenne 91 % de la production totale pendant la période 1996-2005. Les États-Unis en fabriquent, de façon intermittente, entre 2 et 3 tonnes par an, et la Pologne quelques centaines de kilogrammes chaque année, principalement pour la consommation intérieure.

112. Le plus gros importateur est les États-Unis, qui ont importé en 2005 plus de 7 tonnes de témazépam, suivis par l'Allemagne, l'Australie, le Canada, la Finlande, l'Irlande, les Pays-Bas et le Royaume-Uni, qui en importent chacun plus de 1 tonne par an. Une trentaine de pays déclarent en importer plus de 1 kg par an. Comme les années précédentes, les États-Unis sont demeurés le principal consommateur en 2005, représentant 60 % de la consommation mondiale calculée (682 millions de S-DDD).

Brotizolam

113. En 1995, le brotizolam, hypnotique puissant dont la S-DDD (0,25 mg) est la même que celle du triazolam, a été inscrit au Tableau IV de la Convention de 1971. La fabrication de cette substance a été déclarée pour la première fois en 1997 (par l'Allemagne). Le brotizolam n'est fabriqué que par l'Allemagne, en quantités représentant plusieurs centaines de kilogrammes par an, ainsi que par l'Italie et le Japon, en quantités ne représentant que quelques dizaines de kilogrammes par an. En 2005, la fabrication totale a atteint 451 kg. Le principal importateur est le Japon, mais la Suisse en importe également des quantités significatives pour la réexportation. En 2005, douze pays ont signalé avoir importé plus de 1 kg de brotizolam, leurs importations totales se situant à 477 kg. La consommation totale calculée a représenté 1,4 milliard de S-DDD en 2005, le Japon (532 millions de S-DDD,), l'Allemagne (324 millions de S-DDD) et la Colombie (324 millions de S-DDD) représentant 84 % de la consommation mondiale de cette substance.

Estazolam

114. Pendant la période 1995-2004, la fabrication totale d'estazolam a varié entre 1,5 tonne et 2,6 tonnes par an, les principaux fabricants étant la Chine, le Japon et les États-Unis. En 2005, elle a atteint un nouveau record avec 3 tonnes, 2,4 tonnes étant imputables à la Chine. Le Japon en a fabriqué 341 kg et la Pologne et l'Italie en ont produit ensemble 261 kg. Les États-Unis n'en ont pas fabriqué en 2005. Sur les dix pays qui importent cette substance en quantités supérieures à 1 kg, le Brésil, les États-Unis, la France, les Pays-Bas et le Portugal ont représenté 60 % des importations totales en 2005.

Midazolam

115. La fabrication totale déclarée de midazolam, qui était restée stable (environ 2,6 tonnes par an) pendant la période 2000-2004, a brutalement augmenté pour atteindre 8,7 tonnes en 2005, chiffre qui n'a précédemment été dépassé qu'une seule fois. Cette hausse a été imputable à l'augmentation marquée de la production de la Suisse, qui est passée de 2,8 tonnes en 2004 à 6,3 tonnes en 2005. Israël, avec

1,4 tonne, s'est placé au deuxième rang, suivi par le Brésil, l'Inde et l'Italie, dans cet ordre. En revanche, les échanges internationaux de midazolam sont tombés à 3,5 tonnes en 2005, chiffre le plus faible qui ait été enregistré depuis 1998, ce qui a entraîné une augmentation record des stocks des principaux fabricants mondiaux, lesquels se sont montés à 6,8 tonnes. Le midazolam est largement utilisé, et environ 80 pays ont déclaré en avoir importé en 2005. Les principaux importateurs ont été l'Allemagne, le Brésil, les États-Unis et la République de Corée, qui ont représenté ensemble 40 % des importations mondiales en 2005.

Flurazépam

116. Après avoir baissé régulièrement pour tomber de 10,6 tonnes en 1997 à 3,6 tonnes en 2004, la fabrication mondiale de flurazépam a à nouveau légèrement augmenté en 2005 pour se monter à 4,1 tonnes. Le flurazépam n'est actuellement fabriqué que par le Brésil, la Chine et l'Italie. Le plus gros fabricant et le plus gros exportateur est l'Italie, alimentant près de 90 % de la demande mondiale. En 2005, 25 pays ont signalé avoir importé du flurazépam en quantités supérieures à 1 kg. Les principaux importateurs ont été la Suisse et l'Espagne, avec 1,7 tonne et 1,5 tonne respectivement, soit 50 % des importations mondiales de 2005. Des quantités significatives de flurazépam ont également été importées par le Canada et les États-Unis, chacun en ayant importé environ 750 kg pendant l'année.

Loprazolam

117. La fabrication totale déclarée de loprazolam a été de 72 kg en 2005, la France étant le seul fabricant et le principal exportateur de cette substance. L'Espagne (202 kg en 1993) et le Royaume-Uni (25 kg en 2000) ont été les seuls autres pays à fabriquer cette substance au cours des dernières années. En 2005, neuf pays ont déclaré avoir importé du loprazolam en quantités comprises entre 1 kg et 10 kg.

Antiépileptiques de type benzodiazépine

Clonazépam

118. Le clonazépam est une benzodiazépine qui est principalement utilisée comme antiépileptique. La fabrication totale déclarée, qui n'avait pas dépassé une moyenne annuelle d'environ 4 tonnes pour la période 1998-2003, a commencé à augmenter en 2004 et a atteint 6,4 tonnes en 2005, chiffre record. Cette hausse a été due à l'augmentation de la production en Suisse, principal fabricant mondial de clonazépam, qui est passée de 1,9 tonne en 2004 à près de 3 tonnes en 2005. L'Inde, avec 1,8 tonne, est demeurée le deuxième fabricant mondial en 2005, suivie par l'Italie avec 500 kg. En 2005, des quantités significatives de clonazépam ont également été fabriquées par le Brésil, la Chine, Israël et la Pologne.

119. Les échanges mondiaux de clonazépam n'ont cessé d'augmenter, passant d'environ 0,5 tonne en 1995 à 6,8 tonnes en 2005. Une centaine de pays ont déclaré importer cette substance en quantités supérieures à 1 kg. Les États-Unis sont demeurés le plus gros importateur mondial, avec 1,2 tonne, suivis par le Brésil (934 kg) et le Canada (707 kg). En outre, des quantités supérieures à 100 kg ont été importées par les pays suivants, par ordre décroissant: l'Argentine,

la Suisse, la France, l'Italie, le Japon, la République islamique d'Iran, l'Espagne et le Chili. La consommation mondiale a elle aussi fait apparaître une tendance à la hausse depuis le milieu des années 90, augmentant régulièrement pour passer de 273 millions de S-DDD en 1996 à 720 millions de S-DDD en 2005, ce qui constitue un nouveau record. Le principal consommateur est resté les États-Unis d'Amérique, avec 131 millions de S-DDD, suivi par le Brésil, l'Argentine et le Canada.

Sédatifs-hypnotiques et antiépileptiques de type barbiturique

Allobarbital, barbital, butobarbital, méthylphénobarbital, phénobarbital, secbutabarbital et vinylbital

120.   Les sept barbituriques inscrits au Tableau IV sont, du point de vue pharmacologique, proches de ceux qui sont inscrits au Tableau III. Cinq d'entre eux, à savoir l'allobarbital, le barbital, le butobarbital, le secbutabarbital et le vinylbital, sont des barbituriques à action intermédiaire qui sont utilisés principalement comme hypnotiques pour le traitement des insomnies rebelles. Ils ne sont plus utilisés comme sédatifs de jour. Les deux autres, le méthylphénobarbital et le phénobarbital[7], ont d'autres propriétés et sont également utilisés comme antiépileptiques (barbituriques à action prolongée). Le barbital, le méthylphénobarbital et le phénobarbital ont été inscrits au Tableau IV lors de l'adoption de la Convention de 1971, alors que les quatre autres substances y ont été inscrites en 1987.

121.   Le phénobarbital reste la substance la plus largement utilisée et est considéré comme le médicament de prédilection pour le traitement de l'épilepsie. La fabrication totale déclarée de ces barbituriques (pour les utilisations médicales directes et la fabrication de substances non psychotropes) a progressivement augmenté pour atteindre 653 tonnes en 1998 (5,4 milliards de S-DDD); elle a brièvement passé au-dessous de la barre des 4 milliards de S-DDD pendant la période 1999-2000, avant de se rétablir à 5 milliards de S-DDD en moyenne pendant la période 2004-2005. Pendant la période 2001-2005, en moyenne, le phénobarbital a représenté plus de 95 % de la fabrication totale des barbituriques inscrits au Tableau IV (en S-DDD). Le barbital se situe au deuxième rang, avec 4 % de la production totale, suivi par le méthylphénobarbital et l'allobarbital. Il n'a pas été signalé de fabrication de vinylbital depuis 1996 ni de butobarbital depuis 1999.

122.   Ces dernières années, dans l'ordre décroissant, la Pologne, la Chine et le Japon sont les pays où les taux calculés d'utilisation de sédatifs-hypnotiques du type barbiturique ont été les plus élevés, représentant en moyenne entre 0,3 et 0,45 S-DDD pour 1 000 habitants et par jour. En ce qui concerne les antiépileptiques de type barbiturique inscrits au Tableau IV, le Brésil, la Bulgarie, la Croatie, la Fédération de Russie, le Kazakhstan, la Roumanie et l'Ukraine ont été les pays où la consommation a été la plus forte entre 2001 et 2005, avec une moyenne comprise entre 6 et 15,7 S-DDD pour 1 000 habitants et par jour.

---
[7]Voir le Tableau IV pour plus de détails.

123.   La fabrication totale déclarée de phénobarbital a représenté en moyenne 438 tonnes par an pendant la période 2001-2005, après avoir culminé à 508 tonnes en 1998. En 2005, la Chine a fabriqué 56,8 % de la production totale de phénobarbital. La même année, les autres principaux pays producteurs ont été la Hongrie (84 tonnes), la Fédération de Russie (66 tonnes), l'Inde (35 tonnes) et le Brésil (10 tonnes). Pendant la période 2001-2005, la Hongrie (principalement pour l'exportation), l'Allemagne, l'Iraq, le Japon, le Kazakhstan, la Suisse et les États-Unis ont également déclaré avoir fabriqué du phénobarbital (voir la figure 28).

124.   Le phénobarbital reste l'une des substances psychotropes faisant l'objet des échanges les plus importants. Pendant la période 2001-2005, 163 pays et territoires ont déclaré avoir importé cette substance au moins une fois. Les importations totales déclarées se sont montées à 270 tonnes en 2005, les principaux importateurs étant le Brésil (36 tonnes), la Suisse (34 tonnes), l'Ukraine (29 tonnes), le Danemark (25 tonnes), l'Allemagne (20 tonnes), le Japon (10 tonnes) et les États-Unis (18 tonnes), ces pays représentant ensemble 60 % du total.

125.   Depuis 2001, 52 pays ont déclaré avoir exporté du phénobarbital, et les exportations totales ont fluctué entre 173 et 367 tonnes pendant la période 2001-2005, l'Allemagne, le Danemark, la Hongrie et la Suisse représentant jusqu'à 90 % des exportations totales. Les exportations de phénobarbital de la Hongrie ont peu à peu diminué et sont tombées de 116 tonnes en 2001 à 71 tonnes en 2005, année pendant laquelle ce pays a représenté 20 % des exportations totales.

126.   Le barbital est utilisé non seulement en médecine comme sédatif-hypnotique, mais aussi dans l'industrie pour la fabrication de substances non psychotropes. La consommation mondiale calculée, aussi bien pour la médecine que pour l'industrie, est passée d'une moyenne annuelle de 95 tonnes pendant la période 2001-2002 à 106 tonnes pendant la période 2003-2005. La fabrication totale déclarée de

Figure 28.   Phénobarbital: fabrication totale déclarée, 1996-2005

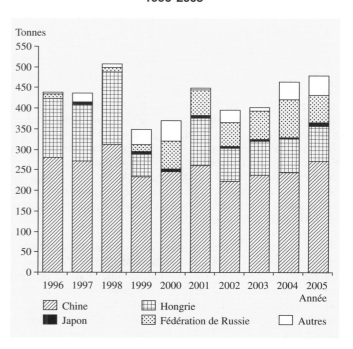

79

barbital a chuté pendant la période 1993-2001, perdant les deux tiers de son volume. Par la suite, la production totale s'est légèrement redressée, passant de 87 tonnes en 2001 à 111 tonnes en 2005. La Chine est demeurée le principal fabricant de la substance, avec en moyenne 96 % du total entre 2000 et 2005. Le Japon (2,7 tonnes) est le seul autre pays à avoir signalé la fabrication de barbital en 2005.

127.   Depuis 1997, le volume des échanges de barbital, comme celui de sa fabrication, a progressivement diminué, de 72 tonnes en 1998 à 11 tonnes en 2002. Au cours des trois années suivantes, les importations totales de cette substance ont été en moyenne de 16 tonnes par an. En 2005, les exportations déclarées par l'Allemagne et la Chine ont représenté 92,6 % des exportations mondiales. Pendant la période 2001-2005, 52 pays ont importé du barbital au moins une fois. Au cours des cinq dernières années, les principaux importateurs de cette substance ont été l'Allemagne (surtout pour la réexportation), l'Inde et le Japon.

128.   Près de 8 tonnes de méthylphénobarbital ont été fabriquées en Allemagne en 1990. Depuis lors, la Suisse est le principal fabricant de cette substance; sa production a fluctué autour d'une moyenne de 2,7 tonnes par an entre 1999 et 2002, et a été nulle en 2003. La fabrication totale de méthylphénobarbital a nettement diminué, tombant de 3,8 tonnes en 2004 (75 % de ce chiffre étant imputable à la Suisse) à 884 kg en 2005 (les deux tiers d'origine suisse et le reste provenant des États-Unis). En 2005, les principaux consommateurs de méthylphénobarbital ont été la Croatie, les États-Unis, l'Italie et la Suisse.

129.   Le commerce international de méthylphénobarbital a varié entre 1,7 tonne et 5,2 tonnes par an et a été en moyenne de 3,2 tonnes par an pendant la période 2001-2005. Des sept pays qui ont signalé avoir exporté du méthylphénobarbital pendant la période 2001-2005, la Suisse a été à l'origine, en moyenne, de 49 % des exportations mondiales, l'autre gros exportateur de cette substance en 2005 ayant été l'Allemagne (702 kg). Pendant la période 2001-2005, 16 pays ont importé du méthylphénobarbital au moins une fois. En 2005, le plus gros importateur régulier de méthylphénobarbital a été l'Allemagne (entièrement pour la réexportation) et 44 % des importations totales ont été absorbées par la Croatie.

130.   Depuis que le Danemark et la Pologne ont cessé de fabriquer de l'allobarbital pendant la période 1994-1995, l'Allemagne est le seul pays à avoir déclaré la fabrication de cette substance. Sa production a sensiblement augmenté, passant de 393 kg en 1998, année où elle a recommencé à en fabriquer, à 4 tonnes environ en 2000. Depuis, cette production a progressivement diminué, jusqu'à 1,6 tonne en 2002. Aucune fabrication n'a été déclarée en 2003, mais l'Allemagne a fabriqué 1 tonne d'allobarbital en moyenne pendant la période 2004-2005. Les stocks de la substance ont diminué en conséquence, passant d'une moyenne de 2,5 tonnes pendant la période 2001-2002 à un peu plus d'une tonne en 2004 puis à 509 kg en 2005.

131.   Les exportations totales d'allobarbital ont fluctué entre 2,4 tonnes en 2001 et 1,5 tonne en 2005, s'élevant en moyenne à 2,3 tonnes par an pendant cette période de cinq ans. L'Allemagne était le plus gros exportateur, avec environ 67 % du total mondial pendant cette période. Pendant la période 2001-2005, 17 pays ont importé cette substance au moins une fois. En 2005, les principaux importateurs ont été

Sri Lanka (701 kg), la Suisse (202 kg pour la réexportation), la Pologne (200 kg), la Turquie (200 kg) et la Hongrie (60 kg). Ces dernières années, la consommation mondiale d'allobarbital a diminué de près de moitié, tombant de 21,4 millions de S-DDD en 2001 à 11 millions de S-DDD en 2005. Ce recul est imputable à la baisse significative de la consommation en Hongrie, en Pologne et en République tchèque. En Pologne, par exemple, la consommation calculée d'allobarbital est tombée de 2,3 S-DDD pour 1 000 habitants et par jour en 2000 à 1 S-DDD pour 1 000 habitants et par jour en 2005.

132.   La fabrication totale de secbutabarbital a beaucoup diminué, tombant de 653 kg en 2002 (dont 78 % aux États-Unis) à 128 kg en 2003, aucune fabrication n'ayant été déclarée pendant la période 2004-2005. Pendant la période 2002-2003, l'Allemagne a signalé avoir fabriqué en moyenne 136 kg de secbutabarbital. Les seuls pays à avoir signalé des importations ou des exportations de cette substance au cours des cinq dernières années ont été l'Allemagne, les États-Unis, le Liban, le Royaume-Uni et la Suisse.

133.   Pendant la période 1996-2005, deux pays seulement ont signalé avoir fabriqué du butobarbital: le Danemark (1,3 tonne en 1998) et l'Allemagne (304 kg en 1997). Depuis lors, aucune fabrication n'a été déclarée. Les stocks mondiaux ont donc continué à baisser progressivement, passant de 1,7 tonne en 1998 à 311 kg en 2005. Le volume du commerce international de butobarbital a lui aussi reculé d'environ 96 %, tombant de 3,7 tonnes en 1998 à 53 kg en 2005. La consommation de butobarbital a été environ huit fois moindre en 2005 que ce qu'elle avait été en 2004.

134.   Des douze barbituriques inscrits aux Tableaux II, III et IV de la Convention de 1971, cinq, à savoir le phénobarbital (67 %), le barbital (15 %), le butalbital (7 %), le pentobarbital (6 %) et l'amobarbital (3 %) ont représenté

Figure 29.   Barbituriques inscrits aux Tableaux II, III et IV: fabrication totale déclarée, par substance, 2005

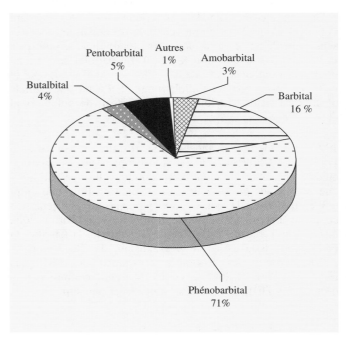

**Figure 30. Barbituriques inscrits
aux Tableaux II, III et IV: fabrication totale déclarée
par des pays sélectionnés, 2005**

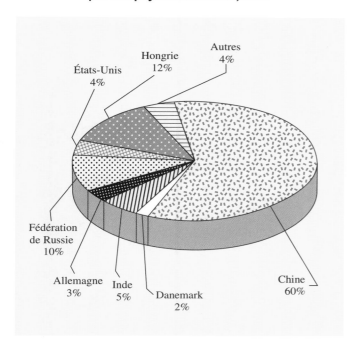

98 % de la fabrication totale déclarée entre 2001 et 2005. La répartition des barbituriques fabriqués en 2005 est indiquée à la figure 29. En 2005, la Chine (60 %), la Hongrie (12 %), la Fédération de Russie (10 %), l'Inde (5 %), les États-Unis (4 %), l'Allemagne (3 %) et le Danemark (2 %) ont représenté 96 % de la fabrication totale de tout ce groupe de barbituriques (voir la figure 30). Le changement le plus notable à cet égard est que la part de la Chine est passée de 54 % de la fabrication totale déclarée en 2004 à 60 % en 2005.

Autres sédatifs-hypnotiques

135. Cinq substances du groupe des sédatifs-hypnotiques inscrits au Tableau IV ne sont ni des barbituriques ni des benzodiazépines. L'ethchlorvynol, l'éthinamate et le méthyprylone sont inscrits au Tableau IV depuis l'adoption de la Convention de 1971, mais les deux autres substances, à savoir l'acide *gamma*-hydroxybutirique (GHB) et le zolpidem ont été incluses dans le groupe des sédatifs-hypnotiques inscrits au Tableau IV en 2001.

136. La fabrication d'ethchlorvynol a été déclarée pour la dernière fois par les États-Unis en 1999 (1,3 tonne) et cette substance n'est plus utilisée depuis 2001. La fabrication d'éthinamate a été déclarée pour la dernière fois par l'Allemagne en 1988 (500 kg), et celle de méthyprylone

par les États-Unis en 1990 (2,1 tonnes). Aucune fabrication ni aucun commerce international d'éthinamate ou de méthyprylone n'est signalé depuis 1991.

137. En ce qui concerne le GHB, des données très limitées sont disponibles pour l'année 2001, lorsque cette substance a été soumise à un contrôle international. Grâce à l'application de mesures nationales de contrôle, les pays à même de communiquer des informations sur la fabrication et les échanges de GHB sont plus nombreux. En 2005, l'Allemagne (5,7 tonnes) et la Lettonie (3,6 tonnes) ont été les principaux fabricants de GHB, représentant à elles deux 86 % de la production mondiale. Les autres principaux fabricants pendant la période 2001-2005 ont été les États-Unis (3,9 tonnes en moyenne) et l'Ukraine (3,8 tonnes en moyenne), suivis, avec des quantités bien moindres, par la Chine, la France et l'Azerbaïdjan. En 2005, les principaux exportateurs étaient l'Allemagne, les États-Unis et la Lettonie, et les plus gros importateurs étaient l'Italie avec 4,6 tonnes et le Royaume-Uni avec 1,8 tonne. Pendant la période 2003-2005, 25 pays ont déclaré au moins une fois avoir importé plus de 1 kg de GHB.

138. Des informations concernant le zolpidem ont été fournies par plusieurs pays pour la période 2001-2005. Le principal fabricant est la France avec 86 % de la production mondiale (32 tonnes), suivie par la République tchèque (3,5 tonnes) et l'Inde (709 kg). Les autres pays ayant signalé avoir fabriqué du zolpidem ces dernières années ont été l'Allemagne, l'Argentine, la Chine, l'Espagne, les États-Unis, Israël et la Slovaquie. Le principal exportateur a également été la France, avec 55 % des exportations mondiales (19 tonnes). Le zolpidem est une substance largement utilisée, et les principaux consommateurs ont été la France, les États-Unis, le Japon et la République tchèque. Pendant la période 2001-2005, plus de 100 pays ont signalé avoir importé au moins une fois plus de 1 kg de zolpidem.

Analgésiques

139. La léfétamine est le seul analgésique inscrit au Tableau IV. Ni fabrication ni commerce de cette substance n'ont été déclarés depuis 1996. L'Italie en détient actuellement 1 kg en stock.

Antidépresseurs

140. La seule substance représentative de ce groupe est l'amineptine, qui a été inscrite au Tableau II de la Convention de 1971 en 2003. Les informations communiquées au sujet de cette substance sont rares. Le seul pays ayant déclaré détenir en stock de petites quantités de cette substance au cours des deux dernières années a été le Brésil.

COMENTARIOS SOBRE LAS ESTADÍSTICAS COMUNICADAS RELATIVAS A SUSTANCIAS SICOTRÓPICAS

Resumen

La utilización de sustancias de la Lista I del Convenio sobre Sustancias Sicotrópicas de 1971 es muy limitada y está restringida a la investigación científica y, excepcionalmente, a la fabricación de sustancias sicotrópicas de otras listas. Tal es el caso también del *delta*-8-tetrahidrocannabinol, cuya fabricación ha aumentado considerablemente en los últimos años, que se produce para obtener dronabinol, una de las variantes estereoquímicas del *delta*-9-tetrahidrocannabinol (*delta*-9-THC) incluida en la Lista II. Los preparados que contienen dronabinol se utilizan en unos pocos países como antiemético para aliviar las naúseas. Los volúmenes de la fabricación y las existencias de *delta*-9-THC, que se habían mantenido estables hasta hace unos pocos años, han aumentado recientemente.

El uso de las anfetaminas, estimulantes del sistema nervioso central incluidos en la Lista II, está muy extendido sobre todo para la fabricación de otras sustancias sicotrópicas y sustancias que no están sometidas a fiscalización internacional, pero también para fines médicos como el tratamiento del trastorno de la concentración y la narcolepsia. La producción mundial de anfetaminas, que se fabrican en su mayor parte en los Estados Unidos y Francia, alcanzó en 2005 su nivel máximo de 45 toneladas, como consecuencia del aumento del consumo en los Estados Unidos. A ese país, que es, con mucho, el mayor consumidor de anfetaminas, correspondió en 2005 el 80% del consumo mundial estimado de anfetaminas. Las anfetaminas (principalmente el metilfenidato) se utilizan en un número cada vez mayor de países, en particular Alemania, el Canadá y España.

El consumo de buprenorfina, analgésico opioide incluido en la Lista III del Convenio de 1971, ha aumentado considerablemente en los últimos años como consecuencia de su utilización en la desintoxicación y el tratamiento de sustitución que se practican en los casos de adicción a la heroína desde comienzos del decenio de 1990. Más de 40 países importan actualmente buprenorfina con ese fin, siendo los principales importadores Alemania y Francia.

Actualmente hay 35 benzodiazepinas sometidas a fiscalización internacional. En la práctica médica las benzodiazepinas se utilizan para tratar a corto plazo el insomnio y como medicación para la preparación e inducción de la anestesia general. Las benzodiazepinas se clasifican como ansiolíticos y sedantes hipnóticos. El consumo de ansiolíticos de tipo benzodiazepínico, en particular de diazepam, es más alto en Europa que en cualquier otra región del mundo. En cambio, la fabricación y el consumo totales comunicados de sedantes hipnóticos de tipo benzodiazepínico, incluido el flunitrazepam, han fluctuado considerablemente. En los últimos años, se ha registrado una tendencia descendente en el consumo mundial comunicado de flunitrazepam, mientras que ha aumentado el consumo de brotizolam. El comercio internacional de flunitrazepam fluctuó en torno a 1 tonelada por año. Al Japón, que sigue siendo el principal país importador de flunitrazepam, le corresponde más de la mitad del volumen mundial de importaciones anuales.

De los 12 barbitúricos incluidos en el Convenio de 1971, el fenobarbital es el de uso más difundido, en particular para el tratamiento de la epilepsia. En 2005 esa sustancia representó el 71% de la fabricación combinada de todos los barbitúricos. Otros barbitúricos importantes son el barbital, el pentobarbital, el butalbital y el amobarbital, que representaron en conjunto aproximadamente el 28% de la fabricación total comunicada. A China, que es el mayor fabricante, le corresponde aproximadamente el 60% del volumen mundial de producción. Le siguen la Federación de Rusia y la India. La mayor parte de los barbitúricos se consumen en América, Asia y Europa, alcanzando el consumo medio en cada región aproximadamente 1.700 millones de S-DDD por año.

Los estimulantes incluidos en la Lista IV del Convenio de 1971 se utilizan esencialmente como anorexígenos o para el tratamiento del trastorno de la concentración. Tras pronunciadas fluctuaciones en el decenio de 1990, la fabricación total comunicada de ese grupo de sustancias se estableció en una cifra media anual de aproximadamente 1.800 millones de S-DDD durante el período comprendido 2001-2005. En 2005, las principales sustancias fabricadas fueron fentermina (45%), fenproporex (23%), y anfepramona (18%). La fentermina fue la sustancia más utilizada de ese grupo. El consumo per cápita más alto de estimulantes de la Lista IV se ha registrado tradicionalmente en América. Si bien el consumo de esos estimulantes en esa región ha seguido aumentando, los niveles de consumo en Asia, Europa y Oceanía han disminuido notablemente desde 2000.

---

1.   La finalidad de los presentes comentarios es facilitar el estudio de la información estadística sobre sustancias sicotrópicas fabricadas lícitamente que se presenta en los cuadros estadísticos (véanse las páginas [109-256] *infra*). Los cuadros contienen la información presentada por los gobiernos a la Junta Internacional de Fiscalización de Estupefacientes (JIFE) de conformidad con lo dispuesto en el artículo 16 del Convenio sobre Sustancias Sicotrópicas de 1971.

2.   En las cuatro listas del Convenio de 1971 figuran actualmente 116 sustancias. Se formulan comentarios sobre las sustancias que, según la información recibida, se utilizaron con fines médicos y científicos. Dado que solamente unos pocos gobiernos han comunicado la fabricación de sustancias de la Lista I y que el comercio internacional de éstas ha sido muy limitado, en un cuadro de la sección correspondiente a los cuadros de las estadísticas comunicadas a la Junta se presenta información resumida sobre el movimiento

de las sustancias incluidas en la Lista I en 2005. Con respecto a las sustancias incluidas en las Listas II y III, en los cuadros estadísticos se presenta información pertinente sobre el quinquenio 2001-2005. En cuanto a las sustancias de la Lista IV, se presenta en los cuadros estadísticos información sobre el trienio 2003-2005. No se incluye en los cuadros estadísticos información sobre algunas sustancias, a saber, la meclocualona y la fenciclidina, ambas incluidas en la Lista II, ni sobre la amineptina o la lefetamina, sustancias de la Lista IV, aunque se mencionan en los comentarios.

Sustancias incluidas en la Lista I

3. La Lista I contiene actualmente 28 sustancias. De conformidad con lo dispuesto en el artículo 7 del Convenio de 1971, debe prohibirse todo uso de esas sustancias, excepto el que con fines científicos y fines médicos muy limitados hagan personas debidamente autorizadas en establecimientos médicos o científicos que estén bajo el control directo de sus gobiernos o hayan sido expresamente aprobados por ellos. Esta restricción se debe a que todas las sustancias de la Lista I son alucinógenos o estimulantes del sistema nervioso central, de valor terapéutico muy escaso o nulo. Por lo tanto, la fabricación, las existencias y el comercio de esas sustancias han sido muy limitados. Las excepciones se indican más adelante.

4. En el Convenio de 1971 no se prevé ningún uso industrial de sustancias sicotrópicas de la Lista I para la fabricación de sustancias o productos no sicotrópicos. No obstante, la sustancia 2,5-dimetoxianfetamina (DMA) se ha empleado con ese fin en los Estados Unidos, único fabricante de la sustancia, donde se utiliza en la elaboración de películas fotográficas especiales. La fabricación de DMA en ese país se mantuvo estable, en un nivel medio anual de 8 toneladas hasta 2001, momento en que el volumen disminuyó alrededor del 50%. En 2005, la fabricación de DMA comunicada por los Estados Unidos ascendió a 520 kilogramos. Durante los cinco últimos años, la fabricación de DMA en los Estados Unidos ha ascendido en promedio a 1.603 kilogramos. A finales de 2005, las existencias de DMA en los Estados Unidos ascendían a 236 kilogramos. No existe, por lo que se ha informado, ningún sucedáneo de la sustancia para el proceso de elaboración mencionado anteriormente. A pesar de que en los Estados Unidos ha disminuido sustancialmente la utilización de la sustancia, parece que no se ha descontinuado su uso industrial en la elaboración de un tinte de película fotográfica[1].

5. En los cinco últimos años, ocho países comunicaron la fabricación de MDMA: Australia, Dinamarca, Estados Unidos, Hungría, Irlanda, Israel, Polonia y Suiza. A finales de 2005, las existencias mundiales de MDMA eran de menos de 500 gramos, en parte en Australia, los Estados Unidos y Suiza. En el período 2001-2005, cuatro países, a saber, Australia, los Estados Unidos, Israel y Suiza, comunicaron la fabricación de apenas unos cuantos gramos de tenanfetamina (MDA). Las existencias de esa sustancia se concentran sobre todo en los Estados Unidos y Suiza. En 2005, Dinamarca comunicó por primera vez la fabricación de casi 25 kilogramos de PMA (p-metoxi-α-metilfenetilamina) y al final del año se concentraban en ese país existencias de esa sustancia que ascendían a unos 40 kilogramos.

6. Las partes en el Convenio de 1971 pueden autorizar el uso limitado de sustancias de la Lista I para la fabricación de sustancias sicotrópicas que figuran en otras listas. Los isómeros del tetrahidrocannabinol (THC) incluidos en la Lista I, principalmente el *delta*-8-tetrahidrocannabinol, se han fabricado en los Estados Unidos y se han utilizado en la elaboración de *delta*-9-tetrahidrocannabinol (*delta*-9-THC), sustancia sicotrópica incluida en la Lista II desde 1991. Únicamente una variante estereoquímica del *delta*-9-THC, el dronabinol, se utiliza en la fabricación de preparados farmacéuticos para fines terapéuticos. Los Estados Unidos son el único país fabricante de los isómeros del THC incluidos en la Lista I. La fabricación de esos isómeros del THC aumentó en cerca del 140% en 1998 y 1999. En los cinco últimos años, ha seguido aumentando la fabricación de isómeros del THC, aproximadamente en un promedio del 16% por año. En 2005, la fabricación total en los Estados Unidos ascendió a 308 kilogramos. A finales de 2005, únicamente los Estados Unidos mantenían existencias, que ascendían a 445 kilogramos.

7. En 2005, sólo cuatro países comunicaron la fabricación, con fines científicos, de apenas unos gramos de otras sustancias de la Lista I no mencionadas anteriormente: Alemania (metcatinona), Estados Unidos (N-etil-MDA, psilocina y tenanfetamina), Irlanda (catinona, N-etil-MDA y tenanfetamina) y Suiza (mescalina, N-etil-MDA y psilocibina).

8. A finales de 2005 se registraban existencias de algunas sustancias de la Lista I que oscilaban entre unos pocos gramos y varios cientos de gramos, principalmente en los Estados Unidos. Las existencias de la mayoría de esas sustancias se han mantenido relativamente estables en los últimos años. Otros países que comunicaron existencias de unos pocos gramos de sustancias de la Lista I a finales de 2005 fueron Australia, el Reino Unido y Suiza. En los párrafos 4 a 6 *supra* se hace referencia a las existencias de DMA y THC.

9. El comercio internacional de sustancias de la Lista I siempre se ha limitado a transacciones ocasionales de apenas unos gramos. En el período 2001-2005, los países indicados a continuación comunicaron pequeñas importaciones o exportaciones de algunas de tales sustancias: Alemania, Australia, Canadá, China, Dinamarca, Francia, Estados Unidos, Irlanda, Israel, Nueva Zelandia, Reino Unido y Suiza.

---

[1] Véase el *Informe de la Junta Internacional de Fiscalización de Estupefacientes correspondiente a 1994* (publicación de las Naciones Unidas, núm. de venta: S.95.XI.4), párr. 75.

Sustancias incluidas en la Lista II

10. En la Lista II figuran 17 sustancias, de valor terapéutico escaso o moderado, cuyo potencial riesgo de abuso constituye un grave peligro para la salud pública. Esas sustancias pertenecen a los siguientes grupos: estimulantes del sistema nervioso central, antieméticos, alucinógenos, sedantes hipnóticos, antitusígenos y antidepresivos. Además de sus diversas aplicaciones en medicina o veterinaria, algunas de esas sustancias se utilizan en la industria para fabricar otras sustancias sicotrópicas o para transformarlas en sustancias no sicotrópicas.

Estimulantes del sistema nervioso central

Anfetaminas

11. Los dos isómeros ópticos de la anfetamina (levanfetamina y dexanfetamina) y su mezcla racémica (anfetamina), así como los dos isómeros ópticos de la metanfetamina (levometan-fetamina y metanfetamina) y su mezcla racémica (racemato de metanfetamina), están incluidos en la Lista II. Desde el decenio de 1970 la JIFE viene recibiendo de los gobiernos informes estadísticos sobre la anfetamina, la dexanfetamina y la metanfetamina. Se dispone de estadísticas sobre la levanfetamina y la levometanfetamina desde 1986 y sobre el racemato de metanfetamina desde 1988, debido a las distintas fechas en que esas sustancias se sometieron a fiscalización en virtud del Convenio de 1971.

12. Las anfetaminas de la Lista II no solo se utilizan direc-tamente con fines médicos, sino que también se emplean en la industria como productos intermedios para la fabricación de otras sustancias. Esas nuevas sustancias pueden dividirse en dos grupos: otras sustancias sicotrópicas, incluidas las que son isómeros ópticos de la sustancia original, y sustancias no sometidas a fiscalización en virtud del Convenio de 1971. En los últimos años las anfetaminas se han transformado principalmente en sustancias utilizadas como anorexígenos (benzfetamina, clobenzorex, fenproporex y levopropil-hexedrina) y antiparkinsonianos (selegilina). Ocasionalmente, también se transforman pequeñas cantidades en otras sustan-cias, como la famprofazona (un analgésico) y el anfetaminilo (un psicoestimulante). La benzfetamina y el fenproporex figuran en la Lista IV del Convenio de 1971, pero el anfeta-minilo, el clobenzorex, la famprofazona, la levopropil-hexedrina y la selegilina no están sometidas a fiscalización internacional.

Utilización como sustancias intermedias

13. En los Estados Unidos se utilizan precursores importados (fenilacetona y norefedrina) y racemato de metanfetamina para la fabricación de anfetamina y dexanfetamina, que se procesan ulteriormente para fabricar preparados farmacéuti-cos. En 2005 se fabricaron en ese país en total 6,7 toneladas de anfetamina y 6,2 toneladas de dexanfetamina. En 2005 los Estados Unidos importaron (de Francia) 2,4 toneladas de racemato de metanfetamina, de las cuales 1,9 toneladas se transformaron en 1,2 toneladas de metanfetamina y 580 kilo-gramos de levometanfetamina. Unos 542 kilogramos de la metanfetamina obtenida se utilizaron luego para fabricar 719 kilogramos de benzfetamina, mientras que la levometan-fetamina se utilizó para fabricar inhaladores nasales que se venden sin receta médica. Como consecuencia de ello, en los Estados Unidos se dispuso de 6,7 toneladas de anfetamina, 6,2 toneladas de dexanfetamina, 452 kilogramos de racemato de metanfetamina y 612 kilogramos de metanfetamina para usos terapéuticos directos.

14. En 2005 se fabricaron en Francia 10,9 toneladas de anfetamina, de las cuales 2,9 toneladas se utilizaron para fabricar unas 2,2 toneladas de dexanfetamina, 7,5 toneladas se utilizaron para fabricar 6,5 toneladas de levanfetamina y la cantidad restante se añadió a las existencias de esa sustancia. En total 4,9 toneladas de levanfetamina se volvieron a trans-formar en 4,7 toneladas de anfetamina. De las 2,9 toneladas de racemato de metanfetamina fabricadas en Francia en 2005, unas 2,4 toneladas se exportaron a los Estados Unidos y los 533 kilogramos restantes se transformaron en 500 kilogra-mos de metanfetamina, que se añadieron a las existencias.

Uso terapéutico directo

15. Con fines terapéuticos directos, las anfetaminas se utilizan principalmente en el tratamiento del trastorno de la concentración (denominado en los Estados Unidos trastorno de déficit de atención con hiperactividad), la narcolepsia y la obesidad, aunque en la mayoría de los países se ha descontinuado o reducido considerablemente el uso genera-lizado de esas sustancias como anorexígenos para tratar la obesidad.

16. En 2005, la cantidad de anfetaminas de la Lista II fabri-cada en todo el mundo ascendió a un total de 45,1 toneladas (más de 3.000 millones de dosis diarias definidas con fines estadísticos (S-DDD)), lo que representa un aumento de 636 kilogramos con respecto al año anterior. La fabricación de anfetamina (41,4%), dexanfetamina (25,3%) y levanfeta-mina (14,3%) representó un 81% de la producción mundial de este grupo de sustancias (véase la figura 1). La produc-ción correspondió casi íntegramente a Francia (58%) y a los

Figura 1. Estimulantes de la Lista II: fabricación total comunicada, 1996 a 2005

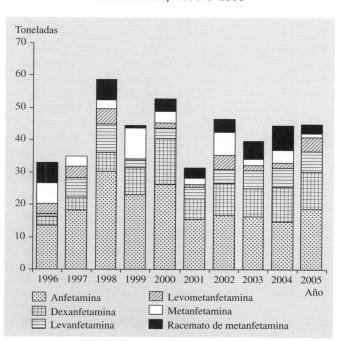

85

Estados Unidos (33%), en tanto que Alemania contribuyó al total con 977 kilogramos de anfetamina y 3,1 toneladas de levometanfetamina que se utilizaron para fabricar sustancias no sicotrópicas.

17. El aumento de la fabricación de anfetaminas en los últimos años se puede atribuir al rápido aumento del uso terapéutico de la anfetamina y la dexanfetamina en los Estados Unidos desde 1998, año en que los productos que contenían ambas sustancias empezaron a utilizarse principalmente para tratar el trastorno de la concentración. En 2005 se fabricaron en los Estados Unidos 6,7 toneladas de anfetamina y 6,2 toneladas de dexanfetamina con esos fines. A Francia, que ha sido, tradicionalmente, uno de los principales fabricantes de anfetaminas, le correspondió en el período 2001-2005 una media de 52,6% de la producción mundial de anfetamina, 44% de la de dexanfetamina y casi el 100% de la producción mundial de levanfetamina.

18. La fabricación de anfetamina aumentó gradualmente, alcanzando en 1998 el nivel máximo de más de 30 toneladas. En los cinco últimos años, la producción mundial de esa sustancia disminuyó considerablemente, aunque la fabricación total comunicada de anfetamina aumentó de 14,6 toneladas en 2004 a 18,7 toneladas en 2005. Las existencias mundiales de la sustancia aumentaron también, alcanzando en 2005 las 6 toneladas, 71% de las cuales se mantenían en los Estados Unidos. En 2005 el comercio internacional de anfetamina ascendía a 63 kilogramos y los principales importadores fueron Chile (35%), el Canadá (30%), Suecia (12%), Bélgica (9%) y la Federación de Rusia (7%).

19. Si bien la fabricación de dexanfetamina se mantuvo estable durante el decenio de 1980, en un nivel de aproximadamente 350 kilogramos por año, después de 1991 empezó a aumentar marcadamente y alcanzó a un total de casi 1,7 toneladas en 1995. A partir de entonces, la fabricación de esa sustancia aumentó sostenidamente, alcanzando el nivel máximo de 14,3 toneladas en 2000 y descendiendo a 6,6 toneladas en 2001, para estabilizarse luego en una media anual de 10,2 toneladas en el período 2002-2005. Francia y los Estados Unidos son los principales países consumidores de dexanfetamina, que se receta para el tratamiento del trastorno de la concentración, la obesidad y la narcolepsia, si bien otros países como Alemania, Australia, el Canadá, Chile y el Reino Unido también han comunicado que utilizan la sustancia considerablemente con fines terapéuticos. Las existencias mundiales de dexanfetamina aumentaron de 1 tonelada en 1995 a 7,3 toneladas en 2003 y descendieron a 5,9 toneladas en 2005. Con 16,4 y 4,3 S-DDD por cada 1.000 habitantes por día, respectivamente, Francia y los Estados Unidos tuvieron el nivel de consumo calculado más alto de dexanfetamina. Si bien 25 países comunicaron importaciones de la sustancia en 2005, más del 91% de los 492 kilogramos de las importaciones de dexanfetamina a nivel mundial correspondió al Canadá (54,6%), Australia (26,8%) y el Reino Unido (10,3%).

20. Además de sus usos terapéuticos directos, la metanfetamina se emplea también para fabricar benzfetamina, recetada para el tratamiento de la obesidad. En 1999, la fabricación total comunicada de metanfetamina ascendió a 9,5 toneladas. Desde ese momento, la producción mundial fluctuó considerablemente, descendiendo en 2005 a 1,4 toneladas y habiéndose fabricado en los Estados Unidos el 80% de ese volumen. Francia es otro país en el que se fabrica

regularmente metanfetamina, aunque comunicó que su producción se redujo de 642 kilogramos en 2004 a 289 kilogramos en 2005. La fabricación de metanfetamina en Alemania ha sido sumamente irregular, habiendo fluctuado entre las 5,2 toneladas en 2002 y los 2 gramos en 2005, lo que se refleja en las tendencias mundiales. Los Estados Unidos son el principal consumidor regular de metanfetamina. En 2005 el nivel de consumo calculado de ese país se elevó de 0,26 a 0,42 S-DDD por cada 1.000 habitantes por día. En total once países comunicaron importaciones de metanfetamina en 2005, habiendo sido los principales importadores Chile y Suiza. En años anteriores, Irlanda y el Reino Unido comunicaron también la importación de grandes cantidades de metanfetamina.

21. En los Estados Unidos, la levometanfentamina se utiliza para fabricar inhaladores nasales que se venden sin receta médica, productos que en ese país están exentos de ciertas medidas de fiscalización previstas con arreglo al artículo 3 del Convenio de 1971. En el último decenio, la fabricación total comunicada de levometanfetamina fue sumamente dispar, fluctuando apreciablemente entre 433 kilogramos y 5,1 toneladas. En 2005, la fabricación total volvió a aumentar marcadamente, triplicándose hasta alcanzar las 4,3 toneladas. Alemania, los Estados Unidos, Francia y la República Checa son los principales países que fabrican la sustancia y sus principales consumidores. La levometanfetamina se utiliza también en Irlanda e Italia, que son los principales importadores de la sustancia.

22. Francia y Hungría son los principales fabricantes de racemato de metanfetamina. La sustancia se ha destinado principalmente a la exportación (un total de 20,1 toneladas desde 1996) o se ha transformado en levometanfetamina y metanfetamina. En los cinco últimos años, la fabricación total comunicada por esos dos países aumentó gradualmente de 3,3 toneladas en 2001 a 7,5 toneladas en 2004. En 2005, sin embargo, la cantidad fabricada se redujo a 2,8 toneladas, una disminución del 62%, debido a un marcado descenso del volumen de fabricación en Hungría, que comunicó una disminución de más de 4 toneladas en 2004 a menos de 2 kilogramos en 2005. Se registró una tendencia análoga en las existencias mundiales, que descendieron de una media de 3,7 toneladas en el período 2001-2004 a 1,9 toneladas en 2005. En Francia la fabricación de racemato de metanfetamina se mantuvo estable en los últimos años, registrando una media anual de 3 toneladas en el período 2001-2005, lo que representa el 64% de la producción mundial en ese período. Los Estados Unidos, el único país importador de la sustancia, importó entre 2,5 y 3 toneladas de racemato de metanfetamina por año en los cinco últimos años.

23. En el cuadro 1 figuran los diez países que tienen los niveles más altos de consumo, para fines médicos e industriales, de las anfetaminas consideradas como grupo, niveles que han sido calculados sobre la base de las estadísticas suministradas en relación con los años 2001, 2003 y 2005[2] y se expresan en dosis S-DDD por cada 1.000 habitantes por día[3].

---

[2] En la nota aclaratoria del cuadro III de la presente publicación se explica el método de cálculo de los niveles de consumo de sustancias sicotrópicas.

[3] En el cuadro IV de la presente publicación figura la lista de las dosis diarias definidas con fines estadísticos (S-DDD) utilizadas en estos cálculos.

Cuadro 1. Cálculo del consumo de estimulantes de la Lista II (excluido el metilfenidato), 2001, 2003 y 2005

	S-DDD por cada 1.000 habitantes por día		
País[a]	2001	2003	2005
Estados Unidos	6,07	6,86	10,22
Canadá	0,42	0,81	1,95
Australia	1,54	1,76	1,24
Bélgica	0,08	0,03	0,26
Chile	0,28	0,18	0,25
Suiza	4,04	0,04	0,23
Suecia	0,20	0,22	0,20
Noruega	0,07	0,14	0,19
Reino Unido	0,23	0,14	0,15
Nueva Zelandia	0,14	0,14	0,11

[a] Los países están ordenados según su nivel de consumo de estimulantes de la Lista II en 2005.

Fenetilina

24. La fenetilina está sometida a fiscalización internacional desde 1986. La última vez que se comunicó la fabricación de la sustancia fue en 1987. Las existencias mundiales de fenetilina, que eran de casi 4 toneladas en 1987, disminuyeron considerablemente tras la destrucción voluntaria de todas las existencias de Suiza en 1991 y del 50% de las existencias de Alemania en 1992. Esas existencias se destruyeron para poner fin a los intentos de los narcotraficantes por desviar la fenetilina hacia canales ilícitos utilizando autorizaciones de importación falsificadas[4]. En 2000 Alemania ya había terminado de exportar gradualmente a los Países Bajos la mitad restante de sus existencias. Los Países Bajos son el único país que todavía conserva existencias importantes de fenetilina (212 kilogramos a finales de 2005) y son el principal exportador de la sustancia, con el 90% de las exportaciones mundiales. El principal importador en 2005 fue Bélgica (68 kilogramos), que reexportó una parte reducida de sus importaciones (7,6 kilogramos) a Alemania y Francia. Ningún otro país ha comunicado desde 2003 la utilización de fenetilina con fines médicos.

Metilfenidato

25. La utilización de metilfenidato[5] con fines terapéuticos aumentó considerablemente en el decenio de 1990. Ese gran aumento se debió principalmente a la evolución de la situación en los Estados Unidos, donde la sustancia es objeto de grandes campañas publicitarias, incluida la publicidad directa a posibles consumidores. La sustancia suele recetarse para el tratamiento del trastorno de la concentración, principalmente en niños. Sin embargo, desde fines del decenio de 1990, el uso de metilfenidato para el tratamiento de ese trastorno ha aumentado marcadamente en muchos otros países. El cálculo del consumo mundial de la sustancia aumentó de 18,5 toneladas en 2001 a 30,4 toneladas en 2005. Si bien el metilfenidato se utiliza principalmente para el tratamiento del trastorno de la concentración, también se receta para tratar la narcolepsia.

---

[4] Véase el *Informe de la Junta Internacional de Fiscalización de Estupefacientes correspondiente a 1999* (publicación de las Naciones Unidas, núm. de venta: S.00.XI.1), párr. 85.

[5] Para los detalles véase el cuadro IV.

Figura 2. Fabricación de metilfenidato, 1996 a 2005

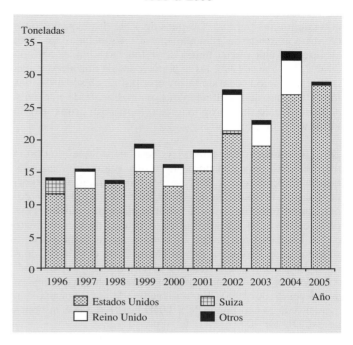

26. La fabricación mundial de metilfenidato aumentó muy rápidamente en la primera mitad del decenio de 1990 (de 2,8 toneladas en 1990 a 19,1 toneladas en 1999). Como consecuencia del uso creciente de anfetaminas para el tratamiento del trastorno de la concentración, la fabricación de metilfenidato disminuyó a 16 toneladas en 2000 (véase la figura 2). A partir de entonces, la fabricación total comunicada de la sustancia fluctuó, si bien siguiendo una tendencia general ascendente y alcanzó su nivel máximo de 33,5 toneladas en 2004, antes de disminuir a 28,8 toneladas en 2005. Los Estados Unidos han sido el principal fabricante de metilfenidato; su producción aumentó de 1,8 toneladas en 1990 a 28,3 toneladas en 2005. Si bien casi todo el metilfenidato fabricado en ese país se había destinado al consumo interno, las exportaciones aumentaron gradualmente de 33 kilogramos en 1996 a 2,7 toneladas en 2005. Las existencias mundiales de metilfenidato siguieron la tendencia de la fabricación, aumentando de 15,5 toneladas en 2001 a 23,4 toneladas en 2005. Ese año, el 83% de las existencias mundiales correspondieron a los Estados Unidos, que contribuyeron apreciablemente a aumentarlas, de 500 kilogramos en 1992 a 19,5 toneladas en 2005. En ese país es motivo de grave preocupación la posible tendencia a diagnosticar en demasía el trastorno de la concentración y a recetar en exceso metilfenidato.

27. Fuera de los Estados Unidos, las necesidades de metilfenidato con fines médicos se satisfacen principalmente mediante importaciones, habiendo aumentado el número de países que comunicaron importaciones de la sustancia de 70 en 1996 a 88 en 2005. El comercio internacional de metilfenidato disminuyó de una media anual de 11,5 toneladas en el período 2003-2004 a 9,2 toneladas en 2005. Alemania, Australia, el Canadá, España, los Países Bajos, el Reino Unido, Sudáfrica y Suiza son los principales países importadores de metilfenidato, que se destina en su mayor parte a la reexportación, representando el total combinado de esos países el 84% del volumen mundial de importaciones. España, los Estados Unidos, el Reino Unido y Suiza son los

principales proveedores de la sustancia en el mercado mundial. En el decenio de 1980, el volumen de exportaciones de metilfenidato de Suiza se mantuvo estable en menos de 400 kilogramos por año. Después de 1991, las exportaciones de Suiza aumentaron gradualmente a 1,4 toneladas en 1996, alcanzando una media anual de 4 toneladas en el período 2003-2005. Hasta 1996, las exportaciones de Suiza provenían de la fabricación local de la materia prima. Desde 1997, las importaciones de metilfenidato, principalmente de España y el Reino Unido, han proporcionado la materia prima para la fabricación de preparados.

28. El número de países y territorios que importan metilfenidato para consumo interno ha venido aumentando. Desde 1995, en total 121 gobiernos han comunicado importaciones de la sustancia. En 2005, en total 33 gobiernos comunicaron importaciones de metilfenidato en cantidades superiores a los 10 kilogramos. El consumo de metilfenidato en los Estados Unidos, que es, con mucho, el principal consumidor de la sustancia, representó en 2005 el 80% del consumo calculado de la sustancia a nivel mundial y se ha caracterizado por un aumento firme y constante desde comienzos del decenio de 1990. La utilización de la sustancia aún aumentó de 317 millones de S-DDD en 1996 a 808 millones de S-DDD en 2005 (véase la figura 3).

29. El nivel de consumo de metilfenidato en el resto del mundo alcanzó una media anual de unos 200 millones de S-DDD en los tres últimos años. Entre los cambios recientes cabe mencionar la disminución del consumo en el Canadá, donde el consumo de metilfenidato descendió de 48 millones de S-DDD en el período 2003-2004 a 29 millones de S-DDD en 2005, y el aumento en 2005 del consumo en Alemania, de 33 millones de S-DDD en 2004 a 44 millones de S-DDD en 2005. El Reino Unido y España son los otros dos principales países consumidores de la sustancia. En los últimos años el consumo de metilfenidato ha aumentado en esos dos países, alcanzando la cifra de 27 y 17 millones de S-DDD, respectivamente, en 2005.

Figura 3. Cálculo del consumo de metilfenidato con fines terapéuticos, 1996 a 2005

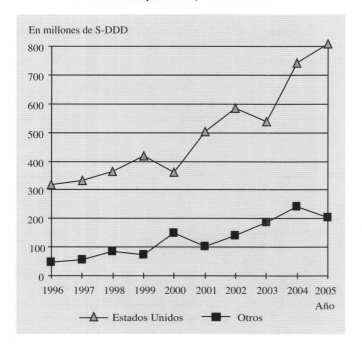

Cuadro 2. Cálculo del consumo de metilfenidato con fines terapéuticos, en 2001, 2003 y 2005

País[a]	En S-DDD por cada 1.000 inhabitantes por día		
	2001	20003	2005
Estados Unidos	5,11	5,21	7,61
Israel	0,72	5,27	2,69
Noruega	0,78	2,13	2,61
Canadá	0,29	4,24	2,55
Países Bajos	1,11	1,38	1,81
Alemania	0,67	0,99	1,47
Australia	0,89	1,34	1,44
Suiza	2,82	2,23	1,36
Bélgica	0,51	1,12	1,24
Nueva Zelandia	1,29	1,35	1,23
Reino Unido	1,04	0,95	1,23
España	0,66	0,78	1,11
Suecia	0,16	0,35	0,89
Dinamarca	0,22	0,40	0,88
Finlandia	0,07	0,29	0,57
Sudáfrica	0,16	0,27	0,51
Panamá	0,10	—	0,45
Chile	0,24	0,35	0,44
Islandia	2,35	5,21	0,01

[a] Los países están ordenados por su nivel de consumo de metilfenidato en 2005.

30. En el cuadro 2 figuran los países que tuvieron los niveles más altos de consumo de metilfenidato con fines terapéuticos en 2005; niveles que han sido calculados sobre la base de las estadísticas suministradas en relación con los años 2001, 2003 y 2005 y se expresan en S-DDD por cada 1.000 habitantes por día.

Fenmetracina

31. En todos los países se han descontinuado la utilización de fenmetracina con fines médicos y su fabricación. Se conservan pequeñas existencias de la sustancia en el Reino Unido (14 gramos) y los Estados Unidos (1 gramo). El comercio internacional de fenmetracina se limita a transacciones ocasionales de unos pocos gramos.´

Antieméticos

Delta-9-tetrahidrocannabinol y sus variantes estereoquímicas

32. La sustancia *delta*-9-THC, junto con sus variantes estereoquímicas, figuraba inicialmente en la Lista I, pero fue transferida a la Lista II en 1991 en vista de la utilización de una de sus variantes estereoquímicas (dronabinol) para aliviar las náuseas. Los Estados Unidos son el único país que ha comunicado la fabricación de cantidades importantes de *delta*-9-THC. La fabricación de *delta*-9-THC en ese país se mantuvo relativamente estable, en un promedio anual de 66 kilogramos a finales del decenio del 1990. No obstante, la cantidad fabricada ha venido aumentando considerablemente desde 2000, con un promedio de 170 kilogramos en los cinco últimos años (180 kilogramos en 2005). Los otros dos países

que han comunicado la fabricación de la sustancia en los últimos cinco años, aunque en cantidades mucho más pequeñas, son Alemania (un promedio de 7 kilogramos) y el Reino Unido (un promedio de 2 kilogramos). En 2005, el Canadá y Suiza comunicaron por primera vez la fabricación de *delta*-9-THC, también en cantidades pequeñas, a saber, 3 y 13 kilogramos, respectivamente.

33.   Casi todo el *delta*-9-THC fabricado en Alemania, el Canadá y los Estados Unidos se destinó al consumo interno. El Reino Unido y Suiza comunicaron el consumo de pequeñas cantidades o no comunicaron consumo alguno pese a lo cual aumentaron las existencias de ambos países. Las existencias comunicadas totales de la sustancia en 2005 (385 kilogramos) se concentraban casi íntegramente en los Estados Unidos y el Reino Unido y representaron un aumento del 65% en comparación con las existencias de 2004. Varios países comunicaron importaciones de la sustancia en 2005; las más importantes correspondieron a Alemania (2.461 gramos) y el Canadá (2.187 gramos), que, junto a los Estados Unidos, han sido los principales consumidores de *delta*-9-THC.

Alucinógenos

Fenciclidina

34.   La fenciclidina se utiliza principalmente como anestésico en veterinaria. En ocasiones anteriores comunicaron la fabricación de esa sustancia en pequeñas cantidades Australia, los Estados Unidos, Francia, Hungría, Israel, el Reino Unido y Suiza (4,5 kilogramos en total en el período 1996-2005). Los Estados Unidos e Israel fueron los únicos países que comunicaron la fabricación de la sustancia en 2005 (2 kilogramos y 146 gramos, respectivamente). Diez países comunicaron que mantenían existencias de fenciclidina en 2005, correspondiendo a los Estados Unidos el 84% del total mundial (3,1 kilogramos). Otros países que mantenían existencias de fenciclidina fueron Francia (210 gramos) e Israel (146 gramos), seguidos por el Reino Unido, Suiza, Dinamarca, el Canadá, Hungría, Australia y Finlandia, en orden decreciente según los niveles de existencias. El comercio internacional de fenciclidina se ha limitado a transacciones ocasionales de unos pocos gramos.

Sedantes hipnóticos

Meclocualona

35.   Desde 1980 no se fabrica meclocualona, aunque todavía se conservan existencias de esa sustancia. El Reino Unido comunicó poseer 152 gramos de meclocualona en 2001. Desde entonces, los Estados Unidos son el único país que comunica existencias de esa sustancia, que seguían siendo de 35 gramos en 2005.

Metacualona

36.   En los últimos años ha disminuido marcadamente la fabricación de metacualona, que en el decenio de 1980 había alcanzado el nivel máximo de más de 50 toneladas por año. En 1997, Suiza (340 kilogramos) y la República Checa (43 kilogramos) comunicaron la fabricación de las últimas

cantidades importantes de la sustancia. Desde entonces, la fabricación mundial siguió disminuyendo, dado que únicamente en los Estados Unidos se fabricaron cantidades muy pequeñas de metacualona (4 gramos en 2003 y 3 gramos en 2004) y no se comunicó fabricación alguna de la sustancia en 2005. En el período 1997-2005, las existencias mundiales de metacualona, concentradas casi íntegramente en Suiza, disminuyeron de 2,4 toneladas en 1997 a 257 kilogramos en 2005, debido a que la sustancia se sigue utilizando mundialmente con fines médicos. En los últimos años, su utilización a nivel mundial fluctuó significativamente y disminuyó de una media anual de 1,1 millones de S-DDD en el bienio 1999-2000 a menos de 6.000 S-DDD en 2005. Se sigue consumiendo metacualona, aunque no en cantidades importantes, prácticamente sólo en Suiza.

Secobarbital

37.   La fabricación de secobarbital, sustancia que anteriormente solía desviarse de la fabricación y el comercio lícitos, ha disminuido en gran medida desde 1988, cuando la sustancia fue transferida de la Lista III a la Lista II. Ese año se comunicó la fabricación de más de 11 toneladas en todo el mundo. El total disminuyó a 2,6 toneladas en 1990 y siguió disminuyendo hasta alcanzar un promedio anual de 1,8 toneladas en el período 1997-2001. La fabricación de secobarbital ascendió en 2001 a 4,2 toneladas (véase la figura 4), su nivel más alto desde 1989, y tuvo lugar en dos países: Alemania (2,3 toneladas) y los Estados Unidos (1,9 toneladas). La fabricación total de secobarbital aumentó ligeramente de 811 kilogramos en 2004 a 817 kilogramos en 2005. Las existencias mundiales de secobarbital disminuyeron de 1,4 toneladas en 2004 a 736 kilogramos en 2005, concentrándose el 65% en Alemania y el 30% en los Estados Unidos.

38.   Durante el período 2001-2005, cinco países comunicaron la fabricación de secobarbital por lo menos una vez, a saber, en orden decreciente según las cantidades fabricadas: Alemania

Figura 4.   Secobarbital: fabricación y existencias totales comunicadas, 1996 a 2005

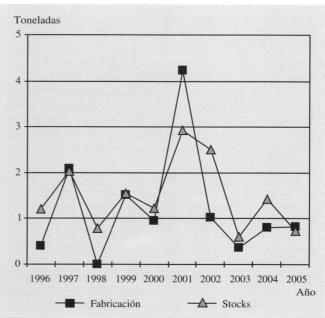

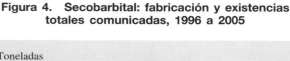

(para el consumo interno y la exportación), los Estados Unidos (principalmente para consumo interno), Dinamarca (casi exclusivamente para la exportación) y el Japón y China (para consumo interno). En 2005, sólo dos países, Alemania (817 kilogramos) e Irlanda (79 kilogramos), comunicaron la fabricación de secobarbital. Las existencias de la sustancia que conservaban los Estados Unidos disminuyeron significativamente de 2001 (1,7 toneladas) a 2005 (220 kilogramos). Tras alcanzar un volumen máximo de 1,7 toneladas en 2001, las importaciones mundiales registraron una media anual de 670 kilogramos en el período 2003-2005. Los principales países que han comerciado con la sustancia en los últimos años han sido Alemania (el principal exportador) y el Reino Unido (el principal importador). Entre los otros países importadores de secobarbital figuran Bélgica, el Canadá, Dinamarca, Irlanda, los Países Bajos y Suecia.

Antitusígenos

Zipeprol

39. El zipeprol, antitusígeno de acción broncoespasmolítica y mucolítica, está sometido a fiscalización internacional desde 1995, razón por la cual sólo se dispone de estadísticas sobre la sustancia a partir de ese año. En 2001 se comunicó por última vez la fabricación de zipeprol, habiendo sido Francia el único país fabricante (666 kilogramos). Las existencias de zipeprol en 2005 se concentraban en Suiza (588 kilogramos), seguida por Chile (10 kilogramos). En 2005, únicamente Suiza (168 kilogramos) comunicó exportaciones de la sustancia. Chile, México y la República de Corea son los únicos países que han comunicado la utilización de la sustancia durante los últimos años.

Sustancias incluidas en la Lista III

40. En la Lista III figuran nueve sustancias. Conforme a los criterios adoptados por el Comité de Expertos de la Organización Mundial de la Salud (OMS) en Farmacodependencia para la inclusión de sustancias en las listas, las sustancias de la Lista III son sustancias cuyo consumo puede ser abusivo y significar un riesgo notable para la salud pública y cuyo valor terapéutico va de moderado a grande. Una de las sustancias, la catina, pertenece al grupo de estimulantes del sistema nervioso central; seis de ellas pertenecen al grupo de los sedantes hipnóticos, cuatro barbitúricos (amobarbital, butalbital, ciclobarbital y pentobarbital), la glutetimida y el flunitrazepam; y las dos sustancias restantes, la buprenorfina y la pentazocina, pertenecen al grupo de los analgésicos.

Estimulantes del sistema nervioso central

Catina

41. Además de su consumo como estimulante, la catina se utiliza también con fines industriales. En los últimos cinco años, el volumen total de fabricación de esa sustancia ha fluctuado enormemente al ritmo de la producción de Alemania, único país en que se producía hasta 2003. En 2004, la India fue el único país que comunicó la fabricación de la sustancia, con una producción de 56 kilogramos, y en 2005 la totalidad de la fabricación mundial de catina correspondió a Alemania (2,2 toneladas). En el período 2001-2005 la fabricación mundial de la sustancia fluctuó entre 6,4 toneladas y 56 kilogramos al año, con una media anual de 2 toneladas.

42. En el período 2001-2005, nueve países comunicaron importaciones de catina y las importaciones mundiales de la sustancia ascendieron a una media anual de 4 toneladas. En ese mismo período, correspondieron a Sudáfrica e Italia el 44% y el 26% de las importaciones mundiales de catina, respectivamente, mientras que Sudáfrica importó en promedio 1,8 toneladas por año (para consumo interno) e Italia importó un promedio de 1 tonelada por año (en su mayor parte para la reexportación). Otros países importadores regulares de la sustancia fueron Francia, México y Suiza. En 2004, las importaciones de México y Suiza descendieron

en comparación con los niveles registrados en el período 1997-2001, disminuyendo a alrededor de 850 kilogramos y 40 kilogramos, respectivamente, y ninguno de los dos países comunicó importación alguna de la sustancia en 2005. Las importaciones de catina de Francia fueron en promedio de más de 300 kilogramos por año en el período 2001-2005. De los siete países que comunicaron exportaciones de catina en los últimos años, Alemania siguió siendo el principal exportador, con una media anual de exportación de 2,4 toneladas en el período 2001-2005.

Sedantes hipnóticos

43. Los barbitúricos son un grupo de agentes depresivos del sistema nervioso central estrechamente relacionados en lo que respecta a su estructura química. Clasificados como sedantes hipnóticos, se solían recetar para el tratamiento del insomnio, la ansiedad, el estrés y la epilepsia. Algunos barbitúricos también se utilizaban como anestésicos en intervenciones quirúrgicas cortas (sustancias de acción ultrabreve), en tanto que otros tienen una acción anticonvulsiva selectiva. Cada barbitúrico es diferente en lo que respecta a la rapidez con que actúa, la duración de la acción y la potencia. Una pequeña dosis de 50 miligramos puede aliviar la ansiedad y la tensión, en tanto que una dosis mayor de 100 a 200 miligramos, suele inducir el sueño. Como en el caso de las benzodiazepinas, los barbitúricos que se encuentran en el mercado ilícito suelen haber sido desviados de los canales lícitos y no sintetizados en laboratorios clandestinos. El riesgo de abuso es alto y los efectos a largo plazo incluyen el desarrollo de tolerancia y de una fuerte dependencia física y psicológica.

Amobarbital, butalbital, ciclobarbital y pentobarbital

44. El amobarbital, el ciclobarbital y el pentobarbital se sometieron a fiscalización al aprobarse el Convenio de 1971, en tanto que el butalbital se añadió en 1987 a la Lista III del Convenio. Tres de esos barbitúricos (el amobarbital, el butalbital y el ciclobarbital) se utilizan principalmente como

Figura 5. Barbitúricos incluidos en la Lista III: fabricación total comunicada, 1996 a 2005

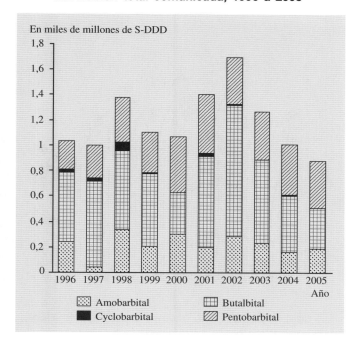

Figura 6. Barbitúricos incluidos en la Lista III: fabricación total comunicada por países, 2001 a 2005

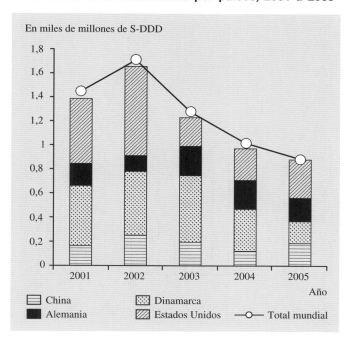

hipnóticos (para inducir sueño) y, en consecuencia, forman parte del tratamiento del insomnio incurable. El pentobarbital, también se ha utilizado como medicación de preparación para la anestesia. En el período 2001-2005, las tasas calculadas más altas de utilización per cápita de esas cuatro sustancias se registraron en Dinamarca, los Estados Unidos y el Canadá, con tasas de 17,2, 6,7 y 2,8 S-DDD por cada 1.000 habitantes por día, respectivamente. La fabricación total comunicada de esas sustancias osciló en torno a los 1.400 millones de S-DDD en el período 2002-2003 y disminuyó luego gradualmente a 881 millones de S-DDD en 2005 (véase la figura 5). En la figura 6 se indica la distribución de la producción total en el período 2001-2005 por países fabricantes.

45. Los Estados Unidos han sido tradicionalmente el principal país fabricante de butalbital, habiéndoles correspondido hasta tres cuartas partes de la producción total. La fabricación mundial de la sustancia disminuyó gradualmente de 76 toneladas en 2002 a 24 toneladas en 2005 (véase la figura 7). Además de los Estados Unidos, los únicos otros países en los que se fabricó butalbital regularmente en el último decenio fueron Alemania y Dinamarca. El butalbital se ha utilizado para la fabricación de diversos preparados que en los Estados Unidos están exentos de ciertas medidas de fiscalización de conformidad con lo dispuesto en el artículo 3 del Convenio de 1971. En los últimos años la fabricación de butalbital de los Estados Unidos ha fluctuado, disminuyendo pronunciadamente de 40 toneladas en 2002 a una media de 7,4 toneladas en el período 2003-2005. Las cantidades fabricadas en Dinamarca disminuyeron a un ritmo constante de 38,7 toneladas en 2003 a 12,8 toneladas en 2005, para volver a casi el mismo nivel de producción media anual registrado en el período 1996-2000 (14 toneladas). En 2005, correspondieron a los Estados Unidos y Dinamarca el 38% y el 53%, respectivamente, de la producción mundial, y Alemania fabricó algo más de 2 toneladas de la sustancia.

46. Diez países comunicaron exportaciones de butalbital en el quinquenio 2001-2005. A Dinamarca correspondió hasta el 96% del volumen mundial de exportaciones en 2001 y ese país siguió siendo el principal exportador en 2005, ya que suministró el 86% de las 22,1 toneladas exportadas en todo el mundo. Las exportaciones de butalbital de los Estados Unidos fueron muy dispares; y fluctuaron entre cero y 2 toneladas en el decenio 1996-2005. Italia y Suiza, cuyo volumen medio de exportaciones fue de 179,4 y 103 kilogramos, por año, respectivamente, figuraron entre los exportadores menores de la sustancia en el período 2001-2005. Los Estados Unidos, Italia y el Canadá siguieron siendo los principales importadores de butalbital. En los últimos años, Dinamarca, los Estados Unidos, Italia y el Canadá han sido los países con las tasas más altas de consumo de la sustancia.

47. La fabricación total comunicada de pentobarbital disminuyó en los últimos años, pasando de 45 toneladas en 2001 a un promedio de 37,7 toneladas en el período 2002-2005 (véase la figura 8). Los Estados Unidos, Alemania, Dinamarca y Suiza fueron los principales fabricantes de la sustancia en los últimos diez años, habiendo fabricado en 2005 los tres primeros países el 52,5%, el 44,5% y el 2,8%, respectivamente, de la producción mundial. En los cinco últimos años, Australia, Dinamarca, Irlanda y Nueva Zelandia alcanzaron las tasas más altas de consumo de la sustancia, que oscilaron entre 2,5 y 3,8 S-DDD por cada 1.000 habitantes por día.

48. El comercio internacional de pentobarbital en el quinquenio 2001-2005 registró una media anual de 26 toneladas aproximadamente. Los principales países exportadores fueron (en orden decreciente por volumen de exportaciones) Alemania, los Estados Unidos, el Canadá, Dinamarca y Francia y sus exportaciones representaron en conjunto más del 92% de las exportaciones mundiales en dicho período. En el período 2001-2005, las exportaciones de Alemania se estabilizaron en una media anual de 11 toneladas, mientras que las exportaciones de pentobarbital de los Estados Unidos

Figura 7. Butalbital: fabricación total comunicada, 1996 a 2005

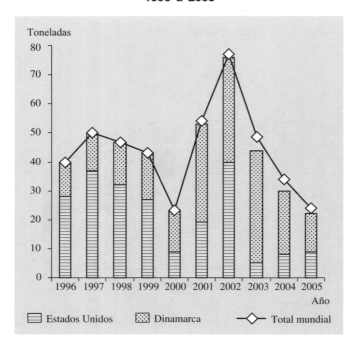

Figura 9. Amobarbital: fabricación total comunicada, 1996 a 2005

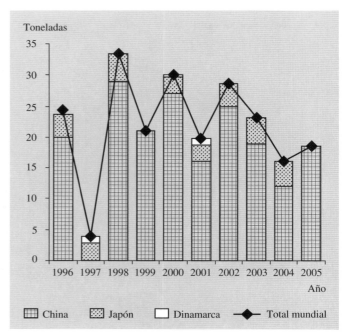

Figura 8. Pentobarbital: fabricación total comunicada, 1996 a 2005

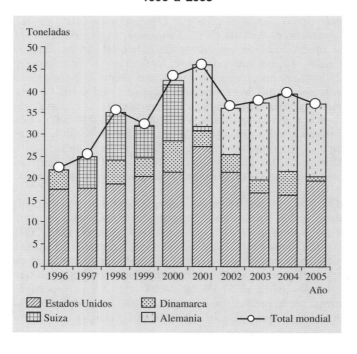

Figura 10. Ciclobarbital: fabricación total comunicada, 1996 a 2005

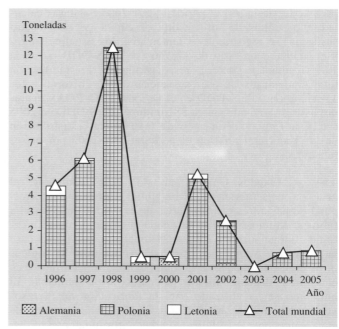

fluctuaron entre las 3,5 toneladas y las 6 toneladas. Según las estadísticas comunicadas, 67 países importaron pentobarbital en ese período. Los principales importadores de la sustancia en 2005 fueron China (45,5 toneladas), el Canadá (6,7 toneladas), Francia (4,5 toneladas), Australia (2,6 toneladas) y el Reino Unido (2,1 toneladas), países a los que correspondió el 86% de las importaciones mundiales.

49. En el período 2001-2004, los principales países fabricantes de amobarbital fueron China, Dinamarca y el Japón,

en tanto que en 2005 únicamente China comunicó la fabricación de la sustancia (18 toneladas) (véase la figura 9). Las existencias mundiales de amobarbital, tras disminuir gradualmente de más de 2 toneladas en 2001 a 1,7 toneladas en 2003, volvieron a aumentar hasta alcanzar las 3,2 toneladas en 2004 y las 7,3 toneladas en 2005. El consumo mundial calculado de la sustancia fluctuó en torno a una media de 21,7 toneladas en el período 2001-2005, registrándose en Rumania, el Japón y China las tasas calculadas más altas de consumo de amobarbital en ese período.

50. Las exportaciones mundiales de amobarbital fluctuaron, si bien registraron una tendencia ascendente, con una media anual de 5,6 toneladas, en el período 2001-2005. Las importaciones anuales mundiales de la sustancia alcanzaron un volumen máximo de 10,2 toneladas en 2005. En orden decreciente, Rumania, los Países Bajos (para la reexportación), Irlanda y Hungría fueron a nivel mundial los principales importadores de amobarbital en los últimos años. En los Países Bajos se registró una disminución marcada de las importaciones de amobarbital, de una media anual de 2,3 toneladas en el período 2002-2003 a 52 kilogramos en 2005. Las importaciones de Rumania también disminuyeron, de 7,1 toneladas en 2002 a 2 toneladas en 2004, sólo para volver a aumentar a 9,7 toneladas en 2005.

51. El ciclobarbital se utiliza principalmente en algunos países de Europa central y oriental y, en el período 2001-2005, las tasas más altas de consumo per cápita se registraron en Polonia y Letonia, con 0,26 y 0,3 S-DDD por cada 1.000 habitantes por día, respectivamente. En los últimos años, Polonia ha sido el principal fabricante de ciclobarbital, habiéndole correspondido hasta el 100% del total mundial en el período 2004-2005 (véase la figura 10), y tras una disminución de unas 5 toneladas en 2001 a una producción nula en 2003, el volumen de fabricación de ciclobarbital de ese país aumentó de 755 kilogramos en 2004 a 914 kilogramos en 2005. Ni Alemania ni Letonia comunicaron fabricación alguna de ciclobarbital en los tres últimos años. Siguiendo la tendencia registrada en la fabricación, las existencias mundiales de la sustancia comunicadas disminuyeron de 2,6 toneladas en 2002 a 110 kilogramos en 2004, para decuplicarse en 2005, año en que alcanzaron las 1,1 toneladas.

52. Las exportaciones mundiales de ciclobarbital disminuyeron de una media anual de 1,1 toneladas durante el período 2003-2004 a 711 kilogramos en 2005. Las exportaciones de Polonia disminuyeron en un 50%, de una media anual de 1,5 toneladas en el período 2001-2004 a 707 kilogramos en 2005, aunque ese país sigue siendo el principal exportador de la sustancia. Otros importantes exportadores de ciclobarbital en el período 2003-2005 fueron, Belarús, Georgia, Letonia, Lituania y Suiza.

Glutetimida

53. Como en los últimos años, no se comunicó a la JIFE fabricación alguna de glutetimida respecto de 2005. A comienzos del decenio de 1980, se fabricaron anualmente varias docenas de toneladas de esa sustancia, en su mayor parte para transformarla en aminoglutetimida, sustancia no sicotrópica utilizada como agente antineoplásico. La fabricación mundial disminuyó sostenidamente en el decenio de 1990 y se detuvo en 1998. Desde entonces, han comunicado la fabricación de la sustancia únicamente Hungría, que fabricó unos 700 kilogramos de glutetimida en 2001, y China, que fabricó 240 kilogramos en 2005.

54. Paralelamente a la disminución de la fabricación de glutetimida, el volumen del comercio internacional de la sustancia, se redujo un nivel máximo de unas 15 toneladas por año en el período 1997-1998 hasta varios cientos de kilogramos en 2002. Desde 2003, las únicas transacciones comerciales comunicadas a la JIFE de cantidades superiores a 1 kilogramo fueron las efectuadas por Hungría, que exportó 300 kilogramos a Rumania en 2003 e importó 200 kilogramos tanto en 2004 como en 2005 de China. Bulgaria y

Suiza, que fueron los principales importadores en el decenio de 1990, no han importado glutetimida desde 2002 y 2001, respectivamente.

Flunitrazepam

55. El flunitrazepam sigue siendo una de las benzodiazepinas que con más frecuencia son objeto de uso indebido. El mercado ilícito de flunitrazepam parece abastecerse principalmente mediante la desviación de la sustancia de los canales de distribución internos y no del comercio internacional. Los preparados de flunitrazepam se suelen pasar de contrabando de los países en que se ha producido la desviación a otros países en que existe un mercado ilícito para ellos. Habida cuenta de las frecuentes desviaciones y del uso indebido de que era objeto, el flunitrazepam fue transferido en 1995 de la Lista IV a la Lista III. Varios países, incluidos los principales fabricantes e importadores de la sustancia, han adoptado políticas rigurosas de fiscalización del flunitrazepam, en estrecha cooperación con la industria farmacéutica.

56. Al igual que el diazepam, el flunitrazepam se utiliza para fines terapéuticos con la finalidad de tratar el insomnio por períodos breves y, en algunos países, como medicación para la preparación e inducción de la anestesia general. Hasta 1996, varios países, entre ellos la Argentina, el Brasil, Dinamarca, España, Italia, el Japón, la República Checa y Turquía, comunicaron la fabricación de flunitrazepam. Desde entonces, únicamente Italia y Suiza, que comenzaron a fabricar la sustancia en 1997, siguieron fabricándola. Si bien en 2004, la fabricación de esos dos países en conjunto ascendió a más de 1,5 toneladas, el volumen de flunitrazepam más alto que jamás se haya comunicado, en 2005 la fabricación mundial de la sustancia bajó a 84 kilogramos, su nivel más bajo hasta ahora. La disminución se produjo debido a que Suiza dejó de fabricar flunitrazepam en 2005 debido a las cuantiosas existencias de la sustancia que aún conservaba (véanse las figuras 22 y 23 y el párrafo 105 *infra*.)

57. El comercio internacional de flunitrazepam se mantuvo relativamente estable en el período 1990-2003, fluctuando en torno a las 1,1 toneladas por año. En 2004, el comercio comenzó a disminuir y siguió descendiendo hasta reducirse a 700 kilogramos en 2005. A Suiza, el principal país exportador de la sustancia desde 1997, e Italia les correspondió en conjunto el 96% de las exportaciones mundiales en 2005. Además, en ese año, algunos países reexportaron flunitrazepam, en particular Alemania, el Brasil, Francia, Irlanda y la República Checa.

58. Las importaciones mundiales de flunitrazepam, que alcanzaron el nivel máximo de más de 1,4 toneladas en 1995, han disminuido a un ritmo constante desde entonces, muy probablemente gracias a las estrictas medidas de fiscalización nacional y a la transferencia de la sustancia, en 1995, a la Lista III del Convenio de 1971. El Japón sigue siendo el principal país importador de flunitrazepam, correspondiéndole más de la mitad del volumen anual mundial de importaciones (421 kilogramos en 2005). Además, 25 países comunicaron importaciones de flunitrazepam en cantidades superiores a 1 kilogramo, incluidos, Alemania, Australia, Austria, Bélgica, el Brasil, Francia, Grecia, la República de Corea y Suecia, que comunicaron importaciones de entre 10 kilogramos y 40 kilogramos.

Analgésicos

Buprenorfina

59.   La buprenorfina[6], que figura en la Lista III desde 1989, pertenece a la familia de los opioides utilizados principalmente como analgésicos. La buprenorfina se emplea también en varios países para en la desintoxicación y el tratamiento de sustitución que se practican en casos de adicción a la heroína. La fabricación total de la sustancia, que ha venido aumentando sostenidamente desde 1993, alcanzó una media de cerca de 2 toneladas en el período 2003-2005, cifra que representa el doble de la cantidad fabricada a fines del decenio de 1990, cuando la sustancia comenzó a utilizarse en dosis más altas para el tratamiento de la adicción a los opioides. Al Reino Unido, que continuó siendo el principal fabricante de buprenorfina, le correspondió, en promedio, el 75% del total mundial durante el período de 2001-2005; la fabricación de la sustancia por ese país aumentó considerablemente, pasando de 274 kilogramos en 1996 a 1.542 kilogramos en 2005. El segundo fabricante en importancia de buprenorfina durante los últimos cinco años fue Australia, que fabricó 383 kilogramos en 2005, destinados principalmente a exportación. La fabricación en ese país ha venido aumentando desde 1999, cuando la notificó por primera vez. La India ha sido también un fabricante regular de buprenorfina, con una fabricación media anual de 15 kilogramos durante el período 2001-2005. En 2005, entre otros fabricantes de buprenorfina figuraron los Países Bajos (30 kilogramos), Bélgica (12 kilogramos), la República Checa (10 kilogramos) y China (9,5 kilogramos). Como era de prever, las existencias totales de la sustancia aumentaron también acentuadamente pasando de 115 kilogramos en 1996 a 1.614 kilogramos en 2005. En 2005, las existencias de buprenorfina estaban principalmente en poder del Reino Unido (728 kilogramos), Alemania (246 kilogramos), Francia (192 kilogramos), Australia (108 kilogramos) y los Países Bajos (49 kilogramos).

60.   El total de las exportaciones de buprenorfina aumentó considerablemente, pasando de 100 kilogramos en 1996 a 1.236 kilogramos en 2005. Esa tendencia obedeció al aumento de las exportaciones de buprenorfina provenientes de Alemania, Australia y el Reino Unido, los exportadores principales de la sustancia. Bélgica, Dinamarca, Francia, la India y los Países Bajos han comunicado también exportaciones de buprenorfina en años recientes.

61.   Alemania y Francia fueron los importadores más grandes (correspondiéndoles el 60% de las importaciones totales) entre los 43 países que comunicaron importaciones anuales de más de 1 kilogramos de buprenorfina en el período 2001-2005. Otros importadores importantes de buprenorfina en 2005 fueron los Estados Unidos (176 kilogramos), España (70 kilogramos), Italia (57 kilogramos), Bélgica (24 kilogramos), Portugal (13 kilogramos), Suiza (12 kilogramos) y Malasia (11 kilogramos), importaciones destinadas en todos los casos al consumo interno. Se refleja un mayor aumento del empleo de la sustancia en los informes estadísticos recibidos de Alemania, Australia, Austria, Bélgica, España, los Estados Unidos, Francia, Italia, Malasia, Portugal, el Reino Unido, la República Checa, Suecia y Suiza, al mismo tiempo han comunicado también la utilización en pequeñas cantidades con ese propósito varios países, entre ellos China, Dinamarca, Estonia, Finlandia, Grecia, Islandia, India, Indonesia, Irlanda, Israel, Letonia, México, Noruega, Pakistán y Singapur.

Pentazocina

62.   La pentazocina es un analgésico opioide de acción análoga a la de la morfina y que se utiliza con fines similares. Fue incluida en la Lista III en 1984. La fabricación total comunicada de pentazocina mostró marcadas fluctuaciones en el período 1996-2005, con una media anual de 4,5 toneladas. En 2005, la fabricación estuvo encabezada por la India (3.027 kilogramos) e Italia (1.446 kilogramos). Mientras que prácticamente toda la fabricación de la India estaba destinada al consumo interno, toda la pentazocina fabricada en Italia se destinó a la exportación. En 2005, a Italia le correspondió más del 50% de las exportaciones mundiales de pentazocina. Otros tres países, Hungría (136 kilogramos en 2001), el Reino Unido (258 kilogramos en 2002) y los Estados Unidos (171 kilogramos en 2001 y 316 kilogramos en 2002), han fabricado también la sustancia en años recientes, aunque en cantidades muchos más pequeñas. Las existencias totales de pentazocina fluctuaron también durante el período 2001-2005, con una media de 3,4 toneladas. Además de los fabricantes principales, la India e Italia, unos pocos países comunicaron que mantenían grandes existencias de la sustancia a fines de 2005: los Estados Unidos (762 kilogramos), el Pakistán (357 kilogramos) y Eslovenia (173 kilogramos).

63.   Los principales importadores de pentazocina en 2005 fueron los Estados Unidos (1.357 kilogramos), el Pakistán (598 kilogramos), el Japón (450 kilogramos), el Canadá (177 kilogramos) y Nigeria (120 kilogramos). Importaron también cantidades significativas Suiza (451 kilogramos) y Portugal (229 kilogramos), principalmente para la reexportación. Entre los principales consumidores de pentazocina se contaban el Canadá, la India, el Japón, Nigeria, el Pakistán y los Estados Unidos.

Sustancias incluidas en la Lista IV

64.   Según los criterios adoptados por la OMS para la inclusión de sustancias en la Lista IV del Convenio de 1971, se incluirán en esa Lista sustancias cuyo consumo pueda ser abusivo y significar un menor riesgo para la salud pública que las sustancias incluidas en la Lista III y cuyo valor terapéutico varíe entre escaso y grande. En la Lista IV figuran 63 sustancias que tienen diversas aplicaciones en medicina. Las sustancias incluidas en esa Lista pertenecen a los siguientes grupos: estimulantes del sistema nervioso central (14 sustancias); ansiolíticos de tipo benzodiazepínico (22 sustancias); otros ansiolíticos (1 sustancia); sedantes hipnóticos de tipo benzodiazepínico (11 sustancias); antiepilépticos de tipo benzodiazepínico (1 sustancia); barbitúricos empleados como sedantes hipnóticos y antiepilépticos (7 sustancias); otros sedantes hipnóticos (5 sustancias); analgésicos (1 sustancia) y antidepresivos (1 sustancia).

---

[6] Para los detalles, véase el cuadro IV.

Estimulantes del sistema nervioso central

65. En la Lista IV figuran los 14 estimulantes siguientes: anfepramona, aminorex, benzfetamina, etilanfetamina, fencanfamina, fendimetracina, fenproporex, fentermina, mazindol, mefenorex, mesocarbo, pemolina, pipradrol y pirovalerona. Sólo la anfepramona y el pipradrol habían sido incluidos originalmente en la Lista, mientras que todos los demás estimulantes se fueron añadiendo posteriormente. Los estimulantes de la Lista IV se utilizan esencialmente como anorexígenos o para el tratamiento del trastorno de la concentración.

66. La fabricación total comunicada de estimulantes del sistema nervioso central que figuran en la Lista IV registró fluctuaciones extremas a finales del decenio de 1990 y se estabilizó en una media anual de cerca de 1.800 millones de S-DDD durante el período 2000-2005 (véase la figura 11). En 1996 la fabricación alcanzó un volumen sin precedentes (3.900 millones de S-DDD). Empezó a disminuir en 1997 y descendió a un volumen sin precedentes en 1998 (356 millones de S-DDD). Después de 1998, la fabricación total comunicada aumentó gradualmente, alcanzando a nivel mundial la cifra de 2.200 millones de S-DDD en 2001. Aunque la fabricación mundial disminuyó ligeramente, a 1.600 millones de S-DDD en 2003, aumentó gradualmente hasta alcanzar los 2.000 millones de S-DDD en 2005.

67. En 2005, de la fabricación total comunicada de los 14 estimulantes de la Lista IV, la fabricación de fentermina (923 millones de S-DDD) constituyó el 45%, la de fenproporex (474 millones de S-DDD) el 23% y la de anfepramona (371 millones de S-DDD) representó el 18% (véase la figura 12). Al mazindol (175 millones de S-DDD) y la fendimetracina (100 millones de S-DDD) les correspondieron el 9% y el 4%, respectivamente, en tanto que a la benzfetamina (10 millones de S-DDD) le correspondió el 0,5%. En 2005 no se comunicó ninguna fabricación de pemolina ni de ninguno de los demás estimulantes del sistema nervioso central incluidos en la Lista IV.

68. Las fluctuaciones de la fabricación y utilización totales comunicadas de estimulantes del sistema nervioso central incluidos en la Lista IV reflejan principalmente las novedades en la utilización de fentermina en los Estados Unidos (véase la figura 13). El marcado aumento del consumo de fentermina en los Estados Unidos en 1996 y 1997 obedeció a su formulación para el tratamiento de la obesidad en combinación con otro anorexígeno (la fenfluramina). A raíz del retiro de la fenfluramina del mercado de los Estados Unidos en septiembre de 1997 debido a sus graves efectos adversos, la utilización de fentermina disminuyó también apreciablemente. Desde 2000, la fabricación y el consumo han repuntado de nuevo y la fentermina se ha convertido una vez más en el anorexígeno más utilizado en los Estados Unidos. De los 1.900 millones de S-DDD de sustancias de este grupo utilizadas a nivel mundial en 2005, la más ampliamente utilizada fue la fentermina (795 millones de S-DDD), seguida por el fenproporex (456 millones de S-DDD), la anfepramona (378 millones de S-DDD) y la fendimetracina (87 millones de S-DDD).

69. El consumo per cápita más elevado de estimulantes de la Lista IV en el decenio de 1990 se registró en América. La disminución temporal del consumo de fentermina en los Estados Unidos y las medidas adoptadas contra el uso inapropiado de algunos estimulantes en varios países de América del Sur (en particular, en la Argentina y Chile) se tradujo en la disminución de las tasas de consumo. Sin embargo, desde 2000 el consumo de fentermina en los Estados Unidos ha venido aumentando de nuevo. Al mismo tiempo, el consumo de estimulantes de la Lista IV continúo aumentando significativamente en algunos países de América (como la Argentina, el Brasil y los Estados Unidos. En general, durante el período 2003-2005, se consumieron en América, en promedio, 10,4 S-DDD por cada 1.000 habitantes por día (véase la figura 14).

Figura 11. Estimulantes del sistema nervioso central incluidos en la Lista IV: fabricación total comunicada, 1996 a 2005

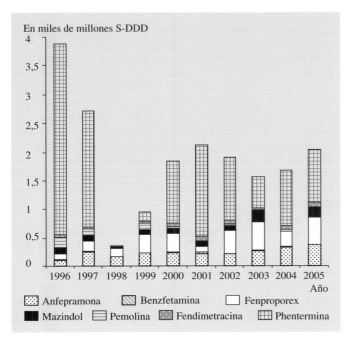

Figura 12. Estimulantes del sistema nervioso central incluidos en la Lista IV: fabricación total comunicada de diversas sustancias, 2005

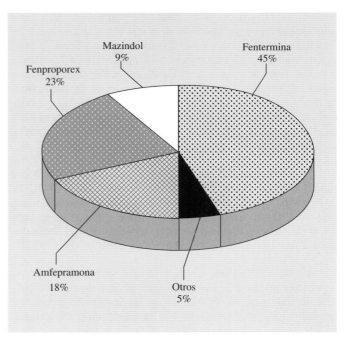

Figura 13. Estimulantes del sistema nervioso central incluidos en la Lista IV: consumo mundial calculado[a], 1996 a 2005

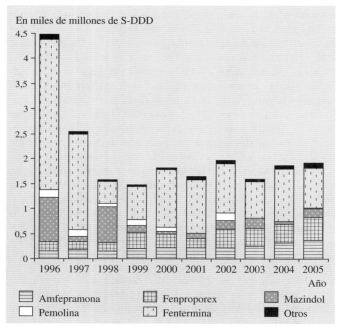

En miles de millones de S-DDD

Año

- ⊟ Amfepramona
- ⊞ Fenproporex
- ▨ Mazindol
- ☐ Pemolina
- ⣿ Fentermina
- ■ Otros

[a] Para calcular el consumo mundial aproximado de cada año se utiliza la información estadística presentada por los gobiernos. Las cifras se expresan en dosis diarias definidas con fines estadísticos (S-DDD).

Figura 14. Estimulantes del sistema nervioso central incluidos en la Lista IV: consumo nacional medio por regiones[a], 1997 a 1999, 2000 a 2002 y 2003 a 2005

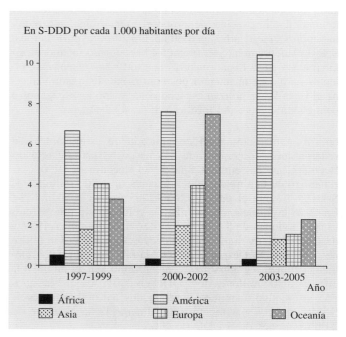

En S-DDD por cada 1.000 habitantes por día

Año

- ■ África
- ⊟ América
- ▨ Asia
- ⊞ Europa
- ▨ Oceanía

[a] Para calcular el consumo medio anual en un trienio se utiliza la información estadística proporcionada por los gobiernos.

70. En el resto del mundo se experimentó una disminución del consumo de esos estimulantes. En Asia la tasa de consumo aumentó ligeramente entre finales del decenio de 1990 y el período 2000-2002, en particular en Malasia, la República de Corea y Singapur. Sin embargo, la tasa media anual de consumo fue 32% más baja durante el período 2003-2005: 1,7 S-DDD por cada 1.000 habitantes por día. En forma similar, en Europa, tras tasas de consumo relativamente estables durante el período 1997-2002, la tasa media disminuyó de 4 S-DDD a 1,6 S-DDD por cada 1.000 habitantes por día en el período 2003-2005. Ese cambio es atribuible principalmente a la marcada disminución del consumo de fentermina en Bélgica y en el Reino Unido, así como al consumo más bajo de fenproporex y anfrepramona en Alemania, Bélgica, Dinamarca y Suiza. La disminución de la tasa calculada de consumo fue aún más dramática en Oceanía, donde disminuyó de 7,5 a 2,3 S-DDD durante el mismo período. Esa disminución se debió a la reducción del 72% y el 76% en el consumo de fentermina en Australia y Nueva Zelandia, respectivamente.

71. A nivel mundial, en 2005 el Brasil (12,5 S-DDD por cada 1.000 habitantes por día), la Argentina (11,8 S-DDD), la República de Corea (9,8 S-DDD) y los Estados Unidos (4,9 S-DDD) tuvieron las tasas calculadas más altas de consumo de estimulantes del sistema nervioso central incluidos en la Lista IV.

72. La fentermina ha sido la principal sustancia del grupo de estimulantes de la Lista IV y, en años recientes, su porcentaje del total de estimulantes fabricados ha fluctuado ampliamente, entre cero y 76%. La fabricación total comunicada de esta sustancia aumentó de un promedio de 9,5 tone-

ladas anuales durante el período 1991-1995 a 50 toneladas en 1996, el volumen más alto comunicado hasta entonces. A partir de 1996, la fabricación mundial comunicada ha fluctuado entre 2,6 toneladas y 30 toneladas, con una media de 14,2 toneladas en el período 2004-2005, siendo los principales fabricantes Alemania, Italia y los Estados Unidos.

73. Diez países han comunicado que exportaron por lo menos 100 kilogramos de fentermina como mínimo una vez en el período 2001-2005. Alemania fue una vez más el mayor exportador de la sustancia en 2005 (4,4 toneladas), seguida por Italia (3,5 toneladas), los Estados Unidos (3 toneladas), Australia, Suiza y los Países Bajos, correspondiendo a los tres primeros países el 84% de las exportaciones mundiales. Cuarenta y seis países comunicaron importaciones de fentermina por lo menos una vez durante el quinquenio 2001-2005. A los Estados Unidos, que fueron el principal importador de la sustancia en 2005 (5,3 toneladas), les correspondió el 47% de las importaciones mundiales, de las que reexportaron más de la mitad. Los otros importadores principales de fentermina en 2005 fueron la República de Corea (2,2 toneladas) y Australia (1,1 toneladas), y el total combinado de esos dos países aumentó en el 23% con respecto al año anterior.

74. El fenproporex, sustancia que fue sometida a fiscalización internacional en 1986, se utiliza principalmente como inhibidor del apetito. Desde 1986, sólo el Brasil, Francia y Suiza y más recientemente, Alemania y la India han comunicado su fabricación. Tras un crecimiento sostenido, de 3 toneladas en 1998 a 10 toneladas en 2003, la fabricación total comunicada de fenproporex disminuyó a 5 toneladas en 2004. Sin embargo, en 2005 la producción

96

mundial aumentó en el 82%, hasta alcanzar las 9,5 toneladas. Alemania y el Brasil fueron los únicos fabricantes de la sustancia en 2005, correspondiendo al Brasil el 87% del total. En el período 1995-1999, la fabricación de fenproporex en Francia varió considerablemente, situándose en una media de alrededor de 1,3 toneladas al año, lo que representa una reducción considerable de la media anual de cerca de 3 toneladas en ese país en el período 1992-1994. La última vez que Francia comunicó la fabricación de fenproporex fue en 2003 (2,6 toneladas), en tanto que Suiza lo hizo por última vez en 2000 (4,9 toneladas). El fenproporex fabricado en el Brasil se destinaba al consumo interno y ese país fue también el principal importador de la sustancia en 2005 (1,6 toneladas), correspondiéndole el 98% de las importaciones mundiales.

75. En 2005, el total de la fabricación comunicada de anfepramona, sustancia que se utiliza principalmente como anorexígeno, ascendió a cerca de 28 toneladas. Tres países comunicaron la fabricación de anfepramona en 2005: el Brasil (27,6 toneladas), Italia (251 kilogramos) y Suiza (22 kilogramos). el volumen de fabricación de Suiza ha disminuido considerablemente desde 2004, año en que fabricó 3,9 toneladas de anfepramona. Sin embargo, Suiza sigue siendo, con mucho, el principal exportador de la sustancia y sus exportaciones aumentaron de una media anual de 2,8 toneladas durante el período 2002-2004 a 5,8 toneladas en 2005. Alemania, Italia y el Brasil fueron los otros exportadores principales de anfepramona. Mientras que Italia exportó casi toda la sustancia que fabricó, la anfepramona fabricada en el Brasil se destinó casi exclusivamente al consumo interno. El Brasil fue, con mucho, el principal país consumidor (5,3 S-DDD por cada 1.000 habitantes por día); en 2005, el consumo de la sustancia en el Brasil representó el 90% del total mundial. Las importaciones más grandes de anfepramona en 2005 fueron comunicadas por los Estados Unidos (1,4 toneladas), Alemania (1,2 toneladas) y Suiza (913 kilogramos). Otros 16 países comunicaron importaciones de anfepramona en cantidades superiores a 1 kilogramos en 2005, y de ellos dos comunicaron importaciones de más de 200 kilogramos: Chile (297 kilogramos) y Australia (255 kilogramos).

76. Italia fue el principal fabricante de fendimetracina. En 2005, la fabricación mundial de esa sustancia ascendió a 7 toneladas, un aumento del 44% respecto del año anterior. Los únicos otros fabricantes de la sustancia en 2005 fueron China (700 kilogramos para la exportación) y Alemania (5 kilogramos). Los Estados Unidos comunicaron la fabricación de fendimetracina en 1999 y 2001 únicamente, en cantidades comparativamente pequeñas (560 kilogramos y 274 kilogramos, respectivamente). La fendimetracina fabricada en Italia está destinada principalmente a la exportación (80% en 2005). Los Estados Unidos han sido tradicionalmente el principal importador de la sustancia (3,1 toneladas en 2005), seguidos por la República de Corea (1,7 toneladas anuales en el período 2004-2005, un aumento de 20 veces desde 2001). Desde 2000, otros cinco países han comunicado importaciones de fendimetracina en cantidades de más de 1 kilogramo: Colombia, Dinamarca, Italia, Malasia y Sudáfrica. De los países que han comunicado la utilización de fendimetracina en 2005, la República de Corea fue, con mucho, el consumidor más importante de la sustancia (1,4 S-DDD por cada 1.000 habitantes por día), seguida por Italia (0,7 S-DDD), Malasia (0,6 S-DDD), los Estados Unidos (0,4 S-DDD) y otros tres países.

77. La fabricación mundial de pemolina, sustancia sometida a fiscalización internacional desde 1989, fluctuó considerablemente durante el período 1996-2005. La producción mundial ascendió a un total de 8,7 toneladas en 1995 y disminuyó luego marcadamente, a 4,6 toneladas en 1997. No se comunicó fabricación de la sustancia en 1998 ni en 2005. En 2001, únicamente los Estados Unidos comunicaron la fabricación de la sustancia (35 kilogramos). Tanto en 2002 como en 2004, Suiza comunicó la fabricación de cerca 1,1 toneladas de pemolina. Los únicos otros fabricantes de la sustancia en el período 2001-2005 fueron los Estados Unidos (465 kilogramos en 2002) y China (6 kilogramos en 2003). Los únicos exportadores de la sustancia en 2005 fueron Suiza (312 kilogramos) y los Países Bajos (128 kilogramos). Los principales importadores de pemolina en 2005 fueron los Estados Unidos (300 kilogramos), Alemania (45 kilogramos), Suiza (23 kilogramos), los Países Bajos (21 kilogramos) y Chile (15 kilogramos). Además de su utilización como estimulante, la pemolina se emplea también para el tratamiento del trastorno de la concentración.

78. El mazindol se ha fabricado hasta ahora casi exclusivamente en el Brasil: una media de 75 kilogramos durante el período 1999-2003, de los que casi la mitad se destinaba al consumo interno y el resto a la exportación. Otros dos países comunicaron la fabricación de mazindol en el período 1996-2005: Polonia en 1998 (25 kilogramos) y 1999 (1 kilogramo) y la Argentina en 2002 (22 kilogramos), 2003 (165 kilogramos) y 2005 (175 kilogramos). En 2004 no se comunicó ninguna fabricación de la sustancia. La utilización de mazindol a nivel mundial disminuyó marcadamente, de 702 kilogramos en 1998 a una media anual de 150 kilogramos durante el período de 2001-2005. Durante el mismo período, 17 países comunicaron haber importado mazindol en cantidades de por lo menos 1 kilogramo, siendo los principales importadores México (49% de las importaciones mundiales) y Suiza (28%). En 2005, el Japón (3 kilogramos) y Suiza (1 kilogramo) fueron los únicos importadores de mazindol.

79. En el período 1997-2004, sólo los Estados Unidos comunicaron la fabricación de benzfetamina, que fue en promedio de 1,1 toneladas anuales durante el período 2000-2004. En 2005, los Estados Unidos fabricaron 729 kilogramos de benzfetamina y Suiza fabricó 29 kilogramos. Desde 1997, no se ha comunicado ningún comercio internacional de benzfetamina, salvo la importación de 31 kilogramos de la sustancia por el Perú en 2003. En el período 2004-2005, el consumo de benzfetamina tuvo lugar únicamente en los Estados Unidos: 1,2 toneladas en 2004 y 1,8 toneladas en 2005.

80. La fabricación y el comercio comunicados de los demás estimulantes incluidos en la Lista IV han sido esporádicos. Desde 1995, únicamente Francia ha comunicado la fabricación de pipradrol: 20 kilogramos en 1999 y 8 kilogramos en 2004, de los cuales 2 kilogramos se exportaron al Canadá. Australia comunicó importaciones de 2 kilogramos de pipradrol en 1999 y 2002 y la fabricación de 3 kilogramos de etilanfetamina (para consumo interno) en 2002. En el período 2001-2005, no se comunicó ninguna fabricación de aminorex, fencanfamina, mefenorex, mesocarbo o pirovalerona. Se comunicaron pequeñas transacciones comerciales ocasionales de benzfetamina, fencanfamina, mefenorex y pipradrol, mientras que no se comunicó ningún comercio internacional de aminorex, etilanfetamina, mesocarbo y pirovalerona.

Benzodiazepinas

81. En 1984 se incluyeron 33 benzodiazepinas en la Lista IV. El midazolam fue agregado a la Lista en 1990 y el brotizolam en 1995. El flunitrazepam fue trasladado en 1995 de la Lista IV a la Lista III.

82. El número de países y territorios que comunican la fabricación y el comercio de benzodiazepinas, o ambas cosas, ha venido aumentando considerablemente. Desde 1990, cerca de 200 países y territorios han comunicado por lo menos una vez la fabricación o el comercio de benzodiazepinas en cantidades de más de 1 kilogramo. No se disponía de información completa sobre la fabricación y el comercio de benzodiazepinas a nivel mundial hasta hace poco, cuando varios importantes países fabricantes y exportadores o importadores implantaron medidas de fiscalización nacional de esas sustancias. Suiza ha suministrado datos sobre las benzodiazepinas únicamente desde 1997, Austria desde 1998, Bélgica en 1999 y el Canadá en 2001.

Ansiolíticos de tipo benzodiazepínico

83. Hay 22 benzodiazepinas que se suelen clasificar como ansiolíticos. La fabricación total comunicada de sustancias de ese grupo aumentó sostenidamente entre 1996 y 2001, cuando alcanzó su volumen más alto de 29.000 millones de S-DDD. La fabricación a nivel mundial disminuyó luego ligeramente, a un total de 22.000 millones de S-DDD en 2005 (véase la figura 15). Las fluctuaciones del volumen de fabricación de ansiolíticos de tipo benzodiazepínico suelen reflejar las fluctuaciones de la fabricación de diazepam, la principal sustancia de ese grupo, que en 2005 representó el 31% (o 6.900 millones de S-DDD) del total. En ese mismo año, el porcentaje correspondiente al alprazolam (6.600 millones de S-DDD) aumentó al 30%, al tiempo que la fabricación de

lorazepam (4.200 millones de S-DDD) representó el 19% de la producción mundial. El bromazepam, el clordiazepóxido y el oxazepam representaron cada uno el 3%, el clorazepato el 2% y el nordazepam el 1% de la fabricación total comunicada de ansiolíticos de tipo benzodiazepínico en 2005 (véase la figura 16). A cada una de las 12 sustancias restantes de ese grupo (clobazam, clotiazepam, cloxazolam, delorazepam, loflazepato de etilo, fludiazepam, halazepam, ketazolam,

Figura 16. Ansiolíticos de tipo benzodiazepínico: porcentaje de la fabricación total comunicada, 2005

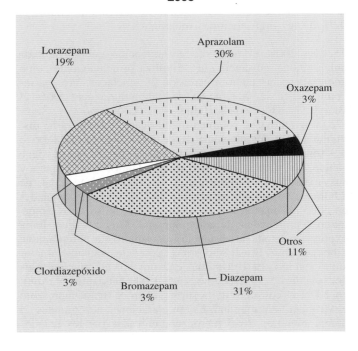

Figura 15. Ansiolíticos de tipo benzodiazepínico: fabricación total comunicada, 1996 a 2005

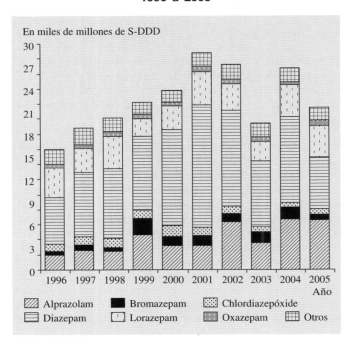

Figura 17. Ansiolíticos de tipo benzodiazepínico: porcentaje de la fabricación total comunicada correspondiente a cada país, 2005

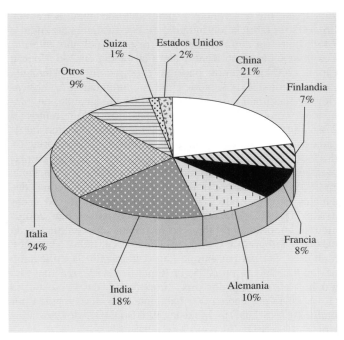

medazepam, pinazepam, prazepam y tetrazepam) correspondió menos del 1% de la fabricación total comunicada calculada en S-DDD. En 2005 no se comunicó ninguna fabricación de camazepam ni oxazepam. Como se observa en las figuras 17 y 18, China e Italia fueron los principales fabricantes de ansiolíticos de tipo benzodiazepínico en el decenio 1995-2004 y en 2005, a estos dos países correspondió, junto con la India y Alemania, el 73% de la fabricación total.

Figura 18.   Ansiolíticos de tipo benzodiazepínico: fabricación comunicada por determinados países, 1996 a 2005

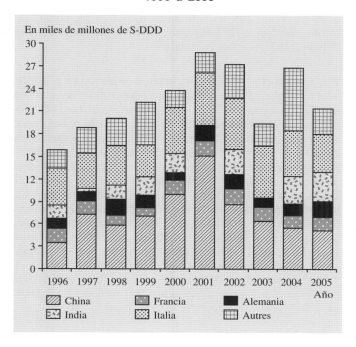

Figura 19.   Ansiolíticos de tipo benzodiazepínico: consumo mundial calculado, 1996-2005[a]

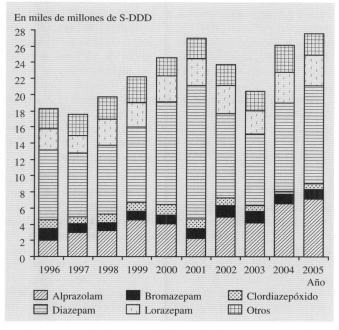

[a] Para calcular el consumo mundial aproximado de cada año se utiliza la información estadística proporcionada por los gobiernos. Las cifras del consumo se expresan en dosis diarias definidas con fines estadísticos (S-DDD).

84.   Aunque los niveles aproximados de consumo, calculados por la JIFE, suelen guardar relación con la tendencia de la fabricación, en 2005 el consumo total de este grupo de sustancias ascendió a 27.700 millones de S-DDD (véase la figura 19), cifra considerablemente mayor a la de la cantidad fabricada ese año. El consumo nacional medio calculado de los ansiolíticos de tipo benzodiazepínico es mayor en Europa que en las demás regiones (véase la figura 20).

Figura 20.   Ansiolíticos de tipo benzodiazepínico: consumo nacional medio[a]**, por región, 1997 a 1999, 2000 a 2002 y 2003 a 2005**

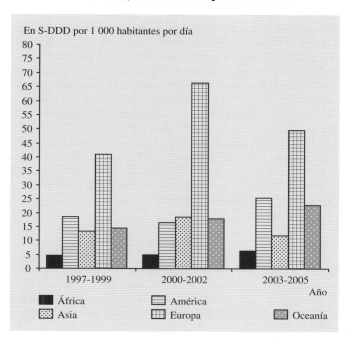

[a] Para calcular el consumo mundial aproximado de cada año se utiliza la información estadística proporcionada por los gobiernos. Las cifras del consumo se expresan en dosis diarias definidas con fines estadísticos (S-DDD).

Diazepam

85.   El diazepam, la sustancia del grupo de los ansiolíticos de tipo benzodiacepínico que más se vende, se consume en todas las regiones del mundo. Durante el período 1990-1999, la fabricación mundial de diazepam siguió una tendencia ascendente, con una media de más de 76 toneladas al año. Durante el período 2000-2004, la fabricación mundial fue en promedio de 123 toneladas. En 2005, disminuyó a 69 toneladas, debido principalmente a que los Estados Unidos, tras haber fabricado más de 29 toneladas de diazepam en 2004, no fabricaron la sustancia en 2005. China, que ha sido tradicionalmente el principal fabricante y exportador de esa sustancia y a la que correspondió cerca del 70% de la fabricación mundial durante el período 2000-2004, fabricó 45 toneladas en 2005. Italia comunicó en 2005 el segundo volumen de fabricación, que ascendió a 12 toneladas. Además, el Brasil y la India comunicaron la fabricación de cantidades de diazepam del orden de toneladas. Suiza, que desde 1997 había fabricado anualmente varias toneladas de diazepam, no fabricó dicha sustancia en 2005. Polonia y la Federación de Rusia fabricaron varios cientos de kilogramos de diazepam.

86. Los volúmenes de exportación disminuyeron ligeramente, de 61 toneladas en 2004 a 60 toneladas en 2005. Con 21 toneladas, a China le correspondió el 35% de esa cantidad. Las exportaciones de Italia se mantuvieron estables, en más de 16 toneladas en 2005, y Suiza exportó 7 toneladas.

87. El diazepam es objeto de amplio consumo y cerca de 120 países y territorios comunicaron importaciones en cantidades de más de 1 kilogramo cada año. En 2005, los mayores importadores fueron Dinamarca (6,7 toneladas), Alemania (4,2 toneladas), los Estados Unidos (3,6 toneladas), Suiza (2,8 toneladas) y España (2 toneladas), países a los que correspondió en conjunto más del 40% de las importaciones mundiales. Importaron cantidades de entre 1 y 2 toneladas, en orden del volumen de importación, el Pakistán, Ghana, Irlanda, el Canadá, la República Islámica del Irán, Tailandia y Nigeria. España, anteriormente el principal importador de diazepam, redujo sus importaciones de la sustancia de 29 toneladas (utilizadas principalmente para aplicaciones veterinarias) en 1989 a 10 toneladas en 1997 y a 2 toneladas en 2005. El consumo mundial de diazepam se mantuvo estable, ascendiendo a 12.000 millones de S-DDD en 2005. De acuerdo con las cifras de consumo calculado, los principales consumidores de esa sustancia en el mundo fueron el Reino Unido (5.200 millones de S-DDD), China (2.500 millones de S-DDD), los Estados Unidos (664 millones de S-DDD) y el Brasil (611 millones de-S-DDD).

Alprazolam

88. La fabricación total comunicada de alprazolam creció sostenidamente, pasando de 1 tonelada en 1986 a 6,7 toneladas en 2005. Después de 2002, la producción mundial se mantuvo en más de 6 toneladas cada año, con excepción de 2003, cuando disminuyó a 3,6 toneladas debido a que los Estados Unidos no fabricaron la sustancia. Las fluctuaciones del volumen de fabricación mundial reflejan, en gran medida, los volúmenes de fabricación en la India y en los Estados Unidos, que son los principales fabricantes de alprazolam. En 2005, la India fabricó 2,3 toneladas, la mayor cantidad fabricada hasta ahora en ese país, mientras que la producción de los Estados Unidos disminuyó de 1,7 toneladas en 2004 a 302 kilogramos en 2005. En 2005, Italia fabricó 1,5 toneladas; Finlandia, 1,2 toneladas; y Francia, alrededor de 1 tonelada. A esos países correspondió en conjunto el 94% de la fabricación mundial de alprazolam en 2005. Fueron asimismo los principales exportadores de la sustancia, correspondiéndoles en conjunto más del 74% de las exportaciones totales en 2005.

89. En 2005, más de 70 países y territorios de todas las regiones del mundo comunicaron importaciones de alprazolam en cantidades superiores a 1 kilogramo. El total de las importaciones aumentó de 1,6 toneladas en 1998 a una media anual de 5,7 toneladas en el período 1999-2004 y alcanzó una nueva cifra sin precedentes en 2004 (6,8 toneladas); a ello siguió una producción ligeramente más baja en 2005, con 6,7 toneladas. En 2005, los principales importadores de alprazolam fueron los Estados Unidos (2 toneladas), Bélgica (970 kilogramos) y España (628 kilogramos), a los que correspondió en conjunto más del 53% del volumen total de importaciones. El consumo a nivel mundial durante el período 2000-2005 fue en promedio de 4.800 millones de S-DDD y los Estados Unidos siguieron siendo el mayor consumidor (1.800 millones de S-DDD en 2005).

Lorazepam

90. La fabricación total comunicada de lorazepam disminuyó de 11,1 toneladas en 2001 a 6,5 toneladas en 2003, volumen comparable al volumen medio registrado durante el período 1999-2000. En 2004, los volúmenes de fabricación aumentaron de nuevo, y alcanzaron más de 10 toneladas tanto en 2004 como en 2005. Esas fluctuaciones son atribuibles a cambios significativos en los volúmenes de fabricación de Italia y Alemania, los dos principales fabricantes de lorazepam. En 2005, Italia y Alemania fabricaron más de 5 toneladas y 3 toneladas, respectivamente. Junto con la India (1,6 toneladas), a esos países correspondió alrededor del 97% de la fabricación total. Otros países que comunicaron la fabricación de lorazepam en 2005 fueron el Brasil y Polonia (105 kilogramos cada uno).

91. Las exportaciones de lorazepam ascendieron en promedio a 10 toneladas al año en el período 2000-2004 y aumentaron a 11,7 toneladas en 2005. Alemania e Italia han sido los principales exportadores de la sustancia. A esos países, junto con Irlanda, un importante reexportador, les correspondió más del 80% de las exportaciones totales de la sustancia en 2005. Aproximadamente 100 países importaron más de 1 kilogramo de lorazepam al menos una vez durante el período 2001-2005. De esos países, los Estados Unidos e Irlanda importaron la mayor parte, y sus importaciones combinadas de la sustancia representaron el 40% del total. Entre los otros importadores principales de lorazepam en 2005 figuran España (924 kilogramos), Francia (758 kilogramos) y Alemania (742 kilogramos). El consumo mundial calculado fue en promedio de 3.500 millones de S-DDD en el período 2001-2005, siendo Alemania el principal consumidor (987 millones de S-DDD en 2005).

Bromazepam

92. La fabricación total comunicada de bromazepam fluctuó considerablemente en el período 1999-2005. Tras haber aumentado marcadamente de una media anual de 6 toneladas durante el período 1997-1998, la producción mundial de la sustancia alcanzó su volumen máximo de más de 21 toneladas en 1999 y disminuyó a una media de 13,5 toneladas en los años posteriores. En 2005, la producción mundial disminuyó a 7,3 toneladas. Esa disminución se debió a que Suiza, el principal fabricante desde 1998 (en promedio 7,8 toneladas por año), no fabricó bromazepam en 2005, a causa de las elevadas existencias que mantenía. Por ello, en 2005 el principal fabricante fue Italia (4,8 toneladas), seguida por el Brasil (1,6 toneladas) y la India (554 kilogramos).

93. En 2005, las exportaciones mundiales de bromazepam, que ascendieron a 15,0 toneladas, se mantuvieron ligeramente por debajo de la media de 15,4 toneladas al año registrada en el período 1997-2004. Al igual que en años anteriores, los principales exportadores fueron Suiza (6,8 toneladas) e Italia (5,2 toneladas), a los que correspondió en conjunto el 80% de las exportaciones totales de la sustancia. De los 84 países que comunicaron importaciones de bromazepam en cantidades de más de 1 kilogramo en 2005, a cinco correspondió el 51% de las importaciones mundiales, a saber, Francia, Suiza, el Brasil, Alemania e Italia, en ese orden. Durante el período 2000-2005, todo el bromazepam importado por Suiza e Italia fue reexportado; durante el mismo período, Francia y el Brasil

importaron bromazepam principalmente para el consumo interno, aunque también reexportaron varios cientos de kilogramos al año. El consumo mundial calculado de bromazepam, que había fluctuado en torno a los 1.300 millones de S-DDD anualmente durante el período 2000-2004, disminuyó ligeramente, a 1.200 millones de S-DDD, en 2005.

Clordiazepóxido

94. La fabricación total comunicada del clordiazepóxido disminuyó sostenidamente, de 43 toneladas en 2000 a 21 toneladas en 2005. Esa disminución refleja las reducciones de las cantidades de clordiazepóxido fabricadas en China, la India e Italia, los principales países fabricantes. En 2005, China fabricó 11 toneladas de clordiazepóxido, correspondiéndole el 52% de la producción mundial, y la India comunicó la fabricación de 6,3 toneladas (30%). La mayor parte del clordiazepóxido fabricado en China e Italia estaba destinado a la reexportación, mientras que la mayor parte de la producción de la India estaba destinada al consumo interno.

95. Las importaciones mundiales de clordiazepóxido disminuyeron de 24 toneladas en 2000 a 13 toneladas en 2005; después de 1997, más de 100 países comunicaron al menos una vez importaciones de la sustancia en cantidades superiores a 1 kilogramo. Los principales importadores de clordiazepóxido en 2005 fueron Suiza (1,7 toneladas, destinadas en su totalidad a la reexportación) y Cuba, los Estados Unidos y Egipto (1,3 toneladas, 1,2 toneladas y 1 tonelada, respectivamente, para consumo interno). En el período 2001-2005, el consumo mundial de la sustancia disminuyó de 1.200 millones de S-DDD a 678 millones de S-DDD.

Oxazepam

96. La fabricación total de oxazepam se mantuvo bastante estable en el período 1998-2002, con una media de aproximadamente 30 toneladas por año. En 2003, aumentó a 34 toneladas, disminuyó a 22 toneladas al año siguiente y alcanzó 27 toneladas en 2005. Los principales fabricantes de oxazepam en 2005 fueron Italia (14,3 toneladas) y Francia (10,4 toneladas), a los que en conjunto correspondió el 91% de la producción mundial. El volumen del comercio de oxazepam fue en promedio de alrededor de 40 toneladas anuales durante el quinquenio 2000-2005. Irlanda y Francia fueron los principales importadores de oxazepam. Mientras que Irlanda importó la sustancia principalmente para la reexportación, Francia utilizó también grandes cantidades para consumo interno, que representó el 25% del consumo mundial calculado en el período 2001-2005.

Clorazepato

97. La fabricación comunicada total de clorazepato se mantuvo estable, en una media de 8,4 toneladas durante el período 2001-2005. A Francia (5,8 toneladas) e Italia (1,1 toneladas) les correspondió el 86% de la producción total de clorazepato en 2005. Cincuenta y cuatro países importaron un total de 8,8 toneladas de clorazepato. Los principales importadores fueron España (que reexportó cerca de la mitad de sus importaciones) y Francia (que reexportó la totalidad de sus importaciones).

Clobazam

98. El total de la fabricación comunicada de clobazam disminuyó de 5,5 toneladas en 2004 a 3,5 toneladas en 2005, siendo los principales fabricantes Alemania (1,2 toneladas) y Francia (1,4 toneladas). El volumen del comercio internacional ascendió a 5 toneladas aproximadamente, y 58 países comunicaron importaciones de más de 1 kilogramo.

Otros

99. El total de la fabricación comunicada combinada de fludiazepam, halazepam, nordazepam, pinazepam y prazepam aumentó de 435 millones de S-DDD en 2004 a 478 millones de S-DDD en 2005. La fabricación combinada de camazepam, clotiazepam, cloxazolam, delorazepam, loflazepato de etilo, ketazolam, medazepam y tetrazepam aumentó de 680 millones de S-DDD en 2004 a 778 millones de S-DDD en 2005.

Otros ansiolíticos

Meprobamato

100. Debido a su sustitución gradual por las benzodiazepinas, la fabricación de meprobamato, la única sustancia de la Lista IV utilizada como ansiolítico que no es de tipo benzodiazepínico, disminuyó continuamente, pasando de un volumen sin precedentes de casi 1.000 toneladas a fines del decenio de 1970 a una media anual de un poco más de la cuarta parte de esa cantidad en el decenio 1993-2003 (véase la figura 21). La fabricación mundial disminuyó de 260 toneladas en 2003 a 103 toneladas en 2005. Esa disminución es atribuible a China, que había fabricado casi la mitad de la oferta mundial en años anteriores pero no fabricó la sustancia en 2005. A Dinamarca, el otro proveedor importante, le

Figura 21. Meprobamato: fabricación comunicada, 1996 a 2005

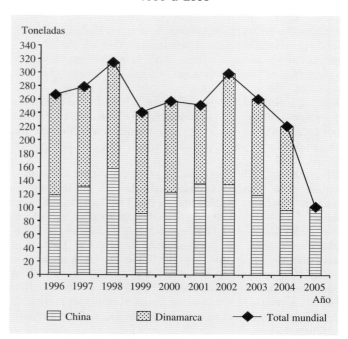

101

correspondió casi la mitad de la producción mundial en ese año. Además, la India y España reanudaron la fabricación de meprobamato después de más de diez años, y fabricaron 400 kilogramos y 107 kilogramos, respectivamente, en 2005. La mayor parte del meprobamato que fabricó Dinamarca se exportó a más de 20 países. Durante el período 2001-2005, Francia y Dinamarca mantenían el volumen más alto de existencias de meprobamato (una media anual de 53 toneladas y 48 toneladas, respectivamente). Hungría ocupó el tercer lugar, con una media de 17 toneladas. China no ha comunicado nunca datos sobre existencias de meprobamato.

101. El volumen de las importaciones de meprobamato fue en promedio de alrededor de 250 toneladas al año en el quinquenio 2001-2005; cerca de 80 países comunicaron importaciones de la sustancia al menos una vez durante ese período. Francia fue el principal importador de meprobamato, habiendo adquirido en promedio 90 toneladas al año durante el período 2001-2005, casi en su totalidad para el consumo interno. Los otros importadores principales de la sustancia en 2005 fueron Cuba (25 toneladas), Hungría (15 toneladas), Sudáfrica (14 toneladas), los Estados Unidos y Rumania (6 toneladas cada uno) y Turquía (5 toneladas).

Sedantes hipnóticos de tipo benzodiazepínico

102. Hay 12 benzodiazepinas que se suelen utilizar como sedantes hipnóticos: brotizolam, estazolam, flunitrazepam (la única benzodiazepina incluida en la Lista III), flurazepam, haloxazolam, loprazolam, lormetazepam, midazolam, nimetazepam, nitrazepam, temazepam y triazolam. Las observaciones sobre el flunitrazepam, sustancia que fue trasladada de la Lista IV a la Lista III en 1995, figuran en los párrafos 55 a 58 *supra*.

103. Tras un aumento del total de la fabricación comunicada de las 12 sustancias del grupo de una media de 6.300 millones de S-DDD al año durante el período 1997-2001 a 7.800 millones de S-DDD en 2002, los volúmenes de fabricación volvieron a su nivel anterior en el período 2003-2004, con una media de 6.400 millones de S-DDD al año. En 2005, la fabricación mundial aumentó de nuevo hasta alcanzar 7.300 millones de S-DDD, la segunda cifra más alta comunicada hasta ahora. Durante el período 1998-2002, Bélgica, el Canadá y Suiza empezaron a presentar a la JIFE informes sobre su fabricación de benzodiazepinas, con lo cual los volúmenes calculados de consumo anual se aproximan más a los volúmenes de fabricación total (véanse las figuras 22 y 23).

104. La media del consumo nacional calculada de sedantes hipnóticos del tipo de la benzodiazepina, expresada en S-DDD por cada 1.000 habitantes por año, es más alta en Europa que en las demás regiones (véase la figura 24).

105. Desde 2000, el porcentaje correspondiente al flunitrazepam en la fabricación combinada de esas 12 benzodiazepinas ha fluctuado considerablemente. Tras haber disminuido del 21% (1.400 millones de S-DDD) del total en ese año al 3% (207 millones de S-DDD) en 2001, la fabricación de flunitrazepam repuntó en 2003, alcanzó en 2004 el porcentaje más alto de ese grupo, con un 23% (1.500 millones de S-DDD), pero cayó en picado de nuevo en 2005, bajando a su volumen más bajo hasta ahora, 1% (84 millones de S-DDD). Esa disminución se debió a que Suiza, el principal fabricante de flunitrazepam, no fabricó la sustancia en 2005 (véanse también los párrafos 57 y 58 *supra*). En cambio, puesto que

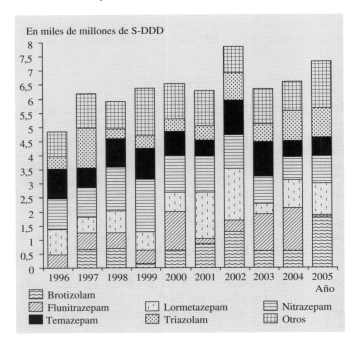

Figure 22. Sedantes hipnóticos de tipo benzodiazepínico, fabricación total comunicada, por sustancia, 1996 a 2005

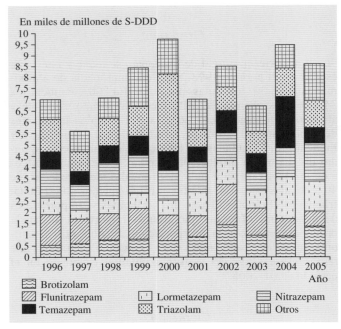

Figura 23. Sedantes hipnóticos de tipo benzodiazepínico: consumo mundial calculado[a], 1996 a 2005

[a]Para calcular el consumo mundial aproximado de cada año se utiliza la información estadística proporcionada por los gobiernos. Las cifras del consumo se expresan en dosis diarias definidas con fines estadísticos (S-DDD).

la fabricación mundial de brotizolam aumentó en más del triple entre 2004 y 2005, de 580 millones de S-DDD a 1.800 millones de S-DDD (véase el párrafo 113 *infra*), a esa sustancia le correspondió el mayor porcentaje (25%) de la fabricación total de sedantes hipnóticos de tipo benzodiazepínico en 2005. El lormetazepam ocupó el segundo lugar

Figura 24. Sedantes hipnóticos de tipo benzodiazepínico: consumo nacional medio[a], por región, 1997 a 1999; 2000 a 2002 y 2003 a 2005

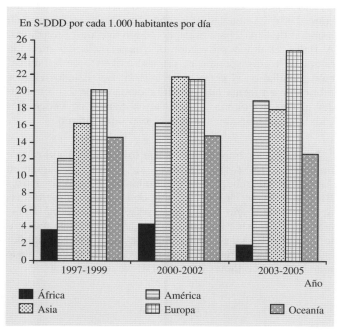

En S-DDD por cada 1.000 habitantes por día

■ África ▦ América
▦ Asia ▦ Europa ▦ Oceanía

[a] Para calcular el consumo anual medio durante un período de tres años se utiliza la información estadística presentada por los gobiernos.

Figura 26. Sedantes hipnóticos de tipo benzodiazepínico: fabricación total comunicada de determinados países, 1996 a 2005

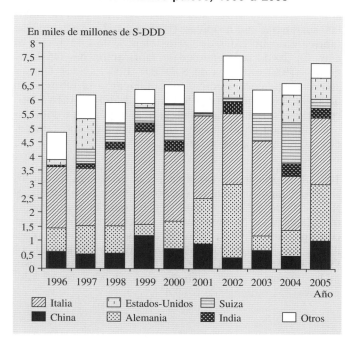

En miles de millones de S-DDD

▨ Italia ▢ Estados-Unidos ▤ Suiza
■ China ▦ Alemania ▨ India ▢ Otros

Figura 25. Sedantes hipnóticos de tipo benzodiazepínico: porcentaje de la fabricación total comunicada correspondiente a distintas sustancias, 2005

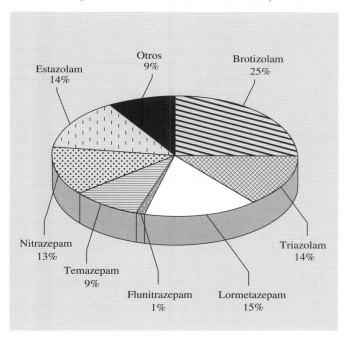

Otros 9%
Brotizolam 25%
Estazolam 14%
Nitrazepam 13%
Temazepam 9%
Flunitrazepam 1%
Lormetazepam 15%
Triazolam 14%

Figura 27. Sedantes hipnóticos de tipo benzodiazepínico: porcentajes de la fabricación total comunicada correspondiente a cada país, 2005

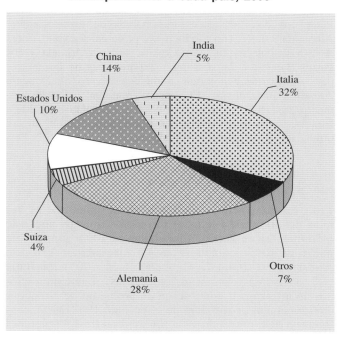

India 5%
China 14%
Estados Unidos 10%
Italia 32%
Suiza 4%
Alemania 28%
Otros 7%

con el 15% (1.100 millones de S-DDD); le siguieron el estazolam y el triazolam, con el 14% (1.000 millones de S-DDD) cada uno, el nitrazepam, con el 13% (946 millones de S-DDD) y el temazepam con el 9% (664 millones de S-DDD). Al midazolam (435 millones de S-DDD), el flurazepam (138 millones de S-DDD) y el loprazolam (72 millones de S-DDD) les correspondió en conjunto el 9% del total (véase la figura 25). La fabricación de haloxazolam y nimetazepam representó me-

nos del 1% de la fabricación mundial de sedantes hipnóticos de tipo benzodiazepínico.

106. La figura 26 muestra los principales fabricantes durante el período 1996-2005. En 2005, Italia continuó siendo el principal fabricante de ese grupo de sustancias (2.400 millones de S-DDD), correspondiéndole el 32% de la fabricación mundial (véase la figura 27).

Triazolam

107. El triazolam es un hipnótico potente que, junto con el brotizolam, registra la S-DDD más baja de todas las sustancias sicotrópicas (0,25 mg). La sustancia se fabrica en cantidades de varios cientos de kilogramos al año. En 2005, se comunicó la fabricación de 245 kilogramos (980 millones de S-DDD). Los Estados Unidos son el fabricante principal y comunicaron la fabricación de 190 kilogramos en 2005. China e Italia también fabrican triazolam. España, Francia y el Japón, que fabricaron triazolam en el pasado, no han comunicado fabricación alguna en años recientes.

108. Los principales exportadores de triazolam fueron los Estados Unidos e Italia, en ese orden. Además, Australia, el Reino Unido y Suiza importan y reexportan regularmente triazolam. El Japón fue el mayor importador y consumidor, correspondiéndole casi la mitad de las importaciones mundiales. Los Estados Unidos, que utilizaron 94 kilogramos (376 millones de S-DDD) en 2005, fueron el mayor consumidor durante ese año, seguidos por el Japón, con 88 kilogramos (352 millones de S-DDD).

Lormetazepam

109. La fabricación de lormetazepam aumentó sostenidamente después de 1991, alcanzando el volumen máximo de 1,9 toneladas en 2002. Tras una breve caída a 380 kilogramos en 2003, la fabricación repuntó de nuevo en 2004 y ascendió a un total de 1,1 toneladas en 2005. Esos totales reflejan las fluctuaciones de la fabricación en Alemania e Italia, los dos fabricantes importantes de lormetazepam. Alemania e Italia son también los principales exportadores de esa sustancia. Además, España, Francia, Irlanda y los Países Bajos son importantes reexportadores de lormetazepam, e importan y exportan cantidades de aproximadamente 200 kilogramos al año. El consumo mundial calculado aumentó de 415 kilogramos en 1997 a 1,3 toneladas en 2005. España, Italia, Bélgica, Francia, y Alemania fueron, en ese orden, los principales consumidores.

Nitrazepam

110. La fabricación mundial de nitrazepam, que ha venido disminuyendo lentamente en los últimos años, de 6,5 toneladas en 2000 a 4 toneladas en 2004, aumentó de nuevo en 2005, situándose en 4,7 toneladas. Fabricaron esa sustancia Italia (2,4 toneladas en 2005), la India (1,7 toneladas) y China (0,7 toneladas). Las exportaciones de nitrazepam, que fueron en promedio de alrededor de 6 toneladas al año durante el período 1998-2002, continuaron disminuyendo y fueron en total de 3,9 toneladas en 2005. Al igual que en años anteriores, Italia siguió siendo el principal exportador de la sustancia, correspondiéndole el 65% del total de las exportaciones en 2005. Muchos países importan nitrazepam. Desde 1998, alrededor de 80 países han comunicado, al menos una vez, importaciones de nitrazepam superiores a 1 kilogramo. El Japón, que siguió siendo el mayor importador individual, comunicó importaciones de 1,6 toneladas en 2005; seguido por Cuba (550 kilogramos) y el Reino Unido (317 kilogramos).

Temazepam

111. El temazepam es fabricado por Italia, Polonia y los Estados Unidos en cantidades que ascienden a un total de entre 10 y 25 toneladas al año. En 2005, la fabricación mundial de temazepam ascendió a algo más de 13 toneladas. A Italia, el único proveedor de importancia del mercado mundial, le correspondió en promedio el 91% de la fabricación mundial en el período 1996-2005. Los Estados Unidos fabricaron en forma intermitente cantidades de 2 a 3 toneladas al año, y Polonia fabricó varios cientos de kilogramos cada año, principalmente para el consumo interno.

112. El mayor importador fueron los Estados Unidos, que importaron más de 7 toneladas en 2005; les siguieron Alemania, Australia, el Canadá, Finlandia, Irlanda, los Países Bajos y el Reino Unido, cada uno de los cuales importó más de 1 tonelada al año. Cerca de 30 países comunicaron importaciones de más de 1 kilogramo por año. Como en años anteriores, los Estados Unidos fueron el principal consumidor en 2005, y les correspondió el 60% del consumo calculado mundial (682 millones de S-DDD).

Brotizolam

113. El brotizolam, un hipnótico potente con la misma S-DDD que el triazolam (S-DDD de 0,25 mg), fue incluido en la Lista IV del Convenio de 1971 en 1995. La fabricación de esa sustancia fue comunicada por primera vez en 1997, por Alemania. Alemania fabrica brotizolam en cantidades de varios cientos de kilogramos al año e Italia y el Japón en cantidades de varias docenas de kilogramos al año. En 2005, la fabricación total fue de 451 kilogramos. El Japón es el mayor importador. Suiza importa también cantidades considerables para la reexportación. En 2005, 12 países comunicaron importaciones de más de 1 kilogramo de brotizolam, que en total ascendieron a 477 kilogramos. El consumo mundial calculado ascendió a 1.400 millones de S-DDD y al Japón (532 millones de S-DDD), Alemania (324 millones de S-DDD) y Colombia (324 millones de S-DDD) les correspondió el 84% del consumo mundial de la sustancia en 2005.

Estazolam

114. Durante el período 1995-2004, la fabricación mundial de estazolam fluctuó entre 1,5 toneladas y 2,6 toneladas por año, que correspondieron principalmente a China, los Estados Unidos y el Japón. En 2005, la fabricación aumentó a un volumen sin precedentes de 3 toneladas, de las que 2,4 toneladas correspondieron a China. El Japón fabricó 341 kilogramos y entre Polonia e Italia fabricaron 261 kilogramos. Los Estados Unidos no fabricaron estazolam en 2005. De los 10 países que importaron la sustancia en cantidades de más de 1 kilogramo, al Brasil, los Estados Unidos, Francia, los Países Bajos y Portugal les correspondió el 60% de las importaciones totales en 2005.

Midazolam

115. El total de la fabricación comunicada de midazolam, que se había mantenido estable en cerca de 2,6 toneladas al año durante el período 2000-2004, dio un salto a 8,7 tonela-

das en 2005, la segunda cantidad más alta registrada hasta ahora. El aumento fue atribuible al marcado incremento de la fabricación por Suiza, que pasó de 2,8 toneladas en 2004 a 6,3 toneladas en 2005. Israel ocupó el segundo lugar, con 1,4 toneladas, seguido por el Brasil, la India e Italia, en ese orden. En cambio, el volumen del comercio internacional de midazolam disminuyó a 3,5 toneladas en 2005, el nivel más bajo desde 1998, lo cual se tradujo en un aumento sin precedentes de las existencias de los fabricantes mundiales, que ascendieron a 6,8 toneladas. El midazolam es ampliamente utilizado y alrededor de 80 países comunicaron importaciones de esa sustancia en 2005. Los mayores importadores en ese año fueron Alemania, el Brasil, los Estados Unidos y la República de Corea, a los que les correspondió en conjunto el 40% de las importaciones mundiales.

Flurazepam

116. Tras haber disminuido gradualmente de 10,6 toneladas en 1997 a 3,6 toneladas en 2004, la fabricación mundial de flurazepam aumentó de nuevo ligeramente, a 4,1 toneladas, en 2005. Actualmente sólo fabrican flurazepam el Brasil, China e Italia. Italia es el mayor fabricante y exportador y satisface casi el 90% de la demanda mundial de esa sustancia. En 2005, 25 países comunicaron importaciones de flurazepam en cantidades de más de 1 kilogramo. Los principales importadores fueron Suiza (1,7 toneladas) y España (1,5 toneladas), a los que correspondió en conjunto el 50% de las importaciones mundiales en 2005. Importaron también cantidades significativas el Canadá y los Estados Unidos, que importaron aproximadamente 750 kilogramos cada uno durante ese año.

Loprazolam

117. El total de la fabricación comunicada de loprazolam ascendió a 72 kilogramos en 2005, siendo Francia el único fabricante y el principal exportador de esa sustancia. El Reino Unido (25 kilogramos en 2000) y España (202 kilogramos en 1993) son los únicos otros países que han comunicado alguna vez la fabricación de loprazolam. En 2005, nueve países comunicaron importaciones de loprazolam, en cantidades de entre 1 kilogramo y 10 kilogramos cada uno.

Antiepilépticos de tipo benzodiazepínico

Clonazepam

118. El clonazepam es una benzodiazepina que se utiliza principalmente como antiepiléptico. El total de la fabricación comunicada de clonazepam, que se había mantenido en una media anual de alrededor de 4 toneladas durante el período 1998-2003, empezó a aumentar en 2004 y alcanzó la cifra de 6,4 toneladas en 2005, el volumen más alto registrado hasta ahora. Ese aumento refleja el incremento de la producción de Suiza, el principal fabricante de clonazepam en el mundo, de 1,9 toneladas en 2004 a casi 3 toneladas en 2005. La India (1,8 toneladas) siguió ocupando ese año el segundo lugar entre los principales fabricantes de clonazepam, seguida por Italia (500 kilogramos). En 2005 fabricaron también cantidades importantes de esa sustancia el Brasil, China, Israel y Polonia.

119. El comercio mundial de clonazepam aumentó sostenidamente, pasando de cerca de 0,5 toneladas en 1995 a 6,8 toneladas en 2005. El clonazepam es objeto de amplio comercio y cerca de 100 países comunicaron importaciones de la sustancia en cantidades superiores a 1 kilogramo. En 2005, los Estados Unidos fueron una vez más el mayor importador de clonazepam del mundo (1,2 tonelada); los siguieron el Brasil (934 kilogramos) y el Canadá (707 kilogramos). Además, importaron también cantidades de más de 100 kilogramos, en orden descendente, la Argentina, Suiza, Francia, Italia, el Japón, la República Islámica del Irán, España y Chile. En el consumo mundial calculado se ha observado asimismo una sostenida tendencia ascendente desde mediados del decenio de 1990, pasando de 273 millones de S-DDD en 1996 a la nueva cifra sin precedentes de más de 720 millones de S-DDD en 2005. Los Estados Unidos siguieron siendo el mayor consumidor (131 millones de S-DDD), seguidos por el Brasil, la Argentina y el Canadá.

Barbitúricos empleados como sedantes hipnóticos y antiepilépticos

Alobarbital, barbital, butobarbital, metilfenobarbital, fenobarbital, secbutabarbital y vinilbital

120. Los siete barbitúricos enumerados en la Lista IV están farmacológicamente relacionados con los que figuran en la Lista III. Cinco de esas sustancias, a saber, el alobarbital, el barbital, el butobarbital, el secbutabarbital y el vinilbital, son barbitúricos de acción intermedia y se utilizan principalmente como hipnóticos (para inducir el sueño) en el tratamiento del insomnio incurable. Ya no se utilizan como sedantes diurnos. Las otras dos sustancias, el metilfenobarbital y el fenobarbital[7] tienen otras propiedades y se utilizan también como antiepilépticos (barbitúricos de acción prolongada). El barbital, el metilfenobarbital y el fenobarbital fueron incorporados en la Lista IV cuando se aprobó el Convenio de 1971, y las otras cuatro sustancias se incorporaron a la Lista en 1987.

121. La sustancia más ampliamente utilizada del grupo de los barbitúricos sigue siendo el fenobarbital, al que se ha considerado como el medicamento de preferencia para el tratamiento de la epilepsia. El total de la fabricación comunicada de esos barbitúricos (tanto para aplicaciones terapéuticas directas como para la fabricación de sustancias no sicotrópicas) aumentó gradualmente, hasta alcanzar las 653 toneladas en 1998 (5.400 millones de S-DDD). Cayó por breve tiempo por debajo de los 4.000 millones de S-DDD en el período 1999-2000 para aumentar luego gradualmente a una media de 5.000 millones de S-DDD en el período 2004-2005. Durante el período 2001-2005, al fenobarbital correspondió en promedio más del 95% de la fabricación total de barbitúricos incluidos en la Lista IV (en S-DDD). El barbital ocupó el segundo lugar y le correspondió el 4% de la fabricación total; le siguieron el metilfenobarbital y el alobarbital. No se ha comunicado la fabricación de vinilbital desde 1996 ni la de butobarbital desde 1999.

---

[7] Para los detalles, véase el cuadro IV.

Figura 28. Fenobarbital: fabricación total comunicada, 1996 a 2005

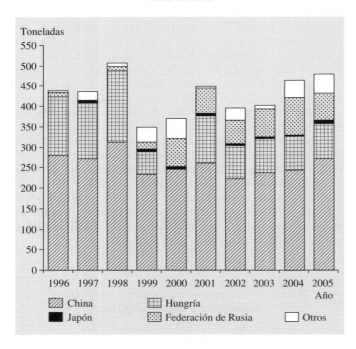

Toneladas

China   Hungría
Japón   Federación de Rusia   Otros

122. En los últimos años, Polonia, seguida por China y el Japón, ha registrado las tasas calculadas más altas de utilización de barbitúricos empleados como sedantes hipnóticos, con una media de entre 0,3 y 0,45 S-DDD por cada 1.000 habitantes por día. En lo que respecta a los barbitúricos utilizados como antiepilépticos enumerados en la Lista IV, el Brasil, Bulgaria, Croacia, la Federación de Rusia, Kazajstán, Rumania y Ucrania fueron los países que registraron las tasas más altas de utilización durante el período 2001-2005, y su consumo fue en promedio de entre 6 y 15,7 S-DDD por cada 1.000 habitantes por día.

123. El total de la fabricación comunicada de fenobarbital fue en promedio de 38 toneladas anuales en el período 2001-2005, habiendo disminuido de su volumen máximo de 508 toneladas en 1998. En 2005, el 56,8% del volumen total de fenobarbital se fabricó en China. Otros países que se contaron entre los principales fabricantes de fenobarbital en 2005 fueron Hungría (84 toneladas), la Federación de Rusia (66 toneladas), la India (35 toneladas) y el Brasil (10 toneladas). En el período 2001-2005 comunicaron también la fabricación de fenobarbital Alemania, los Estados Unidos, Hungría (principalmente para la exportación), el Iraq, el Japón, Kazajstán y Suiza (véase la figura 28).

124. El fenobarbital continúa siendo una de las sustancias sicotrópicas que son objeto de más amplio comercio. Durante el período 2001-2005, 163 países y territorios comunicaron haber importado la sustancia al menos una vez. El total de las importaciones comunicadas ascendió a 270 toneladas en 2005, siendo los importadores principales el Brasil (36 toneladas), Suiza (34 toneladas), Ucrania (29 toneladas), Dinamarca (25 toneladas), Alemania (20 toneladas), los Estados Unidos (18 toneladas), y el Japón (10 toneladas) y países a los que en conjunto correspondió el 60% del total.

125. Desde 2001, 52 países han comunicado exportaciones de fenobarbital y el total de esas exportaciones fluctuó entre 173 y 367 toneladas durante el período 2001-2005, correspondiendo a Alemania, Dinamarca, Hungría y Suiza el 90% de las corrientes de exportación. Las exportaciones de fenobarbital provenientes de Hungría disminuyeron gradualmente, de 116 toneladas en 2001 a 71 toneladas en 2005, cuando a ese país le correspondió el 20% de las exportaciones mundiales.

126. Además de su utilización terapéutica como sedante hipnótico, el barbital se emplea también en la industria para la fabricación de sustancias no sicotrópicas. La utilización calculada de barbital a nivel mundial, comprendida su aplicación tanto terapéutica como industrial, aumentó de una media de 95 toneladas anuales durante el período 2001-2002 a 106 toneladas en el período 2003-2005. El total de la fabricación comunicada de barbital disminuyó pronunciadamente en el período 1993-2001, habiéndose reducido su volumen en dos tercios. La producción total de barbital aumentó luego un poco, de 87 toneladas en 2001 a 111 toneladas en 2005. A China, que siguió siendo el principal fabricante de la sustancia, le correspondió, en promedio, el 96% de la fabricación mundial durante el período 2000-2005. Aparte de China, el Japón (2,7 toneladas) fue el único otro país que comunicó la fabricación de barbital en 2005.

127. Después de 1997, el volumen del comercio de barbital descendió gradualmente, de 72 toneladas en 1998 a 11 toneladas en 2002 y, en los tres años siguientes, las importaciones totales de la sustancia ascendieron en promedio a 16 toneladas por año. En 2005, el 92,6% de las exportaciones mundiales correspondió a Alemania y China. Durante el período 2001-2005, 52 países importaron barbital al menos una vez. En ese período los importadores principales de la sustancia fueron Alemania (principalmente para la reexportación), la India y el Japón.

128. Alemania fabricó casi 8 toneladas de metilfenobarbital en 1990. Desde ese año, Suiza ha sido el principal fabricante de la sustancia. Su producción fluctuó en torno a una media de 2,7 toneladas por año durante el cuatrienio 1999-2002, en tanto que en 2003 no comunicó ninguna fabricación. En 2004, el total de la fabricación comunicada de metilfenobarbital disminuyó pronunciadamente de 3,8 toneladas (de las que el 75% fueron fabricadas en Suiza) a 884 kilogramos (de los que dos terceras partes se fabricaron en Suiza y el resto en los Estados Unidos). Croacia, los Estados Unidos, Italia y Suiza fueron los principales consumidores de metilfenobarbital en 2005.

129. Durante el período 2001-2005, el comercio internacional de metilfenobarbital osciló entre 1,7 toneladas y 5,2 toneladas por año, con una media de 3,2 toneladas anuales. De los siete países que comunicaron exportaciones de metilfenobarbital durante el período 2001-2005, Suiza suministró, en promedio, el 49% de las exportaciones mundiales, siendo el otro exportador principal de metilfenobarbital en 2005 Alemania (702 kilogramos). Durante ese mismo período, 16 países importaron la sustancia al menos una vez. Alemania fue el principal importador regular de metilfenobarbital (importaciones destinadas en su totalidad a la reexportación), y en 2005 cerca del 44% de las importaciones totales correspondieron a Croacia.

130. Únicamente Alemania ha comunicado la fabricación de alobarbital desde que Dinamarca y Polonia descontinuaron la fabricación de esa sustancia en el período 1994-1995. La fabricación de alobarbital por Alemania aumentó considerablemente, de 393 kilogramos en 1998, cuando reanudó la fabricación de esa sustancia, a cerca de 4 toneladas en 2000. Posteriormente, la fabricación de alobarbital en Alemania se fue reduciendo gradualmente para ser de cerca de 1,6 toneladas en 2002. Aunque no se comunicó ninguna fabricación en 2003, Alemania fabricó en promedio 1 tonelada anualmente durante el período 2004-2005. En consecuencia, las existencias totales de la sustancia disminuyeron de una media de 2,5 toneladas en el período 2001-2002 a algo más de 1 tonelada en 2004, antes de disminuir aún más, a 509 kilogramos en 2005.

131. Las exportaciones totales de alobarbital fluctuaron entre 2,4 toneladas en 2001 y 1,5 toneladas en 2005, con una media de 2,3 toneladas por año en ese quinquenio. A Alemania, que fue el mayor exportador, le correspondió cerca del 67% del total mundial durante ese período. Durante el período 2001-2005, 17 países importaron la sustancia al menos una vez. En 2005, los importadores principales fueron Sri Lanka (701 kilogramos), Suiza (202 kilogramos, para la reexportación), Polonia (200 kilogramos), Turquía (200 kilogramos) y Hungría (60 kilogramos). El consumo mundial de alobarbital disminuyó en casi la mitad, de 21,4 millones de S-DDD en 2001 a 11 millones de S-DDD en 2005. La reducción es atribuible a las tasas considerablemente más bajas de utilización en Hungría, Polonia y la República Checa. En Polonia, por ejemplo, la utilización calculada de alobarbital disminuyó de 2,3 S-DDD por cada 1.000 habitantes por día a 1 S-DDD por cada 1.000 habitantes por día en 2005.

132. La fabricación total de secbutabarbital disminuyó pronunciadamente, pasando de 653 kilogramos en 2002 (de

los que los Estados Unidos fabricaron el 78%) a 128 kilogramos en 2003, y no se comunicó ninguna fabricación de esa sustancia en el período 2004-2005. Alemania había comunicado la fabricación de 136 kilogramos de secbutabarbital, en promedio, durante el período 2002-2003. Alemania, los Estados Unidos, el Líbano, el Reino Unido y Suiza son los únicos países que han comunicado el comercio de esa sustancia en los últimos cinco años.

133. Sólo dos países han comunicado la fabricación de butobarbital en el período 1996-2005: Dinamarca (1,3 toneladas en 1998) y Alemania (304 kilogramos en 1997). Después de ello, no se comunicó ninguna fabricación de butobarbital. En consecuencia, las existencias mundiales de la sustancia continuaron disminuyendo, reduciéndose gradualmente de 1,7 toneladas en 1998 a 311 kilogramos en 2005. El volumen del comercio internacional de butobarbital también se ha reducido, en cerca del 96%, de 3,7 toneladas en 1998 a 53 kilogramos en 2005. El consumo de butobarbital disminuyó en ocho veces entre 2004 y 2005.

134. De los 12 barbitúricos incluidos en las Listas II, III y IV del Convenio de 1971, a cinco sustancias correspondió el 98% de la fabricación total comunicada en el quinquenio 2001-2005: fenobarbital (67%), barbital (15%), butalbital (7%), pentobarbital (6%) y amobarbital (3%). En la figura 29 se presenta la distribución de los barbitúricos fabricados en 2005. En 2005, a China (60%), Hungría (12%), la Federación de Rusia (10%), la India (5%), los Estados Unidos (4%), Alemania (3%) y Dinamarca (2%) les correspondió en conjunto el 96% de la fabricación total de todo el grupo de los barbitúricos (véase la figura 30). El cambio significativo a ese respecto es que el porcentaje de China aumentó del 54% de la fabricación total comunicada en 2004 al 60% en 2005.

Figura 29.   Barbitúricos de las Listas II, III y IV:
fabricación total comunicada,
por sustancia, 2005

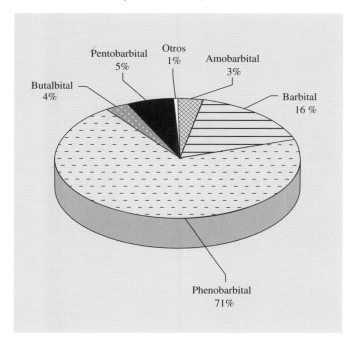

Figura 30.   Barbitúricos de las Listas II, III y IV:
fabricación total comunicada
de determinados países, 2005

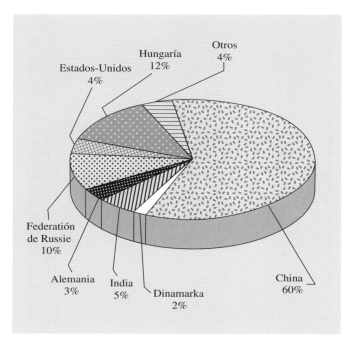

Otros sedantes hipnóticos

135.   Cinco sustancias del grupo de los sedantes hipnóticos de la Lista IV no son ni barbitúricos ni benzodiazepinas. Mientras que el etclorvinol, el etinamato y la metiprilona han figurado en la Lista IV desde la aprobación del Convenio de 1971, las otras dos sustancias, el ácido *gamma*-hidroxibutírico (GHB) y el zolpidem, fueron añadidos al grupo de sedantes hipnóticos de la Lista IV en 2001.

136.   La fabricación de etclorvinol fue comunicada por última vez por los Estados Unidos, en 1999 (1,3 toneladas), y la utilización de la sustancia fue descontinuada en 2001. La fabricación de etinamato fue comunicada por última vez por Alemania, en 1988 (500 kilogramos), y la de metiprilona por los Estados Unidos, en 1990 (2,1 toneladas). Desde 1991 no ha habido informes de fabricación o comercio internacional de etinamato ni metiprilona.

137.   Son muy limitados los datos de que se dispone sobre el GHB respecto del 2001, cuando la sustancia quedó sometida a fiscalización internacional. Gracias a la introducción de medidas de fiscalización a nivel nacional, ha aumentado el número de países que han podido informar sobre la fabricación y el comercio del GHB. En 2005, Alemania (5,7 toneladas) y Letonia (3,6 toneladas) fueron los principales fabricantes de GHB, y a esos dos países les correspondió el 86% de la fabricación mundial. Los otros fabricantes principales en el período 2001-2005 fueron los Estados Unidos (3,9 toneladas en promedio) y Ucrania (3,8 toneladas en promedio), seguidos, con cantidades muy inferiores, por China, Francia y Azerbaiyán. Los principales exportadores en 2005 fueron Alemania, los Estados Unidos y Letonia y los principales importadores Italia (4,6 toneladas) y el Reino Unido (1,8 toneladas). En el período 2003-2005, 25 países

comunicaron haber importado más de 1 kilogramo de GHB al menos una vez.

138.   Se dispone de datos sobre el zolpidem correspondientes al período 2001-2005 respecto de varios países. El principal fabricante fue Francia, al que correspondió el 86% de la producción mundial (32 toneladas), seguido por la República Checa (3,5 toneladas) y la India (709 kilogramos). Alemania, Argentina, China, Eslovaquia, España, Estados Unidos e Israel han comunicado también la fabricación de zolpidem en años recientes. El principal exportador de zolpidem fue Francia, a la que correspondió el 55% de las exportaciones mundiales (19 toneladas). El zolpidem es una sustancia ampliamente utilizada, siendo sus principales consumidores Francia, los Estados Unidos, el Japón y la República Checa. Durante el quinquenio 2001-2005, más de 100 países comunicaron haber importado más de 1 kilogramo de zolpidem al menos en una ocasión.

Analgésicos

139.   La lefetamina es el único analgésico incluido en la Lista IV. No se ha comunicado la fabricación ni el comercio de lefetamina desde 1996. Actualmente, Italia mantiene existencias de 1 kilogramo de la sustancia.

Antidepresivos

140.   La única sustancia representativa de este grupo es la amineptina, que fue incluida en la Lista II del Convenio de 1971 en 2003. No se ha comunicado mucha información sobre esta sustancia. El Brasil es el único país que ha comunicado que mantenía pequeñas cantidades de existencias en los dos últimos años.

Tables of reported statistics

The tables in the present section contain the statistical information on psychotropic substances in Schedules I-IV of the 1971 Convention furnished to INCB by Governments in accordance with article 16 of the Convention. As few Governments have reported the movement of substances listed in Schedule I, a brief statistical table, including statistics on total manufacture of those substances for the three-year period 2003-2005 and on stocks of and international trade in those substances for 2005, is provided. With regard to the statistical tables for substances in Schedules III and IV, it should be noted that, although the majority of countries and territories reported on substances in all schedules, some Governments have not yet extended control measures of the 1971 Convention to all of the substances listed in Schedules III and IV. Therefore, for certain substances, the statistical data available to the Board may only present a partial picture of the global manufacture of and trade in those substances.

With respect to substances in Schedules I and II, Governments are requested by INCB to report quantities in grams. While the gram (g) is the unit of weight used in the statistics on substances in Schedule I, the kilogram (kg) is the unit of weight used for the statistics on substances in Schedules II, III and IV. If a country has reported the movement of less than 500 grams of a substance in Schedule II that has not been included in the statistical tables. However, such small quantities, as well as fractions of kilograms, have been considered when calculating the total manufacture, import and export of each substance. Therefore, for substances in Schedule II, the total generally exceeds the sum of the individual quantities expressed in full kilograms.

For substances in Schedule II, the presentation of the statistical data is made substance by substance. For each substance, the first part refers exclusively to data obtained from manufacturing countries. The second and third parts refer to international trade. For substances in Schedule III, the manufacture of all substances is presented in the first part, while the second and third parts show international trade in all substances. For Schedules II and III, data for the years 2001-2005 are presented. Tables for substances in Schedule IV contain data for the years 2003-2005 only. For technical reasons, substances in Schedule IV were divided into the following five groups for the presentation of data on manufacture and international trade:

Group I: Central nervous system stimulants;

Group II: Anxiolytics, first part: main benzodiazepines and meprobamate;

Group III: Anxiolytics, second part: less common benzodiazepines;

Group IV: Benzodiazepines: sedative-hypnotics and anti-epileptics;

Group V: Sedative-hypnotics and barbiturate-type anti-epileptics.

Lefetamine (SPA), phenmetrazine, and amineptine were not included in any table since reports on these substances have been very limited.

The following symbols are used in the tables:

A dash (—) indicates nil or less than 500 grams; in the case of substances in Schedule II, III or IV (less than 500 milligrams in the case of substances in Schedule I);

A question mark (?) indicates statistical report not furnished;

Two dots (. .) indicate that a statistical report was furnished but the data are not available for the substance in question.

Tableaux statistiques

Les tableaux de la présente section contiennent les renseignements statistiques sur les substances psychotropes inscrites aux Tableaux I à IV de la Convention de 1971 qui ont été fournis à l'OICS par les pays conformément à l'article 16 de la Convention. Les pays ayant signalé un mouvement de substances inscrites au Tableau I étant peu nombreux, on a indiqué dans un tableau statistique sommaire les quantités totales de ces substances fabriquées au cours de la période triennale 2003-2005, ainsi que les stocks et les échanges internationaux en 2005. Il convient de noter que, bien que la plupart des pays et territoires aient communiqué des informations sur les substances de tous les tableaux, un certain nombre de gouvernements n'ont pas encore étendu les mesures de contrôle au titre de la Convention de 1971 à toutes les substances inscrites aux Tableaux III et IV. Il se peut donc que les renseignements statistiques dont dispose l'OICS ne donnent qu'une image partielle de l'ensemble de la fabrication et du commerce de certaines substances.

Concernant les substances inscrites aux Tableaux I et II, l'OICS demande aux États d'indiquer les quantités en grammes. Les poids sont exprimés en grammes dans les statistiques concernant les substances du Tableau I et en kilogrammes dans les statistiques concernant celles inscrites aux Tableaux II, III et IV. Le mouvement d'une quantité inférieure à 500 grammes d'une substance inscrite au Tableau II n'a pas été tenu compte dans les tableaux. Toutefois, les quantités inférieures à un kilogramme ont été prises en compte lors du calcul de la quantité totale fabriquée, importée et exportée pour chaque substance. Pour les substances inscrites au Tableau II, les totaux dépassent donc généralement la somme des quantités exprimées en kilogrammes prises individuellement.

Pour les substances inscrites au Tableau II, les données statistiques sont présentées substance par substance. Pour chaque substance, la première partie porte exclusivement sur les renseignements fournis par les pays fabricants. La deuxième et la troisième partie portent sur le commerce international. Pour les substances inscrites au Tableau III, le total de la fabrication pour toutes les substances est présenté dans la première partie, alors que le commerce international de toutes les substances est indiqué dans les deuxième et troisième parties. Pour les Tableaux II et III, les renseignements sont indiqués pour les années 2001 à 2005. Les tableaux portant sur les substances inscrites au Tableau IV contiennent des renseignements pour les années 2003 à 2005 seulement. Pour des raisons techniques, les données sur la fabrication et le commerce international des substances inscrites au Tableau IV ont été réparties en cinq groupes:

Groupe I: Stimulants du système nerveux central;

Groupe II: Anxiolytiques, première partie: principales benzodiazépines et méprobamate;

Groupe III: Anxiolytiques, deuxième partie: benzodiazépines moins courantes;

Groupe IV: Benzodiazépines: sédatifs-hypnotiques et antiépileptiques;

Groupe V: Sédatifs-hypnotiques et antiépileptiques de type barbiturique.

La léfétamine (SPA), la phenmétrazine et l'amineptine ne sont incluses dans aucun tableau. Très peu de rapports ont été reçus concernant ces substances.

Les symboles suivants sont utilisés dans les tableaux:

Un tiret (—) indique une quantité nulle ou inférieure à 500 grammes dans le cas des substances des Tableaux II, III ou IV, ou inférieure à 500 milligrammes dans le cas des substances du Tableau I;

Un point d'interrogation (?) indique que le rapport statistique n'a pas été communiqué;

Deux points (. .) indiquent que le rapport statistique a été communiqué, mais qu'aucune information n'est disponible pour la substance en question.

Cuadros estadísticos

Los cuadros de la presente sección contienen la información estadística sobre las sustancias sicotrópicas de las Listas I a IV del Convenio de 1971 suministradas a la JIFE por los gobiernos de conformidad con lo dispuesto en el artículo 16 del Convenio. Dado que muy pocos gobiernos han informado del movimiento de sustancias de la Lista I, sólo se presenta un breve cuadro estadístico sobre esas sustancias, en que se incluyen estadísticas sobre su fabricación total en el trienio comprendido entre 2003 y 2005 y sobre las existencias y el comercio internacionales de esas sustancias en 2005. Con respecto a los cuadros estadísticos sobre las sustancias de las Listas III y IV, cabe observar que, si bien la mayoría de los países y territorios informan sobre las sustancias de todas las listas, algunos gobiernos aún no aplican las medidas de fiscalización del Convenio de 1971 a todas las sustancias de las Listas III y IV. Por consiguiente, la información estadística de que dispone la JIFE en relación con determinadas sustancias puede dar solamente una visión parcial de su fabricación y comercio a nivel mundial.

Con respecto a las sustancias de las Listas I y II, la JIFE solicita a los gobiernos que comuniquen las cantidades en gramos. Si bien la unidad de peso utilizada en las estadísticas sobre las sustancias de la Lista I es el gramo (g), la utilizada en las estadísticas sobre las sustancias de las Listas II, III y IV es el kilogramo (kg). Si su país ha declarado un movimiento de menos de 500 gramos de una sustancia de la Lista II, esa información no se ha incluido en los cuadros estadísticos. No obstante, tanto esas pequeñas cantidades como las fracciones de kilogramo se han tomado en consideración al calcular la fabricación, importación y exportación de cada sustancia. En consecuencia, con respecto a las sustancias de la Lista II, el total suele ser superior a la suma de las cantidades expresadas en kilogramos enteros.

Con respecto a las sustancias de la Lista II, la presentación de los datos estadísticos se hace sustancia por sustancia. Para cada sustancia, la primera parte se refiere exclusivamente a los datos obtenidos de los países fabricantes. Las partes segunda y tercera se refieren al comercio internacional. Para las sustancias de la Lista III, la fabricación de todas las sustancias se presenta en la primera parte, mientras que las partes segunda y tercera indican el comercio internacional de todas las sustancias. Para las Listas II y III, se presentan datos correspondientes a los años 2001 a 2005. En los cuadros correspondientes a las sustancias de la Lista IV figuran datos correspondientes a los años 2003 a 2005 solamente. Por razones técnicas, las sustancias de la Lista IV se dividieron en los cinco grupos siguientes para fines de presentación de los datos sobre fabricación y comercio internacionales:

Grupo I: Estimulantes del sistema nervioso central;

Grupo II: Ansiolíticos, primera parte: principales benzodiazepinas y meprobamato;

Grupo III: Ansiolíticos, segunda parte: benzodiazepinas menos comunes;

Grupo IV: Benzodiazepinas: sedantes-hipnóticos y antiepilépticos;

Grupo V: Sedantes-hipnóticos y antiepilépticos de tipo barbitúrico.

La lefetamina (SPA), fenmetracina y amineptina no han sido incluidas en ningún cuadro, ya que la información sobre esas sustancias ha sido muy limitada.

En los cuadros se utilizan los siguientes símbolos:

El guión largo (—) indica cero o una cantidad inferior a 500 gramos en el caso de las sustancias de las Listas II, III o IV, o inferior a 500 miligramos en el caso de las sustancias de la Lista I;

El signo de interrogación (?) indica un informe estadístico no comunicado;

Los dos puntos suspensivos (. .) indican que el informe estadístico fue comunicado, pero no se dispone de información sobre la sustancia en cuestión.

A.   Substances listed in Schedule I

A.   Substances inscrites au Tableau I

A.   Sustancias incluidas en la Lista I

Table A. Reported statistics on substances in Schedule I of the 1971 Convention

Tableau A. Statistiques communiquées sur les substances inscrites au Tableau I de la Convention de 1971

Cuadro A. Estadísticas comunicadas en relación con las sustancias de la Lista I del Convenio de 1971

Movement in manufacturing countries and territories (grams)
Mouvements dans les pays et territoires fabricants (en grammes)
Movimiento de sustancias en los países y territorios fabricantes (en gramos)

Substance / Substance / Sustancia	Country or territory / Pays ou territoire / País o territorio	Total quantity manufactured, 2003-2005 / Quantité totale fabriquée, 2003-2005 / Cantidad total fabricada (2003 a 2005)	Manufacturers' stocks at the end of 2005 / Stocks des fabricants à la fin de 2005 / Existencias de los fabricantes a fines de 2005	Exports Exportations Exportaciones	Imports Importations Importaciones
				of countries manufacturing or holding manufacturers' stocks in 2005 / des pays fabricants ou détenteurs de stocks en 2005 / de los países fabricantes o con existencias de los fabricantes en 2005	
Brolamfetamine (DOB) Brolamfétamine (DOB) Brolanfetamina (DOB)	Australia — Australie United States — États-Unis — Estados Unidos **Total**	— — **—**	2 30 **32**	— — **—**	— — **—**
Cathinone Catinone Catinona	Australia — Australie Ireland — Irlande — Irlanda United States — États-Unis — Estados Unidos **Total**	— 4 2 **6**	1 4 80 **85**	— — — **—**	— — — **—**
DET DET DET	United States — États-Unis — Estados Unidos **Total**	— **—**	6 **6**	— **—**	— **—**
DMA DMA DMA	Australia — Australie United States — États-Unis — Estados Unidos **Total**	— 3 872 500 **3 872 500**	1 236 345 **236 346**	—` — **—**	— — **—**
DMT DMT DMT	Switzerland — Suisse — Suiza United States — États-Unis — Estados Unidos **Total**	— — **—**	2 57 **59**	— — **—**	— — **—**
DOET DOET DOET	United States — États-Unis — Estados Unidos **Total**	— **—**	35 **35**	— **—**	— **—**
Eticyclidine (PCE) Éticyclidine (PCE) Eticiclidina (PCE)	United States — États-Unis — Estados Unidos **Total**	— **—**	60 **60**	— **—**	— **—**

Table A.   Reported statistics on substances in Schedule I of the 1971 Convention *(continued)*

Tableau A.   Statistiques communiquées sur les substances inscrites au Tableau I de la Convention de 1971 *(suite)*

Cuadro A.   Estadísticas comunicadas en relación con las sustancias de la Lista I del Convenio de 1971 *(continuación)*

		Movement in manufacturing countries and territories (grams) Mouvements dans les pays et territoires fabricants (en grammes) Movimiento de sustancias en los países y territorios fabricantes (en gramos)			
Substance Substance Sustancia	Country or territory Pays ou territoire País o territorio	Total quantity manufactured, 2003-2005 Quantité totale fabriquée, 2003-2005 Cantidad total fabricada (2003 a 2005)	Manufacturers' stocks at the end of 2005 Stocks des fabricants à la fin de 2005 Existencias de los fabricantes a fines de 2005	Exports Exportations Exportaciones of countries manufacturing or holding manufacturers' stocks in 2005 des pays fabricants ou détenteurs de stocks en 2005 de los países fabricantes o con existencias de los fabricantes en 2005	Imports Importations Importaciones
MDMA .... MDMA MDMA	Australia — Australie Ireland — Irlande — Irlanda Israel — Israël Poland — Pologne — Polonia Switzerland — Suisse — Suiza United States — États-Unis — Estados Unidos **Total**	50 15 22 65 38 31 **221**	14 7 6 9 92 310 **438**	6 4 16 18 10 **54**	4 5 — 7 **16**
Mescaline .... Mescaline Mescalina	Australia — Australie Sweden — Suède — Suecia Switzerland — Suisse — Suiza United Kingdom — Royaume-Uni — Reino Unido United States — États-Unis — Estados Unidos **Total**	— — 12 — — **12**	1 2 9 — 34 **46**	— — — 2 — **2**	— — — — — **—**
Methcathinone .... Methcathinone Metcatinona	Australia — Australie Germany — Allemagne — Alemania United States — États-Unis — Estados Unidos **Total**	— 2 — **2**	1 2 80 **83**	— — — **—**	— — 20 **20**
4-Methylaminorex .... Méthyl-4 aminorex 4-metilaminorex	United States — États-Unis Estados Unidos **Total**	— **—**	168 **168**	— **—**	— **—**
4-MTA 4-MTA 4-MTA	Australia — Australie **Total**	— **—**	1 **1**	— **—**	— **—**
MMDA .... MMDA MMDA	United States — États-Unis — Estados Unidos **Total**	— **—**	17 **17**	— **—**	— **—**

Table A. Reported statistics on substances in Schedule I of the 1971 Convention *(continued)*

Tableau A. Statistiques communiquées sur les substances inscrites au Tableau I de la Convention de 1971 *(suite)*

Cuadro A. Estadísticas comunicadas en relación con las sustancias de la Lista I del Convenio de 1971 *(continuación)*

Movement in manufacturing countries and territories (grams)
Mouvements dans les pays et territoires fabricants (en grammes)
Movimiento de sustancias en los países y territorios fabricantes (en gramos)

Substance / Substance / Sustancia	Country or territory / Pays ou territoire / País o territorio	Total quantity manufactured, 2003-2005 / Quantité totale fabriquée, 2003-2005 / Cantidad total fabricada (2003 a 2005)	Manufacturers' stocks at the end of 2005 / Stocks des fabricants à la fin de 2005 / Existencias de los fabricantes a fines de 2005	Exports Exportations Exportaciones	Imports Importations Importaciones
				of countries manufacturing or holding manufacturers' stocks in 2005 / des pays fabricants ou détenteurs de stocks en 2005 / de los países fabricantes o con existencias de los fabricantes en 2005	
N-ethyl MDA N-éthyl MDA N-etil MDA	Ireland — Irlande — Irlanda	16	11	4	—
	Israel — Israël	—	1	—	—
	Switzerland — Suisse — Suiza	44	13	2	—
	United States — États-Unis — Estados Unidos	9	149	—	—
	Total	**69**	**174**	**6**	**—**
N-hydroxy MDA N-hydroxy MDA N-hidroxi MDA	United States — États-Unis — Estados Unidos	—	38	—	—
	Total	**—**	**38**	**—**	**—**
(+)-Lysergide (LSD) (+)–Lysergide (LSD) (+)-Lisérgida (LSD)	Israel — Israël	—	2	—	—
	Switzerland — Suisse — Suiza	—	396	—	—
	United States — États-Unis — Estados Unidos	13	54	—	—
	Total	**13**	**452**	**—**	**—**
PMA PMA PMA	Australia — Australie	—	8	—	—
	Denmark—Danemark—Dinamarca	25	40	—	—
	Poland — Pologne — Polonia	2	—	—	—
	Switzerland — Suisse — Suiza	—	13	—	—
	United States — États-Unis — Estados Unidos	3	36	—	—
	Total	**30**	**97**	**—**	**—**
Psilocine Psilocine Psilocina	Switzerland — Suisse — Suiza	9	2	—	—
	United States — États-Unis — Estados Unidos	8	23	—	—
	Total	**17**	**25**	**—**	**—**
Psilocybine Psilocybine Psilocibina	Switzerland — Suisse — Suiza	3	302	—	—
	United States — États-Unis — Estados Unidos	—	56	—	—
	Total	**3**	**358**	**—**	**—**

Table A. Reported statistics on substances in Schedule I of the 1971 Convention *(concluded)*

Tableau A. Statistiques communiquées sur les substances inscrites au Tableau I de la Convention de 1971 *(fin)*

Cuadro A. Estadísticas comunicadas en relación con las sustancias de la Lista I del, Convention de 1971 *(conclusión)*

Movement in manufacturing countries and territories (grams)
Mouvements dans les pays et territoires fabricants (en grammes)
Movimiento de sustancias en los países y territorios fabricantes (en gramos)

Substance / Substance / Sustancia	Country or territory / Pays ou territoire / País o territorio	Total quantity manufactured, 2003-2005 / Quantité totale fabriquée, 2003-2005 / Cantidad total fabricada (2003 a 2005)	Manufacturers' stocks at the end of 2005 / Stocks des fabricants à la fin de 2005 / Existencias de los fabricantes a fines de 2005	Exports Exportations Exportaciones	Imports Importations Importaciones
				of countries manufacturing or holding manufacturers' stocks in 2005 / des pays fabricants ou détenteurs de stocks en 2005 / de los países fabricantes o con existencias de los fabricantes en 2005	
Rolicyclidine (PHP, PCPY) .. Rolicyclidine (PHP, PCPY) Roliciclidina (PHP, PCPY)	United States — États-Unis — Estados Unidos **Total**	— —	30 **30**	— —	— —
STP, DOM .... STP, DOM STP, DOM	United States — États-Unis — Estados Unidos **Total**	— —	58 **58**	— —	— —
Tenamfetamine (MDA) ...... Tenamfétamine (MDA) Tenanfetamina (MDA)	Australia — Australie	43	5	1	—
	Ireland — Irlande — Irlanda	23	18	4	—
	Israel — Israël	7		1	—
	Switzerland — Suisse — Suiza	187	131	4	—
	United States — États-Unis — Estados Unidos	10	184	—	1
	Total	**270**	**338**	**10**	**1**
Tenocyclidine (TCP)........ Ténocyclidine (TCP) Tenociclidina (TCP)	United States — États-Unis — Estados Unidos **Total**	— —	15 **15**	— —	— —
Tetrahydrocannabinol .... Tétrahydrocannabinol Tetrahidrocannabinol	Israel — Israël	—	2	—	2
	United States — États-Unis — Estados Unidos	807 176	445 312	—	—
	Total	**807 176**	**445 314**	—	**2**
TMA .... TMA TMA	Australia — Australie	—	2	—	—
	United States — États-Unis — Estados Unidos	—	8	—	—
	Total	—	**10**	—	—

Note: A dash (—) indicates nil or less than 500 milligrams.
Note: Un tiret (—) indique une quantité nulle ou inférieure à 500 milligrammes.
Nota: El guión largo (—) indica cero o una cantidad inferior a 500 miligramos.

B. Substances listed in Schedule II, 2001-2005

B. Substances inscrites au Tableau II, 2001-2005

B. Sustancias incluidas en la Lista II, 2001-2005

Schedule II. B.1. Manufacturing countries
Tableau II. B.1. Pays fabricants
Lista II. B.1. Países fabricantes

Country / Pays / País	Year / Année / Año	Quantity manufactured / Quantité fabriquée / Cantidad fabricada	Quantities used for the manufacture of non-psychotropic substances or products / Quantités utilisées pour la fabrication de substances ou produits non psychotropes / Cantidades utilizadas para la fabricación de sustancias o productos no sicotrópicos	Manufacturers' stocks / Stocks des fabricants / Existencias de los fabricantes	Exports / Exportations / Exportaciones	Imports / Importations / Importaciones

Amfetamine — Amfétamine — Anfetamina

Country	Year	kg	kg	kg	kg	kg
Argentina / Argentine	2001	—	—	4	—	—
	2002	—	—	2	—	—
	2003	—	—	1	—	—
	2004	—	—	—	—	—
	2005	—	—	—	—	—
Canada / Canadá	2001	—	—	—	—	—
	2002	—	—	—	—	9
	2003	—	—	8	—	1
	2004	—	—	—	—	47
	2005	—	—	114	—	19
Chile / Chili	2001	—	—	—	—	14
	2002	—	—	5	—	14
	2003	—	—	4	—	10
	2004	—	—	—	—	10
	2005	—	—	2	—	21
Denmark / Danemark / Dinamarca	2001	—	—	—	—	—
	2002	—	—	1	—	1
	2003	—	—	—	—	—
	2004	—	—	—	—	1
	2005	—	—	—	—	—
France / Francia	2001	5 892[a,b]	—	1 417	64	—
	2002	7 723[a,b]	—	131	74	—
	2003	10 262[a,b]	—	1 321	31	—
	2004	8 384[a]	—	1 156	70	—
	2005	10 930[a]	—	1 585	37	—
Germany / Allemagne / Alemania	2001	—	—	—	—	36
	2002	1 624[b]	—	88	—	39
	2003	2 518	—	6	—	1
	2004	—	—	—	—	38
	2005	977	953	24	—	1
Israel / Israël	2001	—	—	—	—	—
	2002	—	—	—	—	—
	2003	—	—	2	—	2
	2004	—	—	1	—	—
	2005	—	—	—	—	—
Netherlands / Pays-Bas / Países Bajos	2001	—	—	—	—	—
	2002	—	—	—	1	1
	2003	—	—	1	—	1
	2004	—	—	4	3	6
	2005	—	—	3	—	—

Schedule II. B.1. Manufacturing countries *(continued)*
Tableau II. B.1. Pays fabricants *(suite)*
Lista II. B.1. Países fabricantes *(continuación)*

Country / Pays / País	Year / Année / Año	Quantity manufactured / Quantité fabriquée / Cantidad fabricada	Quantities used for the manufacture of non-psychotropic substances or products / Quantités utilisées pour la fabrication de substances ou produits non psychotropes / Cantidades utilizadas para la fabricación de sustancias o productos no sicotrópicos	Manufacturers' stocks / Stocks des fabricants / Existencias de los fabricantes	Exports / Exportations / Exportaciones	Imports / Importations / Importaciones

Amfetamine — Amfétamine — Anfetamina *(continued — suite — continuación)*

		kg	kg	kg	kg	kg
Sweden .... Suède Suecia	2001	—	—	3	—	7
	2002	—	—	5	—	11
	2003	—	—	4	—	8
	2004	—	—	4	—	7
	2005	—	—	5	—	7
Switzerland .... Suisse Suiza	2001	—	—	11	—	—
	2002	—	—	11	—	—
	2003	—	—	11	—	—
	2004	—	—	11	—	—
	2005	—	—	3	—	—
United Kingdom .... Royaume-Uni Reino Unido	2001	—	—	2	—	—
	2002	—	—	3	—	1
	2003	—	—	6	—	—
	2004	—	—	12	1	1
	2005	—	—	—	—	—
United States.............. États-Unis Estados Unidos	2001	9 612[a]	—	2 390	—	—
	2002	7 442[a]	—	4 177	9	—
	2003	3 527[a]	—	3 953	2	—
	2004	6 208[a]	—	4 542	79	—
	2005	6 746[a]	—	4 247	41	—
Total	2001	15 504	—	3 827	64	57
	2002	16 789	—	4 423	84	76
	2003	16 307	—	5 317	33	23
	2004	14 592	—	5 730	153	110
	2005	18 653	953	5 983	78	48

Dexamfetamine — Dexamfétamine — Dexanfetamina

		kg	kg	kg	kg	kg
Canada .... Canadá	2001	—	—	82	—	152
	2002	—	—	90	—	173
	2003	—	—	54	—	99
	2004	—	—	103	—	176
	2005	—	—	39	—	268
France .... Francia	2001	1 397	1 199[c]	621	207	—
	2002	3 990	1 599[c]	826	197	—
	2003	5 404	1 599[c]	1 497	255	—
	2004	5 576	2 832[c]	734	250	—
	2005	5 229	400[c]	798	206	—

Schedule II. B.1. Manufacturing countries (continued)
Tableau II. B.1. Pays fabricants (suite)
Lista II. B.1. Países fabricantes (continuación)

Country Pays País	Year Année Año	Quantity manufactured Quantité fabriquée Cantidad fabricada	Quantities used for the manufacture of non-psychotropic substances or products Quantités utilisées pour la fabrication de substances ou produits non psychotropes Cantidades utilizadas para la fabricación de sustancias o productos no sicotrópicos	Manufacturers' stocks Stocks des fabricants Existencias de los fabricantes	Exports Exportations Exportaciones	Imports Importations Importaciones
Dexamfetamine — Dexamfétamine — Dexanfetamina *(continued — suite — continuación)*						
		kg	kg	kg	kg	kg
Israel	2001	—	—	—	—	—
Israël	2002	—	—	—	—	—
	2003	—	—	2	—	2
	2004	—	—	2	—	—
	2005	—	—	—	—	—
Netherlands	2001	—		3	—	7
Pays-Bas	2002	—		5	—	7
Países Bajos	2003	—		3	—	5
	2004	—		9	6	21
	2005	—		8	9	16
Sweden	2001	—		2	—	—
Suède	2002	—		—	—	—
Suecia	2003	—		2	—	3
	2004	—		5	—	3
	2005	—		1	—	—
Switzerland	2001	249	—	100	3	2
Suisse	2002	—	—	98	4	2
Suiza	2003	—	—	99	3	5
	2004	—	—	1	3	2
	2005	—	—	4	2	5
United Kingdom	2001	—	—	12	1	76
Royaume-Uni	2002	—	—	25	2	52
Reino Unido	2003	—	—	26	1	48
	2004	—	—	33	—	1
	2005	—	—	44	3	50
United States	2001	4 919	—	4 969	152	—
États-Unis	2002	5 962	—	5 567	152	1
Estados Unidos	2003	3 459	—	5 567	123	—
	2004	5 163	—	4 531	157	—
	2005	6 199	—	4 968	104	—
Total	2001	6 565	1 199	5 789	363	237
	2002	9 952	1 599	6 611	355	235
	2003	8 863	1 599	7 250	382	162
	2004	10 739	2 832	5 418	416	203
	2005	11 428	400	5 862	324	339

Schedule II.   B.1. Manufacturing countries *(continued)*
Tableau II.   B.1. Pays fabricants *(suite)*
Lista II.   B.1. Países fabricantes *(continuación)*

Country Pays País	Year Année Año	Quantity manufactured Quantité fabriquée Cantidad fabricada	Quantities used for the manufacture of non-psychotropic substances or products Quantités utilisées pour la fabrication de substances ou produits non psychotropes Cantidades utilizadas para la fabricación de sustancias o productos no sicotrópicos	Manufacturers' stocks Stocks des fabricants Existencias de los fabricantes	Exports Exportations Exportaciones	Imports Importations Importaciones
Fenetylline — Fénétylline — Fenetilina						
		kg	kg	kg	kg	kg
Netherlands	2001	—	—	4	60	526
Pays-Bas	2002	—	—	406	59	—
Países Bajos	2003	—	—	316	90	—
	2004	—	—	280	36	—
	2005	—	—	212	68	—
Total	2001	—	—	4	60	526
	2002	—	—	406	59	—
	2003	—	—	316	90	—
	2004	—	—	280	36	—
	2005	—	—	212	68	—
Levamfetamine — Lévamfétamine — Levanfetamina						
		kg	kg	kg	kg	kg
France	2001	3 510^d	—	8	—	—
Francia	2002	4 286^d	—	—	—	—
	2003	5 555^d	—	1	—	—
	2004	6 010^d	—	1	—	—
	2005	6 453^d	—	194	—	—
United States	2001	—	—	—	—	—
États-Unis	2002	17	—	158	—	—
Estados Unidos	2003	2	—	140	—	—
	2004	—	—	115	—	—
	2005	—	—	140	—	—
Total	2001	3 510	—	8	—	—
	2002	4 303	—	158	—	—
	2003	5 557	—	141	—	—
	2004	6 010	—	116	—	—
	2005	6 453	—	334	—	—
Levomethamphetamine — Lévométhamphétamine — Levometanfetamina						
		kg	kg	kg	kg	kg
Czech Republic	2001	—	—	—	—	—
République tchèque	2002	—	—	—	—	—
República Checa	2003	48	46	1	—	—
	2004	194	196	—	—	—
	2005	100	—	100	—	—

Schedule II. B.1. Manufacturing countries *(continued)*
Tableau II. B.1. Pays fabricants *(suite)*
Lista II. B.1. Países fabricantes *(continuación)*

Country / Pays / País	Year / Année / Año	Quantity manufactured / Quantité fabriquée / Cantidad fabricada	Quantities used for the manufacture of non-psychotropic substances or products / Quantités utilisées pour la fabrication de substances ou produits non psychotropes / Cantidades utilizadas para la fabricación de sustancias o productos no sicotrópicos	Manufacturers' stocks / Stocks des fabricants / Existencias de los fabricantes	Exports / Exportations / Exportaciones	Imports / Importations / Importaciones

Levomethamphetamine — Lévométhamphétamine — Levometanfetamina *(continued — suite — continuación)*

		kg	kg	kg	kg	kg
France	2001	—	—	23	—	—
Francia	2002	1 102	161	—	400	—
	2003	820	—	—	393	—
	2004	637	—	—	300	—
	2005	416	—	64	—	—
Germany	2001	—	2 156	1 501	—	—
Allemagne	2002	2 853	—	4 336	—	—
Alemania	2003	—	1 985	2 315	—	—
	2004	—	—	2 315	—	—
	2005	3 102	2 143	3 272	—	—
Ireland	2001	—	—	—	—	—
Irlande	2002	—	400	—	—	400
Irlanda	2003	—	—	—	—	400
	2004	—	—	—	—	—
	2005	—	—	—	—	—
United States	2001	841	—	536	—	—
États-Unis	2002	353	—	141	100	—
Estados Unidos	2003	606	—	258	—	—
	2004	640	—	424	—	—
	2005	682	—	198	200	—
Total	2001	841	2 156	2 060	—	—
	2002	4 308	561	4 477	500	400
	2003	1 474	2 031	2 574	393	400
	2004	1 471	196	2 739	300	—
	2005	4 300	2 143	3 634	200	—

Metamfetamine — Métamfétamine — Metanfetamina[e]

		kg	kg	kg	kg	kg
Chile	2001	—	—	—	—	4
Chili	2002	—	—	—	—	4
	2003	—	—	2	—	4
	2004	—	—	—	—	—
	2005	—	—	—	—	1
France	2001	3 285	—	4 324	3 005	—
Francia	2002	2 195	—	4 634	505	—
	2003	4 380	—	5 925	2 505	—
	2004	4 085	—	6 546	2 582	—
	2005	3 104	—	6 831	2 352	—

Schedule II.   B.1. Manufacturing countries *(continued)*
Tableau II.   B.1. Pays fabricants *(suite)*
Lista II.   B.1. Países fabricantes *(continuación)*

Country / Pays / País	Year / Année / Año	Quantity manufactured / Quantité fabriquée / Cantidad fabricada	Quantities used for the manufacture of non-psychotropic substances or products / Quantités utilisées pour la fabrication de substances ou produits non psychotropes / Cantidades utilizadas para la fabricación de sustancias o productos no sicotrópicos	Manufacturers' stocks / Stocks des fabricants / Existencias de los fabricantes	Exports / Exportations / Exportaciones	Imports / Importations / Importaciones

Metamfetamine — Métamfétamine — Metanfetamina[e] *(continued — suite — continuación)*

		kg	kg	kg	kg	kg
Germany	2001	—	—	—	—	—
Allemagne	2002	5 120[f]	5 120	—	—	—
Alemania	2003	—	—	—	—	—
	2004	2 523	2 523	—	—	—
	2005	—	—	—	—	—
Hungary	2001	—	—	1 200	—	—
Hongrie	2002	2 282	—	464	—	—
Hungría	2003	1 867	2 069	262	—	—
	2004	4 053	—	2 245	—	—
	2005	1 807	1 380	2 672	—	—
Ireland	2001	—	—	—	—	—
Irlande	2002	—	—	—	—	—
Irlanda	2003	—	—	—	—	—
	2004	—	—	475	—	81
	2005	475	—	475	—	—
Japan	2001	—	—	1	—	—
Japon	2002	—	—	1	—	—
Japón	2003	—	—	1	—	—
	2004	—	—	1	—	—
	2005	—	—	1	—	—
Switzerland	2001	—	—	5	—	—
Suisse	2002	—	—	5	—	—
Suiza	2003	—	—	5	—	—
	2004	—	—	5	—	—
	2005	—	—	5	—	—
United Kingdom	2001	—	—	101	—	—
Royaume-Uni	2002	—	—	2	—	100
Reino Unido	2003	—	—	—	—	—
	2004	—	—	3	—	—
	2005	—	—	2	—	—
United States	2001	1 692[g]	1 230	3 126	—	3 250
États-Unis	2002	1 385[g]	—	4 316	—	2 500
Estados Unidos	2003	1 164[g]	—	4 102	—	2 500
	2004	983[g]	—	3 772	—	2 500
	2005	1 153[g]	—	4 072	—	2 350
Total	2001	4 977	1 230	8 757	3 005	3 254
	2002	10 982	5 120	9 422	505	2 604
	2003	7 411	2 069	10 297	2 505	2 504
	2004	11 644	2 523	13 047	2 588	2 581
	2005	6 540	1 380	14 060	2 352	2 351

Schedule II.   B.1. Manufacturing countries *(continued)*
Tableau II.   B.1. Pays fabricants *(suite)*
Lista II.   B.1. Países fabricantes *(continuación)*

Country / Pays / País	Year / Année / Año	Quantity manufactured / Quantité fabriquée / Cantidad fabricada	Quantities used for the manufacture of non-psychotropic substances or products / Quantités utilisées pour la fabrication de substances ou produits non psychotropes / Cantidades utilizadas para la fabricación de sustancias o productos no sicotrópicos	Manufacturers' stocks / Stocks des fabricants / Existencias de los fabricantes	Exports / Exportations / Exportaciones	Imports / Importations / Importaciones
Methaqualone — Méthaqualone — Metacualona						
		kg	kg	kg	kg	kg
Switzerland	2001	—	—	1 292	—	—
Suisse	2002	—	—	810	—	—
Suiza	2003	—	—	501	1	—
	2004	—	—	258	—	—
	2005	—	—	257	—	—
Total	2001	—	—	1 292	—	—
	2002	—	—	810	—	—
	2003	—	—	501	1	—
	2004	—	—	258	—	—
	2005	—	—	257	—	—
Methylphenidate — Méthylphénidate — Metilfenidato						
		kg	kg	kg	kg	kg
Argentina	2001	—	—	6	6	24
Argentine	2002	—	—	4	5	27
	2003	—	—	4	3	19
	2004	—	—	1	—	59
	2005	—	—	17	—	38
Austria	2001	—	—	—	—	5
Autriche	2002	—	—	—	—	7
	2003	—	—	3	—	12
	2004	—	—	3	—	15
	2005	—	—	3	—	18
Brazil	2001	34	—	4	—	22
Brésil	2002	40	—	—	—	10
Brasil	2003	86	—	28	—	36
	2004	87	—	3	—	75
	2005	167	—	35	—	133
Canada	2001	—	—	553	199	849
Canadá	2002	—	—	1 218	285	1 481
	2003	—	—	579	360	1 150
	2004	—	—	725	325	1 909
	2005	—	—	888	217	1 254
Chile	2001	—	—	13	—	29
Chili	2002	—	—	6	—	29
	2003	—	—	5	—	56
	2004	—	—	8	—	58
	2005	—	—	30	—	98

Schedule II.   B.1. Manufacturing countries *(continued)*
Tableau II.   B.1. Pays fabricants *(suite)*
Lista II.   B.1. Países fabricantes *(continuación)*

Country / Pays / País	Year / Année / Año	Quantity manufactured / Quantité fabriquée / Cantidad fabricada	Quantities used for the manufacture of non-psychotropic substances or products / Quantités utilisées pour la fabrication de substances ou produits non psychotropes / Cantidades utilizadas para la fabricación de sustancias o productos no sicotrópicos	Manufacturers' stocks / Stocks des fabricants / Existencias de los fabricantes	Exports / Exportations / Exportaciones	Imports / Importations / Importaciones
Methylphenidate — Méthylphénidate — Metilfenidato *(continued — suite — continuación)*						
		kg	kg	kg	kg	kg
China	2001	34	—	—	—	—
Chine	2002	—	—	—	—	—
	2003	52	—	—	—	—
	2004	—	—	—	—	—
	2005	58	—	—	—	11
Colombia	2001	—	—	12	—	8
Colombie	2002	—	—	8	—	12
	2003	—	—	8	—	13
	2004	—	—	4	—	21
	2005	—	—	—	—	18
Denmark................	2001	—	—	—	7	18
Danemark	2002	—	—	2	10	28
Dinamarca	2003	—	—	29	7	56
	2004	—	—	35	7	50
	2005	—	—	38	4	59
Ecuador	2001	—	—	1	—	6
Équateur	2002	—	—	—	—	4
	2003	—	—	—	—	1
	2004	—	—	—	—	4
	2005	—	—	1	—	5
France	2001	—	—	1	—	21
Francia	2002	—	—	8	—	38
	2003	—	—	14	—	57
	2004	—	—	124	—	174
	2005	—	—	13	—	38
Germany	2001	—	—	76	34	610
Allemagne	2002	—	—	120	20	763
Alemania	2003	—	—	278	116	1 164
	2004	—	—	405	218	1 348
	2005	—	—	467	185	1 571
Hungary	2001	—	—	—	—	4
Hongrie	2002	—	—	2	—	5
Hungría	2003	—	—	—	—	1
	2004	—	—	1	—	3
	2005	—	—	1	—	3
India	2001	—	—	—	—	—
Inde	2002	117	—	6	96	—
	2003	—	—	—	294	—
	2004	493	—	11	332	69
	2005	5	—	65	10	21

Country / Pays / País	Year / Année / Año	Quantity manufactured / Quantité fabriquée / Cantidad fabricada	Quantities used for the manufacture of non-psychotropic substances or products / Quantités utilisées pour la fabrication de substances ou produits non psychotropes / Cantidades utilizadas para la fabricación de sustancias o productos no sicotrópicos	Manufacturers' stocks / Stocks des fabricants / Existencias de los fabricantes	Exports / Exportations / Exportaciones	Imports / Importations / Importaciones
Methylphenidate — Méthylphénidate — Metilfenidato *(continued — suite — continuación)*						
		kg	kg	kg	kg	kg
Ireland	2001	—	—	2	—	5
Irlande	2002	—	—	—	2	14
Irlanda	2003	—	—	—	—	15
	2004	—	—	—	—	27
	2005	—	—	—	—	15
Israel	2001	—	—	15	—	51
Israël	2002	—	—	18	—	67
	2003	—	—	23	—	92
	2004	—	—	37	—	128
	2005	—	—	18	—	166
Japan	2001	—	55	77	—	209
Japon	2002	—	—	80	—	261
Japón	2003	92	—	86	—	313
	2004	—	—	10	—	263
	2005	—	—	96	—	316
Lebanon	2001	—	—	—	—	2
Liban	2002	—	—	—	—	2
Líbano	2003	—	—	—	—	2
	2004	—	—	1	—	4
	2005	—	—	4	—	5
Luxembourg	2001	—	—	—	—	—
Luxemburgo	2002	—	—	1	—	5
	2003	?	?	?	?	?
	2004	?	?	?	?	?
	2005	—	—	2	—	—
Mexico	2001	—	—	23	—	108
Mexique	2002	—	—	—	—	118
México	2003	—	—	30	—	127
	2004	—	—	84	—	258
	2005	?	?	?	?	?
Netherlands	2001	—	—	20	8	201
Pays-Bas	2002	—	—	27	5	222
Países Bajos	2003	—	—	89	5	307
	2004	—	—	160	6	397
	2005	—	—	133	12	305
Peru	2001	—	—	—	—	1
Pérou	2002	?	?	?	?	?
Perú	2003	—	—	1	—	2
	2004	—	—	—	—	2
	2005	—	—	—	—	3

Schedule II. B.1. Manufacturing countries *(continued)*
Tableau II. B.1. Pays fabricants *(suite)*
Lista II. B.1. Países fabricantes *(continuación)*

Country Pays País	Year Année Año	Quantity manufactured Quantité fabriquée Cantidad fabricada	Quantities used for the manufacture of non-psychotropic substances or products Quantités utilisées pour la fabrication de substances ou produits non psychotropes Cantidades utilizadas para la fabricación de sustancias o productos no sicotrópicos	Manufacturers' stocks Stocks des fabricants Existencias de los fabricantes	Exports Exportations Exportaciones	Imports Importations Importaciones

Methylphenidate — Méthylphénidate — Metilfenidato *(continued — suite — continuación)*

		kg	kg	kg	kg	kg
Portugal	2001	—	—	—	—	2
	2002	—	—	—	—	2
	2003	—	—	—	—	24
	2004	—	—	19	—	34
	2005	—	—	16	—	23
South Africa	2001	—		30	—	56
Afrique du Sud	2002	—		—	—	78
Sudáfrica	2003	—		—	—	129
	2004	—		52	1	107
	2005	—		—	1	201
Spain	2001	231	—	—	164	—
Espagne	2002	524	—	—	346	58
España	2003	426	—	—	1 033	946
	2004	770	—	218	1 643	1 308
	2005	282	—	—	1 313	1 313
Sweden	2001	—	—	1	—	11
Suède	2002	—	—	6	—	25
Suecia	2003	—	—	9	—	37
	2004	—	—	33	—	80
	2005	—	—	58	—	112
Switzerland	2001	—	—	1 230	3 278	2 233
Suisse	2002	463	—	1 918	2 864	3 301
Suiza	2003	—	—	3 031	4 455	5 743
	2004	—	—	2 965	3 684	3 775
	2005	—	—	1 764	3 707	2 612
Turkey	2001	—	—	—	—	15
Turquie	2002	—	—	—	—	23
Turquía	2003	—	—	—	—	21
	2004	—	—	—	—	27
	2005	—	—	20	—	58
United Kingdom	2001	2 898	—	1 298	2 292	1 216
Royaume-Uni	2002	5 666	—	2 653	3 553	122
Reino Unido	2003	3 280	—	238	5 176	105
	2004	5 358	—	1 746	3 160	211
	2005	—	—	292	881	225
United States	2001	15 009	—	12 117	329	—
États-Unis	2002	20 725	—	14 747	501	—
Estados Unidos	2003	18 882	—	16 189	1 288	—
	2004	26 760	—	18 078	2 599	—
	2005	28 318	—	19 469	2 690	—

Schedule II. B.1. Manufacturing countries *(continued)*
Tableau II. B.1. Pays fabricants *(suite)*
Lista II. B.1. Países fabricantes *(continuación)*

Country / Pays / País	Year / Année / Año	Quantity manufactured / Quantité fabriquée / Cantidad fabricada	Quantities used for the manufacture of non-psychotropic substances or products / Quantités utilisées pour la fabrication de substances ou produits non psychotropes / Cantidades utilizadas para la fabricación de sustancias o productos no sicotrópicos	Manufacturers' stocks / Stocks des fabricants / Existencias de los fabricantes	Exports / Exportations / Exportaciones	Imports / Importations / Importaciones

Methylphenidate — Méthylphénidate — Metilfenidato *(continued — suite — continuación)*

		kg	kg	kg	kg	kg
Total	2001	18 206	55	15 479	6 317	5 706
	2002	27 535	—	20 824	7 687	6 702
	2003	22 818	—	20 644	12 737	10 428
	2004	33 468	—	24 723	11 975	10 406
	2005	28 830	—	23 430	9 020	8 621

Phencyclidine (PCP) — Fenciclidina (PCP)

		kg	kg	kg	kg	kg
United States .... États-Unis Estados Unidos	2001	—	—	—	—	—
	2002	—	—	1	—	—
	2003	—	—	1	—	—
	2004	1	—	2	—	—
	2005	2	—	2	—	—
Total	2001	—	—	—	—	—
	2002	—	—	1	—	—
	2003	—	—	1	—	—
	2004	1	—	2	—	—
	2005	2	—	2	—	—

Secobarbital — Sécobarbital

		kg	kg	kg	kg	kg
Canada .... Canadá	2001	—	—	75	—	71
	2002	—	—	84	—	138
	2003	—	—	83	—	—
	2004	—	—	3	—	3
	2005	—	—	—	—	—
Denmark .... Danemark Dinamarca	2001	—	—	48	369	—
	2002	—	—	44	4	—
	2003	—	—	—	—	—
	2004	—	—	—	—	—
	2005	—	—	—	—	—
Germany .... Allemagne Alemania	2001	2 281	—	827	1 949	736
	2002	1 022	—	846	761	—
	2003	354	—	251	599	—
	2004	807	—	428	511	—
	2005	817	—	477	556	—

Schedule II.   B.1. Manufacturing countries *(continued)*
Tableau II.   B.1. Pays fabricants *(suite)*
Lista II.   B.1. Países fabricantes *(continuación)*

Country Pays País	Year Année Año	Quantity manufactured Quantité fabriquée Cantidad fabricada	Quantities used for the manufacture of non-psychotropic substances or products Quantités utilisées pour la fabrication de substances ou produits non psychotropes Cantidades utilizadas para la fabricación de sustancias o productos no sicotrópicos	Manufacturers' stocks Stocks des fabricants Existencias de los fabricantes	Exports Exportations Exportaciones	Imports Importations Importaciones
Secobarbital — Sécobarbital *(continued — suite — continuación)*						
		kg	kg	kg	kg	kg
Ireland	2001	—	—	—	88	355
Irlande	2002	—	—	244	52	3
Irlanda	2003	—	—	235	6	—
	2004	—	—	151	84	2
	2005	78	—	78	60	1
Japan	2001	—	—	3	—	—
Japon	2002	3	—	1	—	—
Japón	2003	8	—	4	—	—
	2004	3	—	—	—	—
	2005	4	—	4	—	—
Mexico	2001	—	—	10	—	—
Mexique	2002	—	—	10	—	—
México	2003	—	—	—	—	—
	2004	—	—	—	—	—
	2005	?	?	?	?	?
Netherlands	2001	—	—	17	—	15
Pays-Bas	2002	—	—	10	1	4
Países Bajos	2003	—	—	14	—	9
	2004	—	—	61	81	136
	2005	—	—	31	28	—
Sweden	2001	—	—	4	53	19
Suède	2002	—	—	11	—	41
Suecia	2003	—	—	22	—	50
	2004	—	—	18	21	46
	2005	—	—	6	—	27
United Kingdom	2001	—	—	270	765	466
Royaume-Uni	2002	—	—	445	70	57
Reino Unido	2003	—	—	—	74	552
	2004	—	487	385	74	368
	2005	—	—	—	37	568
United States	2001	1 945	—	1 672	—	—
États-Unis	2002	—	—	813	—	—
Estados Unidos	2003	—	—	—	—	—
	2004	—	—	385	—	—
	2005	—	—	219	—	—
Total	2001	4 226	—	2 926	3 224	1 662
	2002	1 025	—	2 508	888	243
	2003	362	—	609	679	611
	2004	810	487	1 431	771	555
	2005	899	—	815	681	596

Schedule II.   B.1. Manufacturing countries *(continued)*
Tableau II.   B.1. Pays fabricants *(suite)*
Lista II.   B.1. Países fabricantes *(continuación)*

Country / Pays / País	Year / Année / Año	Quantity manufactured / Quantité fabriquée / Cantidad fabricada	Quantities used for the manufacture of non-psychotropic substances or products / Quantités utilisées pour la fabrication de substances ou produits non psychotropes / Cantidades utilizadas para la fabricación de sustancias o productos no sicotrópicos	Manufacturers' stocks / Stocks des fabricants / Existencias de los fabricantes	Exports / Exportations / Exportaciones	Imports / Importations / Importaciones

Delta-9-tetrahydrocannabinol — *Delta*-9-tétrahydrocannabinol — *Delta*-9-tetrahidrocannabinol

		kg	kg	kg	kg	kg
Canada	2001	—	—	—	—	—
Canadá	2002	—	—	—	—	1
	2003	—	—	1	—	1
	2004	—	—	2	—	1
	2005	2	—	4	—	2
Germany	2001	1	—	—	—	—
Allemagne	2002	4	—	1	—	—
Alemania	2003	10	—	2	2	5
	2004	13	—	5	1	—
	2005	5	—	6	—	2
Switzerland	2001	—	—	—	—	—
Suisse	2002	—	—	—	—	—
Suiza	2003	—	—	—	—	—
	2004	—	—	—	—	—
	2005	12	—	12	—	—
United Kingdom	2001	3	—	4	—	—
Royaume-Uni	2002	4	—	8	—	—
Reino Unido	2003	—	—	54	5	—
	2004	—	—	71	—	—
	2005	2	—	167	2	—
United States	2001	313	—	184	2	—
États-Unis	2002	109	—	145	2	—
Estados Unidos	2003	109	—	147	1	—
	2004	136	—	172	2	—
	2005	179	—	195	3	—
Total	2001	317	—	188	2	—
	2002	117	—	154	2	1
	2003	119	—	204	8	6
	2004	149	—	250	3	1
	2005	200	—	384	5	4

Zipeprol — Zipéprol

		kg	kg	kg	kg	kg
Chile	2001	—	—	53	—	—
Chili	2002	—	—	33	—	—
	2003	—	—	33	—	—
	2004	—	—	10	—	—
	2005	—	—	10	—	—

Schedule II. B.1. Manufacturing countries *(concluded)*
Tableau II. B.1. Pays fabricants *(fin)*
Lista II. B.1. Países fabricantes *(conclusión)*

Country Pays País	Year Année Año	Quantity manufactured Quantité fabriquée Cantidad fabricada	Quantities used for the manufacture of non-psychotropic substances or products Quantités utilisées pour la fabrication de substances ou produits non psychotropes Cantidades utilizadas para la fabricación de sustancias o productos no sicotrópicos	Manufacturers' stocks Stocks des fabricants Existencias de los fabricantes	Exports Exportations Exportaciones	Imports Importations Importaciones
		Zipeprol — Zipéprol *(continued — suite — continuación)*				
		kg	kg	kg	kg	kg
Colombia	2001	—	—	74	—	—
Colombie	2002	—	—	—	—	—
	2003	—	—	—	—	—
	2004	—	—	—	—	—
	2005	—	—	—	—	—
France	2001	666	—	166	420	—
Francia	2002	—	—	166	—	—
	2003	—	—	—	—	—
	2004	—	—	—	—	—
	2005	—	—	—	—	—
Mexico	2001	—	—	419	—	—
Mexique	2002	—	—	134	—	—
México	2003	—	—	26	—	50
	2004	—	—	125	—	117
	2005	?	?	?	?	?
Switzerland	2001	—	—	2	846	420
Suisse	2002	—	—	—	—	—
Suiza	2003	—	—	—	—	—
	2004	—	—	756	873	1629
	2005	—	—	588	168	—
Total	2001	666	—	714	1266	420
	2002	—	—	333	—	—
	2003	—	—	59	—	50
	2004	—	—	891	873	1 746
	2005	—	—	598	168	—

[a]Partially converted into dexamfetamine. — Partiellement transformés en dexamfétamine. —Parcialmente transformados en dexanfetamina.

[b]Used for the manufacture of fenproporex. — Utilisés pour la fabrication de fenproporex. — Utilizados para la fabricación de fenproporex.

[c]Used for the manufacture of clobenzorex. — Utilisée pour la fabrication de clobenzorex. — Utilizada para la fabricación de clobenzorex.

[d]Used for the manufacture of amfetamine. — Utilisée pour la fabrication d'amfétamine. — Utilizada para la fabricación de anfetamina.

[e]Including metamfetamine racemate. — Y compris le racémate de métamfétamine. — Incluye racemato de metanfetamina.

[f]Used for the manufacture of levopropylhexedrine. — Utilisée pour la fabrication de lévopropylhéxédrine. — Utilizada para la fabricación de levopropilhexedrina.

[g]Partially used for the manufacture of benzfetamine. — Partiellement utilisée pour la fabrication de benzfétamine. — Parcialmente utilizada para la fabricación de benzfetamina.

Schedule II.   B.2.   Exports
Tableau II.   B.2.   Exportations
Lista II.   B.2.   Exportaciones

Country / Pays / País	Year / Année / Año	Amfetamine / Amfétamine / Anfetamina	Dexamfetamine / Dexamfétamine / Dexanfetamina	Fenetylline / Fénétylline / Fenetilina	Metamfetamine[a] / Métamfétamine[a] / Metanfetamina[a]	Methaqualone / Méthaqualone / Metacualona	Methylphenidate / Méthylphénidate / Metilfenidato	Secobarbital / Sécobarbital	Zipeprol / Zipéprol
		kg	kg	kg	kg	kg	kg	kg	kg
Argentina / Argentine	2001	—	—	—	—	—	6	—	—
	2002	—	—	—	—	—	5	—	—
	2003	—	—	—	—	—	3	—	—
	2004	—	—	—	—	—	—	—	—
	2005	—	—	—	—	—	—	—	—
Belgium / Belgique / Bélgica	2001	—	—	—	—	—	—	—	—
	2002	—	—	—	—	—	—	—	—
	2003	—	—	5	—	—	3	9	—
	2004	—	—	6	—	—	1	—	—
	2005	—	—	7	—	—	2	—	—
Canada / Canadá	2001	—	—	—	—	—	199	—	..
	2002	—	—	—	—	—	285	—	—
	2003	—	—	—	—	—	360	—	—
	2004	—	—	—	—	—	325	—	—
	2005	—	—	—	—	—	217	—	—
Denmark / Danemark / Dinamarca	2001	—	—	—	—	—	7	369	—
	2002	—	—	—	—	—	10	4	—
	2003	—	—	—	—	—	7	—	—
	2004	—	—	—	—	—	7	—	—
	2005	—	—	—	—	—	4	—	—
France / Francia	2001	64	207	—	3 000	—	—	—	420
	2002	74	197	—	900	—	—	—	—
	2003	31	255	—	2 894	—	—	—	—
	2004	70	250	—	2 882	—	—	—	—
	2005	37	206	—	2 503	—	—	—	—
Germany / Allemagne / Alemania	2001	—	—	553	—	—	34	1 949	—
	2002	—	—	—	—	—	20	761	—
	2003	—	—	—	—	—	116	599	—
	2004	—	—	—	—	—	218	511	—
	2005	—	—	—	—	—	185	556	—
India / Inde	2001	—	—	—	—	—	—	—	—
	2002	—	—	—	—	—	96	—	—
	2003	—	—	—	—	—	294	—	—
	2004	—	—	—	—	—	332	—	—
	2005	—	—	—	—	—	10	—	—
Ireland / Irlande / Irlanda	2001	—	—	—	—	—	—	88	—
	2002	—	—	—	—	—	2	52	—
	2003	—	—	—	—	—	—	6	—
	2004	—	—	—	—	—	—	84	—
	2005	—	—	—	—	—	—	60	—
Netherlands / Pays-Bas / Países Bajos	2001	—	—	60	—	—	8	—	—
	2002	1	—	59	—	—	5	1	—
	2003	—	—	90	—	—	5	—	—
	2004	3	6	36	—	6	6	81	—
	2005	—	9	68	—	—	12	28	—

Country / Pays / País	Year / Année / Año	Amfe-tamine / Amfé-tamine / Anfe-tamina	Dexam-fetamine / Dexam-fétamine / Dexan-fetamina	Fenetylline / Fénétylline / Fenetilina	Metam-fetamine[a] / Métam-fétamine[a] / Metan-fetamina[a]	Metha-qualone / Métha-qualone / Meta-cualona	Methyl-phenidate / Méthyl-phénidate / Metil-fenidato	Secobarbital / Sécobarbital	Zipeprol / Zipéprol
		kg	kg	kg	kg	kg	kg	kg	kg
New Zealand	2001	—	—	—	—	—	—	—	..
Nouvelle-Zélande	2002	—	—	—	—	—	—	—	—
Nueva Zelandia	2003	—	—	—	—	—	16	—	—
	2004	—	—	—	—	—	15	—	—
	2005	—	—	—	—	—	6	—	—
Norway	2001	1	—	—	—	—	—	—	—
Norvège	2002	—	—	—	—	—	—	—	—
Noruega	2003	—	—	—	—	—	—	—	—
	2004	—	—	—	—	—	—	—	—
	2005	—	—	—	—	—	—	—	—
Panama	2001	—	—	—	—	—	31	—	—
Panamá	2002	—	—	—	—	—	12	—	—
	2003	—	—	—	—	—	10	—	—
	2004	—	—	—	—	—	25	—	—
	2005	—	—	—	—	—	28	—	—
South Africa	2001	—	—	—	—	—	—	—	—
Afrique du Sud	2002	—	—	—	—	—	—	—	—
Sudáfrica	2003	—	—	—	—	—	—	—	—
	2004	—	—	—	—	—	1	—	—
	2005	—	—	—	—	—	1	—	—
Spain	2001	—	—	—	—	—	164	—	—
Espagne	2002	—	—	—	—	—	346	—	—
España	2003	—	—	—	—	—	1 033	—	—
	2004	—	—	—	—	—	1 643	—	—
	2005	—	—	—	—	—	1 313	—	—
Sweden	2001	—	—	—	—	—	—	53	—
Suède	2002	—	—	—	—	—	—	—	—
Suecia	2003	—	—	—	—	—	—	—	—
	2004	—	—	—	—	—	—	21	—
	2005	—	—	—	—	—	—	—	—
Switzerland	2001	—	3	—	—	—	3 278	—	846
Suisse	2002	—	4	—	—	—	2 864	—	—
Suiza	2003	—	3	—	—	1	4 455	—	—
	2004	—	3	—	—	—	3 684	—	873
	2005	—	2	—	—	—	3 707	—	168
United Kingdom	2001	—	1	—	—	—	2 292	765	—
Royaume-Uni	2002	—	2	—	—	—	3 553	70	—
Reino Unido	2003	—	1	—	—	—	5 176	74	—
	2004	1	—	—	—	—	3 160	74	—
	2005	—	3	—	—	—	881	37	—
United States	2001	—	152	—	—	—	329	—	—
États-Unis	2002	9	152	—	100	—	501	—	—
Estados Unidos	2003	2	123	—	—	—	1 288	—	—
	2004	79	157	—	—	—	2 599	—	—
	2005	41	104	—	200	—	2 690	—	—

Schedule II.   B.2.   Exports *(concluded)*
Tableau II.   B.2.   Exportations *(fin)*
Lista II.   B.2.   Exportaciones *(conclusión)*

Country / Pays / País	Year / Année / Año	Amfe-tamine / Amfé-tamine / Anfe-tamina	Dexam-fetamine / Dexam-fétamine / Dexan-fetamina	Fenetylline / Fénétylline / Fenetilina	Metam-fetamine[a] / Métam-fétamine[a] / Metan-fetamina[a]	Metha-qualone / Métha-qualone / Meta-cualona	Methyl-phenidate / Méthyl-phénidate / Metil-fenidato	Secobarbital / Sécobarbital	Zipeprol / Zipéprol
		kg	kg	kg	kg	kg	kg	kg	kg
Total	2001	65	363	613	3 000	—	6 348	3 224	1 266
	2002	84	355	59	1 500	—	7 699	888	—
	2003	33	382	95	2 894	1	12 766	688	—
	2004	153	416	42	2 882	6	12 016	771	873
	2005	78	324	75	2 703	—	9 057	681	191

[a] Including levomethamphetamine and metamfetamine racemate. — Y compris la lévométhamphétamine et le racémate de métamfétamine. — Incluye levometanfetamina y racemato de metanfetamina.

Schedule II.   B.3.   Imports
Tableau II.   B.3.   Importations
Lista II.   B.3.   Importaciones

Country or territory / Pays ou territoire / País o territorio	Year / Année / Año	Amfe-tamine / Amfé-tamine / Anfe-tamina	Dexam-fetamine / Dexam-fétamine / Dexan-fetamina	Fenetylline / Fénétylline / Fenetilina	Metam-fetamine[a] / Métam-fétamine[a] / Metan-fetamina[a]	Metha-qualone / Métha-qualone / Meta-cualona	Methyl-phenidate / Méthyl-phénidate / Metil-fenidato	Secobarbital / Sécobarbital	Zipeprol / Zipéprol
		kg	kg	kg	kg	kg	kg	kg	kg
Argentina .... Argentine	2001	—	—	—	—	—	24	—	—
	2002	—	—	—	—	—	27	—	—
	2003	—	—	—	—	—	19	—	—
	2004	—	—	—	—	—	59	—	—
	2005	—	—	—	—	—	38	—	—
Australia .... Australie	2001	—	157	—	—	—	182	—	—
	2002	—	145	—	—	—	163	—	—
	2003	—	184	—	—	—	281	1	—
	2004	—	230	—	—	—	212	2	—
	2005	—	131	—	—	—	307	4	—
Austria .... Autriche	2001	—	—	—	—	—	5	—	—
	2002	—	—	—	—	—	7	—	—
	2003	—	—	—	—	—	12	—	—
	2004	—	—	—	—	—	15	—	—
	2005	—	—	—	—	—	18	—	—
Barbados .... Barbade	2001	—	—	—	—	—	—	—	—
	2002	—	—	—	—	—	—	—	—
	2003	—	—	—	—	—	—	—	—
	2004	—	—	—	—	—	—	—	—
	2005	—	—	—	—	—	1	—	—
Belgium .... Belgique Bélgica	2001	4	—	54	—	—	57	—	—
	2002	7	3	27	—	—	88	72	—
	2003	1	—	90	—	—	129	46	—
	2004	6	8	36	—	—	113	81	—
	2005	5	9	68	—	—	141	28	—
Botswana	2001	—	—	—	—	—	—	—	—
	2002	—	—	—	—	—	—	—	—
	2003	?	?	?	?	?	?	?	?
	2004	?	?	?	?	?	?	?	?
	2005	—	—	—	—	—	—	—	—
Brazil .... Brésil Brasil	2001	—	—	—	—	—	22	—	—
	2002	—	—	—	—	—	10	—	—
	2003	—	—	—	—	—	36	—	—
	2004	—	—	—	—	—	75	—	—
	2005	—	—	—	—	—	133	—	—
Canada .... Canadá	2001	—	152	—	—	—	849	71	..
	2002	9	173	—	—	—	1 481	138	—
	2003	1	99	—	—	—	1 150	—	—
	2004	47	176	—	—	—	1 909	3	—
	2005	19	268	—	—	—	1 254	—	—
Chile .... Chili	2001	14	—	—	4	—	29	—	—
	2002	14	—	—	4	—	29	—	—
	2003	10	—	—	4	—	56	—	—
	2004	10	—	—	—	—	58	—	—
	2005	21	—	—	1	—	98	—	—

Country or territory / Pays ou territoire / País o territorio	Year / Année / Año	Amfe-tamine / Amfé-tamine / Anfe-tamina	Dexam-fetamine / Dexam-fétamine / Dexan-fetamina	Fenetylline / Fénétylline / Fenetilina	Metam-fetamine[a] / Métam-fétamine[a] / Metan-fetamina[a]	Metha-qualone / Métha-qualone / Meta-cualona	Methyl-phenidate / Méthyl-phénidate / Metil-fenidato	Secobarbital / Sécobarbital	Zipeprol / Zipéprol
		kg	kg	kg	kg	kg	kg	kg	kg
China	2001	—	—	—	—	—	—	—	—
Chine	2002	—	—	—	—	—	—	—	—
	2003	—	—	—	—	—	—	—	—
	2004	—	—	—	—	—	—	—	—
	2005	—	—	—	—	—	11	—	—
Hong Kong SAR of China	2001	—	—	—	—	—	5	1	—
RAS de Hong Kong (Chine)	2002	—	—	—	—	—	8	—	—
RAE de Hong Kong	2003	—	—	—	—	—	8	1	—
de China	2004	—	—	—	—	—	11	2	—
	2005	—	—	—	—	—	14	—	—
Colombia	2001	—	—	—	—	—	8	—	—
Colombie	2002	—	—	—	—	—	12	—	—
	2003	—	—	—	—	—	13	—	—
	2004	—	—	—	—	—	21	—	—
	2005	—	—	—	—	—	18	—	—
Costa Rica	2001	—	—	—	—	—	22	—	—
	2002	—	—	—	—	—	9	—	—
	2003	—	—	—	—	—	5	—	—
	2004	—	—	—	—	—	16	—	—
	2005	—	—	—	—	—	12	—	—
Cuba	2001	—	—	—	—	—	6	—	—
	2002	—	—	—	—	—	—	—	—
	2003	—	—	—	—	—	26	—	—
	2004	—	—	—	—	—	26	—	—
	2005	—	—	—	—	—	17	—	—
Cyprus	2001	—	—	—	—	—	—	9	—
Chypre	2002	—	—	—	—	—	—	27	—
Chipre	2003	—	—	—	—	—	1	23	—
	2004	—	—	—	—	—	—	27	—
	2005	—	—	—	—	—	1	9	—
Czech Republic	2001	—	—	—	—	—	4	—	—
République tchèque	2002	—	—	—	—	—	9	—	—
República Checa	2003	—	—	—	—	—	3	—	—
	2004	—	—	—	—	—	5	—	—
	2005	—	—	—	—	—	13	—	—
Denmark	2001	—	—	—	—	—	18	—	—
Danemark	2002	1	—	—	—	—	28	—	—
Dinamarca	2003	—	—	—	—	—	56	—	—
	2004	1	—	—	—	—	50	—	—
	2005	—	—	—	—	—	59	—	—
Dominican Republic	2001	—	—	—	—	—	1	—	—
République dominicaine	2002	—	—	—	—	—	—	—	—
República Dominicana	2003	—	—	—	—	—	—	—	—
	2004	—	—	—	—	—	1	—	—
	2005	—	—	—	—	—	2	—	—

Schedule II. B.3. Imports *(continued)*
Tableau II. B.3. Importations *(suite)*
Lista II. B.3. Importaciones *(continuación)*

Country or territory Pays ou territoire País o territorio	Year Année Año	Amfe- tamine Amfé- tamine Anfe- tamina	Dexam- fetamine Dexam- fétamine Dexan- fetamina	Fenetylline Fénétylline Fenetilina	Metam- fetamine[a] Métam- fétamine[a] Metan- fetamina[a]	Metha- qualone Métha- qualone Meta- cualona	Methyl- phenidate Méthyl- phénidate Metil- fenidato	Secobarbital Sécobarbital	Zipeprol Zipéprol
		kg	kg	kg	kg	kg	kg	kg	kg
Ecuador	2001	—	—	—	—	—	6	—	—
Équateur	2002	—	—	—	—	—	4	—	—
	2003	—	—	—	—	—	1	—	—
	2004	—	—	—	—	—	4	—	—
	2005	—	—	—	—	—	5	—	—
El Salvador	2001	—	—	—	—	—	1	—	—
	2002	—	—	—	—	—	2	—	—
	2003	—	—	—	—	—	2	—	—
	2004	—	—	—	—	—	3	—	—
	2005	—	—	—	—	—	4	—	—
Finland	2001	—	—	—	—	—	4	—	—
Finlande	2002	—	—	—	—	—	3	—	—
Finlandia	2003	—	—	—	—	—	16	—	—
	2004	—	—	—	—	—	18	—	—
	2005	—	1	—	—	—	33	—	—
France	2001	—	—	—	—	—	21	—	—
Francia	2002	—	—	—	—	—	38	—	—
	2003	—	—	—	—	—	57	—	—
	2004	—	—	—	—	—	174	—	—
	2005	—	—	1	—	—	38	—	—
Germany	2001	36	—	33	—	—	610	736	—
Allemagne	2002	39	—	32	—	—	763	—	—
Alemania	2003	1	—	4	—	—	1 164	—	—
	2004	38	—	5	—	—	1 348	—	—
	2005	1	—	6	—	—	1 571	—	—
Greece	2001	—	—	—	—	—	—	—	—
Grèce	2002	—	—	—	—	—	—	—	—
Grecia	2003	—	—	—	—	—	—	—	—
	2004	—	—	—	—	—	6	—	—
	2005	—	—	—	—	—	5	—	—
Honduras	2001	—	—	—	—	—	—	—	—
	2002	?	?	?	?	?	?	?	?
	2003	—	—	—	—	—	—	—	—
	2004	—	—	—	—	—	1	—	—
	2005	?	?	?	?	?	?	?	?
Hungary	2001	—	—	—	—	—	4	—	—
Hongrie	2002	—	—	—	—	—	5	—	—
Hungría	2003	—	—	—	—	—	1	—	—
	2004	—	—	—	—	—	3	—	—
	2005	—	—	—	—	—	3	—	—
Iceland	2001	1	—	—	—	—	7	—	—
Islande	2002	—	—	—	—	—	10	—	—
Islandia	2003	1	—	—	—	—	16	—	—
	2004	1	—	—	—	—	23	—	—
	2005	—	—	—	—	—	—	—	—

Schedule II. B.3. Imports *(continued)*
Tableau II. B.3. Importations *(suite)*
Lista II. B.3. Importaciones *(continuación)*

Country or territory Pays ou territoire País o territorio	Year Année Año	Amfe- tamine Amfé- tamine Anfe- tamina	Dexam- fetamine Dexam- fétamine Dexan- fetamina	Fenetylline Fénétylline Fenetilina	Metam- fetamine[a] Métam- fétamine[a] Metan- fetamina[a]	Metha- qualone Métha- qualone Meta- cualona	Methyl- phenidate Méthyl- phénidate Metil- fenidato	Secobarbital Sécobarbital	Zipeprol Zipéprol
		kg	kg	kg	kg	kg	kg	kg	kg
India	2001	—	—	—	—	—	—	—	—
Inde	2002	—	—	—	—	—	—	—	—
	2003	—	—	—	—	—	—	—	—
	2004	—	—	—	—	—	69	—	—
	2005	—	—	—	—	—	21	—	—
Indonesia	2001	—	—	—	—	—	3	—	—
Indonésie	2002	—	—	—	—	—	3	—	—
	2003	—	—	—	—	—	8	—	—
	2004	—	—	—	—	—	4	—	—
	2005	—	—	—	—	—	6	—	—
Iran (Islamic Republic of) ...	2001	—	—	—	—	—	29	—	—
Iran (Rép. islamique d')	2002	—	—	—	—	—	52	—	—
Irán (Rep. Islámica del)	2003	—	—	—	—	—	1	—	—
	2004	—	—	—	—	—	—	—	—
	2005	—	—	—	—	—	40	—	—
Ireland	2001	—	—	—	—	—	5	355	—
Irlande	2002	—	—	—	—	—	14	3	—
Irlanda	2003	—	—	—	—	—	15	—	—
	2004	—	—	—	81	—	27	2	—
	2005	—	—	—	—	—	15	1	—
Israel	2001	—	—	—	—	—	51	—	—
Israël	2002	—	—	—	—	—	67	—	—
	2003	2	2	—	—	—	92	—	—
	2004	—	—	—	—	—	128	—	—
	2005	—	—	—	—	—	166	—	—
Jamaica	2001	—	—	—	—	—	—	—	—
Jamaïque	2002	—	—	—	—	—	—	—	—
	2003	—	—	—	—	—	1	—	—
	2004	—	—	—	—	—	—	—	—
	2005	—	—	—	—	—	1	—	—
Japan	2001	—	—	—	—	—	209	—	—
Japon	2002	—	—	—	—	—	261	—	—
Japón	2003	—	—	—	—	—	313	—	—
	2004	—	—	—	—	—	263	—	—
	2005	—	—	—	—	—	316	—	—
Jordan	2001	—	—	—	—	—	—	—	—
Jordanie	2002	—	—	—	—	—	—	—	—
Jordania	2003	—	—	—	—	—	1	—	—
	2004	—	—	—	—	—	1	—	—
	2005	—	—	—	—	—	1	—	—
Kenya	2001	—	—	—	—	—	—	—	—
	2002	—	—	—	—	—	—	—	—
	2003	—	—	—	—	—	—	—	—
	2004	—	—	—	—	—	1	—	—
	2005	?	?	?	?	?	?	?	?

Schedule II. B.3. Imports *(continued)*
Tableau II. B.3. Importations *(suite)*
Lista II. B.3. Importaciones *(continuación)*

Country or territory / Pays ou territoire / País o territorio	Year / Année / Año	Amfe-tamine / Amfé-tamine / Anfe-tamina	Dexam-fetamine / Dexam-fétamine / Dexan-fetamina	Fenetylline / Fénétylline / Fenetilina	Metam-fetamine[a] / Métam-fétamine[a] / Metan-fetamina[a]	Metha-qualone / Métha-qualone / Meta-cualona	Methyl-phenidate / Méthyl-phénidate / Metil-fenidato	Secobarbital / Sécobarbital	Zipeprol / Zipéprol
		kg	kg	kg	kg	kg	kg	kg	kg
Lebanon	2001	—	—	—	—	—	2	—	—
Liban	2002	—	—	—	—	—	2	—	—
Líbano	2003	—	—	—	—	—	2	—	—
	2004	—	—	—	—	—	4	—	—
	2005	—	—	—	—	—	5	—	—
Luxembourg	2001	—	—	—	—	—	—	—	—
Luxemburgo	2002	—	—	—	—	—	5	—	—
	2003	?	?	?	?	?	?	?	?
	2004	?	?	?	?	?	?	?	?
	2005	—	—	—	—	—	—	—	—
Malaysia	2001	—	—	—	—	—	1	—	—
Malaisie	2002	—	—	—	—	—	3	—	—
Malasia	2003	—	—	—	—	—	2	—	—
	2004	—	—	—	—	—	5	—	—
	2005	—	—	—	—	—	6	—	—
Mauritius	2001	—	—	—	—	—	—	—	—
Maurice	2002	—	—	—	—	—	—	—	—
Mauricio	2003	—	—	—	—	—	—	—	—
	2004	—	—	—	—	—	—	—	—
	2005	—	—	—	—	—	2	—	—
Mexico	2001	—	—	—	—	—	108	—	—
Mexique	2002	—	—	—	—	—	118	—	—
México	2003	—	—	—	—	—	127	—	50
	2004	—	—	—	—	—	258	—	117
	2005	?	?	?	?	?	?	?	?
Namibia	2001	?	?	?	?	?	?	?	?
Namibie	2002	?	?	?	?	?	?	?	?
	2003	—	—	—	—	—	—	—	—
	2004	—	—	—	—	—	1	—	—
	2005	—	—	—	—	—	—	—	—
Netherlands	2001	—	7	526	—	—	201	15	—
Pays-Bas	2002	1	7	—	—	—	222	4	—
Países Bajos	2003	1	5	—	—	—	307	9	—
	2004	6	21	—	—	397	397	136	—
	2005	—	16	—	—	—	305	—	—
Netherlands Antilles	2001	—	—	—	—	—	—	—	—
Antilles néerlandaises	2002	—	—	—	—	—	—	—	—
Antillas Neerlandesas	2003	—	—	—	—	—	—	—	—
	2004	—	—	—	—	—	—	—	—
	2005	—	—	—	—	—	1	—	—
New Zealand	2001	—	2	—	—	—	53	—	..
Nouvelle-Zélande	2002	—	1	—	—	—	64	—	—
Nueva Zelandia	2003	—	2	—	—	—	72	—	—
	2004	—	2	—	—	—	96	—	—
	2005	—	2	—	—	—	57	—	—

Schedule II.   B.3. Imports *(continued)*
Tableau II.   B.3. Importations *(suite)*
Lista II.   B.3. Importaciones *(continuación)*

Country or territory Pays ou territoire País o territorio	Year Année Año	Amfe-tamine Amfé-tamine Anfe-tamina	Dexam-fetamine Dexam-fétamine Dexan-fetamina	Fenetylline Fénétylline Fenetilina	Metam-fetamine[a] Métam-fétamine[a] Metan-fetamina[a]	Metha-qualone Métha-qualone Meta-cualona	Methyl-phenidate Méthyl-phénidate Metil-fenidato	Secobarbital Sécobarbital	Zipeprol Zipéprol
		kg	kg	kg	kg	kg	kg	kg	kg
Nicaragua.............	2001	—	—	—	—	—	2	—	—
	2002	—	—	—	—	—	2	—	—
	2003	—	—	—	—	—	2	—	—
	2004	—	—	—	—	—	2	—	—
	2005	—	—	—	—	—	3	—	—
Norway.............	2001	1	1	—	—	—	38	—	—
Norvège	2002	—	1	—	—	—	46	—	—
Noruega	2003	1	1	—	—	—	105	—	—
	2004	1	1	—	—	—	109	—	—
	2005	1	3	—	—	—	128	—	—
Oman.............	2001	—	—	—	—	—	—	—	—
Omán	2002	—	—	—	—	—	0	—	—
	2003	—	—	—	—	—	—	—	—
	2004	—	—	—	—	—	—	—	—
	2005	—	—	—	—	—	—	—	—
Pakistan.............	2001	?	?	?	?	?	?	?	?
Pakistán	2002	—	—	—	—	—	—	—	—
	2003	—	—	—	—	—	—	—	—
	2004	—	—	—	—	—	—	—	—
	2005	—	—	—	—	—	5	—	—
Panama.............	2001	—	—	—	—	—	34	—	—
Panamá	2002	—	—	—	—	—	28	—	—
	2003	—	—	—	—	—	9	—	—
	2004	—	—	—	—	—	40	—	—
	2005	—	—	—	—	—	43	—	—
Paraguay.............	2001	—	—	—	—	—	—	—	—
	2002	—	—	—	—	—	1	—	—
	2003	—	—	—	—	—	2	—	—
	2004	?	?	?	?	?	?	?	?
	2005	?	?	?	?	?	?	?	?
Peru.............	2001	—	—	—	—	—	1	—	—
Pérou	2002	?	?	?	?	?	?	?	?
Perú	2003	—	—	—	—	—	2	—	—
	2004	—	—	—	—	—	2	—	—
	2005	—	—	—	—	—	3	—	—
Poland.............	2001	—	—	—	—	—	—	—	—
Pologne	2002	—	—	—	—	—	—	—	—
Polonia	2003	—	—	—	—	—	—	—	—
	2004	—	—	—	—	—	—	—	—
	2005	—	—	—	—	—	7	—	—
Portugal.............	2001	—	—	—	—	—	2	—	—
	2002	—	—	—	—	—	2	—	—
	2003	—	—	—	—	—	24	—	—
	2004	—	—	—	—	—	34	—	—
	2005	—	—	—	—	—	23	—	—

Country or territory / Pays ou territoire / País o territorio	Year / Année / Año	Amfetamine / Amfétamine / Anfetamina	Dexamfetamine / Dexamfétamine / Dexanfetamina	Fenetylline / Fénétylline / Fenetilina	Metamfetamine[a] / Métamfétamine[a] / Metanfetamina[a]	Methaqualone / Méthaqualone / Metacualona	Methylphenidate / Méthylphénidate / Metilfenidato	Secobarbital / Sécobarbital	Zipeprol / Zipéprol
		kg	kg	kg	kg	kg	kg	kg	kg
Republic of Korea	2001	—	—	—	—	—	33	—	182
République de Corée	2002	—	—	—	—	—	52	—	—
República de Corea	2003	—	—	—	—	—	52	—	84
	2004	—	—	—	—	—	73	—	—
	2005	—	—	—	—	—	—	—	—
Russian Federation	2001	—	—	—	—	—	—	—	—
Fédération de Russie	2002	—	—	—	—	—	—	—	—
Federación de Rusia	2003	—	—	—	—	—	—	—	—
	2004	—	—	—	—	—	—	—	—
	2005	4	—	—	—	—	—	—	—
Saudi Arabia	2001	—	—	—	—	—	3	—	—
Arabie saoudite	2002	—	—	—	—	—	4	—	—
Arabia Saudita	2003	—	—	·	—	—	4	—	—
	2004	—	—	—	—	—	6	—	—
	2005	—	—	—	—	—	5	—	—
Singapore	2001	—	—	—	—	—	—	—	—
Singapour	2002	—	—	—	—	—	2	—	—
Singapur	2003	—	—	—	—	—	3	—	—
	2004	—	—	—	—	—	6	—	—
	2005	—	—	—	—	—	4	—	—
Slovenia	2001	—	—	—	—	—	1	—	—
Slovénie	2002	—	—	—	—	—	—	—	—
Eslovenia	2003	—	—	—	—	—	1	—	—
	2004	—	—	—	—	—	1	—	—
	2005	—	—	—	—	—	1	—	—
South Africa	2001	—	—	—	—	—	56	—	—
Afrique du Sud	2002	—	—	—	—	—	78	—	—
Sudáfrica	2003	—	—	—	—	—	129	—	—
	2004	—	—	—	—	—	107	—	—
	2005	—	—	—	—	—	201	—	—
Spain	2001	—	—	—	—	—	—	—	—
Espagne	2002	—	—	—	—	—	58	—	—
España	2003	—	—	—	—	—	946	—	—
	2004	—	—	—	—	—	1 308	—	—
	2005	—	—	—	—	—	1 313	—	—
Sri Lanka	2001	—	—	—	—	—	—	—	—
	2002	—	—	—	—	—	—	—	—
	2003	—	—	—	—	—	1	—	—
	2004	—	—	—	—	—	2	—	—
	2005	—	—	—	—	—	3	—	—
Sweden	2001	7	—	—	—	—	11	19	—
Suède	2002	11	—	—	—	—	25	41	—
Suecia	2003	8	3	—	—	—	37	50	—
	2004	7	3	—	—	—	80	46	—
	2005	7	—	—	—	—	112	27	—

Schedule II.   B.3.   Imports *(continued)*
Tableau II.   B.3.   Importations *(suite)*
Lista II.   B.3.   Importaciones *(continuación)*

Country or territory / Pays ou territoire / País o territorio	Year / Année / Año	Amfetamine / Amfétamine / Anfetamina	Dexamfetamine / Dexamfétamine / Dexanfetamina	Fenetylline / Fénétylline / Fenetilina	Metamfetamine[a] / Métamfétamine[a] / Metanfetamina[a]	Methaqualone / Méthaqualone / Metacualona	Methylphenidate / Méthylphénidate / Metilfenidato	Secobarbital / Sécobarbital	Zipeprol / Zipéprol
		kg	kg	kg	kg	kg	kg	kg	kg
Switzerland	2001	—	2	—	—	—	2 233	—	420
Suisse	2002	—	2	—	—	—	3 301	—	—
Suiza	2003	—	5	—	—	—	5 743	—	—
	2004	—	2	—	—	—	3 775	—	1 629
	2005	—	5	—	—	—	2 612	—	—
Thailand	2001	—	—	—	—	—	9	—	—
Thaïlande	2002	—	—	—	—	—	8	—	—
Tailandia	2003	—	—	—	—	—	23	—	—
	2004	—	—	—	—	—	36	—	—
	2005	—	—	—	—	—	17	—	—
Trinidad and Tobago	2001	—	—	—	—	—	—	—	—
Trinité-et-Tobago	2002	—	—	—	—	—	—	—	—
Trinidad y Tobago	2003	—	—	—	—	—	—	—	—
	2004	—	—	—	—	—	1	—	—
	2005	—	—	—	—	—	—	—	—
Turkey	2001	—	—	—	—	—	15	—	—
Turquie	2002	—	—	—	—	—	23	—	—
Turquía	2003	—	—	—	—	—	21	—	—
	2004	—	—	—	—	—	27	—	—
	2005	—	—	—	—	—	59	—	—
United Arab Emirates	2001	—	—	—	—	—	1	—	—
Émirats arabes unis	2002	—	—	—	—	—	1	—	—
Emiratos Árabes Unidos	2003	—	—	—	—	—	—	—	—
	2004	—	—	—	—	—	1	—	—
	2005	—	—	—	—	—	—	—	—
United Kingdom	2001	—	76	—	—	—	1 216	466	—
Royaume-Uni	2002	1	52	—	100	—	122	57	—
Reino Unido	2003	—	48	—	—	—	105	552	—
	2004	1	1	—	—	—	211	368	—
	2005	—	50	—	—	—	225	568	—
United States	2001	—	—	—	3 251	—	—	—	—
États-Unis	2002	—	1	—	2 500	—	—	—	—
Estados Unidos	2003	—	—	—	2 500	—	—	—	—
	2004	—	—	—	2 500	—	—	—	—
	2005	—	—	—	2 350	—	—	—	—
Uruguay	2001	—	—	—	—	—	5	—	—
	2002	—	—	—	—	—	4	—	—
	2003	?	?	?	?	?	?	?	?
	2004	?	?	?	?	?	?	?	?
	2005	?	?	?	?	?	?	?	?
Venezuela (Bolivarian Rep. of).	2001	—	—	—	—	—	9	—	—
Venezuela (Rép.	2002	—	—	—	—	—	13	—	—
bolivarienne du)	2003	—	—	—	—	—	4	—	—
Venezuela (Rep.	2004	—	—	—	—	—	22	—	—
Bolivariana de)	2005	—	—	—	—	—	11	—	—

Country or territory / Pays ou territoire / País o territorio	Year / Année / Año	Amfe-tamine / Amfé-tamine / Anfe-tamina	Dexam-fetamine / Dexam-fétamine / Dexan-fetamina	Fenetylline / Fénétylline / Fenetilina	Metamfetamine[a] / Métam-fétamine[a] / Metan-fetamina[a]	Metha-qualone / Métha-qualone / Meta-cualona	Methyl-phenidate / Méthyl-phénidate / Metil-fenidato	Secobarbital / Sécobarbital	Zipeprol / Zipéprol
		kg	kg	kg	kg	kg	kg	kg	kg
Zimbabwe	2001	—	—	—	—	—	1	—	—
	2002	—	—	—	—	—	—	—	—
	2003	—	—	—	—	—	—	—	—
	2004	—	—	—	—	—	—	—	—
	2005	—	—	—	—	—	—	—	—
Total	2001	63	397	613	3 254	—	6 217	1 672	602
	2002	83	385	59	3 000	—	7 277	342	—
	2003	26	349	94	2 904	—	11 206	682	134
	2004	118	444	41	2 582	397	11 248	667	1 746
	2005	58	485	75	2 351	—	9 620	637	—

[a]Including levomethamphetamine and metamfetamine racemate. — Y compris la lévométhamphétamine et le racémate de métamfétamine. — Incluye levometanfetamina y racemato de metanfetamina.

C. Substances listed in Schedule III, 2001-2005

C. Substances inscrites au Tableau III, 2001-2005

C. Sustancias incluidas en la Lista III, 2001-2005

Country / Pays / País	Year / Année / Año	Amo-barbital	Buprenor-phine / Buprénor-phine / Buprenor-fina	Butal-bital	Cathine / Catina	Cyclo-barbital / Ciclo-barbital	Flunitra-zepam / Flunitra-zépam	Glute-thimide / Gluté-thimide / Glute-timida	Penta-zocine / Penta-zocina	Pento-barbital
		kg	kg	kg	kg	kg	kg	kg	kg	kg
Australia	2001	—	132	—	—	—	—	—	—	—
Australie	2002	—	173	—	—	—	—	—	—	—
	2003	—	329	—	—	—	—	—	—	—
	2004	—	282	—	—	—	—	—	—	—
	2005	—	383	—	—	—	—	—	—	—
Belgium	2001	—	—	—	—	—	—	—	—	—
Belgique	2002	—	—	—	—	—	—	—	—	—
Bélgica	2003	—	—	—	—	—	—	—	—	—
	2004	—	314	—	—	—	—	—	—	—
	2005	—	12	—	—	—	—	—	—	—
China	2001	16 460	1	—	—	—	—	—	—	—
Chine	2002	25 140	2	—	—	—	—	—	—	—
	2003	19 420	2	—	—	—	—	—	—	—
	2004	12 125	4	—	—	—	—	—	—	—
	2005	18 571	9	—	—	—	—	240	—	—
Czech Republic	2001	—	—	—	—	—	—	—	—	—
République tchèque	2002	—	10	—	—	—	—	—	—	—
República Checa	2003	—	—	—	—	—	—	—	—	—
	2004	—	—	—	—	—	—	—	—	—
	2005	—	10	—	—	—	—	—	—	—
Denmark	2001	1 037	—	33 506	—	—	—	—	—	3 554
Danemark	2002	—	—	36 300	—	—	—	—	—	4 086
Dinamarca	2003	—	—	38 750	—	—	—	—	—	3 140
	2004	—	—	21 800	—	—	—	—	—	5 447
	2005	—	—	12 800	—	—	—	—	—	1 024
Germany	2001	—	—	1 337	6 365	7	—	—	—	14 176
Allemagne	2002	—	—	1 058	4 380	207	—	—	—	10 489
Alemania	2003	—	—	4 692	211	—	—	—	—	17 698
	2004	—	—	3 813	—	—	—	—	—	17 909
	2005	—	—	2 014	2 207	—	—	—	—	16 524
Hungary	2001	—	—	—	—	—	—	732	136	—
Hongrie	2002	—	—	—	—	—	—	—	—	—
Hungría	2003	—	—	—	—	—	—	—	—	—
	2004	—	—	—	—	—	—	—	—	—
	2005	—	—	—	—	—	—	—	—	—
India	2001	—	—	—	—	—	—	—	—	—
Inde	2002	—	28	—	—	—	—	—	2 956	—
	2003	—	—	—	—	—	—	—	—	—
	2004	—	26	—	56	—	—	—	3 400	—
	2005	—	19	—	—	—	—	—	3 027	—
Italy	2001	—	—	—	—	—	207	—	2 608	—
Italie	2002	—	—	—	—	—	134	—	3 025	—
Italia	2003	—	—	—	—	—	477	—	2 675	—
	2004	—	—	—	—	—	246	—	1 688	—
	2005	—	—	—	—	—	82	—	1 446	—
Japan	2001	2 745	—	—	—	—	—	—	—	—
Japon	2002	3 619	—	—	—	—	—	—	—	559
Japón	2003	4 092	—	—	—	—	—	—	—	492
	2004	4 152	—	—	—	—	—	—	—	—
	2005	4 818	—	—	—	—	2	—	—	—

Schedule III. C.1. Manufacture *(concluded)*
Tableau III. C.1. Fabrication *(fin)*
Lista III. C.1. Fabricación *(conclusión)*

Country / Pays / País	Year / Année / Año	Amo-barbital	Buprenorphine / Buprénorphine / Buprenorfina	Butal-bital	Cathine / Catina	Cyclo-barbital / Ciclo-barbital	Flunitra-zepam / Flunitra-zépam	Glute-thimide / Gluté-thimide / Glute-timida	Penta-zocine / Penta-zocina	Pento-barbital
		kg	kg	kg	kg	kg	kg	kg	kg	kg
Latvia	2001	—	—	—	—	279	—	—	—	—
Lettonie	2002	—	—	—	—	93	—	—	—	—
Letonia	2003	—	—	—	—	—	—	—	—	—
	2004	—	—	—	—	—	—	—	—	18
	2005	—	—	—	—	—	—	—	—	30
Morocco	2001	—	—	—	—	—	—	—	—	—
Maroc	2002	—	—	—	—	—	—	—	—	—
Marruecos	2003	—	—	—	—	—	—	—	—	—
	2004	—	—	—	—	—	—	—	—	—
	2005	—	—	—	—	—	—	—	—	—
Netherlands	2001	—	—	—	—	—	—	—	—	—
Pays-Bas	2002	—	—	—	—	—	—	—	—	—
Países Bajos	2003	—	—	—	—	—	—	—	—	—
	2004	—	73	—	—	—	—	—	—	—
	2005	—	30	—	—	—	—	—	—	—
Poland	2001	—	—	—	—	4 951	—	—	—	—
Pologne	2002	—	—	—	—	2 324	—	—	—	—
Polonia	2003	—	—	—	—	—	—	—	—	—
	2004	—	—	—	—	755	—	—	—	—
	2005	—	—	—	—	914	—	—	—	—
Russian Federation	2001	—	1	—	—	—	—	—	—	—
Fédération de Russie	2002	—	—	—	—	—	—	—	—	—
Federación de Rusia	2003	—	—	—	—	—	—	—	—	—
	2004	—	—	—	—	—	—	—	—	—
	2005	—	—	—	—	—	—	—	—	—
Switzerland	2001	—	—	—	—	—	—	—	—	901
Suisse	2002	—	—	—	—	—	275	—	—	—
Suiza	2003	—	—	—	—	—	815	—	—	—
	2004	—	—	—	—	—	1 296	—	—	—
	2005	—	—	—	—	—	—	—	—	—
United Kingdom	2001	—	337	—	—	—	—	—	—	—
Royaume-Uni	2002	—	619	—	—	—	—	—	258	—
Reino Unido	2003	—	1 347	—	—	—	—	—	—	—
	2004	—	1 598	—	—	—	—	—	—	—
	2005	—	1 542	—	—	—	—	—	—	—
United States	2001	—	—	18 613	—	—	—	—	171	27 241
États-Unis	2002	—	—	39 595	—	—	—	—	316	21 416
Estados Unidos	2003	—	—	5 398	—	—	—	—	—	16 601
	2004	—	3	7 572	—	—	—	—	—	16 160
	2005	—	—	9 216	—	—	—	—	—	19 492
Total	2001	20 242	471	53 456	6 365	5 237	207	732	2 915	45 872
	2002	28 759	832	76 953	4 380	2 624	409	—	6 555	36 550
	2003	23 512	1 678	48 840	211	—	1 292	—	2 675	37 931
	2004	16 277	2 300	33 185	56	755	1 542	—	5 088	39 534
	2005	23 389	2 005	24 030	2 207	914	84	240	4 473	37 086

Quantities used for the manufacture of exempted preparations
Quantités utilisées pour la fabrication de préparations exemptées
Cantidades utilizadas para la fabricación de preparados exentos

Country Pays País	Year Année Año	Butalbital	Cathine Catina	Flunitrazepam Flunitrazépam	Pentobarbital
		kg	kg	kg	kg
Germany .... Allemagne Alemania	2001 2002 2003 2004 2005	— — — — —	7 — — 98 123	32 25 35 19 29	— — — — —
United States .... États-Unis Estados Unidos	2001 2002 2003 2004 2005	7 664 8 553 7 251 5 726 8 255	— — — — —	— — — — —	12 — — — —
Total	2001 2002 2003 2004 2005	7 664 8 553 7 251 5 726 8 255	7 — — 98 123	32 25 35 19 29	12 — — — —

Quantities used for the manufacture of non-psychotropic substances or products
Quantités utilisées pour la fabrication de substances ou produits non psychotropes
Cantidades utilizadas para la fabricación de sustancias o productos no sicotrópicos

Country Pays País	Year Année Año	Buprenorphine Buprénorphine Buprenorfina	Pentobarbital
		kg	kg
Germany .... Allemagne Alemania	2001 2002 2003 2004 2005	— — — — —	— — — — —
United Kingdom .... Royaume-Uni Reino Unido	2001 2002 2003 2004 2005	— 1 1 — —	— 545 — — —
United States .... États-Unis Estados Unidos	2001 2002 2003 2004 2005	— — — — —	— — — — —
Total	2001 2002 2003 2004 2005	— 1 1 — —	— 545 — — —

Schedule III.   C.2.   Exports
Tableau III.   C.2.   Exportations
Lista III.   C.2.   Exportaciones

Country or territory Pays ou territoire País o territorio	Year Année Año	Amo- barbital	Buprenor- phine Buprénor- phine Buprenor- fina	Butal- bital	Cathine Catina	Cyclo- barbital Ciclo- barbital	Flunitra- zepam Flunitra- zépam	Glute- thimide Gluté- thimide Glute- timida	Penta- zocine Penta- zocina	Pento- barbital
		kg	kg	kg	kg	kg	kg	kg	kg	kg
Argentina .... Argentine	2001 2002 2003 2004 2005	— — — — —	— — — — —	28 30 25 — —	— — — — —	— — — — —	7 — — 45 —	— — — — —	— — — — —	— — — — 14
Australia .... Australie	2001 2002 2003 2004 2005	— — — — —	87 227 237 330 320	— — — — —	— — — — —	— — — — —	— — — — —	— — — — —	5 3 16 3 16	50 28 52 14 29
Austria .... Autriche	2001 2002 2003 2004 2005	— — — — —	— — — — —	— — — — —	— — — — —	— — — — —	1 2 4 3 1	— — — — —	— — — — —	63 46 35 17 —
Barbados .... Barbade	2001 2002 2003 2004 2005	— — — — ?	— — — — ?	— — — — ?	— — — — ?	— — — — ?	— — — — ?	— — — — ?	— — — — ?	— 1 2 2 ?
Belgium .... Belgique Bélgica	2001 2002 2003 2004 2005	— 23 — — —	— — — — 5	— 1 5 1 —	— — — — —	— — — — —	2 2 1 — 1	— — — — —	3 9 6 7 9	— — 3 — —
Brazil .... Brésil Brasil	2001 2002 2003 2004 2005	— — — — —	— — — — —	— — — — —	— — — — —	— — — — —	2 8 8 5 5	— — — — —	— — — — —	— — — — —
Canada .... Canadá	2001 2002 2003 2004 2005	— — — — —	— — — — —	— — 500 — —	— — — — —	— — — — —	— — — — —	— — — — —	— — — — 51	5 207 4 633 5 388 3 159 5 446
Chile .... Chili	2001 2002 2003 2004 2005	— — — — —	— — — . —	— — — — —	— — — — —	— — — — —	2 — — 1 1	— — — — —	— — — — —	— — — — —
China .... Chine	2001 2002 2003 2004 2005	2 380 2 800 240 5 025 6 840	— — — — —	— — — — —	— — — — —	— — — — —	— — — — —	— 200 — 200 201	— — — — —	— — — — —

Schedule III. C.2. Exports *(continued)*
Tableau III. C.2. Exportations *(suite)*
Lista III. C.2. Exportaciones *(continuación)*

Country or territory / Pays ou territoire / País o territorio	Year / Année / Año	Amo-barbital	Buprenor-phine / Buprénor-phine / Buprenor-fina	Butal-bital	Cathine / Catina	Cyclo-barbital / Ciclo-barbital	Flunitra-zepam / Flunitra-zépam	Glute-thimide / Gluté-thimide / Glute-timida	Penta-zocine / Penta-zocina	Pento-barbital
		kg	kg	kg	kg	kg	kg	kg	kg	kg
Hong Kong SAR of China	2001	—	—	5	—	—	—	—	—	2
RAS de Hong Kong (Chine)	2002	—	—	—	—	—	—	—	—	1
RAE de Hong Kong	2003	—	—	—	—	—	—	—	—	8
de China	2004	—	—	—	—	—	—	—	—	5
	2005	—	—	—	—	—	—	—	—	4
Cyprus	2001	—	—	—	—	—	—	—	—	—
Chypre	2002	—	—	—	—	—	2	—	—	—
Chipre	2003	—	—	—	—	—	1	—	—	—
	2004	—	—	—	—	—	—	—	—	—
	2005	—	—	—	—	—	—	—	—	—
Czech Republic...........	2001	—	—	—	—	—	13	—	—	—
République tchèque	2002	—	—	—	—	—	8	—	—	—
República Checa	2003	—	—	—	—	—	6	—	—	—
	2004	—	—	—	—	—	7	—	—	—
	2005	—	—	—	—	—	—	—	—	—
Denmark.................	2001	1 310	—	30 407	—	—	1	—	1	3 928
Danemark	2002	—	1	35 576	—	—	2	—	3	4 058
Dinamarca	2003	—	—	32 251	—	—	—	—	—	2 633
	2004	—	1	18 701	—	—	—	—	2	2 710
	2005	—	2	19 000	—	—	—	—	—	2 004
France	2001	—	5	—	234	—	6	—	56	2 723
Francia	2002	—	1	—	321	—	7	229	30	1 959
	2003	—	10	—	81	—	6	—	44	1 485
	2004	—	7	—	473	—	5	—	26	1 698
	2005	—	23	—	313	—	6	—	13	1 695
Germany	2001	468	14	920	3 038	5	13	—	2	10 361
Allemagne	2002	296	74	1 533	2 835	86	11	—	6	11 456
Alemania	2003	206	114	4 137	1 499	9	12	—	—	10 373
	2004	99	122	3 423	2 349	5	18	—	—	9 974
	2005	302	152	2 976	2 066	—	8	—	—	13 043
Hungary	2001	—	—	—	—	—	—	1 000	1	—
Hongrie	2002	200	—	—	—	—	9	300	93	—
Hungría	2003	—	—	—	—	—	—	300	—	—
	2004	—	—	—	—	—	3	—	—	—
	2005	—	—	—	—	—	3	—	—	—
India	2001	—	2	—	—	—	—	—	159	—
Inde	2002	—	2	—	—	—	—	—	468	—
	2003	—	14	—	—	—	—	—	656	—
	2004	—	12	—	425	—	—	—	531	—
	2005	—	16	—	405	—	—	—	908	—
Ireland	2001	686	—	—	—	—	22	—	—	18
Irlande	2002	580	—	—	—	—	21	—	—	—
Irlanda	2003	—	—	—	—	—	18	—	—	—
	2004	183	—	—	—	—	8	—	—	—
	2005	43	—	—	—	—	14	—	—	—

Country or territory / Pays ou territoire / País o territorio	Year / Année / Año	Amo-barbital	Buprenor-phine / Buprénor-phine / Buprenor-fina	Butal-bital	Cathine / Catina	Cyclo-barbital / Ciclo-barbital	Flunitra-zepam / Flunitra-zépam	Glute-thimide / Gluté-thimide / Glute-timida	Penta-zocine / Penta-zocina	Pento-barbital
		kg	kg	kg	kg	kg	kg	kg	kg	kg
Italy	2001	—	—	246	1 210	—	204	—	2 274	—
Italie	2002	—	—	255	730	—	240	—	2 972	—
Italia	2003	—	—	186	1 121	—	181	—	2 918	—
	2004	—	—	150	1 037	—	285	—	1 682	—
	2005	—	—	60	1 115	—	170	—	2 208	—
Japan	2001	—	—	—	—	—	—	—	44	—
Japon	2002	—	—	—	—	—	—	—	—	—
Japón	2003	—	—	—	—	—	—	—	—	—
	2004	—	—	—	—	—	—	—	—	—
	2005	—	—	—	—	—	—	—	—	—
Latvia	2001	—	—	—	—	292	2	—	—	—
Lettonie	2002	—	—	—	—	98	1	—	—	—
Letonia	2003	—	—	—	—	5	—	—	—	—
	2004	—	—	—	—	—	—	—	—	18
	2005	—	—	—	—	—	—	—	—	27
Lithuania	2001	—	—	—	—	28	—	—	—	—
Lituanie	2002	—	—	—	—	52	—	—	—	—
Lituania	2003	—	—	—	—	37	—	—	—	—
	2004	—	—	—	—	22	—	—	—	—
	2005	—	—	—	—	4	—	—	—	—
Malta	2001	—	—	—	—	—	—	—	13	—
Malte	2002	—	—	—	—	—	—	—	1	—
	2003	—	—	—	—	—	—	—	7	—
	2004	—	—	—	—	—	—	—	—	—
	2005	—	—	—	—	—	—	—	—	—
Netherlands	2001	1 202	9	—	—	—	2	—	10	335
Pays-Bas	2002	2 300	9	1	—	—	38	—	24	87
Países Bajos	2003	2 401	7	—	—	—	5	—	13	97
	2004	46	6	20	—	—	2	—	4	270
	2005	40	13	15	—	—	2	—	10	282
Norway	2001	—	—	—	—	—	2	—	4	—
Norvège	2002	—	—	—	—	—	2	—	6	—
Noruega	2003	—	—	—	—	—	2	—	1	—
	2004	—	—	—	—	—	1	—	—	—
	2005	—	—	—	—	—	2	—	—	—
Panama	2001	—	—	—	—	—	—	—	—	—
Panamá	2002	—	—	—	—	—	—	—	1	—
	2003	—	—	—	—	—	—	—	—	—
	2004	—	—	—	—	—	—	—	—	—
	2005	—	—	—	—	—	—	—	—	—
Poland	2001	—	—	—	—	1 721	—	—	—	97
Pologne	2002	—	—	—	—	1 044	—	—	—	2
Polonia	2003	—	1	—	—	1 333	—	—	—	—
	2004	—	—	—	—	734	—	—	—	—
	2005	—	—	—	—	707	—	—	—	—

Country or territory / Pays ou territoire / País o territorio	Year / Année / Año	Amo-barbital	Buprenor-phine / Buprénor-phine / Buprenor-fina	Butal-bital	Cathine / Catina	Cyclo-barbital / Ciclo-barbital	Flunitra-zepam / Flunitra-zépam	Glute-thimide / Gluté-thimide / Glute-timida	Penta-zocine / Penta-zocina	Pento-barbital
		kg	kg	kg	kg	kg	kg	kg	kg	kg
Portugal	2001	—	—	—	—	—	2	—	158	—
	2002	—	—	—	—	—	—	—	386	—
	2003	—	—	—	—	—	—	—	335	—
	2004	—	—	—	—	—	—	—	159	—
	2005	—	—	—	—	—	—	—	175	—
Romania................. Roumanie Rumania	2001	—	—	—	—	—	—	—	—	—
	2002	—	—	—	—	—	—	—	—	—
	2003	9	—	—	—	—	—	—	—	—
	2004	34	—	—	—	—	—	—	—	—
	2005	—	—	—	—	—	—	—	—	—
Singapore .... Singapour Singapur	2001	—	—	—	—	—	—	—	—	—
	2002	—	—	—	—	—	—	—	—	—
	2003	—	—	—	—	—	—	—	—	—
	2004	—	1	—	—	—	—	—	—	—
	2005	—	—	—	—	—	—	—	—	—
Slovakia .... Slovaquie Eslovaquia	2001	—	—	—	—	—	—	—	—	—
	2002	—	—	—	—	—	—	—	—	—
	2003	—	—	—	—	—	—	—	—	—
	2004	?	?	?	?	?	?	?	?	?
	2005	—	9	—	—	—	—	—	—	—
Slovenia .... Slovénie Eslovenia	2001	—	—	—	—	—	—	—	261	—
	2002	—	—	—	—	—	—	—	198	—
	2003	—	—	—	—	—	—	—	141	—
	2004	—	—	—	—	—	—	—	174	—
	2005	—	—	—	—	—	—	—	90	—
South Africa .... Afrique du Sud Sudáfrica	2001	—	—	—	54	—	—	—	—	49
	2002	—	—	—	7	—	—	—	1	33
	2003	—	—	—	4	—	—	—	—	20
	2004	—	—	—	8	—	—	—	1	22
	2005	—	—	—	8	—	—	—	—	24
Spain .... Espagne España	2001	—	—	3	—	—	1	—	—	—
	2002	—	—	—	—	—	—	—	—	—
	2003	—	—	9	—	—	2	—	—	—
	2004	—	—	2	—	—	—	—	—	—
	2005	—	2	—	—	—	—	—	—	—
Sweden .... Suède Suecia	2001	—	—	—	—	—	—	—	—	18
	2002	—	—	—	—	—	1	—	—	—
	2003	—	—	—	—	—	—	—	—	—
	2004	—	—	—	—	—	—	—	—	—
	2005	—	1	—	—	—	—	—	—	—
Switzerland .... Suisse Suiza	2001	—	—	195	344	279	714	500	328	5 627
	2002	240	—	125	—	93	693	—	377	210
	2003	—	—	127	—	—	737	—	404	109
	2004	—	2	63	—	—	536	—	203	150
	2005	—	3	7	23	—	508	—	451	323

Schedule III. C.2. Exports *(concluded)*
Tableau III. C.2. Exportations *(fin)*
Lista III. C.2. Exportaciones *(conclusión)*

Country or territory Pays ou territoire País o territorio	Year Année Año	Amo- barbital	Buprenor- phine Buprénor- phine Buprenor- fina	Butal- bital	Cathine Catina	Cyclo- barbital Ciclo- barbital	Flunitra- zepam Flunitra- zépam	Glute- thimide Gluté- thimide Glute- timida	Penta- zocine Penta- zocina	Pento- barbital
		kg	kg	kg	kg	kg	kg	kg	kg	kg
Thailand	2001	—	—	—	—	—	—	—	—	—
Thaïlande	2002	—	—	—	—	—	—	—	—	—
Tailandia	2003	—	—	—	—	—	—	—	1	—
	2004	—	—	—	—	—	—	—	—	—
	2005	—	—	—	—	—	—	—	—	—
United Kingdom	2001	—	286	—	—	—	2	—	564	66
Royaume-Uni	2002	—	380	—	—	—	2	—	710	26
Reino Unido	2003	—	441	—	—	—	2	—	444	7
	2004	—	564	—	—	—	2	—	262	—
	2005	2	690	—	—	—	—	—	128	11
United States..............	2001	4	—	—	—	—	—	—	221	5 956
États-Unis	2002	—	—	825	—	—	—	—	227	—
Estados Unidos	2003	—	—	801	—	—	—	—	1	3 827
	2004	—	—	103	—	—	—	—	352	6 812
	2005	1	—	75	—	—	—	—	268	3 507
Total	2001	6 050	403	31 804	4 880	2 325	998	1 500	4 104	34 500
	2002	6 439	694	38 346	3 893	1 373	1 049	729	5 515	22 540
	2003	2 856	824	38 041	2 705	1 384	985	300	4 987	24 039
	2004	5 387	1 045	22 463	4 292	761	921	200	3 406	24 851
	2005	7 228	1 236	22 133	3 930	711	721	201	4 327	26 409

Schedule III.   C.3.   Imports
Tableau III.   C.3.   Importations
Lista III.   C.3.   Importaciones

Country or territory / Pays ou territoire / País o territorio	Year / Année / Año	Amo-barbital	Buprenor-phine / Buprénor-phine / Buprenor-fina	Butal-bital	Cathine / Catina	Cyclo-barbital / Ciclo-barbital	Flunitra-zepam / Flunitra-zépam	Glute-thimide / Gluté-thimide / Glute-timida	Penta-zocine / Penta-zocina	Pento-barbital
		kg	kg	kg	kg	kg	kg	kg	kg	kg
Algeria	2001	—	—	—	—	—	—	—	—	—
Algérie	2002	—	—	—	—	—	—	—	—	—
Argelia	2003	—	1	—	—	—	—	—	—	—
	2004	—	—	—	—	—	—	—	—	—
	2005	—	—	—	—	—	—	—	—	—
Angola	2001	—	—	—	—	—	—	—	—	—
	2002	—	—	—	—	—	—	—	1	—
	2003	—	—	—	—	—	—	—	1	—
	2004	—	—	—	—	—	—	—	—	—
	2005	?	?	?	?	?	?	?	?	?
Antigua and Barbuda	2001	—	—	—	—	—	—	—	—	—
Antigua-et-Barbuda	2002	—	—	—	—	—	—	—	—	1
Antigua y Barbuda	2003	?	?	?	?	?	?	?	?	?
	2004	?	?	?	?	?	?	?	?	?
	2005	?	?	?	?	?	?	?	?	?
Argentina	2001	—	—	—	—	—	18	—	—	—
Argentine	2002	—	—	—	—	—	9	—	—	—
	2003		—	100	—	—	11	—	—	100
	2004	—	1	—	—	—	13	—	—	50
	2005	—	—	—	—	—	6	—	—	101
Armenia	2001	—	—	—	—	1	—	—	—	8
Arménie	2002	?	?	?	?	?	?	?	?	?
	2003	?	?	?	?	?	?	?	?	?
	2004	?	?	?	?	?	?	?	?	?
	2005	?	?	?	?	?	?	?	?	?
Australia	2001	—	9	—	—	—	15	—	9	1 866
Australie	2002	—	17	—	—	—	10	—	12	1 366
	2003	—	26	—	—	—	—	—	14	1 822
	2004	—	30	—	—	—	5	—	5	1 412
	2005	—	35	—	—	—	10	—	27	2 594
Austria	2001	—	2	—	—	—	18	—	—	139
Autriche	2002	—	6	—	—	—	16	—	—	61
	2003	—	14	—	—	—	17	—	—	56
	2004	—	15	—	—	—	22	—	—	47
	2005	—	6	—	—	—	11	—	—	22
Bahrain	2001	—	—	—	—	—	—	—	—	—
Bahreïn	2002	—	—	—	—	—	—	—	—	—
Bahrein	2003	—	—	—	—	—	—	—	—	1
	2004	—	—	—	—	—	—	—	—	—
	2005	—	—	—	—	—	—	—	—	—
Barbados	2001	—	—	—	—	—	—	—	—	13
Barbade	2002	—	—	—	—	—	—	—	—	8
	2003	—	—	—	—	—	—	—	—	3
	2004	—	—	—	—	—	—	—	—	9
	2005	—	—	—	—	—	—	—	—	6

Country or territory / Pays ou territoire / País o territorio	Year / Année / Año	Amo-barbital	Buprenor-phine / Buprénor-phine / Buprenor-fina	Butal-bital	Cathine / Catina	Cyclo-barbital / Ciclo-barbital	Flunitra-zepam / Flunitra-zépam	Glute-thimide / Gluté-thimide / Glute-timida	Penta-zocine / Penta-zocina	Pento-barbital
		kg	kg	kg	kg	kg	kg	kg	kg	kg
Belarus	2001	—	—	—	—	78	—	—	—	—
Bélarus	2002	—	—	—	—	61	—	—	—	—
Belarús	2003	—	—	—	—	57	—	—	—	—
	2004	—	—	—	—	56	—	—	—	—
	2005	—	—	—	—	41	—	—	—	—
Belgium	2001	48	—	25	11	5	17	—	59	246
Belgique	2002	96	4	25	—	—	18	—	66	265
Bélgica	2003	50	15	25	—	—	12	—	77	175
	2004	44	23	17	—	—	10	—	58	334
	2005	39	24	12	—	—	11	—	32	191
Bolivia	2001	—	—	—	—	—	1	—	—	—
Bolivie	2002	—	—	—	—	—	1	—	—	—
	2003	—	—	—	—	—	—	—	—	—
	2004	—	—	—	—	—	1	—	—	—
	2005	—	—	7	—	—	1	—	—	—
Bosnia and Herzegovina	2001	?	?	?	?	?	?	?	?	?
Bosnie-Herzégovine	2002	?	?	?	?	?	?	?	?	?
Bosnia y Herzegovina	2003	—	—	—	—	—	—	—	1	—
	2004	—	—	—	—	—	—	—	—	—
	2005	?	?	?	?	?	?	?	?	?
Botswana	2001	—	—	—	—	—	—	—	—	—
	2002	—	—	—	—	—	—	—	—	—
	2003	?	?	?	?	?	?	?	?	?
	2004	?	?	?	?	?	?	?	?	?
	2005	—	—	—	—	—	—	—	—	1
Brazil	2001	23	—	—	—	—	31	—	—	—
Brésil	2002	—	—	—	—	—	52	—	—	—
Brasil	2003	—	—	—	—	—	41	—	—	—
	2004	—	—	—	—	—	45	—	—	—
	2005	—	—	—	—	—	40	—	—	—
Brunei Darussalam	2001	—	—	—	—	—	—	—	—	—
Brunéi Darussalam	2002	—	—	—	—	—	—	—	—	—
	2003	—	—	—	—	—	—	—	—	—
	2004	—	—	—	—	—	—	—	—	—
	2005	—	—	—	—	—	—	—	—	2
Bulgaria	2001	—	—	—	—	6	1	650	—	—
Bulgarie	2002	—	—	—	—	1	—	—	—	—
	2003	—	—	—	—	1	—	—	—	—
	2004	—	—	—	—	1	—	—	—	—
	2005	—	—	—	—	1	—	—	—	—
Cameroon	2001	?	?	?	?	?	?	?	?	?
Cameroun	2002	—	—	—	—	—	—	—	2	—
Camerún	2003	—	—	—	—	—	—	—	—	—
	2004	—	—	—	—	—	—	—	1	—
	2005	?	?	?	?	?	?	?	?	?

Country or territory / Pays ou territoire / País o territorio	Year / Année / Año	Amo-barbital	Buprenor-phine / Buprénor-phine / Buprenor-fina	Butal-bital	Cathine / Catina	Cyclo-barbital / Ciclo-barbital	Flunitra-zepam / Flunitra-zépam	Glute-thimide / Gluté-thimide / Glute-timida	Penta-zocine / Penta-zocina	Pento-barbital
		kg	kg	kg	kg	kg	kg	kg	kg	kg
Canada / Canadá	2001	47	—	1 575	—	—	—	—	219	6 173
	2002	1	1	1 350	—	—	—	—	209	7 413
	2003	—	1	1 576	—	—	—	—	197	5 814
	2004	25	—	500	—	—	—	—	96	6 900
	2005	—	—	1 150	—	—	—	—	128	6 667
Chile / Chili	2001	—	—	27	—	—	10	—	—	—
	2002	—	—	24	—	—	3	—	—	—
	2003	—	—	28	—	—	5	—	—	—
	2004	—	—	18	—	—	2	—	—	—
	2005	—	—	6	—	—	3	—	—	—
China / Chine	2001	—	—	—	—	—	—	—	—	46
	2002	—	—	—	—	—	—	—	—	109
	2003	—	—	—	—	—	—	—	—	46
	2004	—	—	—	—	—	—	—	—	55
	2005	—	—	—	—	—	—	—	—	45
Hong Kong SAR of China / RAS de Hong Kong (Chine) / RAE de Hong Kong de China	2001	—	—	5	—	—	1	—	—	38
	2002	—	—	—	—	—	2	—	—	71
	2003	—	—	—	—	—	1	—	—	72
	2004	—	—	—	—	—	1	—	—	1
	2005	2	—	—	—	—	—	—	—	43
Macao SAR of China / RAS de Macao (Chine) / RAE de Macao de China	2001	—	—	—	—	—	—	—	—	10
	2002	—	—	—	—	—	—	—	—	—
	2003	—	—	—	—	—	—	—	—	4
	2004	—	—	—	—	—	—	—	—	5
	2005	—	—	—	—	—	—	—	—	5
Colombia / Colombie	2001	—	—	—	—	—	—	—	—	68
	2002	—	—	—	—	—	—	—	—	278
	2003	—	—	—	—	—	—	—	—	91
	2004	—	—	—	—	—	—	—	—	91
	2005	—	—	—	—	—	—	—	—	91
Costa Rica	2001	—	—	—	—	—	1	—	—	—
	2002	—	—	—	—	—	—	—	—	—
	2003	—	—	—	—	—	—	—	—	1
	2004	—	—	—	—	—	—	—	—	66
	2005	—	—	—	—	—	—	—	—	—
Croatia / Croatie / Croacia	2001	—	—	—	—	—	—	—	3	—
	2002	—	—	—	—	—	—	—	4	—
	2003	—	—	—	—	—	—	—	3	—
	2004	?	?	?	?	?	?	?	?	?
	2005	—	1	—	—	—	—	—	—	—
Cuba	2001	—	—	—	—	—	—	—	—	—
	2002	—	—	—	—	—	1	—	—	—
	2003	—	—	—	—	—	1	—	—	—
	2004	—	—	—	—	—	—	—	—	—
	2005	—	—	—	—	—	—	—	—	—

Country or territory / Pays ou territoire / País o territorio	Year / Année / Año	Amo-barbital	Buprenor-phine / Buprénor-phine / Buprenor-fina	Butal-bital	Cathine / Catina	Cyclo-barbital / Ciclo-barbital	Flunitra-zepam / Flunitra-zépam	Glute-thimide / Gluté-thimide / Glute-timida	Penta-zocine / Penta-zocina	Pento-barbital
		kg	kg	kg	kg	kg	kg	kg	kg	kg
Cyprus	2001	—	—	—	—	—	—	—	—	—
Chypre	2002	—	—	—	—	—	4	—	—	—
Chipre	2003	—	—	—	—	—	—	—	—	—
	2004	—	—	—	—	—	1	—	—	—
	2005	—	—	—	—	—	—	—	—	—
Czech Republic	2001	—	—	—	—	—	41	—	44	—
République tchèque	2002	—	—	—	—	—	33	—	53	—
República Checa	2003	—	4	—	—	—	20	—	35	—
	2004	—	4	—	—	—	7	—	51	—
	2005	—	10	—	—	—	—	—	45	—
Dem. Rep. of the Congo	2001	—	—	—	—	—	—	—	1	—
Rép. dém. du Congo	2002	?	?	?	?	?	?	?	?	?
Rep. Dem. del Congo	2003	—	—	—	—	—	—	—	2	—
	2004	—	—	—	—	—	—	—	1	—
	2005	—	—	—	—	—	—	—	1	—
Denmark	2001	2	2	112	—	—	3	—	16	1 001
Danemark	2002	—	4	845	—	—	4	—	16	91
Dinamarca	2003	—	6	595	20	—	3	—	14	—
	2004	1	8	139	20	—	3	—	2	—
	2005	—	8	77	—	—	2	—	—	—
Ecuador	2001	—	—	15	—	—	1	—	7	—
Équateur	2002	—	—	8	—	—	1	—	10	—
	2003	—	—	9	—	—	—	—	4	—
	2004	—	—	—	—	—	—	—	4	—
	2005	—	—	—	—	—	—	—	6	—
Egypt	2001	—	—	—	—	—	—	—	—	—
Égypte	2002	—	—	—	—	—	—	—	—	455
Egipto	2003	—	—	—	—	—	—	—	—	455
	2004	—	—	—	—	—	—	—	—	455
	2005	—	—	—	86	—	—	—	—	—
El Salvador	2001	—	—	—	—	—	—	—	—	6
	2002	—	1	—	—	—	—	—	—	20
	2003	—	—	—	—	—	—	—	—	26
	2004	—	—	—	—	—	—	—	—	9
	2005	—	—	—	—	—	—	—	—	33
Estonia	2001	—	—	—	—	—	1	—	—	4
Estonie	2002	—	—	—	—	—	1	—	—	—
	2003	—	—	—	—	—	—	—	—	—
	2004	—	1	—	—	—	—	—	—	4
	2005	—	1	—	—	—	—	—	—	4
Ethiopia	2001	—	—	—	—	—	—	—	1	—
Éthiopie	2002	—	—	—	—	—	—	—	—	—
Etiopía	2003	—	—	—	—	—	—	—	—	—
	2004	—	—	—	—	—	—	—	—	—
	2005	—	—	—	—	—	—	—	—	—

Country or territory / Pays ou territoire / País o territorio	Year / Année / Año	Amo-barbital	Buprenor-phine / Buprénor-phine / Buprenor-fina	Butal-bital	Cathine / Catina	Cyclo-barbital / Ciclo-barbital	Flunitra-zepam / Flunitra-zépam	Glute-thimide / Gluté-thimide / Glute-timida	Penta-zocine / Penta-zocina	Pento-barbital
		kg	kg	kg	kg	kg	kg	kg	kg	kg
Falkland Islands (Malvinas) ...	2001	—	—	—	—	—	—	—	—	—
Îles Falkland (Malvinas)	2002	—	—	—	—	—	—	—	—	—
Islas Malvinas	2003	—	—	—	—	—	·	—	—	—
(Falkland Islands)	2004	—	—	—	—	—	—	—	—	—
	2005	—	—	—	—	—	—	—	—	1
Finland	2001	1	1	—	—	—	—	—	—	23
Finlande	2002	—	2	—	—	—	—	—	—	46
Finlandia	2003	1	2	—	—	—	—	—	—	—
	2004	—	4	—	—	—	—	—	—	46
	2005	—	4	—	—	—	—	—	—	27
France	2001	—	239	—	243	—	26	—	80	5 371
Francia	2002	—	254	—	324	—	11	—	—	5 052
	2003	5	293	—	324	—	20	—	96	3 733
	2004	1	292	—	243	—	13	—	—	3 369
	2005	—	346	—	405	—	16	1	20	4 551
Georgia	2001	—	—	—	—	4	—	—	—	—
Géorgie	2002	—	—	—	—	10	—	—	—	—
	2003	—	—	—	—	18	—	—	—	—
	2004	—	—	—	—	43	—	—	—	—
	2005	—	—	—	—	65	—	—	—	—
Germany	2001	—	89	—	344	—	56	—	19	2 137
Allemagne	2002	223	246	—	—	—	43	—	31	38
Alemania	2003	—	265	—	—	—	66	—	15	35
	2004	—	356	—	—	—	30	—	9	98
	2005	1	361	—	—	—	45	—	6	229
Gibraltar	2001	—	—	—	—	—	—	—	—	1
	2002	—	—	—	—	—	—	—	—	1
	2003	—	—	—	—	—	—	—	—	—
	2004	—	—	—	—	—	—	—	—	—
	2005	—	—	—	—	—	—	—	—	—
Greece	2001	—	—	—	—	—	22	—	—	30
Grèce	2002	—	1	—	—	—	17	—	—	38
Grecia	2003	—	—	—	—	—	20	—	—	27
	2004	—	4	—	—	—	18	—	—	42
	2005	—	2	—	—	—	22	—	—	65
Haiti	2001	—	—	—	—	—	—	—	—	—
Haïti	2002	—	—	—	—	—	—	—	11	—
Haití	2003	—	—	—	—	—	—	—	5	—
	2004	—	—	—	—	—	—	—	4	—
	2005	—	—	—	—	—	—	—	—	—
Hungary	2001	100	—	—	—	—	—	—	—	12
Hongrie	2002	440	—	—	—	—	10	200	—	—
Hungría	2003	310	—	—	—	—	2	—	—	4
	2004	—	—	—	—	—	5	200	—	55
	2005	250	—	—	—	—	5	200	—	4

Country or territory Pays ou territoire País o territorio	Year Année Año	Amo- barbital	Buprenor- phine Buprénor- phine Buprenor- fina	Butal- bital	Cathine Catina	Cyclo- barbital Ciclo- barbital	Flunitra- zepam Flunitra- zépam	Glute- thimide Gluté- thimide Glute- timida	Penta- zocine Penta- zocina	Pento- barbital
		kg	kg	kg	kg	kg	kg	kg	kg	kg
Iceland Islande Islandia	2001 2002 2003 2004 2005	— — — — —	— — — 1 —	1 1 — 1 —	— — — — —	— — — — —	2 1 — — 1	— — — — —	1 1 — — —	8 4 5 7 6
Indonesia Indonésie	2001 2002 2003 2004 2005	— — — — —	— — — — 1	— — — — —	— — — — —	— — — — —	— — — — —	— — — — —	— — — — —	— — — — —
Iran (Islamic Republic of) Iran (Rép.islamique d') Irán (Rep. Islámica del)	2001 2002 2003 2004 2005	— — — — —	— 13 — — —	— — — — —	— — — — —	— — — — —	— — — — —	— — — — —	— 13 20 — 10	— — — — —
Ireland Irlande Irlanda	2001 2002 2003 2004 2005	2 3 2 3 2	— 1 2 2 4	— — — — —	— — — — —	— — — — —	30 22 11 22 8	— — — — —	— — — — —	359 356 197 384 270
Israel Israël	2001 2002 2003 2004 2005	— — — — —	1 — — 1 1	— — — — —	— — — — —	— — — — —	— — — — 2	— — — — —	— — — — —	91 100 46 91 91
Italy Italie Italia	2001 2002 2003 2004 2005	— — — — —	20 33 38 50 57	5 450 3 250 3 600 3 700 3 425	927 1 215 851 1 093 1 175	— — — — —	7 29 4 5 3	— — — — —	— 3 — 113 —	1 1 — — —
Jamaica Jamaïque	2001 2002 2003 2004 2005	— — — — —	— — — — —	— — — — —	— — — — —	— — — — —	— — — — —	— — — — —	2 1 1 3 —	17 — — — —
Japan Japon Japón	2001 2002 2003 2004 2005	— — — — —	2 2 2 1 1	— — — — —	— — — — —	— — — — —	472 587 569 461 421	— — — — —	370 288 405 205 450	272 24 110 74 111
Kazakhstan Kazajstán	2001 2002 2003 2004 2005	— — — — —	— — — — —	— — — — —	— — — — —	3 — — — —	— — — — —	— — — — —	— — — — —	— — — — —

Schedule III.　C.3. Imports *(continued)*
Tableau III.　C.3. Importations *(suite)*
Lista III.　C.3. Importaciones *(continuación)*

Country or territory Pays ou territoire País o territorio	Year Année Año	Amo- barbital	Buprenor- phine Buprénor- phine Buprenor- fina	Butal- bital	Cathine Catina	Cyclo- barbital Ciclo- barbital	Flunitra- zepam Flunitra- zépam	Glute- thimide Gluté- thimide Glute- timida	Penta- zocine Penta- zocina	Pento- barbital
		kg	kg	kg	kg	kg	kg	kg	kg	kg
Kenya	2001	—	—	—	—	—	—	—	2	9
	2002	—	—	—	—	—	1	—	—	—
	2003	—	—	—	—	—	1	—	—	—
	2004	—	—	—	—	—	1	—	2	1
	2005	?	?	?	?	?	?	?	?	?
Kuwait	2001	—	—	—	—	—	—	—	2	—
Koweït	2002	—	—	—	—	—	—	—	2	—
	2003	—	—	—	—	—	—	—	—	—
	2004	—	—	—	—	—	—	—	—	—
	2005	—	—	—	—	—	—	—	—	—
Latvia	2001	—	—	—	—	83	2	—	—	11
Lettonie	2002	—	—	—	—	62	1	—	—	11
Letonia	2003	—	—	—	—	58	—	—	—	—
	2004	—	—	—	—	53	—	—	—	—
	2005	—	1	—	—	38	—	—	—	17
Libyan Arab Jamahiriya	2001	—	—	—	—	—	—	—	—	—
Jamahiriya arabe libyenne	2002	—	—	—	—	—	—	—	2	—
Jamahiriya Árabe Libia	2003	—	—	—	—	—	—	—	—	—
	2004	—	—	—	—	—	—	—	—	—
	2005	—	—	—	—	—	—	—	—	—
Lithuania	2001	—	—	—	—	28	1	—	2	5
Lituanie	2002	—	—	—	—	52	—	—	2	8
Lituania	2003	—	—	—	—	37	—	—	3	15
	2004	—	—	—	—	26	—	—	—	22
	2005	—	—	—	—	—	—	—	—	25
Madagascar	2001	—	1	—	—	—	—	—	—	—
	2002	—	—	—	—	—	—	—	—	—
	2003	—	—	—	—	—	—	—	—	—
	2004	—	—	—	—	—	—	—	—	—
	2005	—	—	—	—	—	—	—	—	—
Malaysia	2001	—	—	—	—	—	—	—	—	39
Malaisie	2002	—	1	—	—	—	—	—	—	16
Malasia	2003	—	2	—	—	—	—	—	1	35
	2004	—	9	—	—	—	—	—	—	—
	2005	—	11	—	—	—	—	—	—	45
Malta	2001	—	—	—	—	—	—	—	—	7
Malte	2002	—	—	—	—	—	—	—	10	8
	2003	—	—	—	—	—	—	—	—	9
	2004	—	—	—	—	—	—	—	—	6
	2005	—	—	—	—	—	—	—	—	3
Mauritania	2001	?	?	?	?	?	?	?	?	?
Mauritanie	2002	—	—	—	—	—	—	—	—	—
	2003	—	—	—	—	—	—	—	—	15
	2004	?	?	?	?	?	?	?	?	?
	2005	?	?	?	?	?	?	?	?	?

Schedule III.   C.3. Imports *(continued)*
Tableau III.   C.3. Importations *(suite)*
Lista III.   C.3. Importaciones *(continuación)*

Country or territory Pays ou territoire País o territorio	Year Année Año	Amo- barbital	Buprenor- phine Buprénor- phine Buprenor- fina	Butal- bital	Cathine Catina	Cyclo- barbital Ciclo- barbital	Flunitra- zepam Flunitra- zépam	Glute- thimide Gluté- thimide Glute- timida	Penta- zocine Penta- zocina	Pento- barbital
		kg	kg	kg	kg	kg	kg	kg	kg	kg
Mauritius .... Maurice Mauricio	2001 2002 2003 2004 2005	— — — — —	— — — — —	— — — — —	— — — — —	— — — — —	— — — — —	— — — — —	— 1 — 1 2	— — — — —
Mexico .... Mexique México	2001 2002 2003 2004 2005	— — — — ?	1 2 3 1 ?	— — — — ?	1 215 810 405 851 ?	— — — — ?	27 31 30 19 ?	— — — — ?	— — — — ?	214 396 155 227 ?
Morocco .... Maroc Marruecos	2001 2002 2003 2004 2005	— — — — —	— — — — —	— — — — —	— — — — —	— — — — —	1 — — — —	— — — — —	— — — — —	9 18 9 21 23
Mozambique	2001 2002 2003 2004 2005	? — — — ?	? — — — ?	? — — — ?	? — — — ?	? — — — ?	? 1 — — ?	? — — — ?	? — — — ?	? — — — ?
Myanmar	2001 2002 2003 2004 2005	— — — — —	— — — — —	— — — — —	— — — — —	— — — — —	— — — — —	— — — — —	1 — — — —	— — — — —
Namibia .... Namibie	2001 2002 2003 2004 2005	? ? — — —	? ? — — —	? ? — — —	? ? 3 8 9	? ? — — —	? ? — — —	? ? — — —	? ? — — —	? ? — — 6
Netherlands .... Pays-Bas Países Bajos	2001 2002 2003 2004 2005	1 219 2 300 2 400 92 52	4 — 2 1 —	— 5 — 32 20	— — — — —	— 86 9 5 —	28 36 4 6 4	— — — — —	68 34 74 16 54	1 112 1 114 337 1 231 1 256
Netherlands Antilles .... *Antilles néerlandaises* *Antillas Neerlandesas*	2001 2002 2003 2004 2005	— — — — —	— — — — —	— — — — —	— — — — —	— — — — —	— — — — —	— — — — —	— — — — —	4 20 9 13 9
New Zealand .... Nouvelle-Zélande Nueva Zelandia	2001 2002 2003 2004 2005	— — — — —	— — 17 — —	— — — — —	— — — — —	— — — — —	.. .. — — —	— — — — —	.. .. — — —	364 364 390 388 462

Country or territory / Pays ou territoire / País o territorio	Year / Année / Año	Amo-barbital	Buprenor-phine / Buprénor-phine / Buprenor-fina	Butal-bital	Cathine / Catina	Cyclo-barbital / Ciclo-barbital	Flunitra-zepam / Flunitra-zépam	Glute-thimide / Gluté-thimide / Glute-timida	Penta-zocine / Penta-zocina	Pento-barbital
		kg	kg	kg	kg	kg	kg	kg	kg	kg
Nigeria	2001	—	—	—	—	—	2	—	30	—
Nigéria	2002	—	—	—	—	—	1	—	35	—
	2003	—	—	—	—	—	2	—	18	—
	2004	—	—	—	—	—	2	—	79	—
	2005	—	—	—	—	—	4	—	120	—
Norway	2001	—	1	1	—	—	13	—	83	125
Norvège	2002	—	3	1	—	—	11	—	55	220
Noruega	2003	—	4	1	—	—	9	—	44	159
	2004	—	5	1	—	—	3	—	2	97
	2005	—	9	1	—	—	4	—	5	214
Pakistan	2001	?	?	?	?	?	?	?	?	?
Pakistán	2002	—	7	—	—	—	—	—	674	—
	2003	—	8	—	—	—	—	—	632	—
	2004	—	6	—	—	—	—	—	660	—
	2005	—	8	—	—	—	—	—	955	144
Panama	2001	—	—	—	—	—	—	—	—	—
Panamá	2002	—	—	—	—	—	—	—	1	—
	2003	—	—	—	—	—	—	—	—	—
	2004	—	—	—	—	—	—	—	—	—
	2005	—	—	—	—	—	—	—	1	—
Papua New Guinea	2001	—	—	—	—	—	—	—	—	—
Papouasie-Nouvelle-Guinée	2002	—	—	—	—	—	—	—	—	—
Papua Nueva Guinea	2003	—	—	—	—	—	1	—	—	—
	2004	?	?	?	?	?	?	?	?	?
	2005	?	?	?	?	?	?	?	?	?
Paraguay	2001	—	—	—	—	—	1	—	—	—
	2002	—	—	—	—	—	10	—	—	—
	2003	—	—	—	—	—	5	—	—	—
	2004	?	?	?	?	?	?	?	?	?
	2005	?	?	?	?	?	?	?	?	?
Peru	2001	—	—	—	—	—	—	—	—	—
Pérou	2002	?	?	?	?	?	?	?	?	?
Perú	2003	—	—	—	—	—	1	—	—	—
	2004	—	—	—	—	—	1	—	—	55
	2005	—	—	—	—	—	—	—	—	36
Poland	2001	—	—	—	—	—	1	—	15	369
Pologne	2002	—	—	—	—	—	2	—	8	458
Polonia	2003	—	5	—	—	—	1	—	13	313
	2004	—	—	—	—	—	—	—	9	—
	2005	—	—	—	—	—	—	—	7	393
Portugal	2001	—	2	—	—	—	2	—	255	67
	2002	—	10	—	—	—	—	—	347	34
	2003	—	7	—	—	—	—	—	285	80
	2004	—	11	—	—	—	—	—	219	87
	2005	—	13	—	—	—	—	—	229	128

Country or territory / Pays ou territoire / País o territorio	Year / Année / Año	Amo-barbital	Buprenor-phine / Buprénor-phine / Buprenor-fina	Butal-bital	Cathine / Catina	Cyclo-barbital / Ciclo-barbital	Flunitra-zepam / Flunitra-zépam	Glute-thimide / Gluté-thimide / Glute-timida	Penta-zocine / Penta-zocina	Pento-barbital
		kg	kg	kg	kg	kg	kg	kg	kg	kg
Qatar.....................	2001	—	—	—	—	—	—	—	—	—
	2002	—	—	—	—	—	—	—	—	—
	2003	—	—	—	—	—	—	—	—	5
	2004	—	—	—	—	—	—	—	—	—
	2005	—	—	—	—	—	—	—	—	—
Republic of Korea	2001	—	—	—	—	—	7	—	19	42
République de Corée	2002	—	—	—	—	—	7	—	24	—
República de Corea	2003	—	19	—	—	—	59	—	18	46
	2004	—	—	—	—	—	13	—	20	9
	2005	—	—	—	—	—	11	—	18	9
Republic of Moldova	2001	—	—	—	—	24	—	—	1	—
République de Moldova	2002	3	—	—	—	14	—	—	—	—
República de Moldova	2003	9	—	—	—	44	—	—	—	—
	2004	42	—	—	—	8	—	—	1	—
	2005	?	?	?	?	?	?	?	?	?
Romania..................	2001	1 230	—	—	—	300	—	600	480	30
Roumanie	2002	7 100	—	—	—	100	3	300	384	120
Rumania	2003	2 400	—	—	—	—	—	300	152	—
	2004	2 000	—	—	—	—	—	1	75	—
	2005	9 700	—	—	—	—	—	—	—	—
Russian Federation	2001	—	—	—	—	1 359	7	—	—	—
Fédération de Russie	2002	—	—	—	—	1 074	4	—	—	—
Federación de Rusia	2003	—	—	—	—	958	5	—	—	—
	2004	—	—	—	—	564	—	—	—	—
	2005	—	1	—	—	—	—	—	—	—
Rwanda	2001	—	—	—	—	—	—	—	—	—
	2002	—	—	—	—	—	—	—	1	—
	2003	—	—	—	—	—	—	—	1	—
	2004	—	—	—	—	—	—	—	1	—
	2005	—	—	—	—	—	—	—	—	—
Sierra Leone	2001	—	—	—	—	—	—	—	2	—
Sierra Leona	2002	—	—	—	—	—	—	—	2	—
	2003	—	—	—	—	—	—	—	—	—
	2004	?	?	?	?	?	?	?	?	?
	2005	—	—	—	—	—	—	—	—	—
Singapore	2001	—	—	—	—	—	—	—	1	19
Singapour	2002	—	—	—	—	—	—	—	—	13
Singapur	2003	—	2	—	—	—	—	—	—	28
	2004	—	4	—	—	—	—	—	—	11
	2005	—	6	—	—	—	—	—	—	572
Slovakia	2001	—	—	—	—	—	13	—	41	—
Slovaquie	2002	—	—	—	—	—	8	—	21	—
Eslovaquia	2003	—	1	—	—	—	6	—	19	—
	2004	?	?	?	?	?	?	?	?	?
	2005	—	3	—	—	—	—	—	8	—

Country or territory / Pays ou territoire / País o territorio	Year / Année / Año	Amo-barbital	Buprenor-phine / Buprénor-phine / Buprenor-fina	Butal-bital	Cathine / Catina	Cyclo-barbital / Ciclo-barbital	Flunitra-zepam / Flunitra-zépam	Glute-thimide / Gluté-thimide / Glute-timida	Penta-zocine / Penta-zocina	Pento-barbital
		kg	kg	kg	kg	kg	kg	kg	kg	kg
Slovenia / Slovénie / Eslovenia	2001	—	—	—	—	—	—	—	150	—
	2002	—	—	—	—	—	—	—	390	—
	2003	—	—	—	—	—	—	—	190	—
	2004	—	—	—	—	—	—	—	50	—
	2005	—	—	—	—	—	—	—	115	—
South Africa / Afrique du Sud / Sudáfrica	2001	—	—	—	1 918	—	2	—	4	546
	2002	—	—	9	1 487	—	1	—	8	819
	2003	—	—	—	1 397	—	1	—	5	455
	2004	—	—	—	2 096	—	9	—	2	911
	2005	—	—	—	1 897	—	2	—	—	546
Spain / Espagne / España	2001	—	—	123	—	—	10	—	6	422
	2002	—	9	86	—	—	10	—	8	357
	2003	—	42	78	—	—	12	—	1	319
	2004	—	45	9	—	—	12	—	5	533
	2005	—	70	—	—	—	5	—	1	384
Sri Lanka	2001	—	—	—	—	—	..	—	..	—
	2002	—	—	—	—	—	..	—	..	—
	2003	—	—	—	—	—	..	—	..	—
	2004	—	—	—	—	—	—	—	1	—
	2005	—	—	—	—	—	—	—	—	—
Swaziland / Swazilandia	2001	—	—	—	—	—	—	—	—	1
	2002	—	—	—	—	—	—	—	—	—
	2003	—	—	—	—	—	—	—	—	—
	2004	—	—	—	—	—	—	—	—	—
	2005	?	?	?	?	?	?	?	?	?
Sweden / Suède / Suecia	2001	3	2	—	—	—	25	—	4	528
	2002	—	5	—	—	—	18	—	6	510
	2003	—	5	—	—	—	15	—	1	546
	2004	10	20	3	—	—	10	—	3	546
	2005	—	9	—	—	—	15	—	2	546
Switzerland / Suisse / Suiza	2001	—	3	245	229	279	54	250	338	546
	2002	240	6	258	40	93	48	—	379	686
	2003	—	7	186	81	—	39	—	406	648
	2004	—	13	152	182	—	72	—	203	543
	2005	—	12	62	—	—	26	—	451	921
Syrian Arab Republic / République arabe syrienne / República Árabe Siria	2001	—	—	—	—	—	—	—	21	—
	2002	—	—	—	—	—	—	—	14	—
	2003	—	—	—	—	—	—	—	30	—
	2004	—	—	—	—	—	—	—	10	10
	2005	—	—	—	—	—	—	—	—	—
Thailand / Thaïlande / Tailandia	2001	73	—	—	—	—	—	—	33	224
	2002	240	—	—	—	—	—	—	6	229
	2003	80	—	—	—	—	1	—	17	—
	2004	—	—	—	—	—	1	—	13	—
	2005	140	—	—	—	—	1	—	6	—

Schedule III. C.3. Imports (continued)
Tableau III. C.3. Importations (suite)
Lista III. C.3. Importaciones (continuación)

Country or territory / Pays ou territoire / País o territorio	Year / Année / Año	Amo-barbital	Buprenor-phine / Buprénor-phine / Buprenor-fina	Butal-bital	Cathine / Catina	Cyclo-barbital / Ciclo-barbital	Flunitra-zepam / Flunitra-zépam	Glute-thimide / Gluté-thimide / Glute-timida	Penta-zocine / Penta-zocina	Pento-barbital
		kg	kg	kg	kg	kg	kg	kg	kg	kg
The former Yugoslav	2001	—	—	—	—	—	—	—	2	—
Rep. of Macedonia	2002	—	—	—	—	—	—	—	1	—
L'ex-Rép. yougoslave	2003	—	—	—	—	—	—	—	1	—
de Macédoine	2004	—	—	—	—	—	—	—	1	—
La ex Rep. Yugoslava de Macedonia	2005	—	—	—	—	—	—	—	—	—
Togo	2001	—	—	—	—	—	—	—	1	—
	2002	—	—	—	—	—	—	—	—	—
	2003	—	—	—	—	—	—	—	—	—
	2004	—	—	—	—	—	—	—	—	—
	2005	—	—	—	—	—	—	—	—	—
Trinidad and Tobago	2001	—	—	—	—	—	—	—	—	2
Trinité-et-Tobago	2002	—	—	—	—	—	—	—	—	—
Trinidad y Tobago	2003	—	—	—	—	—	—	—	1	—
	2004	—	—	—	—	—	—	—	—	—
	2005	—	—	—	—	—	—	—	—	11
Ukraine	2001	—	—	—	—	5	—	—	—	—
Ucrania	2002	—	—	—	—	46	—	—	—	—
	2003	—	—	—	—	9	—	—	—	—
	2004	—	—	—	—	11	—	—	—	—
	2005	—	1	—	—	10	—	—	—	—
United Arab Emirates	2001	—	—	—	—	—	—	—	—	—
Émirats arabes unis	2002	—	—	—	—	—	—	—	—	—
Emiratos Árabes Unidos	2003	—	—	—	—	—	—	—	—	—
	2004	—	—	—	—	—	—	—	—	8
	2005	—	—	—	—	—	—	—	—	—
United Kingdom	2001	1 412	—	—	—	—	3	—	210	4 773
Royaume-Uni	2002	—	21	—	—	—	3	—	411	656
Reino Unido	2003	—	23	—	—	—	2	—	198	—
	2004	—	31	—	—	—	2	—	284	2 968
	2005	—	4	—	—	—	1	—	74	2 105
United Rep. of Tanzania	2001	—	1	—	—	—	—	—	—	—
Rép.-Unie de Tanzanie	2002	—	—	—	—	—	—	—	—	—
Rep. Unida de Tanzanía	2003	—	—	—	—	—	—	—	—	—
	2004	—	—	—	—	—	—	—	—	—
	2005	—	—	—	—	—	—	—	—	—
United States	2001	—	18	27 109	—	—	—	—	223	2 896
États-Unis	2002	—	35	28 226	—	—	—	—	1 792	3 779
Estados Unidos	2003	—	—	39 961	—	—	—	—	1 122	2 751
	2004	—	114	10 415	—	—	—	—	1 154	4 123
	2005	1	176	7 005	—	—	—	—	1 549	681
Uruguay	2001	—	—	16	—	—	17	—	—	38
	2002	—	—	6	—	—	20	—	—	18
	2003	?	?	?	?	?	?	?	?	?
	2004	?	?	?	?	?	?	?	?	?
	2005	?	?	?	?	?	?	?	?	?

Country or territory / Pays ou territoire / País o territorio	Year / Année / Año	Amo-barbital	Buprenor-phine / Buprénor-phine / Buprenor-fina	Butal-bital	Cathine / Catina	Cyclo-barbital / Ciclo-barbital	Flunitra-zepam / Flunitra-zépam	Glute-thimide / Gluté-thimide / Glute-timida	Penta-zocine / Penta-zocina	Pento-barbital
		kg	kg	kg	kg	kg	kg	kg	kg	kg
Uzbekistan Ouzbékistan Uzbekistán	2001	—	—	—	—	—	1	—	—	—
	2002	—	—	—	—	—	—	—	—	—
	2003	—	—	—	—	—	—	—	—	—
	2004	—	—	—	—	—	—	—	—	—
	2005	—	—	—	—	—	—	—	—	—
Yemen Yémen	2001	—	—	—	—	—	—	—	—	—
	2002	?	?	?	?	?	?	?	?	?
	2003	—	—	—	—	—	—	—	1	—
	2004	—	—	—	—	—	—	—	—	—
	2005	—	—	—	—	—	—	—	—	—
Zimbabwe	2001	—	—	—	—	—	—	—	—	16
	2002	—	—	—	—	—	—	—	—	27
	2003	—	—	—	—	—	—	—	—	11
	2004	—	—	—	—	—	—	—	—	14
	2005	—	—	—	—	—	—	—	—	—
Total	2001	4 160	398	34 704	4 887	2 175	991	1 500	2 825	30 358
	2002	10 646	684	34 094	3 876	1 599	1 091	500	5 339	25 679
	2003	5 257	816	46 159	3 081	1 191	997	300	4 123	19 158
	2004	2 218	1 053	14 987	4 493	767	815	201	3 363	25 428
	2005	10 187	1 186	11 765	3 572	155	690	201	4 322	23 151

D. Substances listed in Schedule IV

Manufacture — Exports — Imports

D. Substances inscrites au Tableau IV

Fabrication — Exportations — Importations

D. Sustancias incluidas en la Lista IV

Fabricación — Exportaciones — Importaciones

Schedule IV. D.1. Central nervous system stimulants
Tableau IV. D.1. Stimulants du système nerveux central
Lista IV. D.1. Estimulantes del sistema nervioso central

Manufacture — Fabrication — Fabricación

Country or territory / Pays ou territoire / País o territorio	Year / Année / Año	Amfepramone / Amfépramone / Anfepramona (kg)	Aminorex (kg)	Benzfetamine / Benzfétamine / Benzfetamina (kg)	Etilamfetamine / Étilamfétamine / Etilanfetamina (kg)	Fencamfamin / Fencamfamine / Fencanfamina (kg)	Fenproporex (kg)	Mazindol (kg)	Mefenorex / Méfénorex (kg)	Mesocarb / Mésocarbe / Mesocarbo (kg)	Pemoline / Pémoline / Pemolina (kg)	Phendimetrazine / Phendimétrazine / Fendimetracina (kg)	Phentermine / Fentermine / Fentermina (kg)	Pipradrol (kg)	Pyrovalerone / Pyrovalérone / Pirovalerona (kg)
Argentina / Argentine	2003	—	—	—	—	—	—	165	—	—	—	—	—	—	—
	2004	—	—	—	—	—	—	—	—	—	—	—	—	—	—
	2005	—	—	—	—	—	—	175	—	—	—	—	—	—	—
Brazil / Brésil / Brasil	2003	14 892	—	—	—	—	4 055	44	—	—	—	—	—	—	—
	2004	20 775	—	—	—	—	5 197	—	—	—	—	—	—	—	—
	2005	27 568	—	—	—	—	8 265	—	—	—	—	—	—	—	—
China / Chine	2003	—	—	—	—	—	—	—	—	—	—	—	—	—	—
	2004	—	—	—	—	—	—	—	—	—	6	700	—	—	—
	2005	—	—	—	—	—	—	—	—	—	—	—	—	—	—
France / Francia	2003	—	—	—	—	—	2 680	—	—	—	—	—	—	—	—
	2004	—	—	—	—	—	—	—	—	—	—	—	—	—	—
	2005	—	—	—	—	—	—	—	—	—	—	—	—	8	—
Germany / Allemagne / Alemania	2003	—	—	—	—	—	3 317	—	—	—	—	—	2 475	—	—
	2004	—	—	—	—	—	—	—	—	—	—	—	4 962	—	—
	2005	—	—	—	—	—	1 215	—	—	—	—	5	3 358	—	—
Israel / Israël	2003	—	—	—	—	—	—	—	—	—	—	—	5	—	—
	2004	—	—	—	—	—	—	—	—	—	—	—	5	—	—
	2005	—	—	—	—	—	—	—	—	—	—	—	—	—	—
Italy / Italie / Italia	2003	798	—	—	—	—	—	—	—	—	—	2 173	628	—	—
	2004	—	—	—	—	—	—	—	—	—	—	4 862	2 174	—	—
	2005	251	—	—	—	—	—	—	—	—	—	6 317	3 606	—	—

		kg	kg	kg	kg	kg	kg	kg	kg	kg	kg	kg	kg	kg
Switzerland / **Suisse** / **Suiza**	2003	4 003	—	—	—	—	—	—	—	1 100	—	—	—	—
	2004	3 851	—	—	—	—	—	—	—	—	—	—	—	—
	2005	22	—	29	—	—	—	—	—	—	—	—	—	—
United States / **États-Unis** / **Estados Unidos**	2003	—	—	906	—	—	—	—	—	—	—	4 965	—	—
	2004	—	—	1 428	—	—	—	—	—	—	—	7 396	—	—
	2005	—	—	719	—	—	—	—	—	—	—	6 876	—	—
Total	2003	19 693	—	906	—	10 052	209	—	6	—	2 173	8 073	—	—
	2004	24 626	—	1 428	—	5 197	—	—	1 100	—	4 862	14 537	8	—
	2005	27 841	—	748	—	9 480	175	—	—	—	7 022	13 840	—	—

Exports — Exportations — Exportaciones

		kg	kg	kg	kg	kg	kg	kg	kg	kg	kg	kg	kg	kg
Argentina / **Argentine**	2003	—	—	—	—	—	—	—	—	—	—	—	—	—
	2004	—	—	—	—	—	1	—	—	—	—	—	—	—
	2005	—	—	—	—	—	5	—	—	—	—	—	—	—
Australia / **Australie**	2003	16	—	587	—	—	—	—	—	—	—	—	—	—
	2004	—	—	766	—	—	—	—	—	—	—	—	—	—
	2005	16	—	686	—	—	—	—	—	—	—	—	—	—
Austria / **Autriche**	2003	—	—	149	—	—	—	—	—	—	—	—	—	—
	2004	—	—	156	—	—	—	—	—	—	—	—	—	—
	2005	—	—	210	—	—	—	—	—	—	—	—	—	—
Belgium / **Belgique** / **Bélgica**	2003	94	—	314	—	—	—	—	—	—	—	—	—	—
	2004	257	—	232	—	—	—	—	—	—	—	—	—	—
	2005	156	—	304	—	—	—	—	—	—	—	—	—	—
Brazil / **Brésil** / **Brasil**	2003	436	—	—	—	—	49	—	35	—	—	—	—	—
	2004	298	—	—	—	—	49	—	88	—	—	—	—	—
	2005	226	—	—	—	—	21	—	48	—	—	—	—	—
China / **Chine**	2003	—	—	—	—	—	17	—	—	—	—	—	—	—
	2004	—	—	—	—	—	—	—	—	—	—	—	—	—
	2005	—	—	—	700	—	—	—	—	—	—	—	—	—
Hong Kong SAR of China / *RAS de Hong Kong (Chine)* / *RAE de Hong Kong de China*	2003	—	—	—	—	—	—	—	—	—	—	—	—	—
	2004	—	—	—	—	—	—	—	—	—	—	—	—	—
	2005	4	—	—	—	—	—	—	—	—	—	—	—	—
Costa Rica	2003	—	—	—	—	—	—	—	—	—	—	—	—	—
	2004	—	—	—	—	—	—	—	—	—	—	—	—	—
	2005	—	—	9	—	—	1	—	—	—	—	—	—	—

Schedule IV. D.1. Central nervous system stimulants (continued)
Tableau IV. D.1. Stimulants du système nerveux central (suite)
Lista IV. D.1. Estimulantes del sistema nervioso central (continuación)

Exports — Exportations — Exportaciones (continued — suite — continuación)

Country or territory / Pays ou territoire / País o territorio	Year / Année / Año	Amfepramone / Amfépramone / Anfepramona (kg)	Aminorex (kg)	Benzfetamine / Benzfétamine / Benzfetamina (kg)	Etilamfetamine / Étilamfétamine / Etilamfetamina (kg)	Fencamfamin / Fencamfamine / Fencamfamina (kg)	Fenproporex (kg)	Mazindol (kg)	Mefenorex / Méfénorex (kg)	Mesocarb / Mésocarbe / Mesocarbo (kg)	Pemoline / Pémoline / Pemolina (kg)	Phendimetrazine / Phendimétrazine / Fendimetracina (kg)	Phentermine / Fentermine / Fentermina (kg)	Pipradrol (kg)	Pyrovalerone / Pyrovalérone / Pirovalerona (kg)
France / Francia	2003	—	—	—	—	—	613	—	—	—	—	—	—	—	—
	2004	—	—	—	—	—	912	—	—	—	—	—	—	2	—
	2005	—	—	—	—	—	—	—	—	—	—	—	—	—	—
Germany / Allemagne / Alemania	2003	393	—	—	—	—	2 033	5	—	—	—	—	2 316	—	—
	2004	627	—	—	—	—	848	4	—	—	—	—	2 998	—	—
	2005	652	—	—	—	—	1 602	—	—	—	—	2	4 383	—	—
India / Inde	2003	—	—	—	—	—	966	—	—	—	—	—	400	—	—
	2004	—	—	—	—	—	—	—	—	—	—	—	40	—	—
	2005	—	—	—	—	—	—	—	—	—	—	—	40	—	—
Israel / Israël	2003	—	—	—	—	—	—	—	—	—	—	—	—	—	—
	2004	—	—	—	—	—	—	—	—	—	112	—	—	—	—
	2005	—	—	—	—	—	—	—	—	—	—	—	—	—	—
Italy / Italie / Italia	2003	—	—	—	—	—	—	—	—	—	—	1 498	213	—	—
	2004	510	—	—	—	—	—	—	—	—	—	4 798	2 367	—	—
	2005	336	—	—	—	—	—	—	—	—	—	5 003	3 508	—	—
Malaysia / Malaisie / Malasia	2003	—	—	—	—	—	—	—	—	—	—	—	—	—	—
	2004	—	—	—	—	—	—	—	—	—	—	—	—	—	—
	2005	—	—	—	—	—	—	—	—	—	—	224	1	—	—
Netherlands / Pays-Bas / Países Bajos	2003	—	—	—	—	—	—	—	—	—	182	—	157	—	—
	2004	—	—	—	—	—	—	—	—	—	262	—	309	—	—
	2005	—	—	—	—	—	—	—	—	—	128	—	368	—	—
New Zealand / Nouvelle-Zélande / Nueva Zelandia	2003	—	—	—	—	—	—	—	—	—	—	—	10	—	—
	2004	—	—	—	—	—	—	—	—	—	—	—	14	—	—
	2005	—	—	—	—	—	—	—	—	—	—	—	3	—	—

Imports — Importations — Importaciones

		kg	kg	kg	kg	kg	kg	kg	kg	kg	kg
Panama / Panamá	2003	80	—	—	3	1	—	—	—	62	—
	2004	48	—	—	—	—	—	—	—	71	—
	2005	40	—	—	—	—	—	—	—	53	—
Singapore / Singapour / Singapur	2003	—	—	—	—	—	—	—	—	3	—
	2004	—	—	—	—	—	—	—	—	—	—
	2005	—	—	—	—	—	—	—	—	1	—
South Africa / Afrique du Sud / Sudáfrica	2003	—	—	—	—	—	—	—	—	—	—
	2004	—	—	—	—	—	—	—	—	4	—
	2005	—	—	—	—	—	—	—	—	4	—
Switzerland / Suisse / Suiza	2003	3 635	—	—	861	6	—	549	—	500	—
	2004	2 314	—	—	42	27	—	341	—	433	—
	2005	5 813	9	—	42	25	—	312	—	398	—
United Kingdom / Royaume-Uni / Reino Unido	2003	—	—	—	—	2	—	—	—	134	—
	2004	—	—	—	—	2	—	—	—	—	—
	2005	—	—	—	—	2	—	—	—	—	—
United States / États-Unis / Estados Unidos	2003	62	—	—	—	—	—	9	—	611	—
	2004	7	—	—	—	—	—	—	204	1 244	—
	2005	69	—	—	—	—	—	—	98	2 939	—
Total	2003	4 716	—	—	4 511	63	—	869	1 498	5 456	—
	2004	4 061	—	—	1 890	84	—	807	4 798	8 643	2
	2005	7 312	9	—	1 692	53	—	440	6 027	12 898	—

		kg	kg	kg	kg	kg	kg	kg	kg	kg
Argentina / Argentine	2003	59	—	—	—	—	—	—	—	—
	2004	14	—	—	—	—	—	37	28	—
	2005	40	—	—	—	—	—	20	—	31
Australia / Australie	2003	85	—	—	—	—	—	—	—	464
	2004	170	—	—	—	—	—	—	—	1 043
	2005	255	—	—	—	—	—	—	—	1 135
Austria / Autriche	2003	—	—	—	—	—	—	—	—	216
	2004	—	—	—	—	—	—	—	—	146
	2005	—	—	—	—	—	—	—	—	73
Belgium / Belgique / Bélgica	2003	—	—	—	—	—	—	—	—	40
	2004	252	—	—	—	—	—	—	—	4
	2005	128	—	—	—	—	—	—	—	320

Schedule IV. D.1. Central nervous system stimulants *(continued)*
Tableau IV. D.1. Stimulants du système nerveux central *(suite)*
Lista IV. D.1. Estimulantes del sistema nervioso central *(continuación)*

Imports — Importations — Importaciones *(continued — suite — continuación)*

Country or territory / Pays ou territoire / País o territorio	Year / Année / Año	Amfepramone / Amfépramone / Anfepramona (kg)	Aminorex (kg)	Benzfetamine / Benzfétamine / Benzfetamina (kg)	Etilamfetamine / Étilamfétamine / Etilanfetamina (kg)	Fencamfamin / Fencamfamine / Fencanfamina (kg)	Fenproporex (kg)	Mazindol (kg)	Mefenorex / Méfénorex (kg)	Mesocarb / Mésocarbe / Mesocarbo (kg)	Pemoline / Pémoline / Pemolina (kg)	Phendimetrazine / Phendimétrazine / Fendimetracina (kg)	Phentermine / Fentermina (kg)	Pipradrol (kg)	Pyrovalerone / Pyrovalérone / Pirovalerona (kg)
Belize / Belice	2003	—	—	—	—	—	—	—	—	—	—	—	2	—	—
	2004	—	—	—	—	—	—	—	—	—	—	—	—	—	—
	2005	?	?	?	?	?	?	?	?	?	?	?	?	?	?
Bolivia / Bolivie	2003	—	—	—	—	—	—	—	—	—	—	—	—	—	—
	2004	—	—	—	—	—	—	—	—	—	2	—	—	—	—
	2005	?	?	?	?	?	?	?	?	?	?	?	?	?	?
Brazil / Brésil / Brasil	2003	255	—	—	—	—	3 822	—	—	—	—	—	—	—	—
	2004	—	—	—	—	—	1 626	—	—	—	—	—	—	—	—
	2005	—	—	—	—	—	1 596	—	—	—	—	—	—	—	—
Brunei Darussalam / Brunéi Darussalam	2003	—	—	—	—	—	—	—	—	—	—	—	—	—	—
	2004	—	—	—	—	—	—	—	—	—	—	—	—	—	—
	2005	—	—	—	—	—	—	—	—	—	—	—	2	—	—
Canada / Canadá	2003	88	—	—	—	—	—	—	—	—	3	—	44	—	—
	2004	66	—	—	—	—	—	1	—	—	—	—	56	2	—
	2005	10	—	—	—	—	—	—	—	—	—	—	—	—	—
Chile / Chili	2003	382	—	—	—	—	—	—	—	—	22	—	—	—	—
	2004	127	—	—	—	—	—	—	—	—	13	—	—	—	—
	2005	297	—	—	—	—	2	—	—	—	15	—	—	—	—
China — Chine Hong Kong SAR of China / RAS de Hong Kong (Chine) / RAE de Hong Kong de China	2003	107	—	—	—	—	—	1	—	—	—	—	169	—	—
	2004	33	—	—	—	—	—	—	—	—	—	—	138	—	—
	2005	109	—	—	—	—	—	—	—	—	—	—	152	—	—

Country	Year	1	2	3	4	5	6	7	8	9	10	11	12	13
Costa Rica	2003	—	—	29	—	—	—	—	2	—	—	—	—	62
	2004	—	—	27	—	—	—	—	1	—	—	—	—	83
	2005	—	—	34	—	—	—	—	—	—	—	—	—	19
Côte d'Ivoire	2003	—	—	—	—	—	—	—	—	—	—	—	—	—
	2004	—	—	—	—	—	—	—	—	1	—	—	—	—
	2005	—	—	—	—	—	—	—	—	—	—	—	—	—
Czech Republic / République tchèque / República Checa	2003	—	—	80	—	—	—	—	—	—	—	—	—	—
	2004	—	—	138	—	—	—	—	—	—	—	—	—	—
	2005	—	—	156	—	—	—	—	—	—	—	—	—	—
Denmark / Danemark / Dinamarca	2003	—	—	—	—	—	—	—	—	—	—	—	—	7
	2004	—	—	—	—	—	—	—	—	—	—	—	—	23
	2005	—	—	—	—	—	—	—	—	—	—	—	—	37
Dominican Republic / République dominicaine / República Dominicana	2003	—	—	—	—	—	—	—	—	—	—	—	—	—
	2004	—	—	1	—	—	—	—	—	—	—	—	—	—
	2005	—	—	—	—	—	—	—	—	—	—	—	—	—
Ecuador / Équateur	2003	—	—	9	—	—	—	—	1	60	—	—	—	—
	2004	—	—	7	—	—	—	—	1	—	—	—	—	—
	2005	—	—	10	—	—	—	—	—	2	—	—	—	—
El Salvador	2003	—	—	1	—	—	—	—	—	—	—	—	—	—
	2004	—	—	1	—	—	—	—	—	—	—	—	—	—
	2005	—	—	1	—	—	—	—	—	—	—	—	—	1
Germany / Allemagne / Alemania	2003	—	—	7	—	40	—	—	5	—	—	—	—	825
	2004	—	—	151	—	86	—	—	4	—	—	—	—	551
	2005	—	—	—	—	45	—	—	—	—	—	—	—	1 169
Honduras	2003	—	—	3	—	—	—	—	1	—	—	—	—	—
	2004	—	—	9	—	—	—	—	—	—	—	—	—	—
	2005	?	?	?	?	?	?	?	?	?	?	?	?	?
Indonesia / Indonésie	2003	—	—	—	—	—	—	—	1	—	—	—	—	204
	2004	—	—	—	—	—	—	—	1	—	—	—	—	77
	2005	—	—	—	—	—	—	—	—	—	—	—	—	153
Ireland / Irlande / Irlanda	2003	—	—	—	—	—	—	—	—	—	—	—	—	—
	2004	—	—	—	—	—	—	—	—	—	—	—	—	—
	2005	—	—	1	—	—	—	—	—	—	—	—	—	—
Israel / Israël	2003	—	—	—	—	10	—	—	—	—	—	—	—	—
	2004	—	—	12	—	10	—	—	—	—	—	—	—	—
	2005	—	—	12	—	—	—	—	—	—	—	—	—	—

Schedule IV. D.1. Central nervous system stimulants (continued)
Tableau IV. D.1. Stimulants du système nerveux central (suite)
Lista IV. D.1. Estimulantes del sistema nervioso central (continuación)

Imports — Importations — Importaciones (continued — suite — continuación)

Country or territory / Pays ou territoire / País o territorio	Year / Année / Año	Amfepramone / Amfépramone / Anfepramona	Aminorex	Benzfetamine / Benzfétamine / Benzfetamina	Etilamfetamine / Étilamfétamine / Etilanfetamina	Fencamfamin / Fencamfamine / Fencanfamina	Fenproporex	Mazindol	Mefenorex / Méfénorex	Mesocarb / Mésocarbe / Mesocarbo	Pemoline / Pémoline / Pemolina	Phendimetrazine / Phendimétrazine / Fendimetracina	Phentermine / Fentermine / Fentermina	Pipradrol	Pyrovalerone / Pyrovalérone / Pirovalerona
		kg	kg	kg	kg	kg	kg	kg	kg	kg	kg	kg	kg	kg	kg
Italy / Italie / Italia	2003	—	—	—	—	—	—	—	—	—	—	—	—	—	—
	2004	—	—	—	—	—	—	—	—	—	—	—	160	—	—
	2005	—	—	—	—	—	—	—	—	—	—	224	—	—	—
Jamaica / Jamaïque	2003	—	—	—	—	—	—	—	—	—	—	—	—	—	—
	2004	—	—	—	—	—	—	—	—	—	—	—	1	—	—
	2005	—	—	—	—	—	—	—	—	—	—	—	—	—	—
Japan / Japon / Japón	2003	—	—	—	—	—	—	1	—	—	40	—	—	—	—
	2004	—	—	—	—	—	—	1	—	—	80	—	—	—	—
	2005	—	—	—	—	—	—	3	—	—	40	—	1	—	—
Latvia / Lettonie / Letonia	2003	—	—	—	—	—	—	—	—	—	—	—	—	—	—
	2004	—	—	—	—	—	—	—	—	—	—	—	—	—	—
	2005	—	—	22	—	—	—	—	—	—	—	—	—	—	—
Malaysia / Malaisie / Malasia	2003	—	—	—	—	—	—	—	—	—	—	—	148	—	—
	2004	—	—	—	—	—	—	—	—	—	—	—	471	—	—
	2005	—	—	—	—	—	—	—	—	—	—	616	325	—	—
Mexico / Mexique / México	2003	935	—	—	—	—	—	75	—	—	—	—	523	—	—
	2004	850	—	—	—	—	—	25	—	—	—	—	10	—	—
	2005	?	?	?	?	?	?	?	?	?	?	?	?	?	?
Namibia / Namibie	2003	—	—	—	—	—	—	—	—	—	—	—	—	—	—
	2004	—	—	—	—	—	—	—	—	—	—	—	2	—	—
	2005	—	—	—	—	—	—	—	—	—	—	—	2	—	—

Statistical data table (rotated). Column headers are not printed on this page.

Country	Year	1	2	3	4	5	6	7	8	9	10	11	12	13	14
Netherlands / Pays-Bas / Países Bajos	2003	—	—	481	—	—	—	—	—	—	—	—	—	—	—
	2004	—	—	357	—	—	—	—	—	—	—	—	—	—	—
	2005	—	—	190	—	21	—	—	—	—	—	—	—	—	—
New Zealand / Nouvelle-Zélande / Nueva Zelandia	2003	—	—	23	—	—	—	—	—	—	—	—	—	—	16
	2004	—	—	24	—	—	—	—	—	—	—	—	—	—	—
	2005	—	—	26	—	—	—	—	—	—	—	—	—	—	16
Nicaragua	2003	—	—	—	—	—	—	—	—	7	—	—	—	—	—
	2004	—	—	—	—	—	—	—	—	4	—	—	—	—	—
	2005	—	—	—	—	—	—	—	—	4	—	—	—	—	—
Panama / Panamá	2003	—	—	72	—	—	—	—	1	3	—	—	—	—	80
	2004	—	—	102	—	—	—	—	—	—	—	—	—	—	109
	2005	—	—	118	—	—	—	—	—	1	—	—	—	—	—
Paraguay	2003	—	—	—	—	21	—	—	1	63	—	—	—	—	—
	2004	?	?	?	?	?	?	?	?	?	?	?	?	?	?
	2005	?	?	?	?	?	?	?	?	?	?	?	?	?	?
Peru / Pérou / Perú	2003	—	—	—	—	—	—	—	—	34	—	—	31	8	50
	2004	—	—	—	—	—	—	—	—	2	—	—	—	—	130
	2005	—	—	—	—	—	—	—	—	—	—	—	—	—	54
Philippines / Filipinas	2003	—	—	20	—	—	—	—	20	—	—	—	—	—	—
	2004	—	—	52	—	—	—	—	—	—	—	—	—	—	—
	2005	?	?	?	?	?	?	?	?	—	?	?	?	?	?
Republic of Korea / République de Corée / República de Corea	2003	—	—	—	728	12	—	—	—	—	—	—	—	—	—
	2004	—	—	1 662	1 788	—	—	—	—	—	—	—	—	—	201
	2005	?	?	2 187	1 700	—	?	?	?	—	—	?	?	?	9
Romania / Roumanie / Rumania	2003	—	—	—	—	—	—	—	—	—	—	—	—	—	108
	2004	—	—	—	—	—	—	—	—	—	—	—	—	—	57
	2005	—	—	—	—	—	—	—	—	—	—	—	—	—	—
Singapore / Singapour / Singapur	2003	—	—	93	—	—	—	—	—	—	—	—	—	—	—
	2004	—	—	181	—	—	—	—	—	—	—	—	—	—	—
	2005	—	—	94	—	—	—	—	—	—	—	—	—	—	—
Slovakia / Slovaquie / Eslovaquia	2003	—	—	29	—	—	—	—	—	—	—	—	—	—	—
	2004	?	?	?	?	?	?	?	?	?	?	?	?	?	?
	2005	—	—	—	—	—	—	—	—	—	—	—	—	—	—
South Africa / Afrique du Sud / Sudáfrica	2003	—	—	52	—	20	—	—	—	—	—	—	—	—	43
	2004	—	—	48	6	—	—	—	—	—	—	—	—	—	—
	2005	—	—	83	15	—	—	—	—	—	—	—	—	—	—

Imports — Importations — Importaciones *(continued — suite — continuación)*

Country or territory / Pays ou territoire / País o territorio	Year / Année / Año	Amfepramone / Amfépramone / Anfepramona (kg)	Aminorex (kg)	Benzfetamine / Benzfétamine / Benzfetamina (kg)	Etilamfetamine / Étilamfétamine / Etilanfetamina (kg)	Fencamfamin / Fencamfamine / Fencanfamina (kg)	Fenproporex (kg)	Mazindol (kg)	Mefenorex / Méfénorex (kg)	Mesocarb / Mésocarbe / Mesocarbo (kg)	Pemoline / Pémoline / Pemolina (kg)	Phendimetrazine / Phendimétrazine / Fendimetracina (kg)	Phentermine / Fentermina (kg)	Pipradrol (kg)	Pyrovalerone / Pyrovalérone / Pirovalerona (kg)
Spain / Espagne / España	2003	—	—	—	—	—	—	—	—	—	54	—	—	—	—
	2004	—	—	—	—	—	—	—	—	—	11	—	—	—	—
	2005	—	—	—	—	—	—	—	—	—	—	—	—	—	—
Sri Lanka / Sri Lanka / Sri Lanka	2003	—	—	—	—	—	—	—	—	—	—	—	..	—	—
	2004	—	—	—	—	—	—	—	—	—	—	—	1	—	—
	2005	—	—	—	—	—	—	—	—	—	—	—	1	—	—
Switzerland / Suisse / Suiza	2003	104	—	—	—	—	966	26	—	—	11	—	260	—	—
	2004	249	—	—	—	—	145	20	—	—	211	—	145	—	—
	2005	913	—	—	—	—	—	1	—	—	23	—	367	—	—
Thailand / Thaïlande / Tailandia	2003	107	—	—	—	—	—	—	—	—	—	—	324	—	—
	2004	223	—	—	—	—	—	—	—	—	—	—	354	—	—
	2005	128	—	—	—	—	—	—	—	—	—	—	453	—	—
Trinidad and Tobago / Trinité-et-Tobago / Trinidad y Tobago	2003	—	—	—	—	—	—	—	—	—	—	—	—	—	—
	2004	—	—	—	—	—	—	—	—	—	—	—	1	—	—
	2005	—	—	—	—	—	—	—	—	—	—	—	—	—	—
United Kingdom / Royaume-Uni / Reino Unido	2003	—	—	—	—	—	—	3	—	—	—	—	40	—	—
	2004	85	—	—	—	—	—	3	—	—	—	—	—	—	—
	2005	73	—	—	—	—	—	—	—	—	—	—	246	—	—
United States / États-Unis / Estados Unidos	2003	867	—	—	—	—	—	—	—	—	592	1 078	1 496	—	—
	2004	1 316	—	—	—	—	—	—	—	—	330	2 520	3 108	—	—
	2005	1 360	—	—	—	—	—	—	—	—	300	3 084	5 322	—	—

	Year														
Venezuela (Bolivarian Rep. of)	2003	—	—	—	—	—	8	—	—	—	—	—	27	—	—
Venezuela (Rép. bolivarienne du)	2004	—	—	—	—	—	—	—	—	—	—	—	—	2	—
Venezuela (Rep. Bolivariana de)	2005	—	—	—	—	—	—	—	—	—	—	—	—	—	—
Total	2003	4 384	8	31	—	—	4 963	117	—	—	807	1 806	4 652	—	—
	2004	4 616	—	—	—	—	1 670	78	—	—	789	4 314	8 412	2	—
	2005	4 771	—	22	—	—	1 625	4	—	—	444	5 639	11 342	—	—

179

Schedule IV. D.2. Anxiolytics (first part): main benzodiazepines and meprobamate
Tableau IV. D.2. Anxiolytiques (première partie): principales benzodiazépines et méprobamate
Lista IV. D.2. Ansiolíticos (primera parte): principales benzodiazepinas y meprobamato

Manufacture — Fabrication — Fabricación

Country or territory / Pays ou territoire / País o territorio	Year / Année / Año	Alprazolam	Bromazepam / Bromazépam / Bromazépam	Chlordiazepoxide / Chlordiazépoxide / Clordiazepóxido	Clobazam	Clorazepate / Clorazépate / Clorazepato	Diazepam / Diazépam / Diazépam	Lorazepam / Lorazépam / Lorazépam	Medazepam / Médazépam / Médazépam	Meprobamate / Méprobamate / Meprobamato	Nordazepam / Nordazépam / Nordazépam	Oxazepam / Oxazépam / Oxazépam	Prazepam / Prazépam / Prazépam
		kg	kg	kg	kg	kg	kg	kg	kg	kg	kg	kg	kg
Brazil / Brésil / Brasil	2003	2	1 223	106	—	—	2 777	69	—	—	—	—	—
	2004	8	1 570	338	—	—	5 004	113	—	—	—	2	—
	2005	102	1 630	364	—	—	4 718	105	—	—	—	—	—
China / Chine	2003	125	25	12 004	—	—	58 533	—	—	118 720	—	—	—
	2004	120	402	3 856	—	—	51 804	—	—	96 625	—	—	—
	2005	163	325	10 980	—	—	45 490	4	—	—	—	—	—
Czech Republic / République tchèque / República Checa	2003	28	—	—	—	—	—	—	—	—	—	—	—
	2004	45	—	—	—	—	—	—	—	—	—	—	—
	2005	—	—	—	—	—	—	—	—	—	—	—	—
Denmark / Danemark / Dinamarca	2003	—	—	—	—	—	—	—	—	141 339	—	—	—
	2004	—	—	—	—	—	—	—	—	123 640	—	—	—
	2005	—	—	—	—	—	—	—	—	102 085	—	—	—
Finland / Finlande / Finlandia	2003	—	—	—	—	—	—	—	—	—	883	—	—
	2004	555	—	—	—	—	—	—	—	—	2 044	—	—
	2005	1 213	—	—	—	—	—	—	—	—	2 907	—	—
France / Francia	2003	1 063	—	—	1 351	5 911	—	—	—	—	397	9 653	—
	2004	852	—	—	1 984	5 774	—	—	—	—	679	5 204	—
	2005	981	—	—	1 358	5 764	—	—	—	—	544	10 363	—
Germany / Allemagne / Alemania	2003	—	—	—	2 163	—	—	2 692	—	—	—	—	—
	2004	—	—	—	2 469	—	—	3 712	—	—	—	—	—
	2005	—	—	—	1 201	—	—	5 250	—	—	—	—	—

	Year	D1	D2	D3	D4	D5	D6	D7	D8	D9	D10	D11	D12
India .... Inde	2003	—	—	—	—	—	—	—	—	—	—	—	—
	2004	2 041	349	9 320	846	32	5 961	1 364	—	—	174	2 067	—
	2005	2 291	554	6 275	804	57	5 541	1 611	—	107	174	2 069	—
Iraq	2003	—	—	30	—	—	54	—	—	—	—	—	—
	2004	?	?	?	?	?	?	?	?	?	?	?	?
	2005	?	?	?	?	?	?	?	?	?	?	?	?
Ireland .... Irlande Irlanda	2003	—	—	—	—	—	—	—	—	—	—	—	—
	2004	—	1	4	—	—	—	—	—	—	—	—	—
	2005	—	—	—	—	—	—	—	—	—	—	—	—
Israel .... Israël	2003	17	—	—	—	—	—	—	—	—	—	—	—
	2004	10	—	—	—	175	—	—	—	—	—	—	—
	2005	19	—	—	102	446	—	4	—	—	—	—	—
Italy .... Italie Italia	2003	2 281	5 831	7 951	928	1 268	16 743	3 420	2 096	—	60	22 278	—
	2004	1 319	5 347	5 723	173	1 765	16 890	4 950	1 241	—	—	10 480	—
	2005	1 506	4 771	3 549	75	1 089	11 959	3 247	2 124	—	—	14 278	—
Japan .... Japon Japón	2003	51	—	120	—	—	—	—	—	—	—	—	—
	2004	102	—	—	—	—	—	—	—	—	1	—	—
	2005	—	—	—	—	—	—	—	—	—	—	—	—
Poland .... Pologne Polonia	2003	—	—	—	—	—	—	170	—	—	—	405	—
	2004	—	—	334	—	—	383	151	—	—	—	498	—
	2005	—	—	—	—	—	723	105	—	—	—	—	—
Russian Federation .... Fédération de Russie Federación de Rusia	2003	7	—	—	—	—	172	—	402	—	—	651	—
	2004	14	—	42	—	—	18	—	521	—	—	180	—
	2005	16	—	—	—	—	422	—	202	—	—	341	—
Slovakia .... Slovaquie Eslovaquia	2003	—	—	—	—	—	—	2	—	—	—	—	—
	2004	?	?	?	?	?	?	?	?	?	?	?	?
	2005	—	—	—	—	—	—	—	—	—	—	—	—
Spain .... Espagne España	2003	—	—	—	—	590	—	—	—	—	—	—	—
	2004	—	—	—	—	363	—	8	—	—	—	1 084	—
	2005	—	—	—	—	405	—	7	—	400	—	—	—
Switzerland .... Suisse Suiza	2003	—	7 566	—	—	—	7 931	—	—	—	—	—	4 172
	2004	—	7 540	—	—	—	3 817	—	—	—	1 315	—	4 431
	2005	—	—	—	—	—	—	—	—	—	—	—	3 396
United Kingdom .... Royaume-Uni Reino Unido	2003	—	—	—	—	—	2	91	—	—	—	15	—
	2004	—	—	—	—	—	—	73	—	—	—	—	—
	2005	—	—	—	—	—	—	92	—	—	—	3	—

181

Schedule IV. D.2. Anxiolytics (first part): main benzodiazepines and meprobamate (continued)

Tableau IV. D.2. Anxiolytiques (première partie): principales benzodiazépines et méprobamate (suite)

Lista IV. D.2. Ansiolíticos (primera parte): principales benzodiazepinas y meprobamato (continuación)

Manufacture — Fabrication — Fabricación (continued — suite — continuación)

Country or territory / Pays ou territoire / País o territorio	Year / Année / Año	Alprazolam	Bromazepam	Chlordiazepoxide	Clobazam	Clorazepate	Diazepam	Lorazepam	Medazepam	Meprobamate	Nordazepam	Oxazepam	Prazepam
		kg	kg	kg	kg	kg	kg	kg	kg	kg	kg	kg	kg
United States / États-Unis / Estados Unidos	2003	—	—	—	—	609	20	—	—	—	—	339	—
	2004	1 673	—	—	—	302	29 208	200	—	—	—	3 537	—
	2005	302	—	—	—	265	—	—	—	—	—	—	—
Total	2003	3 574	14 645	20 211	4 442	8 378	86 232	6 452	2 498	260 059	1 340	34 425	4 172
	2004	6 739	15 209	19 575	5 472	8 411	113 085	10 574	1 762	220 265	2 898	21 968	4 431
	2005	6 656	7 331	21 252	3 550	8 029	68 989	10 420	2 327	102 887	4 995	35 054	3 763

Exports — Exportations — Exportaciones

Country or territory / Pays ou territoire / País o territorio	Year / Année / Año	Alprazolam	Bromazepam	Chlordiazepoxide	Clobazam	Clorazepate	Diazepam	Lorazepam	Medazepam	Meprobamate	Nordazepam	Oxazepam	Prazepam
		kg	kg	kg	kg	kg	kg	kg	kg	kg	kg	kg	kg
Argentina / Argentine	2003	13	6	—	5	—	2	2				—	—
	2004	11	11	—	12	—	1	1				—	—
	2005	19	2	—	3	—	—	—				—	—
Australia / Australie	2003	15	—	—	10	—	2	—				43	—
	2004	20	—	—	7	—	2	5				—	—
	2005	20	—	—	7	—	2	5				42	—
Austria / Autriche	2003	—	93	—	37	—	8	2				8	—
	2004	—	77	—	16	—	7	2				38	—
	2005	—	91	—	5	—	3	4				8	—
Barbados / Barbade	2003	—	—	—	—	—	1	—				—	—
	2004	—	—	—	—	—	—	—				—	—
	2005	—	—	—	—	—	2	—				—	—
Belgium / Belgique / Bélgica	2003	856	24	20	15	17	446	15	—	1 026	13	210	7
	2004	958	16	18	1	7	233	12	—	606	25	214	6
	2005	987	13	20	4	11	368	11	—	94	29	70	6

Country	Year	Col1	Col2	Col3	Col4	Col5	Col6	Col7	Col8	Col9	Col10	Col11	Col12
Brazil / Brésil / Brasil	2003	—	691	—	—	—	140	16	—	—	—	—	—
	2004	—	552	—	—	—	245	177	—	—	—	—	—
	2005	17	542	—	—	—	140	135	—	—	—	—	—
Bulgaria / Bulgarie	2003	—	—	—	—	—	14	—	—	—	—	—	—
	2004	—	—	—	—	—	68	—	—	—	—	—	—
	2005	—	—	—	—	—	8	—	—	—	—	—	—
Canada / Canadá	2003	37	2	66	2	2	395	10	—	—	—	1	—
	2004	24	10	61	1	2	446	24	—	—	—	1	—
	2005	95	6	52	2	1	336	19	—	—	—	—	—
Chile / Chili	2003	—	2	4	—	—	25	1	—	—	—	—	—
	2004	3	9	4	—	—	63	3	—	—	—	—	—
	2005	2	—	5	—	—	16	—	—	—	—	—	—
China / Chine	2003	4	1	5 700	—	—	16 280	—	—	115 502	—	—	—
	2004	9	436	4 842	—	—	16 878	—	—	63 500	—	—	—
	2005	3	325	6 721	—	—	20 890	—	—	—	—	—	—
Hong Kong SAR of China / RAS de Hong Kong (Chine) / RAE de Hong Kong de China	2003	—	—	1	—	—	1	—	—	—	—	—	—
	2004	1	—	2	—	—	1	—	—	—	—	—	—
	2005	—	—	1	—	—	2	—	—	—	—	—	—
Colombia / Colombie	2003	1	3	—	—	—	7	—	—	—	—	—	—
	2004	1	—	—	—	—	—	—	—	—	—	—	—
	2005	—	—	—	—	—	—	—	—	—	—	—	—
Costa Rica	2003	16	22	—	—	—	7	—	—	—	—	—	—
	2004	5	13	—	—	—	9	—	—	—	—	—	—
	2005	5	20	—	—	—	8	—	—	—	—	—	—
Croatia / Croatie / Croacia	2003	—	—	—	—	—	—	8	—	28	—	47	—
	2004	?	?	?	?	?	?	?	?	?	?	?	?
	2005	—	—	—	—	—	—	7	—	8	—	28	—
Cuba	2003	—	—	—	—	—	13	—	—	—	—	—	—
	2004	—	—	—	—	—	6	—	—	—	—	—	—
	2005	—	—	—	—	—	—	—	—	—	—	—	—
Cyprus / Chypre / Chipre	2003	—	12	42	—	—	33	19	—	—	—	360	—
	2004	—	24	11	—	—	50	25	—	—	—	224	—
	2005	—	25	97	—	—	26	26	—	—	—	174	—
Czech Republic / République tchèque / República Checa	2003	10	—	28	—	—	2	—	—	—	—	69	—
	2004	10	—	9	—	—	—	—	—	—	—	18	—
	2005	27	—	24	—	—	2	—	—	—	—	84	—

Schedule IV. D.2. Anxiolytics (first part): main benzodiazepines and meprobamate (continued)
Tableau IV. D.2. Anxiolytiques (première partie): principales benzodiazépines et méprobamate (suite)
Lista IV. D.2. Ansiolíticos (primera parte): principales benzodiazepinas y meprobamato (continuación)

Exports — Exportations — Exportaciones (continued — suite — continuación)

Country or territory / Pays ou territoire / País o territorio	Year / Année / Año	Alprazolam (kg)	Bromazepam / Bromazépam (kg)	Chlordiazepoxide / Chlordiazépoxide / Clordiazepóxido (kg)	Clobazam (kg)	Clorazepate / Clorazépate / Clorazepato (kg)	Diazepam / Diazépam (kg)	Lorazepam / Lorazépam (kg)	Medazepam / Médazépam (kg)	Meprobamate / Méprobamate / Meprobamato (kg)	Nordazepam / Nordazépam (kg)	Oxazepam / Oxazépam (kg)	Prazepam / Prazépam (kg)
Denmark / Danemark / Dinamarca	2003	—	7	841	—	—	5 605	—	—	123 373	—	22	—
	2004	11	12	776	—	—	5 720	—	—	109 754	—	30	—
	2005	1	7	606	—	—	5 674	2	—	121 223	—	33	—
El Salvador	2003	—	6	6	2	—	37	26	—	—	—	—	—
	2004	—	7	17	1	—	21	6	—	—	—	—	—
	2005	—	—	—	—	—	—	—	—	—	—	—	—
Finland / Finlande / Finlandia	2003	220	—	—	—	—	4	—	—	—	—	—	—
	2004	559	—	—	—	—	3	—	—	—	—	—	—
	2005	930	—	—	—	—	6	—	—	—	—	—	—
France / Francia	2003	946	281	14	1 657	5 384	300	82	—	5 424	78	7 611	715
	2004	981	290	6	2 183	4 491	240	81	—	4 249	127	6 666	133
	2005	925	361	7	2 150	4 191	237	67	—	5 107	107	9 382	192
Georgia / Géorgie	2003	—	—	—	—	—	—	—	—	—	—	—	—
	2004	—	—	1	—	—	—	—	—	—	—	1	—
	2005	—	—	—	—	—	1	—	—	—	—	1	—
Germany / Allemagne / Alemania	2003	56	370	49	1 780	656	1 394	2 531	569	3 000	—	1 178	2 949
	2004	53	398	46	2 096	665	1 226	2 755	526	446	—	1 297	2 730
	2005	53	340	64	2 082	678	2 346	3 398	764	418	—	1 230	591
Greece / Grèce / Grecia	2003	1	2	—	32	3	31	14	—	—	—	—	—
	2004	3	1	—	29	3	7	14	—	—	—	—	—
	2005	3	3	—	29	3	33	10	—	—	—	—	—
Hungary / Hongrie / Hungría	2003	37	—	—	—	—	392	7	—	—	—	316	—
	2004	38	—	—	—	—	505	13	—	—	—	625	—
	2005	33	—	—	—	48	626	15	—	72	—	798	—

		C1	C2	C3	C4	C5	C6	C7	C8	C9	C10	C11	C12
India	2003	—	2 128	—	—	—	566	682	—	500	2 386	246	639
Inde	2004	—	2 067	174	—	—	855	1 124	39	592	2 763	298	1 047
	2005	—	2 051	50	—	—	859	2 491	45	627	701	654	1 008
Indonesia	2003	—	—	—	—	—	—	87	—	—	—	—	—
Indonésie	2004	—	—	—	—	—	—	—	—	—	—	—	—
	2005	—	—	—	—	—	—	—	—	—	—	—	—
Ireland	2003	9 197	—	—	—	—	2 226	219	—	—	10	—	83
Irlande	2004	8 878	—	—	—	—	2 288	390	—	—	—	—	64
Irlanda	2005	9 709	—	—	—	—	2 645	1 111	—	—	—	—	95
Israel	2003	—	—	—	—	—	9	—	110	104	—	—	—
Israël	2004	—	—	—	—	—	—	—	148	73	—	—	10
	2005	—	—	1	—	—	1	—	421	69	—	—	10
Italy	2003	225	17 050	69	—	1 549	3 694	16 202	1 366	395	7 920	6 133	2 022
Italie	2004	225	13 413	5	—	2 173	3 712	20 042	1 293	251	4 219	4 969	1 523
Italia	2005	129	14 300	—	—	2 107	3 643	16 207	1 305	337	5 406	5 205	1 494
Jordan	2003	—	—	—	—	—	—	—	—	—	58	1	1
Jordanie	2004	—	—	—	—	—	—	2	—	—	33	4	1
Jordania	2005	—	—	—	—	—	—	12	—	—	61	5	2
Latvia	2003	—	79	—	—	—	—	52	14	—	3	22	—
Lettonie	2004	—	85	—	—	1	—	67	—	—	—	24	—
Letonia	2005	—	70	—	—	—	—	52	—	—	—	15	1
Lithuania	2003	—	25	—	—	—	—	41	—	—	21	—	—
Lituanie	2004	—	19	—	—	—	—	26	—	—	11	—	—
Lituania	2005	—	4	—	—	—	—	26	—	—	4	1	—
Malaysia	2003	—	—	—	—	—	—	—	—	—	—	—	—
Malaisie	2004	—	—	—	—	—	—	1	—	—	6	—	—
Malasia	2005	—	—	—	—	—	—	—	—	—	—	—	—
Malta	2003	—	—	—	—	—	—	61	—	—	—	—	—
Malte	2004	—	—	—	—	—	—	25	—	—	—	—	—
	2005	—	—	—	—	—	—	—	—	—	—	—	—
Morocco	2003	—	—	—	—	—	—	—	—	—	11	—	—
Maroc	2004	107	—	—	—	—	—	—	—	—	12	—	—
Marruecos	2005	128	—	—	—	—	—	—	—	—	20	—	—
Netherlands	2003	1	407	—	4 313	—	41	274	2	7	258	9	22
Pays-Bas	2004	6	422	174	779	—	28	93	7	2	102	5	23
Países Bajos	2005	5	524	—	1 297	—	50	67	5	7	44	2	36

Schedule IV. D.2. Anxiolytics (first part): main benzodiazepines and meprobamate *(continued)*

Tableau IV. D.2. Anxiolytiques (première partie): principales benzodiazépines et méprobamate *(suite)*

Lista IV. D.2. Ansiolíticos (primera parte): principales benzodiazepinas y meprobamato *(continuación)*

Exports — Exportations — Exportaciones *(continued — suite — continuación)*

Country or territory / Pays ou territoire / País o territorio	Year / Année / Año	Alprazolam (kg)	Bromazepam / Bromazépam / Bromazépam (kg)	Chlordiazepoxide / Chlordiazépoxide / Clordiazepóxido (kg)	Clobazam (kg)	Clorazepate / Clorazépate / Clorazepato (kg)	Diazepam / Diazépam / Diazépam (kg)	Lorazepam / Lorazépam / Lorazépam (kg)	Medazepam / Médazépam / Médazépam (kg)	Meprobamate / Méprobamate / Meprobamato (kg)	Nordazepam / Nordazépam / Nordazépam (kg)	Oxazepam / Oxazépam / Oxazépam (kg)	Prazepam / Prazépam / Prazépam (kg)
Norway / Norvège / Noruega	2003	—	—	97	—	—	359	—	—	3	—	236	—
	2004	—	—	100	—	—	324	—	—	—	—	251	—
	2005	—	—	104	—	—	318	—	—	—	—	216	—
Panama / Panamá	2003	5	3	16	—	15	4	7	—	—	—	—	—
	2004	1	2	18	—	18	1	7	—	—	—	—	—
	2005	1	3	6	—	9	2	5	—	—	—	—	—
Poland / Pologne / Polonia	2003	—	—	411	—	—	713	35	—	—	—	185	—
	2004	—	—	264	—	—	638	44	9	—	—	225	—
	2005	—	—	195	—	—	519	43	9	—	—	145	—
Portugal	2003	3	—	2	—	9	34	1	—	2	9	—	—
	2004	—	2	2	—	—	27	1	—	2	4	—	—
	2005	1	1	2	—	—	2	1	—	—	—	—	—
Romania / Roumanie / Rumania	2003	—	—	—	—	—	—	—	—	16	—	—	—
	2004	—	—	—	—	—	—	—	—	—	—	—	—
	2005	—	—	—	—	—	—	—	—	—	—	—	—
Russian Federation / Fédération de Russie / Federación de Rusia	2003	—	—	—	—	—	2	—	27	—	—	7	—
	2004	—	—	—	—	—	11	—	11	—	—	29	—
	2005	—	—	—	—	—	—	—	—	—	—	—	—
Serbia and Montenegro / Serbie-et-Monténégro / Serbia y Montenegro	2003	—	274	—	—	—	271	—	—	—	—	—	40
	2004	?	?	?	?	?	?	?	?	?	?	?	?
	2005	?	?	?	?	?	?	?	?	?	?	?	?
Singapore / Singapour / Singapur	2003	—	—	131	—	—	25	—	—	200	—	—	—
	2004	—	1	137	—	—	75	1	—	—	—	—	—
	2005	—	—	89	—	—	—	—	—	—	—	—	—

Country	Year	1	2	3	4	5	6	7	8	9	10	11	12
Slovakia / Slovaquie / Eslovaquia	2003	—	—	1	—	—	211	—	—	—	—	—	—
	2004	?	?	?	?	?	?	?	?	?	?	?	?
	2005	2	—	—	—	—	175	—	—	—	—	—	—
Slovenia / Slovénie / Eslovenia	2003	14	284	—	—	—	181	31	111	—	—	—	—
	2004	14	326	—	—	—	182	32	107	—	—	—	—
	2005	24	295	—	—	—	177	27	103	—	—	—	—
South Africa / Afrique du Sud / Sudáfrica	2003	—	1	1	1	—	6	2	—	369	—	5	—
	2004	—	1	1	—	—	3	2	—	691	—	1	—
	2005	—	1	1	—	—	29	1	—	548	—	1	—
Spain / Espagne / España	2003	—	85	641	3	2 291	193	52	—	441	—	603	—
	2004	—	113	507	—	1 855	515	36	—	—	—	1 038	—
	2005	61	120	723	1	1 533	22	55	—	408	—	619	—
Sweden / Suède / Suecia	2003	—	—	—	—	—	—	—	—	10	—	7	—
	2004	—	—	—	—	—	—	—	—	120	—	39	—
	2005	—	—	—	—	—	—	1	—	88	—	44	—
Switzerland / Suisse / Suiza	2003	201	8 009	3 213	111	453	7 574	242	71	4 623	—	61	4 460
	2004	295	7 249	2 613	171	237	9 846	222	210	5 900	—	82	3 367
	2005	302	6 781	2 310	102	310	7 004	129	125	10 000	—	48	3 588
Thailand / Thaïlande / Tailandia	2003	—	—	6	—	10	10	35	—	—	—	—	—
	2004	—	—	6	—	9	8	18	—	—	—	—	—
	2005	—	—	19	—	13	8	21	—	—	—	—	—
The former Yugoslav Rep. of Macedonia / L'ex-Rép. yougoslave de Macédoine / La ex Rep. Yugoslava de Macedonia	2003	—	142	—	—	—	19	6	2	—	—	—	—
	2004	—	183	—	—	—	22	10	6	—	—	—	—
	2005	—	167	—	—	—	72	8	—	—	—	—	—
Tunisia / Tunisie / Túnez	2003	—	—	—	24	—	—	—	—	—	—	—	—
	2004	—	—	—	15	—	—	—	—	—	—	—	—
	2005	—	—	—	10	—	—	—	—	—	—	—	—
Ukraine / Ucrania	2003	—	—	—	—	—	20	—	—	—	—	—	—
	2004	—	—	—	—	—	16	—	—	—	—	—	—
	2005	—	—	—	—	—	23	—	—	—	—	—	—
United Kingdom / Royaume-Uni / Reino Unido	2003	1	20	322	—	9	437	564	—	—	—	927	—
	2004	2	—	186	—	13	1 182	404	—	401	—	733	—
	2005	49	25	36	1	8	1 296	562	—	—	—	140	—

Schedule IV. D.2. Anxiolytics (first part): main benzodiazepines and meprobamate *(continued)*

Tableau IV. D.2. Anxiolytiques (première partie): principales benzodiazépines et méprobamate *(suite)*

Lista IV. D.2. Ansiolíticos (primera parte): principales benzodiazepinas y meprobamato *(continuación)*

Exports — Exportations — Exportaciones *(continued — suite — continuación)*

Country or territory / Pays ou territoire / País o territorio	Year / Année / Año	Alprazolam	Bromazepam / Bromazé-pam	Chlordiaz-epoxide / Chlordia-zépoxide / Clordia-zepóxido	Clobazam	Clorazepate / Clorazé-pate / Cloraze-pato	Diazepam / Diazépam	Lorazepam / Lorazépam	Medazepam / Médazépam	Mepro-bamate / Mépro-bamate / Mepro-bamato	Nordaze-pam / Nordazé-pam	Oxazepam / Oxazépam	Prazepam / Prazépam
		kg	kg	kg	kg	kg	kg	kg	kg	kg	kg	kg	kg
United States / États-Unis / Estados Unidos	2003	391	—	5	—	36	102	7	—	1251	—	—	—
	2004	630	—	—	—	73	541	—	—	1	—	251	—
	2005	568	—	11	—	73	1	—	—	151	—	1	—
Viet Nam	2003	—	—	—	—	—	4	—	—	—	—	—	—
	2004	—	—	—	—	—	11	—	—	—	—	—	—
	2005	—	—	—	—	—	10	—	—	—	—	—	—
Zambia / Zambie	2003	—	—	—	—	—	1	—	—	—	—	—	—
	2004	—	—	—	—	—	—	—	—	—	—	—	—
	2005	—	—	—	—	—	—	—	—	—	—	—	—
Total	2003	5 594	16 751	22 284	4 685	10 377	52 910	10 251	2 330	259 581	169	40 782	8 397
	2004	6 297	15 032	16 773	5 450	8 860	60 910	10 778	3 042	186 449	509	36 647	6 574
	2005	6 774	15 011	17 329	5 436	8 654	60 354	11 749	3 099	139 414	187	39 722	6 768

Imports — Importations — Importaciones

Country or territory / Pays ou territoire / País o territorio	Year / Année / Año	Alprazolam	Bromazepam / Bromazé-pam	Chlordiaz-epoxide / Chlordia-zépoxide / Clordia-zepóxido	Clobazam	Clorazepate / Clorazé-pate / Cloraze-pato	Diazepam / Diazépam	Lorazepam / Lorazépam	Medazepam / Médazépam	Mepro-bamate / Mépro-bamate / Mepro-bamato	Nordaze-pam / Nordazé-pam	Oxazepam / Oxazépam	Prazepam / Prazépam
		kg	kg	kg	kg	kg	kg	kg	kg	kg	kg	kg	kg
Afghanistan / Afganistán	2003	?	?	?	?	?	?	?	?	?	?	?	?
	2004	—	—	—	—	—	4	—	—	—	—	—	—
	2005	?	?	?	?	?	?	?	?	?	?	?	?
Albania / Albanie	2003	—	3	100	—	—	100	4	—	400	—	—	—
	2004	—	6	50	—	4	64	10	—	400	—	—	—
	2005	—	3	75	—	3	56	10	—	400	—	—	—
Algeria / Algérie / Argelia	2003	—	133	—	—	195	536	65	—	4 268	—	—	335
	2004	—	29	—	—	136	13	76	—	1 512	—	—	—
	2005	—	253	—	—	221	17	101	—	3 162	—	—	250

Country	Year	1	2	3	4	5	6	7	8	9	10	11	12
Andorra / Andorre	2003	—	—	—	—	1	1	—	—	4	—	—	—
	2004	—	1	1	—	1	1	1	—	5	—	—	—
	2005	—	—	1	—	1	1	1	—	1	—	—	—
Angola	2003	9	1	1	—	—	7	—	—	—	—	—	—
	2004	1	—	—	—	—	9	—	—	1	—	—	—
	2005	…	…	…	…	…	…	…	…	…	…	…	…
Argentina / Argentine	2003	330	655	—	10	—	1 174	441	—	—	—	15	—
	2004	440	417	50	75	67	388	280	—	—	—	20	—
	2005	380	421	10	45	35	344	397	—	—	—	20	—
Australia / Australie	2003	126	13	—	38	—	597	13	—	—	—	1 830	—
	2004	28	9	—	21	—	522	20	—	—	—	1 460	—
	2005	27	13	—	19	—	678	20	—	—	—	1 340	—
Austria / Autriche	2003	11	168	16	49	10	92	25	—	2 200	—	580	22
	2004	9	176	15	24	14	161	29	—	1 996	—	453	11
	2005	12	163	5	19	12	172	31	—	1 218	—	610	16
Azerbaijan / Azerbaïdjan / Azerbaiyán	2003	—	—	—	—	—	2	—	—	—	—	—	—
	2004	—	—	3	—	—	15	—	—	—	—	4	—
	2005	—	—	3	—	—	3	—	—	—	—	5	—
Bahrain / Bahreïn / Bahrein	2003	—	—	5	—	—	—	—	—	—	—	—	—
	2004	—	—	2	—	—	3	—	—	—	—	—	—
	2005	—	—	7	—	—	2	—	—	—	—	—	—
Bangladesh	2003	—	—	—	770	—	560	—	—	—	—	—	—
	2004	—	220	—	—	—	—	—	—	—	—	—	—
	2005	25	295	—	325	—	745	—	—	—	—	—	—
Barbados / Barbade	2003	1	—	—	1	—	6	1	—	—	—	—	—
	2004	1	—	1	1	—	3	1	—	—	—	—	—
	2005	1	—	—	2	—	3	1	—	—	—	—	—
Belarus / Bélarus / Belarús	2003	—	—	46	36	—	70	1	33	—	—	59	—
	2004	—	—	38	38	—	84	1	28	—	—	41	—
	2005	—	—	16	43	—	59	1	7	—	—	32	—
Belgium / Belgique / Bélgica	2003	962	511	21	36	214	641	317	—	711	60	356	235
	2004	951	448	19	38	250	448	241	—	1 225	—	390	167
	2005	967	520	22	43	223	644	339	—	1 597	50	458	242
Belize / Belice	2003	—	—	—	—	—	1	1	—	—	—	—	—
	2004	—	—	—	—	—	—	—	—	—	—	—	—
	2005	…	…	…	…	…	…	…	…	…	…	…	…
Benin / Bénin	2003	—	9	—	—	6	268	—	—	23	—	3	—
	2004	—	4	—	—	2	124	—	—	5	—	1	1
	2005	—	5	—	—	5	217	—	—	11	—	2	2

Schedule IV. D.2. Anxiolytics (first part): main benzodiazepines and meprobamate (continued)
Tableau IV. D.2. Anxiolytiques (première partie): principales benzodiazépines et méprobamate (suite)
Lista IV. D.2. Ansiolíticos (primera parte): principales benzodiazepinas y meprobamato (continuación)

Imports — Importations — Importaciones (continued — suite —continuación)

Country or territory / Pays ou territoire / País o territorio	Year / Année / Año	Alprazolam	Bromazepam / Bromazépam	Chlordiazepoxide / Chlordiazépoxide / Clordiazepóxido	Clobazam	Clorazepate / Clorazépate / Clorazepato	Diazepam / Diazépam	Lorazepam / Lorazépam	Medazepam / Médazépam	Meprobamate / Méprobamate / Meprobamato	Nordazepam / Nordazépam	Oxazepam / Oxazépam	Prazepam / Prazépam
		kg	kg	kg	kg	kg	kg	kg	kg	kg	kg	kg	kg
Bolivia / Bolivie	2003	1	1	—	—	—	2	2	—	—	—	—	—
	2004	2	—	—	—	—	30	2	—	—	—	—	—
	2005	3	1	—	—	—	13	2	—	—	—	—	—
Bosnia and Herzegovina / Bosnie-Herzégovine / Bosnia y Herzegovina	2003	—	55	—	—	—	55	3	7	9	—	17	—
	2004	2	78	—	—	—	157	4	6	4	—	11	—
	2005	?	?	?	?	?	?	?	?	?	?	?	?
Botswana	2003	?	?	?	?	?	?	?	?	?	?	?	?
	2004	?	?	?	?	?	?	?	?	?	?	?	?
	2005	—	—	1	—	—	17	—	—	—	—	—	—
Brazil / Brésil / Brasil	2003	79	1 083	822	380	21	1 302	358	4	—	—	—	—
	2004	135	1 070	906	521	22	1 890	536	2	—	—	—	—
	2005	62	1 202	836	395	26	648	248	2	—	—	12	—
Brunei Darussalam / Brunéi Darussalam	2003	—	—	1	—	—	—	—	—	—	—	—	—
	2004	—	—	1	—	—	—	—	—	—	—	—	—
	2005	—	—	1	—	—	—	—	—	—	—	—	—
Bulgaria / Bulgarie	2003	3	105	3	—	—	62	—	50	—	—	2	—
	2004	3	103	2	—	23	161	—	8	—	—	1	—
	2005	3	—	4	—	16	115	—	3	—	—	2	—
Burkina Faso	2003	—	2	7	—	7	10	—	—	21	—	—	4
	2004	—	—	—	—	—	—	—	—	—	—	—	—
	2005	—	3	—	1	6	9	—	—	2	—	—	1
Burundi	2003	?	?	?	?	?	?	?	?	?	?	?	?
	2004	—	—	—	—	—	—	—	—	—	—	—	—
	2005	—	—	—	—	—	6	—	—	—	—	—	—

Country	Year	1	2	3	4	5	6	7	8	9	10	11	12
Cambodia / Cambodge / Camboya	2003	4	—	10	172	—	1	80	5	—	6	15	—
	2004	1	—	2	65	—	—	77	6	—	—	19	—
	2005	—	—	1	48	—	—	29	—	—	—	24	—
Cameroon / Cameroun / Camerún	2003	—	—	—	—	—	1	69	4	—	—	3	—
	2004	—	—	—	33	—	—	12	137	2	—	1	2
	2005	?	?	?	?	?	?	?	?	?	?	?	?
Canada / Canadá	2003	—	2 075	—	2	—	169	678	8	196	10	119	60
	2004	—	2 010	—	800	—	481	139	77	106	31	47	184
	2005	—	2 100	—	200	—	286	1 445	46	197	22	112	62
Cape Verde / Cap-Vert / Cabo Verde	2003	—	—	—	—	—	—	5	—	—	1	2	—
	2004	—	—	—	—	—	—	25	—	—	2	1	—
	2005	—	—	—	—	—	—	—	—	—	2	—	—
Chad / Tchad	2003	—	—	—	—	—	—	—	—	—	—	—	—
	2004	—	—	—	5	—	1	10	2	108	132	312	1
	2005	?	?	?	?	?	?	?	?	?	?	?	?
Chile / Chili	2003	—	6	—	25	—	36	303	8	6	284	41	46
	2004	—	5	—	25	—	29	451	6	—	309	20	46
	2005	—	5	—	25	—	19	342	4	17	375	58	112
China / Chine	2003	—	—	—	—	—	48	1 914	—	—	—	—	—
	2004	—	—	—	—	—	9	—	—	—	—	97	—
	2005	—	—	—	—	—	20	—	—	—	—	—	—
Hong Kong SAR of China / RAS de Hong Kong (Chine) / RAE de Hong Kong de China	2003	—	—	—	50	—	5	42	2	5	12	9	2
	2004	—	—	—	—	—	8	50	2	4	28	10	3
	2005	—	—	—	—	—	9	52	2	5	27	9	2
Macao SAR of China / RAS de Macao (Chine) / RAE de Macao de China	2003	—	—	—	—	—	1	2	—	—	—	—	—
	2004	—	—	—	—	—	—	1	—	—	—	—	1
	2005	—	—	—	—	—	—	2	—	—	—	—	—
Colombia / Colombie	2003	—	—	—	—	—	60	55	—	24	—	15	10
	2004	—	—	—	—	—	29	11	—	26	—	14	11
	2005	—	—	—	—	—	23	6	—	17	—	13	11
Costa Rica	2003	—	—	—	—	—	13	50	—	1	—	16	7
	2004	—	—	—	—	—	12	13	—	2	—	17	6
	2005	—	—	—	—	—	1	13	—	3	—	19	4
Côte d'Ivoire	2003	27	—	—	29	—	—	43	10	—	1	—	—
	2004	7	—	—	—	—	—	14	9	3	2	7	—
	2005	—	—	—	—	—	—	18	8	2	1	6	—

Schedule IV. D.2. Anxiolytics (first part): main benzodiazepines and meprobamate (continued)

Tableau IV. D.2. Anxiolytiques (première partie): principales benzodiazépines et méprobamate (suite)

Lista IV. D.2. Ansiolíticos (primera parte): principales benzodiazepinas y meprobamato (continuación)

Imports — Importations — Importaciones (continued — suite — continuación)

Country or territory / Pays ou territoire / País o territorio	Year / Année / Año	Alprazolam	Bromazepam / Bromazépam	Chlordiazepoxide / Chlordiazépoxide / Clordiazepóxido	Clobazam	Clorazepate / Clorazépate / Clorazepato	Diazepam / Diazépam	Lorazepam / Lorazépam	Medazepam / Médazépam	Meprobamate / Méprobamate / Meprobamato	Nordazepam / Nordazépam	Oxazepam / Oxazépam	Prazepam / Prazépam
		kg	kg	kg	kg	kg	kg	kg	kg	kg	kg	kg	kg
Croatia / Croatie / Croacia	2003	17	63	—	—	—	232	—	6	300	—	908	—
	2004	?	?	?	?	?	?	?	?	?	?	?	?
	2005	21	41	—	—	—	419	10	—	300	—	500	—
Cuba	2003	—	—	975	—	—	350	—	200	18 750	—	—	—
	2004	30	—	400	51	—	270	—	300	10 500	—	—	—
	2005	—	—	1 250	45	—	594	—	125	25 050	—	—	—
Cyprus / Chypre / Chipre	2003	1	21	148	1	1	36	27	—	—	—	307	—
	2004	5	18	102	2	10	71	56	—	—	—	348	—
	2005	7	26	131	1	10	40	30	—	—	—	60	—
Czech Republic / République tchèque / República Checa	2003	19	112	186	—	—	242	—	13	—	—	160	—
	2004	37	137	207	1	—	204	—	11	—	174	240	—
	2005	44	99	5	—	—	206	—	11	—	—	160	—
Dem. People's Rep. of Korea / Rép. populaire dém. de Corée / Rep. Popular Dem. de Corea	2003	?	?	?	?	?	?	?	?	?	?	?	?
	2004	?	?	?	?	?	?	?	?	?	?	?	?
	2005	—	—	—	—	—	500	—	—	—	—	—	—
Dem. Rep. of the Congo / Rép. dém. du Congo / Rep. Dem. del Congo	2003	—	1	3	—	8	758	—	—	1 192	—	—	—
	2004	19	2	1	—	2	1 044	—	—	1 217	—	2	12
	2005	—	2	2	—	—	663	—	—	683	—	—	—
Denmark / Danemark / Dinamarca	2003	22	69	1 071	15	—	6 218	7	—	9 346	—	456	—
	2004	10	41	951	15	—	4 692	10	—	5 004	—	488	—
	2005	12	44	546	10	—	6 708	40	—	543	—	436	—
Djibouti	2003	?	?	?	?	?	?	?	?	?	?	?	?
	2004	?	?	?	?	?	?	?	?	?	?	?	?
	2005	—	1	—	—	1	4	—	—	—	—	—	1

Country	Year	C1	C2	C3	C4	C5	C6	C7	C8	C9	C10	C11
Dominican Rep. / Rép. dominicaine / Rep. Dominicana	2003	—	2	—	—	2	77	—	1	—	2	2
	2004	—	4	—	—	4	58	—	1	—	1	7
	2005	—	—	2	—	9	59	—	1	—	—	11
Ecuador / Équateur	2003	—	—	—	—	4	72	1	4	—	6	2
	2004	—	—	—	—	2	78	1	9	4	6	2
	2005	—	—	—	—	2	76	1	21	5	7	3
Egypt / Égypte / Egipto	2003	—	3	5 600	—	—	300	—	—	368	120	9
	2004	—	—	6 000	—	—	—	—	—	379	90	16
	2005	—	15	—	—	—	325	—	—	982	170	10
El Salvador	2003	—	—	—	—	33	63	—	24	82	24	—
	2004	—	—	—	—	6	118	—	36	110	16	—
	2005	—	—	—	—	13	127	—	31	78	25	1
Eritrea / Érythrée	2003	—	—	—	—	—	5	—	—	—	—	—
	2004	—	—	—	—	—	1	—	—	—	—	—
	2005	—	—	—	—	—	—	—	—	—	—	—
Estonia / Estonie	2003	—	16	—	—	—	28	—	—	—	4	1
	2004	—	10	—	—	—	29	—	—	—	5	2
	2005	—	5	—	—	—	28	—	—	—	5	3
Ethiopia / Éthiopie / Etiopía	2003	—	—	—	—	—	9	—	—	3	1	—
	2004	—	—	—	—	—	15	—	—	3	—	—
	2005	—	—	—	—	—	1	—	—	1	1	—
Finland / Finlande / Finlandia	2003	2 916	942	952	—	17	213	—	6	147	—	17
	2004	2 262	618	908	—	15	208	—	6	145	—	10
	2005	2 419	705	828	—	14	223	—	6	135	—	15
France / Francia	2003	—	6 551	93 448	—	647	1 109	2 419	937	207	3 729	185
	2004	—	5 855	73 255	—	584	791	1 910	1 277	97	3 096	172
	2005	—	7 072	88 215	—	758	758	1 751	944	124	2 641	225
French Polynesia / Polynésie française / Polinesia Francesa	2003	2	—	20	—	—	—	2	—	—	2	—
	2004	2	—	16	?	—	—	—	—	?	2	—
	2005	?	?	?	?	?	?	?	?	?	?	?
Gabon / Gabón	2003	?	?	?	?	?	?	?	?	?	?	?
	2004	?	—	?	—	—	4	2	—	—	1	—
	2005	?	1	?	—	—	6	3	—	—	2	—
Georgia / Géorgie	2003	—	2	—	—	—	21	—	—	2	—	—
	2004	—	6	—	—	—	24	—	—	2	—	—
	2005	—	9	—	—	—	34	—	—	3	1	1

Schedule IV. D.2. Anxiolytics (first part): main benzodiazepines and meprobamate (continued)
Tableau IV. D.2. Anxiolytiques (première partie): principales benzodiazépines et méprobamate (suite)
Lista IV. D.2. Ansiolíticos (primera parte): principales benzodiazepinas y meprobamato (continuación)

Imports — Importations — Importaciones (continued — suite — continuación)

Country or territory / Pays ou territoire / País o territorio	Year / Année / Año	Alprazolam	Bromazepam / Bromazépam / Bromazépam	Chlordiazepoxide / Chlordiazépoxide / Clordiazepóxido	Clobazam	Clorazepate / Clorazépate / Clorazepato	Diazepam / Diazépam / Diazepam	Lorazepam / Lorazépam / Lorazépam	Medazepam / Médazépam / Medazépam	Meprobamate / Méprobamate / Meprobamato	Nordazepam / Nordazépam / Nordazépam	Oxazepam / Oxazépam / Oxazépam	Prazepam / Prazépam / Prazépam
		kg	kg	kg	kg	kg	kg	kg	kg	kg	kg	kg	kg
Germany .... Allemagne Alemania	2003	88	1 120	166	398	833	3 092	343	351	3 396	9	3 920	3 605
	2004	79	904	103	576	912	2 961	596	500	50	5	4 625	2 116
	2005	117	928	205	649	951	4 179	742	850	418	—	4 077	678
Ghana	2003	?	?	?	?	?	?	?	?	?	?	?	?
	2004	—	1	—	—	—	976	1	—	—	—	—	—
	2005	—	—	525	—	—	1 454	—	—	—	—	—	—
Greece .... Grèce Grecia	2003	31	234	41	111	41	111	116	—	—	—	—	80
	2004	39	265	34	39	50	125	103	—	—	—	—	109
	2005	31	250	25	81	73	200	98	—	—	—	—	84
Guatemala	2003	1	2	25	20	—	25	2	—	1 186	—	—	—
	2004	?	?	?	?	?	?	?	?	?	?	?	?
	2005	?	?	?	?	?	?	?	?	?	?	?	?
Guinea .... Guinée	2003	?	?	?	?	?	?	?	?	?	?	?	?
	2004	?	?	?	?	?	?	?	?	?	?	?	?
	2005	4	8	7	5	10	48	10	—	—	—	—	2
Guyana	2003	—	—	8	—	—	16	—	—	—	—	—	—
	2004	?	?	?	?	?	?	?	?	?	?	?	?
	2005	—	—	2	?	—	6	5	—	?	?	?	—
Haiti .... Haïti Haití	2003	—	1	—	—	1	49	3	—	—	—	—	—
	2004	—	1	—	—	—	36	2	—	—	—	—	—
	2005	—	1	—	—	—	15	2	—	—	—	—	—
Honduras	2003	2	7	6	2	—	13	2	—	—	—	—	—
	2004	4	2	12	2	—	3	2	—	—	—	—	—
	2005	?	?	?	?	?	?	?	?	?	?	?	?

Country	Year	1	2	3	4	5	6	7	8	9	10	11	12
Hungary / Hongrie / Hungría	2003	159	—	160	37	—	722	16	551	29 300	—	700	—
	2004	173	—	145	22	—	677	10	731	22 000	—	500	—
	2005	163	20	114	57	66	930	24	308	15 000	—	800	—
Iceland / Islande / Islandia	2003	3	2	11	—	—	16	1	—	10	—	24	—
	2004	1	2	6	—	—	11	—	—	13	—	33	—
	2005	1	2	1	—	—	1	—	—	9	—	34	—
India / Inde	2003	—	—	—	355	—	—	—	—	—	—	—	—
	2004	—	—	—	365	—	350	4	—	—	—	—	—
	2005	61	—	1	585	—	70	—	—	—	—	—	—
Indonesia / Indonésie	2003	15	4	260	120	—	464	15	—	200	—	—	—
	2004	16	8	175	175	—	614	2	—	100	—	—	—
	2005	20	4	143	91	—	380	11	—	—	—	—	—
Iran (Islamic Rep. of) / Iran (Rép. islamique d') / Irán (Rep. Islámica del)	2003	20	—	2 520	210	—	790	300	—	—	—	100	—
	2004	55	—	750	30	—	1 350	270	—	—	—	935	—
	2005	106	—	800	—	—	1 338	290	—	—	—	700	—
Iraq	2003	—	...	22	...	...	49	—	...	...	...	—	—
	2004	...	...	...	...	...	...	...	...	...	...	...	...
	2005	...	...	...	...	...	...	...	...	...	...	...	...
Ireland / Irlande / Irlanda	2003	119	22	3	18	10	465	2 397	—	—	—	10 601	18
	2004	76	20	22	11	16	1 170	2 379	—	—	—	8 551	29
	2005	103	20	84	—	10	1 451	2 726	—	—	—	11 525	14
Israel / Israël	2003	8	3	—	4	2	114	15	—	—	2	240	—
	2004	4	6	30	64	3	103	30	—	—	—	210	—
	2005	5	6	40	4	9	112	36	—	50	—	300	—
Italy / Italie / Italia	2003	115	880	139	68	31	1 162	454	220	250	—	367	424
	2004	132	1 081	118	99	17	1 089	429	10	—	—	737	388
	2005	167	900	27	74	20	506	361	—	150	—	480	388
Jamaica / Jamaïque	2003	2	1	—	6	1	7	1	—	—	—	—	—
	2004	1	1	—	1	—	8	1	—	—	—	—	—
	2005	1	1	—	4	—	10	—	—	—	—	—	—
Japan / Japon / Japón	2003	118	786	510	100	73	1 944	147	140	—	—	—	—
	2004	218	686	400	50	73	1 460	128	140	—	—	—	—
	2005	159	82	150	200	73	1 621	212	130	—	—	—	10
Jordan / Jordanie / Jordania	2003	5	47	255	—	1	37	3	—	—	—	—	—
	2004	35	31	7	—	2	21	1	—	—	—	—	—
	2005	10	30	103	—	—	46	2	—	—	—	—	—
Kazakhstan / Kazajstán	2003	—	—	18	—	—	22	—	—	—	—	20	—
	2004	—	—	—	—	—	5	—	—	—	—	—	—
	2005	—	—	—	—	—	—	—	—	—	—	—	—

Schedule IV. D.2. Anxiolytics (first part): main benzodiazepines and meprobamate (continued)

Tableau IV. D.2. Anxiolytiques (première partie): principales benzodiazépines et méprobamate (suite)

Lista IV. D.2. Ansiolíticos (primera parte): principales benzodiazepinas y meprobamato (continuación)

Imports — Importations (continued — suite — continuación)

Country or territory / Pays ou territoire / País o territorio	Year / Année / Año	Alprazolam	Bromazepam / Bromazépam / Bromazépam	Chlordiazepoxide / Chlordiazépoxide / Clordiazepóxido	Clobazam	Clorazepate / Clorazépate / Clorazepato	Diazepam / Diazépam / Diazepam	Lorazepam / Lorazépam / Lorazepam	Medazepam / Médazépam / Medazépam	Meprobamate / Méprobamate / Meprobamato	Nordazepam / Nordazépam / Nordazépam	Oxazepam / Oxazépam / Oxazépam	Prazepam / Prazépam / Prazépam
		kg	kg	kg	kg	kg	kg	kg	kg	kg	kg	kg	kg
Kenya	2003	1	3	5	—	—	107	—	—	—	—	—	—
	2004	1	2	—	—	—	58	1	—	—	—	—	—
	2005	?	?	?	?	?	?	?	?	?	?	?	?
Kuwait / Koweït	2003	—	1	26	—	—	4	—	—	—	—	—	—
	2004	—	1	26	1	—	3	1	—	—	—	—	—
	2005	—	1	12	—	—	3	—	—	—	—	—	—
Kyrgyzstan / Kirghizistan / Kirguistán	2003	—	—	—	—	—	11	6	—	—	—	—	—
	2004	—	—	—	—	—	8	—	1	—	—	1	—
	2005	—	—	1	—	—	8	—	—	—	—	—	—
Lao People's Dem. Rep. / Rép. dém. populaire lao / Rep. Dem. Popular Lao	2003	—	16	—	—	—	26	—	—	—	—	—	—
	2004	—	5	—	—	—	1	—	—	—	—	—	—
	2005	—	5	1	—	—	—	—	—	—	—	—	—
Latvia / Lettonie / Letonia	2003	3	29	14	—	15	90	1	3	—	—	165	—
	2004	2	40	9	—	—	115	1	1	—	—	140	—
	2005	5	36	9	—	—	80	1	1	—	—	132	—
Lebanon / Liban / Líbano	2003	3	22	10	—	13	4	1	—	800	—	—	—
	2004	5	31	33	—	9	5	4	—	800	—	—	—
	2005	3	27	20	—	10	4	5	—	800	—	—	—
Lesotho	2003	?	?	?	?	?	?	?	?	?	?	?	?
	2004	?	?	?	?	?	?	?	?	?	?	?	?
	2005	—	—	—	—	—	6	—	—	—	—	—	—
Libyan Arab Jamahiriya / Jamahiriya arabe libyenne / Jamahiriya Árabe Libia	2003	—	—	23	—	—	6	—	—	—	—	—	—
	2004	—	—	—	—	—	4	—	—	—	—	—	—
	2005	—	—	14	—	—	3	—	—	—	—	—	—

Country	Year												
Lithuania / Lituanie / Lituania	2003	—	66	—	—	36	39	144	14	—	32	26	3
	2004	—	73	—	—	25	48	112	16	—	28	34	10
	2005	—	29	—	—	33	50	97	16	—	9	41	4
Luxembourg / Luxembourg / Luxemburgo	2003	—	—	—	—	—	—	—	—	—	—	—	—
	2004	...	...	...	...	...	...	...	...	...	...	...	...
	2005	7	5	6			9	4	9	2		14	2
Madagascar	2003	3	—	—	25	—	—	19	5	—	—	2	—
	2004												
	2005												
Malaysia / Malaisie / Malasia	2003	—	—	—	—	—	5	31	7	23	15	17	10
	2004	—	—	—	—	—	11	108	10	8	11	6	5
	2005	—	—	—	—	—	6	64	13	5	29	4	9
Maldives / Maldives / Maldivas	2003	—	—	—	—	—	—	—	—	—	—	—	—
	2004	—	—	—	—	—	—	1	—	—	—	—	—
	2005	—	—	—	—	—	—	—	—	—	—	—	—
Mali / Mali	2003	—	—	—	23	—	—	6	4	2	—	3	—
	2004	1	—	—	24	—	—	6	6	1	1	2	—
	2005	18	—	—	—	—	—	4	7	1	—	1	—
Malta / Malte	2003	—	—	—	—	—	5	7	—	—	7	9	—
	2004	—	—	—	—	—	5	2	—	—	2	11	—
	2005	—	—	—	—	—	4	5	—	—	3	8	—
Mauritania / Mauritanie	2003	—	—	—	4	—	—	5	2	—	—	1	—
	2004	...	...	...	...	...	...	...	...	...	...	...	...
	2005	...	...	...	...	...	...	...	...	...	...	...	...
Mauritius / Maurice / Mauricio	2003	—	—	—	—	—	—	14	—	—	—	2	—
	2004	—	—	—	—	—	—	9	2	—	—	2	1
	2005	1	—	—	—	—	—	9	1	—	—	2	1
Mexico / Mexique / México	2003	—	—	—	—	—	174	739	—	40	—	210	70
	2004	...	...	...	...	...	60	1 452	20	51	...	140	78
	2005	...	...	...	...	...	...	...	...	...	...	...	...
Mongolia / Mongolie	2003	—	—	—	—	—	—	2	—	—	—	—	—
	2004	...	...	...	...	...	...	2	...	...	...	...	...
	2005	...	...	...	...	...	...	...	...	...	...	...	...
Morocco / Maroc / Marruecos	2003	15	—	70	425	—	16	37	23	18	90	102	6
	2004	312	—	120	100	—	16	65	25	18	75	88	4
	2005	288	—	100	807	—	26	11	32	18	100	91	8
Mozambique	2003	—	—	—	—	—	—	—	—	—	1	—	—
	2004	...	...	...	...	...	...	10	...	...	2	...	...
	2005	...	...	...	...	...	...	...	...	...	...	...	...

Schedule IV. D.2. Anxiolytics (first part): main benzodiazepines and meprobamate (continued)

Tableau IV. D.2. Anxiolytiques (première partie): principales benzodiazépines et méprobamate (suite)

Lista IV. D.2. Ansiolíticos (primera parte): principales benzodiazepinas y meprobamato (continuación)

Imports — Importations — Importaciones (continued — suite — continuación)

Country or territory / Pays ou territoire / País o territorio	Year / Année / Año	Alprazolam kg	Bromazepam / Bromazépam kg	Chlordiazepoxide / Chlordiazépoxide / Clordiazepóxido kg	Clobazam kg	Clorazepate / Clorazépate / Clorazepato kg	Diazepam / Diazépam kg	Lorazepam / Lorazépam kg	Medazepam / Médazépam kg	Meprobamate / Méprobamate / Meprobamato kg	Nordazepam / Nordazépam kg	Oxazepam / Oxazépam kg	Prazepam / Prazépam kg
Namibia / Namibie	2003	—	1	—	—	—	4	—	—	184	—	1	—
	2004	—	1	1	—	—	1	—	—	341	—	1	—
	2005	—	1	1	—	—	2	—	—	354	—	4	—
Nepal / Népal	2003	14	—	69	—	—	32	35	—	—	—	—	—
	2004	—	—	—	—	—	—	—	—	—	—	—	—
	2005	?	?	?	?	?	?	?	?	?	?	?	?
Netherlands / Pays-Bas / Países Bajos	2003	42	54	343	35	105	411	90	—	500	—	1 662	15
	2004	38	55	149	43	137	278	63	—	1 125	174	2 132	29
	2005	45	36	146	59	61	256	79	—	872	—	2 173	17
Netherlands Antilles / Antilles néerlandaises / Antillas Neerlandesas	2003	—	1	—	—	—	2	1	—	—	—	—	—
	2004	—	2	—	—	—	1	1	—	—	—	—	—
	2005	—	2	—	—	—	2	—	—	—	—	—	—
New Caledonia / Nouvelle-Calédonie / Nueva Caledonia	2003	—	2	—	—	2	1	—	—	70	—	3	3
	2004	?	?	?	?	?	?	?	?	?	?	?	?
	2005	—	3	—	1	2	—	5	—	58	—	6	3
New Zealand / Nouvelle-Zélande / Nueva Zelandia	2003	—	—	—	10	—	36	4	—	—	—	21	—
	2004	1	—	—	7	—	32	9	—	—	—	25	—
	2005	—	—	—	7	—	31	5	—	—	—	25	—
Nicaragua	2003	2	10	15	1	—	6	2	—	—	—	—	—
	2004	2	12	38	1	—	14	15	—	—	—	—	—
	2005	3	11	54	1	—	43	9	—	—	—	—	—
Niger	2003	?	?	?	?	?	?	?	?	?	?	?	?
	2004	?	?	?	?	?	?	?	?	?	?	?	?
	2005	—	—	—	—	2	12	—	—	—	—	—	—

Country / Year	C1	C2	C3	C4	C5	C6	C7	C8	C9	C10	C11	C12
Nigeria / Nigéria 2003	—	61	—	—	—	531	—	—	—	—	—	—
2004	—	61	—	—	—	441	—	—	—	—	—	—
2005	—	62	—	—	—	1 038	—	—	—	—	—	—
Norway / Norvège / Noruega 2003	4	—	60	3	—	470	—	—	105	—	878	—
2004	4	—	149	4	—	362	—	—	108	—	398	—
2005	6	—	100	5	—	607	—	—	81	—	1 086	—
Oman / Omán 2003	—	1	—	—	—	1	—	—	—	—	—	—
2004	—	—	—	—	—	—	—	—	—	—	—	—
2005	—	—	—	—	—	1	—	—	—	—	—	—
Pakistan / Pakistán 2003	42	644	1 240	200	—	2 924	171	—	2 400	—	15	—
2004	64	731	1 045	236	—	2 287	166	12	—	—	—	—
2005	33	867	890	281	—	1 901	225	—	1 600	—	—	—
Panama / Panamá 2003	6	6	9	3	14	24	8	—	—	—	—	—
2004	4	6	19	3	22	6	5	—	—	—	—	—
2005	2	5	17	2	12	5	2	—	—	—	—	—
Papua New Guinea / Papouasie-Nouvelle-Guinée / Papua Nueva Guinea 2003	—	—	—	—	—	2	—	—	—	—	1	—
2004	...	...	...	...	...	...	...	...	—	...	...	...
2005	...	...	...	...	...	...	...	...	—	...	...	...
Paraguay 2003	8	121	—	—	9	4	2	—	—	—	—	—
2004	...	...	...	...	...	...	...	...	—	...	...	...
2005	...	...	...	...	...	...	...	...	—	...	...	...
Peru / Pérou / Perú 2003	30	8	—	1	—	170	9	—	—	—	—	—
2004	35	44	—	6	—	485	2	...	—	...	—	—
2005	30	34	3	11	—	395	1	...	—	...	—	—
Philippines / Filipinas 2003	2	1	—	—	2	16	—	—	—	—	—	—
2004	1	2	—	—	1	12	—	—	—	—	—	—
2005	...	...	...	...	...	...	...	...	...	—	...	...
Poland / Pologne / Polonia 2003	31	44	50	5	356	601	—	102	—	—	332	—
2004	42	78	—	5	202	876	—	89	—	—	291	—
2005	38	51	800	4	288	501	—	86	—	—	183	—
Portugal 2003	74	251	104	159	44	638	200	—	25	9	511	4
2004	97	255	91	120	108	537	158	—	—	5	538	3
2005	120	251	106	142	144	389	186	—	—	5	697	3
Qatar 2003	—	—	3	—	—	—	—	—	—	—	—	—
2004	—	—	—	—	—	—	—	—	—	—	—	—
2005	—	—	—	—	—	—	—	—	—	—	—	—
Republic of Korea / République de Corée / República de Corea 2003	42	42	60	60	18	600	70	—	—	—	—	—
2004	152	47	111	30	24	710	55	—	—	—	—	—
2005	41	13	111	41	13	650	105	—	—	—	—	—

Schedule IV.   D.2. Anxiolytics (first part): main benzodiazepines and meprobamate *(continued)*

Tableau IV.   D.2. Anxiolytiques (première partie): principales benzodiazépines et méprobamate *(suite)*

Lista IV.   D.2. Ansiolíticos (primera parte): principales benzodiazepinas y meprobamato *(continuación)*

Imports — Importations — Importaciones *(continued — suite — continuación)*

Country or territory / Pays ou territoire / País o territorio	Year / Année / Año	Alprazolam	Bromazepam / Bromazépam	Chlordiazepoxide / Chlordiazépoxide / Clordiazepóxido	Clobazam	Clorazepate / Clorazépate / Clorazepato	Diazepam / Diazépam	Lorazepam / Lorazépam	Medazepam / Médazépam	Meprobamate / Méprobamate / Meprobamato	Nordazepam / Nordazépam	Oxazepam / Oxazépam	Prazepam / Prazépam
		kg	kg	kg	kg	kg	kg	kg	kg	kg	kg	kg	kg
Republic of Moldova / République de Moldova / República de Moldova	2003	—	—	17	—	1	61	—	7	96	—	11	—
	2004	—	—	6	—	—	38	—	2	32	—	17	—
	2005	?	?	?	?	?	?	?	?	?	?	?	?
Romania / Roumanie / Rumania	2003	19	22	—	—	14	626	4	343	4 300	—	—	—
	2004	15	43	—	—	18	350	10	83	1 000	—	—	—
	2005	—	—	—	—	—	—	—	—	—	—	—	—
Russian Federation / Fédération de Russie / Federación de Rusia	2003	3	—	164	—	—	572	1	10	—	—	75	—
	2004	—	—	85	—	—	455	2	21	—	—	82	—
	2005	—	—	—	—	—	—	—	—	—	—	—	—
Rwanda	2003	—	—	—	—	—	5	—	—	2	—	—	—
	2004	—	—	—	—	—	1	—	—	7	—	—	—
	2005	—	—	1	—	—	21	—	—	14	—	—	—
Saint Vincent and the Grenadines / Saint-Vincent-et-les-Grenadines / San Vicente y las Granadinas	2003	—	—	—	—	—	1	—	—	—	—	—	—
	2004	—	—	—	—	—	1	—	—	—	—	—	—
	2005	—	—	61	—	—	681	36	—	—	—	—	—
Samoa	2003	?	?	?	?	?	?	?	?	?	?	?	?
	2004	?	?	?	?	?	?	?	?	?	?	?	?
	2005	—	—	—	—	—	87	—	—	—	—	—	—
Saudi Arabia / Arabie saoudite / Arabia Saudita	2003	2	6	1	—	—	14	1	—	—	—	—	—
	2004	1	4	2	—	—	8	1	—	—	—	—	—
	2005	1	3	—	2	—	7	—	—	—	—	—	—

Country	Year												
Senegal / Sénégal	2003	1	7	—	3	11	23	4	—	5	—	6	79
	2004	—	—	—	—	—	—	—	—	—	—	—	—
	2005	1	4	2	2	12	6	2	—	3	—	2	25
Serbia and Montenegro / Serbie-et-Monténégro / Serbia y Montenegro	2003	28	758	—	—	15	1 250	51	—	—	—	—	155
	2004	?	?	?	?	?	?	?	?	?	?	?	?
	2005	?	?	?	?	?	?	?	?	?	?	?	?
Seychelles	2003	—	—	—	—	—	1	—	—	—	—	—	—
	2004	—	—	—	—	—	1	—	—	—	—	—	—
	2005	?	?	?	?	?	?	?	?	?	?	?	?
Sierra Leone / Sierra Leona	2003	—	—	—	—	—	15	—	—	—	—	—	—
	2004	?	?	?	?	?	?	?	?	?	?	?	?
	2005	—	—	—	—	—	27	1	—	—	—	—	—
Singapore / Singapour / Singapur	2003	1	4	144	—	4	64	3	—	—	1	—	—
	2004	2	5	150	1	4	116	5	—	—	3	—	—
	2005	1	5	89	2	4	39	3	—	20	1	—	—
Slovakia / Slovaquie / Eslovaquia	2003	9	41	51	—	—	307	—	63	—	—	69	—
	2004	?	?	?	?	?	?	?	?	?	?	?	?
	2005	17	48	39	—	—	307	—	33	—	—	84	—
Slovenia / Slovénie / Eslovenia	2003	13	53	—	3	—	200	35	100	5	—	30	—
	2004	21	156	—	3	—	200	45	150	2	—	26	—
	2005	30	476	—	4	—	550	44	250	8	—	23	—
South Africa / Afrique du Sud / Sudáfrica	2003	22	139	46	47	3	1 205	31	—	45 600	—	403	8
	2004	19	81	8	15	2	2 385	27	—	34 050	—	976	4
	2005	30	89	12	37	2	84	31	—	14 550	—	310	12
Spain / Espagne / España	2003	233	473	74	143	3 886	2 090	779	230	450	—	26	182
	2004	312	736	42	120	3 403	1 799	947	220	—	—	25	69
	2005	628	525	196	169	2 929	2 075	924	160	—	—	35	1 694
Sri Lanka	2003	—	..	..	..	—	..	..	—	—	—	—	—
	2004	—	..	43	30	—	104	3	—	—	—	—	—
	2005	701	27	29	40	—	103	3	—	—	—	—	—
Suriname	2003	—	—	—	—	—	11	—	—	—	—	—	—
	2004	—	—	—	—	2	12	1	—	—	—	—	—
	2005	—	—	—	—	—	10	—	—	—	—	—	—
Swaziland / Swazilandia	2003	—	—	—	—	—	—	—	—	98	—	—	—
	2004	—	—	—	—	—	1	—	—	143	—	—	—
	2005	?	?	?	?	?	?	?	?	?	?	?	?

Schedule IV. D.2. Anxiolytics (first part): main benzodiazepines and meprobamate *(continued)*
Tableau IV. D.2. Anxiolytiques (première partie): principales benzodiazépines et méprobamate *(suite)*
Lista IV. D.2. Ansiolíticos (primera parte): principales benzodiazepinas y meprobamato *(continuación)*

Imports — Importations — Importaciones *(continued — suite — continuación)*

Country or territory / Pays ou territoire / País o territorio	Year / Année / Año	Alprazolam	Bromazepam / Bromazépam	Chlordiazepoxide / Chlordiazépoxide / Clordiazepóxido	Clobazam	Clorazepate / Clorazépate / Clorazepato	Diazepam / Diazépam	Lorazepam / Lorazépam	Medazepam / Médazépam	Meprobamate / Méprobamate / Meprobamato	Nordazepam / Nordazépam	Oxazepam / Oxazépam	Prazepam / Prazépam
		kg	kg	kg	kg	kg	kg	kg	kg	kg	kg	kg	kg
Sweden / Suède / Suecia	2003	13	—	1	4	—	182	4	—	253	—	727	—
	2004	17	—	2	4	—	177	4	—	600	—	345	—
	2005	20	—	2	4	—	183	3	—	600	—	964	—
Switzerland / Suisse / Suiza	2003	88	1 687	2 998	129	521	2 540	281	71	6 427	—	742	85
	2004	329	1 681	2 655	180	308	6 384	281	210	11 200	—	605	32
	2005	283	1 270	1 654	131	401	2 755	184	125	2 900	—	501	63
Syrian Arab Rep. / Rép. arabe syrienne / Rep. Árabe Siria	2003	9	24	150	40	—	369	2	—	—	—	—	2
	2004	12	17	400	5	25	19	14	40	1 625	—	—	18
	2005	10	20	100	—	110	255	9	—	700	—	—	15
Thailand / Thaïlande / Tailandia	2003	40	5	424	12	303	1 351	72	—	—	—	—	2
	2004	42	4	329	12	388	800	110	5	—	—	—	18
	2005	36	4	548	16	398	1 121	99	5	—	—	—	15
The former Yugoslav Rep. of Macedonia / L'ex-Rép. yougoslave de Macédoine / La ex Rep. Yugoslava de Macedonia	2003	1	229	—	—	1	272	14	25	20	—	—	26
	2004	1	377	—	—	2	170	14	10	—	—	—	25
	2005	2	252	—	—	1	245	16	17	—	—	—	42
Togo	2003	—	3	—	1	5	20	—	—	2	—	—	2
	2004	—	3	—	—	4	8	—	—	1	—	—	2
	2005	—	5	—	—	6	9	—	—	—	—	—	2
Trinidad and Tobago / Trinité-et-Tobago / Trinidad y Tobago	2003	—	1	1	1	—	5	1	—	—	—	—	—
	2004	1	1	2	1	—	8	2	—	—	—	—	—
	2005	—	1	2	1	—	10	1	—	—	—	—	—

Country	Year	1	2	3	4	5	6	7	8	9	10	11	12
Tristan da Cunha / Tristán da Cunha	2003	—	—	—	—	—	—	—	—	—	—	—	—
	2004	—	—	—	—	—	—	—	—	—	—	—	—
	2005	...	...	...	...	...	...	...	...	...	...	...	...
Tunisia / Tunisie / Túnez	2003	93	—	—	1 496	—	19	17	60	40	12	25	1
	2004	67	—	—	3 367	—	23	13	105	40	12	28	1
	2005	78	—	—	3 065	—	26	23	102	30	18	38	1
Turkey / Turquie / Turquía	2003	—	—	—	5 000	200	1	52	10	—	76	—	19
	2004	—	—	—	6 000	300	2	176	13	—	92	—	30
	2005	—	—	—	5 000	700	2	131	4	—	35	—	26
Turkmenistan / Turkménistan / Turkmenistán	2003	—	—	—	—	—	—	15	—	—	—	—	—
	2004	—	—	—	—	—	—	2	—	—	—	—	—
	2005	...	...	...	...	...	...	...	...	...	...	...	...
Uganda / Ouganda	2003	—	—	—	—	—	—	57	—	—	29	—	—
	2004	—	—	—	—	—	—	40	—	—	—	—	—
	2005	...	...	...	...	...	...	...	...	...	...	...	...
Ukraine / Ucrania	2003	—	13	—	—	1	—	123	—	—	36	—	—
	2004	—	10	—	—	3	—	56	—	—	8	—	—
	2005	—	14	—	—	—	—	203	—	—	6	—	—
United Arab Emirates / Émirats arabes unis / Emiratos Árabes Unidos	2003	—	—	—	—	—	—	28	2	—	—	2	—
	2004	—	—	—	—	—	—	4	—	—	—	2	—
	2005	—	1	—	—	—	—	2	1	—	—	3	1
United Kingdom / Royaume-Uni / Reino Unido	2003	—	1 139	—	—	—	506	1 166	26	69	731	20	3
	2004	—	732	—	401	—	513	3 138	25	65	554	—	3
	2005	—	624	—	—	—	276	225	7	57	33	17	50
United Rep. of Tanzania / Rép.-Unie de Tanzanie / Rep. Unida de Tanzanía	2003	—	—	—	—	—	—	160	—	—	—	—	—
	2004	—	—	—	—	—	—	131	—	1	—	—	—
	2005	—	—	—	—	—	—	675	—	3	—	—	—
United States / États-Unis / Estados Unidos	2003	—	1 830	—	6 400	—	584	4 885	478	—	2 700	4	1 331
	2004	—	920	—	10 800	—	1 499	7 121	493	—	1 142	—	2 411
	2005	—	746	—	6 000	—	1 419	3 564	594	—	1 218	—	2 034
Uzbekistan / Ouzbékistan / Uzbekistán	2003	—	5	—	—	—	—	19	—	—	—	1	—
	2004	—	4	—	—	—	—	19	—	—	—	—	1
	2005	—	10	—	—	4	—	29	—	—	—	—	—
Venezuela (Bolivarian Rep. of) / Venezuela (Rép. bolivarienne du) / Venezuela (Rep. Bolivariana de)	2003	—	—	—	—	—	27	15	9	80	39	283	75
	2004	—	92	—	—	—	33	104	15	80	29	251	51
	2005	—	150	—	—	—	9	73	2	30	5	99	62

Schedule IV. D.2. Anxiolytics (first part): main benzodiazepines and meprobamate *(concluded)*

Tableau IV. D.2. Anxiolytiques (première partie): principales benzodiazépines et méprobamate *(fin)*

Lista IV. D.2. Ansiolíticos (primera parte): principales benzodiazepinas y meprobamato *(conclusión)*

Imports — Importations — Importaciones *(continued — suite — continuación)*

Country or territory / Pays ou territoire / País o territorio	Year / Année / Año	Alprazolam	Bromazepam / Bromazé-pam / Bromazé-pam	Chlordiaz-epoxide / Chlordia-zépoxide / Clordia-zepóxido	Clobazam	Cloraze-pate / Clorazé-pate / Cloraze-pato	Diazepam / Diazépam	Lorazepam / Lorazépam	Medazepam / Médazépam	Mepro-bamate / Mépro-bamate / Mepro-bamato	Nordaze-pam / Nordazé-pam / Nordazé-pam	Oxazepam / Oxazépam / Oxazépam	Prazepam / Prazépam
		kg	kg	kg	kg	kg	kg	kg	kg	kg	kg	kg	kg
Viet Nam	2003	—	—	—	—	4	143	—	—	—	—	—	—
	2004	—	—	—	—	—	103	—	—	—	—	—	—
	2005	—	2	—	—	—	234	—	—	—	—	—	—
Yemen .... / Yémen	2003	5	6	49	—	—	71	7	—	—	—	—	—
	2004	8	8	40	—	—	51	—	—	300	—	—	—
	2005	13	8	89	—	—	43	4	—	200	—	—	—
Zambia .... / Zambie	2003	—	—	—	—	—	3	—	—	—	—	—	—
	2004	—	—	—	—	—	9	—	—	—	—	—	—
	2005	—	—	—	—	—	41	—	—	—	—	—	—
Zimbabwe	2003	—	—	—	—	—	25	—	—	2 000	—	—	—
	2004	—	—	—	—	—	—	—	—	2 025	—	—	—
	2005	—	—	—	—	—	25	—	—	1 975	—	—	—
Total	2003	4 917	15 926	18 592	5 085	9 893	51 332	9 382	2 771	248 579	161	38 994	8 346
	2004	6 791	14 362	13 184	4 854	9 151	57 367	10 561	2 907	200 790	483	34 990	5 665
	2005	7 269	12 898	13 461	5 006	8 765	48 772	10 716	2 846	175 919	163	39 269	6 375

Schedule IV. D.3. Anxiolytics (second part): less common benzodiazepines
Tableau IV. D.3. Anxiolytiques (deuxième partie): benzodiazépines moins courantes
Lista IV. D.3. Ansiolíticos (segunda parte): benzodiazepinas menos comunes

Manufacture — Fabrication — Fabricación

Country or territory / Pays ou territoire / País o territorio	Year / Année / Año	Camazepam / Camazépam	Clotiazepam / Clotiazépam	Cloxazolam	Delorazepam / Délorazépam	Ethyl loflazepate / Loflazépate d'éthyle / Loflazepato de etilo	Fludiazepam / Fludiazépam	Halazepam / Halazépam	Ketazolam / Kétazolam	Oxazolam	Pinazepam / Pinazépam	Tetrazepam / Tétrazépam
		kg	kg	kg	kg	kg	kg	kg	kg	kg	kg	kg
Argentina / Argentine	2003	—	—	20	—	—	—	—	—	—	—	—
	2004	—	—	—	—	—	—	—	—	—	—	—
	2005	—	—	37	—	—	—	—	—	—	—	—
Brazil / Brésil / Brasil	2003	—	—	245	—	—	—	—	—	—	—	—
	2004	—	—	245	—	—	—	—	—	—	—	—
	2005	—	—	308	—	—	—	—	—	—	—	—
China / Chine	2003	—	—	—	—	—	—	—	—	—	—	—
	2004	—	45	—	—	—	—	—	—	—	—	—
	2005	—	—	—	—	—	—	—	—	—	—	—
Czech Republic / République tchèque / República Checa	2003	—	—	—	—	—	—	—	—	—	—	—
	2004	—	—	—	—	—	—	—	—	—	108	—
	2005	—	—	—	—	—	—	—	—	—	—	—
France / Francia	2003	—	111	—	—	94	—	—	—	—	—	21 228
	2004	—	132	—	—	134	—	—	—	—	—	17 937
	2005	—	205	—	—	111	—	—	—	—	—	15 229
Germany / Allemagne / Alemania	2003	—	—	—	—	—	—	—	763	—	—	—
	2004	—	—	—	—	—	—	—	766	—	—	—
	2005	—	—	—	—	—	—	—	904	—	—	—
Italy / Italie / Italia	2003	—	—	—	246	—	—	—	619	—	—	5 099
	2004	—	—	—	—	—	—	—	—	—	—	3 120
	2005	—	—	—	122	—	—	—	—	—	—	2 979
Japan / Japon / Japón	2003	—	2 516	392	—	208	—	—	—	—	—	—
	2004	—	2 196	163	—	160	56	—	—	—	—	—
	2005	—	3 233	—	—	158	—	—	—	2 141	—	—
Spain / Espagne / España	2003	—	—	—	—	—	—	—	273	—	—	—
	2004	—	—	—	—	—	—	—	—	—	—	—
	2005	—	—	—	—	—	—	—	226	—	—	—

Schedule IV. D.3. Anxiolytics (second part): less common benzodiazepines *(continued)*
Tableau IV. D.3. Anxiolytiques (deuxième partie): benzodiazépines moins courantes *(suite)*
Lista IV. D.3. Ansiolíticos (segunda parte): benzodiazepinas menos comunes *(continuación)*

Manufacture — Fabrication — Fabricación *(continued — suite — continuación)*

Country or territory / Pays ou territoire / País o territorio	Year / Année / Año	Camazepam / Camazépam (kg)	Clotiazepam / Clotiazépam (kg)	Cloxazolam (kg)	Delorazepam / Délorazépam (kg)	Ethyl loflazepate / Loflazépate d'éthyle / Loflazepato de etilo (kg)	Fludiazepam / Fludiazépam (kg)	Halazepam / Halazépam (kg)	Ketazolam / Kétazolam (kg)	Oxazolam (kg)	Pinazepam / Pinazépam (kg)	Tetrazepam / Tétrazépam (kg)
Switzerland / Suisse / Suiza	2003	—	—	—	—	10	—	1 197	—	—	—	26 327
	2004	—	—	—	—	10	—	—	—	—	—	21 057
	2005	—	—	—	—	—	—	3 503	—	—	—	18 264
Total	2003	—	2 627	657	246	312	—	1 197	1 655	—	—	26 327
	2004	—	2 373	408	—	304	56	1 197	766	—	108	21 057
	2005	—	3 438	345	122	269	—	3 503	1 130	2 141	—	18 264

Exports — Exportations — Exportaciones

Country or territory / Pays ou territoire / País o territorio	Year / Année / Año	Camazepam / Camazépam (kg)	Clotiazepam / Clotiazépam (kg)	Cloxazolam (kg)	Delorazepam / Délorazépam (kg)	Ethyl loflazepate / Loflazépate d'éthyle / Loflazepato de etilo (kg)	Fludiazepam / Fludiazépam (kg)	Halazepam / Halazépam (kg)	Ketazolam / Kétazolam (kg)	Oxazolam (kg)	Pinazepam / Pinazépam (kg)	Tetrazepam / Tétrazépam (kg)
Argentina / Argentine	2003	—	—	—	—	—	—	—	—	—	—	—
	2004	—	—	16	—	—	—	—	—	—	—	—
	2005	—	—	22	—	—	—	—	—	—	—	—
Belgium / Belgique / Bélgica	2003	—	7	—	—	—	—	—	380	—	—	37
	2004	—	22	—	—	2	—	—	250	—	—	32
	2005	—	5	—	—	3	—	—	160	—	—	55
Brazil / Brésil / Brasil	2003	—	—	27	—	—	—	—	—	—	—	—
	2004	—	—	66	—	—	—	—	—	—	—	—
	2005	—	—	41	—	—	—	—	—	—	—	—
China / Chine	2003	—	—	—	—	—	—	—	—	—	—	—
	2004	—	45	—	—	—	—	—	—	—	—	—
	2005	—	—	—	—	—	—	—	—	—	—	—
Czech Republic / République tchèque / República Checa	2003	—	—	—	—	—	—	—	—	—	—	—
	2004	—	—	—	—	—	—	—	—	—	97	—
	2005	—	—	—	—	—	—	—	—	—	65	—
France / Francia	2003	—	—	—	—	47	—	—	—	—	—	17 182
	2004	—	—	—	—	58	—	—	—	—	—	17 684
	2005	—	78	—	—	70	—	—	—	—	—	17 342

Country	Year	1	2	3	4	5	6	7	8	9	10	11	Total
Germany / Allemagne / Alemania	2003	275	—	—	757	—	—	—	—	—	—	—	
	2004	638	—	—	756	—	—	—	—	—	—	—	
	2005	1 054	—	—	871	—	—	—	—	—	—	—	
Hungary / Hongrie / Hungria	2003	5 412	—	—	—	—	—	—	—	—	—	—	
	2004	—	—	—	—	—	—	—	—	—	—	—	
	2005	114	—	—	—	—	—	—	—	—	—	—	
Ireland / Irlande / Irlanda	2003	—	—	—	—	1 201	—	—	—	—	—	—	
	2004	—	—	—	—	1 558	—	—	—	—	—	—	
	2005	—	—	—	—	3 003	—	—	—	—	—	—	
Italy / Italie / Italia	2003	4 385	—	—	536	—	—	—	4	—	—	—	
	2004	3 103	—	—	14	—	—	—	2	—	—	—	
	2005	3 430	—	—	22	—	—	—	—	—	—	—	
Japan / Japon / Japón	2003	—	—	240	—	—	10	4	—	15	339	—	
	2004	—	—	270	—	—	8	4	—	24	416	—	
	2005	—	—	330	—	—	7	6	—	17	538	—	
Latvia / Lettonie / Letonia	2003	10	—	—	—	—	—	—	—	—	—	—	
	2004	—	—	—	—	—	—	—	—	—	—	—	
	2005	—	—	—	—	—	—	—	—	—	—	—	
Netherlands / Pays-Bas / Paises Bajos	2003	—	29	—	—	—	—	—	—	15	—	—	
	2004	—	45	—	—	—	—	—	—	15	—	—	
	2005	—	103	—	—	—	—	—	—	—	—	—	
Panama / Panamá	2003	56	—	—	—	—	—	3	—	—	—	—	
	2004	56	—	—	—	—	—	4	—	—	—	—	
	2005	36	—	—	—	—	—	3	—	—	—	—	
Paraguay	2003	?	?	?	44	?	?	?	?	?	?	?	
	2004	?	?	?	?	?	?	?	?	?	?	?	
	2005	—	—	—	?	—	—	—	—	—	—	—	
Spain / Espagne / España	2003	9 580	—	—	242	—	—	—	—	—	—	—	
	2004	7 224	—	—	230	—	—	—	—	—	—	—	
	2005	19 930	—	—	206	4	—	—	—	—	—	—	
Switzerland / Suisse / Suiza	2003	—	—	—	150	—	—	6	2	42	—	—	
	2004	—	—	—	116	1 197	—	1	2	58	—	—	
	2005	—	—	—	129	3 503	—	—	—	51	—	—	
Thailand / Thaïlande / Tailandia	2003	—	—	—	—	—	—	—	—	—	—	—	
	2004	—	8	—	—	—	—	—	—	—	—	—	
	2005	—	10	—	—	—	—	—	—	—	—	—	
Total	2003	36 937	29	240	2 109	1 201	10	60	6	99	346	—	
	2004	28 737	150	270	1 366	2 755	8	69	4	179	483	—	
	2005	41 961	178	330	1 388	6 510	7	82	—	131	621	—	

Schedule IV. D.3. Anxiolytics (second part): less common benzodiazepines (continued)
Tableau IV. D.3. Anxiolytiques (deuxième partie): benzodiazépines moins courantes (suite)
Lista IV. D.3. Ansiolíticos (segunda parte): benzodiazepinas menos comunes (continuación)

Imports — Importations — Importaciones

Country or territory / Pays ou territoire / País o territorio	Year / Année / Año	Camazepam / Camazépam (kg)	Clotiazepam / Clotiazépam (kg)	Cloxazolam (kg)	Delorazepam / Délorazépam (kg)	Ethyl loflazepate / Loflazépate d'éthyle / Loflazepato de etilo (kg)	Fludiazepam / Fludiazépam (kg)	Halazepam / Halazépam (kg)	Ketazolam / Kétazolam (kg)	Oxazolam (kg)	Pinazepam / Pinazépam (kg)	Tetrazepam / Tétrazépam (kg)
Algeria Algérie Argelia	2003 2004 2005	— — —	— — —	— — —	— — —	— — —	— — —	— — —	— — —	— — —	— — —	691 671 699
Andorra Andorre	2003 2004 2005	— — —	— — —	— — —	— — —	— — —	— — —	1 — —	1 1 1	— — —	— — —	5 6 7
Argentina Argentine	2003 2004 2005	— — —	— — —	— — —	— — —	— — —	— — —	— — —	9 8 5	— — —	— — —	— — —
Austria Autriche	2003 2004 2005	— — —	— — —	— — —	— — —	— — —	— — —	— — —	— — —	— — —	— — —	258 259 254
Belgium Belgique Bélgica	2003 2004 2005	— — —	320 — 78	15 15 8	— — —	3 4 3	— — —	— — —	508 8 6	— — —	— — —	861 981 879
Benin Bénin	2003 2004 2005	— — —	— — —	— — —	— — —	— — —	— — —	— — —	— — —	— — —	— — —	6 2 5
Bolivia Bolivie	2003 2004 2005	— — —	— — —	— — —	— — —	— — —	— — —	— — —	10 7 10	— — —	— — —	— 1 —
Brazil Brésil Brasil	2003 2004 2005	— — —	— — —	8 15 18	— — —	— — —	— — —	— — —	— — —	— — —	— — —	— — —

Country	Year	1	2	3	4	5	6	7	8	9	10	11
Bulgaria — Bulgarie	2003	2	—	—	—	—	—	—	—	—	—	—
	2004	15	—	—	—	—	—	—	—	—	—	—
	2005	5	—	—	—	—	—	—	—	—	—	—
Burkina Faso	2003	2	—	—	—	—	—	—	—	—	—	—
	2004	—	—	—	—	—	—	—	—	—	—	—
	2005	4	—	—	—	—	—	—	—	—	—	—
Chad — Tchad	2003	—	—	—	—	—	—	—	—	—	—	—
	2004	1	—	—	—	—	—	—	—	—	—	—
	2005	?	?	?	?	?	?	?	?	?	?	?
Chile — Chili	2003	—	—	—	64	—	—	—	—	—	—	—
	2004	5	—	—	30	—	—	—	—	—	1	—
	2005	12	—	—	30	—	—	—	—	—	5	—
China — Chine — Hong Kong SAR of China — RAS de Hong Kong (Chine) — RAE de Hong Kong de China	2003	—	4	—	—	—	—	—	—	—	—	—
	2004	—	2	—	—	—	—	—	—	—	—	—
	2005	—	6	—	—	—	—	—	—	—	—	—
Costa Rica	2003	—	—	—	—	—	—	1	—	—	—	—
	2004	1	—	—	—	—	—	2	—	—	—	—
	2005	1	—	—	—	—	—	2	—	—	—	—
Côte d'Ivoire	2003	14	—	—	—	—	—	1	—	—	—	—
	2004	7	—	—	—	—	—	1	—	—	—	—
	2005	8	—	—	—	—	—	—	—	—	—	—
Cuba	2003	—	—	—	—	—	—	—	—	—	—	—
	2004	—	—	—	—	—	1	—	—	—	—	—
	2005	—	—	—	—	—	—	—	—	—	—	—
Czech Republic — République tchèque — República Checa	2003	393	—	—	—	—	—	—	—	—	—	—
	2004	381	—	—	—	—	—	—	—	—	—	—
	2005	394	65	—	—	—	—	—	—	—	—	—
Dem. Rep. of the Congo — Rép. dém. du Congo — Rep. Dem. del Congo	2003	—	—	—	—	—	—	—	—	—	—	—
	2004	—	—	—	—	—	—	—	—	—	—	—
	2005	1	—	—	—	—	—	—	—	—	—	—
Djibouti	2003	?	?	?	?	?	?	?	?	?	?	?
	2004	?	?	?	?	?	?	?	?	?	?	?
	2005	1	—	—	—	—	—	—	—	—	—	—
Ecuador — Équateur	2003	10	—	—	46	—	—	—	—	—	—	—
	2004	12	—	—	36	—	—	—	—	—	—	—
	2005	8	—	—	60	—	—	—	—	—	—	—
Egypt — Egypte — Egipto	2003	300	—	—	—	—	—	—	2	—	—	—
	2004	550	—	—	—	—	—	—	2	—	—	—
	2005	520	—	—	—	—	—	—	—	—	—	—

Schedule IV. D.3. Anxiolytics (second part): less common benzodiazepines *(continued)*
Tableau IV. D.3. Anxiolytiques (deuxième partie): benzodiazépines moins courantes *(suite)*
Lista IV. D.3. Ansiolíticos (segunda parte): benzodiazepinas menos comunes *(continuación)*

Imports — Importations — Importaciones *(continued — suite — continuación)*

Country or territory / Pays ou territoire / País o territorio	Year / Année / Año	Camazepam / Camazépam	Clotiazepam / Clotiazépam	Cloxazolam	Delorazepam / Délorazépam	Ethyl loflazepate / Loflazépate d'éthyle / Loflazepato de etilo	Fludiazepam / Fludiazépam	Halazepam / Halazépam	Ketazolam / Kétazolam	Oxazolam	Pinazepam / Pinazépam	Tetrazepam / Tétrazépam
		kg	kg	kg	kg	kg	kg	kg	kg	kg	kg	kg
El Salvador	2003	—	—	—	—	—	—	—	—	—	—	—
	2004	—	—	—	—	—	—	—	—	—	—	1
	2005	—	—	—	—	—	—	—	—	—	—	—
France / Francia	2003	—	170	—	—	—	—	—	—	—	—	11 018
	2004	—	18	—	—	—	—	—	—	—	—	7 118
	2005	—	150	—	—	—	—	—	—	—	—	6 752
French Polynesia / Polynésie française / Polinesia Francesa	2003	—	—	—	—	—	—	—	—	—	—	11
	2004	—	—	—	—	—	—	—	—	—	—	12
	2005	?	?	?	?	?	?	?	?	?	?	?
Gabon / Gabón	2003	?	?	?	?	?	?	?	?	?	?	?
	2004	?	?	?	?	?	?	?	?	?	?	5
	2005	—	—	—	—	—	—	—	—	—	—	7
Germany / Allemagne / Alemania	2003	—	—	—	—	—	—	—	—	—	—	4 936
	2004	—	—	—	—	—	—	—	—	—	—	3 953
	2005	—	—	—	—	—	—	—	—	—	—	4 354
Guinea / Guinée	2003	?	?	?	?	?	?	?	?	?	?	?
	2004	?	?	?	?	?	?	?	?	?	?	?
	2005	—	—	—	—	—	—	—	—	—	—	1
Honduras	2003	—	—	—	—	—	—	—	—	—	—	2
	2004	—	—	—	—	—	—	—	—	—	—	2
	2005	?	?	?	?	?	?	?	?	?	?	?
Hungary / Hongrie / Hungría	2003	—	—	—	—	—	—	—	—	—	—	3 489
	2004	—	—	—	—	—	—	—	—	—	—	—
	2005	—	—	—	—	—	—	—	—	—	—	144
Ireland / Irlande / Irlanda	2003	—	—	—	—	—	—	1 197	—	—	—	—
	2004	—	—	—	—	—	—	3 510	—	—	—	—
	2005	—	—	—	—	—	—	—	—	—	—	—

Country	Year	1	2	3	4	5	6	7	8	9	10	11
Italy / Italie / Italia	2003	—	—	—	122	—	—	—	—	—	120	—
	2004	150	—	—	90	—	—	—	—	—	—	—
	2005	257	—	—	107	—	—	—	—	—	—	—
Japan / Japon / Japón	2003	—	—	20	—	—	—	12	—	—	45	—
	2004	—	—	10	—	—	—	28	—	—	—	—
	2005	—	—	200	—	—	—	9	—	—	—	—
Latvia / Lettonie / Letonia	2003	23	—	—	—	—	—	—	—	—	—	—
	2004	13	—	—	—	—	—	—	—	—	—	—
	2005	9	—	—	—	—	—	—	—	—	—	—
Lebanon / Liban / Líbano	2003	8	—	—	—	—	—	—	—	—	—	—
	2004	21	—	—	—	—	—	—	—	—	—	—
	2005	23	—	—	—	—	—	—	—	—	—	—
Lithuania / Lituanie / Lituania	2003	13	—	—	—	—	—	—	—	—	—	—
	2004	12	—	—	—	—	—	—	—	—	—	—
	2005	13	—	—	—	—	—	—	—	—	—	—
Luxembourg / Luxemburgo	2003	—	—	—	—	—	—	—	—	—	?	—
	2004	?	?	?	?	?	?	?	?	?	5	?
	2005	34	—	—	—	—	—	—	—	—	—	—
Mali / Malí	2003	1	—	—	—	—	—	—	—	—	—	—
	2004	2	—	—	—	—	—	—	—	—	—	—
	2005	7	—	—	—	—	—	—	—	—	—	—
Mauritania / Mauritanie	2003	1	—	—	—	—	—	—	—	—	—	—
	2004	?	?	?	?	?	?	?	?	?	?	?
	2005	?	?	?	?	?	?	?	?	?	?	?
Mexico / Mexique / México	2003	25	—	—	—	—	—	—	—	—	—	—
	2004	45	?	?	?	?	?	10	?	?	?	?
	2005	?	—	—	—	—	—	—	—	—	—	—
Morocco / Maroc / Marruecos	2003	200	—	—	—	—	—	—	—	—	—	—
	2004	280	—	—	—	—	—	—	—	—	—	—
	2005	595	—	—	—	—	—	—	—	—	—	—
Netherlands / Pays-Bas / Países Bajos	2003	—	—	—	—	—	—	—	—	15	—	—
	2004	—	104	—	—	—	—	—	—	15	—	—
	2005	—	73	—	—	—	—	—	—	—	—	—
New Caledonia / Nouvelle-Calédonie / Nueva Caledonia	2003	11	—	—	—	—	—	—	—	—	—	—
	2004	?	?	?	?	?	?	?	?	?	?	?
	2005	12	—	—	—	—	—	—	—	—	—	—
Niger / Niger	2003	?	?	?	?	?	?	?	?	?	?	?
	2004	?	?	?	?	?	?	?	?	?	?	?
	2005	1	—	—	—	—	—	—	—	—	—	—

Schedule IV. D.3. Anxiolytics (second part): less common benzodiazepines (concluded)
Tableau IV. D.3. Anxiolytiques (deuxième partie): benzodiazépines moins courantes (fin)
Lista IV. D.3. Ansiolíticos (segunda parte): benzodiazepinas menos comunes (conclusión)

Imports — Importations — Importaciones (continued — suite — continuación)

Country or territory / Pays ou territoire / País o territorio	Year / Année / Año	Camazepam / Camazépam (kg)	Clotiazepam / Clotiazépam (kg)	Cloxazolam (kg)	Delorazepam / Délorazépam (kg)	Ethyl loflazepate / Loflazépate d'éthyle / Loflazepato de etilo (kg)	Fludiazepam / Fludiazépam (kg)	Halazepam / Halazépam (kg)	Ketazolam / Kétazolam (kg)	Oxazolam (kg)	Pinazepam / Pinazépam (kg)	Tetrazepam / Tétrazépam (kg)
Pakistan / Pakistán	2003	—	—	—	—	—	—	—	—	—	4	—
	2004	—	—	—	—	—	—	—	—	—	4	—
	2005	—	—	—	—	—	—	—	—	—	—	—
Panama / Panamá	2003	—	—	—	—	3	—	—	—	—	—	66
	2004	—	—	—	—	4	—	—	—	—	—	51
	2005	—	—	—	—	3	—	—	—	—	—	43
Paraguay	2003	—	—	—	—	—	—	—	60	—	—	2
	2004	?	?	?	?	?	?	?	?	?	?	?
	2005	?	?	?	?	?	?	?	?	?	?	?
Peru / Pérou / Perú	2003	—	—	—	—	—	—	—	4	—	—	1
	2004	—	—	—	—	—	—	—	26	—	—	1
	2005	—	—	—	—	—	—	—	24	—	—	—
Poland / Pologne / Polonia	2003	—	—	—	—	—	—	—	—	—	—	1 605
	2004	—	—	—	—	—	—	—	—	—	—	489
	2005	—	—	—	—	—	—	—	—	—	—	1 493
Portugal	2003	—	—	52	—	28	—	376	40	—	—	—
	2004	—	—	68	—	40	—	326	30	—	—	—
	2005	—	—	63	—	40	—	285	—	—	—	—
Republic of Korea / République de Corée / República de Corea	2003	—	126	—	—	8	—	—	—	—	20	—
	2004	—	173	—	—	5	—	—	—	—	20	—
	2005	—	100	—	—	6	—	—	—	—	10	—
Republic of Moldova / République de Moldova / República de Moldova	2003	—	—	—	—	—	—	—	—	—	—	3
	2004	—	—	—	—	—	—	—	—	—	—	1
	2005	?	?	?	?	?	?	?	?	?	?	?

	Year	(1)	(2)	(3)	(4)	(5)	(6)	(7)	(8)	(9)	(10)
Romania / Roumanie / Rumania	2003	50	—	—	—	—	—	—	—	—	—
	2004	26	—	—	—	—	—	—	—	—	—
	2005	—	—	—	—	—	—	—	—	—	—
Senegal / Sénégal	2003	18	—	—	—	—	—	—	—	—	—
	2004	—	—	—	—	—	—	—	—	—	—
	2005	12	—	—	—	—	—	—	—	—	—
Serbia and Montenegro / Serbie-et-Monténégro / Serbia y Montenegro	2003	7	—	—	—	—	—	—	—	—	—
	2004	...	...	...	...	...	...	...	...	...	...
	2005	...	...	...	...	...	...	...	...	...	...
Singapore / Singapour / Singapur	2003	—	—	—	—	—	—	—	—	—	—
	2004	—	2	—	—	—	—	—	—	—	—
	2005	—	—	—	—	—	—	—	—	—	—
Slovakia / Slovaquie / Eslovaquia	2003	111	—	—	—	—	—	—	—	—	—
	2004	...	...	...	...	...	...	...	...	...	...
	2005	110	—	—	—	—	—	—	—	—	—
South Africa / Afrique du Sud / Sudáfrica	2003	—	—	20	—	—	—	—	—	60	—
	2004	—	—	8	—	—	—	—	—	70	—
	2005	—	—	5	—	—	—	—	—	60	—
Spain / Espagne / España	2003	13 172	—	965	895	—	—	—	—	—	—
	2004	18 909	—	1 390	202	—	—	—	—	—	—
	2005	10 686	—	916	896	—	—	—	—	—	—
Switzerland / Suisse / Suiza	2003	—	—	187	—	—	—	2	34	—	—
	2004	—	—	130	211	—	—	2	68	—	—
	2005	—	—	159	1 827	—	—	—	49	—	—
Thailand / Thaïlande / Tailandia	2003	—	—	—	—	—	1	—	—	—	—
	2004	—	16	—	—	—	2	—	—	—	—
	2005	—	22	—	—	—	—	—	—	—	—
Togo	2003	2	—	—	—	—	—	—	—	—	—
	2004	2	—	—	—	—	—	—	—	—	—
	2005	1	—	—	—	—	—	—	—	—	—
Tunisia / Tunisie / Túnez	2003	95	—	—	—	—	—	—	—	—	—
	2004	78	—	—	—	—	—	—	—	—	—
	2005	118	—	—	—	—	—	—	2	—	—
United States / États-Unis / Estados Unidos	2003	—	—	—	—	—	—	—	—	—	—
	2004	—	—	—	—	—	—	—	—	—	—
	2005	—	—	—	—	—	—	—	—	—	—
Total	2003	37 412	28	2 036	1 272	—	57	4	126	841	—
	2004	34 063	146	1 764	1 936	1	96	4	181	262	—
	2005	27 470	178	1 313	6 518	—	63	—	138	398	—

Schedule IV. D.4. Benzodiazepines: sedative-hypnotics + anti-epileptics
Tableau IV. D.4. Benzodiazépines: sédatifs-hypnotiques + antiépileptiques
Lista IV. D.4. Benzodiazepinas: sedantes-hipnóticos + antiepilépticos

Manufacture — Fabrication — Fabricación

Country or territory / Pays ou territoire / País o territorio	Year / Année / Año	Brotizolam (kg)	Clonazepam / Clonazépam (kg)	Estazolam (kg)	Flurazepam / Flurazépam (kg)	Haloxazolam (kg)	Loprazolam (kg)	Lormetazepam / Lormétazépam (kg)	Midazolam (kg)	Nimetazepam / Nimétazépam (kg)	Nitrazepam / Nitrazépam (kg)	Temazepam / Témazépam (kg)	Triazolam (kg)
Brazil / Brésil / Brasil	2003	—	31	—	—	—	—	—	157	—	—	—	—
	2004	—	184	—	531	—	—	—	762	—	—	—	—
	2005	—	253	—	501	—	—	—	468	—	—	—	—
China / Chine	2003	—	400	1 547	38	—	—	—	36	—	87	—	32
	2004	—	300	672	28	—	—	—	35	—	752	—	22
	2005	—	300	2 392	—	—	—	—	64	—	685	—	14
Czech Republic / République tchèque / República Checa	2003	—	—	—	—	—	—	—	104	—	—	—	—
	2004	—	—	—	—	—	—	—	102	—	—	—	—
	2005	—	—	—	—	—	—	—	—	—	—	—	—
France / Francia	2003	—	—	—	—	—	86	—	—	—	—	—	82
	2004	—	—	—	—	—	114	—	—	—	—	—	—
	2005	—	—	—	—	—	72	—	—	—	—	—	—
Germany / Allemagne / Alemania	2003	126	—	—	—	—	—	442	—	—	—	—	—
	2004	114	—	—	—	—	—	437	—	—	—	—	—
	2005	396	—	—	—	—	—	—	—	—	—	—	—
India / Inde	2003	—	—	—	—	—	—	—	—	—	—	—	—
	2004	—	1 126	—	—	—	—	—	399	6	2 195	—	—
	2005	—	1 787	—	—	—	—	—	303	6	1 673	—	—
Israel / Israël	2003	—	—	—	—	—	—	—	1 589	—	—	—	—
	2004	—	25	—	—	—	—	—	532	—	—	—	—
	2005	—	367	2	—	—	—	—	1 352	—	—	—	—
Italy / Italie / Italia	2003	25	1 591	25	3 788	—	—	380	142	—	4 744	23 429	45
	2004	31	1 620	19	3 089	—	—	569	249	—	1 071	9 196	53
	2005	22	512	59	3 624	—	—	685	238	—	2 375	13 280	55

		kg	kg	kg	kg	kg	kg	kg	kg	kg	kg	kg	kg
Japan	2003	—	—	498	—	149	—	—	—	—	—	—	—
Japon	2004	—	—	289	—	303	—	—	—	62	—	—	—
Japón	2005	33	—	341	—	—	—	—	—	—	—	—	—
Poland	2003	—	84	178	—	—	—	—	—	—	—	1 150	—
Pologne	2004	—	92	188	—	—	—	—	—	—	—	147	—
Polonia	2005	—	171	202	—	—	—	5	—	—	—	—	—
Switzerland	2003	—	1 684	—	—	—	—	—	3 239	—	—	—	—
Suisse	2004	—	1 888	—	—	—	—	—	2 758	—	—	—	—
Suiza	2005	—	2 975	—	—	—	—	—	6 268	—	—	—	—
United Kingdom	2003	—	24	—	—	—	—	—	—	—	—	—	—
Royaume-Uni	2004	—	2	—	—	—	—	—	—	—	—	—	—
Reino Unido	2005	—	11	—	—	—	—	—	—	—	—	—	—
United States	2003	—	42	—	—	—	—	—	—	—	—	1 900	190
États-Unis	2004	—	—	377	—	—	—	—	—	—	—	5	190
Estados Unidos	2005	—	—	—	—	—	—	—	—	—	—	—	—
Total	2003	151	3 856	2 248	3 826	149	86	380	5 267	—	4 831	24 579	159
	2004	145	5 237	1 545	3 648	303	114	1 011	4 837	68	4 018	11 243	265
	2005	451	6 377	3 046	4 125	—	72	1 127	8 694	6	4 734	13 285	259

Exports — Exportations — Exportaciones

		kg	kg	kg	kg	kg	kg	kg	kg	kg	kg	kg	kg
Argentina	2003	—	17	—	—	—	—	—	1	—	—	—	1
Argentine	2004	—	24	—	—	—	—	—	10	—	—	—	1
	2005	—	23	—	—	—	—	—	4	—	—	—	1
Australia	2003	—	18	—	—	—	—	—	13	2	—	46	8
Australie	2004	—	21	—	—	—	—	—	12	4	—	79	8
	2005	—	35	—	—	—	—	—	1	1	—	69	8
Austria	2003	2	—	—	—	—	—	—	137	—	2	—	—
Autriche	2004	2	—	—	—	—	—	—	146	—	4	—	—
	2005	2	—	—	—	—	—	—	72	—	1	—	—
Belgium	2003	—	11	—	—	—	1	5	2	9	—	10	46
Belgique	2004	—	6	—	—	—	—	4	8	9	—	—	40
Bélgica	2005	—	2	—	—	—	1	3	2	4	—	—	39
Brazil	2003	—	154	—	—	—	—	—	210	—	3	—	—
Brésil	2004	—	248	—	—	—	—	—	212	—	2	—	—
Brasil	2005	—	214	—	—	—	—	—	251	—	4	—	—
Canada	2003	2	152	—	8	—	—	—	—	3	—	—	—
Canadá	2004	2	480	—	9	—	—	—	—	2	—	—	—
	2005	2	469	—	5	—	—	—	—	4	—	—	—
Chile	2003	—	—	—	—	—	—	—	—	—	—	—	—
Chili	2004	—	2	—	—	—	—	—	—	—	—	—	—
	2005	—	2	—	—	—	—	—	7	—	—	—	—

215

Schedule IV. D.4. Benzodiazepines: sedative-hypnotics + anti-epileptics (continued)
Tableau IV. D.4. Benzodiazépines: sédatifs-hypnotiques + antiépileptiques (suite)
Lista IV. D.4. Benzodiazepinas: sedantes-hipnóticos + antiepilépticos (continuación)

Exports — Exportations — Exportaciones (continued — suite — continuación)

Country or territory / Pays ou territoire / País o territorio	Year / Année / Año	Brotizolam (kg)	Clonazepam / Clonazépam (kg)	Estazolam (kg)	Flurazepam / Flurazépam (kg)	Haloxazolam (kg)	Loprazolam (kg)	Lormetazepam / Lormétazépam (kg)	Midazolam (kg)	Nimetazepam / Nimétazépam (kg)	Nitrazepam / Nitrazépam (kg)	Temazepam / Témazépam (kg)	Triazolam (kg)
China Chine	2003	—	17	—	—	—	—	—	5	—	450	—	—
	2004	—	5	—	—	—	—	—	—	—	300	—	1
	2005	—	19	52	—	—	—	—	3	—	550	—	1
Hong Kong SAR of China RAS de Hong Kong (Chine) RAE de Hong Kong de China	2003	—	—	—	—	—	—	—	6	—	—	—	—
	2004	—	—	—	—	—	—	—	2	—	—	—	—
	2005	—	—	—	—	—	—	—	5	—	—	—	—
Colombia Colombie	2003	—	—	—	—	—	—	—	—	—	—	—	—
	2004	—	—	—	—	—	—	—	—	—	—	—	—
	2005	1	—	—	—	—	—	—	—	—	—	—	—
Costa Rica	2003	—	18	—	—	—	—	—	42	—	—	—	—
	2004	—	10	—	—	—	—	—	26	—	—	—	—
	2005	—	20	—	—	—	—	—	29	—	—	—	—
Croatia Croatie Croacia	2003	—	—	—	—	—	—	—	—	—	6	—	—
	2004	?	?	?	?	?	?	?	?	?	?	?	?
	2005	—	—	—	—	—	—	—	—	—	13	—	—
Cuba	2003	—	—	—	—	—	—	—	—	—	—	—	—
	2004	—	—	—	—	—	—	—	—	—	—	—	—
	2005	—	—	—	—	—	—	—	3	—	—	—	—
Cyprus Chypre Chipre	2003	—	2	—	73	—	—	—	—	—	10	315	—
	2004	—	—	—	66	—	—	1	—	—	16	658	—
	2005	—	3	—	98	—	—	—	—	—	18	404	—
Czech Republic République tchèque República Checa	2003	—	—	—	—	—	—	—	—	—	—	—	—
	2004	—	—	—	—	—	—	—	102	—	—	—	—
	2005	—	—	—	—	—	—	—	—	—	—	—	—
Denmark Danemark Dinamarca	2003	—	7	—	2	—	—	—	11	—	3	—	—
	2004	—	5	—	2	—	—	—	4	—	51	—	—
	2005	—	6	—	2	—	—	—	5	—	101	—	—

Country	Year												
Estonia / Estonie	2003	—	—	1	—	—	—	—	—	—	—	—	—
	2004	—	—	—	—	—	—	—	—	—	—	—	—
	2005	—	—	—	—	—	—	—	—	—	—	—	—
Finland / Finlande / Finlandia	2003	—	247	—	—	—	—	—	—	—	—	—	—
	2004	—	320	—	—	—	—	—	—	—	—	—	—
	2005	—	434	—	—	—	—	—	—	—	—	—	—
France / Francia	2003	82	221	17	—	200	199	70	—	—	—	76	—
	2004	—	130	3	—	180	220	55	—	—	—	83	—
	2005	—	225	3	—	219	256	55	—	—	—	123	—
Germany / Allemagne / Alemania	2003	—	742	77	—	78	493	—	—	197	—	7	236
	2004	—	835	46	—	133	688	—	—	144	—	8	289
	2005	—	688	47	—	206	729	—	—	193	—	25	263
Greece / Grèce / Grecia	2003	—	—	—	—	—	9	—	—	—	—	—	—
	2004	—	—	—	—	—	9	—	—	—	—	1	—
	2005	—	—	—	—	—	9	—	—	—	—	1	—
Hungary / Hongrie / Hungría	2003	—	949	17	—	—	—	—	—	—	—	—	—
	2004	—	279	48	—	1	—	—	—	—	—	—	—
	2005	—	585	85	—	1	—	—	—	—	—	—	—
India / Inde	2003	—	—	288	—	123	—	—	—	—	—	920	—
	2004	—	—	84	10	229	—	—	—	—	—	974	—
	2005	—	—	120	—	246	—	—	—	—	—	1 276	—
Ireland / Irlande / Irlanda	2003	1	1 758	136	—	6	144	—	—	—	—	—	—
	2004	—	878	75	—	2	153	—	—	—	—	—	—
	2005	—	367	32	—	—	99	—	—	—	1	—	—
Israel / Israël	2003	—	—	—	—	935	—	—	—	—	—	259	—
	2004	—	—	—	—	918	—	—	—	—	—	98	—
	2005	—	—	—	—	1 147	—	—	—	—	—	391	—
Italy / Italie / Italia	2003	55	18 951	2 652	—	197	345	—	—	3 144	25	1 566	27
	2004	40	14 594	2 897	—	210	483	—	—	2 598	24	1 401	20
	2005	34	13 284	2 519	—	251	700	5	—	3 559	62	1 402	9
Japan / Japon / Japón	2003	2	—	—	6	5	—	—	—	—	159	—	—
	2004	—	—	—	5	—	—	—	—	—	19	—	—
	2005	—	—	—	6	—	—	—	—	—	183	—	—
Jordan / Jordanie / Jordania	2003	—	—	—	—	—	—	—	—	—	—	—	—
	2004	—	—	—	—	—	—	—	—	—	—	—	—
	2005	—	—	—	—	—	—	—	—	—	—	2	—
Latvia / Lettonie / Letonia	2003	—	—	4	—	3	—	—	—	—	—	2	—
	2004	—	—	3	—	5	—	—	—	—	—	3	—
	2005	—	—	3	—	3	—	—	—	—	—	1	—

Schedule IV. D.4. Benzodiazepines: sedative-hypnotics + anti-epileptics *(continued)*
Tableau IV. D.4. Benzodiazépines: sédatifs-hypnotiques + antiépileptiques *(suite)*
Lista IV. D.4. Benzodiazepinas: sedantes-hipnóticos + antiepilépticos *(continuación)*

Exports — Exportations — Exportaciones *(continued — suite — continuación)*

Country or territory / Pays ou territoire / País o territorio	Year / Année / Año	Brotizolam (kg)	Clonazepam Clonazépam (kg)	Estazolam (kg)	Flurazepam Flurazépam (kg)	Haloxazolam (kg)	Loprazolam (kg)	Lormetazepam Lormétazépam (kg)	Midazolam (kg)	Nimetazepam Nimétazépam (kg)	Nitrazepam Nitrazépam (kg)	Temazepam Témazépam (kg)	Triazolam (kg)
Lithuania / Lituanie / Lituania	2003	—	6	—	—	—	—	—	—	—	—	—	—
	2004	—	6	—	—	—	—	—	—	—	—	—	—
	2005	—	1	—	—	—	—	—	—	—	—	—	—
Malaysia / Malaisie / Malasia	2003	—	—	—	—	—	—	—	—	—	—	—	—
	2004	—	—	—	—	—	—	—	—	—	—	—	—
	2005	—	—	—	—	—	—	—	2	—	—	—	—
Netherlands / Pays-Bas / Países Bajos	2003	—	—	12	520	—	—	56	374	—	170	145	—
	2004	—	—	18	117	—	—	52	312	—	80	148	—
	2005	—	—	20	2	—	—	91	139	—	39	50	—
New Zealand / Nouvelle-Zélande / Nueva Zelandia	2003	—	—	—	—	—	—	—	—	—	4	—	—
	2004	—	—	—	—	—	—	—	—	—	6	—	—
	2005	—	—	—	—	—	—	—	—	—	6	—	—
Norway / Norvège / Noruega	2003	—	—	—	—	—	—	—	4	—	17	—	—
	2004	—	—	—	—	—	—	—	2	—	18	—	—
	2005	—	—	—	—	—	—	—	4	—	14	—	—
Panama / Panamá	2003	—	6	—	—	—	—	—	4	—	—	—	1
	2004	—	1	—	—	—	—	—	2	—	—	—	—
	2005	—	1	—	—	—	—	—	4	—	—	—	—
Poland / Pologne / Polonia	2003	—	49	16	—	—	—	—	—	—	—	8	—
	2004	—	52	35	—	—	—	—	—	—	—	9	—
	2005	—	55	23	—	—	—	—	3	—	—	3	—
Portugal	2003	—	—	—	—	—	—	—	—	—	—	—	—
	2004	—	—	—	—	—	—	—	2	—	—	—	—
	2005	—	—	—	1	—	2	—	5	—	—	—	—

Romania / Roumanie / Rumania	2003	—	—	—	—	—	—	—	—	—	—	—	—
	2004	—	—	—	—	—	—	—	—	—	40	—	—
	2005	—	—	—	—	—	—	—	—	—	—	—	—
Russian Federation / Fédération de Russie / Federación de Rusia	2003	—	—	—	—	—	—	—	—	—	1	—	—
	2004	—	—	—	—	—	—	—	—	—	—	—	—
	2005	—	—	—	—	—	—	—	—	—	—	—	—
Singapore / Singapour / Singapur	2003	—	—	—	—	—	—	—	—	—	—	—	—
	2004	—	—	—	—	—	—	—	1	—	—	—	—
	2005	—	—	—	—	—	—	—	—	—	—	—	—
Slovakia / Slovaquie / Eslovaquia	2003	—	—	—	—	—	—	—	—	—	41	—	—
	2004	?	?	?	?	?	?	?	?	?	?	?	?
	2005	—	—	—	—	—	—	—	—	—	21	—	—
Slovenia / Slovénie / Eslovenia	2003	—	—	—	29	—	—	—	—	—	—	—	—
	2004	—	—	—	22	—	—	—	—	—	—	—	—
	2005	—	—	—	23	—	—	—	—	—	—	—	—
South Africa / Afrique du Sud / Sudáfrica	2003	—	—	—	—	—	—	—	—	—	1	—	—
	2004	—	—	—	—	—	—	—	1	—	—	—	—
	2005	—	—	—	—	—	—	—	1	—	—	—	—
Spain / Espagne / España	2003	6	7	—	622	—	—	202	4	—	139	—	—
	2004	—	1	—	814	—	—	218	2	—	134	—	—
	2005	—	7	—	1 171	—	1	226	—	—	205	—	—
Sweden / Suède / Suecia	2003	—	—	—	—	—	—	—	—	—	—	—	—
	2004	—	—	—	—	—	—	—	—	—	—	—	—
	2005	—	—	—	—	—	—	—	1	—	—	—	—
Switzerland / Suisse / Suiza	2003	116	2 350	—	1 797	—	—	10	2 672	—	130	538	14
	2004	152	2 586	—	1 572	—	—	10	2 577	—	141	525	15
	2005	105	2 712	—	1 617	—	—	11	898	—	30	522	10
Tunisia / Tunisie / Túnez	2003	—	—	—	—	—	—	—	—	—	—	—	—
	2004	—	—	—	—	—	—	—	1	—	—	—	—
	2005	—	—	—	—	—	—	—	—	—	—	—	—
United Kingdom / Royaume-Uni / Reino Unido	2003	—	108	—	169	—	9	3	7	—	25	2	—
	2004	—	103	—	171	—	6	2	6	—	69	3	—
	2005	—	10	—	151	—	7	2	2	—	115	40	10
United States / États-Unis / Estados Unidos	2003	—	—	—	22	—	—	—	1	—	—	—	77
	2004	—	1	—	—	—	—	—	2	—	—	—	101
	2005	—	—	—	—	—	—	—	—	—	—	—	102
Total	2003	387	5 752	212	6 583	—	80	1 466	5 036	6	4 203	23 932	287
	2004	463	6 119	96	5 516	—	61	1 840	5 108	15	4 026	18 458	206
	2005	380	6 800	341	6 821	—	71	2 126	3 507	6	3 930	16 671	205

Schedule IV. D.4. Benzodiazepines: sedative-hypnotics + anti-epileptics (continued)
Tableau IV. D.4. Benzodiazépines: sédatifs-hypnotiques + antiépileptiques (suite)
Lista IV. D.4. Benzodiazepinas: sedantes-hipnóticos + antiepilépticos (continuación)

Imports — Importations — Importaciones

Country or territory / Pays ou territoire / País o territorio	Year / Année / Año	Brotizolam (kg)	Clonazepam / Clonazépam (kg)	Estazolam (kg)	Flurazepam / Flurazépam (kg)	Haloxazolam (kg)	Loprazolam (kg)	Lormetazepam / Lormétazépam (kg)	Midazolam (kg)	Nimetazepam / Nimétazépam (kg)	Nitrazepam / Nitrazépam (kg)	Temazepam / Témazépam (kg)	Triazolam (kg)
Albania / Albanie / Albania	2003	—	—	—	—	—	—	—	—	—	—	—	—
	2004	—	1	—	—	—	—	—	—	—	—	—	—
	2005	—	1	—	—	—	—	—	—	—	—	—	—
Algeria / Algérie / Argelia	2003	—	77	—	—	—	—	—	—	—	—	—	—
	2004	—	30	—	—	—	—	—	—	—	—	—	—
	2005	—	69	—	—	—	—	—	1	—	3	—	—
Angola / Angola / Angola	2003	—	—	—	—	—	—	—	1	—	—	—	—
	2004	—	—	—	—	—	—	—	1	—	—	—	—
	2005	?	?	?	?	?	?	?	?	?	?	?	?
Argentina / Argentine / Argentina	2003	—	422	—	26	—	—	1	156	—	10	—	—
	2004	—	305	—	20	—	1	—	106	—	—	—	—
	2005	—	479	—	5	—	—	—	135	—	—	—	—
Australia / Australie / Australia	2003	—	40	—	—	—	—	1	66	—	110	1 323	18
	2004	—	44	—	—	—	—	1	32	—	150	960	5
	2005	—	87	—	—	—	—	—	27	—	51	1 053	10
Austria / Autriche / Austria	2003	3	3	—	—	—	—	—	266	—	21	—	4
	2004	2	3	—	—	—	—	—	160	—	12	—	4
	2005	3	5	—	—	—	—	—	127	—	11	—	5
Azerbaijan / Azerbaïdjan / Azerbaiyán	2003	—	—	—	—	—	—	—	—	—	—	—	—
	2004	—	1	—	—	—	—	—	—	—	—	—	—
	2005	—	—	—	1	—	—	—	—	—	—	5	—
Bahrain / Bahreïn / Bahrein	2003	—	—	—	—	—	—	—	1	—	—	—	—
	2004	—	—	—	—	—	—	—	1	—	—	—	—
	2005	—	—	—	—	—	—	—	1	—	1	—	—

Country	Year	1	2	3	4	5	6	7	8	9	10	11	12
Bangladesh	2003	—	—	—	—	70	—	—	—	—	—	10	—
	2004	—	—	—	—	—	—	—	—	—	—	—	—
	2005	—	—	—	—	91	—	—	—	—	—	55	—
Barbados / Barbade	2003	—	—	2	—	—	—	—	—	—	—	—	—
	2004	—	—	3	—	—	—	—	—	—	—	—	—
	2005	—	—	—	—	1	—	—	—	—	—	—	—
Belarus / Bélarus / Belarús	2003	—	—	8	—	—	—	—	—	—	—	2	2
	2004	—	—	8	—	—	—	—	—	—	—	1	2
	2005	—	—	5	—	—	—	—	—	—	—	1	2
Belgium / Belgique / Bélgica	2003	97	—	22	—	26	155	9	—	189	—	27	—
	2004	25	—	19	—	20	165	6	—	123	—	21	—
	2005	26	—	19	—	19	223	9	—	174	—	18	—
Benin / Bénin	2003	—	—	—	—	—	—	—	—	—	—	1	—
	2004	—	—	—	—	—	—	—	—	—	—	—	—
	2005	—	—	—	—	—	—	—	—	—	—	1	—
Bolivia / Bolivie	2003	—	—	—	—	—	—	—	—	—	—	3	—
	2004	—	—	—	—	1	—	—	—	—	—	3	—
	2005	—	—	—	—	10	—	—	—	—	—	3	—
Bosnia and Herzegovina / Bosnie-Herzégovine / Bosnia y Herzegovina	2003	—	—	11	—	1	—	—	—	2	—	—	—
	2004	—	—	11	—	—	—	—	—	3	—	—	—
	2005	?	?	?	?	?	?	?	?	?	?	?	?
Brazil / Brésil / Brasil	2003	—	—	114	—	502	—	—	—	364	12	641	—
	2004	—	—	68	—	758	—	—	—	2	14	612	—
	2005	—	—	106	—	587	—	—	—	—	24	934	—
Bulgaria / Bulgarie	2003	—	—	3	—	2	—	—	—	—	—	14	—
	2004	—	—	3	—	2	—	—	—	—	—	13	—
	2005	—	—	6	—	4	—	—	—	—	—	16	—
Burundi	2003	?	?	?	?	?	?	?	?	?	?	?	?
	2004	—	—	—	—	—	—	—	—	—	—	—	—
	2005	—	—	—	—	—	—	—	—	—	—	1	—
Cambodia / Cambodge / Camboya	2003	—	—	—	—	—	—	—	—	—	—	2	—
	2004	—	—	—	—	—	—	—	—	—	—	1	—
	2005	—	—	—	—	—	1	—	—	—	—	4	—
Canada / Canadá	2003	9	1 753	75	—	39	—	—	—	356	—	426	—
	2004	2	762	95	—	37	—	—	—	252	—	659	—
	2005	2	1 251	95	—	40	—	—	—	757	—	707	—
Chad / Tchad	2003	—	—	—	—	—	—	—	—	—	—	—	—
	2004	—	—	24	—	—	—	—	—	—	—	40	—
	2005	?	?	?	?	?	?	?	?	?	?	?	?

Schedule IV. D.4. Benzodiazepines: sedative-hypnotics + anti-epileptics (continued)
Tableau IV. D.4. Benzodiazépines: sédatifs-hypnotiques + antiépileptiques (suite)
Lista IV. D.4. Benzodiazepinas: sedantes-hipnóticos + antiepilépticos (continuación)

Imports — Importations — Importaciones (continued — suite — continuación)

Country or territory / Pays ou territoire / País o territorio	Year / Année / Año	Brotizolam	Clonazepam / Clonazépam	Estazolam	Flurazepam / Flurazépam	Haloxazolam	Loprazolam	Lor-metazepam / Lor-métazépam	Midazolam	Nimetazepam / Nimétazépam	Nitrazepam / Nitrazépam	Temazepam / Témazépam	Triazolam
		kg	kg	kg	kg	kg	kg	kg	kg	kg	kg	kg	kg
Chile / Chili	2003	—	60	—	—	—	—	—	62	—	—	—	—
	2004	—	71	—	—	—	—	—	61	—	—	—	—
	2005	—	109	—	—	—	—	—	81	—	—	—	—
China / Chine	2003	—	—	—	—	—	—	—	150	—	—	—	—
	2004	—	—	—	—	—	—	—	145	—	—	—	—
	2005	—	—	—	—	—	—	—	144	—	—	—	—
Hong Kong SAR of China / RAS de Hong Kong (Chine) / RAE de Hong Kong de China	2003	—	2	—	3	—	—	1	12	—	4	—	—
	2004	—	3	—	3	—	—	—	12	—	2	—	1
	2005	—	3	—	1	—	—	—	15	—	2	—	1
Macao SAR of China / RAS de Macao (Chine) / RAE de Macao de China	2003	—	—	—	—	—	—	—	1	—	—	—	1
	2004	—	—	—	1	—	—	—	1	—	—	—	1
	2005	—	—	—	—	—	—	—	1	—	—	—	1
Colombia / Colombie	2003	72	26	—	—	—	—	—	23	—	—	—	1
	2004	—	26	—	—	—	—	—	23	—	—	—	1
	2005	82	27	—	—	—	—	—	22	—	—	—	—
Costa Rica	2003	—	22	—	—	—	—	—	30	—	—	—	1
	2004	—	16	—	—	—	—	—	29	—	—	—	2
	2005	—	34	—	—	—	—	—	38	—	—	—	12
Côte d'Ivoire	2003	—	3	—	—	—	—	—	—	—	—	—	1
	2004	—	6	10	—	—	1	—	—	—	1	—	—
	2005	—	6	—	—	—	—	—	—	—	1	—	—
Croatia / Croatie / Croacia	2003	?	3	?	9	?	?	?	10	—	30	—	—
	2004	?	?	?	?	?	?	?	?	?	?	?	?
	2005	—	3	—	10	—	—	—	12	—	30	—	—

Country	Year												
Cuba	2003	—	13	—	—	—	—	—	3	—	450	—	—
	2004	—	—	—	—	—	—	—	7	—	300	—	—
	2005	—	15	—	—	—	—	—	7	—	550	—	—
Cyprus / **Chypre** / **Chipre**	2003	—	15	—	55	—	—	—	1	—	20	395	—
	2004	—	5	—	115	—	—	1	1	—	40	700	—
	2005	—	10	—	50	—	—	1	—	—	15	290	1
Czech Republic / **République tchèque** / **República Checa**	2003	—	26	—	—	—	—	—	45	—	41	—	—
	2004	—	27	—	—	—	—	—	60	—	42	—	—
	2005	—	26	—	—	—	—	—	30	—	21	—	—
Dem. Rep. of the Congo / **Rép. dém. du Congo** / **Rep. Dem. del Congo**	2003	—	—	—	—	—	—	—	—	—	—	—	—
	2004	—	10	—	—	—	—	3	1	—	—	—	—
	2005	—	60	—	—	—	—	2	—	—	—	—	—
Denmark / **Danemark** / **Dinamarca**	2003	—	22	—	2	—	—	1	16	—	208	—	5
	2004	—	13	—	2	—	—	1	6	—	58	—	—
	2005	—	16	—	2	—	—	1	9	—	107	—	—
Dominican Republic / **République dominicaine** / **República Dominicana**	2003	—	4	—	—	—	—	—	2	—	3	—	—
	2004	—	10	—	—	—	—	—	2	—	10	—	—
	2005	—	7	—	—	—	—	—	2	—	10	—	—
Ecuador / **Équateur**	2003	—	5	—	—	—	—	—	3	—	—	—	—
	2004	—	9	—	—	—	—	—	4	—	—	—	—
	2005	—	11	—	—	—	—	—	4	—	—	—	—
Egypt / **Égypte** / **Egipto**	2003	—	69	—	—	—	—	—	4	—	—	—	—
	2004	—	109	—	—	—	—	—	14	—	—	—	—
	2005	—	44	—	—	—	—	—	13	—	—	—	—
El Salvador	2003	—	5	—	—	—	—	—	6	—	—	—	—
	2004	—	4	—	—	—	—	—	5	—	—	—	—
	2005	—	8	—	—	—	—	—	8	—	—	—	—
Estonia / **Estonie**	2003	—	1	—	—	—	—	—	1	—	9	—	—
	2004	—	2	—	—	—	—	—	3	—	5	—	—
	2005	—	2	—	—	—	—	—	4	—	8	—	—
Finland / **Finlande** / **Finlandia**	2003	—	14	16	—	—	—	—	17	—	21	909	—
	2004	9	12	10	—	—	2	—	20	—	—	643	—
	2005	—	14	25	—	—	2	2	18	—	—	1 326	—
France / **Francia**	2003	—	386	—	—	—	—	253	440	—	77	191	—
	2004	—	427	—	—	—	—	429	307	—	84	321	—
	2005	—	366	—	—	—	—	500	317	—	54	275	—
French Polynesia / *Polynésie française* / *Polinesia Francesa*	2003	—	—	—	—	—	—	—	2	—	—	—	—
	2004	—	1	—	—	—	—	—	1	—	—	—	—
	2005	?	?	?	?	?	?	?	?	?	?	?	?

Schedule IV. D.4. Benzodiazepines: sedative-hypnotics + anti-epileptics (continued)
Tableau IV. D.4. Benzodiazépines: sédatifs-hypnotiques + antiépileptiques (suite)
Lista IV. D.4. Benzodiazepinas: sedantes-hipnóticos + antiepilépticos (continuación)

Imports — Importations — Importaciones (continued — suite — continuación)

Country or territory / Pays ou territoire / País o territorio	Year / Année / Año	Brotizolam (kg)	Clonazepam / Clonazépam (kg)	Estazolam (kg)	Flurazepam / Flurazépam (kg)	Haloxazolam (kg)	Loprazolam (kg)	Lormetazepam / Lormétazépam (kg)	Midazolam (kg)	Nimetazepam / Nimétazépam (kg)	Nitrazepam / Nitrazépam (kg)	Temazepam / Témazépam (kg)	Triazolam (kg)
Georgia / Géorgie	2003	—	1	—	—	—	—	—	—	—	—	—	—
	2004	—	1	—	—	—	—	—	—	—	—	—	—
	2005	—	1	—	—	—	—	—	—	—	—	—	—
Germany / Allemagne / Alemania	2003	117	39	—	694	—	—	128	379	—	124	1 447	1
	2004	151	28	—	259	—	1	150	425	—	274	1 072	1
	2005	110	47	—	500	—	—	175	592	—	169	966	1
Ghana	2003	?	?	?	?	?	?	?	?	?	?	?	?
	2004	—	—	—	—	—	—	—	1	—	—	—	—
	2005	—	—	—	—	—	—	—	1	—	—	—	—
Greece / Grèce / Grecia	2003	—	6	—	—	—	—	9	29	—	—	37	1
	2004	—	7	—	—	—	—	8	30	—	—	40	1
	2005	—	7	—	—	—	—	14	35	—	—	10	—
Guatemala	2003	—	2	—	—	—	3	—	4	—	—	—	—
	2004	?	?	?	?	?	?	?	?	?	?	?	?
	2005	?	?	?	?	?	?	?	?	?	?	?	?
Guyana	2003	—	—	—	1	—	—	—	—	—	1	—	—
	2004	?	?	?	?	?	?	?	?	?	?	?	?
	2005	—	—	—	—	—	—	—	—	—	—	—	—
Haiti / Haïti / Haití	2003	—	—	—	—	—	—	—	—	—	—	—	—
	2004	—	—	—	—	—	—	—	1	—	—	—	—
	2005	—	—	—	—	—	—	—	—	—	—	—	—
Honduras	2003	—	3	—	—	—	—	—	4	—	—	—	1
	2004	—	3	—	—	—	—	—	3	—	—	—	—
	2005	?	?	?	?	?	?	?	?	?	?	?	?

224

Country	Year												
Hungary / Hongrie / Hungría	2003	1	87	—	—	—	—	—	256	—	100	• 1 080	—
	2004	1	117	—	—	—	—	—	182	—	138	405	—
	2005	1	97	—	—	—	—	—	191	—	130	554	—
Iceland / Islande / Islandia	2003	—	1	—	2	—	—	—	—	—	2	—	—
	2004	—	1	—	2	—	—	—	—	—	1	—	—
	2005	—	1	—	2	—	—	—	—	—	1	—	—
India / Inde	2003	—	53	—	—	—	—	—	4	—	—	—	—
	2004	—	75	—	—	—	—	—	—	—	—	—	—
	2005	—	20	—	—	—	—	—	2	—	6	—	—
Indonesia / Indonésie	2003	—	2	9	—	—	—	—	3	—	3	—	—
	2004	—	1	7	7	—	—	—	5	—	3	—	—
	2005	—	2	6	5	—	—	—	5	—	5	—	—
Iran (Islamic Rep. of) / Iran (Rép. islamique d') / Irán (Rep. Islámica del)	2003	—	188	—	—	—	—	—	3	—	—	—	3
	2004	—	355	—	—	—	—	—	7	—	—	—	1
	2005	—	220	—	—	—	—	—	3	—	—	—	1
Ireland / Irlande / Irlanda	2003	—	1	—	177	—	—	152	16	—	10	2 460	—
	2004	—	2	—	157	—	13	184	8	—	58	32	—
	2005	—	2	—	175	—	8	114	6	—	59	415	—
Israel / Israël	2003	6	251	—	—	—	—	—	15	—	15	—	—
	2004	8	—	—	—	—	—	—	20	30	30	—	—
	2005	8	6	—	—	—	—	—	15	—	30	—	—
Italy / Italie / Italia	2003	6	270	22	199	—	—	190	22	—	47	566	21
	2004	9	343	16	288	—	—	203	25	—	31	100	14
	2005	9	251	20	91	—	—	181	29	—	3	129	21
Jamaica / Jamaïque	2003	—	—	—	—	—	—	—	2	—	—	—	—
	2004	—	—	—	—	—	—	—	1	—	—	—	—
	2005	1	—	—	1	—	—	—	1	—	—	—	—
Japan / Japon / Japón	2003	119	121	3	163	—	—	63	120	—	830	—	104
	2004	117	151	13	171	—	—	55	110	—	1 620	—	110
	2005	749	250	12	161	—	—	36	93	—	1 200	—	88
Jordan / Jordanie / Jordania	2003	—	2	—	—	—	—	—	2	—	—	—	—
	2004	—	3	—	—	—	—	—	3	—	—	—	—
	2005	—	6	—	—	—	—	—	4	—	—	—	—
Kazakhstan / Kazajstán	2003	—	1	—	—	—	—	—	—	2 370	2	—	—
	2004	—	—	—	—	—	—	—	—	—	—	—	—
	2005	—	—	—	—	—	—	—	—	—	—	—	—
Kenya	2003	~	1	~	~	~	~	~	4	~	~	~	~
	2004	~	—	~	~	~	~	~	3	~	~	~	~
	2005	~	~	~	~	~	~	~	~	~	~	~	~

Schedule IV. D.4. Benzodiazepines: sedative-hypnotics + anti-epileptics (continued)
Tableau IV. D.4. Benzodiazépines: sédatifs-hypnotiques + antiépileptiques (suite)
Lista IV. D.4. Benzodiazepinas: sedantes-hipnóticos + antiepilépticos (continuación)

Imports — Importations — Importaciones (continued — suite — continuación)

Country or territory / Pays ou territoire / País o territorio	Year / Année / Año	Brotizolam (kg)	Clonazepam / Clonazépam (kg)	Estazolam (kg)	Flurazepam / Flurazépam (kg)	Haloxazolam (kg)	Loprazolam (kg)	Lor-metazepam / Lor-métazépam (kg)	Midazolam (kg)	Nimetazepam / Nimétazépam (kg)	Nitrazepam / Nitrazépam (kg)	Temazepam / Témazépam (kg)	Triazolam (kg)
Kuwait / Koweït	2003	—	—	—	—	—	—	—	1	—	—	—	—
	2004	—	1	—	—	—	—	—	2	—	1	—	—
	2005	—	1	—	—	—	—	—	—	—	—	—	—
Kyrgyzstan / Kirghizistan / Kirguistán	2003	—	—	—	—	—	—	—	—	—	—	—	—
	2004	—	1	—	—	—	—	—	—	—	—	—	—
	2005	—	1	—	—	—	—	—	—	—	—	—	—
Lao People's Dem. Rep. / Rép. dém. populaire lao / Rep. dem. Popular Lao	2003	—	—	—	—	—	—	—	—	—	—	—	—
	2004	—	—	—	—	—	—	—	2	—	—	—	—
	2005	—	—	—	—	—	—	—	—	—	—	—	—
Latvia / Lettonie / Letonia	2003	—	14	—	—	—	—	—	3	—	16	—	—
	2004	—	15	—	—	—	—	—	6	—	6	—	—
	2005	—	14	—	—	—	—	—	4	—	7	—	—
Lebanon / Liban / Líbano	2003	—	3	—	—	—	—	—	3	—	—	—	—
	2004	—	4	—	—	—	—	—	4	—	—	—	—
	2005	—	4	—	—	—	—	—	3	—	—	—	—
Libyan Arab Jamahiriya / Jamahiriya arabe libyenne / Jamahiriya Árabe Libia	2003	—	1	—	—	—	—	—	1	—	1	—	—
	2004	—	1	—	—	—	—	—	2	—	2	—	—
	2005	—	1	—	—	—	—	—	2	—	2	—	—
Lithuania / Lituanie / Lituania	2003	—	23	—	—	—	—	—	3	—	17	1	—
	2004	—	28	—	—	—	—	—	2	—	17	—	—
	2005	—	21	—	—	—	—	—	2	—	16	—	—
Luxembourg / Luxemburgo	2003	—	—	—	—	—	—	—	—	—	—	—	—
	2004	?	?	?	?	?	?	?	?	?	?	?	?
	2005	—	1	—	—	—	1	4	2	—	—	—	—

Malaysia	2003	—	3	—	—	—	—	—	109	—	5	—	—
Malaisie	2004	—	2	—	1	—	—	—	260	—	5	—	1
Malasia	2005	—	6	—	1	—	—	—	263	—	—	—	—
Mali	2003	—	—	—	—	—	—	—	—	—	—	—	—
Malí	2004	—	—	—	—	—	—	—	—	—	—	—	—
	2005	—	1	—	—	—	—	—	—	—	—	—	—
Malta	2003	—	—	—	4	—	—	—	1	—	3	1	—
Malte	2004	—	—	—	5	—	—	—	—	—	2	1	—
	2005	—	—	—	—	—	—	—	—	—	3	3	—
Mauritius	2003	—	1	—	—	—	—	—	—	—	2	—	—
Maurice	2004	—	1	—	—	—	—	—	—	—	2	—	—
Mauricio	2005	—	1	—	—	—	—	—	—	—	2	—	—
Mexico	2003	38	216	10	—	—	—	—	27	—	—	—	3
Mexique	2004	—	324	15	—	—	—	—	63	—	—	—	3
México	2005	?	?	?	?	?	?	?	?	?	?	?	?
Morocco	2003	—	—	—	—	—	—	—	1	—	—	—	—
Maroc	2004	—	—	—	—	—	—	—	2	—	—	—	—
Marruecos	2005	—	—	—	—	—	—	—	1	—	—	—	—
Namibia	2003	—	—	—	—	—	—	—	—	—	—	—	—
Namibie	2004	—	—	—	—	—	—	—	—	—	—	—	—
	2005	—	—	—	—	—	—	—	1	—	—	—	—
Nepal	2003	—	25	—	—	—	—	—	—	—	—	—	—
Népal	2004	—	—	—	—	—	—	—	—	—	—	—	—
	2005	?	?	?	?	?	?	?	?	?	?	?	?
Netherlands	2003	—	10	16	304	—	1	78	461	—	175	1 332	—
Pays-Bas	2004	—	14	16	240	—	2	81	427	—	118	1 331	—
Países Bajos	2005	—	14	22	166	—	1	135	223	—	107	1 177	—
Netherlands Antilles	2003	—	—	—	—	—	—	—	2	—	—	—	—
Antilles néerlandaises	2004	—	—	—	—	—	—	—	2	—	—	—	—
Antillas Neerlandesas	2005	—	—	—	—	—	—	—	2	—	—	—	—
New Caledonia	2003	—	—	—	—	—	—	—	1	—	—	—	—
Nouvelle-Calédonie	2004	?	?	?	?	?	?	?	?	?	?	?	?
Nueva Caledonia	2005	—	—	—	—	—	—	23	—	—	—	—	—
New Zealand	2003	—	4	—	—	—	—	—	7	—	4	49	1
Nouvelle-Zélande	2004	—	5	—	—	—	—	—	6	—	13	71	1
Nueva Zelandia	2005	—	5	—	—	—	—	—	8	—	13	69	1
Nicaragua	2003	—	1	—	—	—	—	—	7	—	—	—	—
	2004	—	1	—	—	—	—	—	7	—	—	—	—
	2005	—	3	—	—	—	—	—	8	—	—	—	—

Schedule IV. D.4. Benzodiazepines: sedative-hypnotics + anti-epileptics (continued)
Tableau IV. D.4. Benzodiazépines: sédatifs-hypnotiques + antiépileptiques (suite)
Lista IV. D.4. Benzodiazepinas: sedantes-hipnóticos + antiepilépticos (continuación)

Imports — Importations — Importaciones (continued — suite — continuación)

Country or territory / Pays ou territoire / País o territorio	Year / Année / Año	Brotizolam	Clonazepam / Clonazépam	Estazolam	Flurazepam / Flurazépam	Haloxazolam	Loprazolam	Lormetazepam / Lormétazépam	Midazolam	Nimetazepam / Nimétazépam	Nitrazepam / Nitrazépam	Temazepam / Témazépam	Triazolam
		kg	kg	kg	kg	kg	kg	kg	kg	kg	kg	kg	kg
Nigeria / Nigéria	2003	—	—	—	—	—	—	—	—	—	112	—	—
	2004	—	—	—	—	—	—	—	—	—	102	—	—
	2005	—	—	—	—	—	—	—	—	—	—	—	—
Norway / Norvège / Noruega	2003	—	9	—	—	—	—	—	6	—	43	—	—
	2004	—	8	—	—	—	—	—	4	—	162	—	—
	2005	—	11	—	—	—	—	—	6	—	14	—	—
Oman / Omán	2003	—	—	—	—	—	—	—	1	—	—	—	—
	2004	—	—	—	—	—	—	—	1	—	—	—	—
	2005	—	1	—	—	—	—	—	2	—	—	—	—
Pakistan / Pakistán	2003	—	—	5	—	—	—	16	33	—	10	32	—
	2004	—	—	3	—	—	—	14	33	—	12	20	—
	2005	—	10	5	—	—	—	14	51	—	12	612	—
Panama / Panamá	2003	—	7	—	—	—	1	—	7	—	—	—	—
	2004	—	2	—	—	—	1	—	8	—	—	—	—
	2005	—	3	—	—	—	1	—	6	—	—	—	—
Paraguay	2003	—	7	—	—	—	—	—	3	—	—	—	—
	2004	?	?	?	?	?	?	?	?	?	?	?	?
	2005	?	?	?	?	?	?	?	?	?	?	?	?
Peru / Pérou / Perú	2003	—	13	—	—	—	—	—	3	—	—	—	—
	2004	—	24	—	—	—	—	—	8	—	—	—	—
	2005	—	29	—	—	—	—	—	12	—	—	—	—
Philippines / Filipinas	2003	—	5	—	20	—	—	—	21	—	—	—	—
	2004	—	5	1	—	—	—	—	19	—	—	—	—
	2005	?	?	?	?	?	?	?	?	?	?	?	?

Country	Year	1	2	3	4	5	6	7	8	9	10	11	12
Poland / Pologne / Polonia	2003	—	1	—	—	—	—	—	52	—	150	—	—
	2004	—	3	—	—	—	—	—	71	—	100	—	—
	2005	—	4	52	—	—	7	—	75	—	100	125	—
Portugal	2003	2	10	40	143	—	2	1	129	—	—	65	1
	2004	2	8	40	97	—	2	1	102	—	—	52	1
	2005	2	21	40	193	—	10	1	102	—	15	2	1
Qatar	2003	—	—	—	—	—	—	—	—	—	—	—	—
	2004	—	—	—	—	—	—	—	1	—	—	—	—
	2005	—	—	—	—	—	—	—	1	—	—	—	—
Republic of Korea / République de Corée / República de Corea	2003	6	12	1	46	—	—	—	9	—	—	90	14
	2004	36	15	2	100	—	—	—	17	—	—	242	4
	2005	14	16	—	82	—	—	—	516	—	—	116	1
Republic of Moldova / République de Moldova / República de Moldova	2003	—	1	—	—	—	—	—	—	—	3	—	—
	2004	—	—	—	—	—	—	—	—	—	1	—	—
	2005	?	?	?	?	?	?	?	?	?	?	?	?
Romania / Roumanie / Rumania	2003	—	6	—	—	—	—	—	13	—	75	—	—
	2004	—	14	—	—	—	—	—	22	—	155	—	—
	2005	—	—	—	—	—	—	—	—	—	—	—	—
Russian Federation / Fédération de Russie / Federación de Rusia	2003	—	20	—	—	—	—	—	2	—	3	3	—
	2004	—	15	—	—	—	—	—	5	—	13	2	—
	2005	—	—	—	—	—	—	—	—	—	—	—	—
Rwanda	2003	—	1	—	—	—	—	—	—	—	—	—	—
	2004	—	—	—	—	—	—	—	—	—	—	—	—
	2005	—	—	—	—	—	—	—	—	—	—	—	—
Saint Vincent and the Grenadines / Saint-Vincent-et-les-Grenadines / San Vicente y las Granadinas	2003	—	—	—	—	—	—	—	—	—	—	—	—
	2004	—	—	—	—	—	—	—	—	—	—	—	—
	2005	—	1	—	—	—	—	—	4	—	—	—	—
Samoa	2003	?	?	?	?	?	?	?	?	?	?	?	?
	2004	?	?	?	?	?	?	?	?	?	?	?	?
	2005	—	—	—	—	—	1	—	—	—	—	—	1
Saudi Arabia / Arabie saoudite / Arabia Saudita	2003	—	6	—	—	—	—	—	7	—	—	1	—
	2004	—	6	—	—	—	—	—	6	—	—	—	—
	2005	—	1	—	—	—	—	—	4	—	—	1	—
Senegal / Sénégal	2003	—	2	—	—	—	—	—	—	—	—	—	—
	2004	—	—	—	—	—	—	—	—	—	—	—	—
	2005	—	2	—	—	—	—	—	—	—	—	—	—

Schedule IV. D.4. Benzodiazepines: sedative-hypnotics + anti-epileptics *(continued)*
Tableau IV. D.4. Benzodiazépines: sédatifs-hypnotiques + antiépileptiques *(suite)*
Lista IV. D.4. Benzodiazepinas: sedantes-hipnóticos + antiepilépticos *(continuación)*

Imports — Importations — Importaciones *(continued — suite — continuación)*

Country or territory / Pays ou territoire / País o territorio	Year / Année / Año	Brotizolam (kg)	Clonazepam / Clonazépam (kg)	Estazolam (kg)	Flurazepam / Flurazépam (kg)	Haloxazolam (kg)	Loprazolam (kg)	Lormetazepam / Lormétazépam (kg)	Midazolam (kg)	Nimetazepam / Nimétazépam (kg)	Nitrazepam / Nitrazépam (kg)	Temazepam / Témazépam (kg)	Triazolam (kg)
Serbia and Montenegro / Serbie-et-Monténégro / Serbia y Montenegro	2003	—	8	—	—	—	—	—	69	—	—	—	—
	2004	?	?	?	?	?	?	?	?	?	?	?	?
	2005	?	?	?	?	?	?	?	?	?	?	?	?
Sierra Leone / Sierra Leona	2003	—	—	—	—	—	—	—	—	—	1	—	—
	2004	?	?	?	?	?	?	?	?	?	?	?	?
	2005	—	—	—	—	—	—	—	—	—	—	—	—
Singapore / Singapour / Singapur	2003	—	1	—	7	—	—	1	32	2	9	—	—
	2004	—	1	—	6	—	—	1	30	2	10	—	—
	2005	—	1	—	3	—	—	—	30	2	11	—	—
Slovakia / Slovaquie / Eslovaquia	2003	—	4	—	—	—	—	—	3	—	85	—	—
	2004	?	?	?	?	?	?	?	?	?	?	?	?
	2005	—	6	—	—	—	—	—	6	—	—	—	—
Slovenia / Slovénie / Eslovenia	2003	—	1	—	50	—	—	—	24	—	3	—	—
	2004	—	1	—	50	—	—	—	19	—	3	—	—
	2005	—	1	—	—	—	—	—	27	—	2	—	—
South Africa / Afrique du Sud / Sudáfrica	2003	—	15	—	5	—	9	1	55	—	13	54	1
	2004	—	20	—	3	—	3	1	55	—	23	26	1
	2005	—	20	—	4	—	9	—	82	—	21	72	2
Spain / Espagne / España	2003	4	106	—	952	—	12	362	155	—	—	—	1
	2004	1	110	—	1 149	—	29	780	279	—	—	—	141
	2005	1	123	—	1 452	—	6	645	194	—	—	—	1
Sri Lanka	2003	—	..	—	—	—	—	—	..	—	..	—	—
	2004	—	7	—	—	—	—	—	1	—	2	—	—
	2005	—	12	—	—	—	—	—	2	—	3	—	—

Country	Year												
Sweden / Suède / Suecia	2003	—	—	18	—	4	—	—	—	—	—	6	—
	2004	—	—	70	—	5	—	—	—	—	—	8	—
	2005	—	—	41	—	4	—	—	—	—	—	6	—
Switzerland / Suisse / Suiza	2003	15	991	150	—	258	14	—	—	1 725	—	395	120
	2004	16	633	122	—	255	18	—	—	1 529	—	370	156
	2005	12	168	40	—	293	13	—	—	1 722	—	458	145
Syrian Arab Republic / République arabe syrienne / República Árabe Siria	2003	—	—	—	—	36	—	—	—	—	—	5	—
	2004	—	—	3	—	46	—	—	—	—	—	5	—
	2005	—	—	8	—	45	—	—	—	—	—	25	—
Thailand / Thaïlande / Tailandia	2003	—	20	1	—	37	—	—	—	—	—	31	—
	2004	—	20	3	—	18	—	—	—	—	—	21	—
	2005	—	—	—	—	32	—	—	—	—	—	27	—
The former Yugoslav Rep. of Macedonia / L'ex-Rép. yougoslave de Macédoine / La ex Rep. Yugoslava de Macedonia	2003	—	—	1	—	4	—	—	—	4	—	—	—
	2004	—	—	1	—	1	—	—	—	7	—	—	—
	2005	—	—	—	—	—	—	—	—	7	—	1	—
Trinidad and Tobago / Trinité-et-Tobago / Trinidad y Tobago	2003	—	—	—	—	1	—	—	—	—	—	—	—
	2004	—	—	—	—	1	—	—	—	—	—	—	—
	2005	—	—	—	—	1	—	—	—	—	—	1	—
Tunisia / Tunisie / Túnez	2003	—	—	—	—	2	—	—	—	—	—	2	—
	2004	—	—	—	—	8	—	—	—	—	—	2	—
	2005	—	—	—	—	5	—	—	—	—	—	1	—
Turkey / Turquie / Turquía	2003	—	—	—	—	10	—	—	—	—	—	21	—
	2004	—	—	—	—	75	—	—	—	—	—	24	11
	2005	—	—	—	—	19	—	—	—	—	—	14	—
Ukraine / Ucrania	2003	—	—	—	—	—	—	—	—	—	—	2	—
	2004	—	—	22	—	—	—	—	—	—	—	—	—
	2005	—	—	—	—	—	—	—	—	—	—	1	—
United Arab Emirates / Émirats arabes unis / Emiratos Árabes Unidos	2003	—	—	—	—	5	—	—	—	—	—	1	—
	2004	—	—	—	—	5	—	—	—	—	—	1	—
	2005	—	—	—	—	5	—	—	—	—	—	1	—
United Kingdom / Royaume-Uni / Reino Unido	2003	—	2 679	409	—	23	12	33	—	181	—	118	—
	2004	1	1 176	315	—	43	11	5	—	221	—	171	—
	2005	10	864	317	—	27	4	—	—	172	—	21	—
United Rep. of Tanzania / Rép.-Unie de Tanzanie / Rep. Unida de Tanzanía	2003	—	—	—	—	—	—	—	—	—	—	—	—
	2004	—	—	—	—	103	—	—	—	—	—	—	—
	2005	—	—	—	—	—	—	—	—	—	—	—	—

Schedule IV. D.4. Benzodiazepines: sedative-hypnotics + anti-epileptics (concluded)
Tableau IV. D.4. Benzodiazépines: sédatifs-hypnotiques + antiépileptiques (fin)
Lista IV. D.4. Benzodiazepinas: sedantes-hipnóticos + antiepilépticos (conclusión)

Country or territory / Pays ou territoire / País o territorio	Year / Année / Año	Brotizolam (kg)	Clonazepam / Clonazépam (kg)	Estazolam (kg)	Flurazepam / Flurazépam (kg)	Haloxazolam (kg)	Loprazolam (kg)	Lormetazepam / Lormétazépam (kg)	Midazolam (kg)	Nimetazepam / Nimétazépam (kg)	Nitrazepam / Nitrazépam (kg)	Temazepam / Témazépam (kg)	Triazolam (kg)
United States / États-Unis / Estados Unidos	2003	—	973	46	451	—	—	—	330	—	—	7 846	5
	2004	—	940	11	626	—	—	—	329	—	1	16 890	6
	2005	—	1 240	30	788	—	—	—	436	—	2	7 032	6
Uzbekistan / Ouzbékistan / Uzbekistán	2003	—	—	—	—	—	—	—	3	—	—	—	—
	2004	—	—	—	—	—	—	—	1	—	—	—	—
	2005	—	—	—	—	—	—	—	3	—	1	—	—
Venezuela (Bolivarian Rep. of) / Venezuela (Rép. bolivarienne du) / Venezuela (Rep. Bolivariana de)	2003	—	8	—	—	—	—	—	5	—	—	—	—
	2004	—	39	—	—	—	—	—	12	—	8	—	—
	2005	—	22	—	55	—	—	—	25	—	—	—	—
Viet Nam	2003	—	—	—	—	—	—	—	1	—	—	—	—
	2004	—	1	—	—	—	—	—	1	—	—	—	—
	2005	—	—	—	—	—	—	—	2	—	—	—	—
Yemen / Yémen	2003	—	1	—	—	—	—	—	2	—	—	—	—
	2004	—	1	—	—	—	—	—	1	—	2	—	—
	2005	—	—	—	—	—	—	—	—	—	—	—	—
Zambia / Zambie	2003	—	—	—	—	—	—	—	—	—	—	—	—
	2004	—	—	—	—	—	—	—	—	—	1	—	—
	2005	—	—	—	—	—	—	—	—	—	—	—	—
Zimbabwe	2003	—	—	—	—	—	—	—	—	—	—	—	—
	2004	—	—	—	—	—	—	—	—	—	1	—	—
	2005	—	—	—	—	—	—	—	—	—	—	—	—
Total	2003	496	5 472	180	6 084	—	70	1 439	4 794	2 372	3 596	23 325	306
	2004	505	5 789	158	5 440	—	65	2 107	5 010	32	4 376	25 499	345
	2005	1 126	6 205	236	6 629	—	48	2 096	5 296	2	3 537	16 515	202

Schedule IV. D.5. Sedative-hypnotics + barbiturate-type anti-epileptics
Tableau IV. D.5. Sédatifs-hypnotiques + antiépileptiques de type barbiturique
Lista IV. D.5. Sedantes-hipnóticos + antiepilépticos de tipo barbitúrico

Manufacture — Fabrication — Fabricación

Country / Pays / País	Year / Année / Año	Allobarbital / Alobarbital (kg)	Barbital (kg)	Butobarbital (kg)	Ethchlorvynol / Etclorvinol (kg)	Ethinamate / Éthinamate / Etinamato (kg)	Methylphenobarbital / Méthylphénobarbital / Metilfenobarbital (kg)	Methyprylon / Méthyprylone / Metiprilona (kg)	Phenobarbital / Phénobarbital / Fenobarbital (kg)	Secbutabarbital (kg)	Vinylbital / Vinilbital (kg)	Zolpidem (kg)
Argentina / Argentine	2003	—	—	—	—	—	—	—	—	—	—	991
	2004	—	—	—	—	—	—	—	—	—	—	—
	2005	—	—	—	—	—	—	—	—	—	—	—
Brazil / Brésil / Brasil	2003	—	103 456	—	—	—	—	—	4 947	—	—	17
	2004	—	100 151	—	—	—	—	—	8 794	—	—	112
	2005	—	109 001	—	—	—	—	—	10 149	—	—	148
China / Chine	2003	—	—	—	—	—	—	—	237 966	—	—	2 485
	2004	—	—	—	—	—	—	—	244 733	—	—	2 611
	2005	—	—	—	—	—	—	—	272 202	—	—	3 532
Czech Republic / République tchèque / República Checa	2003	—	—	—	—	—	—	—	—	—	—	—
	2004	—	—	—	—	—	—	—	—	—	—	—
	2005	—	—	—	—	—	—	—	—	—	—	—
France / Francia	2003	—	—	—	—	—	—	—	—	—	—	30 596
	2004	—	—	—	—	—	—	—	—	—	—	22 281
	2005	—	—	—	—	—	—	—	—	—	—	27 760
Germany / Allemagne / Alemania	2003	—	—	—	—	—	—	—	1 166	—	—	—
	2004	1 182	—	—	—	—	—	—	3 005	128	—	—
	2005	878	—	—	—	—	—	—	2 156	—	—	—
Hungary / Hongrie / Hungría	2003	—	—	—	—	—	—	—	82 703	—	—	14
	2004	—	—	—	—	—	—	—	82 640	—	—	—
	2005	—	—	—	—	—	—	—	—	—	—	—
India / Inde	2003	—	—	—	—	—	—	—	—	—	—	—
	2004	—	—	—	—	—	485	—	30 567	—	—	833
	2005	—	—	—	—	—	735	—	35 070	—	—	709
Iraq	2003	—	—	—	—	—	—	—	208	—	—	—
	2004	?	?	?	?	?	?	?	?	?	?	?
	2005	?	?	?	?	?	?	?	?	?	?	?

Schedule IV. D.5. Sedative-hypnotics + barbiturate-type anti-epileptics (continued)
Tableau IV. D.5. Sédatifs-hypnotiques + antiépileptiques de type barbiturique (suite)
Lista IV. D.5. Sedantes-hipnóticos + antiepilépticos de tipo barbitúrico (continuación)

Manufacture — Fabrication — Fabricación (continued — suite — continuación)

Country / Pays / País	Year / Année / Año	Allobarbital / Alobarbital	Barbital	Butobarbital	Ethchlorvynol / Etclorvinol	Ethinamate / Éthinamate / Etinamato	Methylphenobarbital / Méthylphénobarbital / Metilfenobarbital	Methyprylon / Méthyprylone / Metiprilona	Phenobarbital / Phénobarbital / Fenobarbital	Secbutabarbital	Vinylbital / Vinilbital	Zolpidem
		kg	kg	kg	kg	kg	kg	kg	kg	kg	kg	kg
Israel / Israël	2003	—	—	—	—	—	—	—	—	—	—	11
	2004	—	—	—	—	—	—	—	—	—	—	24
	2005	—	—	—	—	—	—	—	—	—	—	72
Japan / Japon / Japón	2003	—	2 061	—	—	—	—	—	5 017	—	—	—
	2004	—	2 030	—	—	—	—	—	1 172	—	—	—
	2005	—	2 764	—	—	—	—	—	9 196	—	—	31
Kazakhstan / Kazajstán	2003	—	—	—	—	—	—	—	87	—	—	—
	2004	—	—	—	—	—	—	—	87	—	—	—
	2005	—	—	—	—	—	—	—	—	—	—	—
Russian Federation / Fédération de Russie / Federación de Rusia	2003	—	—	—	—	—	—	—	67 835	—	—	—
	2004	—	—	—	—	—	—	—	92 616	—	—	—
	2005	—	—	—	—	—	—	—	65 933	—	—	—
Spain / Espagne / España	2003	—	—	—	—	—	—	—	—	—	—	—
	2004	—	—	—	—	—	—	—	—	—	—	26
	2005	—	—	—	—	—	—	—	—	—	—	—
Switzerland / Suisse / Suiza	2003	—	—	—	—	—	—	—	—	—	—	—
	2004	—	—	—	—	—	2 910	—	—	—	—	—
	2005	—	—	—	—	—	584	—	—	—	—	—
United States / États-Unis / Estados Unidos	2003	—	2	—	—	—	792	—	2 650	—	—	102
	2004	—	—	—	—	—	417	—	—	—	—	—
	2005	—	—	—	—	—	300	—	—	—	—	106
Total	2003	—	105 519	—	—	—	792	—	402 579	128	—	34 216
	2004	1 182	102 181	—	—	—	3 812	—	463 614	—	—	25 887
	2005	878	111 771	—	—	—	1 619	—	395 314	—	—	32 359

234

Exports — Exportations — Exportaciones

		kg	kg	kg	kg	kg	kg	kg	kg	kg	kg	kg
Argentina .... Argentine	2003	873	—	—	76	—	—	—	—	—	4	—
	2004	11	—	—	119	—	—	—	—	—	—	—
	2005	—	—	—	—	—	—	—	—	—	—	—
Australia .... Australie	2003	—	—	—	6	—	—	—	—	—	—	—
	2004	—	—	—	6	—	—	—	—	—	—	—
	2005	—	—	—	15	—	—	—	—	—	—	—
Austria .... Autriche	2003	—	—	—	195	—	—	—	—	—	7	—
	2004	—	—	—	176	—	—	—	—	—	3	—
	2005	—	—	—	142	—	—	—	—	—	—	—
Barbados .... Barbade	2003	—	—	—	6	—	—	—	—	—	—	—
	2004	—	—	—	20	—	—	—	—	—	—	—
	2005	—	—	—	9	—	—	—	—	—	—	—
Belarus .... Bélarus .... Belarús	2003	—	—	—	—	—	—	—	—	—	—	—
	2004	—	—	—	500	—	—	—	—	—	—	—
	2005	—	—	—	—	—	—	—	—	—	—	—
Belgium .... Belgique .... Bélgica	2003	35	—	—	492	—	—	—	—	—	—	—
	2004	23	—	—	765	—	—	—	—	—	—	—
	2005	29	—	—	242	—	—	—	—	—	—	—
Brazil .... Brésil .... Brasil	2003	—	—	—	72	—	—	—	—	—	—	—
	2004	—	—	—	25	—	—	—	—	—	—	—
	2005	—	—	—	25	—	—	—	—	—	—	—
Bulgaria .... Bulgarie	2003	—	—	—	9	—	—	—	—	—	—	—
	2004	—	—	—	4	—	—	—	—	—	—	—
	2005	—	—	—	500	—	—	—	—	—	—	—
Canada .... Canadá	2003	—	—	—	200	—	—	—	—	—	—	—
	2004	—	—	—	—	—	—	—	—	—	—	—
	2005	—	—	—	—	—	—	—	—	—	—	—
Chile .... Chili	2003	—	—	—	2	—	—	—	—	—	—	—
	2004	—	—	—	1	—	—	—	—	—	—	3
	2005	4	—	—	—	—	—	—	—	—	—	—
China .... Chine	2003	—	—	—	97 232	—	—	—	—	—	11 500	—
	2004	—	—	—	143 331	—	—	—	—	—	7 800	—
	2005	2	—	—	168 542	—	—	—	—	—	12 175	—
Hong Kong SAR of China .... RAS de Hong Kong (Chine) RAE de Hong Kong de China	2003	1	—	—	1	—	—	—	—	—	—	—
	2004	1	—	—	1	—	—	—	—	—	—	—
	2005	1	—	—	1	—	—	—	—	—	—	—

Schedule IV. D.5. Sedative-hypnotics + barbiturate-type anti-epileptics (continued)
Tableau IV. D.5. Sédatifs-hypnotiques + antiépileptiques de type barbiturique (suite)
Lista IV. D.5. Sedantes-hipnóticos + antiepilépticos de tipo barbitúrico (continuación)

Exports — Exportations — Exportaciones (continued — suite — continuación)

Country or territory / Pays ou territoire / País o territorio	Year / Année / Año	Allo-barbital Alo-barbital	Barbital	Buto-barbital	Ethchlor-vynol Etclor-vinol	Ethinamate Éthinamate Etinamato	Methylpheno-barbital Méthylphéno-barbital Metifeno-barbital	Methy-prylon Méthy-prylone Meti-prilona	Pheno-barbital Phéno-barbital Feno-barbital	Secbuta-barbital	Vinylbital Vinilbital	Zolpidem
		kg	kg	kg	kg	kg	kg	kg	kg	kg	kg	kg
Costa Rica	2003	—	—	—	—	—	—	—	—	—	—	1
	2004	—	—	—	—	—	—	—	—	—	—	1
	2005	—	—	—	—	—	—	—	—	—	—	—
Croatia Croatie Croacia	2003	—	—	—	—	—	150	—	364	—	—	5
	2004	?	?	?	?	?	?	?	?	?	?	?
	2005	—	—	—	—	—	93	—	262	—	—	5
Cuba	2003	—	—	—	—	—	—	—	156	—	—	—
	2004	—	—	—	—	—	—	—	117	—	—	—
	2005	—	—	—	—	—	—	—	—	—	—	—
Cyprus Chypre Chipre	2003	—	—	—	—	—	—	—	38	—	—	—
	2004	—	—	—	—	—	—	—	23	—	—	—
	2005	—	—	—	—	—	—	—	98	—	—	—
Czech Republic République tchèque República Checa	2003	5	5	—	—	—	—	—	347	—	—	1 802
	2004	—	—	—	—	—	—	—	307	—	—	2 782
	2005	—	—	—	—	—	—	—	721	—	—	2 887
Denmark Danemark Dinamarca	2003	50	113	—	—	—	—	—	20 167	—	—	132
	2004	25	197	—	—	—	—	—	19 939	—	—	146
	2005	—	250	—	—	—	—	—	24 059	—	—	93
El Salvador	2003	—	—	—	—	—	—	—	3	—	—	—
	2004	—	—	—	—	—	—	—	2	—	—	—
	2005	—	—	—	—	—	—	—	—	—	—	—
Estonia Estonie	2003	—	—	—	—	—	—	—	—	—	—	—
	2004	—	—	—	—	—	—	—	—	—	—	1
	2005	—	—	—	—	—	—	—	2	—	—	—

Country	Year	(1)	(2)	(3)	(4)	(5)	(6)	(7)	(8)	(9)	(10)	(11)
France — Francia	2003	12 616	—	—	5 868	—	—	—	—	—	—	—
	2004	12 068	—	—	6 220	—	—	—	—	—	—	—
	2005	10 590	—	—	4 405	—	—	—	—	—	—	—
Germany — Allemagne — Alemania	2003	197	—	97	16 989	—	1 310	—	—	4	6 376	1 510
	2004	508	—	108	19 246	—	560	—	—	180	5 300	1 383
	2005	546	—	13	21 436	—	702	—	—	—	6 481	1 169
Greece — Grèce — Grecia	2003	36	—	—	—	—	—	—	—	—	—	—
	2004	74	—	—	—	—	—	—	—	—	—	—
	2005	67	—	—	—	—	—	—	—	—	—	—
Hungary — Hongrie — Hungría	2003	43	—	—	90 360	—	—	—	—	—	—	—
	2004	2	—	—	83 271	—	—	—	—	—	—	—
	2005	159	—	—	71 558	—	—	—	—	—	—	—
India — Inde	2003	9	—	—	8 956	—	1 310	—	—	—	—	—
	2004	593	—	—	18 033	—	560	—	—	31	—	—
	2005	520	—	—	25 301	—	702	—	—	6	—	—
Ireland — Irlande — Irlanda	2003	14	—	—	1 236	—	—	—	—	—	—	—
	2004	49	—	—	816	—	—	—	—	—	—	—
	2005	39	—	—	914	—	—	—	—	—	—	—
Israel — Israël	2003	10	—	—	12	—	—	—	—	—	—	—
	2004	7	—	—	9	—	—	—	—	—	—	—
	2005	81	—	—	—	—	—	—	—	—	—	—
Italy — Italie — Italia	2003	1	—	—	4	—	—	—	—	—	4	—
	2004	1	—	—	1	—	—	—	—	—	4	—
	2005	1	—	—	3	—	—	—	—	—	1	—
Japan — Japon — Japón	2003	—	—	—	—	—	—	—	—	—	—	—
	2004	—	—	—	—	—	—	—	—	—	—	—
	2005	3	—	—	—	—	—	—	—	—	—	—
Jordan — Jordanie — Jordania	2003	—	—	—	233	—	—	—	—	—	—	190
	2004	—	—	—	323	—	—	—	—	—	—	234
	2005	—	—	—	1 907	—	—	—	—	—	—	163
Latvia — Lettonie — Letonia	2003	1	—	—	—	—	—	—	—	—	—	—
	2004	—	—	—	—	—	—	—	—	—	—	—
	2005	—	—	—	186	—	—	—	—	—	—	—
Lithuania — Lituanie — Lituania	2003	—	—	—	62	—	—	—	—	—	—	—
	2004	—	—	—	312	—	—	—	—	—	—	—
	2005	—	—	—	51	—	—	—	—	—	—	—
Malaysia — Malaisie — Malasia	2003	—	—	—	—	—	—	—	—	—	—	—
	2004	—	—	—	—	—	—	—	—	—	—	—
	2005	—	—	—	4	—	—	—	—	—	—	—

Schedule IV. D.5. Sedative-hypnotics + barbiturate-type anti-epileptics (continued)
Tableau IV. D.5. Sédatifs-hypnotiques + antiépileptiques de type barbiturique (suite)
Lista IV. D.5. Sedantes-hipnóticos + antiepilépticos de tipo barbitúrico (continuación)

Exports — Exportations — Exportaciones (continued — suite — continuación)

Country or territory / Pays ou territoire / Pais o territorio	Year / Année / Año	Allobarbital / Alobarbital (kg)	Barbital (kg)	Butobarbital (kg)	Ethchlorvynol / Etclorvinol (kg)	Ethinamate / Éthinamate / Etinamato (kg)	Methylphenobarbital / Méthylphénobarbital / Metilfenobarbital (kg)	Methyprylon / Méthyprylone / Metiprilona (kg)	Phenobarbital / Phénobarbital / Fenobarbital (kg)	Secbutabarbital (kg)	Vinylbital / Vinilbital (kg)	Zolpidem (kg)
Malta / Malte	2003	—	—	—	—	—	—	—	1 752	—	—	572
	2004	—	—	—	—	—	—	—	—	—	—	1 160
	2005	—	—	—	—	—	—	—	—	—	—	65
Netherlands / Pays-Bas / Países Bajos	2003	—	3	—	—	—	—	—	5 485	—	—	—
	2004	8	4	18	—	—	—	—	2 968	—	—	—
	2005	6	1	7	—	—	—	—	1 732	—	—	—
New Zealand / Nouvelle-Zélande / Nueva Zelandia	2003	—	—	—	—	—	—	—	3	—	—	—
	2004	—	—	—	—	—	—	—	3	—	—	—
	2005	—	—	—	—	—	—	—	2	—	—	—
Norway / Norvège / Noruega	2003	—	—	—	—	—	—	—	—	—	—	22
	2004	—	—	—	—	—	—	—	—	—	—	38
	2005	—	—	—	—	—	—	—	—	—	—	51
Panama / Panamá	2003	—	—	—	—	—	—	—	—	—	—	33
	2004	—	—	—	—	—	—	—	—	—	—	43
	2005	—	—	—	—	—	—	—	—	—	—	31
Paraguay	2003	—	—	—	—	—	—	—	—	—	—	9
	2004	?	?	?	?	?	?	?	?	?	?	?
	2005	?	?	?	?	?	?	?	?	?	?	?
Poland / Pologne / Polonia	2003	—	—	—	—	—	—	—	28	—	—	—
	2004	—	—	—	—	—	—	—	55	—	—	—
	2005	—	—	—	—	—	—	—	—	—	—	—
Portugal	2003	—	—	—	—	—	—	—	35	—	—	—
	2004	—	—	—	—	—	—	—	74	—	—	—
	2005	—	—	—	—	—	—	—	77	—	—	1

Country	Year	(1)	(2)	(3)	(4)	(5)	(6)	(7)	(8)	(9)	(10)	(11)
Romania / Roumanie / Rumania	2003	—	—	—	—	—	—	—	102	—	—	—
	2004	—	—	—	—	—	—	—	13	—	—	—
	2005	—	—	—	—	—	—	—	—	—	—	—
Russian Federation / Fédération de Russie / Federación de Rusia	2003	—	—	—	—	—	—	—	37	—	—	—
	2004	—	—	—	—	—	—	—	224	—	—	—
	2005	—	—	—	—	—	—	—	—	—	—	—
Serbia and Montenegro / Serbie-et-Monténégro / Serbia y Montenegro	2003	—	—	—	—	—	—	—	13	—	—	—
	2004	?	?	?	?	?	?	?	?	?	?	?
	2005	?	?	?	?	?	?	?	?	?	?	?
Singapore / Singapour / Singapur	2003	—	—	—	—	—	—	—	1 046	—	—	—
	2004	—	—	—	—	—	—	—	1 150	—	—	—
	2005	—	—	—	—	—	—	—	626	—	—	—
Slovakia / Slovaquie / Eslovaquia	2003	26	—	18	—	—	—	—	686	—	—	—
	2004	?	?	?	?	?	?	?	?	?	?	?
	2005	—	—	—	—	—	—	—	824	—	—	13
Slovenia / Slovénie / Eslovenia	2003	—	—	—	—	—	—	—	—	—	—	70
	2004	—	—	—	—	—	—	—	—	—	—	123
	2005	—	—	—	—	—	—	—	—	—	—	162
South Africa / Afrique du Sud / Sudáfrica	2003	—	—	—	—	—	—	—	24	—	—	2
	2004	—	1	—	—	—	—	—	136	—	—	2
	2005	—	—	—	—	—	—	—	13	—	—	—
Spain / Espagne / España	2003	—	94	—	—	—	—	—	11	—	—	1 460
	2004	—	2	—	—	—	—	—	8	—	—	2 237
	2005	—	87	—	—	—	—	—	5	—	—	3 184
Sweden / Suède / Suecia	2003	—	—	—	—	—	—	—	1	—	—	—
	2004	—	—	—	—	—	—	—	4	—	—	—
	2005	—	—	—	—	—	—	—	7	—	—	—
Switzerland / Suisse / Suiza	2003	405	67	—	—	—	951	—	25 701	2	—	—
	2004	470	22	—	—	—	1 446	—	32 397	25	—	—
	2005	200	65	—	—	—	982	—	40 515	13	—	—
Thailand / Thaïlande / Tailandia	2003	—	—	—	—	—	—	—	7	—	—	—
	2004	—	—	—	—	—	—	—	—	—	—	—
	2005	—	—	—	—	—	—	—	11	—	—	—
Ukraine / Ucrania	2003	—	—	—	—	—	—	—	75	—	—	—
	2004	—	—	—	—	—	—	—	—	—	—	—
	2005	—	—	—	—	—	—	—	—	—	—	—
United Kingdom / Royaume-Uni / Reino Unido	2003	—	34	—	—	—	—	—	12 664	—	—	—
	2004	—	8	—	—	—	—	—	5 083	—	—	—
	2005	—	23	—	—	—	—	—	3 539	38	—	2

Schedule IV. D.5. Sedative-hypnotics + barbiturate-type anti-epileptics (continued)
Tableau IV. D.5. Sédatifs-hypnotiques + antiépileptiques de type barbiturique (suite)
Lista IV. D.5. Sedantes-hipnóticos + antiepilépticos de tipo barbitúrico (continuación)

Exports — Exportations — Exportaciones (continued — suite — continuación)

Country or territory / Pays ou territoire / País o territorio	Year / Année / Año	Allobarbital / Allo-barbital / Alo-barbital (kg)	Barbital (kg)	Butobarbital (kg)	Ethchlorvynol / Etchlorvynol / Etclorvinol (kg)	Ethinamate / Éthinamate / Etinamato (kg)	Methylphenobarbital / Méthylphéno-barbital / Metilfenobarbital (kg)	Methyprylon / Méthyprylone / Metilprilona (kg)	Phenobarbital / Phéno-barbital / Feno-barbital (kg)	Secbutabarbital / Secbuta-barbital (kg)	Vinylbital / Vinilbital (kg)	Zolpidem (kg)
United States / États-Unis / Estados Unidos	2003	—	75	—	—	—	—	—	53	—	—	7
	2004	—	129	—	—	—	—	—	30	—	—	8
	2005	—	85	—	—	—	—	—	723	—	—	556
Total	2003	2 186	18 279	22	—	—	3 721	—	290 809	99	—	17 951
	2004	2 120	13 474	229	—	—	2 566	—	335 716	133	—	19 879
	2005	1 541	19 171	13	—	—	2 479	—	368 453	64	—	19 091

Imports — Importations — Importaciones

Country or territory / Pays ou territoire / País o territorio	Year / Année / Año	Allobarbital / Allo-barbital / Alo-barbital (kg)	Barbital (kg)	Butobarbital (kg)	Ethchlorvynol / Etchlorvynol / Etclorvinol (kg)	Ethinamate / Éthinamate / Etinamato (kg)	Methylphenobarbital / Méthylphéno-barbital / Metilfenobarbital (kg)	Methyprylon / Méthyprylone / Metilprilona (kg)	Phenobarbital / Phéno-barbital / Feno-barbital (kg)	Secbutabarbital / Secbuta-barbital (kg)	Vinylbital / Vinilbital (kg)	Zolpidem (kg)
Afghanistan / Afganistán	2003	?	?	?	?	?	?	?	?	?	?	?
	2004	—	—	—	—	—	—	—	6	—	—	—
	2005	?	?	?	?	?	?	?	?	?	?	?
Albania / Albanie	2003	—	100	—	—	—	—	—	129	—	—	1
	2004	—	100	—	—	—	—	—	129	—	—	1
	2005	—	100	—	—	—	—	—	129	—	—	—
Algeria / Algérie / Argelia	2003	—	—	—	—	—	—	—	1 915	—	—	—
	2004	—	5	—	—	—	—	—	609	—	—	—
	2005	—	—	—	—	—	—	—	1 928	—	—	—
Andorra / Andorre	2003	—	—	—	—	—	—	—	1	—	—	1
	2004	—	—	—	—	—	—	—	2	—	—	—
	2005	—	—	—	—	—	—	—	2	—	—	—
Angola	2003	—	—	—	—	—	—	—	60	—	—	1
	2004	—	—	—	—	—	—	—	38	—	—	—
	2005	?	?	?	?	?	?	?	?	?	?	?

Country	Year	(1)	(2)	(3)	(4)	(5)	(6)	(7)	(8)	(9)	(10)
Argentina / Argentine	2003	26	—	—	3 496	—	150	—	—	1	—
	2004	24	—	—	2 513	—	103	—	—	—	—
	2005	—	—	—	3 025	—	250	—	—	1	—
Australia / Australie	2003	82	—	—	695	—	—	—	—	35	—
	2004	116	—	—	768	—	—	—	—	14	—
	2005	136	—	—	775	—	—	—	—	34	—
Austria / Autriche	2003	—	—	—	241	—	1	—	—	30	—
	2004	—	—	—	229	—	—	—	—	3	—
	2005	68	—	—	247	—	—	—	—	5	—
Azerbaijan / Azerbaidjan / Azerbaiyán	2003	—	—	—	—	—	—	—	—	—	—
	2004	—	—	—	119	—	—	—	—	—	—
	2005	5	—	—	76	—	—	—	—	—	—
Bahrain / Bahreïn / Bahrein	2003	—	—	—	15	—	—	—	—	—	—
	2004	—	—	—	7	—	—	—	—	—	—
	2005	—	—	—	6	—	—	—	—	—	1
Barbados / Barbade	2003	—	—	—	21	—	—	—	—	—	—
	2004	—	—	—	28	—	—	—	—	—	—
	2005	—	—	—	7	—	—	—	—	—	—
Belarus / Bélarus / Belarús	2003	—	—	—	867	—	—	—	—	—	—
	2004	—	—	—	1 478	—	—	—	—	—	—
	2005	1	—	—	1 369	—	—	—	—	—	—
Belgium / Belgique / Bélgica	2003	343	—	—	845	—	—	—	—	6	8
	2004	426	—	—	1 812	—	—	—	3	5	6
	2005	453	—	—	1 266	—	—	—	7	8	—
Belize / Belice	2003	—	—	—	9	—	—	—	—	—	—
	2004	—	—	—	—	—	—	—	—	—	—
	2005	?	?	?	?	?	?	?	?	?	?
Benin / Bénin	2003	1	—	—	484	—	—	—	—	—	—
	2004	1	—	—	525	—	—	—	—	—	—
	2005	1	—	—	839	—	—	—	—	—	—
Bolivia / Bolivie	2003	—	—	—	26	—	—	—	—	—	—
	2004	5	—	—	104	—	—	—	—	—	—
	2005	4	—	—	128	—	—	—	—	—	—
Bosnia and Herzegovina / Bosnie-Herzégovine / Bosnia y Herzegovina	2003	—	—	—	136	—	40	—	—	—	—
	2004	3	—	—	89	—	31	—	—	—	—
	2005	?	?	?	?	?	?	?	?	?	?
Botswana	2003	?	?	?	?	?	?	?	?	?	?
	2004	?	?	?	?	?	?	?	?	?	?
	2005	—	—	—	3	—	—	—	—	—	—

Schedule IV. D.5. Sedative-hypnotics + barbiturate-type anti-epileptics (continued)
Tableau IV. D.5. Sédatifs-hypnotiques + antiépileptiques de type barbiturique (suite)
Lista IV. D.5. Sedantes-hipnóticos + antiepilépticos de tipo barbitúrico (continuación)

Imports — Importations — Importaciones (continued — suite — continuación)

Country or territory / Pays ou territoire / País o territorio	Year / Année / Año	Allobarbital / Alobarbital (kg)	Barbital (kg)	Butobarbital (kg)	Ethchlorvynol / Etclorvinol (kg)	Ethinamate / Éthinamate / Etinamato (kg)	Methylphenobarbital / Méthylphénobarbital / Metilfenobarbital (kg)	Methyprylon / Méthyprylone / Metiprilona (kg)	Phenobarbital / Phénobarbital / Fenobarbital (kg)	Secbutabarbital (kg)	Vinylbital / Vinilbital (kg)	Zolpidem (kg)
Brazil / Brésil / Brasil	2003	—	1	—	—	—	—	—	22 677	—	—	9
	2004	—	—	—	—	—	—	—	39 850	—	—	76
	2005	—	—	—	—	—	—	—	35 775	—	—	120
Brunei Darussalam / Brunéi Darussalam	2003	—	—	—	—	—	—	—	—	—	—	—
	2004	—	—	—	—	—	—	—	1	—	—	—
	2005	—	—	—	—	—	—	—	1	—	—	1
Bulgaria / Bulgarie	2003	—	—	—	—	—	—	—	4 125	—	—	3
	2004	—	—	—	—	—	—	—	4 775	—	—	2
	2005	—	—	—	—	—	—	—	4 564	—	—	2
Burkina Faso	2003	—	—	—	—	—	—	—	444	—	—	—
	2004	—	—	—	—	—	—	—	—	—	—	—
	2005	—	—	—	—	—	—	—	674	—	—	—
Burundi	2003	?	?	?	?	?	?	?	?	?	?	?
	2004	—	—	—	—	—	—	—	—	—	—	—
	2005	—	—	—	—	—	—	—	9	—	—	—
Cambodia / Cambodge / Camboya	2003	—	—	—	—	—	—	—	28	—	—	1
	2004	—	—	—	—	—	—	—	66	—	—	2
	2005	—	—	—	—	—	—	—	7	—	—	2
Cameroon / Cameroun / Camerún	2003	—	—	—	—	—	—	—	—	—	—	—
	2004	—	—	—	—	—	—	—	1 296	—	—	?
	2005	?	?	?	?	?	?	?	?	?	?	?
Canada / Canadá	2003	—	23	—	—	—	1	—	1 142	—	—	—
	2004	—	2	—	—	—	—	—	706	—	—	4
	2005	—	4	—	—	—	—	—	1 596	—	—	20

Country	Year	Col 1	Col 2	Col 3	Col 4	Col 5	Col 6	Col 7	Col 8	Col 9	Col 10
Cape Verde / **Cap-Vert** / **Cabo Verde**	2003	—	—	—	6	—	—	—	—	—	—
	2004	—	—	—	25	—	—	—	—	—	—
	2005	—	—	—	100	—	—	—	—	—	—
Cayman Islands / *Îles Caïmanes* / *Islas Caimanes*	2003	—	—	—	1	—	—	—	—	—	—
	2004	?	?	?	?	?	?	?	?	?	?
	2005	?	?	?	?	?	?	?	?	?	?
Chad / **Tchad**	2003	—	—	—	—	—	—	—	—	—	—
	2004	—	—	—	11	—	—	—	—	—	—
	2005	?	?	?	?	?	?	?	?	?	?
Chile / **Chili**	2003	65	—	—	1 035	—	—	—	—	—	—
	2004	75	—	—	1 533	—	—	—	—	—	—
	2005	71	—	—	1 764	—	—	—	—	—	—
China / **Chine**	2003	17	—	—	—	—	—	—	—	—	—
	2004	32	—	—	—	—	—	—	—	—	—
	2005	191	—	—	—	—	—	—	—	—	—
Hong Kong SAR of China / *RAS de Hong Kong (Chine)* / *RAE de Hong Kong de China*	2003	27	—	—	92	—	—	—	—	2	—
	2004	45	—	—	132	—	—	—	—	1	—
	2005	37	—	1	77	—	—	—	—	—	—
Macao SAR of China / *RAS de Macao (Chine)* / *RAE de Macao de China*	2003	1	—	—	4	—	—	—	—	—	—
	2004	1	—	—	1	—	—	—	—	—	—
	2005	1	—	—	2	—	—	—	—	—	—
Colombia / **Colombie**	2003	18	—	—	3 200	—	—	—	—	—	—
	2004	42	—	—	3 000	—	—	—	—	—	—
	2005	44	—	—	600	—	—	—	—	—	—
Costa Rica	2003	2	—	—	56	—	—	—	—	—	—
	2004	3	—	—	—	—	—	—	—	—	—
	2005	8	—	—	401	—	—	—	—	—	—
Côte d'Ivoire	2003	—	—	—	130	—	—	—	—	—	—
	2004	1	1	—	106	—	1	—	—	—	—
	2005	1	—	—	—	—	—	—	—	—	—
Croatia / **Croatie** / **Croacia**	2003	61	—	—	900	—	1 310	—	—	5	—
	2004	?	?	?	?	?	?	?	?	?	?
	2005	82	—	—	—	—	1 203	—	—	3	—
Cuba	2003	—	—	—	2 400	—	—	—	—	12	—
	2004	—	—	—	2 493	—	—	—	—	2	—
	2005	—	—	—	2 177	—	—	—	—	—	—

Schedule IV. D.5. Sedative-hypnotics + barbiturate-type anti-epileptics (continued)
Tableau IV. D.5. Sédatifs-hypnotiques + antiépileptiques de type barbiturique (suite)
Lista IV. D.5. Sedantes-hipnóticos + antiepilépticos de tipo barbitúrico (continuación)

Imports — Importations — Importaciones (continued — suite — continuación)

Country or territory / Pays ou territoire / País o territorio	Year / Année / Año	Allo-barbital / Alo-barbital (kg)	Barbital (kg)	Buto-barbital (kg)	Ethchlor-vynol / Etclor-vinol (kg)	Ethinamate / Éthinamate / Etinamato (kg)	Methylpheno-barbital / Méthylphéno-barbital / Metilfeno-barbital (kg)	Methy-prylon / Méthyprylone / Meti-prilona (kg)	Pheno-barbital / Phéno-barbital / Feno-barbital (kg)	Secbuta-barbital (kg)	Vinylbital / Vinilbital (kg)	Zolpidem (kg)
Cyprus / Chypre / Chipre	2003	—	—	—	—	—	—	—	55	—	—	2
	2004	—	—	—	—	—	—	—	40	—	—	3
	2005	—	—	—	—	—	—	—	110	—	—	5
Czech Republic / République tchèque / República Checa	2003	31	41	17	—	—	—	—	1 091	—	—	212
	2004	—	37	—	—	—	—	—	1 592	—	—	224
	2005	—	—	—	—	—	—	—	609	—	—	215
Dem. Rep. of the Congo / Rép. dém. du Congo / Rep. Dem. del Congo	2003	—	—	—	—	—	—	—	790	—	—	—
	2004	—	—	—	—	—	—	—	908	—	—	—
	2005	—	—	—	—	—	—	—	320	—	—	—
Denmark / Danemark / Dinamarca	2003	25	31	—	—	—	—	—	19 359	—	—	220
	2004	25	70	—	—	—	—	—	28 253	—	—	315
	2005	—	199	—	—	—	—	—	27 215	—	—	289
Djibouti	2003	?	?	?	?	?	?	?	?	?	?	?
	2004	?	?	?	?	?	?	?	?	?	?	?
	2005	—	1	—	—	—	—	—	20	—	—	1
Dominica / Dominique	2003	?	?	?	?	?	?	?	?	?	?	?
	2004	—	—	—	—	—	—	—	1	—	—	—
	2005	—	—	—	—	—	—	—	2	—	—	—
Dominican Republic / République dominicaine / República Dominicana	2003	—	—	—	—	—	—	—	182	—	—	14
	2004	—	—	—	—	—	—	—	592	—	—	10
	2005	—	—	—	—	—	—	—	637	—	—	9
Ecuador / Équateur	2003	—	—	—	—	—	—	—	2	—	—	5
	2004	—	—	—	—	—	—	—	49	—	—	6
	2005	—	—	—	—	—	—	—	23	—	—	7

Country	Year	(1)	(2)	(3)	(4)	(5)	(6)	(7)	(8)	(9)	(10)
Egypt / Égypte / Egipto	2003	10	—	—	6 014	—	—	—	—	—	—
	2004	—	—	—	6 714	—	—	—	—	—	—
	2005	—	—	—	11 400	—	—	—	—	—	—
El Salvador	2003	1	—	—	335	—	—	—	—	—	—
	2004	1	—	—	250	—	—	—	—	—	—
	2005	1	—	—	519	—	—	—	—	—	—
Eritrea / Érythrée	2003	—	—	—	79	—	—	—	—	—	—
	2004	—	—	—	54	—	—	—	—	—	—
	2005	—	—	—	328	—	—	—	—	—	—
Estonia / Estonie	2003	2	—	—	22	—	—	—	—	—	—
	2004	4	—	—	23	—	—	—	—	—	—
	2005	4	—	—	28	—	—	—	—	—	—
Ethiopia / Éthiopie / Etiopía	2003	—	—	—	3 944	—	—	—	—	—	—
	2004	—	—	—	1 535	—	—	—	—	—	—
	2005	—	—	—	2 276	—	—	—	—	—	—
Finland / Finlande / Finlandia	2003	127	—	—	177	—	—	—	—	32	—
	2004	79	—	—	60	—	—	—	—	46	—
	2005	80	—	—	81	—	—	—	—	14	—
France / Francia	2003	—	—	—	17 333	—	—	—	—	1 009	—
	2004	1 112	—	—	10 306	—	—	—	—	1 229	—
	2005	1 288	—	—	11 137	—	—	—	—	1 125	—
French Polynesia / Polynésie française / Polinesia Francesa	2003	2	—	—	12	—	—	—	—	—	—
	2004	1	—	—	10	—	—	—	—	—	—
	2005	?	?	?	?	?	?	?	?	?	?
Gabon / Gabón	2003	?	?	?	?	?	?	?	?	?	?
	2004	1	—	—	—	—	—	—	—	—	—
	2005	1	—	—	23	—	—	—	—	—	—
Georgia / Géorgie	2003	1	—	—	10	—	—	—	—	—	—
	2004	—	—	—	44	—	—	—	—	89	—
	2005	—	—	—	—	—	—	—	—	—	—
Germany / Allemagne / Alemania	2003	1 092	—	83	20 356	—	1 310	—	—	10 005	—
	2004	1 259	—	—	23 809	—	560	—	15	5 006	—
	2005	1 125	—	—	20 303	—	702	—	—	10 003	—
Ghana	2003	?	?	?	?	?	?	?	?	?	?
	2004	—	—	—	—	—	—	—	—	—	—
	2005	—	—	—	1 251	—	—	—	—	—	—

Schedule IV. D.5. Sedative-hypnotics + barbiturate-type anti-epileptics (continued)
Tableau IV. D.5. Sédatifs-hypnotiques + antiépileptiques de type barbiturique (suite)
Lista IV. D.5. Sedantes-hipnóticos + antiepilépticos de tipo barbitúrico (continuación)

Imports — Importations — Importaciones (continued — suite — continuación)

Country or territory / Pays ou territoire / País o territorio	Year / Année / Año	Allobarbital / Allo-barbital / Alo-barbital (kg)	Barbital (kg)	Buto-barbital (kg)	Ethchlor-vynol / Etclor-vinol (kg)	Ethinamate / Éthinamate / Etinamato (kg)	Methylpheno-barbital / Méthylphéno-barbital / Metilfeno-barbital (kg)	Methy-prylon / Méthy-prylone / Meti-prilona (kg)	Pheno-barbital / Phéno-barbital / Feno-barbital (kg)	Secbuta-barbital (kg)	Vinylbital / Vinilbital (kg)	Zolpidem (kg)
Greece / Grèce / Grecia	2003	—	—	—	—	—	—	—	433	—	—	258
	2004	—	—	—	—	—	—	—	370	—	—	258
	2005	—	1	—	—	—	—	—	407	—	—	325
Grenada / Grenade / Granada	2003	—	—	—	—	—	—	—	1	—	—	—
	2004	—	—	—	—	—	—	—	5	—	—	—
	2005	—	—	—	—	—	—	—	—	—	—	—
Guatemala	2003	—	—	—	—	—	—	—	1 253	—	—	—
	2004	?	?	?	?	?	?	?	?	?	?	?
	2005	?	?	?	?	?	?	?	?	?	?	?
Guinea / Guinée	2003	?	?	?	?	?	?	?	?	?	?	?
	2004	?	?	?	?	?	?	?	?	?	?	?
	2005	—	—	—	—	—	—	—	21	—	—	2
Guyana	2003	—	—	—	—	—	—	—	13	—	—	—
	2004	?	?	?	?	?	?	?	?	?	?	?
	2005	—	—	—	—	—	—	—	—	—	—	—
Haiti / Haïti / Haití	2003	—	—	—	—	—	—	—	284	—	—	—
	2004	—	—	—	—	—	—	—	91	—	?	—
	2005	—	—	—	—	—	—	—	341	—	—	—
Honduras	2003	—	—	—	—	—	—	—	800	—	—	1
	2004	?	?	?	?	?	?	?	—	?	—	1
	2005	—	—	—	—	—	—	—	?	—	?	?
Hungary / Hongrie / Hungría	2003	570	96	—	—	—	—	—	50	—	—	230
	2004	130	97	—	—	—	—	—	347	—	?	416
	2005	60	9	—	—	—	—	—	543	—	—	469

Country / Pays / País	Year	1	2	3	4	5	6	7	8	9	10
Iceland / Islande / Islandia	2003	7	—	—	5	—	—	—	—	—	—
	2004	11	—	—	6	—	—	—	2	—	—
	2005	12	—	—	6	—	—	—	—	—	—
India / Inde	2003	—	—	—	—	—	—	—	1	—	—
	2004	3	—	—	—	—	—	—	5	—	—
	2005	—	—	—	—	—	—	—	—	—	—
Indonesia / Indonésie	2003	—	—	—	2 025	—	—	—	—	—	—
	2004	—	—	—	4 121	—	—	—	—	—	—
	2005	6	—	—	3 686	—	—	—	—	—	—
Iran (Islamic Republic of) / Iran (Rép. islamique d') / Irán (Rep. Islámica del)	2003	—	—	—	3 910	—	—	—	—	—	—
	2004	—	—	—	1 500	—	—	—	—	—	—
	2005	—	—	—	1 500	—	—	—	—	—	—
Iraq	2003	—	...	...	148	...	...	...	...	...	...
	2004	...	...	...	...	...	...	...	...	...	...
	2005	...	...	...	...	...	...	...	...	...	...
Ireland / Irlande / Irlanda	2003	99	—	—	1 002	—	—	—	3	—	—
	2004	159	—	—	1 176	—	—	—	2	—	—
	2005	52	—	—	1 402	—	—	—	2	—	—
Israel / Israël	2003	4	—	—	359	—	—	—	—	50	—
	2004	58	—	—	432	—	—	—	1	25	—
	2005	58	—	—	155	—	—	40	—	—	—
Italy / Italie / Italia	2003	516	—	—	7 636	300	—	—	2 209	—	—
	2004	506	—	—	9 726	700	—	—	903	—	—
	2005	491	—	—	7 128	212	—	—	1 807	—	—
Jamaica / Jamaïque	2003	1	—	—	50	—	—	—	—	—	—
	2004	1	—	—	75	—	—	—	—	—	—
	2005	1	—	—	54	—	—	—	—	—	—
Japan / Japon / Japón	2003	1 400	—	—	12 502	—	—	—	2 055	—	—
	2004	1 461	—	—	13 018	—	—	—	2 848	—	—
	2005	1 874	—	—	10 182	—	—	—	2 549	—	—
Jordan / Jordanie / Jordania	2003	3	—	—	1 956	—	—	4	—	—	—
	2004	3	—	—	274	—	—	6	—	—	200
	2005	5	—	—	2 480	—	—	6	—	—	400
Kazakhstan / Kazajstán	2003	—	—	—	3 825	—	—	—	—	—	—
	2004	—	—	—	1 500	—	—	—	—	—	—
	2005	—	—	—	4 000	—	—	—	—	—	—
Kenya	2003	1	—	—	1	—	—	—	—	—	—
	2004	2	—	—	2	—	—	—	—	—	—
	2005	...	...	...	...	...	...	...	...	...	...

Schedule IV. D.5. Sedative-hypnotics + barbiturate-type anti-epileptics (continued)
Tableau IV. D.5. Sédatifs-hypnotiques + antiépileptiques de type barbiturique (suite)
Lista IV. D.5. Sedantes-hipnóticos + antiepilépticos de tipo barbitúrico (continuación)

Imports — Importations — Importaciones (continued — suite — continuación)

Country or territory / Pays ou territoire / País o territorio	Year / Année / Año	Allo-barbital / Alo-barbital	Barbital	Buto-barbital	Ethchlor-vynol / Etclor-vinol	Ethinamate / Éthinamate / Etinamato	Methylpheno-barbital / Méthylphéno-barbital / Metilfeno-barbital	Methy-prylon / Méthy-prylone / Meti-prilona	Pheno-barbital / Phéno-barbital / Feno-barbital	Secbuta-barbital	Vinylbital / Vinilbital	Zolpidem
		kg	kg	kg	kg	kg	kg	kg	kg	kg	kg	kg
Kuwait / Koweit	2003	—	—	—	—	—	—	—	9	—	—	9
	2004	—	—	—	—	—	—	—	17	—	—	6
	2005	—	—	—	—	—	—	—	4	—	—	7
Kyrgyzstan / Kirghizistan / Kirguistán	2003	—	—	—	—	—	—	—	5	—	—	16
	2004	—	—	—	—	—	—	—	87	—	—	12
	2005	—	—	—	—	—	—	—	5	—	—	25
Lao People's Dem. Rep. / Rép. dém. populaire lao / Rep. dem. Popular Lao	2003	—	—	—	—	—	—	—	25	—	—	—
	2004	—	—	—	—	—	—	—	—	—	—	—
	2005	—	—	—	—	—	—	—	25	—	—	—
Latvia / Lettonie / Letonia	2003	—	22	—	—	—	—	—	674	—	—	—
	2004	—	—	—	—	—	—	—	319	—	—	—
	2005	—	22	—	—	—	—	—	883	—	—	—
Lebanon / Liban / Líbano	2003	—	—	—	—	—	—	—	160	—	—	—
	2004	—	—	—	—	—	—	—	70	—	—	—
	2005	—	—	—	—	—	—	—	122	13	—	—
Lesotho	2003	?	?	?	?	?	?	?	?	?	?	?
	2004	?	?	?	?	?	?	?	?	?	?	?
	2005	—	—	—	—	—	—	—	76	—	—	—
Libyan Arab Jamahiriya / Jamahiriya arabe libyenne / Jamahiriya Árabe Libia	2003	—	—	—	—	—	—	—	8	—	—	—
	2004	—	—	—	—	—	—	—	158	—	—	—
	2005	—	—	—	—	—	—	—	89	—	—	—
Lithuania / Lituanie / Lituania	2003	—	45	—	—	—	—	—	372	—	—	8
	2004	—	45	—	—	—	—	—	535	—	—	10
	2005	—	45	—	—	—	—	—	149	—	—	11

		1	2	3	4	5	6	7	8	9	10
Luxembourg Luxemburgo	2003	—	—	—	—	—	—	—	—	—	—
	2004	?	?	?	?	?	?	?	?	?	?
	2005	22	—	—	15	—	—	—	—	—	—
Madagascar	2003	—	—	—	36	—	—	—	—	—	—
	2004	—	—	—	—	—	—	—	—	—	—
	2005	—	—	—	—	—	—	—	—	—	—
Malaysia Malaisie Malasia	2003	37	—	—	2	—	—	—	—	4	—
	2004	20	—	—	200	—	—	—	—	—	—
	2005	21	—	—	103	—	—	—	—	—	—
Maldives Maldivas	2003	—	—	—	5	—	—	—	—	—	—
	2004	—	—	—	—	—	—	—	—	—	—
	2005	—	—	—	—	—	—	—	—	—	—
Mali Mali	2003	—	—	—	98	—	—	—	—	—	—
	2004	—	—	—	76	—	—	—	—	—	—
	2005	—	—	—	84	—	—	—	—	—	—
Malta Malte	2003	4	—	—	1 000	—	—	—	—	—	—
	2004	5	—	—	—	—	—	—	—	—	—
	2005	5	—	—	1	—	—	—	—	—	—
Mauritius Maurice Mauricio	2003	1	—	—	41	—	—	—	—	—	—
	2004	2	—	—	72	—	—	—	—	—	—
	2005	2	—	—	72	—	—	—	—	—	—
Mexico Mexique México	2003	—	—	—	2 350	—	—	—	—	—	—
	2004	23	—	—	2 550	—	—	—	—	—	—
	2005	?	?	?	?	?	?	?	?	?	?
Micronesia (Fed. States of) Micronésie (États féd. de) Micronesia (Estados Fed. de)	2003	—	—	—	3	—	—	—	—	—	—
	2004	—	—	—	2	—	—	—	—	—	—
	2005	—	—	—	1	—	—	—	—	—	—
Mongolia Mongolie	2003	—	—	—	2	—	—	—	—	2	—
	2004	—	—	—	—	—	—	—	—	—	—
	2005	?	?	?	?	?	?	?	?	?	?
Morocco Maroc Marruecos	2003	32	—	—	784	—	—	—	—	—	—
	2004	32	—	—	1 391	—	—	—	—	—	—
	2005	64	—	—	1 217	—	—	—	—	—	—
Mozambique	2003	—	—	—	4	—	—	—	—	—	—
	2004	—	—	—	252	—	—	—	—	—	—
	2005	?	?	?	?	?	?	?	?	?	?

Schedule IV. D.5. Sedative-hypnotics + barbiturate-type anti-epileptics (continued)
Tableau IV. D.5. Sédatifs-hypnotiques + antiépileptiques de type barbiturique (suite)
Lista IV. D.5. Sedantes-hipnóticos + antiepilépticos de tipo barbitúrico (continuación)

Imports — Importations — Importaciones (continued — suite — continuación)

Country or territory / Pays ou territoire / País o territorio	Year / Année / Año	Allobarbital / Alobarbital (kg)	Barbital (kg)	Butobarbital (kg)	Ethchlorvynol / Etchlorvinol / Etclorvinol (kg)	Ethinamate / Éthinamate / Etinamato (kg)	Methylphenobarbital / Méthylphénobarbital / Metilfenobarbital (kg)	Methyprylon / Méthyprylone / Metiprilona (kg)	Phenobarbital / Phénobarbital / Fenobarbital (kg)	Secbutabarbital (kg)	Vinylbital / Vinilbital (kg)	Zolpidem (kg)
Namibia / Namibie	2003	—	—	—	—	—	—	—	5	—	—	2
	2004	—	—	—	—	—	—	—	7	—	—	1
	2005	—	—	—	—	—	—	—	11	—	—	1
Nepal / Népal	2003	—	—	—	—	—	—	—	50	—	—	—
	2004	—	—	—	—	—	—	—	—	—	—	—
	2005	?	?	?	?	?	?	?	?	?	?	?
Netherlands / Pays-Bas / Países Bajos	2003	—	35	—	—	—	—	—	5 283	—	—	673
	2004	8	38	30	—	—	—	—	3 836	—	—	949
	2005	7	22	—	—	—	—	—	917	—	—	173
Netherlands Antilles / Antilles néerlandaises / Antillas Neerlandesas	2003	—	—	—	—	—	—	—	7	—	—	2
	2004	—	—	—	—	—	—	—	4	—	—	2
	2005	—	—	—	—	—	—	—	4	—	—	2
New Caledonia / Nouvelle-Calédonie / Nueva Caledonia	2003	—	—	—	—	—	—	—	13	—	—	3
	2004	?	?	?	?	?	?	?	?	?	?	?
	2005	—	—	—	—	—	—	—	15	—	—	3
New Zealand / Nouvelle-Zélande / Nueva Zelandia	2003	—	—	—	—	—	—	—	56	—	—	—
	2004	—	11	—	—	—	—	—	85	—	—	—
	2005	—	11	—	—	—	—	—	57	—	—	—
Nicaragua	2003	—	—	—	—	—	—	—	41	—	—	1
	2004	—	—	—	—	—	—	—	22	—	—	1
	2005	—	—	—	—	—	—	—	89	—	—	1
Niger	2003	?	?	?	?	?	?	?	?	?	?	?
	2004	?	?	?	?	?	?	?	?	?	?	?
	2005	—	—	—	—	—	—	—	34	—	—	—

Country	Year										
Nigeria / Nigéria	2003	—	—	—	—	—	—	279	—	—	—
	2004	—	—	—	—	—	—	750	—	—	—
	2005	—	—	—	—	—	—	500	—	—	—
Norway / Norvège / Noruega	2003	—	9	—	—	—	—	171	—	—	36
	2004	—	3	—	—	—	—	146	—	—	105
	2005	—	6	—	—	—	—	150	—	—	77
Oman / Omán	2003	—	—	—	—	—	—	7	—	—	—
	2004	—	—	—	—	—	—	3	—	—	—
	2005	—	—	—	—	—	—	9	—	—	—
Pakistan / Pakistán	2003	—	—	—	—	—	—	814	—	—	—
	2004	—	—	—	—	—	—	648	—	—	20
	2005	—	—	—	—	—	—	772	—	—	—
Palau / Palaos	2003	—	—	—	—	—	—	—	—	—	—
	2004	—	—	—	—	—	—	1	—	—	—
	2005	—	—	—	—	—	—	—	—	—	—
Panama / Panamá	2003	—	—	—	—	—	—	1	—	—	63
	2004	—	—	—	—	—	—	552	—	—	50
	2005	—	—	—	—	—	—	150	—	—	35
Papua New Guinea / Papouasie-Nouvelle Guinée / Papua Nueva Guinea	2003	—	—	—	—	—	—	58	—	—	—
	2004	?	?	?	?	?	?	?	?	?	?
	2005	?	?	?	?	?	?	?	?	?	?
Paraguay	2003	—	—	—	—	—	—	200	—	—	2
	2004	?	?	?	?	?	?	?	?	?	?
	2005	?	?	?	?	?	?	?	?	?	?
Peru / Pérou / Perú	2003	41	—	—	—	—	—	500	—	—	4
	2004	—	—	—	—	—	—	31	—	—	3
	2005	—	—	—	—	—	—	875	—	—	8
Philippines / Filipinas	2003	—	—	—	—	—	—	922	—	—	22
	2004	—	—	—	—	—	—	804	—	—	12
	2005	?	?	?	?	?	?	?	?	?	?
Poland / Pologne / Polonia	2003	600	—	—	—	—	—	3 161	—	—	201
	2004	550	—	—	—	—	—	1 995	—	—	269
	2005	200	—	—	—	—	—	1 013	—	—	224
Portugal	2003	—	—	—	—	—	—	975	—	—	38
	2004	—	—	—	—	—	—	895	—	—	164
	2005	—	—	—	—	—	—	226	—	—	162

Schedule IV. D.5. Sedative-hypnotics + barbiturate-type anti-epileptics (continued)
Tableau IV. D.5. Sédatifs-hypnotiques + antiépileptiques de type barbiturique (suite)
Lista IV. D.5. Sedantes-hipnóticos + antiepilépticos de tipo barbitúrico (continuación)

Imports — Importations — Importaciones (continued — suite — continuación)

Country or territory / Pays ou territoire / País o territorio	Year / Année / Año	Allobarbital / Alobarbital	Barbital	Butobarbital	Ethchlorvynol / Etclorvinol	Ethinamate / Éthinamate / Etinamato	Methylphenobarbital / Méthylphénobarbital / Metilfenobarbital	Methyprylon / Méthyprylone / Metiprilona	Phenobarbital / Phénobarbital / Fenobarbital	Secbutabarbital	Vinylbital / Vinilbital	Zolpidem
		kg	kg	kg	kg	kg	kg	kg	kg	kg	kg	kg
Qatar............	2003	—	—	—	—	—	—	—	5	—	—	—
	2004	—	—	—	—	—	—	—	3	—	—	—
	2005	—	—	—	—	—	—	—	3	—	—	—
Republic of Korea.......... / République de Corée / República de Corea	2003	—	1 335	—	—	—	—	—	300	—	—	105
	2004	—	—	—	—	—	—	—	1 100	—	—	135
	2005	—	1 336	—	—	—	—	—	600	—	—	218
Republic of Moldova....... / République de Moldova / República de Moldova	2003	—	—	—	—	—	—	—	153	—	—	—
	2004	—	—	—	—	—	—	—	257	—	—	—
	2005	?	?	?	?	?	?	?	?	?	?	?
Romania.......... / Roumanie / Rumania	2003	—	—	—	—	—	—	—	4 005	—	—	87
	2004	—	—	—	—	—	—	—	5 811	—	—	31
	2005	—	—	—	—	—	—	—	—	—	—	—
Russian Federation.......... / Fédération de Russie / Federación de Rusia	2003	—	—	—	—	—	—	—	10 053	—	—	28
	2004	—	—	—	—	—	—	—	3 761	—	—	9
	2005	—	—	—	—	—	—	—	—	—	—	—
Rwanda..........	2003	—	—	—	—	—	—	—	30	—	—	—
	2004	—	—	—	—	—	—	—	40	—	—	—
	2005	—	—	—	—	—	—	—	95	—	—	—
Saint Lucia.......... / Sainte-Lucie / Santa Lucía	2003	—	—	—	—	—	—	—	4	—	—	—
	2004	—	—	—	—	—	—	—	2	—	—	—
	2005	—	—	—	—	—	—	—	—	—	—	—
Sao Tome and Principe..... / Sao Tomé-et-Principe / Santo Tomé y Príncipe	2003	—	—	—	—	—	—	—	1	—	—	—
	2004	—	—	—	—	—	—	—	—	—	—	—
	2005	—	—	—	—	—	—	—	—	—	—	—

Country	Year	1	2	3	4	5	6	7	8	9	10	11
Saudi Arabia / Arabie saoudite / Arabia Saudita	2003	2	—	—	191	—	—	—	—	—	—	—
	2004	—	—	—	228	—	—	—	—	—	—	—
	2005	—	—	—	182	—	—	—	—	—	—	—
Senegal / Sénégal	2003	3	—	—	2 174	—	—	—	—	—	—	—
	2004	—	—	—	—	—	—	—	—	—	—	—
	2005	—	—	—	482	—	—	—	—	—	—	—
Serbia and Montenegro / Serbie-et-Monténégro / Serbia y Montenegro	2003	1	—	—	1 309	—	—	—	—	—	5	—
	2004	?	?	?	?	?	?	?	?	?	?	?
	2005	?	?	?	?	?	?	?	?	?	?	?
Seychelles	2003	—	—	—	2	—	—	—	—	—	—	—
	2004	—	—	—	1	—	—	—	—	—	—	—
	2005	?	?	?	?	?	?	?	?	?	?	?
Sierra Leone	2003	—	—	—	15	—	—	—	—	—	—	—
	2004	?	?	?	?	?	?	?	?	?	?	?
	2005	—	—	—	49	—	—	—	—	—	—	—
Singapore / Singapour / Singapur	2003	3	—	—	1 071	—	—	—	—	—	1	—
	2004	6	—	—	1 175	—	—	—	—	—	—	—
	2005	11	—	—	642	—	—	—	—	—	—	—
Slovakia / Slovaquie / Eslovaquia	2003	47	—	—	905	—	—	—	—	4	5	13
	2004	?	?	?	?	?	?	?	?	?	?	?
	2005	92	—	—	622	—	—	—	—	—	1	—
Slovenia / Slovénie / Eslovenia	2003	194	—	—	50	—	94	—	—	—	6	—
	2004	219	—	—	44	—	95	—	—	—	8	—
	2005	263	—	—	65	—	41	—	—	—	1	—
South Africa / Afrique du Sud / Sudáfrica	2003	206	—	—	1 000	—	—	—	—	—	2	—
	2004	157	—	—	1 958	—	—	—	—	—	2	—
	2005	—	—	—	2 025	—	—	—	—	—	—	—
Spain / Espagne / España	2003	3 008	—	—	3 400	—	—	—	—	—	..	—
	2004	4 063	—	—	2 710	—	—	—	—	—	5	—
	2005	3 662	—	—	2 552	—	—	—	—	—	1	—
Sri Lanka	2003	—	—	—	..	—	—	—	—	—	..	—
	2004	2	—	—	802	—	—	—	—	—	—	701
	2005	2	—	—	3	—	—	—	—	—	—	—
Suriname	2003	—	—	—	—	—	—	—	—	—	—	—
	2004	—	—	—	30	—	—	—	—	—	—	—
	2005	—	—	—	—	—	—	—	—	—	—	—
Swaziland / Swazilandia	2003	—	—	—	—	—	—	—	—	—	—	—
	2004	—	—	—	1	—	—	—	—	—	—	—
	2005	?	?	?	?	?	?	?	?	?	?	?

Schedule IV. D.5. Sedative-hypnotics + barbiturate-type anti-epileptics (continued)
Tableau IV. D.5. Sédatifs-hypnotiques + antiépileptiques de type barbiturique (suite)
Lista IV. D.5. Sedantes-hipnóticos + antiepilépticos de tipo barbitúrico (continuación)

Imports — Importations — Importaciones (continued — suite — continuación)

Country or territory / Pays ou territoire / País o territorio	Year / Année / Año	Allobarbital / Alobarbital (kg)	Barbital (kg)	Butobarbital (kg)	Ethchlorvynol / Etclorvinol (kg)	Ethinamate / Éthinamate / Etinamato (kg)	Methylphenobarbital / Méthylphénobarbital / Metilfenobarbital (kg)	Methyprylon / Méthyprylone / Metiprilona (kg)	Phenobarbital / Phénobarbital / Fenobarbital (kg)	Secbutabarbital (kg)	Vinylbital / Vinilbital (kg)	Zolpidem (kg)
Sweden / Suède / Suecia	2003	—	51	—	—	—	1	—	201	—	—	266
	2004	—	78	—	—	—	—	—	405	—	—	284
	2005	—	15	—	—	—	1	—	210	—	—	354
Switzerland / Suisse / Suiza	2003	307	68	—	—	—	—	—	35 027	2	—	258..4
	2004	470	54	—	—	—	—	—	35 459	25	—	247
	2005	202	73	—	—	—	—	—	34 463	13	—	—
Syrian Arab Republic / Rép. arabe syrienne / Rep. Árabe Siria	2003	—	—						2 175	—	—	—
	2004	—	—						2 055	—	—	—
	2005	—	—						25	—	—	15
Thailand / Thaïlande / Tailandia	2003	—	—						1 468	—	—	4
	2004	—	—						4 875	—	—	3
	2005	—	—						1 809	—	—	7
The former Yugoslav Rep. of Macedonia / L'ex-Rép. yougoslave de Macédoine / La ex Rep. Yugoslava de Macedonia	2003	—	—						151	—	—	—
	2004	—	—						90	—	—	—
	2005	—	—						254	—	—	11
Togo	2003	—	—						217	—	—	—
	2004	—	—						115	—	—	—
	2005	—	—						103	—	—	—
Tonga	2003	?	?	?	?	?	?	?	?	?	?	?
	2004	—	—	—	—	—	—	—	2	—	—	—
	2005	—	—	—	—	—	—	—	1	—	—	—

Country	Year											
Trinidad and Tobago / Trinité-et-Tobago / Trinidad y Tobago	2003	—	—	—	—	—	—	—	4	—	—	—
	2004	—	—	—	—	—	—	—	41	—	—	—
	2005	—	—	—	—	—	—	—	51	—	—	—
Tunisia / Tunisie / Túnez	2003	—	—	—	—	—	—	—	682	—	—	14
	2004	—	—	—	—	—	—	—	722	—	—	11
	2005	—	—	—	—	—	—	—	796	—	—	12
Turkey / Turquie / Turquía	2003	400	—	—	—	—	—	—	2 745	—	—	—
	2004	470	—	—	—	—	—	—	1 025	—	—	1
	2005	200	—	—	—	—	—	—	900	—	—	—
Uganda / Ouganda	2003	?	?	?	?	?	?	?	167	?	?	?
	2004	?	?	?	?	?	?	?	540	?	?	?
	2005	?	?	?	?	?	?	?	?	?	?	?
Ukraine / Ucrania	2003	—	—	—	—	—	—	—	22 709	—	—	—
	2004	—	—	—	—	—	—	—	26 275	—	—	1
	2005	—	—	—	—	—	—	—	28 700	—	—	—
United Arab Emirates / Émirats arabes unis / Emiratos Árabes Unidos	2003	—	—	—	—	—	—	—	27	—	—	—
	2004	—	—	—	—	—	—	—	7	—	—	—
	2005	—	—	—	—	—	—	—	—	—	—	—
United Kingdom / Royaume-Uni / Reino Unido	2003	—	324	—	—	—	—	—	1 690	—	—	—
	2004	—	425	150	—	—	—	—	8 135	—	—	76
	2005	—	355	—	—	—	—	—	2 162	—	—	—
United Rep. of Tanzania / Rép.-Unie de Tanzanie / Rep. Unida de Tanzanía	2003	—	—	—	—	—	—	—	2 526	—	—	—
	2004	—	—	—	—	—	—	—	1 545	—	—	—
	2005	—	—	—	—	—	—	—	1 041	—	—	—
United States / États-Unis / Estados Unidos	2003	—	1 338	—	—	—	500	—	15 745	—	—	7 831
	2004	—	2 340	3	—	—	335	—	33 711	—	—	2 726
	2005	—	1 596	—	—	—	300	—	18 113	—	—	4 441
Uzbekistan / Ouzbékistan / Uzbekistán	2003	—	—	—	—	—	—	—	40	—	—	—
	2004	—	—	—	—	—	—	—	64	—	—	—
	2005	—	—	—	—	—	—	—	36	—	—	—
Vanuatu	2003	?	?	?	?	?	?	?	?	?	?	?
	2004	?	?	?	?	?	?	?	2	?	?	?
	2005	?	?	?	?	?	?	?	2	?	?	?
Venezuela (Bolivarian Rep. of) / Venezuela (Rép. bolivarienne du) / Venezuela (Rep. Bolivariana de)	2003	—	—	—	—	—	—	—	2 349	—	—	—
	2004	—	—	3	—	—	—	—	2 655	—	—	51
	2005	—	—	—	—	—	—	—	933	—	—	19

Schedule IV. D.5. Sedative-hypnotics + barbiturate-type anti-epileptics *(concluded)*
Tableau IV. D.5. Sédatifs-hypnotiques + antiépileptiques de type barbiturique *(fin)*
Lista IV. D.5. Sedantes-hipnóticos + antiepilépticos de tipo barbitúrico *(conclusión)*

Imports — Importations — Importaciones *(continued — suite — continuación)*

Country or territory / Pays ou territoire / País o territorio	Year / Année / Año	Allo-barbital / Alo-barbital kg	Barbital kg	Buto-barbital kg	Ethchlorvynol / Etclorvinol kg	Ethinamate / Éthinamate / Etinamato kg	Methylphenobarbital / Méthylphénobarbital / Metilfenobarbital kg	Methyprylon / Méthyprylone / Metiprilona kg	Phenobarbital / Phéno-barbital / Fenobarbital kg	Secbuta-barbital kg	Vinylbital / Vinilbital kg	Zolpidem kg
Viet Nam	2003	—	—	—	—	—	—	—	4 910	—	—	10
	2004	—	—	—	—	—	—	—	4 200	—	—	3
	2005	—	—	—	—	—	—	—	5 020	—	—	—
Yemen / Yémen	2003	—	—	—	—	—	—	—	10	—	—	—
	2004	—	—	—	—	—	—	—	37	—	—	—
	2005	—	—	—	—	—	—	—	25	—	—	—
Zambia / Zambie	2003	—	—	—	—	—	—	—	345	—	—	—
	2004	—	—	—	—	—	—	—	175	—	—	—
	2005	—	—	—	—	—	—	—	151	—	—	—
Zimbabwe	2003	—	—	—	—	—	—	—	275	—	—	—
	2004	—	—	—	—	—	—	—	350	—	—	—
	2005	—	—	—	—	—	—	—	680	—	—	—
Total	2003	2 037	18 949	28	—	—	3 707	—	287 447	85	—	18 087
	2004	1 886	13 476	207	—	—	1 825	—	325 248	25	1	16 374
	2005	1 777	19 348	53	—	—	2 709	—	276 196	27	—	17 607

Table IV. Levels of consumption of groups of psychotropic substances in defined daily doses for statistical purposes (S-DDD) per thousand inhabitants per day

Levels of consumption of groups of psychotropic substances in defined daily doses for statistical purposes (S-DDD) per thousand inhabitants per day are calculated on the basis of statistics on manufacture and trade provided by Governments. To exclude the impact of yearly fluctuations on the calculated annual consumption, the average for the three-year period 2003-2005 was calculated. In countries that do not manufacture and export psychotropic substances, quantities declared as imported are considered to be destined for consumption. For countries with manufacture and exports of psychotropic substances, the average annual manufacture is added to the average annual import; the average annual export and amounts of psychotropic substances used for conversion into other psychotropic or non-psychotropic substances are deducted. Countries and territories are presented in order of descending levels of consumption expressed in numbers of defined daily doses consumed on average per day and per thousand inhabitants. The names of territories appear in italics.

Conclusions on the actual level of consumption of psychotropic substances should be drawn with caution, as data on manufacture and trade reported by Governments may not be complete or may not cover all substances. High levels of consumption may, however, indicate overprescription and/or diversion into illicit channels. The Governments concerned should review the data. The groups of psychotropic substances are presented in table III.2.

Tableau IV. Niveaux de consommation des substances psychotropes par groupes en doses quotidiennes déterminées à des fins statistiques (S-DDD) par millier d'habitants et par jour

Les niveaux de consommation des substances psychotropes par groupes en doses quotidiennes déterminées à des fins statistiques (S-DDD) par millier d'habitants et par jour sont calculés d'après les statistiques sur la fabrication et le commerce fournies par les gouvernements. Pour pallier l'impact des fluctuations d'une année à l'autre de la fabrication et du commerce sur la consommation annuelle déterminée, on a calculé la moyenne pour la période de trois ans 2003 à 2005. Dans les pays qui ne fabriquent pas ou n'exportent pas de substances psychotropes, les quantités importées qu'ils signalent sont considérées comme étant destinées à la consommation. Pour les pays fabricants et exportateurs de substances psychotropes, les quantités annuelles moyennes fabriquées sont ajoutées aux quantités annuelles moyennes importées; les exportations annuelles moyennes et les quantités de substances psychotropes servant à la transformation en d'autres substances psychotropes ou non psychotropes sont déduites. Les pays et territoires sont présentés par ordre de consommation décroissant exprimé en nombre de doses quotidiennes déterminées consommées en moyenne par jour et par millier d'habitants. Les noms des territoires sont en italique.

Il faut être prudent si l'on tire des conclusions sur les niveaux réels de la consommation de substances psychotropes, car les renseignements sur la fabrication et le commerce fournis par les gouvernements peuvent être incomplets ou ne pas porter sur toutes les substances. Toutefois, des niveaux de consommation élevés peuvent indiquer qu'il y a eu exagération dans les prescriptions et/ou qu'il y a eu un détournement vers des circuits illicites. Les gouvernements intéressés devraient vérifier ces données. Les groupes de substances psychotropes sont présentés au tableau III.2.

Cuadro IV. Niveles de consumo de sustancias sicotrópicas por grupos en dosis diarias definidas con fines estadísticos (S-DDD) por millar de habitantes por día

Los niveles de consumo de sustancias sicotrópicas por grupos se calculan en dosis diarias definidas con fines estadísticos (S-DDD) por millar de habitantes por día, en base a las estadísticas sobre fabricación y comercio suministradas por los gobiernos. A fin de excluir la repercusión de las fluctuaciones anuales de la fabricación y el comercio en el cálculo del consumo anual, se ha tomado el promedio correspondiente al trienio comprendido entre 2003 y 2005. En el caso de los países que no fabrican ni exportan sustancias sicotrópicas, las cantidades importadas declaradas se consideran destinadas al consumo. En cuanto a los países que fabrican y exportan dichas sustancias, la fabricación anual media se suma a la importación anual media; se deducen la exportación anual media y las cantidades de sustancias sicotrópicas utilizadas para su transformación en otras sustancias sicotrópicas o no sicotrópicas. Los países y territorios se presentan por orden decreciente de niveles de consumo, expresados en número de S-DDD consumidas en promedio por día y por millar de habitantes. Los nombres de los territorios figuran en letra cursiva.

Conviene ser prudente al deducir conclusiones sobre el nivel real de consumo de sustancias sicotrópicas, pues es posible que los datos sobre fabricación y comercio comunicados por los gobiernos no sean completos o no abarquen todas las sustancias. En cambio, unos niveles de consumo elevados pueden ser indicio de un exceso de prescripciones médicas y/o de desviación hacia los canales ilícitos. Los gobiernos interesados deben examinar los datos. Los grupos de sustancias sicotrópicas se presentan en el cuadro III.2.

Tables

Tableaux

Cuadros

Table IV.1. Consumption of stimulants
Tableau IV.1. Consommation de stimulants
Cuadro IV.1. Consumo de estimulantes

Country or territory Pays ou territoire País o territorio	All stimulants (groups A–D)[a] Tous les stimulants (groupes A à D)[a] Todos los estimulantes (grupos A a D)[a]	Schedule II (groups A and B)[a] Tableau II (groupes A et B)[a] Lista II (grupos A y B)[a]	Schedules III and IV (groups C and D)[a] Tableaux III et IV (groupes C et D)[a] Listas III y IV (grupos C y D)[a]
United States of America — États-Unis d'Amérique — Estados Unidos de América	22.35	18.02	4.33
Ireland — Irlande — Irlanda	21.00	21.00	0.00
Brazil — Brésil — Brasil	12.53	0.14	12.39
Argentina — Argentine	11.74	0.05	11.69
South Africa — Afrique du Sud — Sudáfrica	8.57	0.51	8.06
Republic of Korea — République de Corée — República de Corea	8.43	0.00	8.43
Australia — Australie	7.33	2.68	4.65
Switzerland — Suisse — Suiza	6.80	1.58	5.22
Canada — Canadá	5.39	5.05	0.34
Panama — Panamá	4.75	0.45	4.30
Hong Kong SAR of China — RAS de Hong Kong (Chine) — RAE de Hong Kong de China	4.70	0.19	4.51
Singapore — Singapour — Singapur	4.13	0.09	4.04
Israel — Israël	3.66	2.80	0.86
Germany — Allemagne — Alemania	3.58	1.48	2.10
Czech Republic — République tchèque — República Checa	2.91	0.12	2.79
Norway — Norvège — Noruega	2.80	2.80	0.00
Malaysia — Malaisie — Malasia	2.49	0.02	2.47
New Zealand — Nouvelle-Zélande — Nueva Zelandia	2.45	1.34	1.11
United Kingdom — Royaume-Uni — Reino Unido	2.23	1.38	0.85
Belgium — Belgique — Bélgica	2.20	1.82	0.38
Costa Rica	1.95	0.27	1.68
Netherlands — Pays-Bas — Países Bajos	1.91	1.91	0.00
Chile — Chili	1.48	0.69	0.79
Thailand — Thaïlande — Tailandia	1.44	0.03	1.41
Denmark — Danemark — Dinamarca	1.13	0.92	0.21
Spain — Espagne — España	1.12	1.12	0.00
Sweden — Suède — Suecia	1.09	1.09	0.00
Italy — Italie — Italia	1.00	0.00	1.00
Namibia — Namibie	0.84	0.04	0.80
Finland — Finlande — Finlandia	0.61	0.61	0.00
Netherlands Antilles — Antilles néerlandaises — Antillas Neerlandesas	0.47	0.47	0.00
Andorra — Andorre	0.39	0.39	0.00
Norfolk Island — Île Norfolk — Isla Norfolk	0.32	0.32	0.00
Ecuador — Équateur	0.31	0.03	0.28
Austria — Autriche	0.27	0.22	0.05
Japan — Japon — Japón	0.26	0.17	0.09

Table IV.1. Consumption of stimulants
Tableau IV.1. Consommation de stimulants
Cuadro IV.1. Consumo de estimulantes
(continued — suite — continuación)

Country or territory Pays ou territoire País o territorio	All stimulants (groups A–D)[a] Tous les stimulants (groupes A à D)[a] Todos los estimulantes (grupos A a D)[a]	Schedule II (groups A and B)[a] Tableau II (groupes A et B)[a] Lista II (grupos A y B)[a]	Schedules III and IV (groups C and D)[a] Tableaux III et IV (groupes C et D)[a] Listas III y IV (grupos C y D)[a]
Portugal	0.25	0.25	0.00
Cyprus — Chypre — Chipre	0.22	0.22	0.00
Gibraltar	0.22	0.22	0.00
Bahamas	0.19	0.19	0.00
Dominica — Dominique	0.19	0.19	0.00
Christmas Island — Île Christmas — Isla Christmas	0.18	0.18	0.00
Saint Helena — Sainte-Hélène — Santa Elena	0.18	0.18	0.00
Nicaragua	0.15	0.05	0.10

[a]The groups of psychotropic substances are presented in table III.2. — Les groupes de substances psychotropes sont présentés dans le tableau III.2. — Los grupos de sustancias sicotrópicas se presentan en el cuadro III.2.

Table IV.2. Consumption of sedative-hypnotics
Tableau IV.2. Consommation de sédatifs-hypnotiques
Cuadro IV.2. Consumo de sedantes-hipnóticos
(continued — suite — continuación)

Country or territory Pays ou territoire País o territorio	All sedative-hypnotics (groups E–J)[a] Tous les sédatifs-hypnotiques (groupes E à J)[a] Todos los sedantes-hipnóticos (grupos E a J)[a]	Benzodiazepines (group G)[a] Benzodiazépines (groupe G)[a] Benzodiazepinas (grupo G)[a]	Others Autres Otros
Japan — Japon — Japón	96.58	91.26	5.32
Belgium — Belgique — Bélgica	93.87	81.83	12.04
United Kingdom — Royaume-Uni — Reino Unido	83.64	82.24	1.39
France — Francia	75.90	12.09	63.81
Switzerland — Suisse — Suiza	58.57	56.31	2.26
Spain — Espagne — España	36.68	33.22	3.46
Costa Rica	32.91	32.38	0.53
Cyprus — Chypre — Chipre	32.52	30.48	2.04
Finland — Finlande — Finlandia	30.77	26.40	4.38
Italy — Italie — Italia	28.29	23.53	4.76
Cuba	26.72	26.72	0.00
Czech Republic — République tchèque — República Checa	24.63	1.53	23.10
Ireland — Irlande — Irlanda	23.10	19.87	3.23
Denmark — Danemark — Dinamarca	22.70	11.06	11.64
Netherlands — Pays-Bas — Países Bajos	22.29	19.65	2.64
Germany — Allemagne — Alemania	22.28	18.12	4.15
Israel — Israël	19.95	16.79	3.16
Portugal	18.44	12.53	5.92
United States of America — États-Unis d'Amérique — Estados Unidos de América	17.90	7.95	9.95
Sweden — Suède — Suecia	17.62	6.99	10.64
Hungary — Hongrie — Hungría	16.57	11.66	4.91
Australia — Australie	16.56	11.03	5.53
Iceland — Islande — Islandia	13.94	2.44	11.51
Greece — Grèce — Grecia	13.87	7.29	6.59
Austria — Autriche	13.86	13.78	0.08
Canada — Canadá	13.19	9.47	3.72
New Zealand — Nouvelle-Zélande — Nueva Zelandia	10.02	6.67	3.35
Poland — Pologne — Polonia	10.02	8.00	2.01
Malta — Malte	8.77	5.14	3.63
Slovenia — Slovénie — Eslovenia	7.54	2.60	4.93
Republic of Korea — République de Corée — República de Corea	7.35	6.09	1.27
Romania — Roumanie — Rumania	7.28	0.64	6.64
Singapore — Singapour — Singapur	7.19	2.74	4.45
Netherlands Antilles — Antilles néerlandaises — Antillas Neerlandesas	5.04	1.28	3.76
Estonia — Estonie	4.72	3.79	0.93
Norway — Norvège — Noruega	4.30	1.40	2.90
Lithuania — Lituanie — Lituania	3.73	2.58	1.14
Brazil — Brésil — Brasil	3.53	3.37	0.16
South Africa — Afrique du Sud — Sudáfrica	3.16	2.94	0.22
China — Chine	2.57	1.84	0.73
Latvia — Lettonie — Letonia	2.31	1.01	1.30
Chile — Chili	2.13	0.93	1.20
Hong Kong SAR of China — RAS de Hong Kong (Chine) — RAE de Hong Kong de China	1.93	0.37	1.56
Argentina — Argentine	1.91	1.85	0.06
Malaysia — Malaisie — Malasia	1.74	1.50	0.24
Lebanon — Liban — Líbano	1.59	0.11	1.48
Mauritius — Maurice — Mauricio	1.37	0.91	0.46
Panama — Panamá	1.33	0.97	0.35

Table IV.2. Consumption of sedative-hypnotics
Tableau IV.2. Consommation de sédatifs-hypnotiques
Cuadro IV.2. Consumo de sedantes-hipnóticos
(continued — suite — continuación)

Country or territory Pays ou territoire País o territorio	All sedative-hypnotics (groups E–J)[a] Tous les sédatifs-hypnotiques (groupes E à J)[a] Todos los sedantes-hipnóticos (grupos E a J)[a]	Benzodiazepines (group G)[a] Benzodiazépines (groupe G)[a] Benzodiazepinas (grupo G)[a]	Others Autres Otros
Macao SAR of China — RAS de Macao (Chine) — RAE de Macao de China	1.20	0.30	0.90
Dominican Republic — République dominicaine — República Dominicana	0.96	0.67	0.29
India — Inde	0.89	0.84	0.05
Pakistan — Pakistán	0.89	0.89	0.00
Syrian Arab Republic — République arabe syrienne — República Árabe Siria	0.61	0.61	0.00
Bulgaria — Bulgarie	0.60	0.31	0.29
Nigeria — Nigéria	0.55	0.55	0.00
Morocco — Maroc — Marruecos	0.50	0.01	0.49
Tunisia — Tunisie — Túnez	0.41	0.07	0.34
Colombia — Colombie	0.40	0.07	0.33
Ecuador — Équateur	0.36	0.18	0.17
El Salvador	0.36	0.17	0.18
Venezuela (Bolivarian Republic of) — Venezuela (République bolivarienne du) — Venezuela (República Bolivariana de)	0.34	0.14	0.21
Belarus — Bélarus — Belarús	0.33	0.28	0.06
The former Yugoslav Republic of Macedonia — L'ex-République yougoslave de Macédoine — La ex República Yugoslava de Macedonia	0.32	0.32	0.00
Nicaragua	0.26	0.21	0.05
United Arab Emirates — Émirats arabes unis — Emiratos Árabes Unidos	0.24	0.24	0.00
Qatar	0.23	0.23	0.00
Gabon — Gabón	0.21	0.00	0.21
Bahrain — Bahreïn — Bahrein	0.20	0.20	0.00
Libyan Arab Jamahiriya — Jamahiriya arabe libyenne — Jamahiriya Árabe Libia	0.20	0.20	0.00
Peru — Pérou — Perú	0.18	0.06	0.12
Georgia — Géorgie	0.17	0.00	0.17
Jamaica — Jamaïque	0.16	0.05	0.11
Albania — Albanie	0.15	0.00	0.15
Thailand — Thaïlande — Tailandia	0.15	0.11	0.03

[a] The groups of psychotropic substances are presented in table III.2. — Les groupes de substances psychotropes sont présentés dans le tableau III.2. — Los grupos de sustancias sicotrópicas se presentan en el cuadro III.2.

Table IV.3.   Consumption of anxiolytics
Tableau IV.3.   Consommation d'anxiolytiques
Cuadro IV.3.   Consumo de ansiolíticos
(continued — suite — continuación)

Country or territory Pays ou territoire País o territorio	All anxiolytics (groups K and L)[a] Tous les anxiolytiques (groupes K et L)[a] Todos los ansiolíticos (grupos K y L)[a]	Benzodiazepines (group K)[a] Benzodiazépines (groupe K)[a] Benzodiazepinas (grupo K)[a]	Meprobamate (group L)[a] Méprobamate (groupe L)[a] Meprobamato (grupo L)[a]
France — Francia	58.26	55.19	3.06
Hungary — Hongrie — Hungría	54.02	49.05	4.97
Ireland — Irlande — Irlanda	52.00	51.40	0.60
Belgium — Belgique — Bélgica	51.00	50.20	0.80
Cyprus — Chypre — Chipre	47.99	47.99	0.00
Germany — Allemagne — Alemania	43.16	43.16	0.00
Finland — Finlande — Finlandia	35.40	35.18	0.22
Italy — Italie — Italia	35.02	35.01	0.00
Canada — Canadá	32.72	32.72	0.00
Norway — Norvège — Noruega	31.96	31.92	0.04
Lithuania — Lituanie — Lituania	29.92	29.92	0.00
Greece — Grèce — Grecia	27.83	27.83	0.00
Denmark — Danemark — Dinamarca	23.97	23.87	0.11
Switzerland — Suisse — Suiza	23.76	23.75	0.01
United States — États-Unis — Estados Unidos	23.33	23.33	0.00
Andorra — Andorre	23.20	23.16	0.03
Romania — Roumanie — Rumania	20.58	20.10	0.47
Chile — Chili	20.57	20.57	0.00
Malta — Malte	19.86	19.86	0.00
Lebanon — Liban — Líbano	19.76	19.19	0.57
Ghana	19.43	19.43	0.00
Austria — Autriche	18.92	18.51	0.41
Brazil — Brésil — Brasil	18.46	18.46	0.00
Iceland — Islande — Islandia	18.46	18.39	0.07
Spain — Espagne — España	17.30	17.00	0.30
Israel — Israël	17.29	17.28	0.01
Portugal	16.50	16.10	0.40

Iran (Islamic Republic of) —
  Iran (République islamique d') —
  Irán (República Islámica del)
	15.95	15.95	0.00

South Africa — Afrique du Sud — Sudáfrica	15.74	14.01	1.73
Netherlands — Pays-Bas — Países Bajos	15.65	15.61	0.03
United Kingdom — Royaume-Uni — Reino Unido	15.50	15.00	0.50
Australia — Australie	15.15	15.15	0.00
Sweden — Suède — Suecia	14.24	14.16	0.08
Estonia — Estonie	13.49	13.49	0.00
Czech Republic — République tchèque — República Checa	13.43	13.43	0.00
Latvia — Lettonie — Letonia	12.97	12.97	0.00
Japan — Japon — Japón	12.27	12.27	0.00
Slovenia — Slovénie — Eslovenia	12.00	11.50	0.50
Albania — Albanie	11.04	10.86	0.18
El Salvador	9.85	9.85	0.00
Poland — Pologne — Polonia	9.74	9.74	0.00
Thailand — Thaïlande — Tailandia	9.57	9.57	0.00

Venezuela (Bolivarian Republic of) —
  Venezuela (République bolivarienne du) —
  Venezuela (República Bolivariana de)
	9.36	9.36	0.00

Benin — Bénin	9.34	9.34	0.00
Republic of Korea — République de Corée — República de Corea	9.09	9.09	0.00
Cape Verde — Cap-Vert — Cabo Verde	8.58	8.58	0.00
Bulgaria — Bulgarie	8.56	8.56	0.00
Tunisia — Tunisie — Túnez	8.01	7.29	0.72

Table IV.3.   Consumption of anxiolytics
Tableau IV.3.   Consommation d'anxiolytiques
Cuadro IV.3.   Consumo de ansiolíticos
(continued — suite — continuación)

Country or territory Pays ou territoire País o territorio	All anxiolytics (groups K and L)[a] Tous les anxiolytiques (groupes K et L)[a] Todos los ansiolíticos (grupos K y L)[a]	Benzodiazepines (group K)[a] Benzodiazépines (groupe K)[a] Benzodiazepinas (grupo K)[a]	Meprobamate (group L)[a] Méprobamate (groupe L)[a] Meprobamato (grupo L)[a]
Syrian Arab Republic — République arabe syrienne — República Árabe Siria	7.95	7.86	0.09
Algeria — Algérie — Argelia	7.93	7.70	0.23
Peru — Pérou — Perú	7.58	7.58	0.00
Nicaragua	7.13	7.13	0.00
Dominican Republic — République dominicaine — República Dominicana	6.53	6.53	0.00
China — Chine	5.86	5.86	0.00
Morocco — Maroc — Marruecos	5.31	5.21	0.10
Pakistan — Pakistán	5.29	5.28	0.01
Mauritius — Maurice — Mauricio	5.14	5.14	0.00
Netherlands Antilles — Antilles néerlandaises — Antillas Neerlandesas	5.10	5.10	0.00
Hong Kong SAR of China — RAS de Hong Kong (Chine) — RAE de Hong Kong de China	5.04	5.04	0.00
United Republic of Tanzania — République-Unie de Tanzanie — República Unida de Tanzanía	5.02	5.02	0.00
India — Inde	4.96	4.96	0.00
Singapore — Singapour — Singapur	4.41	4.41	0.00
New Zealand — Nouvelle-Zélande — Nueva Zelandia	4.04	4.04	0.00
Democratic Republic of the Congo — République démocratique du Congo — República Democrática del Congo	3.60	3.57	0.03
Ecuador — Équateur	3.34	3.34	0.00
Trinidad and Tobago — Trinité-et-Tobago — Trinidad y Tabago	3.30	3.30	0.00
Sri Lanka	3.13	3.13	0.00
Panama — Panamá	2.84	2.84	0.00
Cambodia — Cambodge — Camboya	2.56	2.55	0.01
Egypt — Égypte — Egipto	2.52	2.52	0.00
Nigeria — Nigéria	2.49	2.49	0.00
Bangladesh	2.46	2.46	0.00
Belarus — Bélarus — Belarús	2.44	2.44	0.00
Malaysia — Malaisie — Malasia	2.26	2.26	0.00
Jamaica — Jamaïque	2.21	2.21	0.00
Costa Rica	2.00	2.00	0.00
Gabon — Gabón	2.00	2.00	0.00
Turkey — Turquie — Turquía	1.98	1.85	0.13
Georgia — Géorgie	1.88	1.88	0.00
Bahrain — Bahreïn — Bahrein	1.70	1.70	0.00
Russian Federation — Fédération de Russie — Federación de Rusia	1.45	1.45	0.00
Colombia — Colombie	1.39	1.39	0.00
Macao SAR of China — RAS de Macao (Chine) — RAE de Macao de China	1.20	1.20	0.00
Zambia — Zambie	1.05	1.05	0.00
Senegal — Sénégal	1.02	1.02	0.00
Togo	1.01	1.01	0.00

[a]The groups of psychotropic substances are presented in table III.2. — Les groupes de substances psychotropes sont présentés dans le tableau III.2. — Los grupos de sustancias sicotrópicas se presentan en el cuadro III.2.

Table IV.4.   Consumption of anti-epileptics
Tableau IV.4.   Consommation d'antiépileptiques
Cuadro IV.4.   Consumo de antiepilépticos

(continued — suite — continuación)

Country or territory Pays ou territoire País o territorio	All anti-epileptics (groups M and N)[b] Tous les antiépileptiques (groupes M et N)[b] Todos los antiepilépticos (grupos M y N)[b]	Barbiturates[a] (group M)[b] Barbituriques[a] (groupe M)[b] Barbitúricos[a] (grupo M)[b]	Benzodiazepines (group N)[b] Benzodiazépines (groupe N)[b] Benzodiazepinas (grupo N)[b]
Ukraine — Ucrania	14.35	14.35	0.00
Bulgaria — Bulgarie	14.29	13.64	0.90

Russian Federation —
  Fédération de Russie —
  Federación de Rusia
	12.54	12.54	0.00

Latvia — Lettonie — Letonia	10.24	8.30	1.94
Argentina — Argentine	8.80	3.99	4.81
Brazil — Brésil — Brasil	7.45	5.79	1.65
Canada — Canadá	6.44	2.44	4.00
Hungary — Hongrie — Hungría	6.00	5.40	0.60
Italy — Italie — Italia	5.29	4.71	0.58
France — Francia	5.02	3.28	1.74
Chile — Chili	4.99	2.79	2.20
Switzerland — Suisse — Suiza	4.89	3.65	1.24
Egypt — Égypte — Egipto	4.88	4.62	0.26
Japan — Japon — Japón	4.84	4.16	0.67
Romania — Roumanie — Rumania	3.77	3.76	0.02
Belarus — Bélarus — Belarús	3.73	3.69	0.03
Benin — Bénin	3.48	3.48	0.00
Cyprus — Chypre — Chipre	3.41	0.41	3.00
Belgium — Belgique — Bélgica	3.26	2.27	0.53

United States of America —
  États-Unis d'Amérique —
  Estados Unidos de América
	3.03	1.79	1.23

South Africa — Afrique du Sud — Sudáfrica	2.73	2.49	0.24
Lithuania — Lituanie — Lituania	2.72	0.77	1.96
Spain — Espagne — España	2.67	1.70	0.97
El Salvador	2.65	2.22	0.43
Algeria — Algérie — Argelia	2.63	1.87	0.75
Ireland — Irlande — Irlanda	2.44	2.27	0.18
Israel — Israël	2.42	1.11	1.30

Dominican Republic —
  République dominicaine —
  República Dominicana
	2.31	2.03	0.28

Tunisia — Tunisie — Túnez	2.28	2.25	0.04
China — Chine	2.27	2.19	0.07
Viet Nam	2.26	2.26	0.00
Eritrea — Érythrée	2.25	2.25	0.00
United Kingdom — Royaume-Uni — Reino Unido	2.23	1.16	1.07
Australia — Australie	1.98	1.07	0.91
Mauritius — Maurice — Mauricio	1.93	1.64	0.29
Netherlands — Pays-Bas — Países Bajos	1.84	1.55	0.30
Morocco — Maroc — Marruecos	1.75	1.75	0.00
Norway — Norvège — Noruega	1.75	0.91	0.84
Iran (Islamic Rep. of) — Iran (Rép. islamique d') — Irán (Rep. Islámica del)	1.71	0.60	1.11
Panama — Panamá	1.55	1.33	0.22
Burkina Faso	1.47	1.47	0.00
Zimbabwe	1.46	1.46	0.00
Senegal — Sénégal	1.40	1.33	0.07
Finland — Finlande — Finlandia	1.35	0.43	0.92
Lebanon — Liban — Líbano	1.35	0.88	0.48

Venezuela (Bolivarian Republic of) —
  Venezuela (République bolivarienne du) —
  Venezuela (República Bolivariana de)
	1.31	1.01	0.30

Table IV.4.   Consumption of anti-epileptics
Tableau IV.4.   Consommation d'antiépileptiques
Cuadro IV.4.   Consumo de antiepilépticos
(continued — suite — continuación)

Country or territory Pays ou territoire País o territorio	All anti-epileptics (groups M and N)[b] Tous les antiépileptiques (groupes M et N)[b] Todos los antiepilépticos (grupos M y N)[b]	Barbiturates[a] (group M)[b] Barbituriques[a] (groupe M)[b] Barbitúricos[a] (grupo M)[b]	Benzodiazepines (group N)[b] Benzodiazépines (groupe N)[b] Benzodiazepinas (grupo N)[b]
Peru — Pérou — Perú	1.27	0.89	0.37
Greece — Grèce — Grecia	1.20	1.01	0.19
Costa Rica	1.17	0.00	1.17
Czech Republic — République tchèque — República Checa	1.17	0.30	0.87
Haiti — Haïti — Haití	1.14	1.14	0.00
Portugal	1.13	0.41	0.72
Sri Lanka	1.12	0.89	0.24
Sweden — Suède — Suecia	1.09	0.82	0.27
Estonia — Estonie	1.07	0.55	0.53
Trinidad and Tobago — Trinité-et-Tobago — Trinidad y Tabago	1.07	1.07	0.00

[a]The elevated consumption levels of barbiturates are partly due to other uses of phenobarbital (sedative-hypnotic or in combination preparations prescribed for various indications). — Les niveaux de consommation élevés des barbituriques sont imputables en partie aux autres utilisations du phénobarbital (comme sédatif-hypnotique ou dans des préparations combinées prescrites pour diverses indications). — Los elevados niveles de consumo de barbitúricos se deben en parte a otros usos del fenobarbital (como sedante-hipnótico o en preparados combinados prescritos para diversas indicaciones).

[b]The groups of psychotropic substances are presented in table III.2. — Les groupes de substances psychotropes sont présentés dans le tableau III.2. — Los grupos de sustancias sicotrópicas se presentan en el cuadro III.2.

Table IV.5. Comparision of trends in consumption of specific substances and groups, 1993-1995 and 2003-2005

Tableau IV.5. Comparaison des tendances dans la consommation de certaines substances et groupes, 1993-1995 et 2003-2005

Cuadro IV.5. Comparacion de las tendencias en el consumo de algunas sustancias y grupos, 1993-1995 y 2003-2005

(continued — suite — continuación)

Country or territory Pays ou territoire País o territorio	1993-1995	2003-2005
Buprenorphine — Buprénorphine — Buprenorfina		
France — Francia	0.18	10.52
Germany — Allemagne — Alemania	0.08	4.64
Australia — Australie	0.00	3.81
New Zealand — Nouvelle-Zélande — Nueva Zelandia	0.00	3.38
Austria — Autriche	0.00	3.10
Norway — Norvège — Noruega	0.00	3.04
Netherlands — Pays-Bas — Países Bajos	0.00	2.94
Spain — Espagne — España	0.00	2.92
Iceland — Islande — Islandia	0.00	2.67
Portugal	0.00	2.66
Sweden — Suède — Suecia	0.00	2.65
Italy — Italie — Italia	0.04	2.17
Denmark — Danemark — Dinamarca	0.29	2.13
Czech Republic — République tchèque — República Checa	0.07	2.09
Singapore — Singapour — Singapur	0.00	2.01
Switzerland — Suisse — Suiza	0.00	1.69
Ireland — Irlande — Irlanda	0.00	1.57
Methylphenidate — Méthylphénidate — Metilfenidato		
United States — États-Unis — Estados Unidos	2.51	6.65
Iceland — Islande — Islandia	0.13	4.27
Canada — Canadá	1.11	3.67
Norway — Norvège — Noruega	0.23	2.32
Israel — Israël	0.31	1.87
Switzerland — Suisse — Suiza	0.59	1.85
Netherlands — Pays-Bas — Países Bajos	0.08	1.67
New Zealand — Nouvelle-Zélande — Nueva Zelandia	0.23	1.51
Australia — Australie	0.34	1.26
Germany — Allemagne — Alemania	0.05	1.19
United Kingdom — Royaume-Uni — Reino Unido	0.45	1.19
Belgium — Belgique — Bélgica	0.10	1.12
Spain — Espagne — España	0.10	0.80
Denmark — Danemark — Dinamarca	0.06	0.64
Sweden — Suède — Suecia	0.02	0.61
Ireland — Irlande — Irlanda	0.10	0.46
Finland — Finlande — Finlandia	0.00	0.40
Chile — Chili	0.11	0.37
Panama — Panamá	0.14	0.30
Phenobarbital — Phénobarbital — Fenobarbital		
Ukraine — Ucrania	6.75	17.16
Russian Federation — Fédération de Russie — Federación de Rusia	7.00	15.20
Bulgaria — Bulgarie	13.62	14.81
Kazakhstan — Kazajstán	0.00	9.73

Table IV.5.   Comparision of trends in consumption of specific substances and groups, 1993-1995 and 2003-2005
Tableau IV.5.   Comparaison des tendances dans la consommation de certaines substances et groupes, 1993-1995 et 2003-2005
Cuadro IV.5.   Comparacion de las tendencias en el consumo de algunas sustancias y grupos, 1993-1995 y 2003-2005

(continued — suite — continuación)

Country or territory Pays ou territoire País o territorio	1993-1995	2003-2005
Phenobarbital — Phénobarbital — Fenobarbital *(continued — suite — continuación)*		
Latvia — Lettonie — Letonia	1.76	6.53
Brazil — Brésil — Brasil	3.82	6.25
Cuba	15.41	5.52
Romania — Roumanie — Rumania	5.99	4.97
Italy — Italie — Italia	3.96	4.17
Cape Verde —Cap-Vert — Cabo Verde	0.86	3.87
Senegal — Sénégal	0.74	3.81
Japan — Japon — Japón	2.63	3.67
Egypt — Égypte — Egipto	0.20	3.24
Jordan — Jordanie — Jordania	1.03	3.20
France — Francia	10.91	3.18
Belarus —Bélarus — Belarús	0.53	2.82
Argentina — Argentine	2.00	2.74
Benin — Bénin	0.49	2.62
Stimulants in Schedule IV — Stimulants au Tableau IV — Estimulantes de la Lista IV		
Brazil — Brésil — Brasil	5.14	10.52
Argentina — Argentine	11.12	8.37
United States — États-Unis — Estados Unidos	4.98	6.92
Republic of Korea — République de Corée — República de Corea	0.11	6.16
Singapore — Singapour — Singapur	4.57	5.34
Hong Kong SAR of China — RAS de Hong Kong (Chine) — RAE de Hong Kong de China	12.09	4.68
Switzerland — Suisse — Suiza	0.15	2.93
Malaysia — Malaisie — Malasia	1.60	2.64
Australia — Australie	3.61	2.57
Panama — Panamá	0.07	2.41
Costa Rica	1.28	2.24
Czech Republic — République tchèque — República Checa	1.06	2.22
Germany — Allemagne — Alemania	0.29	1.66
Mexico — Mexique — México	3.01	1.22
Paraguay	0.14	1.20
Thailand — Thaïlande — Tailandia	1.17	1.19
France — Francia	1.22	1.16
Chile — Chili	10.07	0.86
New Zealand — Nouvelle-Zélande — Nueva Zelandia	0.76	0.83
Israel — Israël	0.69	0.79
Italy — Italie — Italia	0.84	0.66
Belize — Belice	0.00	0.48
Ecuador — Équateur	0.72	0.43
Netherlands — Pays-Bas — Países Bajos	5.76	0.43
Brunei Darussalam — Brunéi Darussalam	0.13	0.40
Azerbaijan — Azerbaïdjan — Azerbaiyán	0.00	0.39
Canada — Canadá	0.44	0.37
United Kingdom — Royaume-Uni — Reino Unido	4.93	0.33
Slovakia — Slovaquie — Eslovaquia	0.34	0.32

Table IV.5. Comparision of trends in consumption of specific substances and groups, 1993-1995 and 2003-2005

Tableau IV.5. Comparaison des tendances dans la consommation de certaines substances et groupes, 1993-1995 et 2003-2005

Cuadro IV.5. Comparacion de las tendencias en el consumo de algunas sustancias y grupos, 1995-1993 y 2005-2003

(concluded — fin — conclusión)

Country or territory Pays ou territoire País o territorio	1995-1995	2003-2005
Stimulants in Schedule IV — Stimulants au Tableau IV — Estimulantes de la Lista IV *(continued — suite — continuación)*		
South Africa — Afrique du Sud — Sudáfrica	0.47	0.30
Philippines — Filipinas	0.03	0.29
Honduras	0.13	0.25
Peru — Pérou — Perú	0.85	0.18
Denmark — Danemark — Dinamarca	0.77	0.14
Nicaragua	0.06	0.13
Namibia — Namibie	0.06	0.12
Romania — Roumanie — Rumania	0.00	0.10
Belgium — Belgique — Bélgica	0.00	0.09
Venezuela (Bolivarian Rep. of) — Venezuela (Rép. bolivarienne du) — Venezuela (Rep. Bolivariana de)	0.95	0.08
Japan — Japon — Japón	0.04	0.06
Spain — Espagne — España	2.43	0.03

Table V.   Assessments of annual medical and scientific requirements for substances listed in Schedules II, III and IV of the Convention on Psychotropic Substances of 1971

Assessments of annual medical and scientific requirements for substances listed in Schedules II, III and IV of the Convention on Psychotropic Substances of 1971 are published in accordance with the provisions of Economic and Social Council resolutions 1981/7 of 6 May 1981 and 1991/44 of 21 June 1991. The Council requested Governments to assess, from time to time, their annual requirements and to submit the assessments to INCB for publication.

The reported medical and scientific requirements are intended to supplement the import and export control system for international trade established in article 12 of the 1971 Convention. The reported assessments are intended to assist the national authorities of exporting countries in ascertaining whether a requested import appears to be excessive in comparison with a reported annual requirement for that country. If that is the case, the export should be denied until the designated national authorities of the importing country confirm the legitimacy of the import request and authenticate the import documents. It is expected that scrupulous adherence to this procedure will substantially diminish attempts at diversion, especially those involving very large quantities.

The countries and territories that have submitted assessments for psychotropic substances are presented in English alphabetical order. The names of territories appear in italics. The names of countries and territories are those that were in official use at the time the data were collected (in 2005).

Pursuant to Economic and Social Council resolution 1996/30 of 24 June 1996, INCB established assessments of annual licit requirements of psychotropic substances for countries that have not yet submitted such information. In the table below, assessments established by INCB are indicated by footnote (^{a}).

> The assessments established by INCB reflect previous patterns of use of psychotropic substances in the respective countries. They should not be considered recommended consumption levels. The only objective of these assessments is to provide exporting countries with approximate information on the legitimate requirements of the importing country. INCB encourages all Governments concerned to establish their own assessments as soon as possible.

Exporting countries should note that importing countries are free to replace any substance for which an assessment has been established by INCB with another substance from the same therapeutic group and the same schedule, provided that the quantity to be imported, expressed in defined daily doses for statistical purposes (S-DDD), does not exceed the equivalent of the assessment also expressed in S-DDD. The composition of the respective therapeutic groups and the S-DDD of the substances in those groups are indicated in table III.2 of the present publication.

Tableau V. Prévisions des besoins annuels médicaux et scientifiques concernant les substances énumérées aux Tableaux II, III et IV de la Convention de 1971 sur les substances psychotropes

Les prévisions des besoins annuels médicaux et scientifiques concernant les substances énumérées aux Tableaux II, III et IV de la Convention de 1971 sur les substances psychotropes sont communiquées conformément aux dispositions des résolutions 1981/7, en date du 6 mai 1981, et 1991/44, en date du 21 juin 1991, du Conseil économique et social. Le Conseil a prié les gouvernements d'effectuer de temps à autre des prévisions de leurs besoins annuels et de communiquer ces prévisions à l'Organe international de contrôle des stupéfiants (OICS) afin qu'elles soient publiées.

Les indications relatives aux besoins médicaux et scientifiques sont destinées à compléter le système de contrôle du commerce international à l'importation et à l'exportation prévu à l'article 12 de la Convention de 1971. Les prévisions doivent permettre d'aider les autorités des pays exportateurs à déterminer si une importation demandée par un pays semble excessive par rapport aux besoins annuels signalés par ce pays. Dans ce cas, il ne faudra pas que l'exportation ait lieu tant que les services officiels du pays importateur n'auront pas confirmé la validité de la demande d'importation et authentifié les documents d'importation. On pense qu'en se conformant scrupuleusement à cette procédure on parviendra à éliminer les tentatives de détournement, notamment celles qui impliquent de très grandes quantités des substances visées.

Les pays et territoires qui ont soumis des prévisions pour des substances psychotropes sont présentés dans l'ordre alphabétique anglais. Les noms des territoires sont en italique. Les noms des pays et territoires sont ceux qui étaient officiellement en usage au moment où les données ont été recueillies (en 2005).

En application de la résolution 1996/30, en date du 24 juin 1996, du Conseil économique et social, l'Organe a évalué les besoins annuels en substances psychotropes utilisées à des fins licites pour les pays qui ne les ont pas encore communiqués. Dans le tableau ci-après, les évaluations ainsi établies par l'Organe comportent un renvoi à une note de bas de page indiquée par une lettre ([a]).

L'OICS a évalué les besoins en substances psychotropes des différents pays en se fondant sur les profils d'utilisation propres à ces pays. Les prévisions indiquées ne sont pas des niveaux de consommation recommandés. Elles ont été établies dans le seul but de fournir aux pays exportateurs des renseignements approximatifs sur les besoins légitimes des pays importateurs. L'OICS encourage tous les gouvernements visés à établir leurs propres prévisions aussitôt que possible.

Les pays exportateurs doivent noter que les pays importateurs sont libres de remplacer toute substance, pour laquelle l'Organe a évalué les besoins, par une autre substance appartenant au même groupe thérapeutique et inscrite au même tableau, à condition que la quantité à importer, exprimée en doses quotidiennes déterminées à des fins statistiques (S-DDD), ne dépasse pas l'équivalent de la prévision (également exprimé en S-DDD). La composition des différents groupes thérapeutiques et la valeur des S-DDD des substances appartenant à ces groupes sont indiquées au tableau III.2 de la présente publication.

Cuadro V.   Previsiones de las necesidades anuales para fines médicos y científicos de las sustancias incluidas en las Listas II, III y IV del Convenio sobre Sustancias Sicotrópicas de 1971

Las previsiones de las necesidades anuales para fines médicos y científicos de las sustancias incluidas en las Listas II, III y IV del Convenio sobre Sustancias Sicotrópicas de 1971 se publican de conformidad con las disposiciones de las resoluciones del Consejo Económico y Social 1981/7, de 6 de mayo de 1981, y 1991/44, de 21 de junio de 1991. El Consejo pidió a los gobiernos que evaluaran periódicamente sus necesidades anuales y que presentaran las previsiones a la JIFE con miras a publicarlas.

Los informes sobre las necesidades para fines médicos y científicos complementan el sistema de control de importaciones y exportaciones en el comercio internacional establecido en el artículo 12 del Convenio de 1971. Las previsiones presentadas tienen por objeto ayudar a las autoridades nacionales de los países exportadores a determinar si la importación solicitada parece excesiva en comparación con las necesidades anuales declaradas por el país en cuestión. En esos casos, debe negarse la exportación hasta que las autoridades competentes del país importador confirmen la legitimidad de la petición de importación y autentifiquen los documentos de importación. Cabe esperar que si se sigue escrupulosamente este procedimiento disminuyan considerablemente los intentos de desviación, especialmente los que entrañan grandes cantidades de sustancias.

Los países y territorios que han suministrado previsiones para las sustancias sicotrópicas se presentan en orden alfabético inglés. Los nombres de los territoriros figuran en letra cursiva. Los nombres de los países y territorios son los que se utilizaban oficialmente en el momento en que se obtuvo la información (en 2005).

De conformidad con la resolución 1996/30 del Consejo Económico y Social, de 24 de junio de 1996, la JIFE estableció previsiones de las necesidades anuales lícitas de sustancias sicotrópicas para los países que aún no habían presentado tal información. En el siguiente cuadro, las previsiones establecidas por la JIFE se indican en una nota de pie de página (^{a}).

> Las previsiones establecidas por la JIFE reflejan los patrones previos de consumo de sustancias sicotrópicas en los países respectivos. Estas previsiones no deben ser consideradas niveles de consumo recomendados. Su único objetivo es proporcionar a los países exportadores información aproximada sobre las necesidades legítimas del país importador. La JIFE exhorta a todos los gobiernos interesados a establecer sus propias previsiones tan pronto como sea posible.

Los países exportadores deberán tener en cuenta que los países importadores pueden reemplazar cualquier sustancia para la cual la JIFE ha establecido una previsión por otra sustancia perteneciente al mismo grupo terapéutico y a la misma lista, siempre y cuando la cantidad que se vaya a importar, expresada en dosis diarias definidas con fines estadísticos (S-DDD), no exceda de la cantidad equivalente de la previsión, expresada también en S-DDD. En el cuadro III.2 de la presente publicación se indican la composición de los respectivos grupos terapéuticos y las S-DDD de las sustancias de esos grupos.

Table V. Assessments of annual domestic medical and scientific requirements
Tableau V. Évaluations des besoins annuels médicaux et scientifiques intérieurs
Cuadro V. Previsiones de las necesidades anuales internas para fines médicos y científicos

Country (or territory) and substance Pays (ou territoire) et substance País (o territorio) y sustancia	Assessment (grams) Évaluation (en grammes) Previsión (en gramos)
Afghanistan — Afganistán	
Alprazolam	15 000
Bromazepam — Bromazépam	10 000
Buprenorphine — Buprénorphine — Buprenorfina	10
Chlordiazepoxide — Chlordiazépoxide — Clordiazepóxido	60 000
Clonazepam — Clonazépam	2 000
Clorazepate — Clorazépate — Clorazepato	60 000
Diazepam — Diazépam	40 000
Lorazepam — Lorazépam	2 000
Nitrazepam — Nitrazépam	3 000
Oxazepam — Oxazépam	2 000
Pentazocine — Pentazocina	6 000
Phenobarbital — Phénobarbital — Fenobarbital	1 000 000
Temazepam — Témazépam	4 000
Albania — Albanie	
Alprazolam	500
Barbital	100 000
Bromazepam — Bromazépam	5 000
Brotizolam	100
Chlordiazepoxide — Chlordiazépoxide — Clordiazepóxido	50 000
Clonazepam — Clonazépam	1 500
Clorazepate — Clorazépate — Clorazepato	4 000
Diazepam — Diazépam	80 000
Flunitrazepam — Flunitrazépam	20
Lorazepam — Lorazépam	12 000
Meprobamate — Méprobamate — Meprobamato	300 000
Methylphenidate — Méthylphénidate — Metilfenidato	500
Midazolam	200
Nitrazepam — Nitrazépam	200
Phenobarbital — Phénobarbital — Fenobarbital	130 000
Temazepam — Témazépam	100
Zolpidem	1 000
Algeria — Algérie — Argelia	
Barbital	5 000
Bromazepam — Bromazépam	1 000 000
Buprenorphine — Buprénorphine — Buprenorfina	2 500
Chlordiazepoxide — Chlordiazépoxide — Clordiazepóxido	50 000
Clonazepam — Clonazépam	130 000
Clorazepate — Clorazépate — Clorazepato	550 000
Diazepam — Diazépam	500 000
Flunitrazepam — Flunitrazépam	500
Lorazepam — Lorazépam	300 000
Meprobamate — Méprobamate — Meprobamato	5 000 000
Midazolam	1 500
Nitrazepam — Nitrazépam	40 000
Nordazepam — Nordazépam	1
Phenobarbital — Phénobarbital — Fenobarbital	4 000 000
Prazepam — Prazépam	800 000
Temazepam — Témazépam	500
Tetrazepam — Tétrazépam	2 000 000
Zolpidem	250 000
Andorra — Andorre	
Alprazolam	1 300
Amfetamine — Amfétamine — Anfetamina	5
Bromazepam — Bromazépam	2 000
Brotizolam	10
Buprenorphine — Buprénorphine — Buprenorfina	10
Butalbital	500
Butobarbital	1 000
Chlordiazepoxide — Chlordiazépoxide — Clordiazepóxido	100
Clobazam	300
Clonazepam — Clonazépam	100
Clorazepate — Clorazépate — Clorazepato	3 000
Clotiazepam — Clotiazépam	100
Delta-9-tetrahydrocannabinol — Delta-9-tétrahydrocannabinol — Delta-9-tetrahidrocannabinol	10
Diazepam — Diazépam	3 000
Estazolam	10
Ethyl loflazepate — Loflazépate d'éthyle — Loflazepato de etilo	20
Flunitrazepam — Flunitrazépam	50
Flurazepam — Flurazépam	1 000
Halazepam — Halazépam	2 000
Ketazolam — Kétazolam	2 000
Loprazolam	50
Lorazepam — Lorazépam	2 000
Lormetazepam — Lormétazépam	1 000
Medazepam — Médazépam	300
Meprobamate — Méprobamate — Meprobamato	15 000
Metamfetamine racemate — Racémate de métamfétamine — Racemato de metanfetamina	5
Methylphenidate — Méthylphénidate — Metilfenidato	500
Midazolam	100
Nitrazepam — Nitrazépam	200
Nordazepam — Nordazépam	200
Oxazepam — Oxazépam	1 000
Pemoline — Pémoline — Pemolina	100
Pentazocine — Pentazocina	50
Phenobarbital — Phénobarbital — Fenobarbital	5 000
Pinazepam — Pinazépam	100
Prazepam — Prazépam	1 000
Temazepam — Témazépam	100
Tetrazepam — Tétrazépam	15 000
Triazolam	10
Zolpidem	1 000
Angola	
Alprazolam	3 000
Bromazepam — Bromazépam	600
Brotizolam	600
Buprenorphine — Buprénorphine — Buprenorfina	300
Chlordiazepoxide — Chlordiazépoxide — Clordiazepóxido	600
Clobazam	100
Clonazepam — Clonazépam	50
Clorazepate — Clorazépate — Clorazepato	60
Cloxazolam	50
Diazepam — Diazépam	40 000

Table V. Assessments of annual domestic medical and scientific requirements
Tableau V. Évaluations des besoins annuels médicaux et scientifiques intérieurs
Cuadro V. Previsiones de las necesidades anuales internas para fines médicos y científicos

Country (or territory) and substance Pays (ou territoire) et substance País (o territorio) y sustancia	Assessment (grams) Évaluation (en grammes) Previsión (en gramos)
Estazolam	50
Flunitrazepam — Flunitrazépam	600
Flurazepam — Flurazépam	60
Halazepam — Halazépam	65
Ketazolam — Kétazolam	70
Lorazepam — Lorazépam	1 000
Meprobamate — Méprobamate — Meprobamato	4 000
Midazolam	900
Nitrazepam — Nitrazépam	650
Pentazocine — Pentazocina	900
Phenobarbital — Phénobarbital — Fenobarbital	80 000
Triazolam	50
Anguilla — Anguila	
Clonazepam — Clonazépam	1
Diazepam — Diazépam	55
Lorazepam — Lorazépam	10
Midazolam	10
Pentobarbital — Phénobarbital — Fenobarbital	300
Antigua and Barbuda — Antigua-et-Barbuda — Antigua y Barbuda	
Alprazolam	4 825
Bromazepam — Bromazépam	861
Chlordiazepoxide — Chlordiazépoxide — Clordiazepóxido	40
Clobazam	1
Clonazepam — Clonazépam	6
Diazepam — Diazépam	386
Lorazepam — Lorazépam	1 495
Methylphenidate — Méthylphénidate — Metilfenidato	25
Midazolam	6
Pentazocine — Pentazocina	5
Pentobarbital	637
Phenobarbital — Phénobarbital — Fenobarbital	9 127
Triazolam	1
Argentina — Argentine	
4-Bromo-2,5-dimethoxyphenyl-ethylamine (2C-B) — 4-bromo-2,5-diméthoxyphényléthylamine (2C-B) — 4-bromo-2,5-dimetoxifeniletilamina (2C-B)	10
Allobarbital — Alobarbital	100
Alprazolam	425 000
Amfepramone — Amfépramone — Anfepramona	65 000
Amfetamine — Amfétamine — Anfetamina	100
Amineptin — Amineptine — Amineptina	100
Aminorex	100
Amobarbital	100
Barbital	60 000
Benzfetamine — Benzfétamine — Benzfetamina	10
Bromazepam — Bromazépam	750 000
Brotizolam	1 000
Buprenorphine — Buprénorphine — Buprenorfina	300
Butalbital	140 000
Butobarbital	10
Camazepam — Camazépam	10
Cathine — Catina	10

Country (or territory) and substance Pays (ou territoire) et substance País (o territorio) y sustancia	Assessment (grams) Évaluation (en grammes) Previsión (en gramos)
Chlordiazepoxide — Chlordiazépoxide — Clordiazepóxido	1 000
Clobazam	60 000
Clonazepam — Clonazépam	480 000
Clorazepate — Clorazépate — Clorazepato	60 000
Clotiazepam — Clotiazépam	10
Cloxazolam	10
Cyclobarbital — Ciclobarbital	10
Delorazepam — Délorazépam	10
Delta-9-tetrahydrocannabinol — *Delta*-9-tétrahydrocannabinol — *Delta*-9-tetrahidrocannabinol	10
Dexamfetamine — Dexamfétamine — Dexanfetamina	10
Diazepam — Diazépam	900 000
Estazolam	10
Ethchlorvynol — Etclorvinol	10
Ethinamate — Éthinamate — Etinamato	10
Ethyl loflazepate — Loflazépate d'éthyle — Loflazepato de etilo	400
Etilamfetamine — Étilamfétamine — Etilanfetamina	10
Fencamfamin — Fencamfamine — Fencanfamina	10
Fenetylline — Fénétylline — Fenetilina	10
Fenproporex	35 000
Fludiazepam — Fludiazépam	1 000
Flunitrazepam — Flunitrazépam	100 000
Flurazepam — Flurazépam	22 000
Gamma-hydroxybutyric acid (GHB) — Acide *gamma*-hydroxybutirique (GHB) — Ácido *gamma*-hidroxibutírico (GHB)	10
Glutethimide — Glutéthimide — Glutetimida	10
Halazepam — Halazépam	10
Haloxazolam	50
Ketazolam — Kétazolam	15 000
Lefetamine (SPA) — Léfétamine (SPA) — Lefetamina (SPA)	50
Levamfetamine — Lévamfétamine — Levanfetamina	10
Levomethamphetamine — Lévométhamphétamine — Levometanfetamina	10
Loprazolam	600
Lorazepam — Lorazépam	450 000
Lormetazepam — Lormétazépam	3 000
Mazindol	2 000
Mecloqualone — Mécloqualone — Meclocualona	10
Medazepam — Médazépam	600
Mefenorex — Méfénorex	10
Meprobamate — Méprobamate — Meprobamato	200 000
Mesocarb — Mésocarbe — Mesocarbo	10
Metamfetamine — Métamfétamine — Metanfetamina	10
Metamfetamine racemate — Racémate de métamfétamine — Racemato de metanfetamina	10
Methaqualone — Méthaqualone — Metacualona	10
Methylphenidate — Méthylphénidate — Metilfenidato	60 000
Methylphenobarbital — Méthylphénobarbital — Metilfenobarbital	300 000
Methyprylon — Méthyprylone — Metiprilona	10
Midazolam	180 000
Nimetazepam — Nimétazépam	10
Nitrazepam — Nitrazépam	10 000
Nordazepam — Nordazépam	10

277

Table V.   Assessments of annual domestic medical and scientific requirements
Tableau V.   Évaluations des besoins annuels médicaux et scientifiques intérieurs
Cuadro V.   Previsiones de las necesidades anuales internas
para fines médicos y científicos

Country (or territory) and substance Pays (ou territoire) et substance País (o territorio) y sustancia	Assessment (grams) Évaluation (en grammes) Previsión (en gramos)	Country (or territory) and substance Pays (ou territoire) et substance País (o territorio) y sustancia	Assessment (grams) Évaluation (en grammes) Previsión (en gramos)
Argentina — Argentine		Clobazam	21
(continued — suite — continuación)		Clonazepam — Clonazépam	200
Oxazepam — Oxazépam	45 000	Clorazepate — Clorazépate — Clorazepato	100
Oxazolam	10	Dexamfetamine — Dexamfétamine —	
Pemoline — Pémoline — Pemolina	100 000	Dexanfetamina	5
Pentazocine — Pentazocina	10	Diazepam — Diazépam	1 100
Pentobarbital	100 000	Flunitrazepam — Flunitrazépam	24
Phencyclidine (PCP) — Fenciclidina (PCP)	10	Flurazepam — Flurazépam	416
Phendimetrazine — Phendimétrazine —		Loprazolam	2
Fendimetracina	10	Lorazepam — Lorazépam	320
Phenmetrazine — Phenmétrazine — Fenmetracina	10	Lormetazepam — Lormétazépam	3
Phenobarbital — Phénobarbital — Fenobarbital	3 600 000	Mazindol	1
Phentermine — Fentermina	65 000	Methylphenidate — Méthylphénidate —	
Pinazepam — Pinazépam	10	Metilfenidato	200
Pipradrol	10	Midazolam	2 340
Prazepam — Prazépam	10	Nitrazepam — Nitrazépam	50
Pyrovalerone — Pyrovalérone — Pirovalerona	10	Oxazepam — Oxazépam	500
Secbutabarbital	10	Pentazocine — Pentazocina	345
Secobarbital — Sécobarbital	10	Pentobarbital	9 251
Temazepam — Témazépam	1 000	Phenobarbital — Phénobarbital — Fenobarbital	8 155
Tetrazepam — Tétrazépam	800	Secobarbital — Sécobarbital	15
Triazolam	5 000	Temazepam — Témazépam	500
Vinylbital — Vinilbital	10	Triazolam	5
Zipeprol — Zipéprol	1 000	Zolpidem	300
Zolpidem	25 000		
		Ascension Island — Île de l'Ascension —	
Armenia — Arménie		*Isla de la Ascensión*	
Alprazolam	100	Diazepam — Diazépam	3
Bromazepam — Bromazépam	200	Temazepam — Témazépam	20
Butobarbital	3 000		
Chlordiazepoxide — Chlordiazépoxide —		**Australia — Australie**	
Clordiazepóxido	10 000	Alprazolam	130 000
Clobazam	100	Amfepramone — Amfépramone — Anfepramona	270 000
Clonazepam — Clonazépam	2 000	Amfetamine — Amfétamine — Anfetamina	30
Clorazepate — Clorazépate — Clorazepato	2 000	Amobarbital	50
Cyclobarbital — Ciclobarbital	3 000	Barbital	40 000
Diazepam — Diazépam	30 000	Benzfetamine — Benzfétamine — Benzfetamina	1
Gamma-hydroxybutyric acid (GHB) —		Bromazepam — Bromazépam	16 000
Acide *gamma*-hydroxybutirique (GHB) —		Buprenorphine — Buprénorphine — Buprenorfina	55 000
Ácido *gamma*-hidroxibutírico (GHB)	1 000	Butalbital	30
Lorazepam — Lorazépam	4 000	Cathine — Catina	25 000
Medazepam — Médazépam	1 000	Chlordiazepoxide — Chlordiazépoxide —	
Meprobamate — Méprobamate — Meprobamato	500	Clordiazepóxido	390
Midazolam	500	Clobazam	180 000
Nitrazepam — Nitrazépam	10 000	Clonazepam — Clonazépam	100 000
Nordazepam — Nordazépam	10	Cloxazolam	1
Oxazepam — Oxazépam	15 000	Delorazepam — Délorazépam	5
Pentazocine — Pentazocina	1 000	*Delta*-9-tetrahydrocannabinol —	
Pentobarbital	10 000	*Delta*-9-tétrahydrocannabinol —	
Phenobarbital — Phénobarbital — Fenobarbital	400 000	*Delta*-9-tetrahidrocannabinol	10
Temazepam — Témazépam	100	Dexamfetamine — Dexamfétamine — Dexanfetamina	232 000
Tetrazepam — Tétrazépam	100	Diazepam — Diazépam	760 000
Zolpidem	300	Estazolam	1
		Fenetylline — Fénétylline — Fenetilina	1
Aruba		Flunitrazepam — Flunitrazépam	15 000
Alprazolam	150	Flurazepam — Flurazépam	50
Amfetamine — Amfétamine — Anfetamina	1	*Gamma*-hydroxybutyric acid (GHB) —	
Bromazepam — Bromazépam	1 600	Acide *gamma*-hydroxybutirique (GHB) —	
Chlordiazepoxide — Chlordiazépoxide —		Ácido *gamma*-hidroxibutírico (GHB)	220
Clordiazepóxido	340	Levamfetamine — Lévamfétamine — Levanfetamina	1
		Loprazolam	3

Table V. Assessments of annual domestic medical and scientific requirements
Tableau V. Évaluations des besoins annuels médicaux et scientifiques intérieurs
Cuadro V. Previsiones de las necesidades anuales internas para fines médicos y científicos

Country (or territory) and substance Pays (ou territoire) et substance País (o territorio) y sustancia	Assessment (grams) Évaluation (en grammes) Previsión (en gramos)
Lorazepam — Lorazépam	25 000
Lormetazepam — Lormétazépam	10
Meprobamate — Méprobamate — Meprobamato	1 000
Metamfetamine — Métamfétamine— Metanfetamina	8
Metamfetamine racemate — Racémate de métamfétamine — Racemato de metanfetamina	1
Methaqualone — Méthaqualone — Metacualona	1
Methylphenidate — Méthylphénidate — Metilfenidato	480 000
Methylphenobarbital — Méthylphénobarbital — Metilfenobarbital	500
Midazolam	85 000
Nitrazepam — Nitrazépam	300 000
Nordazepam — Nordazépam	20
Oxazepam — Oxazépam	2 050 000
Pemoline — Pémoline — Pemolina	100
Pentazocine — Pentazocina	30 000
Pentobarbital	3 000 000
Phencyclidine (PCP) — Fenciclidina (PCP)	1
Phenobarbital — Phénobarbital — Fenobarbital	800 000
Phentermine — Fentermina	1 600 000
Prazepam — Prazépam	110
Secobarbital — Sécobarbital	60 000
Temazepam — Témazépam	1 200 000
Tetrazepam — Tétrazépam	40
Triazolam	20 000
Zolpidem	700 000

Austria — Autriche

Allobarbital — Alobarbital	500
Alprazolam	15 000
Amfetamine — Amfétamine — Anfetamina	500
Amobarbital	50
Barbital	40 000
Bromazepam — Bromazépam	200 000
Brotizolam	4 000
Buprenorphine — Buprénorphine — Buprenorfina	35 000
Butalbital	50
Cathine — Catina	1
Chlordiazepoxide — Chlordiazépoxide — Clordiazepóxido	20 000
Clobazam	25 000
Clonazepam — Clonazépam	5 000
Clorazepate — Clorazépate — Clorazepato	20 000
Delta-9-tetrahydrocannabinol — Delta-9-tétrahydrocannabinol — Delta-9-tetrahidrocannabinol	1 500
Diazepam — Diazépam	300 000
Flunitrazepam — Flunitrazépam	20 000
Gamma-hydroxybutyric acid (GHB) — Acide gamma-hydroxybutirique (GHB) — Ácido gamma-hidroxibutírico (GHB)	200 000
Lorazepam — Lorazépam	40 000
Lormetazepam — Lormétazépam	2 000
Medazepam — Médazépam	50
Meprobamate — Méprobamate — Meprobamato	4 000 000
Metamfetamine — Métamfétamine — Metanfetamina	5
Methylphenidate — Méthylphénidate — Metilfenidato	25 000

Country (or territory) and substance Pays (ou territoire) et substance País (o territorio) y sustancia	Assessment (grams) Évaluation (en grammes) Previsión (en gramos)
Methylphenobarbital — Méthylphénobarbital — Metilfenobarbital	500
Midazolam	300 000
Nitrazepam — Nitrazépam	40 000
Nordazepam — Nordazépam	10
Oxazepam — Oxazépam	650 000
Pentobarbital	20 000
Phencyclidine (PCP) — Fenciclidina (PCP)	2
Phendimetrazine — Phendimétrazine — Fendimetracina	1
Phenobarbital — Phénobarbital — Fenobarbital	300 000
Phentermine — Fentermina	500 000
Prazepam — Prazépam	25 000
Secobarbital — Sécobarbital	2
Tetrazepam — Tétrazépam	450 000
Triazolam	5 000
Zolpidem	120 000

Azerbaijan — Azerbaïdjan — Azerbaiyán

Alprazolam	200
Barbital	6 700
Bromazepam — Bromazépam	1 300
Buprenorphine — Buprénorphine — Buprenorfina	20
Camazepam — Camazépam	100
Chlordiazepoxide — Chlordiazépoxide — Clordiazepóxido	7 000
Clobazam	400
Clonazepam — Clonazépam	1 200
Diazepam — Diazépam	25 000
Estazolam	50
Flunitrazepam — Flunitrazépam	150
Flurazepam — Flurazépam	700
Gamma-hydroxybutyric acid (GHB) — Acide gamma-hydroxybutirique (GHB) — Ácido gamma-hidroxibutírico (GHB)	200 500
Lorazepam — Lorazépam	100
Medazepam — Médazépam	1 500
Meprobamate — Méprobamate — Meprobamato	22 000
Midazolam	800
Nitrazepam — Nitrazépam	1 300
Nordazepam — Nordazépam	200
Oxazepam — Oxazépam	8 000
Pentazocine — Pentazocina	60
Pentobarbital	50
Phendimetrazine — Phendimétrazine — Fendimetracina	250
Phenobarbital — Phénobarbital — Fenobarbital	260 000
Secbutabarbital	200
Tetrazepam — Tétrazépam	2 500
Triazolam	25
Zolpidem	20 000

Bahamas

Alprazolam	200
Amfepramone — Amfépramone — Anfepramona	200
Amfetamine — Amfétamine — Anfetamina	70
Bromazepam — Bromazépam	400
Butobarbital	5
Chlordiazepoxide — Chlordiazépoxide — Clordiazepóxido	700

Table V. Assessments of annual domestic medical and scientific requirements
Tableau V. Évaluations des besoins annuels médicaux et scientifiques intérieurs
Cuadro V. Previsiones de las necesidades anuales internas para fines médicos y científicos

Country (or territory) and substance Pays (ou territoire) et substance País (o territorio) y sustancia	Assessment (grams) Évaluation (en grammes) Previsión (en gramos)
Bahamas	
(continued — suite — continuación)	
Clobazam	200
Clonazepam — Clonazépam	100

Delta-9-tetrahydrocannabinol —
  Delta-9-tétrahydrocannabinol —
  Delta-9-tetrahidrocannabinol
	1

Dexamfetamine — Dexamfétamine — Dexanfetamina	50
Diazepam — Diazépam	30 000
Flunitrazepam — Flunitrazépam	6
Lorazepam — Lorazépam	1 270
Meprobamate — Méprobamate — Meprobamato	1 600
Metamfetamine — Métamfétamine — Metanfetamina	1
Methylphenidate — Méthylphénidate — Metilfenidato	920
Midazolam	700
Pentobarbital	9 375
Phenobarbital — Phénobarbital — Fenobarbital	40 000
Temazepam — Témazépam	1
Triazolam	6
Zolpidem	500
Bahrain — Bahreïn — Bahrein	
Allobarbital — Alobarbital	3 000
Alprazolam	500
Bromazepam — Bromazépam	500
Buprenorphine — Buprénorphine — Buprenorfina	1
Chlordiazepoxide — Chlordiazépoxide — Clordiazepóxido	10 000
Clobazam	50
Clonazepam — Clonazépam	750
Diazepam — Diazépam	3 500
Flurazepam — Flurazépam	23
Lorazepam — Lorazépam	200
Methylphenidate — Méthylphénidate — Metilfenidato	350
Midazolam	2 000
Nitrazepam — Nitrazépam	1 000
Pentazocine — Pentazocina	1 500
Pentobarbital	10 000
Phenobarbital — Phénobarbital — Fenobarbital	20 000
Secobarbital — Sécobarbital	1 000
Temazepam — Témazépam	200
Bangladesh	
Alprazolam	200 000
Barbital	200 000
Bromazepam — Bromazépam	1 000 000
Clobazam	1 500 000
Clonazepam — Clonazépam	500 000
Diazepam — Diazépam	2 500 000
Flurazepam — Flurazépam	300 000
Lorazepam — Lorazépam	600 000
Midazolam	700 000
Nitrazepam — Nitrazépam	1 000 000
Phenobarbital — Phénobarbital — Fenobarbital	500 000
Barbados — Barbade	
Alprazolam	292
Amobarbital	364
Bromazepam — Bromazépam	56
Buprenorphine — Buprénorphine — Buprenorfina	46

Country (or territory) and substance Pays (ou territoire) et substance País (o territorio) y sustancia	Assessment (grams) Évaluation (en grammes) Previsión (en gramos)
Chlordiazepoxide — Chlordiazépoxide — Clordiazepóxido	1 234
Clobazam	3 000
Clonazepam — Clonazépam	157
Clorazepate — Clorazépate — Clorazepato	110
Dexamfetamine — Dexamfétamine — Dexanfetamina	4
Diazepam — Diazépam	8 000
Flunitrazepam — Flunitrazépam	130
Flurazepam — Flurazépam	180
Lorazepam — Lorazépam	1 600
Methylphenidate — Méthylphénidate — Metilfenidato	1 400
Midazolam	258
Nitrazepam — Nitrazépam	3 000
Oxazepam — Oxazépam	3
Pentazocine — Pentazocina	107
Pentobarbital	19 000
Phenobarbital — Phénobarbital — Fenobarbital	30 000
Phentermine — Fentermina	135
Triazolam	3
Zolpidem	580
Belarus — Bélarus — Belarús	

4-Bromo-2,5-dimethoxyphenyl-ethylamine (2C-B) —
  4-bromo-2,5-diméthoxyphényléthylamine (2C-B) —
  4-bromo-2,5-dimetoxifeniletilamina (2C-B)
	1

Alprazolam	3 000
Amfetamine — Amfétamine — Anfetamina	2
Barbital	5 000
Bromazepam — Bromazépam	1
Buprenorphine — Buprénorphine — Buprenorfina	200
Cathine — Catina	1
Chlordiazepoxide — Chlordiazépoxide — Clordiazepóxido	125 000
Clonazepam — Clonazépam	2 500
Clorazepate — Clorazépate — Clorazepato	2 000
Cyclobarbital — Ciclobarbital	200 000

Delta-9-tetrahydrocannabinol —
  Delta-9-tétrahydrocannabinol —
  Delta-9-tetrahidrocannabinol
	1

Diazepam — Diazépam	200 000
Fludiazepam — Fludiazépam	1
Flunitrazepam — Flunitrazépam	2 001

Gamma-hydroxybutyric acid (GHB) —
  Acide gamma-hydroxybutirique (GHB) —
  Ácido gamma-hidroxibutírico (GHB)
	200 000

Lorazepam — Lorazépam	2 000
Medazepam — Médazépam	50 000
Meprobamate — Méprobamate — Meprobamato	1 000
Mesocarb — Mésocarbe — Mesocarbo	1 000
Metamfetamine — Métamfétamine — Metanfetamina	1
Midazolam	1 000
Nitrazepam — Nitrazépam	20 000
Nordazepam — Nordazépam	1
Oxazepam — Oxazépam	200 000
Pentazocine — Pentazocina	10 000
Pentobarbital	1
Phencyclidine (PCP) — Fenciclidina (PCP)	1
Phenobarbital — Phénobarbital — Fenobarbital	3 000 000
Temazepam — Témazépam	1 000
Tetrazepam — Tétrazépam	2 000
Triazolam	500
Zolpidem	1 000

Table V.   Assessments of annual domestic medical and scientific requirements
Tableau V.   Évaluations des besoins annuels médicaux et scientifiques intérieurs
Cuadro V.   Previsiones de las necesidades anuales internas para fines médicos y científicos

Country (or territory) and substance Pays (ou territoire) et substance País (o territorio) y sustancia	Assessment (grams) Évaluation (en grammes) Previsión (en gramos)

Belgium — Belgique — Bélgica

Allobarbital — Alobarbital	5 000 000
Alprazolam	600 000
Amfepramone — Amfépramone — Anfepramona	2 000 000
Amfetamine — Amfétamine — Anfetamina	15 000
Amobarbital......................................	350 000
Barbital	100 000
Bromazepam — Bromazépam.....................	700 000
Brotizolam.......................................	15 000
Buprenorphine — Buprénorphine — Buprenorfina	30 000
Butalbital..	600 000
Butobarbital.....................................	80 000
Camazepam — Camazépam......................	3 000
Cathine — Catina................................	200 000
Chlordiazepoxide — Chlordiazépoxide — Clordiazepóxido	50 000
Clobazam	150 000
Clonazepam — Clonazépam	50 000
Clorazepate — Clorazépate — Clorazepato........	500 000
Clotiazepam — Clotiazépam	320 000
Cloxazolam	30 000
Cyclobarbital — Ciclobarbital.....................	120 000

Delta-9-tetrahydrocannabinol —
   Delta-9-tétrahydrocannabinol —
   Delta-9-tetrahidrocannabinol ....
	2 000

Dexamfetamine — Dexamfétamine — Dexanfetamina	30 000
Diazepam — Diazépam	500 000
Ethyl loflazepate — Loflazépate d'éthyle — Loflazepato de etilo	10 000
Fenetylline — Fénétylline — Fenetilina	100 000
Fenproporex	50 000
Flunitrazepam — Flunitrazépam	150 000
Flurazepam — Flurazépam	250 000

Gamma-hydroxybutyric acid (GHB) —
   Acide *gamma*-hydroxybutirique (GHB) —
   Ácido *gamma*-hidroxibutírico (GHB) ....
	50 000

Halazepam — Halazépam	25 000
Ketazolam — Kétazolam	500 000
Levamfetamine — Lévamfétamine — Levanfetamina...	1
Levomethamphetamine — Lévométhamphétamine — Levometanfetamina	1
Loprazolam	20 000
Lorazepam — Lorazépam	600 000
Lormetazepam — Lormétazépam	300 000
Mazindol	10 000
Mecloqualone — Mécloqualone — Meclocualona	1
Medazepam — Médazépam	20 000
Meprobamate — Méprobamate — Meprobamato	5 000 000
Metamfetamine — Métamfétamine — Metanfetamina ..	500

Metamfetamine racemate —
   Racémate de métamfétamine —
   Racemato de metanfetamina ....
	1

Methylphenidate — Méthylphénidate — Metilfenidato ..	200 000
Methylphenobarbital — Méthylphénobarbital — Metilfenobarbital	600 000
Methyprylon — Méthyprylone — Metiprilona	1 000
Midazolam.......................................	50 000
Nitrazepam — Nitrazépam.........................	280 000
Nordazepam — Nordazépam	60 000
Oxazepam — Oxazépam..........................	600 000
Pemoline — Pémoline — Pemolina	50 000

Pentazocine — Pentazocina	200 000
Pentobarbital.....................................	400 000
Phencyclidine (PCP) — Fenciclidina (PCP)	50
Phendimetrazine — Phendimétrazine — Fendimetracina	2 000
Phenmetrazine — Phenmétrazine — Fenmetracina ..	1
Phenobarbital — Phénobarbital — Fenobarbital	2 000 000
Phentermine — Fentermina.......................	900 000
Pinazepam — Pinazépam	50 000
Prazepam — Prazépam...........................	300 000
Secobarbital — Sécobarbital	1 100 000
Temazepam — Témazépam	50 000
Tetrazepam — Tétrazépam	1 600 000
Triazolam	50 000
Zolpidem	1 000 000

Belize — Belice

Alprazolam	200
Bromazepam — Bromazépam.....................	400
Chlordiazepoxide — Chlordiazépoxide — Clordiazepóxido	600
Diazepam — Diazépam	10 000
Loprazolam	4 000
Meprobamate — Méprobamate — Meprobamato	4 000
Methylphenidate — Méthylphénidate — Metilfenidato ..	500
Midazolam.......................................	2 000
Nitrazepam — Nitrazépam	2 000
Phenobarbital — Phénobarbital — Fenobarbital	20 000
Phentermine — Fentermina.......................	8 000
Temazepam — Témazépam	100
Tetrazepam — Tétrazépam	10

Benin — Bénin

Alprazolam	200
Bromazepam — Bromazépam.....................	10 000
Buprenorphine — Buprénorphine — Buprenorfina	50
Chlordiazepoxide — Chlordiazépoxide — Clordiazepóxido	200
Clobazam	1 000
Clonazepam — Clonazépam	100
Clorazepate — Clorazépate — Clorazepato........	8 000
Clotiazepam — Clotiazépam	100
Diazepam — Diazépam...........................	900 000
Ethyl loflazepate — Loflazépate d'éthyle — Loflazepato de etilo	100
Lorazepam — Lorazépam	2 000
Meprobamate — Méprobamate — Meprobamato	10 000
Midazolam.......................................	100
Nitrazepam — Nitrazépam	500
Oxazepam — Oxazépam..........................	3 500
Phenobarbital — Phénobarbital — Fenobarbital	5 000 000
Prazepam — Prazépam...........................	2 500
Tetrazepam — Tétrazépam	7 000
Triazolam	50
Zolpidem	2 000

Bermuda — Bermudes — Bermudas

4-Bromo-2,5-dimethoxyphenyl-ethylamine (2C-B) —
   4-bromo-2,5-diméthoxyphényléthylamine (2C-B) —
   4-bromo-2,5-dimetoxifeniletilamina (2C-B) ....
	1

Alprazolam	500
Amfetamine — Amfétamine — Anfetamina	40

Table V.   Assessments of annual domestic medical and scientific requirements
Tableau V.   Évaluations des besoins annuels médicaux et scientifiques intérieurs
Cuadro V.   Previsiones de las necesidades anuales internas
para fines médicos y científicos

Country (or territory) and substance Pays (ou territoire) et substance País (o territorio) y sustancia	Assessment (grams) Évaluation (en grammes) Previsión (en gramos)
Bermuda — Bermudes — Bermudas *(continued — suite — continuación)*	
Bromazepam — Bromazépam	1 000
Buprenorphine — Buprénorphine — Buprenorfina	200
Butalbital	250
Chlordiazepoxide — Chlordiazépoxide — Clordiazepóxido	500
Clonazepam — Clonazépam	100

Delta-9-tetrahydrocannabinol —
  Delta-9-tétrahydrocannabinol —
  Delta-9-tetrahidrocannabinol
	1

Dexamfetamine — Dexamfétamine — Dexanfetamina	40
Diazepam — Diazépam	500
Flunitrazepam — Flunitrazépam	5
Flurazepam — Flurazépam	100

Gamma-hydroxybutyric acid (GHB) —
  Acide *gamma*-hydroxybutirique (GHB) —
  Ácido *gamma*-hidroxibutírico (GHB)
	1

Loprazolam	200
Lorazepam — Lorazépam	500
Meprobamate — Méprobamate — Meprobamato	2 000
Metamfetamine — Métamfétamine — Metanfetamina	1
Methaqualone — Méthaqualone — Metacualona	1
Methylphenidate — Méthylphénidate — Metilfenidato	4 000
Midazolam	50
Nitrazepam — Nitrazépam	50
Oxazepam — Oxazépam	100
Oxazolam	100
Pemoline — Pémoline — Pemolina	100
Pentazocine — Pentazocina	500
Pentobarbital	5 000
Phencyclidine (PCP) — Fenciclidina (PCP)	1
Phendimetrazine — Phendimétrazine — Fendimetracina	1
Phenobarbital — Phénobarbital — Fenobarbital	3 500
Phentermine — Fentermina	100
Secobarbital — Sécobarbital	700
Temazepam — Témazépam	1 000
Tetrazepam — Tétrazépam	100
Triazolam	1
Zolpidem	100
Bhutan — Bhoutan — Bhután	
Diazepam — Diazépam	35
Midazolam	75
Pentazocine — Pentazocina	728
Phenobarbital — Phénobarbital — Fenobarbital	11 148
Bolivia — Bolivie	
Alprazolam	1 605 629
Bromazepam — Bromazépam	684
Brotizolam	1
Clonazepam — Clonazépam	1 085
Clorazepate — Clorazépate — Clorazepato	115
Diazepam — Diazépam	50 620
Flunitrazepam — Flunitrazépam	11
Ketazolam — Kétazolam	5 767
Lorazepam — Lorazépam	190
Methylphenidate — Méthylphénidate — Metilfenidato	11
Midazolam	3 989
Phenobarbital — Phénobarbital — Fenobarbital	15 000

Country (or territory) and substance Pays (ou territoire) et substance País (o territorio) y sustancia	Assessment (grams) Évaluation (en grammes) Previsión (en gramos)
Tetrazepam — Tétrazépam	600
Zolpidem	20
Bosnia and Herzegovina — Bosnie-Herzégovine — Bosnia y Herzegovina	
Alprazolam	42 261
Bromazepam — Bromazépam	112 606
Brotizolam	19
Clonazepam — Clonazépam	1 439
Clorazepate — Clorazépate — Clorazepato	17 505
Diazepam — Diazépam	326 201
Flurazepam — Flurazépam	3 930
Lorazepam — Lorazépam	17 755
Medazepam — Médazépam	32 766
Midazolam	3 438
Nitrazepam — Nitrazépam	7 350
Nordazepam — Nordazépam	1
Oxazepam — Oxazépam	1 857
Phenobarbital — Phénobarbital — Fenobarbital	371 082
Prazepam — Prazépam	38 760
Tetrazepam — Tétrazépam	750
Zolpidem	60
Botswana	
Alprazolam	130
Bromazepam — Bromazépam	1 000
Buprenorphine — Buprénorphine — Buprenorfina	10
Chlordiazepoxide — Chlordiazépoxide — Clordiazepóxido	6 000
Clobazam	50
Clonazepam — Clonazépam	820
Diazepam — Diazépam	20 000
Flunitrazepam — Flunitrazépam	50
Ketazolam — Kétazolam	1 000
Loprazolam	22
Lorazepam — Lorazépam	280
Meprobamate — Méprobamate — Meprobamato	500 000
Methylphenidate — Méthylphénidate — Metilfenidato	1 000
Midazolam	1 000
Nitrazepam — Nitrazépam	1 000
Oxazepam — Oxazépam	400
Pentazocine — Pentazocina	100
Pentobarbital	1 000
Phenobarbital — Phénobarbital — Fenobarbital	15 000
Phentermine — Fentermina	1 000
Temazepam — Témazépam	500
Triazolam	100
Zolpidem	100
Brazil — Brésil — Brasil	

4-Bromo-2,5-dimethoxyphenyl-ethylamine (2C-B) —
  4-bromo-2,5-diméthoxyphényléthylamine (2C-B) —
  4-bromo-2,5-dimetoxifeniletilamina (2C-B)
	1

Allobarbital — Alobarbital	1
Alprazolam	150 000
Amfepramone — Amfépramone — Anfepramona	21 019 000
Amfetamine — Amfétamine — Anfetamina	1
Amineptin — Aminéptine — Amineptina	300
Aminorex	1
Amobarbital	5
Barbital	4 000
Benzfetamine — Benzfétamine — Benzfetamina	1
Bromazepam — Bromazépam	2 200 000

Table V.   Assessments of annual domestic medical and scientific requirements
Tableau V.   Évaluations des besoins annuels médicaux et scientifiques intérieurs
Cuadro V.   Previsiones de las necesidades anuales internas para fines médicos y científicos

Country (or territory) and substance / Pays (ou territoire) et substance / País (o territorio) y sustancia	Assessment (grams) / Évaluation (en grammes) / Previsión (en gramos)
Brotizolam	1
Buprenorphine — Buprénorphine — Buprenorfina	15
Butalbital	1
Butobarbital	1
Camazepam — Camazépam	1
Cathine — Catina	1
Chlordiazepoxide — Chlordiazépoxide — Clordiazepóxido	1 500 000
Clobazam	450 000
Clonazepam — Clonazépam	1 000 000
Clorazepate — Clorazépate — Clorazepato	30 000
Clotiazepam — Clotiazépam	1
Cloxazolam	200 000
Cyclobarbital — Ciclobarbital	1
Delorazepam — Délorazépam	1
Delta-9-tetrahydrocannabinol — Delta-9-tétrahydrocannabinol — Delta-9-tetrahidrocannabinol	1
Dexamfetamine — Dexamfétamine — Dexanfetamina	1
Diazepam — Diazépam	6 000 000
Estazolam	26 000
Ethchlorvynol — Etclorvinol	1
Ethinamate — Éthinamate — Etinamato	1
Ethyl loflazepate — Loflazépate d'éthyle — Loflazepato de etilo	1
Etilamfetamine — Étilamfétamine — Etilanfetamina	1
Fencamfamin — Fencamfamine — Fencanfamina	1
Fenetylline — Fénétylline — Fenetilina	1
Fenproporex	5 000 000
Fludiazepam — Fludiazépam	1
Flunitrazepam — Flunitrazépam	45 000
Flurazepam — Flurazépam	550 000
Gamma-hydroxybutyric acid (GHB) — Acide gamma-hydroxybutirique (GHB) — Ácido gamma-hidroxibutírico (GHB)	1
Glutethimide — Glutéthimide — Glutetimida	1
Halazepam — Halazépam	1
Haloxazolam	1
Ketazolam — Kétazolam	1
Lefetamine (SPA) — Léfétamine (SPA) — Lefetamina (SPA)	1
Levamfetamine — Lévamfétamine — Levanfetamina	1
Levomethamphetamine — Lévométhamphétamine — Levometanfetamina	1
Loprazolam	1
Lorazepam — Lorazépam	400 000
Lormetazepam — Lormétazépam	1
Mazindol	30 000
Mecloqualone — Mécloqualone — Meclocualona	1
Medazepam — Médazépam	5 000
Mefenorex — Méfénorex	1
Meprobamate — Méprobamate — Meprobamato	1
Mesocarb — Mésocarbe — Mesocarbo	1
Metamfetamine — Métamfétamine — Metanfetamina	1
Metamfetamine racemate — Racémate de métamfétamine — Racemato de metanfetamina	1
Methaqualone — Méthaqualone — Metacualona	1
Methylphenidate — Méthylphénidate — Metilfenidato	300 000
Methylphenobarbital — Méthylphénobarbital — Metilfenobarbital	1
Methyprylon — Méthyprylone — Metiprilona	1
Midazolam	1 100 000
Nimetazepam — Nimétazépam	1
Nitrazepam — Nitrazépam	120 000
Nordazepam — Nordazépam	1
Oxazepam — Oxazépam	15 000
Oxazolam	1
Pemoline — Pémoline — Pemolina	1
Pentazocine — Pentazocina	1
Pentobarbital	12 000
Phencyclidine (PCP) — Fenciclidina (PCP)	1
Phendimetrazine — Phendimétrazine — Fendimetracina	1
Phenmetrazine — Phenmétrazine — Fenmetracina	1
Phenobarbital — Phénobarbital — Fenobarbital	50 000 000
Phentermine — Fentermina	1
Pinazepam — Pinazépam	1
Pipradrol	1
Prazepam — Prazépam	1
Pyrovalerone — Pyrovalérone — Pirovalerona	1
Secbutabarbital	1
Secobarbital — Sécobarbital	1
Temazepam — Témazépam	18
Tetrazepam — Tétrazépam	1
Triazolam	2 000
Vinylbital — Vinilbital	1
Zipeprol — Zipéprol	1
Zolpidem	150 000
British Virgin Islands — Îles Vierges britanniques — Islas Vírgenes Británicas	
Alprazolam	5 000
Chlordiazepoxide — Chlordiazépoxide — Clordiazepóxido	5 000
Diazepam — Diazépam	7 000
Flurazepam — Flurazépam	6 000
Lorazepam — Lorazépam	5 000
Methylphenidate — Méthylphénidate — Metilfenidato	25
Midazolam	100
Nitrazepam — Nitrazépam	5 000
Pentazocine — Pentazocina	7 000
Phenobarbital — Phénobarbital — Fenobarbital	10 000
Brunei Darussalam — Brunéi Darussalam	
Alprazolam	120
Bromazepam — Bromazépam	80
Buprenorphine — Buprénorphine — Buprenorfina	10
Chlordiazepoxide — Chlordiazépoxide — Clordiazepóxido	2 500
Clobazam	600
Clonazepam — Clonazépam	300
Diazepam — Diazépam	800
Flurazepam — Flurazépam	200
Lorazepam — Lorazépam	100
Methylphenidate — Méthylphénidate — Metilfenidato	600
Midazolam	700
Oxazepam — Oxazépam	1
Pentazocine — Pentazocina	150
Pentobarbital	2 500
Phenobarbital — Phénobarbital — Fenobarbital	800
Phentermine — Fentermina	3 000
Temazepam — Témazépam	150
Zolpidem	1 200

Table V. Assessments of annual domestic medical and scientific requirements
Tableau V. Évaluations des besoins annuels médicaux et scientifiques intérieurs
Cuadro V. Previsiones de las necesidades anuales internas para fines médicos y científicos

Country (or territory) and substance Pays (ou territoire) et substance País (o territorio) y sustancia	Assessment (grams) Évaluation (en grammes) Previsión (en gramos)
Bulgaria — Bulgarie	
Alprazolam	12 000
Amfetamine — Amfétamine — Anfetamina	2
Amobarbital	5 000
Barbital	25 000
Bromazepam — Bromazépam....................	200 000
Buprenorphine — Buprénorphine — Buprenorfina	1 000
Butobarbital....................	2
Chlordiazepoxide — Chlordiazépoxide — Clordiazepóxido	25 000
Clobazam	10 000
Clonazepam — Clonazépam	25 000
Clorazepate — Clorazépate — Clorazepato	45 000
Cyclobarbital — Ciclobarbital....................	200 000
Dexamfetamine — Dexamfétamine — Dexanfetamina	2
Diazepam — Diazépam	400 000
Estazolam	1 000
Flunitrazepam — Flunitrazépam	4 000
Flurazepam — Flurazépam	1 000
Glutethimide — Glutéthimide — Glutetimida	100 000
Levamfetamine — Lévamfétamine — Levanfetamina ...	2
Lorazepam — Lorazépam	1 000
Mazindol	1 000
Medazepam — Médazépam	100 000
Metamfetamine — Métamfétamine — Metanfetamina ..	3
Methaqualone — Méthaqualone — Metacualona	1 000
Methylphenidate — Méthylphénidate — Metilfenidato ..	2 000
Midazolam....................	15 000
Nitrazepam — Nitrazépam	10 000
Nordazepam — Nordazépam	4 000
Oxazepam — Oxazépam....................	6 000
Pentazocine — Pentazocina	5 000
Pentobarbital....................	500
Phencyclidine (PCP) — Fenciclidina (PCP)	2
Phenobarbital — Phénobarbital — Fenobarbital	11 000 000
Secobarbital — Sécobarbital	2
Temazepam — Témazépam	2 000
Tetrazepam — Tétrazépam	25 000
Triazolam	1 000
Vinylbital — Vinilbital	1 000
Zolpidem	20 000
Burkina Faso	
Alprazolam	60
Bromazepam — Bromazépam....................	3 240
Buprenorphine — Buprénorphine — Buprenorfina	8
Chlordiazepoxide — Chlordiazépoxide — Clordiazepóxido	2 700
Clobazam	2 500
Clonazepam — Clonazépam	190
Clorazepate — Clorazépate — Clorazepato	6 700
Diazepam — Diazépam	24 000
Flunitrazepam — Flunitrazépam	200

Gamma-hydroxybutyric acid (GHB) —
  Acide gamma-hydroxybutirique (GHB) —
  Ácido gamma-hidroxibutírico (GHB) ....
	1 000

Lorazepam — Lorazépam	1 200
Meprobamate — Méprobamate — Meprobamato	70 500
Midazolam....................	500

Country (or territory) and substance Pays (ou territoire) et substance País (o territorio) y sustancia	Assessment (grams) Évaluation (en grammes) Previsión (en gramos)
Nitrazepam — Nitrazépam	15 000
Oxazepam — Oxazépam....................	600
Phenobarbital — Phénobarbital — Fenobarbital	476 000
Prazepam — Prazépam	6 200
Tetrazepam — Tétrazépam	3 100
Triazolam	5
Zolpidem	60
Burundi	
Alprazolam	12
Bromazepam — Bromazépam....................	36
Clobazam	255
Clonazepam — Clonazépam	4 800
Diazepam — Diazépam	12 085
Phenobarbital — Phénobarbital — Fenobarbital	37 250
Tetrazepam — Tétrazépam	100
Cambodia — Cambodge — Camboya	
Alprazolam	1 000
Bromazepam — Bromazépam....................	23 000
Buprenorphine — Buprénorphine — Buprenorfina	1 000
Chlordiazepoxide — Chlordiazépoxide — Clordiazepóxido	2 000
Clobazam	500
Clonazepam — Clonazépam	3 000
Clorazepate — Clorazépate — Clorazepato	7 000
Diazepam — Diazépam	125 000
Flunitrazepam — Flunitrazépam	1 000
Lorazepam — Lorazépam	2 000
Meprobamate — Méprobamate — Meprobamato	120 000
Midazolam	4 000
Nitrazepam — Nitrazépam	1 000
Nordazepam — Nordazépam	8 000
Pentazocine — Pentazocina	1 000
Phenobarbital — Phénobarbital — Fenobarbital	150 000
Prazepam — Prazépam	4 000
Zolpidem	5 000
Cameroon — Cameroun — Camerún	
Alprazolam	1 800
Bromazepam — Bromazépam....................	5 148
Buprenorphine — Buprénorphine — Buprenorfina	36
Chlordiazepoxide — Chlordiazépoxide — Clordiazepóxido	400
Clobazam	3 964
Clonazepam — Clonazépam	4
Clorazepate — Clorazépate — Clorazepato	5 238
Diazepam — Diazépam	82 340
Ethyl loflazepate — Loflazépate d'éthyle — Loflazepato de etilo	3
Flunitrazepam — Flunitrazépam	1
Lorazepam — Lorazépam	1 702
Meprobamate — Méprobamate — Meprobamato	94 420
Nitrazepam — Nitrazépam	360
Pentazocine — Pentazocina	424
Phenobarbital — Phénobarbital — Fenobarbital	989 119
Prazepam — Prazépam	7 392
Tetrazepam — Tétrazépam	15 048
Triazolam	1
Zolpidem	594

Table V. Assessments of annual domestic medical and scientific requirements
Tableau V. Évaluations des besoins annuels médicaux et scientifiques intérieurs
Cuadro V. Previsiones de las necesidades anuales internas
para fines médicos y científicos

Country (or territory) and substance Pays (ou territoire) et substance País (o territorio) y sustancia	Assessment (grams) Évaluation (en grammes) Previsión (en gramos)
Canada — Canadá	
Allobarbital — Alobarbital	50
Alprazolam	550 000
Amfepramone — Amfépramone — Anfepramona	150 000
Amfetamine — Amfétamine — Anfetamina	60 000
Aminorex	2
Amobarbital	40 000
Barbital	30 000
Benzfetamine — Benzfétamine — Benzfetamina	1
Bromazepam — Bromazépam	600 000
Buprenorphine — Buprénorphine — Buprenorfina	1 000
Butalbital	2 000 000
Butobarbital	1 000
Cathine — Catina	5
Chlordiazepoxide — Chlordiazépoxide — Clordiazepóxido	500 000
Clobazam	300 000
Clonazepam — Clonazépam	1 200 000
Clorazepate — Clorazépate — Clorazepato	120 000
Delorazepam — Délorazépam	110
Delta-9-tetrahydrocannabinol — *Delta*-9-tétrahydrocannabinol — *Delta*-9-tetrahidrocannabinol	25 000
Dexamfetamine — Dexamfétamine — Dexanfetamina	350 000
Diazepam — Diazépam	1 800 000
Ethinamate — Éthinamate — Etinamato	3
Fencamfamin — Fencamfamine — Fencanfamina	1
Fenproporex	5
Flunitrazepam — Flunitrazépam	2
Flurazepam — Flurazépam	950 000
Gamma-hydroxybutyric acid (GHB) — Acide *gamma*-hydroxybutirique (GHB) — Ácido *gamma*-hidroxibutírico (GHB)	500 000
Halazepam — Halazépam	1
Levamfetamine — Lévamfétamine — Levanfetamina	40
Levomethamphetamine — Lévométhamphétamine — Levometanfetamina	2
Lorazepam — Lorazépam	500 000
Lormetazepam — Lormétazépam	5
Mazindol	5 000
Meprobamate — Méprobamate — Meprobamato	1 500 000
Metamfetamine — Métamfétamine — Metanfetamina	40
Methaqualone — Méthaqualone — Metacualona	1
Methylphenidate — Méthylphénidate — Metilfenidato	2 500 000
Methylphenobarbital — Méthylphénobarbital — Metilfenobarbital	1 000
Midazolam	100 000
Nitrazepam — Nitrazépam	200 000
Nordazepam — Nordazépam	10
Oxazepam — Oxazépam	3 000 000
Pemoline — Pémoline — Pemolina	3 000
Pentazocine — Pentazocina	220 000
Pentobarbital	10 600 000
Phencyclidine (PCP) — Fenciclidina (PCP)	15
Phenobarbital — Phénobarbital — Fenobarbital	3 000 000
Phentermine — Fentermina	100 000
Pipradrol	5 000
Prazepam — Prazépam	1
Secbutabarbital	100
Secobarbital — Sécobarbital	100 000
Temazepam — Témazépam	2 000 000

Country (or territory) and substance Pays (ou territoire) et substance País (o territorio) y sustancia	Assessment (grams) Évaluation (en grammes) Previsión (en gramos)
Triazolam	15 000
Zolpidem	625 000
Cape Verde — Cap-Vert — Cabo Verde	
Alprazolam	50
Bromazepam — Bromazépam	3 000
Chlordiazepoxide — Chlordiazépoxide — Clordiazepóxido	4 000
Clorazepate — Clorazépate — Clorazepato	15
Diazepam — Diazépam	15 000
Lorazepam — Lorazépam	400
Midazolam	20
Phenobarbital — Phénobarbital — Fenobarbital	100 000
Cayman Islands — Îles Caïmanes — Islas Caimanes	
Alprazolam	30
Amfetamine — Amfétamine — Anfetamina	25
Amobarbital	100
Bromazepam — Bromazépam	50
Buprenorphine — Buprénorphine — Buprenorfina	3
Butalbital	500
Chlordiazepoxide — Chlordiazépoxide — Clordiazepóxido	200
Clobazam	10
Clonazepam — Clonazépam	30
Dexamfetamine — Dexamfétamine — Dexanfetamina	50
Diazepam — Diazépam	600
Flurazepam — Flurazépam	20
Lorazepam — Lorazépam	150
Mazindol	10
Meprobamate — Méprobamate — Meprobamato	700
Methylphenidate — Méthylphénidate — Metilfenidato	600
Midazolam	60
Nitrazepam — Nitrazépam	150
Oxazepam — Oxazépam	150
Pentazocine — Pentazocina	100
Pentobarbital	8 000
Phenobarbital — Phénobarbital — Fenobarbital	3 000
Phentermine — Fentermina	500
Secobarbital — Sécobarbital	500
Temazepam — Témazépam	800
Triazolam	5
Zolpidem	20
Central African Republic — République centrafricaine — República Centroafricana	
Alprazolam	2
Bromazepam — Bromazépam	810
Buprenorphine — Buprénorphine — Buprenorfina	2
Chlordiazepoxide — Chlordiazépoxide — Clordiazepóxido	200
Clobazam	300
Clonazepam — Clonazépam	10
Clorazepate — Clorazépate — Clorazepato	900
Diazepam — Diazépam	16 600
Estazolam	6
Flunitrazepam — Flunitrazépam	3
Lorazepam — Lorazépam	20

Table V. Assessments of annual domestic medical and scientific requirements
Tableau V. Évaluations des besoins annuels médicaux et scientifiques intérieurs
Cuadro V. Previsiones de las necesidades anuales internas para fines médicos y científicos

Country (or territory) and substance / Pays (ou territoire) et substance / País (o territorio) y sustancia	Assessment (grams) / Évaluation (en grammes) / Previsión (en gramos)
Central African Republic — **République centrafricaine —** **República Centroafricana**	
(continued — suite — continuación)	
Meprobamate — Méprobamate — Meprobamato	3 000
Nitrazepam — Nitrazépam.......................	20
Oxazepam — Oxazépam.........................	4
Phenobarbital — Phénobarbital — Fenobarbital	73 200
Prazepam — Prazépam..........................	40
Tetrazepam — Tétrazépam	600
Triazolam	40
Zolpidem......................................	6
Chad — Tchad	
Bromazepam — Bromazépam.....................	1 200
Clobazam	800
Clonazepam — Clonazépam......................	1 600
Clorazepate — Clorazépate — Clorazepato.........	3 000
Clotiazepam — Clotiazépam......................	500
Diazepam — Diazépam..........................	25 000
Lorazepam — Lorazépam........................	850
Lormetazepam — Lormétazépam	250
Meprobamate — Méprobamate — Meprobamato	6 800
Midazolam.....................................	800
Nimetazepam — Nimétazépam...................	450
Nitrazepam — Nitrazépam.......................	450
Nordazepam — Nordazépam	650
Oxazepam — Oxazépam.........................	650
Phenobarbital — Phénobarbital — Fenobarbital	36 500
Tetrazepam — Tétrazépam	1 750
Zolpidem......................................	150
Chile — Chili	
Alprazolam	120 000
Amfepramone — Amfépramone — Anfepramona	700 000
Amfetamine — Amfétamine — Anfetamina	40 000
Barbital	2 000
Bromazepam — Bromazépam.....................	80 000
Brotizolam.....................................	1 000
Buprenorphine — Buprénorphine — Buprenorfina	3 000
Butalbital......................................	40 000
Chlordiazepoxide — Chlordiazépoxide — Clordiazepóxido	650 000
Clobazam	20 000
Clonazepam — Clonazépam......................	180 000
Clorazepate — Clorazépate — Clorazepato.........	15 000
Clotiazepam — Clotiazépam......................	20 000
Dexamfetamine — Dexamfétamine — Dexanfetamina	3
Diazepam — Diazépam..........................	800 000
Fenproporex	20 000
Flunitrazepam — Flunitrazépam	15 000
Ketazolam — Kétazolam	80 000
Lorazepam — Lorazépam........................	60 000
Lormetazepam — Lormétazépam	5 000
Mazindol	500
Meprobamate — Méprobamate — Meprobamato	100 000
Metamfetamine — Métamfétamine — Metanfetamina ..	10 000
Methylphenidate — Méthylphénidate — Metilfenidato ..	210 000

Country (or territory) and substance / Pays (ou territoire) et substance / País (o territorio) y sustancia	Assessment (grams) / Évaluation (en grammes) / Previsión (en gramos)
Midazolam.....................................	200 000
Nitrazepam — Nitrazépam.......................	3 000
Oxazepam — Oxazépam.........................	15 000
Pemoline — Pémoline — Pemolina	60 000
Pentobarbital	2 000
Phenobarbital — Phénobarbital — Fenobarbital	2 000 000
Phentermine — Fentermina	20 000
Tetrazepam — Tétrazépam	20 000
Triazolam	1 000
Zolpidem......................................	150 000
China — Chine	
Alprazolam	200 000
Amfetamine — Amfétamine — Anfetamina	10
Amobarbital	30 000 000
Barbital	120 000 000
Bromazepam — Bromazépam.....................	100 000
Brotizolam.....................................	100
Buprenorphine — Buprénorphine — Buprenorfina	5 000
Chlordiazepoxide — Chlordiazépoxide — Clordiazepóxido	30 000 000
Clonazepam — Clonazépam......................	200 000
Delta-9-tetrahydrocannabinol — *Delta*-9-tétrahydrocannabinol — *Delta*-9-tetrahidrocannabinol	2
Diazepam — Diazépam..........................	120 000 000
Estazolam	500 000
Flurazepam — Flurazépam	100 000
Gamma-hydroxybutyric acid (GHB) — Acide *gamma*-hydroxybutirique (GHB) — Ácido *gamma*-hidroxibutírico (GHB)	1 000 000
Glutethimide — Glutéthimide — Glutetimida	300 000
Lorazepam — Lorazépam........................	150 000
Meprobamate — Méprobamate — Meprobamato	150 000 000
Methaqualone — Méthaqualone — Metacualona.....	10
Methylphenidate — Méthylphénidate — Metilfenidato ..	20 000
Midazolam.....................................	150 000
Nitrazepam — Nitrazépam.......................	1 500 000
Nordazepam — Nordazépam	1
Pemoline — Pémoline — Pemolina	500 000
Pentazocine — Pentazocina	10 000
Pentobarbital..................................	150 000
Phenobarbital — Phénobarbital — Fenobarbital	300 000 000
Secobarbital — Sécobarbital	10 000
Triazolam	50 000
Zolpidem......................................	150 000
Hong Kong SAR of China — *RAS de Hong Kong (Chine) —* *RAE de Hong Kong de China*	
4-Bromo-2,5-dimethoxyphenyl-ethylamine (2C-B) — 4-bromo-2,5-diméthoxyphényléthylamine (2C-B) — 4-bromo-2,5-dimetoxifeniletilamina (2C-B)	1
Alprazolam	4 500
Amfepramone — Amfépramone — Anfepramona	110 000
Amfetamine — Amfétamine — Anfetamina	1
Aminorex	1
Amobarbital	10 000
Barbital	2 000
Bromazepam — Bromazépam.....................	12 000

Table V. Assessments of annual domestic medical and scientific requirements
Tableau V. Évaluations des besoins annuels médicaux et scientifiques intérieurs
Cuadro V. Previsiones de las necesidades anuales internas
para fines médicos y científicos

Country (or territory) and substance Pays (ou territoire) et substance País (o territorio) y sustancia	Assessment (grams) Évaluation (en grammes) Previsión (en gramos)
Buprenorphine — Buprénorphine — Buprenorfina	200
Butalbital	5 000
Cathine — Catina..........	2 000
Chlordiazepoxide — Chlordiazépoxide — Clordiazepóxido	45 000
Clobazam	6 000
Clonazepam — Clonazépam	3 000
Clorazepate — Clorazépate — Clorazepato..........	3 000
Cloxazolam	100
Delorazepam — Délorazépam..........	1
Delta-9-tetrahydrocannabinol — Delta-9-tétrahydrocannabinol — Delta-9-tetrahidrocannabinol	1
Dexamfetamine — Dexamfétamine — Dexanfetamina ..	20
Diazepam — Diazépam..........	55 000
Estazolam	10
Ethchlorvynol — Etclorvinol	1
Ethyl loflazepate — Loflazépate d'éthyle — Loflazepato de etilo	1
Fencamfamin — Fencamfamine — Fencanfamina ...	1
Fludiazepam — Fludiazépam	2
Flunitrazepam — Flunitrazépam	2 000
Flurazepam — Flurazépam	6 000
Gamma-hydroxybutyric acid (GHB) — Acide gamma-hydroxybutirique (GHB) — Ácido gamma-hidroxibutírico (GHB)	30
Levomethamphetamine — Lévométhamphétamine — Levometanfetamina	1
Lorazepam — Lorazépam	8 000
Lormetazepam — Lormétazépam	1 500
Mazindol	2 000
Medazepam — Médazépam	1
Meprobamate — Méprobamate — Meprobamato	102 000
Metamfetamine — Métamfétamine — Metanfetamina ..	5
Metamfetamine racemate — Racémate de métamfétamine — Racemato de metanfetamina	2
Methaqualone — Méthaqualone — Metacualona.....	1
Methylphenidate — Méthylphénidate — Metilfenidato ..	25 000
Methylphenobarbital — Méthylphénobarbital — Metilfenobarbital	1
Methyprylon — Méthyprylone — Metiprilona	5
Midazolam..........	140 000
Nitrazepam — Nitrazépam..........	7 000
Nordazepam — Nordazépam	1
Oxazepam — Oxazépam..........	1
Oxazolam	2 000
Pentazocine — Pentazocina	1 000
Pentobarbital..........	80 000
Phencyclidine (PCP) — Fenciclidina (PCP)	1
Phenmetrazine — Phenmétrazine — Fenmetracina ..	1
Phenobarbital — Phénobarbital — Fenobarbital	170 000
Phentermine — Fentermina..........	170 000
Pinazepam — Pinazépam	6 000
Prazepam — Prazépam	1 000
Secobarbital — Sécobarbital	2 450
Temazepam — Témazépam	1 000
Tetrazepam — Tétrazépam	10
Triazolam	1 000
Zipeprol — Zipéprol	1
Zolpidem	65 000

Country (or territory) and substance Pays (ou territoire) et substance País (o territorio) y sustancia	Assessment (grams) Évaluation (en grammes) Previsión (en gramos)
Macao SAR of China — RAS de Macao (Chine) — *RAE de Macao de China*	
4-Bromo-2,5-dimethoxyphenyl-ethylamine (2C-B) — 4-bromo-2,5-diméthoxyphényléthylamine (2C-B) — 4-bromo-2,5-dimetoxifeniletilamina (2C-B)	1
Allobarbital — Alobarbital	1
Alprazolam	500
Amfepramone — Amfépramone — Anfepramona	1
Amfetamine — Amfétamine — Anfetamina	1
Aminorex..........	1
Amobarbital..........	2
Barbital	400
Benzfetamine — Benzfétamine — Benzfetamina.....	1
Bromazepam — Bromazépam..........	680
Brotizolam	1
Buprenorphine — Buprénorphine — Buprenorfina	30
Butalbital	1
Butobarbital	1
Camazepam — Camazépam	1
Cathine — Catina..........	45
Chlordiazepoxide — Chlordiazépoxide — Clordiazepóxido	700
Clobazam	500
Clonazepam — Clonazépam	400
Clorazepate — Clorazépate — Clorazepato..........	120
Clotiazepam — Clotiazépam	1
Cloxazolam	10
Cyclobarbital — Ciclobarbital..........	1
Delorazepam — Délorazépam..........	1
Delta-9-tetrahydrocannabinol — Delta-9-tétrahydrocannabinol — Delta-9-tetrahidrocannabinol	1
Dexamfetamine — Dexamfétamine — Dexanfetamina	1
Diazepam — Diazépam..........	4 000
Estazolam	1
Ethchlorvynol — Etclorvinol	1
Ethinamate — Éthinamate — Etinamato	1
Ethyl loflazepate — Loflazépate d'éthyle — Loflazepato de etilo	1
Etilamfetamine — Étilamfétamine — Etilanfetamina ..	1
Fencamfamin — Fencamfamine — Fencanfamina ...	1
Fenetylline — Fénétylline — Fenetilina	1
Fenproporex	1
Fludiazepam — Fludiazépam	1
Flunitrazepam — Flunitrazépam	80
Flurazepam — Flurazépam	3 000
Gamma-hydroxybutyric acid (GHB) — Acide gamma-hydroxybutirique (GHB) — Ácido gamma-hidroxibutírico (GHB)	1
Glutethimide — Glutéthimide — Glutetimida	1
Halazepam — Halazépam	1
Haloxazolam	1
Ketazolam — Kétazolam	1
Lefetamine (SPA) — Léfétamine (SPA) — Lefetamina (SPA)..........	1
Levamfetamine — Lévamfétamine — Levanfetamina ...	1
Levomethamphetamine — Lévométhamphétamine — Levometanfetamina	1

Table V. Assessments of annual domestic medical and scientific requirements
Tableau V. Évaluations des besoins annuels médicaux et scientifiques intérieurs
Cuadro V. Previsiones de las necesidades anuales internas
para fines médicos y científicos

Country (or territory) and substance Pays (ou territoire) et substance País (o territorio) y sustancia	Assessment (grams) Évaluation (en grammes) Previsión (en gramos)
Macao SAR of China — RAS de Macao (Chine) — RAE de Macao de China	
(continued — suite — continuación)	
Loprazolam	1
Lorazepam — Lorazépam	800
Lormetazepam — Lormétazépam	5
Mazindol	1
Mecloqualone — Mécloqualone — Meclocualona	1
Medazepam — Médazépam	1
Mefenorex — Méfénorex	1
Meprobamate — Méprobamate — Meprobamato	1
Mesocarb — Mésocarbe — Mesocarbo	1
Metamfetamine — Métamfétamine — Metanfetamina	1
Metamfetamine racemate — Racémate de métamfétamine — Racemato de metanfetamina	1
Methaqualone — Méthaqualone — Metacualona	1
Methylphenidate — Méthylphénidate — Metilfenidato	90
Methylphenobarbital — Méthylphénobarbital — Metilfenobarbital	1
Methyprylon — Méthyprylone — Metiprilona	1
Midazolam	800
Nimetazepam — Nimétazépam	1
Nitrazepam — Nitrazépam	1
Nordazepam — Nordazépam	1
Oxazepam — Oxazépam	500
Oxazolam	1
Pemoline — Pémoline — Pemolina	1
Pentazocine — Pentazocina	40
Pentobarbital	60 000
Phencyclidine (PCP) — Fenciclidina (PCP)	1
Phendimetrazine — Phendimétrazine — Fendimetracina	1
Phenmetrazine — Phenmétrazine — Fenmetracina	1
Phenobarbital — Phénobarbital — Fenobarbital	5 000
Phentermine — Fentermina	1
Pinazepam — Pinazépam	1
Pipradrol	1
Prazepam — Prazépam	1
Pyrovalerone — Pyrovalérone — Pirovalerona	1
Secbutabarbital	1
Secobarbital — Sécobarbital	1
Temazepam — Témazépam	1
Tetrazepam — Tétrazépam	1
Triazolam	2
Vinylbital — Vinilbital	1
Zipeprol — Zipéprol	1
Zolpidem	1 200
Christmas Island — Île Christmas — Isla Christmas	
Dexamfetamine — Dexamfétamine — Dexanfetamina	20
Methylphenidate — Méthylphénidate — Metilfenidato	10
Cocos (Keeling) Islands — Îles Cocos (Keeling) — Islas Cocos (Keeling)	
Dexamfetamine — Dexamfétamine — Dexanfetamina	1
Colombia — Colombie	
Alprazolam	25 000
Amobarbital	5
Barbital	300
Bromazepam — Bromazépam	40 000
Brotizolam	20 000
Buprenorphine — Buprénorphine — Buprenorfina	1
Cathine — Catina	1
Clobazam	35 000
Clonazepam — Clonazépam	55 000
Delta-9-tetrahydrocannabinol — *Delta*-9-tétrahydrocannabinol — *Delta*-9-tetrahidrocannabinol	3 000
Diazepam — Diazépam	80 000
Gamma-hydroxybutyric acid (GHB) — Acide *gamma*-hydroxybutirique (GHB) — Ácido *gamma*-hidroxibutírico (GHB)	10
Lorazepam — Lorazépam	60 000
Methylphenidate — Méthylphénidate — Metilfenidato	25 000
Midazolam	40 000
Pentobarbital	150 000
Phenobarbital — Phénobarbital — Fenobarbital	3 000 000
Temazepam — Témazépam	5
Triazolam	1 500
Zolpidem	100 000
Comoros — Comores — Comoras	
Diazepam — Diazépam	5 000[a]
Meprobamate — Méprobamate — Meprobamato	20 000[a]
Nitrazepam — Nitrazépam	1 000[a]
Phenobarbital — Phénobarbital — Fenobarbital	35 000[a]
Congo	
Alprazolam	19
Bromazepam — Bromazépam	218
Clorazepate — Clorazépate — Clorazepato	1 920
Diazepam — Diazépam	399
Lorazepam — Lorazépam	308
Meprobamate — Méprobamate — Meprobamato	17
Nitrazepam — Nitrazépam	57
Oxazepam — Oxazépam	166
Phenobarbital — Phénobarbital — Fenobarbital	2 340
Prazepam — Prazépam	480
Tetrazepam — Tétrazépam	1 900
Zolpidem	310
Cook Islands — Îles Cook — Islas Cook	
Alprazolam	1
Amfetamine — Amfétamine — Anfetamina	50
Clobazam	2
Clonazepam — Clonazépam	1
Diazepam — Diazépam	60
Lorazepam — Lorazépam	1
Methylphenidate — Méthylphénidate — Metilfenidato	12
Midazolam	6
Nitrazepam — Nitrazépam	3
Phenobarbital — Phénobarbital — Fenobarbital	280
Phentermine — Fentermina	190
Temazepam — Témazépam	13
Triazolam	1

Table V. Assessments of annual domestic medical and scientific requirements
Tableau V. Évaluations des besoins annuels médicaux et scientifiques intérieurs
Cuadro V. Previsiones de las necesidades anuales internas para fines médicos y científicos

Country (or territory) and substance / Pays (ou territoire) et substance / País (o territorio) y sustancia	Assessment (grams) / Évaluation (en grammes) / Previsión (en gramos)
Costa Rica	
4-Bromo-2,5-dimethoxyphenyl-ethylamine (2C-B) — 4-bromo-2,5-diméthoxyphényléthylamine (2C-B) — 4-bromo-2,5-dimetoxifeniletilamina (2C-B)	1
Alprazolam	10 00
Amfepramone — Amfépramone — Anfepramona	12 000
Amfetamine — Amfétamine — Anfetamina	1
Amobarbital	1 000
Barbital	1 000
Bromazepam — Bromazépam	40 000
Butalbital	1 500
Butobarbital	1 500
Cathine — Catina	1
Chlordiazepoxide — Chlordiazépoxide — Clordiazepóxido	3 000
Clobazam	5 000
Clonazepam — Clonazépam	45 000
Cloxazolam	1
Delta-9-tetrahydrocannabinol — Delta-9-tétrahydrocannabinol — Delta-9-tetrahidrocannabinol	2
Diazepam — Diazépam	80 000
Ethyl loflazepate — Loflazépate d'éthyle — Loflazepato de etilo	6 000
Flunitrazepam — Flunitrazépam	2 000
Glutethimide — Glutéthimide — Glutetimida	1
Loprazolam	2 000
Lorazepam — Lorazépam	25 000
Mazindol	7 000
Meprobamate — Méprobamate — Meprobamato	1 000
Metamfetamine — Métamfétamine — Metanfetamina	1
Metamfetamine racemate — Racémate de métamfétamine — Racemato de metanfetamina	1
Methylphenidate — Méthylphénidate — Metilfenidato	30 000
Midazolam	70 000
Nitrazepam — Nitrazépam	1 000
Nordazepam — Nordazépam	2
Oxazepam — Oxazépam	2
Pentobarbital	90 000
Phencyclidine (PCP) — Fenciclidina (PCP)	1
Phenobarbital — Phénobarbital — Fenobarbital	630 000
Phentermine — Fentermina	60 000
Prazepam — Prazépam	1 000
Temazepam — Témazépam	1
Tetrazepam — Tétrazépam	3 000
Triazolam	20 000
Zolpidem	25 000
Côte d'Ivoire	
Alprazolam	150
Amfepramone — Amfépramone — Anfepramona	1 700
Amobarbital	500
Bromazepam — Bromazépam	14 000
Buprenorphine — Buprénorphine — Buprenorfina	50
Chlordiazepoxide — Chlordiazépoxide — Clordiazepóxido	2 000
Clobazam	7 000
Clonazepam — Clonazépam	403
Clorazepate — Clorazépate — Clorazepato	25 000
Diazepam — Diazépam	40 000
Estazolam	3
Ethyl loflazepate — Loflazépate d'éthyle — Loflazepato de etilo	500
Fenproporex	400
Flunitrazepam — Flunitrazépam	200
Loprazolam	1
Lorazepam — Lorazépam	1 400
Meprobamate — Méprobamate — Meprobamato	120 000
Methylphenidate — Méthylphénidate — Metilfenidato	4
Midazolam	1 400
Nitrazepam — Nitrazépam	5 200
Nordazepam — Nordazépam	250
Oxazepam — Oxazépam	200
Phenobarbital — Phénobarbital — Fenobarbital	152 000
Prazepam — Prazépam	12 000
Temazepam — Témazépam	30
Tetrazepam — Tétrazépam	26 000
Triazolam	1
Zolpidem	803
Croatia — Croatie — Croacia	
4-Bromo-2,5-dimethoxyphenyl-ethylamine (2C-B) — 4-bromo-2,5-diméthoxyphényléthylamine (2C-B) — 4-bromo-2,5-dimetoxifeniletilamina (2C-B)	2
Alprazolam	35 000
Amfetamine — Amfétamine — Anfetamina	10
Barbital	12 000
Bromazepam — Bromazépam	70 000
Buprenorphine — Buprénorphine — Buprenorfina	5 000
Clobazam	100
Clonazepam — Clonazépam	8 000
Dexamfetamine — Dexamfétamine — Dexanfetamina	2
Diazepam — Diazépam	360 000
Flunitrazepam — Flunitrazépam	5
Flurazepam — Flurazépam	12 000
Lorazepam — Lorazépam	50 000
Meprobamate — Méprobamate — Meprobamato	300 000
Metamfetamine — Métamfétamine — Metanfetamina	2
Methylphenidate — Méthylphénidate — Metilfenidato	29
Methylphenobarbital — Méthylphénobarbital — Metilfenobarbital	1 500 000
Midazolam	20 000
Nitrazepam — Nitrazépam	50 000
Nordazepam — Nordazépam	10
Oxazepam — Oxazépam	1 000 000
Phenobarbital — Phénobarbital — Fenobarbital	700 000
Triazolam	2
Zolpidem	200 000
Cuba	
Alprazolam	30 000
Amfetamine — Amfétamine — Anfetamina	2
Barbital	5 000
Benzfetamine — Benzfétamine — Benzfetamina	1
Bromazepam — Bromazépam	1 000
Cathine — Catina	1
Chlordiazepoxide — Chlordiazépoxide — Clordiazepóxido	1 500 000
Clobazam	75 000
Clonazepam — Clonazépam	25 000
Delta-9-tetrahydrocannabinol — Delta-9-tétrahydrocannabinol — Delta-9-tetrahidrocannabinol	1

Table V. Assessments of annual domestic medical and scientific requirements
Tableau V. Évaluations des besoins annuels médicaux et scientifiques intérieurs
Cuadro V. Previsiones de las necesidades anuales internas
para fines médicos y científicos

Country (or territory) and substance Pays (ou territoire) et substance País (o territorio) y sustancia	Assessment (grams) Évaluation (en grammes) Previsión (en gramos)
Cuba	
(continued — suite — continuación)	
Dexamfetamine — Dexamfétamine — Dexanfetamina .	1
Diazepam — Diazépam	570 000
Etilamfetamine — Étilamfétamine — Etilanfetamina ..	1
Fencamfamin — Fencamfamine — Fencanfamina ...	1
Fenetylline — Fénétylline — Fenetilina	1
Fenproporex	1
Flunitrazepam — Flunitrazépam	1 000
Mecloqualone — Mécloqualone — Meclocualona	1
Medazepam — Médazépam	250 000
Mefenorex — Méfénorex	1
Meprobamate — Méprobamate — Meprobamato	65 000
Mesocarb — Mésocarbe — Mesocarbo	1
Metamfetamine — Métamfétamine — Metanfetamina ..	1
Methaqualone — Méthaqualone — Metacualona	1
Methylphenidate — Méthylphénidate — Metilfenidato ..	20 000
Midazolam	70 000
Nitrazepam — Nitrazépam	550 000
Nordazepam — Nordazépam	1
Oxazepam — Oxazépam	1
Pemoline — Pémoline — Pemolina	1
Phencyclidine (PCP) — Fenciclidina (PCP)	1
Phendimetrazine — Phendimétrazine — Fendimetracina	1
Phenmetrazine — Phenmétrazine — Fenmetracina ..	1
Phenobarbital — Phénobarbital — Fenobarbital	3 500 000
Phentermine — Fentermina	1
Pipradrol	1
Pyrovalerone — Pyrovalérone — Pirovalerona	1
Temazepam — Témazépam	1
Zolpidem	1 000
Cyprus — Chypre — Chipre	
Alprazolam	9 000
Amfetamine — Amfétamine — Anfetamina	15
Amobarbital	400
Barbital	500
Bromazepam — Bromazépam	70 000
Buprenorphine — Buprénorphine — Buprenorfina	500
Butobarbital	500
Chlordiazepoxide — Chlordiazépoxide — Clordiazepóxido	180 000
Clobazam	5 000
Clonazepam — Clonazépam	20 000
Clorazepate — Clorazépate — Clorazepato	20 000
Dexamfetamine — Dexamfétamine — Dexanfetamina ..	15
Diazepam — Diazépam	120 000
Flunitrazepam — Flunitrazépam	4 000
Flurazepam — Flurazépam	200 000
Lorazepam — Lorazépam	70 000
Lormetazepam — Lormétazépam	2 000
Mazindol	500
Medazepam — Médazépam	500
Meprobamate — Méprobamate — Meprobamato	500
Metamfetamine — Métamfétamine — Metanfetamina ..	1
Methylphenidate — Méthylphénidate — Metilfenidato ..	1 500
Midazolam	1 500
Nitrazepam — Nitrazépam	50 000
Nordazepam — Nordazépam	10

Country (or territory) and substance Pays (ou territoire) et substance País (o territorio) y sustancia	Assessment (grams) Évaluation (en grammes) Previsión (en gramos)
Oxazepam — Oxazépam	700 000
Phenobarbital — Phénobarbital — Fenobarbital	130 000
Secobarbital — Sécobarbital	30 000
Temazepam — Témazépam	800 000
Triazolam	1 500
Zolpidem	5 000
Czech Republic — République tchèque — República Checa	
4-Bromo-2,5-dimethoxyphenyl-ethylamine (2C-B) — 4-bromo-2,5-diméthoxyphényléthylamine (2C-B) — 4-bromo-2,5-dimetoxifeniletilamina (2C-B)	5
Allobarbital — Alobarbital	100 000
Alprazolam	250 000
Amfetamine — Amfétamine — Anfetamina	50
Amineptin — Amineptine — Amineptina	5
Amobarbital	2 000
Barbital	80 000
Bromazepam — Bromazépam	250 000
Brotizolam	10
Buprenorphine — Buprénorphine — Buprenorfina	40 000
Butalbital	5
Butobarbital	30 000
Cathine — Catina	10
Chlordiazepoxide — Chlordiazépoxide — Clordiazepóxido	350 000
Clobazam	5 000
Clonazepam — Clonazépam	70 000
Clorazepate — Clorazépate — Clorazepato	5 000
Cyclobarbital — Ciclobarbital	5
Delta-9-tetrahydrocannabinol — *Delta*-9-tétrahydrocannabinol — *Delta*-9-tetrahidrocannabinol	10
Dexamfetamine — Dexamfétamine — Dexanfetamina .	10
Diazepam — Diazépam	350 000
Fenetylline — Fénétylline — Fenetilina	10
Flunitrazepam — Flunitrazépam	50 000
Flurazepam — Flurazépam	5 000
Gamma-hydroxybutyric acid (GHB) — Acide *gamma*-hydroxybutirique (GHB) — Ácido *gamma*-hidroxibutírico (GHB)	60 000
Glutethimide — Glutéthimide — Glutetimida	10
Levamfetamine — Lévamfétamine — Levanfetamina ..	10
Levomethamphetamine — Lévométhamphétamine — Levometanfetamina	450 000
Loprazolam	10
Lorazepam — Lorazépam	1 000
Lormetazepam — Lormétazépam	100
Mazindol	10
Medazepam — Médazépam	40 000
Meprobamate — Méprobamate — Meprobamato	40 000
Metamfetamine — Métamfétamine — Metanfetamina	100
Methaqualone — Méthaqualone — Metacualona	10
Methylphenidate — Méthylphénidate — Metilfenidato ..	25 000
Midazolam	270 000
Nitrazepam — Nitrazépam	70 000
Nordazepam — Nordazépam	300 000
Oxazepam — Oxazépam	350 000
Pemoline — Pémoline — Pemolina	10
Pentazocine — Pentazocina	80 000

Table V.   Assessments of annual domestic medical and scientific requirements
Tableau V.   Évaluations des besoins annuels médicaux et scientifiques intérieurs
Cuadro V.   Previsiones de las necesidades anuales internas para fines médicos y científicos

Country (or territory) and substance Pays (ou territoire) et substance País (o territorio) y sustancia	Assessment (grams) Évaluation (en grammes) Previsión (en gramos)
Pentobarbital	2 000
Phencyclidine (PCP) — Fenciclidina (PCP)	10
Phendimetrazine — Phendimétrazine — Fendimetracina	10
Phenmetrazine — Phenmétrazine — Fenmetracina	10
Phenobarbital — Phénobarbital — Fenobarbital	2 000 000
Phentermine — Fentermina	200 000
Pinazepam — Pinazépam	270 000
Prazepam — Prazépam	500
Secobarbital — Sécobarbital	5
Temazepam — Témazépam	500
Tetrazepam — Tétrazépam	600 000
Triazolam	500
Zipeprol — Zipéprol	5
Zolpidem	5 300 000
Democratic People's Republic of Korea — République populaire démocratique de Corée — República Popular Democrática de Corea	
Barbital	40 000
Clonazepam — Clonazépam	1 000
Diazepam — Diazépam	1 000 000
Flunitrazepam — Flunitrazépam	1 000
Lorazepam — Lorazépam	200
Midazolam	500
Nitrazepam — Nitrazépam	3 000
Pentobarbital	3 000
Phenobarbital — Phénobarbital — Fenobarbital	1 500 000
Democratic Republic of the Congo — Républiqe démocratique du Congo — República Democrática del Congo	
Alprazolam	1 000
Amfepramone — Amfépramone — Anfepramona	100
Bromazepam — Bromazépam	2 500
Brotizolam	500
Buprenorphine — Buprénorphine — Buprenorfina	1 000
Chlordiazepoxide — Chlordiazépoxide — Clordiazepóxido	2 500
Clobazam	500
Clonazepam — Clonazépam	1 000
Clorazepate — Clorazépate — Clorazepato	2 500
Diazepam — Diazépam	3 000 000
Lorazepam — Lorazépam	25
Lormetazepam — Lormétazépam	25
Medazepam — Médazépam	500
Meprobamate — Méprobamate — Meprobamato	3 000 000
Methylphenidate — Méthylphénidate — Metilfenidato	10
Methylphenobarbital — Méthylphénobarbital — Metilfenobarbital	1 500
Midazolam	500
Nitrazepam — Nitrazépam	300
Oxazepam — Oxazépam	100
Pentazocine — Pentazocina	2 500
Phenobarbital — Phénobarbital — Fenobarbital	3 000 000
Prazepam — Prazépam	10
Temazepam — Témazépam	100
Tetrazepam — Tétrazépam	200
Triazolam	100
Zolpidem	500

Country (or territory) and substance Pays (ou territoire) et substance País (o territorio) y sustancia	Assessment (grams) Évaluation (en grammes) Previsión (en gramos)
Denmark — Danemark — Dinamarca	
4-Bromo-2,5-dimethoxyphenyl-ethylamine (2C-B) — 4-bromo-2,5-diméthoxyphényléthylamine (2C-B) — 4-bromo-2,5-dimetoxifeniletilamina (2C-B)	5
Allobarbital — Alobarbital	600 000
Alprazolam	20 000
Amfepramone — Amfépramone — Anfepramona	160 000
Amfetamine — Amfétamine — Anfetamina	3 000
Amobarbital	500 000
Barbital	3 000 000
Benzfetamine — Benzfétamine — Benzfetamina	200
Bromazepam — Bromazépam	70 000
Brotizolam	1 000
Buprenorphine — Buprénorphine — Buprenorfina	20 000
Butalbital	100 000
Butobarbital	2 000
Camazepam — Camazépam	5
Cathine — Catina	200
Chlordiazepoxide — Chlordiazépoxide — Clordiazepóxido	1 500 000
Clobazam	20 000
Clonazepam — Clonazépam	25 000
Clorazepate — Clorazépate — Clorazepato	3 000
Clotiazepam — Clotiazépam	5
Cloxazolam	5
Cyclobarbital — Ciclobarbital	200
Delorazepam — Délorazépam	5
Delta-9-tetrahydrocannabinol — Delta-9-tétrahydrocannabinol — Delta-9-tetrahidrocannabinol	1 200
Dexamfetamine —Dexamfétamine —Dexanfetamina	2 000
Diazepam — Diazépam	10 000 000
Estazolam	5 000
Ethchlorvynol — Etclorvinol	5
Ethinamate — Éthinamate — Etinamato	5
Ethyl loflazepate — Loflazépate d'éthyle — Loflazepato de etilo	5
Etilamfetamine — Étilamfétamine — Etilanfetamina	5
Fencamfamin — Fencamfamine — Fencanfamina	5
Fenproporex	5
Fludiazepam — Fludiazépam	5
Flunitrazepam — Flunitrazépam	10 000
Flurazepam — Flurazépam	5 000
Gamma-hydroxybutyric acid (GHB) — Acide gamma-hydroxybutirique (GHB) — Ácido gamma-hidroxibutírico (GHB)	100 000
Halazepam — Halazépam	5
Haloxazolam	5
Ketazolam — Kétazolam	5
Lefetamine (SPA) — Léfétamine (SPA) — Lefetamina (SPA)	5
Levamfetamine —Lévamfétamine —Levanfetamina	10
Loprazolam	1 000
Lorazepam — Lorazépam	14 000
Lormetazepam — Lormétazépam	5 000
Mazindol	200
Medazepam — Médazépam	5
Mefenorex — Méfénorex	5
Meprobamate — Méprobamate — Meprobamato	300 000 000
Mesocarb — Mésocarbe — Mesocarbo	5
Metamfetamine — Métamfétamine —Metanfetamina	10

Table V.   Assessments of annual domestic medical and scientific requirements
Tableau V.   Évaluations des besoins annuels médicaux et scientifiques intérieurs
Cuadro V.   Previsiones de las necesidades anuales internas
para fines médicos y científicos

Country (or territory) and substance Pays (ou territoire) et substance País (o territorio) y sustancia	Assessment (grams) Évaluation (en grammes) Previsión (en gramos)
Denmark — Danemark — Dinamarca	
(continued — suite — continuación)	
Metamfetamine racemate — Racémate de métamfétamine — Racemato de metanfetamina	10
Methaqualone — Méthaqualone — Metacualona	10
Methylphenidate — Méthylphénidate — Metilfenidato	100 000
Methylphenobarbital — Méthylphénobarbital — Metilfenobarbital	1 000
Methyprylon — Méthyprylone — Metiprilona	5
Midazolam	20 000
Nimetazepam — Nimétazépam	5
Nitrazepam — Nitrazépam	200 000
Nordazepam — Nordazépam	100
Oxazepam — Oxazépam	600 000
Oxazolam	5
Pemoline — Pémoline — Pemolina	5
Pentazocine — Pentazocina	5 000
Pentobarbital	2 000 000
Phencyclidine (PCP) — Fenciclidina (PCP)	10
Phendimetrazine — Phendimétrazine — Fendimetracina	10
Phenobarbital — Phénobarbital — Fenobarbital	50 000 000
Phentermine — Fentermina	1 000
Pinazepam — Pinazépam	5
Prazepam — Prazépam	100
Pyrovalerone — Pyrovalérone — Pirovalerona	5
Secbutabarbital	5
Secobarbital — Sécobarbital	2 000
Temazepam — Témazépam	10 000
Tetrazepam — Tétrazépam	5
Triazolam	3 000
Vinylbital — Vinilbital	5
Zolpidem	400 000
Djibouti	
Alprazolam	13
Bromazepam — Bromazépam	485
Chlordiazepoxide — Chlordiazépoxide — Clordiazepóxido	34
Clobazam	6
Clonazepam — Clonazépam	26
Clorazepate — Clorazépate — Clorazepato	770
Diazepam — Diazépam	3 431
Lorazepam — Lorazépam	50
Mesocarb — Mésocarbe — Mesocarbo	112
Midazolam	200
Oxazepam — Oxazépam	15
Phenobarbital — Phénobarbital — Fenobarbital	67 568
Prazepam — Prazépam	311
Tetrazepam — Tétrazépam	1 260
Triazolam	1
Zolpidem	632
Dominica — Dominique	
Clobazam	300
Clonazepam — Clonazépam	100
Diazepam — Diazépam	1 000
Lorazepam — Lorazépam	100

Country (or territory) and substance Pays (ou territoire) et substance País (o territorio) y sustancia	Assessment (grams) Évaluation (en grammes) Previsión (en gramos)
Methylphenidate — Méthylphénidate — Metilfenidato	400
Midazolam	2
Phenobarbital — Phénobarbital — Fenobarbital	6 000
Dominican Republic — République dominicaine — República Dominicana	
Alprazolam	12 000
Bromazepam — Bromazépam	6 000
Buprenorphine — Buprénorphine — Buprenorfina	500
Cathine — Catina	500
Chlordiazepoxide — Chlordiazépoxide — Clordiazepóxido	1 000
Clobazam	3 000
Clonazepam — Clonazépam	10 000
Clorazepate — Clorazépate — Clorazepato	2 000
Cloxazolam	500
Diazepam — Diazépam	100 000
Ethyl loflazepate — Loflazépate d'éthyle — Loflazepato de etilo	1 000
Fenproporex	1 000
Fludiazepam — Fludiazépam	1 000
Flunitrazepam — Flunitrazépam	500
Flurazepam — Flurazépam	1 000
Loprazolam	1 000
Lorazepam — Lorazépam	10 000
Mazindol	1 000
Medazepam — Médazépam	500
Methaqualone — Méthaqualone — Metacualona	1 000
Methylphenidate — Méthylphénidate — Metilfenidato	3 000
Methylphenobarbital — Méthylphénobarbital — Metilfenobarbital	300
Midazolam	5 000
Nitrazepam — Nitrazépam	12 000
Oxazepam — Oxazépam	4 000
Oxazolam	500
Pemoline — Pémoline — Pemolina	500
Pentazocine — Pentazocina	1 000
Pentobarbital	1 000
Phenobarbital — Phénobarbital — Fenobarbital	800 000
Phentermine — Fentermina	1 000
Temazepam — Témazépam	500
Tetrazepam — Tétrazépam	500
Triazolam	3 000
Zolpidem	30 000
Ecuador — Équateur	
Alprazolam	9 131
Bromazepam — Bromazépam	22 000
Brotizolam	2 000
Buprenorphine — Buprénorphine — Buprenorfina	500
Butalbital	33 500
Chlordiazepoxide — Chlordiazépoxide — Clordiazepóxido	33 000
Clobazam	198 000
Clonazepam — Clonazépam	24 000
Clorazepate — Clorazépate — Clorazepato	9 000
Cloxazolam	8 801
Diazepam — Diazépam	150 000
Estazolam	2 500

Table V. Assessments of annual domestic medical and scientific requirements
Tableau V. Évaluations des besoins annuels médicaux et scientifiques intérieurs
Cuadro V. Previsiones de las necesidades anuales internas para fines médicos y científicos

Country (or territory) and substance Pays (ou territoire) et substance País (o territorio) y sustancia	Assessment (grams) Évaluation (en grammes) Previsión (en gramos)	Country (or territory) and substance Pays (ou territoire) et substance País (o territorio) y sustancia	Assessment (grams) Évaluation (en grammes) Previsión (en gramos)
Ethyl loflazepate — Loflazépate d'éthyle —		Fenproporex	2 250
Loflazepato de etilo	8 801	Loprazolam	800
Fenproporex	120 000	Lorazepam — Lorazépam	48 660
Flunitrazepam — Flunitrazépam	4 000	Mazindol	90
Ketazolam — Kétazolam	93 500	Meprobamate — Méprobamate — Meprobamato	50 000
Lorazepam — Lorazépam	12 000	Methylphenidate — Méthylphénidate — Metilfenidato	6 850
Lormetazepam — Lormétazépam	4 600	Midazolam	21 039
Mazindol	3 080	Pentobarbital	352 100
Methylphenidate — Méthylphénidate — Metilfenidato	12 000	Phenobarbital — Phénobarbital — Fenobarbital	1 010 000
Midazolam	18 700	Phentermine — Fentermina	7 807
Nitrazepam — Nitrazépam	25 000	Tetrazepam — Tétrazépam	600
Pentazocine — Pentazocina	18 000	Triazolam	2 000
Pentobarbital	130 000	Zolpidem	7 300
Phenobarbital — Phénobarbital — Fenobarbital	110 000		
Phentermine — Fentermina	75 000	**Equatorial Guinea — Guinée équatoriale — Guinea Ecuatorial**	
Tetrazepam — Tétrazépam	30 000		
Triazolam	5 500	Diazepam — Diazépam	800
Zolpidem	12 000	Pentazocine — Pentazocina	500
		Phenobarbital — Phénobarbital — Fenobarbital	700
Egypt — Égypte — Egipto			
Allobarbital — Alobarbital	5 000	**Eritrea — Érythrée**	
Alprazolam	25 000	Clonazepam — Clonazépam	400
Barbital	1 000	Diazepam — Diazépam	6 000
Bromazepam — Bromazépam	200 000	Pentazocine — Pentazocina	2 315
Buprenorphine — Buprénorphine — Buprenorfina	1 000	Phenobarbital — Phénobarbital — Fenobarbital	105 000
Cathine — Catina	100 000		
Chlordiazepoxide — Chlordiazépoxide —		**Estonia — Estonie**	
Clordiazepóxido	900 000	Alprazolam	5 500
Clonazepam — Clonazépam	100 000	Amfetamine — Amfétamine — Anfetamina	300
Clorazepate — Clorazépate — Clorazepato	1 000	Barbital	1 000
Delorazepam — Délorazépam	1 000	Bromazepam — Bromazépam	7 500
Diazepam — Diazépam	255 000	Brotizolam	200
Lorazepam — Lorazépam	2 000	Buprenorphine — Buprénorphine — Buprenorfina	3 500
Lormetazepam — Lormétazépam	1 000	Chlordiazepoxide — Chlordiazépoxide —	
Meprobamate — Méprobamate — Meprobamato	2 000 000	Clordiazepóxido	100
Methylphenidate — Méthylphénidate — Metilfenidato	1 000	Clonazepam — Clonazépam	5 000
Methylphenobarbital — Méthylphénobarbital —		Dexamfetamine — Dexamfétamine — Dexanfetamina	300
Metilfenobarbital	50 000	Diazepam — Diazépam	35 000
Midazolam	35 000	Flunitrazepam — Flunitrazépam	30
Oxazepam — Oxazépam	30 000	*Gamma*-hydroxybutyric acid (GHB) —	
Pentobarbital	100 000	Acide *gamma*-hydroxybutirique (GHB) —	
Phenobarbital — Phénobarbital — Fenobarbital	10 000 000	Ácido *gamma*-hidroxibutírico (GHB)	85 000
Temazepam — Témazépam	1 000	Lorazepam — Lorazépam	500
Tetrazepam — Tétrazépam	1 000 000	Meprobamate — Méprobamate — Meprobamato	500
Triazolam	1 000	Methylphenidate — Méthylphénidate — Metilfenidato	900
		Midazolam	5 700
El Salvador		Nitrazepam — Nitrazépam	10 000
Alprazolam	15 465	Oxazepam — Oxazépam	11 000
Amfepramone — Amfépramone — Anfepramona	5 625	Pentazocine — Pentazocina	500
Bromazepam — Bromazépam	66 907	Pentobarbital	32 500
Buprenorphine — Buprénorphine — Buprenorfina	5	Phenobarbital — Phénobarbital — Fenobarbital	46 000
Cathine — Catina	3 750	Temazepam — Témazépam	100
Chlordiazepoxide — Chlordiazépoxide —		Tetrazepam — Tétrazépam	250
Clordiazepóxido	144 031	Triazolam	100
Clobazam	65 000	Zolpidem	7 000
Clonazepam — Clonazépam	16 790		
Clorazepate — Clorazépate — Clorazepato	150	**Ethiopia — Éthiopie — Etiopía**	
Diazepam — Diazépam	327 042	Bromazepam — Bromazépam	9 697
Ethyl loflazepate — Loflazépate d'éthyle —		Chlordiazepoxide — Chlordiazépoxide —	
Loflazepato de etilo	200	Clordiazepóxido	225 000

Table V. Assessments of annual domestic medical and scientific requirements
Tableau V. Évaluations des besoins annuels médicaux et scientifiques intérieurs
Cuadro V. Previsiones de las necesidades anuales internas para fines médicos y científicos

Country (or territory) and substance / Pays (ou territoire) et substance / País (o territorio) y sustancia	Assessment (grams) / Évaluation (en grammes) / Previsión (en gramos)
Ethiopia — Éthiopie — Etiopía	
(continued — suite — continuación)	
Clonazepam — Clonazépam	1 235
Diazepam — Diazépam	75 000
Midazolam	11 719
Oxazepam — Oxazépam	125
Pentazocine — Pentazocina	6 236
Pentobarbital	2 000
Phenobarbital — Phénobarbital — Fenobarbital	2 500 000
Falkland Islands (Malvinas) —	
Îles Falkland (Malvinas) —	
Islas Malvinas (Falkland Islands)	
Clonazepam — Clonazépam	1
Diazepam — Diazépam	50
Lorazepam — Lorazépam	1
Methylphenidate — Méthylphénidate — Metilfenidato	5
Midazolam	3
Nitrazepam — Nitrazépam	3
Pentobarbital	1 000
Phenobarbital — Phénobarbital — Fenobarbital	5
Temazepam — Témazépam	20
Fiji — Fidji	
Alprazolam	7
Amobarbital	450
Bromazepam — Bromazépam	310
Buprenorphine — Buprénorphine — Buprenorfina	1
Chlordiazepoxide — Chlordiazépoxide — Clordiazepóxido	8
Clobazam	90
Clonazepam — Clonazépam	130
Dexamfetamine — Dexamfétamine — Dexanfetamina	13
Diazepam — Diazépam	10 000
Flunitrazepam — Flunitrazépam	45
Lorazepam — Lorazépam	175
Mazindol	2
Methylphenidate — Méthylphénidate — Metilfenidato	100
Midazolam	450
Nitrazepam — Nitrazépam	350
Oxazepam — Oxazépam	1 000
Oxazolam	15
Pentazocine — Pentazocina	1 800
Pentobarbital	26 000
Phenobarbital — Phénobarbital — Fenobarbital	32 000
Phentermine — Fentermina	4 200
Temazepam — Témazépam	300
Triazolam	15
Finland — Finlande — Finlandia	
4-Bromo-2,5-dimethoxyphenyl-ethylamine (2C-B) —	
4-bromo-2,5-diméthoxyphényléthylamine (2C-B) —	
4-bromo-2,5-dimetoxifeniletilamina (2C-B)	1
Alprazolam	1 200 000
Amfetamine — Amfétamine — Anfetamina	150
Amobarbital	1 000
Barbital	50 000

Country (or territory) and substance / Pays (ou territoire) et substance / País (o territorio) y sustancia	Assessment (grams) / Évaluation (en grammes) / Previsión (en gramos)
Benzfetamine — Benzfétamine — Benzfetamina	1
Bromazepam — Bromazépam	1
Buprenorphine — Buprénorphine — Buprenorfina	5 000
Butalbital	70
Cathine — Catina	1
Chlordiazepoxide — Chlordiazépoxide — Clordiazepóxido	200 000
Clobazam	14 000
Clonazepam — Clonazépam	20 000
Clorazepate — Clorazépate — Clorazepato	1 000
Delta-9-tetrahydrocannabinol —	
Delta-9-tétrahydrocannabinol —	
Delta-9-tetrahidrocannabinol	1
Dexamfetamine — Dexamfétamine — Dexanfetamina	1 700
Diazepam — Diazépam	300 000
Estazolam	1
Etilamfetamine — Étilamfétamine — Etilanfetamina	1
Fenetylline — Fénétylline — Fenetilina	1
Fludiazepam — Fludiazépam	1
Flunitrazepam — Flunitrazépam	100
Flurazepam — Flurazépam	10
Gamma-hydroxybutyric acid (GHB) —	
Acide *gamma*-hydroxybutirique (GHB) —	
Ácido *gamma*-hidroxibutírico (GHB)	110 000
Levamfetamine — Lévamfétamine — Levanfetamina	1
Levomethamphetamine — Lévométhamphétamine — Levometanfetamina	10
Lorazepam — Lorazépam	30 000
Lormetazepam — Lormétazépam	4 200
Mazindol	10
Mefenorex — Méfénorex	1
Meprobamate — Méprobamate — Meprobamato	1 500 000
Metamfetamine — Métamfétamine — Metanfetamina	10
Metamfetamine racemate —	
Racémate de métamfétamine —	
Racemato de metanfetamina	1
Methaqualone — Méthaqualone — Metacualona	5
Methylphenidate — Méthylphénidate — Metilfenidato	60 000
Midazolam	50 000
Nitrazepam — Nitrazépam	30 000
Nordazepam — Nordazépam	2 500 000
Oxazepam — Oxazépam	1 200 000
Pemoline — Pémoline — Pemolina	1
Pentazocine — Pentazocina	100
Pentobarbital	100 000
Phencyclidine (PCP) — Fenciclidina (PCP)	5
Phenobarbital — Phénobarbital — Fenobarbital	220 000
Secobarbital — Sécobarbital	1
Temazepam — Témazépam	2 000 000
Tetrazepam — Tétrazépam	1
Triazolam	500
Zolpidem	200 000
France — Francia	
4-Bromo-2,5-dimethoxyphenyl-ethylamine (2C-B) —	
4-bromo-2,5-dimethoxyphényléthylamine (2C-B) —	
4-bromo-2,5-dimetoxifeniletilamina (2C-B)	5
Alprazolam	1 500 000
Amfepramone — Amfépramone — Anfepramona	1 000
Amfetamine — Amfétamine — Anfetamina	10 000 000
Aminorex	10

Table V. Assessments of annual domestic medical and scientific requirements
Tableau V. Évaluations des besoins annuels médicaux et scientifiques intérieurs
Cuadro V. Previsiones de las necesidades anuales internas
para fines médicos y científicos

Country (or territory) and substance Pays (ou territoire) et substance País (o territorio) y sustancia	Assessment (grams) Évaluation (en grammes) Previsión (en gramos)	Country (or territory) and substance Pays (ou territoire) et substance País (o territorio) y sustancia	Assessment (grams) Évaluation (en grammes) Previsión (en gramos)
Amobarbital	6 000	Prazepam — Prazépam	3 200 000
Barbital	2 000 000	Secobarbital — Sécobarbital	10
Benzfetamine — Benzfétamine — Benzfetamina	1	Temazepam — Témazépam	700 000
Bromazepam — Bromazépam	4 000 000	Tetrazepam — Tétrazépam	30 000 000
Brotizolam	15 000	Triazolam	1 000
Buprenorphine — Buprénorphine — Buprenorfina	400 000	Zipeprol — Zipéprol	5
Butalbital	50	Zolpidem	60 000 000
Butobarbital	100 000		
Cathine — Catina	400 000	*French Polynesia — Polynésie française —*	
Chlordiazepoxide — Chlordiazépoxide —		*Polinesia Francesa*	
Clordiazepóxido	400 000	Alprazolam	100
Clobazam	3 000 000	Amfepramone — Amfépramone — Anfepramona	5 000
Clonazepam — Clonazépam	400 000	Amfetamine — Amfétamine — Anfetamina	20
Clorazepate — Clorazépate — Clorazepato	9 000 000	Amobarbital	5
Clotiazepam — Clotiazépam	150 000	Bromazepam — Bromazépam	3 300
Cyclobarbital — Ciclobarbital	10	Buprenorphine — Buprénorphine — Buprenorfina	50
Delta-9-tetrahydrocannabinol —		Chlordiazepoxide — Chlordiazépoxide —	
Delta-9-tétrahydrocannabinol —		Clordiazepóxido	60
Delta-9-tetrahidrocannabinol	100	Clobazam	700
Dexamfetamine — Dexamfétamine — Dexanfetamina	5 000 000	Clonazepam — Clonazépam	1 400
Diazepam — Diazépam	1 200 000	Clorazepate — Clorazépate — Clorazepato	2 300
Estazolam	25 000	Clotiazepam — Clotiazépam	10
Ethyl loflazepate — Loflazépate d'éthyle —		*Delta*-9-tetrahydrocannabinol —	
Loflazepato de etilo	100 000	*Delta*-9-tétrahydrocannabinol —	
Etilamfetamine — Étilamfétamine — Etilanfetamina	1	*Delta*-9-tetrahidrocannabinol	1
Fenetylline — Fénétylline — Fenetilina	1 300	Diazepam — Diazépam	1 200
Fenproporex	500 000	Estazolam	3
Flunitrazepam — Flunitrazépam	20 000	Ethyl loflazepate — Loflazépate d'éthyle —	
Flurazepam — Flurazépam	100	Loflazepato de etilo	15
Gamma-hydroxybutyric acid (GHB) —		Fenproporex	10
Acide *gamma*-hydroxybutirique (GHB) —		Flunitrazepam — Flunitrazépam	50
Ácido *gamma*-hidroxibutírico (GHB)	450 000	*Gamma*-hydroxybutyric acid (GHB) —	
Glutethimide — Glutéthimide — Glutetimida	20	Acide *gamma*-hydroxybutirique (GHB) —	
Ketazolam — Kétazolam	10	Ácido *gamma*-hidroxibutírico (GHB)	500
Levamfetamine — Lévamfétamine — Levanfetamina	5 000 000	Loprazolam	10
Levomethamphetamine — Lévométhamphétamine —		Lorazepam — Lorazépam	200
Levometanfetamina	1 500 000	Lormetazepam — Lormétazépam	40
Loprazolam	100 000	Meprobamate — Méprobamate — Meprobamato	40 000
Lorazepam — Lorazépam	2 500 000	Methylphenidate — Méthylphénidate —	
Lormetazepam — Lormétazépam	500 000	Metilfenidato	100
Mazindol	50	Midazolam	1 000
Mecloqualone — Mécloqualone — Meclocualona	10	Nitrazepam — Nitrazépam	60
Meprobamate — Méprobamate — Meprobamato	120 000 000	Nordazepam — Nordazépam	20
Metamfetamine — Métamfétamine — Metanfetamina	1 000 000	Oxazepam — Oxazépam	700
Metamfetamine racemate —		Phenobarbital — Phénobarbital — Fenobarbital	30 000
Racémate de métamfétamine —		Prazepam — Prazépam	4 400
Racemato de metanfetamina	1 500 000	Temazepam — Témazépam	10
Methaqualone — Méthaqualone — Metacualona	10	Tetrazepam — Tétrazépam	14 000
Methylphenidate — Méthylphénidate — Metilfenidato	200 000	Triazolam	10
Methylphenobarbital — Méthylphénobarbital —		Zolpidem	3 000
Metilfenobarbital	30		
Midazolam	400 000	**Gabon — Gabón**	
Nitrazepam — Nitrazépam	400 000	Alprazolam	34 000
Nordazepam — Nordazépam	400 000	Bromazepam — Bromazépam	2 031
Oxazepam — Oxazépam	15 000 000	Buprenorphine — Buprénorphine — Buprenorfina	8
Pentazocine — Pentazocina	120 000	Chlordiazepoxide — Chlordiazépoxide —	
Pentobarbital	6 000 000	Clordiazepóxido	380
Phencyclidine (PCP) — Fenciclidina (PCP)	10	Clobazam	59
Phenmetrazine — Phenmétrazine — Fenmetracina	10	Clonazepam — Clonazépam	25
Phenobarbital — Phénobarbital — Fenobarbital	20 000 000	Clorazepate — Clorazépate — Clorazepato	4 450
Phentermine — Fentermina	10		

Table V. Assessments of annual domestic medical and scientific requirements
Tableau V. Évaluations des besoins annuels médicaux et scientifiques intérieurs
Cuadro V. Previsiones de las necesidades anuales internas para fines médicos y científicos

Country (or territory) and substance / Pays (ou territoire) et substance / País (o territorio) y sustancia	Assessment (grams) / Évaluation (en grammes) / Previsión (en gramos)
Gabon — Gabón	
(continued — suite — continuación)	
Delta-9-tetrahydrocannabinol — *Delta*-9-tétrahydrocannabinol — *Delta*-9-tetrahidrocannabinol	1
Diazepam — Diazépam	5 130
Ethyl loflazepate — Loflazépate d'éthyle — Loflazepato de etilo	39
Fenproporex	213
Lorazepam — Lorazépam	374
Meprobamate — Méprobamate — Meprobamato	19 134
Midazolam	21
Nitrazepam — Nitrazépam	106
Nordazepam — Nordazépam	42
Oxazepam — Oxazépam	347
Pentazocine — Pentazocina	312
Phenobarbital — Phénobarbital — Fenobarbital	61 000
Prazepam — Prazépam	1 885
Tetrazepam — Tétrazépam	6 096
Triazolam	1
Zolpidem	526
Gambia — Gambie	
Allobarbital — Alobarbital	1
Amfetamine — Amfétamine — Anfetamina	1
Amobarbital	1
Barbital	1
Chlordiazepoxide — Chlordiazépoxide — Clordiazepóxido	1
Clonazepam — Clonazépam	500
Delta-9-tetrahydrocannabinol — *Delta*-9-tétrahydrocannabinol — *Delta*-9-tetrahidrocannabinol	1
Diazepam — Diazépam	3 000
Loprazolam	100
Lorazepam — Lorazépam	100
Lormetazepam — Lormétazépam	100
Metamfetamine — Métamfétamine — Metanfetamina	1
Methaqualone — Méthaqualone — Metacualona	1
Midazolam	200
Nitrazepam — Nitrazépam	500
Pentazocine — Pentazocina	650
Pentobarbital	1
Phenobarbital — Phénobarbital — Fenobarbital	40 000
Secbutabarbital	1
Secobarbital — Sécobarbital	1
Georgia — Géorgie	
Alprazolam	1 000
Barbital	100 000
Bromazepam — Bromazépam	2 500
Buprenorphine — Buprénorphine — Buprenorfina	10
Chlordiazepoxide — Chlordiazépoxide — Clordiazepóxido	5 000
Clonazepam — Clonazépam	2 000
Clorazepate — Clorazépate — Clorazepato	10
Cloxazolam	10
Cyclobarbital — Ciclobarbital	70 000
Diazepam — Diazépam	70 000
Flunitrazepam — Flunitrazépam	10

Country (or territory) and substance / Pays (ou territoire) et substance / País (o territorio) y sustancia	Assessment (grams) / Évaluation (en grammes) / Previsión (en gramos)
Gamma-hydroxybutyric acid (GHB) — Acide *gamma*-hydroxybutirique (GHB) — Ácido *gamma*-hidroxibutírico (GHB)	60 000
Lorazepam — Lorazépam	10
Medazepam — Médazépam	2 000
Meprobamate — Méprobamate — Meprobamato	10
Midazolam	1 000
Nitrazepam — Nitrazépam	400
Oxazepam — Oxazépam	17 000
Pentazocine — Pentazocina	10
Phenobarbital — Phénobarbital — Fenobarbital	150 000
Temazepam — Témazépam	10
Tetrazepam — Tétrazépam	10
Triazolam	10
Zolpidem	10
Germany — Allemagne — Alemania	
Allobarbital — Alobarbital	2 002 000
Alprazolam	80 000
Amfepramone — Amfépramone — Anfepramona	1 500 000
Amfetamine — Amfétamine — Anfetamina	100 500
Aminorex	5
Amobarbital	502 000
Barbital	7 000 000
Benzfetamine — Benzfétamine — Benzfetamina	1
Bromazepam — Bromazépam	1 000 000
Brotizolam	160 000
Buprenorphine — Buprénorphine — Buprenorfina	400 000
Butalbital	5 005 000
Butobarbital	201 000
Cathine — Catina	3 150 000
Chlordiazepoxide — Chlordiazépoxide — Clordiazepóxido	250 000
Clobazam	2 500 000
Clonazepam — Clonazépam	36 300
Clorazepate — Clorazépate — Clorazepato	1 200 000
Clotiazepam — Clotiazépam	1
Cyclobarbital — Ciclobarbital	10 100
Delta-9-tetrahydrocannabinol — *Delta*-9-tétrahydrocannabinol — *Delta*-9-tetrahidrocannabinol	17 000
Dexamfetamine — Dexamfétamine — Dexanfetamina	1 400
Diazepam — Diazépam	3 000 000
Estazolam	20
Ethyl loflazepate — Loflazépate d'éthyle — Loflazepato de etilo	1
Etilamfetamine — Étilamfétamine — Etilanfetamina	1
Fencamfamin — Fencamfamine — Fencanfamina	1
Fenetylline — Fénétylline — Fenetilina	10 000
Fenproporex	1 600 000
Fludiazepam — Fludiazépam	1
Flunitrazepam — Flunitrazépam	52 500
Flurazepam — Flurazépam	650 000
Gamma-hydroxybutyric acid (GHB) — Acide *gamma*-hydroxybutirique (GHB) — Ácido *gamma*-hidroxibutírico (GHB)	5 800 000
Glutethimide — Glutéthimide — Glutetimida	5
Ketazolam — Kétazolam	1 005 000
Levamfetamine — Lévamfétamine — Levanfetamina	20
Levomethamphetamine — Lévométhamphétamine — Levometanfetamina	500

Table V. Assessments of annual domestic medical and scientific requirements
Tableau V. Évaluations des besoins annuels médicaux et scientifiques intérieurs
Cuadro V. Previsiones de las necesidades anuales internas para fines médicos y científicos

Country (or territory) and substance Pays (ou territoire) et substance País (o territorio) y sustancia	Assessment (grams) Évaluation (en grammes) Previsión (en gramos)
Loprazolam	1 000
Lorazepam — Lorazépam	3 500 000
Lormetazepam — Lormétazépam	800 000
Mazindol	5 005
Medazepam — Médazépam	800 000
Mefenorex — Méfénorex	1
Meprobamate — Méprobamate — Meprobamato	5 500 200
Metamfetamine —Métamfétamine —Metanfetamina . .	500
Metamfetamine racemate — Racémate de métamfétamine — Racemato de metanfetamina	50
Methaqualone — Méthaqualone — Metacualona	500
Methylphenidate — Méthylphénidate —Metilfenidato . .	2 022 000
Methylphenobarbital — Méthylphénobarbital — Metilfenobarbital	1 100 000
Midazolam	500 000
Nitrazepam — Nitrazépam	300 000
Nordazepam — Nordazépam	10 000
Oxazepam — Oxazépam	4 500 000
Pemoline — Pémoline — Pemolina	20 000
Pentazocine — Pentazocina	10 000
Pentobarbital	13 000 000
Phencyclidine (PCP) — Fenciclidina (PCP)	20
Phendimetrazine — Phendimétrazine — Fendimetracina	100
Phenmetrazine — Phenmétrazine — Fenmetracina . .	20
Phenobarbital — Phénobarbital — Fenobarbital	30 000 000
Phentermine — Fentermina	3 010 000
Prazepam — Prazépam	3 020 000
Secbutabarbital	151 000
Secobarbital — Sécobarbital	602 000
Temazepam — Témazépam	1 400 000
Tetrazepam — Tétrazépam	5 000 000
Triazolam	1 150
Zolpidem	2 000 000
Ghana	
Alprazolam	50
Barbital	1 000
Bromazepam — Bromazépam	1 000
Chlordiazepoxide — Chlordiazépoxide — Clordiazepóxido	1 200 000
Clorazepate — Clorazépate — Clorazepato	500
Delta-9-tetrahydrocannabinol — *Delta*-9-tétrahydrocannabinol — *Delta*-9-tetrahidrocannabinol	2
Diazepam — Diazépam	2 000 000
Flunitrazepam — Flunitrazépam	5
Flurazepam — Flurazépam	20
Lorazepam — Lorazépam	5 000
Meprobamate — Méprobamate — Meprobamato	300 000
Midazolam	700
Nitrazepam — Nitrazépam	500
Pentazocine — Pentazocina	500
Pentobarbital	500
Phenobarbital — Phénobarbital — Fenobarbital	1 800 000
Phentermine — Fentermina	4 000
Pinazepam — Pinazépam	3 000
Temazepam — Témazépam	5
Triazolam	150

Country (or territory) and substance Pays (ou territoire) et substance País (o territorio) y sustancia	Assessment (grams) Évaluation (en grammes) Previsión (en gramos)
Gibraltar	
Alprazolam	80
Bromazepam — Bromazépam	180
Buprenorphine — Buprénorphine — Buprenorfina	6
Butobarbital	180
Chlordiazepoxide — Chlordiazépoxide — Clordiazepóxido	200
Clobazam	30
Clonazepam — Clonazépam	8
Clorazepate — Clorazépate — Clorazepato	20
Diazepam — Diazépam	1 500
Flunitrazepam — Flunitrazépam	80
Flurazepam — Flurazépam	400
Loprazolam	1
Lorazepam — Lorazépam	150
Lormetazepam — Lormétazépam	1
Meprobamate — Méprobamate — Meprobamato	120
Methylphenidate — Méthylphénidate —Metilfenidato . .	90
Midazolam	40
Nitrazepam — Nitrazépam	300
Oxazepam — Oxazépam	30
Pentobarbital	2 000
Phenobarbital — Phénobarbital — Fenobarbital	100
Temazepam — Témazépam	800
Greece — Grèce — Grecia	
Alprazolam	50 000
Amfepramone — Amfépramone — Anfepramona	30 000
Amobarbital	120
Barbital	16 000
Bromazepam — Bromazépam	350 000
Brotizolam	2 000
Buprenorphine — Buprénorphine — Buprenorfina	6 000
Butalbital	50
Chlordiazepoxide — Chlordiazépoxide — Clordiazepóxido	80 000
Clobazam	120 000
Clonazepam — Clonazépam	12 000
Clorazepate — Clorazépate — Clorazepato	100 000
Delorazepam — Délorazépam	50
Delta-9-tetrahydrocannabinol — *Delta*-9-tétrahydrocannabinol — *Delta*-9-tetrahidrocannabinol	5
Dexamfetamine —Dexamfétamine —Dexanfetamina . .	10
Diazepam — Diazépam	240 000
Flunitrazepam — Flunitrazépam	35 000
Lorazepam — Lorazépam	160 000
Lormetazepam — Lormétazépam	10 000
Methaqualone — Méthaqualone — Metacualona	1
Methylphenidate — Méthylphénidate —Metilfenidato . .	21 000
Midazolam	30 000
Nitrazepam — Nitrazépam	10
Nordazepam — Nordazépam	10
Oxazepam — Oxazépam	10
Pentazocine — Pentazocina	1 000
Pentobarbital	80 000
Phenobarbital — Phénobarbital — Fenobarbital	950 000
Prazepam — Prazépam	150 000
Temazepam — Témazépam	100 000
Triazolam	3 000
Zipeprol — Zipéprol	200 000
Zolpidem	400 000

Table V.   Assessments of annual domestic medical and scientific requirements
Tableau V.   Évaluations des besoins annuels médicaux et scientifiques intérieurs
Cuadro V.   Previsiones de las necesidades anuales internas
para fines médicos y científicos

Country (or territory) and substance Pays (ou territoire) et substance País (o territorio) y sustancia	Assessment (grams) Évaluation (en grammes) Previsión (en gramos)
Grenada — Grenade — Granada	
Alprazolam	20
Bromazepam — Bromazépam	40
Buprenorphine — Buprénorphine — Buprenorfina	1 000
Chlordiazepoxide — Chlordiazépoxide — Clordiazepóxido	2 000
Clobazam	60
Clonazepam — Clonazépam	15
Diazepam — Diazépam	4 000
Flurazepam — Flurazépam	1 500
Lorazepam — Lorazépam	500
Methylphenidate — Méthylphénidate — Metilfenidato	100
Midazolam	1 000
Nitrazepam — Nitrazépam	200
Pentazocine — Pentazocina	20
Pentobarbital	1 000
Phenobarbital — Phénobarbital — Fenobarbital	16 000
Triazolam	15
Zolpidem	1 000
Guatemala	
Alprazolam	6 000
Amfepramone — Amfépramone — Anfepramona	35 000
Bromazepam — Bromazépam	16 000
Buprenorphine — Buprénorphine — Buprenorfina	7
Chlordiazepoxide — Chlordiazépoxide — Clordiazepóxido	65 000
Clobazam	30 000
Clonazepam — Clonazépam	5 000
Diazepam — Diazépam	25 000
Ethyl loflazepate — Loflazépate d'éthyle — Loflazepato de etilo	700
Flunitrazepam — Flunitrazépam	10
Loprazolam	2 000
Lorazepam — Lorazépam	6 000
Mazindol	100
Meprobamate — Méprobamate — Meprobamato	650 000
Methylphenidate — Méthylphénidate — Metilfenidato	5 000
Midazolam	10 000
Pentobarbital	15 000
Phenobarbital — Phénobarbital — Fenobarbital	900 000
Phentermine — Fentermina	12 000
Tetrazepam — Tétrazépam	40 000
Triazolam	100
Zolpidem	22 500
Guinea — Guinée	
Alprazolam	120 005
Amfetamine — Amfétamine — Anfetamina	50
Bromazepam — Bromazépam	195 010
Buprenorphine — Buprénorphine — Buprenorfina	20 050
Chlordiazepoxide — Chlordiazépoxide — Clordiazepóxido	130 095
Clobazam	103 045
Clorazepate — Clorazépate — Clorazepato	249 058
Diazepam — Diazépam	254 050
Fenproporex	120 045
Flunitrazepam — Flunitrazépam	95 060
Lorazepam — Lorazépam	18 020
Meprobamate — Méprobamate — Meprobamato	50 037
Nitrazepam — Nitrazépam	25 080
Pentazocine — Pentazocina	105 045
Pentobarbital	80 070
Phenobarbital — Phénobarbital — Fenobarbital	80 012
Tetrazepam — Tétrazépam	227 012
Zolpidem	139 000
Guinea-Bissau — Guinée-Bissau	
Bromazepam — Bromazépam	51
Diazepam — Diazépam	3 000
Lorazepam — Lorazépam	50
Phenobarbital — Phénobarbital — Fenobarbital	25 000
Guyana	
Alprazolam	600
Amfetamine — Amfétamine — Anfetamina	1 000
Bromazepam — Bromazépam	2 000
Chlordiazepoxide — Chlordiazépoxide — Clordiazepóxido	45 000
Clobazam	500
Clonazepam — Clonazépam	1 500
Dexamfetamine — Dexamfétamine — Dexanfetamina	1 000
Diazepam — Diazépam	52 000
Fludiazepam — Fludiazépam	4 000
Flunitrazepam — Flunitrazépam	300
Flurazepam — Flurazépam	4 000
Ketazolam — Kétazolam	1 500
Lorazepam — Lorazépam	21 000
Medazepam — Médazépam	500
Meprobamate — Méprobamate — Meprobamato	20 000
Methaqualone — Méthaqualone — Metacualona	500
Methylphenidate — Méthylphénidate — Metilfenidato	1 000
Midazolam	1 500
Nitrazepam — Nitrazépam	18 000
Oxazepam — Oxazépam	4 000
Oxazolam	1 200
Pentazocine — Pentazocina	3 000
Phenobarbital — Phénobarbital — Fenobarbital	65 000
Phentermine — Fentermina	1 800
Temazepam — Témazépam	200
Triazolam	600
Haiti — Haïti — Haití	
Alprazolam	25
Bromazepam — Bromazépam	1 500
Chlordiazepoxide — Chlordiazépoxide — Clordiazepóxido	900
Clobazam	250
Clonazepam — Clonazépam	20
Clorazepate — Clorazépate — Clorazepato	2 800
Diazepam — Diazépam	55 500
Flunitrazepam — Flunitrazépam	30
Lorazepam — Lorazépam	4 300
Methylphenidate — Méthylphénidate — Metilfenidato	300
Midazolam	600
Pentazocine — Pentazocina	7 500
Phenobarbital — Phénobarbital — Fenobarbital	625 000
Tetrazepam — Tétrazépam	3 500
Zolpidem	250

Table V. Assessments of annual domestic medical and scientific requirements
Tableau V. Évaluations des besoins annuels médicaux et scientifiques intérieurs
Cuadro V. Previsiones de las necesidades anuales internas para fines médicos y científicos

Country (or territory) and substance Pays (ou territoire) et substance País (o territorio) y sustancia	Assessment (grams) Évaluation (en grammes) Previsión (en gramos)
Honduras	
Alprazolam	53 031
Amfepramone — Amfépramone — Anfepramona	6 075
Bromazepam — Bromazépam	74 656
Cathine — Catina	12 054
Chlordiazepoxide — Chlordiazépoxide —	
Clordiazepóxido	47 759
Clobazam	16 615
Clonazepam — Clonazépam	39 098
Diazepam — Diazépam	294 089
Ethyl loflazepate — Loflazépate d'éthyle —	
Loflazepato de etilo	1 863
Fenproporex	12 006
Loprazolam	872
Lorazepam — Lorazépam	61 035
Mazindol	1 911
Methylphenidate — Méthylphénidate — Metilfenidato . .	10 007
Midazolam	7 644
Phenobarbital — Phénobarbital — Fenobarbital	2 823 227
Phentermine — Fentermina	12 006
Tetrazepam — Tétrazépam	34 106
Triazolam	2 751
Zolpidem	6 564
Hungary — Hongrie — Hungría	
Allobarbital — Alobarbital	100 000
Alprazolam	350 000
Amfetamine — Amfétamine — Anfetamina	10
Amobarbital	250 000
Barbital	105 000
Bromazepam — Bromazépam	300 000
Brotizolam	2 000
Buprenorphine — Buprénorphine — Buprenorfina	50 020
Chlordiazepoxide — Chlordiazépoxide —	
Clordiazepóxido	170 000
Clobazam	80 000
Clonazepam — Clonazépam	130 000
Clorazepate — Clorazépate — Clorazepato	100 000
Delta-9-tetrahydrocannabinol —	
Delta-9-tétrahydrocannabinol —	
Delta-9-tetrahidrocannabinol	5
Diazepam — Diazépam	2 200 000
Flunitrazepam — Flunitrazépam	6 000
Gamma-hydroxybutyric acid (GHB) —	
Acide *gamma*-hydroxybutirique (GHB) —	
Ácido *gamma*-hidroxibutírico (GHB)	200
Glutethimide — Glutéthimide — Glutetimida	300 000
Lorazepam — Lorazépam	450 001
Mazindol	2
Medazepam — Médazépam	970 000
Meprobamate — Méprobamate — Meprobamato	25 250 000
Metamfetamine — Métamfétamine — Metanfetamina . .	10
Metamfetamine racemate —	
Racémate de métamfétamine —	
Racemato de metanfetamina	2 500 000
Methylphenidate — Méthylphénidate — Metilfenidato . .	14 700
Methylphenobarbital — Méthylphénobarbital —	
Metilfenobarbital	1
Midazolam	220 000
Nitrazepam — Nitrazépam	510 000

Country (or territory) and substance Pays (ou territoire) et substance País (o territorio) y sustancia	Assessment (grams) Évaluation (en grammes) Previsión (en gramos)
Nordazepam — Nordazépam	10
Oxazepam — Oxazépam	1 500 026
Pentobarbital	54 600
Phenobarbital — Phénobarbital — Fenobarbital	102 100 500
Temazepam — Témazépam	2 104 000
Tetrazepam — Tétrazépam	1 280 000
Triazolam	1
Zolpidem	35 004 000
Iceland — Islande — Islandia	
Alprazolam	2 000
Amfetamine — Amfétamine — Anfetamina	2 500
Barbital	1 000
Bromazepam — Bromazépam	2 500
Buprenorphine — Buprénorphine — Buprenorfina	350
Butalbital	500
Chlordiazepoxide — Chlordiazépoxide —	
Clordiazepóxido	10 000
Clobazam	500
Clonazepam — Clonazépam	2 000
Delta-9-tetrahydrocannabinol —	
Delta-9-tétrahydrocannabinol —	
Delta-9-tetrahidrocannabinol	10
Dexamfetamine — Dexamfétamine — Dexanfetamina . .	2
Diazepam — Diazépam	15 000
Flunitrazepam — Flunitrazépam	1 400
Flurazepam — Flurazépam	3 500
Lorazepam — Lorazépam	100
Meprobamate — Méprobamate — Meprobamato	15 000
Methylphenidate — Méthylphénidate — Metilfenidato . .	50 000
Midazolam	500
Nitrazepam — Nitrazépam	2 000
Oxazepam — Oxazépam	45 000
Pemoline — Pémoline — Pemolina	100
Pentazocine — Pentazocina	400
Pentobarbital	8 000
Phenobarbital — Phénobarbital — Fenobarbital	10 000
Phentermine — Fentermina	5
Triazolam	200
Zolpidem	25 000
India — Inde	
Allobarbital — Alobarbital	10 000
Alprazolam	10 000
Amfetamine — Amfétamine — Anfetamina	10
Amobarbital	250
Barbital	25 000 000
Bromazepam — Bromazépam	10
Buprenorphine — Buprénorphine — Buprenorfina	50
Butalbital	1
Butobarbital	65 000
Cathine — Catina	1
Chlordiazepoxide — Chlordiazépoxide —	
Clordiazepóxido	304 802
Clobazam	500 000
Clonazepam — Clonazépam	150 000
Clorazepate — Clorazépate — Clorazepato	10
Delorazepam — Délorazépam	2 201
Diazepam — Diazépam	2 040 000
Etilamfetamine — Étilamfétamine — Etilanfetamina . . .	1

Table V. Assessments of annual domestic medical and scientific requirements
Tableau V. Évaluations des besoins annuels médicaux et scientifiques intérieurs
Cuadro V. Previsiones de las necesidades anuales internas
para fines médicos y científicos

Country (or territory) and substance Pays (ou territoire) et substance País (o territorio) y sustancia	Assessment (grams) Évaluation (en grammes) Previsión (en gramos)
India — Inde	
(continued — suite — continuación)	
Lorazepam — Lorazépam	500 000
Meprobamate — Méprobamate — Meprobamato	3 000
Metamfetamine — Métamfétamine — Metanfetamina	10
Methylphenidate — Méthylphénidate — Metilfenidato	200
Midazolam	36 000
Nimetazepam — Nimétazépam	10
Nitrazepam — Nitrazépam	126 000
Nordazepam — Nordazépam	500
Oxazepam — Oxazépam	500 000
Pentazocine — Pentazocina	25 000
Pentobarbital	1 000 000
Phendimetrazine — Phendimétrazine — Fendimetracina	1
Phenobarbital — Phénobarbital — Fenobarbital	300 000
Phentermine — Fentermina	100 240
Temazepam — Témazépam	10
Triazolam	10
Zolpidem	37 201
Indonesia — Indonésie	
Alprazolam	21 000
Amfepramone — Amfépramone — Anfepramona	200 000
Amfetamine — Amfétamine — Anfetamina	2
Bromazepam — Bromazépam	15 000
Buprenorphine — Buprénorphine — Buprenorfina	3 528
Chlordiazepoxide — Chlordiazépoxide — Clordiazepóxido	350 000
Clobazam	200 000
Clonazepam — Clonazépam	1 900
Diazepam — Diazépam	600 000
Estazolam	7 700
Flunitrazepam — Flunitrazépam	25
Flurazepam — Flurazépam	12 000
Glutethimide — Glutéthimide — Glutetimida	50
Lorazepam — Lorazépam	11 000
Mazindol	750
Meprobamate — Méprobamate — Meprobamato	300 000
Metamfetamine — Métamfétamine — Metanfetamina	2
Methylphenidate — Méthylphénidate — Metilfenidato	10 000
Midazolam	4 000
Nitrazepam — Nitrazépam	5 000
Phenobarbital — Phénobarbital — Fenobarbital	5 000 000
Triazolam	900
Zolpidem	20 000
Iran (Islamic Republic of) — **Iran (République islamique d') —** **Irán (República Islámica del)**	
Alprazolam	140 000
Amfetamine — Amfétamine — Anfetamina	500
Bromazepam — Bromazépam	500
Buprenorphine — Buprénorphine — Buprenorfina	20 000
Chlordiazepoxide — Chlordiazépoxide — Clordiazepóxido	4 000 000
Clobazam	60 000
Clonazepam — Clonazépam	400 000
Dexamfetamine — Dexamfétamine — Dexanfetamina	100
Diazepam — Diazépam	2 200 000

Country (or territory) and substance Pays (ou territoire) et substance País (o territorio) y sustancia	Assessment (grams) Évaluation (en grammes) Previsión (en gramos)
Estazolam	10
Flunitrazepam — Flunitrazépam	100
Flurazepam — Flurazépam	550 000
Lorazepam — Lorazépam	400 000
Meprobamate — Méprobamate — Meprobamato	100
Metamfetamine — Métamfétamine — Metanfetamina	10

Metamfetamine racemate —
    Racémate de métamfétamine —
    Racemato de metanfetamina
	1

Methylphenidate — Méthylphénidate — Metilfenidato	120 000
Midazolam	20 000
Nitrazepam — Nitrazépam	3 000
Oxazepam — Oxazépam	1 200 000
Pentazocine — Pentazocina	20 000
Phenobarbital — Phénobarbital — Fenobarbital	5 000 000
Temazepam — Témazépam	500
Triazolam	50
Zolpidem	15 000
Iraq	
Alprazolam	410
Bromazepam — Bromazépam	1 804
Buprenorphine — Buprénorphine — Buprenorfina	272
Chlordiazepoxide — Chlordiazépoxide — Clordiazepóxido	565 790
Clobazam	4 716
Clonazepam — Clonazépam	58 101
Dexamfetamine — Dexamfétamine — Dexanfetamina	245
Diazepam — Diazépam	602 998
Flurazepam — Flurazépam	1 912
Lorazepam — Lorazépam	3 172
Lormetazepam — Lormétazépam	26
Mazindol	919
Medazepam — Médazépam	19 575
Meprobamate — Méprobamate — Meprobamato	2 000 000
Methylphenidate — Méthylphénidate — Metilfenidato	509
Midazolam	3 208
Nitrazepam — Nitrazépam	1 510
Pentazocine — Pentazocina	7 500
Phenobarbital — Phénobarbital — Fenobarbital	3 261 179
Triazolam	7 630
Vinylbital — Vinilbital	2 288
Ireland — Irlande — Irlanda	

4-Bromo-2,5-dimethoxyphenyl-ethylamine (2C-B) —
    4-bromo-2,5-diméthoxyphényléthylamine (2C-B) —
    4-bromo-2,5-dimetoxifeniletilamina (2C-B)
	10

Allobarbital — Alobarbital	10
Alprazolam	100 000
Amfepramone — Amfépramone — Anfepramona	10
Amfetamine — Amfétamine — Anfetamina	1 500
Aminorex	10
Amobarbital	1 000 000
Barbital	110 000
Benzfetamine — Benzfétamine — Benzfetamina	100 500
Bromazepam — Bromazépam	35 000
Brotizolam	1 000
Buprenorphine — Buprénorphine — Buprenorfina	5 000
Butalbital	10
Butobarbital	10
Camazepam — Camazépam	10
Cathine — Catina	10

Table V. Assessments of annual domestic medical and scientific requirements
Tableau V. Évaluations des besoins annuels médicaux et scientifiques intérieurs
Cuadro V. Previsiones de las necesidades anuales internas para fines médicos y científicos

Country (or territory) and substance Pays (ou territoire) et substance País (o territorio) y sustancia	Assessment (grams) Évaluation (en grammes) Previsión (en gramos)
Chlordiazepoxide — Chlordiazépoxide — Clordiazepóxido	100 000
Clobazam	25 000
Clonazepam — Clonazépam	5 000
Clorazepate — Clorazépate — Clorazepato	30 000
Clotiazepam — Clotiazépam	10
Cloxazolam	10
Cyclobarbital — Ciclobarbital	10
Delorazepam — Délorazépam	10
Delta-9-tetrahydrocannabinol — Delta-9-tétrahydrocannabinol — Delta-9-tetrahidrocannabinol	1 500
Dexamfetamine — Dexamfétamine — Dexanfetamina	1 000
Diazepam — Diazépam	1 500 000
Estazolam	10
Ethchlorvynol — Etclorvinol	10
Ethinamate — Éthinamate — Etinamato	10
Ethyl loflazepate — Loflazépate d'éthyle — Loflazepato de etilo	10
Etilamfetamine — Étilamfétamine — Etilanfetamina	10
Fencamfamin — Fencamfamine — Fencanfamina	10
Fenetylline — Fénétylline — Fenetilina	10
Fenproporex	10
Fludiazepam — Fludiazépam	1 000
Flunitrazepam — Flunitrazépam	50 000
Flurazepam — Flurazépam	300 000
Gamma-hydroxybutyric acid (GHB) — Acide gamma-hydroxybutirique (GHB) — Ácido gamma-hidroxibutírico (GHB)	27 000
Glutethimide — Glutéthimide — Glutetimida	10
Halazepam — Halazépam	3 500 000
Haloxazolam	10
Ketazolam — Kétazolam	10
Lefetamine (SPA) — Léfétamine (SPA) — Lefetamina (SPA)	10
Levamfetamine — Lévamfétamine — Levanfetamina	200
Levomethamphetamine — Lévométhamphétamine — Levometanfetamina	485 000
Loprazolam	2 000
Lorazepam — Lorazépam	3 000 000
Lormetazepam — Lormétazépam	300 000
Mazindol	1 000
Mecloqualone — Mécloqualone — Meclocualona	10
Medazepam — Médazépam	1 000
Mefenorex — Méfénorex	10
Meprobamate — Méprobamate — Meprobamato	5 000
Mesocarb — Mésocarbe — Mesocarbo	10
Metamfetamine — Métamfétamine — Metanfetamina	200 000
Metamfetamine racemate — Racémate de métamfétamine — Racemato de metanfetamina	10
Methaqualone — Méthaqualone — Metacualona	10
Methylphenidate — Méthylphénidate — Metilfenidato	35 000
Methylphenobarbital — Méthylphénobarbital — Metilfenobarbital	1 000
Methyprylon — Méthyprylone — Metiprilona	10
Midazolam	50 000
Nimetazepam — Nimétazépam	10
Nitrazepam — Nitrazépam	200 000
Nordazepam — Nordazépam	10 000
Oxazepam — Oxazépam	13 000 000
Oxazolam	10
Pemoline — Pémoline — Pemolina	500

Country (or territory) and substance Pays (ou territoire) et substance País (o territorio) y sustancia	Assessment (grams) Évaluation (en grammes) Previsión (en gramos)
Pentazocine — Pentazocina	1 000
Pentobarbital	450 000
Phencyclidine (PCP) — Fenciclidina (PCP)	10
Phendimetrazine — Phendimétrazine — Fendimetracina	10
Phenmetrazine — Phenmétrazine — Fenmetracina	10
Phenobarbital — Phénobarbital — Fenobarbital	1 650 000
Phentermine — Fentermina	2 000
Pinazepam — Pinazépam	10
Pipradrol	10
Prazepam — Prazépam	50 000
Pyrovalerone — Pyrovalérone — Pirovalerona	10
Secbutabarbital	10
Secobarbital — Sécobarbital	250 000
Temazepam — Témazépam	3 000 000
Tetrazepam — Tétrazépam	50 000
Triazolam	10 000
Vinylbital — Vinilbital	10
Zipeprol — Zipéprol	10
Zolpidem	170 000
Israel — Israël	
Allobarbital — Alobarbital	18 000
Alprazolam	19 000
Amfetamine — Amfétamine — Anfetamina	1 700
Amobarbital	500
Barbital	3 000
Bromazepam — Bromazépam	14 000
Brotizolam	11 000
Buprenorphine — Buprénorphine — Buprenorfina	2 500
Chlordiazepoxide — Chlordiazépoxide — Clordiazepóxido	86 000
Clobazam	110 000
Clonazepam — Clonazépam	530 000
Clorazepate — Clorazépate — Clorazepato	20 000
Delorazepam — Délorazépam	500
Delta-9-tetrahydrocannabinol — Delta-9-tétrahydrocannabinol — Delta-9-tetrahidrocannabinol	20
Dexamfetamine — Dexamfétamine — Dexanfetamina	2 800
Diazepam — Diazépam	270 000
Estazolam	3
Flunitrazepam — Flunitrazépam	500
Gamma-hydroxybutyric acid (GHB) — Acide gamma-hydroxybutirique (GHB) — Ácido gamma-hidroxibutírico (GHB)	1
Lorazepam — Lorazépam	40 000
Mazindol	250
Meprobamate — Méprobamate — Meprobamato	50 000
Metamfetamine — Métamfétamine — Metanfetamina	10
Methylphenidate — Méthylphénidate — Metilfenidato	250 000
Methylphenobarbital — Méthylphénobarbital — Metilfenobarbital	1 000
Midazolam	27 000
Nitrazepam — Nitrazépam	60 000
Nordazepam — Nordazépam	10
Oxazepam — Oxazépam	400 000
Pemoline — Pémoline — Pemolina	500
Pentazocine — Pentazocina	300
Pentobarbital	100 720
Phencyclidine (PCP) — Fenciclidina (PCP)	75
Phenobarbital — Phénobarbital — Fenobarbital	500 000

Table V. Assessments of annual domestic medical and scientific requirements
Tableau V. Évaluations des besoins annuels médicaux et scientifiques intérieurs
Cuadro V. Previsiones de las necesidades anuales internas para fines médicos y científicos

Country (or territory) and substance Pays (ou territoire) et substance País (o territorio) y sustancia	Assessment (grams) Évaluation (en grammes) Previsión (en gramos)
Israel — Israël	
(continued — suite — continuación)	
Phentermine — Fentermina	30 000
Triazolam	60
Zolpidem	160 000
Italy — Italie — Italia	
Alprazolam	250 000
Amfepramone — Amfépramone — Anfepramona	5
Amfetamine — Amfétamine — Anfetamina	6
Amobarbital	15
Barbital	3 000 000
Bromazepam — Bromazépam	1 500 000
Brotizolam	2 000 000
Buprenorphine — Buprénorphine — Buprenorfina	60 000
Butalbital	4 000 000
Cathine — Catina	2 200 000
Chlordiazepoxide — Chlordiazépoxide — Clordiazepóxido	2 000 000
Clobazam	150 000
Clonazepam — Clonazépam	150 000
Clorazepate — Clorazépate — Clorazepato	300 000
Clotiazepam — Clotiazépam	200 000
Delorazepam — Délorazépam	100 000
Delta-9-tetrahydrocannabinol — *Delta*-9-tétrahydrocannabinol — *Delta*-9-tetrahidrocannabinol	500
Dexamfetamine — Dexamfétamine — Dexanfetamina	8
Diazepam — Diazépam	2 000 000
Estazolam	50 000
Etilamfetamine — Étilamfétamine — Etilanfetamina	1
Fenetylline — Fénétylline — Fenetilina	1
Fenproporex	1
Flunitrazepam — Flunitrazépam	100 000
Flurazepam — Flurazépam	2 000 000
Gamma-hydroxybutyric acid (GHB) — Acide *gamma*-hydroxybutirique (GHB) — Ácido *gamma*-hidroxibutírico (GHB)	7 000 000
Halazepam — Halazépam	2
Ketazolam — Kétazolam	300 000
Lefetamine (SPA) — Léfétamine (SPA) — Lefetamina (SPA)	20 000
Levomethamphetamine — Lévométhamphétamine — Levometanfetamina	1 000 000
Loprazolam	10 000
Lorazepam — Lorazépam	1 000 000
Lormetazepam — Lormétazépam	1 000 000
Mazindol	1
Medazepam — Médazépam	400 000
Mefenorex — Méfénorex	1
Meprobamate — Méprobamate — Meprobamato	750 000
Metamfetamine — Métamfétamine — Metanfetamina	100 000
Methylphenidate — Méthylphénidate — Metilfenidato	50 000
Methylphenobarbital — Méthylphénobarbital — Metilfenobarbital	600 000
Midazolam	100 000
Nitrazepam — Nitrazépam	300 000
Oxazepam — Oxazépam	1 000 000
Pentazocine — Pentazocina	450 000
Pentobarbital	91 000
Phencyclidine (PCP) — Fenciclidina (PCP)	6
Phendimetrazine — Phendimétrazine — Fendimetracina	1 000 000
Phenobarbital — Phénobarbital — Fenobarbital	13 000 000
Phentermine — Fentermina	80 000
Pinazepam — Pinazépam	6 000
Prazepam — Prazépam	2 200 000
Temazepam — Témazépam	3 200 000
Triazolam	100 000
Zolpidem	500 000
Jamaica — Jamaïque	
Alprazolam	1 650
Bromazepam — Bromazépam	1 100
Chlordiazepoxide — Chlordiazépoxide — Clordiazepóxido	961
Clobazam	5 000
Clonazepam — Clonazépam	220
Clorazepate — Clorazépate — Clorazepato	560
Dexamfetamine — Dexamfétamine — Dexanfetamina	1
Diazepam — Diazépam	15 000
Flunitrazepam — Flunitrazépam	25
Flurazepam — Flurazépam	743
Lorazepam — Lorazépam	1 320
Metamfetamine — Métamfétamine — Metanfetamina	1
Methylphenidate — Méthylphénidate — Metilfenidato	2 500
Midazolam	2 000
Pentazocine — Pentazocina	1 000
Pentobarbital	18 889
Phenmetrazine — Phenmétrazine — Fenmetracina	1
Phenobarbital — Phénobarbital — Fenobarbital	111 000
Phentermine — Fentermina	1 200
Triazolam	9
Zolpidem	1 150
Japan — Japon — Japón	
Allobarbital — Alobarbital	100 000
Alprazolam	550 000
Amfetamine — Amfétamine — Anfetamina	40
Amobarbital	4 000 000
Barbital	14 500 000
Benzfetamine — Benzfétamine — Benzfetamina	10 000
Bromazepam — Bromazépam	800 000
Brotizolam	150 000
Buprenorphine — Buprénorphine — Buprenorfina	10 000
Butalbital	370 000
Cathine — Catina	1 000
Chlordiazepoxide — Chlordiazépoxide — Clordiazepóxido	1 500 000
Clobazam	1 000 000
Clonazepam — Clonazépam	200 000
Clorazepate — Clorazépate — Clorazepato	200 000
Clotiazepam — Clotiazépam	4 000 000
Cloxazolam	400 000
Cyclobarbital — Ciclobarbital	1 000
Delta-9-tetrahydrocannabinol — *Delta*-9-tétrahydrocannabinol — *Delta*-9-tetrahidrocannabinol	50
Dexamfetamine — Dexamfétamine — Dexanfetamina	10
Diazepam — Diazépam	2 200 000
Estazolam	1 000 000
Ethinamate — Éthinamate — Etinamato	50 000

Table V. Assessments of annual domestic medical and scientific requirements
Tableau V. Évaluations des besoins annuels médicaux et scientifiques intérieurs
Cuadro V. Previsiones de las necesidades anuales internas para fines médicos y científicos

Country (or territory) and substance / Pays (ou territoire) et substance / País (o territorio) y sustancia	Assessment (grams) / Évaluation (en grammes) / Previsión (en gramos)
Ethyl loflazepate — Loflazépate d'éthyle — Loflazepato de etilo	300 000
Fludiazepam — Fludiazépam	100 000
Flunitrazepam — Flunitrazépam	600 000
Flurazepam — Flurazépam	500 000
Gamma-hydroxybutyric acid (GHB) — Acide gamma-hydroxybutirique (GHB) — Ácido gamma-hidroxibutírico (GHB)	200
Halazepam — Halazépam	50 000
Haloxazolam	200 000
Lefetamine (SPA) — Léfétamine (SPA) — Lefetamina (SPA)	50 000
Levamfetamine — Lévamfétamine — Levanfetamina	10
Levomethamphetamine — Lévométhamphétamine — Levometanfetamina	10
Lorazepam — Lorazépam	150 000
Lormetazepam — Lormétazépam	100 000
Mazindol	10 000
Medazepam — Médazépam	500 000
Meprobamate — Méprobamate — Meprobamato	300 000
Metamfetamine — Métamfétamine — Metanfetamina	500
Metamfetamine racemate — Racémate de métamfétamine — Racemato de metanfetamina	10
Methaqualone — Méthaqualone — Metacualona	1
Methylphenidate — Méthylphénidate — Metilfenidato	400 000
Methylphenobarbital — Méthylphénobarbital — Metilfenobarbital	900 000
Midazolam	250 000
Nimetazepam — Nimétazépam	110 000
Nitrazepam — Nitrazépam	2 150 000
Oxazepam — Oxazépam	100 000
Oxazolam	4 600 000
Pemoline — Pémoline — Pemolina	100 000
Pentazocine — Pentazocina	700 000
Pentobarbital	1 300 000
Phencyclidine (PCP) — Fenciclidina (PCP)	21
Phenobarbital — Phénobarbital — Fenobarbital	23 000 000
Phentermine — Fentermina	6 000
Pipradrol	1 500
Prazepam — Prazépam	150 000
Secbutabarbital	12 000
Secobarbital — Sécobarbital	5 000
Triazolam	200 000
Zolpidem	1 700 000
Jordan — Jordanie — Jordania	
Allobarbital — Alobarbital	1 150 000
Alprazolam	15 500
Amfetamine — Amfétamine — Anfetamina	150
Barbital	2 300
Bromazepam — Bromazépam	35 000
Buprenorphine — Buprénorphine — Buprenorfina	1 150
Butobarbital	10 000
Chlordiazepoxide — Chlordiazépoxide — Clordiazepóxido	345 000
Clobazam	6 000
Clonazepam — Clonazépam	6 000
Clorazepate — Clorazépate — Clorazepato	5 000
Delta-9-tetrahydrocannabinol — Delta-9-tétrahydrocannabinol — Delta-9-tetrahidrocannabinol	150
Dexamfetamine — Dexamfétamine — Dexanfetamina	150
Diazepam — Diazépam	115 000
Lorazepam — Lorazépam	3 250
Lormetazepam — Lormétazépam	1 150
Metamfetamine — Métamfétamine — Metanfetamina	150
Methylphenidate — Méthylphénidate — Metilfenidato	1 200
Midazolam	2 300
Nitrazepam — Nitrazépam	1 150
Oxazepam — Oxazépam	1 150
Pentazocine — Pentazocina	2 300
Pentobarbital	150
Phendimetrazine — Phendimétrazine — Fendimetracina	150
Phenmetrazine — Phenmétrazine — Fenmetracina	150
Phenobarbital — Phénobarbital — Fenobarbital	2 500 000
Secobarbital — Sécobarbital	150
Zolpidem	30 000
Kazakhstan — Kazajstán	
Allobarbital — Alobarbital	1
Alprazolam	600
Amfepramone — Amfépramone — Anfepramona	1
Amfetamine — Amfétamine — Anfetamina	800
Amobarbital	1
Barbital	1
Benzfetamine — Benzfétamine — Benzfetamina	1
Bromazepam — Bromazépam	63
Brotizolam	1 000
Buprenorphine — Buprénorphine — Buprenorfina	3
Butobarbital	15
Chlordiazepoxide — Chlordiazépoxide — Clordiazepóxido	50 000
Clonazepam — Clonazépam	5 000
Clorazepate — Clorazépate — Clorazepato	4 000
Cyclobarbital — Ciclobarbital	13 000
Delta-9-tetrahydrocannabinol — Delta-9-tétrahydrocannabinol — Delta-9-tetrahidrocannabinol	80
Diazepam — Diazépam	400 355
Fenetylline — Fénétylline — Fenetilina	320
Flunitrazepam — Flunitrazépam	2 000
Gamma-hydroxybutyric acid (GHB) — Acide gamma-hydroxybutirique (GHB) — Ácido gamma-hidroxibutírico (GHB)	528 868
Lorazepam — Lorazépam	2 000
Medazepam — Médazépam	9 000
Meprobamate — Méprobamate — Meprobamato	300
Mesocarb — Mésocarbe — Mesocarbo	8 000
Metamfetamine — Métamfétamine — Metanfetamina	800
Metamfetamine racemate — Racémate de métamfétamine — Racemato de metanfetamina	800
Methaqualone — Méthaqualone — Metacualona	800
Methylphenidate — Méthylphénidate — Metilfenidato	800
Midazolam	800
Nitrazepam — Nitrazépam	9 000
Oxazepam — Oxazépam	100 000
Pentazocine — Pentazocina	653
Pentobarbital	1
Phencyclidine (PCP) — Fenciclidina (PCP)	8
Phenobarbital — Phénobarbital — Fenobarbital	10 318 800
Temazepam — Témazépam	11 000
Tetrazepam — Tétrazépam	500
Zolpidem	11 000

Table V. Assessments of annual domestic medical and scientific requirements
Tableau V. Évaluations des besoins annuels médicaux et scientifiques intérieurs
Cuadro V. Previsiones de las necesidades anuales internas para fines médicos y científicos

Country (or territory) and substance Pays (ou territoire) et substance País (o territorio) y sustancia	Assessment (grams) Évaluation (en grammes) Previsión (en gramos)
Kenya	
Alprazolam	1 000
Bromazepam — Bromazépam	20 500
Buprenorphine — Buprénorphine — Buprenorfina	270
Chlordiazepoxide — Chlordiazépoxide — Clordiazepóxido	21 000
Clonazepam — Clonazépam	3 000
Delta-9-tetrahydrocannabinol — Delta-9-tétrahydrocannabinol — Delta-9-tetrahidrocannabinol	1
Diazepam — Diazépam	1 320 000
Flunitrazepam — Flunitrazépam	870
Lorazepam — Lorazépam	1 500
Meprobamate — Méprobamate — Meprobamato	3 600
Methylphenidate — Méthylphénidate — Metilfenidato	705
Midazolam	8 500
Nitrazepam — Nitrazépam	350
Pentazocine — Pentazocina	1 500
Pentobarbital	5 500
Phenobarbital — Phénobarbital — Fenobarbital	3 205 000
Phentermine — Fentermina	20 000
Zolpidem	2 000
Kiribati	
Diazepam — Diazépam	1 000
Midazolam	500
Phenobarbital — Phénobarbital — Fenobarbital	1 500
Kuwait — Koweït	
Alprazolam	1 000
Amfetamine — Amfétamine — Anfetamina	100
Barbital	1 000
Bromazepam — Bromazépam	4 000
Chlordiazepoxide — Chlordiazépoxide — Clordiazepóxido	40 000
Clobazam	1 000
Clonazepam — Clonazépam	1 000
Clorazepate — Clorazépate — Clorazepato	1 000
Dexamfetamine — Dexamfétamine — Dexanfetamina	200
Diazepam — Diazépam	6 000
Flunitrazepam — Flunitrazépam	1 000
Loprazolam	1 000
Lorazepam — Lorazépam	1 000
Lormetazepam — Lormétazépam	1 000
Methylphenidate — Méthylphénidate — Metilfenidato	700
Midazolam	1 000
Nitrazepam — Nitrazépam	1 000
Pentazocine — Pentazocina	1 000
Pentobarbital	1 000
Phenobarbital — Phénobarbital — Fenobarbital	17 000
Temazepam — Témazépam	1 000
Kyrgyzstan — Kirghizistan — Kirguistán	
Alprazolam	200
Bromazepam — Bromazépam	200
Chlordiazepoxide — Chlordiazépoxide — Clordiazepóxido	1 000
Clonazepam — Clonazépam	1 500
Diazepam — Diazépam	40 000
Medazepam — Médazépam	500
Nitrazepam — Nitrazépam	1 000
Oxazepam — Oxazépam	2 000
Phenobarbital — Phénobarbital — Fenobarbital	170 000
Lao People's Democratic Republic — République démocratique populaire lao — República Democrática Popular Lao	
Barbital	2 000
Bromazepam — Bromazépam	5 000
Chlordiazepoxide — Chlordiazépoxide — Clordiazepóxido	500
Clonazepam — Clonazépam	500
Clorazepate — Clorazépate — Clorazepato	2 000
Diazepam — Diazépam	10 000
Flurazepam — Flurazépam	200
Meprobamate — Méprobamate — Meprobamato	15 000
Midazolam	500
Nitrazepam — Nitrazépam	500
Phendimetrazine — Phendimétrazine — Fendimetracina	200
Phenobarbital — Phénobarbital — Fenobarbital	25 000
Latvia — Lettonie — Letonia	
Alprazolam	10 000
Barbital	25 000
Bromazepam — Bromazépam	60 000
Brotizolam	1 000
Buprenorphine — Buprénorphine — Buprenorfina	1 500
Chlordiazepoxide — Chlordiazépoxide — Clordiazepóxido	1 500
Clobazam	500
Clonazepam — Clonazépam	30 000
Clorazepate — Clorazépate — Clorazepato	10 000
Cyclobarbital — Ciclobarbital	50 000
Diazepam — Diazépam	200 000
Estazolam	1 000
Flunitrazepam — Flunitrazépam	4 000
Gamma-hydroxybutyric acid (GHB) — Acide gamma-hydroxybutirique (GHB) — Ácido gamma-hidroxibutírico (GHB)	3 000 000
Lorazepam — Lorazépam	1 000
Medazepam — Médazépam	5 000
Meprobamate — Méprobamate — Meprobamato	400
Mesocarb — Mésocarbe — Mesocarbo	1 000
Methylphenidate — Méthylphénidate — Metilfenidato	2 000
Midazolam	15 000
Nitrazepam — Nitrazépam	30 000
Oxazepam — Oxazépam	300 000
Pentazocine — Pentazocina	1 000
Pentobarbital	40 000
Phenobarbital — Phénobarbital — Fenobarbital	650 000
Temazepam — Témazépam	3 000
Tetrazepam — Tétrazépam	15 000
Triazolam	1 000
Zolpidem	15 000

Table V. Assessments of annual domestic medical and scientific requirements
Tableau V. Évaluations des besoins annuels médicaux et scientifiques intérieurs
Cuadro V. Previsiones de las necesidades anuales internas para fines médicos y científicos

Country (or territory) and substance / Pays (ou territoire) et substance / País (o territorio) y sustancia	Assessment (grams) / Évaluation (en grammes) / Previsión (en gramos)
Lebanon — Liban — Líbano	
Alprazolam	6 000
Bromazepam — Bromazépam	70 000
Chlordiazepoxide — Chlordiazépoxide — Clordiazepóxido	50 000
Clonazepam — Clonazépam	6 000
Clorazepate — Clorazépate — Clorazepato	50 000
Diazepam — Diazépam	15 000
Lorazepam — Lorazépam	20 000
Meprobamate — Méprobamate — Meprobamato	1 200 000
Methylphenidate — Méthylphénidate — Metilfenidato	9 000
Midazolam	10 000
Nitrazepam — Nitrazépam	9 000
Nordazepam — Nordazépam	1 500
Phenobarbital — Phénobarbital — Fenobarbital	160 000
Secbutabarbital	50 000
Tetrazepam — Tétrazépam	60 000
Zolpidem	50 000
Lesotho	
Chlordiazepoxide — Chlordiazépoxide — Clordiazepóxido	10 000
Clonazepam — Clonazépam	1 010
Diazepam — Diazépam	25 000[a]
Methylphenidate — Méthylphénidate — Metilfenidato	1 004
Nitrazepam — Nitrazépam	1 000[a]
Pentazocine — Pentazocina	1 000[a]
Phenmetrazine — Phenmétrazine — Fenmetracina	30
Phenobarbital — Phénobarbital — Fenobarbital	363 800
Liberia — Libéria	
Diazepam — Diazépam	20 000
Pentazocine — Pentazocina	15 000
Pentobarbital	10 000
Phenobarbital — Phénobarbital — Fenobarbital	15 000
Libyan Arab Jamahiriya — Jamahiriya arabe libyenne — Jamahiriya Árabe Libia	
Alprazolam	85
Bromazepam — Bromazépam	600
Buprenorphine — Buprénorphine — Buprenorfina	1
Chlordiazepoxide — Chlordiazépoxide — Clordiazepóxido	250 000
Clonazepam — Clonazépam	1 680
Diazepam — Diazépam	9 500
Lorazepam — Lorazépam	1 020
Methylphenidate — Méthylphénidate — Metilfenidato	520
Midazolam	750
Nitrazepam — Nitrazépam	2 350
Pentazocine — Pentazocina	1 100
Phenobarbital — Phénobarbital — Fenobarbital	250 000
Zolpidem	800
Lithuania — Lituanie — Lituania	
Alprazolam	5 000
Barbital	50 000
Bromazepam — Bromazépam	65 000
Brotizolam	200
Buprenorphine — Buprénorphine — Buprenorfina	2 200
Chlordiazepoxide — Chlordiazépoxide — Clordiazepóxido	50 000
Clonazepam — Clonazépam	30 000
Clorazepate — Clorazépate — Clorazepato	25 000
Cyclobarbital — Ciclobarbital	50 000
Diazepam — Diazépam	200 000
Estazolam	350
Flunitrazepam — Flunitrazépam	1 000
Gamma-hydroxybutyric acid (GHB) — Acide *gamma*-hydroxybutirique (GHB) — Ácido *gamma*-hidroxibutírico (GHB)	400 000
Lorazepam — Lorazépam	50 000
Medazepam — Médazépam	50 000
Methylphenidate — Méthylphénidate — Metilfenidato	100
Midazolam	3 000
Nitrazepam — Nitrazépam	40 000
Oxazepam — Oxazépam	100 000
Pentazocine — Pentazocina	4 000
Pentobarbital	35 000
Phenobarbital — Phénobarbital — Fenobarbital	600 000
Temazepam — Témazépam	1 000
Tetrazepam — Tétrazépam	17 000
Triazolam	100
Zolpidem	20 000
Luxembourg — Luxemburgo	
Alprazolam	3 000
Amfetamine — Amfétamine — Anfetamina	35
Bromazepam — Bromazépam	30 000
Brotizolam	300
Buprenorphine — Buprénorphine — Buprenorfina	150
Clobazam	3 800
Clonazepam — Clonazépam	1 000
Clorazepate — Clorazépate — Clorazepato	16 000
Clotiazepam — Clotiazépam	10 000
Cloxazolam	300
Diazepam — Diazépam	8 000
Ethyl loflazepate — Loflazépate d'éthyle — Loflazepato de etilo	200
Fenetylline — Fénétylline — Fenetilina	300
Flunitrazepam — Flunitrazépam	30
Flurazepam — Flurazépam	2 100
Ketazolam — Kétazolam	300
Loprazolam	1 500
Lorazepam — Lorazépam	15 000
Lormetazepam — Lormétazépam	7 200
Meprobamate — Méprobamate — Meprobamato	4 600
Methylphenidate — Méthylphénidate — Metilfenidato	12 000
Midazolam	2 600
Nitrazepam — Nitrazépam	150
Nordazepam — Nordazépam	9 050
Oxazepam — Oxazépam	9 300
Pentazocine — Pentazocina	100
Phenobarbital — Phénobarbital — Fenobarbital	21 000
Prazepam — Prazépam	10 200
Tetrazepam — Tétrazépam	46 200
Triazolam	100
Zolpidem	33 000

Table V. Assessments of annual domestic medical and scientific requirements
Tableau V. Évaluations des besoins annuels médicaux et scientifiques intérieurs
Cuadro V. Previsiones de las necesidades anuales internas para fines médicos y científicos

Country (or territory) and substance Pays (ou territoire) et substance País (o territorio) y sustancia	Assessment (grams) Évaluation (en grammes) Previsión (en gramos)
Madagascar	
Alprazolam	5 224
Barbital	2 500
Bromazepam — Bromazépam	13 064
Buprenorphine — Buprénorphine — Buprenorfina	150
Butobarbital	2 500
Chlordiazepoxide — Chlordiazépoxide — Clordiazepóxido	5 148
Clobazam	6 200
Clonazepam — Clonazépam	5 964
Clorazepate — Clorazépate — Clorazepato	29 604
Clotiazepam — Clotiazépam	1 150
Diazepam — Diazépam	88 344
Estazolam	250
Ethyl loflazepate — Loflazépate d'éthyle — Loflazepato de etilo	270
Flunitrazepam — Flunitrazépam	1 039
Flurazepam — Flurazépam	1 039
Loprazolam	250
Lorazepam — Lorazépam	6 045
Lormetazepam — Lormétazépam	160
Meprobamate — Méprobamate — Meprobamato	1 009 300
Midazolam	1 045
Nitrazepam — Nitrazépam	6 401
Nordazepam — Nordazépam	100
Oxazepam — Oxazépam	2 740
Pentazocine — Pentazocina	500
Phenobarbital — Phénobarbital — Fenobarbital	1 755 386
Prazepam — Prazépam	32 590
Temazepam — Témazépam	900
Tetrazepam — Tétrazépam	66 550
Triazolam	1 001
Zolpidem	21 766
Malawi	
Amobarbital	364
Bromazepam — Bromazépam	440
Chlordiazepoxide — Chlordiazépoxide — Clordiazepóxido	250
Clonazepam — Clonazépam	30
Diazepam — Diazépam	18 000
Lorazepam — Lorazépam	6 080
Meprobamate — Méprobamate — Meprobamato	95 000
Methylphenidate — Méthylphénidate — Metilfenidato	4
Methylphenobarbital — Méthylphénobarbital — Metilfenobarbital	10 000
Methyprylon — Méthyprylone — Metiprilona	10 000
Midazolam	120
Nitrazepam — Nitrazépam	390
Pentazocine — Pentazocina	450
Pentobarbital	400
Phenobarbital — Phénobarbital — Fenobarbital	1 075 000
Temazepam — Témazépam	150
Malaysia — Malaisie — Malasia	
4-Bromo-2,5-dimethoxyphenyl-ethylamine (2C-B) — 4-bromo-2,5-diméthoxyphényléthylamine (2C-B) — 4-bromo-2,5-dimetoxifeniletilamina (2C-B)	10
Allobarbital — Alobarbital	1 500
Alprazolam	8 000
Amfetamine — Amfétamine — Anfetamina	100
Barbital	5 000
Bromazepam — Bromazépam	6 000
Buprenorphine — Buprénorphine — Buprenorfina	15 000
Cathine — Catina	50
Chlordiazepoxide — Chlordiazépoxide — Clordiazepóxido	29 500
Clobazam	25 000
Clonazepam — Clonazépam	5 000
Clorazepate — Clorazépate — Clorazepato	9 000
Delta-9-tetrahydrocannabinol — Delta-9-tétrahydrocannabinol — Delta-9-tetrahidrocannabinol	1
Dexamfetamine — Dexamfétamine — Dexanfetamina	50
Diazepam — Diazépam	180 000
Flunitrazepam — Flunitrazépam	1
Flurazepam — Flurazépam	3 000
Gamma-hydroxybutyric acid (GHB) — Acide gamma-hydroxybutirique (GHB) — Ácido gamma-hidroxibutírico (GHB)	10
Lorazepam — Lorazépam	45 000
Mazindol	300
Metamfetamine — Métamfétamine — Metanfetamina	100
Mecloqualone — Mécloqualone — Meclocualona	1
Methylphenidate — Méthylphénidate — Metilfenidato	10 500
Midazolam	220 000
Nitrazepam — Nitrazépam	2 500
Nordazepam — Nordazépam	5
Oxazepam — Oxazépam	50
Pentazocine — Pentazocina	10 000
Pentobarbital	45 000
Phencyclidine (PCP) — Fenciclidina (PCP)	500
Phendimetrazine — Phendimétrazine — Fendimetracina	500 000
Phenobarbital — Phénobarbital — Fenobarbital	250 000
Phentermine — Fentermina	615 000
Temazepam — Témazépam	50
Triazolam	1 000
Zolpidem	30 000
Maldives — Maldivas	
Alprazolam	61
Chlordiazepoxide — Chlordiazépoxide — Clordiazepóxido	175
Clonazepam — Clonazépam	120
Clorazepate — Clorazépate — Clorazepato	120
Diazepam — Diazépam	1 110
Lorazepam — Lorazépam	12
Midazolam	50
Pentazocine — Pentazocina	950
Phenobarbital — Phénobarbital — Fenobarbital	5 744
Mali — Malí	
Allobarbital — Alobarbital	20
Alprazolam	400
Amfetamine — Amfétamine — Anfetamina	230
Amobarbital	20
Barbital	20
Bromazepam — Bromazépam	9 626

Table V. Assessments of annual domestic medical and scientific requirements
Tableau V. Évaluations des besoins annuels médicaux et scientifiques intérieurs
Cuadro V. Previsiones de las necesidades anuales internas para fines médicos y científicos

Country (or territory) and substance Pays (ou territoire) et substance País (o territorio) y sustancia	Assessment (grams) Évaluation (en grammes) Previsión (en gramos)
Buprenorphine — Buprénorphine — Buprenorfina	43
Butalbital	20
Butobarbital	20
Cathine — Catina	10
Chlordiazepoxide — Chlordiazépoxide — Clordiazepóxido	5 316
Clobazam	6 200
Clonazepam — Clonazépam	995
Clorazepate — Clorazépate — Clorazepato	20 000
Clotiazepam — Clotiazépam	20
Cyclobarbital — Ciclobarbital	20
Delta-9-tetrahydrocannabinol — Delta-9-tétrahydrocannabinol — Delta-9-tetrahidrocannabinol	10
Dexamfetamine — Dexamfétamine — Dexanfetamina	100
Diazepam — Diazépam	40 000
Estazolam	20
Ethyl loflazepate — Loflazépate d'éthyle — Loflazepato de etilo	12 620
Etilamfetamine — Étilamfétamine — Etilanfetamina . .	20
Fenetylline — Fénétylline — Fenetilina	100
Fludiazepam — Fludiazépam	20
Flunitrazepam — Flunitrazépam	230
Flurazepam — Flurazépam	20
Glutethimide — Glutéthimide — Glutetimida	20
Ketazolam — Kétazolam	4 000
Levamfetamine — Lévamfétamine — Levanfetamina . . .	100
Levomethamphetamine — Lévométhamphétamine — Levometanfetamina	100
Loprazolam	20
Lorazepam — Lorazépam	136
Mecloqualone — Mécloqualone — Meclocualona	100
Meprobamate — Méprobamate — Meprobamato	60 000
Metamfetamine — Métamfétamine — Metanfetamina . .	230
Methaqualone — Méthaqualone — Metacualona	100
Methylphenidate — Méthylphénidate — Metilfenidato . .	10
Midazolam	20
Nitrazepam — Nitrazépam	3 000
Oxazepam — Oxazépam	500
Oxazolam	850
Pentazocine — Pentazocina	20
Pentobarbital	20
Phencyclidine (PCP) — Fenciclidina (PCP)	10
Phendimetrazine — Phendimétrazine — Fendimetracina	20
Phenmetrazine — Phenmétrazine — Fenmetracina . .	10
Phenobarbital — Phénobarbital — Fenobarbital	600 000
Prazepam — Prazépam	90 000
Secobarbital — Sécobarbital	20
Temazepam — Témazépam	20
Tetrazepam — Tétrazépam	7 925
Triazolam	21
Vinylbital — Vinilbital	20
Zolpidem	3
Malta — Malte	
4-Bromo-2,5-dimethoxyphenyl-ethylamine (2C-B) — 4-bromo-2,5-diméthoxyphényléthylamine (2C-B) — 4-bromo-2,5-dimetoxifeniletilamina (2C-B)	1
Alprazolam	800

Country (or territory) and substance Pays (ou territoire) et substance País (o territorio) y sustancia	Assessment (grams) Évaluation (en grammes) Previsión (en gramos)
Amfetamine — Amfétamine — Anfetamina	1
Amobarbital	1 000
Bromazepam — Bromazépam	15 000
Buprenorphine — Buprénorphine — Buprenorfina	200
Cathine — Catina	1
Chlordiazepoxide — Chlordiazépoxide — Clordiazepóxido	800
Clobazam	600
Clonazepam — Clonazépam	400
Dexamfetamine — Dexamfétamine — Dexanfetamina	100
Diazepam — Diazépam	150 000
Flunitrazepam — Flunitrazépam	1
Flurazepam — Flurazépam	11 000
Gamma-hydroxybutyric acid (GHB) — Acide gamma-hydroxybutirique (GHB) — Ácido gamma-hidroxibutírico (GHB)	1
Ketazolam — Kétazolam	200
Loprazolam	50
Lorazepam — Lorazépam	10 000
Lormetazepam — Lormétazépam	300
Metamfetamine — Métamfétamine — Metanfetamina . .	1
Metamfetamine racemate — Racémate de métamfétamine — Racemato de metanfetamina	1
Methylphenidat — Méthylphénidate — Metilfenidato . . .	1 400
Midazolam	1 500
Nitrazepam — Nitrazépam	8 000
Pentazocine — Pentazocina	25 000
Pentobarbital	15 000
Phenobarbital — Phénobarbital — Fenobarbital	1 000 000
Secobarbital — Sécobarbital	900
Temazepam — Témazépam	5 000
Triazolam	100
Zipeprol — Zipéprol	1
Zolpidem	15 000
Marshall Islands — Îles Marshall — Islas Marshall	
Chlordiazepoxide — Chlordiazépoxide — Clordiazepóxido	10
Clonazepam — Clonazépam	20
Clorazepate — Clorazépate — Clorazepato	10
Diazepam — Diazépam	500
Lorazepam — Lorazépam	20
Midazolam	30
Phenobarbital — Phénobarbital — Fenobarbital	500
Temazepam — Témazépam	10
Mauritania — Mauritanie	
Bromazepam — Bromazépam	2 000
Buprenorphine — Buprénorphine — Buprenorfina	10
Chlordiazepoxide — Chlordiazépoxide — Clordiazepóxido	3 000
Clorazepate — Clorazépate — Clorazepato	8 000
Diazepam — Diazépam	8 000
Meprobamate — Méprobamate — Meprobamato	30 000
Nitrazepam — Nitrazépam	1 000
Phenobarbital — Phénobarbital — Fenobarbital	75 000
Prazepam — Prazépam	4 000
Tetrazepam — Tétrazépam	4 000

Table V. Assessments of annual domestic medical and scientific requirements
Tableau V. Évaluations des besoins annuels médicaux et scientifiques intérieurs
Cuadro V. Previsiones de las necesidades anuales internas
para fines médicos y científicos

Country (or territory) and substance Pays (ou territoire) et substance País (o territorio) y sustancia	Assessment (grams) Évaluation (en grammes) Previsión (en gramos)
Mauritius — Maurice — Mauricio	
Alprazolam	1 700
Bromazepam — Bromazépam	3 000
Chlordiazepoxide — Chlordiazépoxide — Clordiazepóxido	4 000
Clonazepam — Clonazépam	971
Clorazepate — Clorazépate — Clorazepato	5 000
Diazepam — Diazépam	16 000
Flunitrazepam — Flunitrazépam	125
Lorazepam — Lorazépam	600
Lormetazepam — Lormétazépam	190
Methylphenidate — Méthylphénidate — Metilfenidato	25
Midazolam	525
Nitrazepam — Nitrazépam	9 000
Pentazocine — Pentazocina	5 000
Pentobarbital	14 000
Phenobarbital — Phénobarbital — Fenobarbital	100 000
Prazepam — Prazépam	1 700
Zolpidem	6 000
Mexico — Mexique — México	
Alprazolam	200 000
Amfepramone — Amfépramone — Anfepramona	2 375 000
Amfetamine — Amfétamine — Anfetamina	2
Amobarbital	1
Barbital	200
Bromazepam — Bromazépam	600 000
Brotizolam	60 000
Buprenorphine — Buprénorphine — Buprenorfina	5 500
Butalbital	1 500 000
Cathine — Catina	2 000 000
Chlordiazepoxide — Chlordiazépoxide — Clordiazepóxido	140 000
Clobazam	150 000
Clonazepam — Clonazépam	1 100 000
Clorazepate — Clorazépate — Clorazepato	40 000
Delta-9-tetrahydrocannabinol — Delta-9-tétrahydrocannabinol — Delta-9-tetrahidrocannabinol	2
Diazepam — Diazépam	2 500 000
Estazolam	30 000
Ethyl loflazepate — Loflazépate d'éthyle — Loflazepato de etilo	20 000
Etilamfetamine — Étilamfétamine — Etilanfetamina	1
Fenproporex	1 000 000
Flunitrazepam — Flunitrazépam	30 000
Flurazepam — Flurazépam	18 000
Ketazolam — Kétazolam	500
Lorazepam — Lorazépam	150 000
Mazindol	150 000
Meprobamate — Méprobamate — Meprobamato	1
Metamfetamine — Métamfétamine — Metanfetamina	2
Methaqualone — Méthaqualone — Metacualona	1
Methylphenidate — Méthylphénidate — Metilfenidato	820 000
Midazolam	300 000
Nitrazepam — Nitrazépam	3
Nordazepam — Nordazépam	25 000
Oxazepam — Oxazépam	1
Pemoline — Pémoline — Pemolina	2
Pentazocine — Pentazocina	1

Country (or territory) and substance Pays (ou territoire) et substance País (o territorio) y sustancia	Assessment (grams) Évaluation (en grammes) Previsión (en gramos)
Pentobarbital	800 000
Phencyclidine (PCP) — Fenciclidina (PCP)	2
Phenobarbital — Phénobarbital — Fenobarbital	1 700 000
Phentermine — Fentermina	1 00 000
Pinazepam — Pinazépam	10 007
Secobarbital — Sécobarbital	2
Temazepam — Témazépam	8
Tetrazepam — Tétrazépam	48 000
Triazolam	10 000
Zipeprol — Zipéprol	95 000
Zolpidem	130 000
Micronesia (Federated States of) — Micronésie (États fédérés de) — Micronesia (Estados Federados de)	
Alprazolam	72
Chlordiazepoxide — Chlordiazépoxide — Clordiazepóxido	10
Diazepam — Diazépam	913
Flurazepam — Flurazépam	182
Meprobamate — Méprobamate — Meprobamato	192
Methylphenidate — Méthylphénidate — Metilfenidato	90
Midazolam	20
Oxazepam — Oxazépam	38
Phenobarbital — Phénobarbital — Fenobarbital	3 676
Triazolam	1
Mongolia — Mongolie	
Diazepam — Diazépam	3 900
Pentazocine — Pentazocina	150
Phenobarbital — Phénobarbital — Fenobarbital	250 700
Montserrat	
Buprenorphine — Buprénorphine — Buprenorfina	1
Diazepam — Diazépam	119
Lorazepam — Lorazépam	7
Methylphenidate — Méthylphénidate — Metilfenidato	22
Midazolam	1
Nitrazepam — Nitrazépam	5
Pentazocine — Pentazocina	3
Pentobarbital	902
Phenobarbital — Phénobarbital — Fenobarbital	500
Morocco — Maroc — Marruecos	
Alprazolam	8 000
Bromazepam — Bromazépam	137 000
Buprenorphine — Buprénorphine — Buprenorfina	110
Chlordiazepoxide — Chlordiazépoxide — Clordiazepóxido	100 000
Clobazam	40 000
Clorazepate — Clorazépate — Clorazepato	48 000
Diazepam — Diazépam	36 730
Flunitrazepam — Flunitrazépam	5
Lorazepam — Lorazépam	43 500
Meprobamate — Méprobamate — Meprobamato	1 300 000
Midazolam	5 160
Nordazepam — Nordazépam	108 000
Oxazepam — Oxazépam	1
Pentobarbital	36 400

Table V. Assessments of annual domestic medical and scientific requirements
Tableau V. Évaluations des besoins annuels médicaux et scientifiques intérieurs
Cuadro V. Previsiones de las necesidades anuales internas para fines médicos y científicos

Country (or territory) and substance Pays (ou territoire) et substance País (o territorio) y sustancia	Assessment (grams) Évaluation (en grammes) Previsión (en gramos)
Phenobarbital — Phénobarbital — Fenobarbital	1 550 000
Prazepam — Prazépam........................	250 002
Tetrazepam — Tétrazépam.....................	340 000
Triazolam	1
Zolpidem	49 600
Mozambique	
Allobarbital — Alobarbital	150
Bromazepam — Bromazépam	150
Chlordiazepoxide — Chlordiazépoxide — Clordiazepóxido	20 000
Clonazepam — Clonazépam...................	200
Diazepam — Diazépam	100 000
Lorazepam — Lorazépam	500
Medazepam — Médazépam	100
Midazolam................................	150
Nitrazepam — Nitrazépam....................	100
Oxazepam — Oxazépam.....................	500
Phenobarbital — Phénobarbital — Fenobarbital	100 000
Zolpidem.................................	250
Myanmar	
Alprazolam	3 000
Bromazepam — Bromazépam	1 000
Buprenorphine — Buprénorphine — Buprenorfina	500
Chlordiazepoxide — Chlordiazépoxide — Clordiazepóxido	1 000
Clobazam	20 000
Clorazepate — Clorazépate — Clorazepato.........	2 000
Diazepam — Diazépam	105 444
Flunitrazepam — Flunitrazépam	3 000
Lorazepam — Lorazépam	3 000
Methylphenidate — Méthylphénidate — Metilfenidato .	15 000
Midazolam................................	1 000
Nimetazepam — Nimétazépam.................	403
Nordazepam — Nordazépam	1 000
Pentazocine — Pentazocina	1 000
Phenobarbital — Phénobarbital — Fenobarbital	25 625
Zolpidem.................................	25 000
Namibia — Namibie	
Alprazolam	1 000
Amfepramone — Amfépramone — Anfepramona	4
Barbital	500
Bromazepam — Bromazépam	1 500
Buprenorphine — Buprénorphine — Buprenorfina	500
Butalbital	50 000
Cathine — Catina..........................	15 000
Chlordiazepoxide — Chlordiazépoxide — Clordiazepóxido	1 000
Clobazam	1 000
Clonazepam — Clonazépam...................	1 000
Clorazepate — Clorazépate — Clorazepato.........	50
Diazepam — Diazépam	15 000
Flunitrazepam — Flunitrazépam	35
Flurazepam — Flurazépam	2 000
Ketazolam — Kétazolam	500
Loprazolam	50
Lorazepam — Lorazépam	2 000
Lormetazepam — Lormétazépam	50

Country (or territory) and substance Pays (ou territoire) et substance País (o territorio) y sustancia	Assessment (grams) Évaluation (en grammes) Previsión (en gramos)
Meprobamate — Méprobamate — Meprobamato	400 000
Methylphenidate — Méthylphénidate — Metilfenidato ..	5 000
Midazolam................................	1 000
Nitrazepam — Nitrazépam....................	1 000
Oxazepam — Oxazépam.....................	4 000
Pentazocine — Pentazocina	30
Pentobarbital..............................	5 000
Phendimetrazine — Phendimétrazine — Fendimetracina..........................	50
Phenobarbital — Phénobarbital — Fenobarbital	15 000
Phentermine — Fentermina...................	5 000
Prazepam — Prazépam......................	1 000
Temazepam — Témazépam	1 000
Triazolam	1 000
Zolpidem.................................	4 000
Nauru	
Clonazepam — Clonazépam...................	2
Diazepam — Diazépam	30
Nitrazepam — Nitrazépam....................	10
Pentazocine — Pentazocina	5
Phenobarbital — Phénobarbital — Fenobarbital	164
Nepal — Népal	
Alprazolam	10 200
Buprenorphine — Buprénorphine — Buprenorfina	250
Chlordiazepoxide — Chlordiazépoxide — Clordiazepóxido	30 000
Clobazam	20 000
Clonazepam — Clonazépam...................	12 000
Diazepam — Diazépam	150 000
Flurazepam — Flurazépam	400
Glutethimide — Glutéthimide — Glutetimida	800
Lorazepam — Lorazépam	20 000
Medazepam — Médazépam	200
Meprobamate — Méprobamate — Meprobamato	1 000
Midazolam................................	5 000
Nitrazepam — Nitrazépam....................	30 000
Oxazepam — Oxazépam.....................	10 000
Oxazolam	600
Pentazocine — Pentazocina	14 500
Pentobarbital..............................	10 000
Phenobarbital — Phénobarbital — Fenobarbital	300 000
Phentermine — Fentermina...................	500
Prazepam — Prazépam......................	500
Triazolam	100
Zolpidem.................................	15 000
Netherlands — Pays-Bas — Países Bajos	
Allobarbital — Alobarbital	2 000
Alprazolam	30 000
Amfetamine — Amfétamine — Anfetamina	1 500
Amobarbital	200 000
Barbital	100 000
Bromazepam — Bromazépam	55 000
Brotizolam	2 000
Buprenorphine — Buprénorphine — Buprenorfina	3 000
Butalbital	50 000
Butobarbital..............................	15 000

309

Table V. Assessments of annual domestic medical and scientific requirements
Tableau V. Évaluations des besoins annuels médicaux et scientifiques intérieurs
Cuadro V. Previsiones de las necesidades anuales internas para fines médicos y científicos

Country (or territory) and substance Pays (ou territoire) et substance País (o territorio) y sustancia	Assessment (grams) Évaluation (en grammes) Previsión (en gramos)
Netherlands — Pays-Bas — Países Bajos	
(continued — suite — continuación)	
Chlordiazepoxide — Chlordiazépoxide —	
Clordiazepóxido	200 000
Clobazam	50 000
Clonazepam — Clonazépam	13 500
Clorazepate — Clorazépate — Clorazepato	180 000
Cloxazolam	20 000
Cyclobarbital — Ciclobarbital	125 000
Delta-9-tetrahydrocannabinol —	
Delta-9-tétrahydrocannabinol —	
Delta-9-tetrahidrocannabinol	150
Dexamfetamine — Dexamfétamine — Dexanfetamina	18 000
Diazepam — Diazépam	400 000
Estazolam	20 000
Fenetylline — Fénétylline — Fenetilina	100 000
Flunitrazepam — Flunitrazépam	10 000
Flurazepam — Flurazépam	300 000
Gamma-hydroxybutyric acid (GHB) —	
Acide *gamma*-hydroxybutirique (GHB) —	
Ácido *gamma*-hidroxibutírico (GHB)	250 000
Loprazolam	3 000
Lorazepam — Lorazépam	80 000
Lormetazepam — Lormétazépam	90 000
Medazepam — Médazépam	500
Meprobamate — Méprobamate — Meprobamato	1 500 000
Metamfetamine — Métamfétamine — Metanfetamina	5
Methylphenidate — Méthylphénidate — Metilfenidato	400 000
Methylphenobarbital — Méthylphénobarbital —	
Metilfenobarbital	5 000
Midazolam	300 000
Nitrazepam — Nitrazépam	100 000
Nordazepam — Nordazépam	1 000
Oxazepam — Oxazépam	2 200 000
Pentazocine — Pentazocina	50 000
Pentobarbital	1 200 000
Phenobarbital — Phénobarbital — Fenobarbital	2 000 000
Phentermine — Fentermina	300 000
Pinazepam — Pinazépam	10 000
Prazepam — Prazépam	20 000
Secobarbital — Sécobarbital	160 000
Temazepam — Témazépam	1 250 000
Tetrazepam — Tétrazépam	5
Triazolam	500
Zolpidem	2 000 000
Netherlands Antilles — Antilles néerlandaises — **Antillas Neerlandesas**	
Alprazolam	300
Bromazepam — Bromazépam	2 000
Brotizolam	3
Buprenorphine — Buprénorphine — Buprenorfina	1
Chlordiazepoxide — Chlordiazépoxide —	
Clordiazepóxido	100
Clobazam	300
Clonazepam — Clonazépam	300
Clorazepate — Clorazépate — Clorazepato	100
Delta-9-tetrahydrocannabinol —	
Delta-9-tétrahydrocannabinol —	
Delta-9-tetrahidrocannabinol	1
Diazepam — Diazépam	3 000

Country (or territory) and substance Pays (ou territoire) et substance País (o territorio) y sustancia	Assessment (grams) Évaluation (en grammes) Previsión (en gramos)
Flunitrazepam — Flunitrazépam	75
Flurazepam — Flurazépam	200
Loprazolam	50
Lorazepam — Lorazépam	1 000
Meprobamate — Méprobamate — Meprobamato	50
Metamfetamine — Métamfétamine — Metanfetamina	1
Methylphenidate — Méthylphénidate — Metilfenidato	1 500
Midazolam	2 750
Nitrazepam — Nitrazépam	150
Oxazepam — Oxazépam	1 500
Pentazocine — Pentazocina	25
Pentobarbital	20 000
Phenobarbital — Phénobarbital — Fenobarbital	15 000
Temazepam — Témazépam	1 500
Triazolam	10
Zolpidem	2 500
New Caledonia — Nouvelle-Calédonie — *Nueva Caledonia*	
Alprazolam	300
Bromazepam — Bromazépam	5 000
Buprenorphine — Buprénorphine — Buprenorfina	60
Chlordiazepoxide — Chlordiazépoxide —	
Clordiazepóxido	200
Clobazam	900
Clonazepam — Clonazépam	400
Clorazepate — Clorazépate — Clorazepato	3 000
Clotiazepam — Clotiazépam	200
Delta-9-tetrahydrocannabinol —	
Delta-9-tétrahydrocannabinol —	
Delta-9-tetrahidrocannabinol	1
Diazepam — Diazépam	700
Estazolam	100
Ethyl loflazepate — Loflazépate d'éthyle —	
Loflazepato de etilo	50
Flunitrazepam — Flunitrazépam	25
Gamma-hydroxybutyric acid (GHB) —	
Acide *gamma*-hydroxybutirique (GHB) —	
Ácido *gamma*-hidroxibutírico (GHB)	1 000
Loprazolam	50
Lorazepam — Lorazépam	600
Lormetazepam — Lormétazépam	100
Meprobamate — Méprobamate — Meprobamato	90 000
Methylphenidate — Méthylphénidate — Metilfenidato	150
Midazolam	1 200
Nitrazepam — Nitrazépam	300
Nordazepam — Nordazépam	50
Oxazepam — Oxazépam	9 000
Phenobarbital — Phénobarbital — Fenobarbital	20 000
Prazepam — Prazépam	4 000
Temazepam — Témazépam	400
Tetrazepam — Tétrazépam	17 000
Triazolam	10
Zolpidem	5 000
New Zealand — Nouvelle-Zélande — **Nueva Zelandia**	
Alprazolam	1 000
Amfepramone — Amfépramone — Anfepramona	39 000
Amfetamine — Amfétamine — Anfetamina	50

Table V. Assessments of annual domestic medical and scientific requirements
Tableau V. Évaluations des besoins annuels médicaux et scientifiques intérieurs
Cuadro V. Previsiones de las necesidades anuales internas para fines médicos y científicos

Country (or territory) and substance Pays (ou territoire) et substance País (o territorio) y sustancia	Assessment (grams) Évaluation (en grammes) Previsión (en gramos)
Amobarbital	92
Barbital	15 000
Bromazepam — Bromazépam	40
Brotizolam	10
Buprenorphine — Buprénorphine — Buprenorfina	9 000
Chlordiazepoxide — Chlordiazépoxide — Clordiazepóxido	1 000
Clobazam	13 000
Clonazepam — Clonazépam	11 000
Clorazepate — Clorazépate — Clorazepato	5
Delta-9-tetrahydrocannabinol — *Delta*-9-tétrahydrocannabinol — *Delta*-9-tetrahidrocannabinol	1
Dexamfetamine — Dexamfétamine — Dexanfetamina	3 700
Diazepam — Diazépam	45 000
Estazolam	5
Flunitrazepam — Flunitrazépam	100
Flurazepam — Flurazépam	10
Gamma-hydroxybutyric acid (GHB) — Acide *gamma*-hydroxybutirique (GHB) — Ácido *gamma*-hidroxibutírico (GHB)	400 000
Lorazepam — Lorazépam	17 000
Lormetazepam — Lormétazépam	1 000
Mazindol	1
Mefenorex — Méfénorex	1
Meprobamate — Méprobamate — Meprobamato	10
Metamfetamine — Métamfétamine — Metanfetamina	6
Metamfetamine racemate — Racémate de métamfétamine — Racemato de metanfetamina	1
Methaqualone — Méthaqualone — Metacualona	1
Methylphenidate — Méthylphénidate — Metilfenidato	150 000
Methylphenobarbital — Méthylphénobarbital — Metilfenobarbital	200
Midazolam	12 000
Nitrazepam — Nitrazépam	30 000
Nordazepam — Nordazépam	1
Oxazepam — Oxazépam	90 000
Pentazocine — Pentazocina	10 000
Pentobarbital	500 000
Phencyclidine (PCP) — Fenciclidina (PCP)	1
Phenobarbital — Phénobarbital — Fenobarbital	145 000
Phentermine — Fentermina	125 000
Prazepam — Prazépam	5
Secobarbital — Sécobarbital	46
Temazepam — Témazépam	100 000
Tetrazepam — Tétrazépam	10
Triazolam	3 000
Zolpidem	10
Nicaragua	
Alprazolam	7 653
Bromazepam — Bromazépam	19 944
Buprenorphine — Buprénorphine — Buprenorfina	2
Chlordiazepoxide — Chlordiazépoxide — Clordiazepóxido	75 370
Clobazam	1 252
Clonazepam — Clonazépam	3 408
Diazepam — Diazépam	46 221
Fenproporex	6 851
Flunitrazepam — Flunitrazépam	27
Ketazolam — Kétazolam	324
Loprazolam	126
Lorazepam — Lorazépam	20 899
Mazindol	350
Methylphenidate — Méthylphénidate — Metilfenidato	4 178
Midazolam	10 409
Phenobarbital — Phénobarbital — Fenobarbital	156 317
Triazolam	267
Zolpidem	1 537
Niger — Níger	
Alprazolam	5
Bromazepam — Bromazépam	591
Buprenorphine — Buprénorphine — Buprenorfina	16
Chlordiazepoxide — Chlordiazépoxide — Clordiazepóxido	165
Clobazam	78
Clonazepam — Clonazépam	326
Clorazepate — Clorazépate — Clorazepato	3 711
Diazepam — Diazépam	10 857
Ethyl loflazepate — Loflazépate d'éthyle — Loflazepato de etilo	2
Flunitrazepam — Flunitrazépam	2
Lorazepam — Lorazépam	82
Meprobamate — Méprobamate — Meprobamato	2 810
Oxazepam — Oxazépam	25
Pentazocine — Pentazocina	150
Phenobarbital — Phénobarbital — Fenobarbital	166 000
Tetrazepam — Tétrazépam	2 420
Triazolam	1
Nigeria — Nigéria	
Bromazepam — Bromazépam	100 000
Diazepam — Diazépam	840 000
Flunitrazepam — Flunitrazépam	5 000
Lorazepam — Lorazépam	4 800
Midazolam	1[a]
Nitrazepam — Nitrazépam	150 000
Pentazocine — Pentazocina	200 000
Phenobarbital — Phénobarbital — Fenobarbital	800 000
Zolpidem	2 000
Norfolk Island — Île Norfolk — Isla Norfolk	
Dexamfetamine — Dexamfétamine — Dexanfetamina	5
Flunitrazepam — Flunitrazépam	2
Methylphenidate — Méthylphénidate — Metilfenidato	30
Norway — Norvège — Noruega	
Alprazolam	8 200
Amfetamine — Amfétamine — Anfetamina	1 500
Amobarbital	300
Barbital	14 000
Bromazepam — Bromazépam	30
Brotizolam	1
Buprenorphine — Buprénorphine — Buprenorfina	11 100
Butalbital	1 000
Cathine — Catina	1
Chlordiazepoxide — Chlordiazépoxide — Clordiazepóxido	170 000

311

Table V. Assessments of annual domestic medical and scientific requirements
Tableau V. Évaluations des besoins annuels médicaux et scientifiques intérieurs
Cuadro V. Previsiones de las necesidades anuales internas para fines médicos y científicos

Country (or territory) and substance Pays (ou territoire) et substance País (o territorio) y sustancia	Assessment (grams) Évaluation (en grammes) Previsión (en gramos)
Norway — Norvège — Noruega	
(continued — suite — continuación)	
Clobazam	4 300
Clonazepam — Clonazépam	12 221
Clorazepate — Clorazépate — Clorazepato	10
Cyclobarbital — Ciclobarbital	2
Delta-9-tetrahydrocannabinol — *Delta*-9-tétrahydrocannabinol — *Delta*-9-tetrahidrocannabinol	100
Dexamfetamine — Dexamfétamine — Dexanfetamina	4 000
Diazepam — Diazépam	820 000
Estazolam	50
Flunitrazepam — Flunitrazépam	6 100
Flurazepam — Flurazépam	400
Gamma-hydroxybutyric acid (GHB) — Acide *gamma*-hydroxybutirique (GHB) — Ácido *gamma*-hidroxibutírico (GHB)	50 100
Ketazolam — Kétazolam	1
Lorazepam — Lorazépam	150
Meprobamate — Méprobamate — Meprobamato	120 000
Metamfetamine — Métamfétamine — Metanfetamina	1
Metamfetamine racemate — Racémate de métamfétamine — Racemato de metanfetamina	1
Methylphenidate — Méthylphénidate — Metilfenidato	223 500
Midazolam	8 200
Nitrazepam — Nitrazépam	180 000
Nordazepam — Nordazépam	1
Oxazepam — Oxazépam	1 500 000
Pemoline — Pémoline — Pemolina	200
Pentazocine — Pentazocina	35 200
Pentobarbital	340 000
Phencyclidine (PCP) — Fenciclidina (PCP)	1
Phenobarbital — Phénobarbital — Fenobarbital	200 000
Phentermine — Fentermina	20
Secbutabarbital	1
Secobarbital — Sécobarbital	200
Temazepam — Témazépam	2
Tetrazepam — Tétrazépam	20
Triazolam	20
Zolpidem	120 000
Oman — Omán	
Alprazolam	29 000
Amfetamine — Amfétamine — Anfetamina	11
Bromazepam — Bromazépam	1 200
Buprenorphine — Buprénorphine — Buprenorfina	2
Chlordiazepoxide — Chlordiazépoxide — Clordiazepóxido	300
Clonazepam — Clonazépam	1 100
Clorazepate — Clorazépate — Clorazepato	100
Delta-9-tetrahydrocannabinol — *Delta*-9-tétrahydrocannabinol — *Delta*-9-tetrahidrocannabinol	1
Diazepam — Diazépam	4 000
Flunitrazepam — Flunitrazépam	1
Glutethimide — Glutéthimide — Glutetimida	40
Lorazepam — Lorazépam	60
Metamfetamine — Métamfétamine — Metanfetamina	10
Methylphenidate — Méthylphénidate — Metilfenidato	1 500

Country (or territory) and substance Pays (ou territoire) et substance País (o territorio) y sustancia	Assessment (grams) Évaluation (en grammes) Previsión (en gramos)
Midazolam	3 500
Pemoline — Pémoline — Pemolina	450
Pentobarbital	3 000
Phenobarbital — Phénobarbital — Fenobarbital	21 000
Secobarbital — Sécobarbital	500
Temazepam — Témazépam	100
Pakistan — Pakistán	
Alprazolam	150 000
Bromazepam — Bromazépam	1 200 000
Buprenorphine — Buprénorphine — Buprenorfina	15 000
Chlordiazepoxide — Chlordiazépoxide — Clordiazepóxido	2 000 000
Clobazam	390 000
Clonazepam — Clonazépam	50 000
Clorazepate — Clorazépate — Clorazepato	280 000
Diazepam — Diazépam	5 473 000
Estazolam	10 000
Fludiazepam — Fludiazépam	600
Lorazepam — Lorazépam	332 000
Lormetazepam — Lormétazépam	30 000
Medazepam — Médazépam	42 000
Meprobamate — Méprobamate — Meprobamato	3 000 000
Methylphenidate — Méthylphénidate — Metilfenidato	40 000
Midazolam	104 000
Nimetazepam — Nimétazépam	4 000
Nitrazepam — Nitrazépam	70 000
Oxazepam — Oxazépam	30 000
Pentazocine — Pentazocina	1 500 000
Phenobarbital — Phénobarbital — Fenobarbital	5 120 000
Pinazepam — Pinazépam	40 000
Prazepam — Prazépam	30 000
Temazepam — Témazépam	900 000
Triazolam	6 250
Zolpidem	150 000
Palau — Palaos	
Alprazolam	10
Clonazepam — Clonazépam	15
Clorazepate — Clorazépate — Clorazepato	10
Diazepam — Diazépam	500
Lorazepam — Lorazépam	15
Methylphenidate — Méthylphénidate — Metilfenidato	400
Nitrazepam — Nitrazépam	500
Phenobarbital — Phénobarbital — Fenobarbital	300
Temazepam — Témazépam	90
Panama — Panamá	
Alprazolam	10 000
Amfepramone — Amfépramone — Anfepramona	60 000
Bromazepam — Bromazépam	10 000
Chlordiazepoxide — Chlordiazépoxide — Clordiazepóxido	50 000
Clobazam	5 000
Clonazepam — Clonazépam	5 000
Clorazepate — Clorazépate — Clorazepato	25 000
Diazepam — Diazépam	50 000
Ethyl loflazepate — Loflazépate d'éthyle — Loflazepato de etilo	6 000
Fenproporex	6 000

Table V.   Assessments of annual domestic medical and scientific requirements
Tableau V.   Évaluations des besoins annuels médicaux et scientifiques intérieurs
Cuadro V.   Previsiones de las necesidades anuales internas para fines médicos y científicos

Country (or territory) and substance Pays (ou territoire) et substance País (o territorio) y sustancia	Assessment (grams) Évaluation (en grammes) Previsión (en gramos)
Flunitrazepam — Flunitrazépam	500
Loprazolam	2 000
Lorazepam — Lorazépam	15 000
Mazindol	4 000
Methylphenidate — Méthylphénidate — Metilfenidato	60 000
Midazolam	12 000
Pentazocine — Pentazocina	4 000
Phenobarbital — Phénobarbital — Fenobarbital	500 000
Phentermine — Fentermina	130 000
Tetrazepam — Tétrazépam	70 000
Triazolam	1 000
Zolpidem	60 000
Papua New Guinea — **Papouasie-Nouvelle-Guinée —** **Papua Nueva Guinea**	
Alprazolam	10
Amfetamine — Amfétamine — Anfetamina	20
Bromazepam — Bromazépam	30
Buprenorphine — Buprénorphine — Buprenorfina	2
Clonazepam — Clonazépam	10
Dexamfetamine —Dexamfétamine—Dexanfetamina	20
Diazepam — Diazépam	10 000
Flunitrazepam — Flunitrazépam	10
Lorazepam — Lorazépam	300
Meprobamate — Méprobamate — Meprobamato	500
Methylphenidate — Méthylphénidate —Metilfenidato	300
Midazolam	300
Nitrazepam — Nitrazépam	1 000
Oxazepam — Oxazépam	3 000
Pentazocine — Pentazocina	500
Phenobarbital — Phénobarbital — Fenobarbital	200 000
Phentermine — Fentermina	200
Pipradrol	1
Temazepam — Témazépam	2 000
Triazolam	3
Zolpidem	5 000
Paraguay	
Alprazolam	15 000
Bromazepam — Bromazépam	150 000
Chlordiazepoxide — Chlordiazépoxide — Clordiazepóxido	2 000
Clobazam	2 000
Clonazepam — Clonazépam	8 000
Clorazepate — Clorazépate — Clorazepato	6 000
Diazepam — Diazépam	8 000
Ethyl loflazepate — Loflazépate d'éthyle — Loflazepato de etilo	1 000
Fenproporex	5 000
Flunitrazepam — Flunitrazépam	8 000
Ketazolam — Kétazolam	75 000
Lorazepam — Lorazépam	180
Mazindol	3 000
Methylphenidate — Méthylphénidate — Metilfenidato	2 500
Midazolam	3 500
Pemoline — Pémoline — Pemolina	20 000
Phenobarbital — Phénobarbital — Fenobarbital	250 000
Tetrazepam — Tétrazépam	30 000
Zolpidem	40 000

Country (or territory) and substance Pays (ou territoire) et substance País (o territorio) y sustancia	Assessment (grams) Évaluation (en grammes) Previsión (en gramos)
Peru — Pérou — Perú	
Alprazolam	500 000
Amfepramone — Amfépramone — Anfepramona	250 000
Bromazepam — Bromazépam	250 000
Buprenorphine — Buprénorphine — Buprenorfina	2 000
Chlordiazepoxide — Chlordiazépoxide — Clordiazepóxido	7 530
Clobazam	50 000
Clonazepam — Clonazépam	100 000
Diazepam — Diazépam	700 000
Estazolam	2 000
Fenproporex	100 000
Flunitrazepam — Flunitrazépam	20 000
Ketazolam — Kétazolam	90 000
Lorazepam — Lorazépam	100 000
Mazindol	5 000
Methylphenidate — Méthylphénidate — Metilfenidato	15 000
Midazolam	50 000
Pentazocine — Pentazocina	751
Pentobarbital	100 000
Phenobarbital — Phénobarbital — Fenobarbital	1 500 000
Tetrazepam — Tétrazépam	2 000
Triazolam	1 000
Zolpidem	50 000
Philippines — Filipinas	
Alprazolam	5 000
Amfepramone — Amfépramone — Anfepramona	85 000
Bromazepam — Bromazépam	40 000
Buprenorphine — Buprénorphine — Buprenorfina	500
Chlordiazepoxide — Chlordiazépoxide — Clordiazepóxido	3 000
Clobazam	6 000
Clonazepam — Clonazépam	8 500
Clorazepate — Clorazépate — Clorazepato	5 000
Dexamfetamine —Dexamfétamine—Dexanfetamina	1 000
Diazepam — Diazépam	50 000
Estazolam	1 500
Flurazepam — Flurazépam	10 000
Lorazepam — Lorazépam	5 000
Mazindol	50 000
Methylphenidate — Méthylphénidate — Metilfenidato	15 000
Midazolam	50 000
Nitrazepam — Nitrazépam	1 000
Pentobarbital	60 800
Phenobarbital — Phénobarbital — Fenobarbital	1 800 000
Phentermine — Fentermina	100 000
Zolpidem	50 000
Poland — Pologne — Polonia	
4-Bromo-2,5-dimethoxyphenyl-ethylamine (2C-B) — 4-bromo-2,5-diméthoxyphényléthylamine (2C-B) — 4-bromo-2,5-dimetoxifeniletilamina (2C-B)	10
Allobarbital — Alobarbital	2 000 000
Alprazolam	35 000
Amfepramone — Amfépramone — Anfepramona	100
Amfetamine — Amfétamine — Anfetamina	50
Aminorex	100
Amobarbital	1 000
Barbital	2 500 000

313

Table V. Assessments of annual domestic medical and scientific requirements
Tableau V. Évaluations des besoins annuels médicaux et scientifiques intérieurs
Cuadro V. Previsiones de las necesidades anuales internas
para fines médicos y científicos

Country (or territory) and substance Pays (ou territoire) et substance País (o territorio) y sustancia	Assessment (grams) Évaluation (en grammes) Previsión (en gramos)	Country (or territory) and substance Pays (ou territoire) et substance País (o territorio) y sustancia	Assessment (grams) Évaluation (en grammes) Previsión (en gramos)
Poland — Pologne — Polonia		Methaqualone — Méthaqualone — Metacualona	10
(continued — suite — continuación)		Methylphenidate — Méthylphénidate — Metilfenidato	15 000
Benzfetamine — Benzfétamine — Benzfetamina	100	Methylphenobarbital — Méthylphénobarbital —	
Bromazepam — Bromazépam	40 000	Metilfenobarbital	100
Brotizolam	100	Methyprylon — Méthyprylone — Metiprilona	100
Buprenorphine — Buprénorphine — Buprenorfina	8 000	Midazolam	65 000
Butalbital	500	Nimetazepam — Nimétazépam	100
Butobarbital	100	Nitrazepam — Nitrazépam	350 000
Camazepam — Camazépam	100	Nordazepam — Nordazépam	20 000
Cathine — Catina	500	Oxazepam — Oxazépam	800 000
Chlordiazepoxide — Chlordiazépoxide —		Oxazolam	100
Clordiazepóxido	1 500 000	Pemoline — Pémoline — Pemolina	100
Clobazam	5 000	Pentazocine — Pentazocina	30 000
Clonazepam — Clonazépam	350 000	Pentobarbital	500 000
Clorazepate — Clorazépate — Clorazepato	800 000	Phencyclidine (PCP) — Fenciclidina (PCP)	10
Clotiazepam — Clotiazépam	100	Phendimetrazine — Phendimétrazine —	
Cloxazolam	100	Fendimetracina	100
Cyclobarbital — Ciclobarbital	4 000 000	Phenmetrazine — Phenmétrazine — Fenmetracina	10
Delorazepam — Délorazépam	100	Phenobarbital — Phénobarbital — Fenobarbital	4 000 000
Delta-9-tetrahydrocannabinol —		Phentermine — Fentermina	100
Delta-9-tétrahydrocannabinol —		Pinazepam — Pinazépam	100
Delta-9-tetrahidrocannabinol	10	Pipradrol	100
Dexamfetamine — Dexamfétamine — Dexanfetamina	20	Prazepam — Prazépam	100
Diazepam — Diazépam	2 000 000	Pyrovalerone — Pyrovalérone — Pirovalerona	100
Estazolam	220 000	Secbutabarbital	100
Ethchlorvynol — Etclorvinol	100	Secobarbital — Sécobarbital	10
Ethinamate — Éthinamate — Etinamato	100	Temazepam — Témazépam	600 000
Ethyl loflazepate — Loflazépate d'éthyle —		Tetrazepam — Tétrazépam	1 500 000
Loflazepato de etilo	100	Triazolam	100
Etilamfetamine — Étilamfétamine — Etilanfetamina	100	Vinylbital — Vinilbital	100
Fencamfamin — Fencamfamine — Fencanfamina	100	Zipeprol — Zipéprol	10
Fenetylline — Fénétylline — Fenetilina	10	Zolpidem	350 000
Fenproporex	100		
Fludiazepam — Fludiazépam	100	**Portugal**	
Flunitrazepam — Flunitrazépam	2 000	Alprazolam	250 000
Flurazepam — Flurazépam	100	Amfetamine — Amfétamine — Anfetamina	10
Gamma-hydroxybutyric acid (GHB) —		Amobarbital	1 000
Acide *gamma*-hydroxybutirique (GHB) —		Barbital	10 000
Ácido *gamma*-hidroxibutírico (GHB)	5 000	Bromazepam — Bromazépam	320 000
Glutethimide — Glutéthimide — Glutetimida	200	Brotizolam	5 000
Halazepam — Halazépam	100	Buprenorphine — Buprénorphine — Buprenorfina	22 000
Haloxazolam	100	Chlordiazepoxide — Chlordiazépoxide —	
Ketazolam — Kétazolam	100	Clordiazepóxido	180 000
Lefetamine (SPA) — Léfétamine (SPA) —		Clobazam	200 000
Lefetamina (SPA)	100	Clonazepam — Clonazépam	15 000
Levamfetamine — Lévamfétamine — Levanfetamina	10	Clorazepate — Clorazépate — Clorazepato	300 000
Levomethamphetamine — Lévométhamphétamine —		Cloxazolam	120 000
Levometanfetamina	10	*Delta*-9-tetrahydrocannabinol —	
Loprazolam	100	*Delta*-9-tétrahydrocannabinol —	
Lorazepam — Lorazépam	200 000	*Delta*-9-tetrahidrocannabinol	1 000
Lormetazepam — Lormétazépam	10 000	Diazepam — Diazépam	1 200 000
Mazindol	20 000	Estazolam	60 000
Mecloqualone — Mécloqualone — Meclocualona	10	Ethyl loflazepate — Loflazépate d'éthyle —	
Medazepam — Médazépam	250 000	Loflazepato de etilo	100 000
Mefenorex — Méfénorex	100	Etilamfetamine — Étilamfétamine — Etilanfetamina	5
Meprobamate — Méprobamate — Meprobamato	100 000	Fenetylline — Fénétylline — Fenetilina	5
Mesocarb — Mésocarbe — Mesocarbo	100	Flunitrazepam — Flunitrazépam	2 000
Metamfetamine — Métamfétamine — Metanfetamina	20	Flurazepam — Flurazépam	300 000
Metamfetamine racemate —		*Gamma*-hydroxybutyric acid (GHB) —	
Racémate de métamfétamine —		Acide *gamma*-hydroxybutirique (GHB) —	
Racemato de metanfetamina	10	Ácido *gamma*-hidroxibutírico (GHB)	150 000

Table V.   Assessments of annual domestic medical and scientific requirements
Tableau V.   Évaluations des besoins annuels médicaux et scientifiques intérieurs
Cuadro V.   Previsiones de las necesidades anuales internas para fines médicos y científicos

Country (or territory) and substance Pays (ou territoire) et substance País (o territorio) y sustancia	Assessment (grams) Évaluation (en grammes) Previsión (en gramos)
Halazepam — Halazépam	450 000
Ketazolam — Kétazolam	40 000
Loprazolam	20 000
Lorazepam — Lorazépam	220 000
Lormetazepam — Lormétazépam	4 000
Meprobamate — Méprobamate — Meprobamato	75 000
Metamfetamine — Métamfétamine — Metanfetamina	5
Methylphenidate — Méthylphénidate — Metilfenidato	60 000
Midazolam	150 000
Nitrazepam — Nitrazépam	1 000
Nordazepam — Nordazépam	15 000
Oxazepam — Oxazépam	950 000
Pentazocine — Pentazocina	500 000
Pentobarbital	150 000
Phencyclidine (PCP) — Fenciclidina (PCP)	5
Phenmetrazine — Phenmétrazine — Fenmetracina	5
Phenobarbital — Phénobarbital — Fenobarbital	1 200 000
Prazepam — Prazépam	12 000
Temazepam — Témazépam	80 000
Triazolam	3 000
Zipeprol — Zipéprol	2 000
Zolpidem	200 000

Qatar

Alprazolam	10
Bromazepam — Bromazépam	250
Buprenorphine — Buprénorphine — Buprenorfina	1
Chlordiazepoxide — Chlordiazépoxide — Clordiazepóxido	600
Clobazam	150
Clonazepam — Clonazépam	150
Diazepam — Diazépam	650
Flunitrazepam — Flunitrazépam	1
Lorazepam — Lorazépam	12
Methylphenidate — Méthylphénidate — Metilfenidato	750
Midazolam	10
Pentazocine — Pentazocina	20
Phenobarbital — Phénobarbital — Fenobarbital	7 500
Temazepam — Témazépam	10
Zolpidem	20

Republic of Korea — République de Corée — República de Corea

Alprazolam	50 000
Amfepramone — Amfépramone — Anfepramona	800 000
Barbital	1 500 000
Bromazepam — Bromazépam	80 000
Brotizolam	80 000
Buprenorphine — Buprénorphine — Buprenorfina	300
Chlordiazepoxide — Chlordiazépoxide — Clordiazepóxido	150 000
Clobazam	100 000
Clonazepam — Clonazépam	20 000
Clorazepate — Clorazépate — Clorazepato	20 000
Clotiazepam — Clotiazépam	200 000
Dexamfetamine — Dexamfétamine — Dexanfetamina	50
Diazepam — Diazépam	1 000 000
Estazolam	1 000

Country (or territory) and substance Pays (ou territoire) et substance País (o territorio) y sustancia	Assessment (grams) Évaluation (en grammes) Previsión (en gramos)
Ethyl loflazepate — Loflazépate d'éthyle — Loflazepato de etilo	10 000
Flurazepam — Flurazépam	100 000
Gamma-hydroxybutyric acid (GHB) — Acide gamma-hydroxybutirique (GHB) — Ácido gamma-hidroxibutírico (GHB)	100
Loprazolam	100 000
Mazindol	5 000
Meprobamate — Méprobamate — Meprobamato	100
Metamfetamine racemate — Racémate de métamfétamine — Racemato de metanfetamina	100
Methylphenidate — Méthylphénidate — Metilfenidato	260 187
Midazolam	15 000
Nordazepam — Nordazépam	100
Pemoline — Pémoline — Pemolina	10 000
Pentazocine — Pentazocina	20 000
Pentobarbital	20 000
Phendimetrazine — Phendimétrazine — Fendimetracina	1 500 000
Phenmetrazine — Phenmétrazine — Fenmetracina	100
Phenobarbital — Phénobarbital — Fenobarbital	2 000 000
Phentermine — Fentermina	1 500 000
Pinazepam — Pinazépam	50 000
Temazepam — Témazépam	250 000
Triazolam	7 000
Zipeprol — Zipéprol	100 000
Zolpidem	300 000

Republic of Moldova — République de Moldova — República de Moldova

Alprazolam	2 000
Amobarbital	50 000
Bromazepam — Bromazépam	1 000
Buprenorphine — Buprénorphine — Buprenorfina	2 000
Butobarbital	2 000
Camazepam — Camazépam	1 000
Chlordiazepoxide — Chlordiazépoxide — Clordiazepóxido	20 000
Clonazepam — Clonazépam	1 500
Clorazepate — Clorazépate — Clorazepato	1 500
Cyclobarbital — Ciclobarbital	50 000
Diazepam — Diazépam	50 000
Flunitrazepam — Flunitrazépam	1 000
Flurazepam — Flurazépam	500
Gamma-hydroxybutyric acid (GHB) — Acide gamma-hydroxybutirique (GHB) — Ácido gamma-hidroxibutírico (GHB)	145 000
Ketazolam — Kétazolam	500
Medazepam — Médazépam	5 000
Meprobamate — Méprobamate — Meprobamato	125 000
Midazolam	500
Nitrazepam — Nitrazépam	5 000
Oxazepam — Oxazépam	22 500
Pentazocine — Pentazocina	2 000
Phenobarbital — Phénobarbital — Fenobarbital	256 000
Temazepam — Témazépam	2 000
Tetrazepam — Tétrazépam	2 000
Zolpidem	5 000

Table V. Assessments of annual domestic medical and scientific requirements
Tableau V. Évaluations des besoins annuels médicaux et scientifiques intérieurs
Cuadro V. Previsiones de las necesidades anuales internas para fines médicos y científicos

Country (or territory) and substance Pays (ou territoire) et substance País (o territorio) y sustancia	Assessment (grams) Évaluation (en grammes) Previsión (en gramos)
Romania — Roumanie — Rumania	
Alprazolam	100 000
Amfepramone — Amfépramone — Anfepramona	300 000
Barbital	10 000
Bromazepam — Bromazépam	100 000
Clonazepam — Clonazépam	20 000
Clorazepate — Clorazépate — Clorazepato	60 000
Diazepam — Diazépam	1 000 000
Flunitrazepam — Flunitrazépam	2 000
Lorazepam — Lorazépam	15 000
Medazepam — Médazépam	500 000
Meprobamate — Méprobamate — Meprobamato	10 000 000
Midazolam	180 000
Nitrazepam — Nitrazépam	150 000
Pentazocine — Pentazocina	250 000
Phenobarbital — Phénobarbital — Fenobarbital	8 000 000
Tetrazepam — Tétrazépam	150 000
Zolpidem	150 000
Russian Federation — Fédération de Russie — **Federación de Rusia**	
Alprazolam	60 000
Amobarbital	50 000
Bromazepam — Bromazépam	1 000
Buprenorphine — Buprénorphine — Buprenorfina	40 000
Butobarbital	250 000
Chlordiazepoxide — Chlordiazépoxide — Clordiazepóxido	1 000 000
Clonazepam — Clonazépam	150 000
Clorazepate — Clorazépate — Clorazepato	60 000
Cyclobarbital — Ciclobarbital	3 000 000
Diazepam — Diazépam	3 000 000
Flunitrazepam — Flunitrazépam	10 000
Lorazepam — Lorazépam	30 000
Medazepam — Médazépam	1 000 000
Meprobamate — Méprobamate — Meprobamato	50 000
Midazolam	30 000
Nitrazepam — Nitrazépam	1 000 000
Oxazepam — Oxazépam	1 500 000
Pentazocine — Pentazocina	50 000
Phenobarbital — Phénobarbital — Fenobarbital	200 000 000
Temazepam — Témazépam	30 000
Tetrazepam — Tétrazépam	30 000
Triazolam	20 000
Zolpidem	200 000
Rwanda	
Allobarbital — Alobarbital	10
Alprazolam	30
Amobarbital	15
Bromazepam — Bromazépam	850
Buprenorphine — Buprénorphine — Buprenorfina	10
Chlordiazepoxide — Chlordiazépoxide — Clordiazepóxido	50
Clobazam	500
Clonazepam — Clonazépam	500
Clorazepate — Clorazépate — Clorazepato	1 000
Cloxazolam	1
Diazepam — Diazépam	4 500
Flunitrazepam — Flunitrazépam	25
Flurazepam — Flurazépam	10

Country (or territory) and substance Pays (ou territoire) et substance País (o territorio) y sustancia	Assessment (grams) Évaluation (en grammes) Previsión (en gramos)
Ketazolam — Kétazolam	50
Lorazepam — Lorazépam	300
Lormetazepam — Lormétazépam	5
Meprobamate — Méprobamate — Meprobamato	50 000
Midazolam	10
Nitrazepam — Nitrazépam	100
Oxazepam — Oxazépam	200
Pemoline — Pémoline — Pemolina	50
Pentazocine — Pentazocina	4 500
Pentobarbital	1 500
Phendimetrazine — Phendimétrazine — Fendimetracina	50
Phenobarbital — Phénobarbital — Fenobarbital	250 000
Prazepam — Prazépam	100
Temazepam — Témazépam	5
Tetrazepam — Tétrazépam	120
Triazolam	1
Zolpidem	750
Saint Helena — Sainte-Hélène — Santa Elena	
Clonazepam — Clonazépam	25
Diazepam — Diazépam	45
Lorazepam — Lorazépam	8
Methylphenidate — Méthylphénidate — Metilfenidato	20
Midazolam	4
Nitrazepam — Nitrazépam	6
Phenobarbital — Phénobarbital — Fenobarbital	180
Temazepam — Témazépam	70
Saint Kitts and Nevis — Saint-Kitts-et-Nevis — **Saint Kitts y Nevis**	
Alprazolam	10
Amobarbital	3
Chlordiazepoxide — Chlordiazépoxide — Clordiazepóxido	200
Clobazam	50
Clonazepam — Clonazépam	10
Diazepam — Diazépam	500
Lorazepam — Lorazépam	50
Methylphenidate — Méthylphénidate — Metilfenidato	20
Midazolam	10
Nitrazepam — Nitrazépam	150
Pentazocine — Pentazocina	15
Pentobarbital	5 000
Phenobarbital — Phénobarbital — Fenobarbital	1 000
Saint Lucia — Sainte-Lucie — Santa Lucía	
Alprazolam	100
Bromazepam — Bromazépam	100
Buprenorphine — Buprénorphine — Buprenorfina	15
Chlordiazepoxide — Chlordiazépoxide — Clordiazepóxido	500
Clobazam	50
Clonazepam — Clonazépam	50
Clorazepate — Clorazépate — Clorazepato	200
Diazepam — Diazépam	2 000
Flurazepam — Flurazépam	50
Lorazepam — Lorazépam	300
Methylphenidate — Méthylphénidate — Metilfenidato	50
Midazolam	50
Nitrazepam — Nitrazépam	100

Table V. Assessments of annual domestic medical and scientific requirements
Tableau V. Évaluations des besoins annuels médicaux et scientifiques intérieurs
Cuadro V. Previsiones de las necesidades anuales internas
para fines médicos y científicos

Country (or territory) and substance Pays (ou territoire) et substance País (o territorio) y sustancia	Assessment (grams) Évaluation (en grammes) Previsión (en gramos)
Pentazocine — Pentazocina	50
Pentobarbital	2 400
Phenobarbital — Phénobarbital — Fenobarbital	6 000
Saint Vincent and the Grenadines — **Saint-Vincent-et-les-Grenadines —** **San Vicente y las Granadinas**	
Alprazolam	200
Butobarbital	1
Chlordiazepoxide — Chlordiazépoxide — Clordiazepóxido	500
Clobazam	50
Clonazepam — Clonazépam	50
Clorazepate — Clorazépate — Clorazepato	200
Diazepam — Diazépam	2 000
Flurazepam — Flurazépam	50
Lorazepam — Lorazépam	300
Medazepam — Médazépam	200
Meprobamate — Méprobamate — Meprobamato	100
Midazolam	50
Nitrazepam — Nitrazépam	200
Oxazepam — Oxazépam	200
Pentazocine — Pentazocina	300
Pentobarbital	300
Phenobarbital — Phénobarbital — Fenobarbital	6 000
Samoa	
Allobarbital — Alobarbital	1
Alprazolam	10
Amfepramone — Amfépramone — Anfepramona	1
Amfetamine — Amfétamine — Anfetamina	1
Aminorex	1
Amobarbital	2
Barbital	1
Bromazepam — Bromazépam	1
Buprenorphine — Buprénorphine — Buprenorfina	2
Butalbital	2
Butobarbital	1
Camazepam — Camazépam	1
Chlordiazepoxide — Chlordiazépoxide — Clordiazepóxido	200
Clonazepam — Clonazépam	60
Cyclobarbital — Ciclobarbital	2
Delta-9-tetrahydrocannabinol — *Delta*-9-tétrahydrocannabinol — *Delta*-9-tetrahidrocannabinol	1
Dexamfetamine — Dexamfétamine — Dexanfetamina	1
Diazepam — Diazépam	2 000
Flunitrazepam — Flunitrazépam	2
Glutethimide — Glutéthimide — Glutetimida	2
Haloxazolam	1
Levamfetamine — Lévamfétamine — Levanfetamina	1
Lorazepam — Lorazépam	50
Lormetazepam — Lormétazépam	1
Meprobamate — Méprobamate — Meprobamato	1
Mesocarb — Mésocarbe — Mesocarbo	1
Metamfetamine — Métamfétamine — Metanfetamina	1
Methylphenidate — Méthylphénidate — Metilfenidato	300
Midazolam	200
Nitrazepam — Nitrazépam	200
Oxazolam	1

Country (or territory) and substance Pays (ou territoire) et substance País (o territorio) y sustancia	Assessment (grams) Évaluation (en grammes) Previsión (en gramos)
Pentazocine — Pentazocina	50
Pentobarbital	1
Phenobarbital — Phénobarbital — Fenobarbital	3 000
Phentermine — Fentermina	200
Pinazepam — Pinazépam	1
Secbutabarbital	2
Secobarbital — Sécobarbital	1
Temazepam — Témazépam	1
Tetrazepam — Tétrazépam	1
Triazolam	1
Zipeprol — Zipéprol	1
Sao Tome and Principe — Sao Tomé-et-Principe — **Santo Tomé y Príncipe**	
Diazepam — Diazépam	2 000
Phenobarbital — Phénobarbital — Fenobarbital	1 000
Saudi Arabia — Arabie saoudite — Arabia Saudita	
Alprazolam	4 500
Amobarbital	200
Bromazepam — Bromazépam	16 890
Buprenorphine — Buprénorphine — Buprenorfina	1
Chlordiazepoxide — Chlordiazépoxide — Clordiazepóxido	2 500
Clobazam	2 300
Clonazepam — Clonazépam	15 000
Dexamfetamine — Dexamfétamine — Dexanfetamina	25
Diazepam — Diazépam	25 000
Flurazepam — Flurazépam	250
Lorazepam — Lorazépam	2 500
Methylphenidate — Méthylphénidate — Metilfenidato	45 000
Midazolam	28 000
Nitrazepam — Nitrazépam	875
Pemoline — Pémoline — Pemolina	55
Pentazocine — Pentazocina	70
Pentobarbital	30
Phenobarbital — Phénobarbital — Fenobarbital	380 000
Temazepam — Témazépam	2 600
Zolpidem	700
Senegal — Sénégal	
Alprazolam	1 285
Amfepramone — Amfépramone — Anfepramona	1 440
Bromazepam — Bromazépam	6 588
Buprenorphine — Buprénorphine — Buprenorfina	33
Chlordiazepoxide — Chlordiazépoxide — Clordiazepóxido	3 648
Clobazam	2 250
Clonazepam — Clonazépam	4 094
Clorazepate — Clorazépate — Clorazepato	19 000
Diazepam — Diazépam	15 000
Fenproporex	480
Lorazepam — Lorazépam	1 879
Meprobamate — Méprobamate — Meprobamato	190 000
Midazolam	27
Oxazepam — Oxazépam	4 500
Phenobarbital — Phénobarbital — Fenobarbital	1 378 000
Prazepam — Prazépam	46 080
Tetrazepam — Tétrazépam	28 800
Zolpidem	4 220

Table V. Assessments of annual domestic medical and scientific requirements
Tableau V. Évaluations des besoins annuels médicaux et scientifiques intérieurs
Cuadro V. Previsiones de las necesidades anuales internas para fines médicos y científicos

Country (or territory) and substance / Pays (ou territoire) et substance / País (o territorio) y sustancia	Assessment (grams) / Évaluation (en grammes) / Previsión (en gramos)
Serbia and Montenegro — Serbie-et-Monténégro — Serbia y Montenegro	
Alprazolam	28 000
Barbital	5 000
Bromazepam — Bromazépam	760 000
Brotizolam	260
Chlordiazepoxide — Chlordiazépoxide — Clordiazepóxido	1
Clonazepam — Clonazépam	8 000
Clorazepate — Clorazépate — Clorazepato	20 000
Diazepam — Diazépam	1 300 000
Lorazepam — Lorazépam	52 000
Methylphenidate — Méthylphénidate — Metilfenidato	2 000
Midazolam	70 000
Nordazepam — Nordazépam	1
Phenobarbital — Phénobarbital — Fenobarbital	1 310 000
Prazepam — Prazépam	200 000
Tetrazepam — Tétrazépam	200 000
Triazolam	1
Zolpidem	1 000
Seychelles	
Clonazepam — Clonazépam	100
Diazepam — Diazépam	1 000
Lorazepam — Lorazépam	11
Midazolam	50
Nitrazepam — Nitrazépam	2
Phenobarbital — Phénobarbital — Fenobarbital	3 540
Prazepam — Prazépam	100
Sierra Leone — Sierra Leona	
Alprazolam	500
Amfetamine — Amfétamine — Anfetamina	11
Chlordiazepoxide — Chlordiazépoxide — Clordiazepóxido	80
Clorazepate — Clorazépate — Clorazepato	10 000[a]
Diazepam — Diazépam	28 000
Loprazolam	2 000[a]
Lorazepam — Lorazépam	2 000
Meprobamate — Méprobamate — Meprobamato	3 000[a]
Metamfetamine — Métamfétamine — Metanfetamina	1
Nimetazepam — Nimétazépam	2 000[a]
Nitrazepam — Nitrazépam	1 000
Pemoline — Pémoline — Pemolina	1 000[a]
Pentazocine — Pentazocina	1 000
Pentobarbital	1 000[a]
Phenobarbital — Phénobarbital — Fenobarbital	51 000
Temazepam — Témazépam	7 000[a]
Singapore — Singapour — Singapur	
4-Bromo-2,5-dimethoxyphenyl-ethylamine (2C-B) — 4-bromo-2,5-diméthoxyphényléthylamine (2C-B) — 4-bromo-2,5-dimetoxifeniletilamina (2C-B)	5
Alprazolam	4 000
Amfepramone — Amfépramone — Anfepramona	5
Amfetamine — Amfétamine — Anfetamina	10
Amobarbital	50
Barbital	2 200
Benzfetamine — Benzfétamine — Benzfetamina	5
Bromazepam — Bromazépam	10 000
Buprenorphine — Buprénorphine — Buprenorfina	7 700
Butalbital	100
Cathine — Catina	100
Chlordiazepoxide — Chlordiazépoxide — Clordiazepóxido	172 500
Clobazam	5 000
Clonazepam — Clonazépam	5 000
Clorazepate — Clorazépate — Clorazepato	10 000
Delorazepam — Délorazépam	5
Delta-9-tetrahydrocannabinol — *Delta*-9-tétrahydrocannabinol — *Delta*-9-tetrahidrocannabinol	160
Dexamfetamine — Dexamfétamine — Dexanfetamina	25
Diazepam — Diazépam	100 000
Estazolam	5
Ethchlorvynol — Etclorvinol	5
Fenetylline — Fénétylline — Fenetilina	5
Fludiazepam — Fludiazépam	5
Flunitrazepam — Flunitrazépam	10
Flurazepam — Flurazépam	10 000
Gamma-hydroxybutyric acid (GHB) — Acide *gamma*-hydroxybutirique (GHB) — Ácido *gamma*-hidroxibutírico (GHB)	5
Glutethimide — Glutéthimide — Glutetimida	5
Halazepam — Halazépam	5
Loprazolam	5
Lorazepam — Lorazépam	10 000
Lormetazepam — Lormétazépam	3 000
Mazindol	1 000
Meprobamate — Méprobamate — Meprobamato	100 000
Metamfetamine — Métamfétamine — Metanfetamina	10
Methaqualone — Méthaqualone — Metacualona	5
Methylphenidate — Méthylphénidate — Metilfenidato	10 000
Midazolam	70 000
Nimetazepam — Nimétazépam	5 000
Nitrazepam — Nitrazépam	15 000
Nordazepam — Nordazépam	3 000
Oxazepam — Oxazépam	5
Pentazocine — Pentazocina	5 000
Pentobarbital	20 000
Phencyclidine (PCP) — Fenciclidina (PCP)	5
Phendimetrazine — Phendimétrazine — Fendimetracina	5
Phenmetrazine — Phenmétrazine — Fenmetracina	5
Phenobarbital — Phénobarbital — Fenobarbital	2 535 000
Phentermine — Fentermina	150 000
Pinazepam — Pinazépam	2 500
Prazepam — Prazépam	5
Secobarbital — Sécobarbital	505
Temazepam — Témazépam	5
Triazolam	5
Zolpidem	15 000
Slovakia — Slovaquie — Eslovaquia	
Allobarbital — Alobarbital	100 000
Alprazolam	25 000
Amfetamine — Amfétamine — Anfetamina	1
Amobarbital	500
Barbital	15 000
Bromazepam — Bromazépam	70 000
Buprenorphine — Buprénorphine — Buprenorfina	7 000
Butalbital	10

Table V. Assessments of annual domestic medical and scientific requirements
Tableau V. Évaluations des besoins annuels médicaux et scientifiques intérieurs
Cuadro V. Previsiones de las necesidades anuales internas para fines médicos y científicos

Country (or territory) and substance Pays (ou territoire) et substance País (o territorio) y sustancia	Assessment (grams) Évaluation (en grammes) Previsión (en gramos)
Butobarbital....................	50 000
Cathine — Catina.................	10
Chlordiazepoxide — Chlordiazépoxide — Clordiazepóxido..................	120 000
Clobazam.......................	15 000
Clonazepam — Clonazépam...........	20 000
Clorazepate — Clorazépate — Clorazepato.........	10 000
Cyclobarbital — Ciclobarbital..........	1 000
Delta-9-tetrahydrocannabinol — *Delta*-9-tétrahydrocannabinol — *Delta*-9-tetrahidrocannabinol..................	1
Dexamfetamine —Dexamfétamine —Dexanfetamina..	1
Diazepam — Diazépam...............	1 500 000
Flunitrazepam — Flunitrazépam........	30 000
Glutethimide — Glutéthimide — Glutetimida.......	10
Levamfetamine —Lévamfétamine — Levanfetamina..	1
Lorazepam — Lorazépam.............	200 000
Lormetazepam — Lormétazépam.........	5
Mazindol......................	1 000
Medazepam — Médazépam...........	100 000
Metamfetamine —Métamfétamine — Metanfetamina..	1
Methylphenidate —Méthylphénidate — Metilfenidato..	30
Midazolam.....................	25 000
Nitrazepam — Nitrazépam.............	200 000
Nordazepam — Nordazépam...........	1
Oxazepam — Oxazépam.............	200 000
Pentazocine — Pentazocina...........	50 000
Pentobarbital....................	1 000
Phenmetrazine — Phenmétrazine — Fenmetracina..	50
Phenobarbital — Phénobarbital — Fenobarbital	3 000 000
Phentermine — Fentermina.............	60 000
Tetrazepam — Tétrazépam.............	200 000
Triazolam	1
Zolpidem	1 000 000
Slovenia — Slovénie — Eslovenia	
Alprazolam	800 000
Amfetamine — Amfétamine — Anfetamina	5
Barbital	8 140
Bromazepam — Bromazépam.............	550 000
Buprenorphine — Buprénorphine — Buprenorfina	5 500
Clobazam	5 500
Clonazepam — Clonazépam.............	2 200
Clorazepate — Clorazépate — Clorazepato.........	2 200
Delta-9-tetrahydrocannabinol — *Delta*-9-tétrahydrocannabinol — *Delta*-9-tetrahidrocannabinol..................	3
Diazepam — Diazépam...............	660 000
Flurazepam — Flurazépam.............	264 000
Lorazepam — Lorazépam.............	44 000
Medazepam — Médazépam...........	330 000
Meprobamate — Méprobamate — Meprobamato	33 000
Metamfetamine —Métamfétamine — Metanfetamina..	5
Methylphenidate —Méthylphénidate — Metilfenidato..	1 320
Methylphenobarbital — Méthylphénobarbital — Metilfenobarbital......................	330 000
Midazolam.....................	27 500
Nitrazepam — Nitrazépam.............	2 500
Oxazepam — Oxazépam.............	49 500
Pentazocine — Pentazocina...........	660 000
Pentobarbital....................	40 000
Phenobarbital — Phénobarbital — Fenobarbital	165 000
Prazepam — Prazépam...............	30 000

Country (or territory) and substance Pays (ou territoire) et substance País (o territorio) y sustancia	Assessment (grams) Évaluation (en grammes) Previsión (en gramos)
Temazepam — Témazépam	100
Triazolam	200
Zolpidem......................	440 000
Solomon Islands — Îles Salomon — Islas Salomón	
Diazepam — Diazépam................	200
Midazolam.....................	100
Phenobarbital — Phénobarbital — Fenobarbital	4 500
Somalia — Somalie	
Chlordiazepoxide — Chlordiazépoxide — Clordiazepóxido..................	68 000
Diazepam — Diazépam...............	50 000ᵃ
Nitrazepam — Nitrazépam.............	1 000ᵃ
Pentazocine — Pentazocina...........	600
Phenobarbital — Phénobarbital — Fenobarbital	100 000ᵃ
South Africa — Afrique du Sud — Sudáfrica	
Alprazolam	44 000
Amfepramone — Amfépramone — Anfepramona	51 000
Amobarbital	10 000
Barbital	12 000
Benzfetamine — Benzfétamine — Benzfetamina	1 000
Bromazepam — Bromazépam.............	249 000
Brotizolam	1 000
Buprenorphine — Buprénorphine — Buprenorfina	3 000
Butalbital	12 000
Butobarbital	2 000
Cathine — Catina..................	4 354 800
Chlordiazepoxide — Chlordiazépoxide — Clordiazepóxido..................	80 000
Clobazam	60 000
Clonazepam — Clonazépam...........	30 000
Clorazepate — Clorazépate — Clorazepato.........	11 000
Dexamfetamine —Dexamfétamine —Dexanfetamina..	146
Diazepam — Diazépam...............	3 500 000
Fludiazepam — Fludiazépam...........	1 000
Flunitrazepam — Flunitrazépam........	30 000
Flurazepam — Flurazépam.............	26 000
Ketazolam — Kétazolam	54 000
Loprazolam	22 000
Lorazepam — Lorazépam.............	80 000
Lormetazepam — Lormétazépam.........	10 000
Meprobamate — Méprobamate — Meprobamato	65 000 000
Metamfetamine —Métamfétamine — Metanfetamina..	1
Methylphenidate —Méthylphénidate — Metilfenidato..	348 000
Midazolam.....................	140 000
Nitrazepam — Nitrazépam.............	40 000
Oxazepam — Oxazépam.............	1 014 000
Pemoline — Pémoline — Pemolina	80 000
Pentazocine — Pentazocina...........	14 000
Pentobarbital....................	1 360 000
Phendimetrazine — Phendimétrazine — Fendimetracina..................	60 000
Phenobarbital — Phénobarbital — Fenobarbital	7 000 000
Phentermine — Fentermina.............	150 000
Pipradrol	1 000
Prazepam — Prazépam...............	50 000
Secobarbital — Sécobarbital	500
Temazepam — Témazépam	286 000
Triazolam	4 000
Zolpidem......................	360 000

319

Table V.   Assessments of annual domestic medical and scientific requirements
Tableau V.   Évaluations des besoins annuels médicaux et scientifiques intérieurs
Cuadro V.   Previsiones de las necesidades anuales internas
para fines médicos y científicos

Country (or territory) and substance Pays (ou territoire) et substance País (o territorio) y sustancia	Assessment (grams) Évaluation (en grammes) Previsión (en gramos)	Country (or territory) and substance Pays (ou territoire) et substance País (o territorio) y sustancia	Assessment (grams) Évaluation (en grammes) Previsión (en gramos)
Spain — Espagne — España		**Sri Lanka**	
Alprazolam	450 000	Alprazolam	3 500
Amfepramone — Amfépramone — Anfepramona	100	Amfetamine — Amfétamine — Anfetamina	1
Amfetamine — Amfétamine — Anfetamina	1 000	Barbital	1 101
Amobarbital	100	Bromazepam — Bromazépam	1 700
Barbital	100 000	Chlordiazepoxide — Chlordiazépoxide —	
Benzfetamine — Benzfétamine — Benzfetamina	100	Clordiazepóxido	55 000
Bromazepam — Bromazépam	600 000	Clobazam	50 000
Brotizolam	10 000	Clonazepam — Clonazépam	9 625
Buprenorphine — Buprénorphine — Buprenorfina	90 000	Delta-9-tetrahydrocannabinol —	
Butalbital	70 000	Delta-9-tétrahydrocannabinol —	
Camazepam — Camazépam	100	Delta-9-tetrahidrocannabinol	1
Cathine — Catina	10	Diazepam — Diazépam	410 000
Chlordiazepoxide — Chlordiazépoxide —		Flurazepam — Flurazépam	5
Clordiazepóxido	2 000 000	Lorazepam — Lorazépam	4 285
Clobazam	250 000	Metamfetamine — Métamfétamine — Metanfetamina	1
Clonazepam — Clonazépam	80 000	Methylphenidate — Méthylphénidate — Metilfenidato	4 920
Clorazepate — Clorazépate — Clorazepato	10 000 000	Midazolam	9 250
Clotiazepam — Clotiazépam	100 000	Nitrazepam — Nitrazépam	3 800
Cloxazolam	1 000	Nordazepam — Nordazépam	1
Delta-9-tetrahydrocannabinol —		Oxazepam — Oxazépam	1
Delta-9-tétrahydrocannabinol —		Pentazocine — Pentazocina	3 300
Delta-9-tetrahidrocannabinol	15	Phenobarbital — Phénobarbital — Fenobarbital	1 401 000
Dexamfetamine — Dexamfétamine — Dexanfetamina	80	Phentermine — Fentermina	1 200
Diazepam — Diazépam	5 000 000	Temazepam — Témazépam	375
Etilamfetamine — Étilamfétamine — Etilanfetamina	1	Zolpidem	8 000
Fenetylline — Fénétylline — Fenetilina	1		
Fenproporex	1 000	**Sudan — Soudan — Sudán**	
Flunitrazepam — Flunitrazépam	32 000	Allobarbital — Alobarbital	5 000
Flurazepam — Flurazépam	1 500 000	Alprazolam	1 000
Gamma-hydroxybutyric acid (GHB) —		Bromazepam — Bromazépam	80 000
Acide gamma-hydroxybutirique (GHB) —		Chlordiazepoxide — Chlordiazépoxide —	
Ácido gamma-hidroxibutírico (GHB)	10 000	Clordiazepóxido	80 000
Halazepam — Halazépam	1 500 000	Clonazepam — Clonazépam	10 000
Ketazolam — Kétazolam	1 500 000	Diazepam — Diazépam	60 000
Loprazolam	50 000	Lorazepam — Lorazépam	6 000
Lorazepam — Lorazépam	1 300 000	Lormetazepam — Lormétazépam	100
Lormetazepam — Lormétazépam	700 000	Meprobamate — Méprobamate — Meprobamato	100 000
Mazindol	1 000	Methylphenidate — Méthylphénidate — Metilfenidato	600
Medazepam — Médazépam	500 000	Nitrazepam — Nitrazépam	7 000
Mefenorex — Méfénorex	500	Pentazocine — Pentazocina	600
Meprobamate — Méprobamate — Meprobamato	1 500 000	Phenobarbital — Phénobarbital — Fenobarbital	180 000
Metamfetamine — Métamfétamine — Metanfetamina	10		
Methaqualone — Méthaqualone — Metacualona	50	**Suriname**	
Methylphenidate — Méthylphénidate — Metilfenidato	2 000 000	Clonazepam — Clonazépam	300
Methylphenobarbital — Méthylphénobarbital —		Clorazepate — Clorazépate — Clorazepato	3 000
Metilfenobarbital	1 000	Diazepam — Diazépam	45 000
Midazolam	250 000	Lorazepam — Lorazépam	900
Nitrazepam — Nitrazépam	150 000	Methylphenidate — Méthylphénidate — Metilfenidato	250
Nordazepam — Nordazépam	1 000	Phenobarbital — Phénobarbital — Fenobarbital	40 000
Oxazepam — Oxazépam	1 000 000		
Oxazolam	100	**Swaziland — Swazilandia**	
Pemoline — Pémoline — Pemolina	100 000	Alprazolam	1
Pentazocine — Pentazocina	10 000	Amfetamine — Amfétamine — Anfetamina	1
Pentobarbital	500 000	Bromazepam — Bromazépam	1 800
Phencyclidine (PCP) — Fenciclidina (PCP)	1	Brotizolam	50
Phenobarbital — Phénobarbital — Fenobarbital	4 000 000	Cathine — Catina	100
Pinazepam — Pinazépam	1 000	Chlordiazepoxide — Chlordiazépoxide —	
Prazepam — Prazépam	200 000	Clordiazepóxido	120
Secobarbital — Sécobarbital	1 000	Clonazepam — Clonazépam	125
Tetrazepam — Tétrazépam	20 000 000		
Triazolam	2 000		
Zipeprol — Zipéprol	940		
Zolpidem	6 000 000		

Table V. Assessments of annual domestic medical and scientific requirements
Tableau V. Évaluations des besoins annuels médicaux et scientifiques intérieurs
Cuadro V. Previsiones de las necesidades anuales internas para fines médicos y científicos

Country (or territory) and substance Pays (ou territoire) et substance País (o territorio) y sustancia	Assessment (grams) Évaluation (en grammes) Previsión (en gramos)

Delta-9-tetrahydrocannabinol —
  Delta-9-tétrahydrocannabinol —
  Delta-9-tetrahidrocannabinol
	1

Diazepam — Diazépam	2 000
Flunitrazepam — Flunitrazépam	1
Loprazolam	50
Lorazepam — Lorazépam	100
Lormetazepam — Lormétazépam	10
Meprobamate — Méprobamate — Meprobamato	600 000
Metamfetamine — Métamfétamine — Metanfetamina	1
Methylphenidate — Méthylphénidate — Metilfenidato	50
Midazolam	250
Nitrazepam — Nitrazépam	320
Oxazepam — Oxazépam	100
Pentobarbital	1 700
Phenobarbital — Phénobarbital — Fenobarbital	2 000
Temazepam — Témazépam	700
Triazolam	100
Zolpidem	50
Sweden — Suède — Suecia	
Alprazolam	29 000
Amfepramone — Amfépramone — Anfepramona	100
Amfetamine — Amfétamine — Anfetamina	14 600
Amobarbital	3 000
Barbital	50 000
Bromazepam — Bromazépam	100
Buprenorphine — Buprénorphine — Buprenorfina	25 250
Cathine — Catina	10
Chlordiazepoxide — Chlordiazépoxide — Clordiazepóxido	4 000
Clobazam	4 000
Clonazepam — Clonazépam	8 500
Clorazepate — Clorazépate — Clorazepato	500

Delta-9-tetrahydrocannabinol —
  Delta-9-tétrahydrocannabinol —
  Delta-9-tetrahidrocannabinol
	100

Dexamfetamine — Dexamfétamine — Dexanfetamina	11 000
Diazepam — Diazépam	216 000
Flunitrazepam — Flunitrazépam	13 750

Gamma-hydroxybutyric acid (GHB) —
  Acide *gamma*-hydroxybutirique (GHB) —
  Ácido *gamma*-hidroxibutírico (GHB)
	64 080

Lorazepam — Lorazépam	25 935
Medazepam — Médazépam	20
Meprobamate — Méprobamate — Meprobamato	1 200 000
Metamfetamine — Métamfétamine — Metanfetamina	5
Methylphenidate — Méthylphénidate — Metilfenidato	271 530
Methylphenobarbital — Méthylphénobarbital — Metilfenobarbital	1 000
Midazolam	10 500
Nitrazepam — Nitrazépam	100 000
Oxazepam — Oxazépam	868 350
Pentazocine — Pentazocina	2 000
Pentobarbital	680 000
Phencyclidine (PCP) — Fenciclidina (PCP)	10
Phenmetrazine — Phenmétrazine — Fenmetracina	5
Phenobarbital — Phénobarbital — Fenobarbital	400 000
Phentermine — Fentermina	500
Secobarbital — Sécobarbital	41 500
Triazolam	300
Zolpidem	969 000

Country (or territory) and substance Pays (ou territoire) et substance País (o territorio) y sustancia	Assessment (grams) Évaluation (en grammes) Previsión (en gramos)
Switzerland — Suisse — Suiza	

4-Bromo-2,5-dimethoxyphenyl-ethylamine (2C-B) —
  4-bromo-2,5-diméthoxyphényléthylamine (2C-B) —
  4-bromo-2,5-dimetoxifeniletilamina (2C-B)
	10

Allobarbital — Alobarbital	600 000
Alprazolam	500 000
Amfepramone — Amfépramone — Anfepramona	500 000
Amfetamine — Amfétamine — Anfetamina	10 000
Amobarbital	100 000
Barbital	250 000
Bromazepam — Bromazépam	4 000 000
Brotizolam	150 000
Buprenorphine — Buprénorphine — Buprenorfina	10 000
Butalbital	100 000
Cathine — Catina	1 000 000
Chlordiazepoxide — Chlordiazépoxide — Clordiazepóxido	10 000 000
Clobazam	250 000
Clonazepam — Clonazépam	500 000
Clorazepate — Clorazépate — Clorazepato	700 000
Cloxazolam	150 000
Cyclobarbital — Ciclobarbital	10 000
Delorazepam — Délorazépam	5 000

Delta-9-tetrahydrocannabinol —
  Delta-9-tétrahydrocannabinol —
  Delta-9-tetrahidrocannabinol
	5 000

Dexamfetamine — Dexamfétamine — Dexanfetamina	10 000
Diazepam — Diazépam	9 000 000
Ethyl loflazepate — Loflazépate d'éthyle — Loflazepato de etilo	10 000
Etilamfetamine — Étilamfétamine — Etilanfetamina	10 000
Fenetylline — Fénétylline — Fenetilina	10
Fenproporex	1 000 000
Flunitrazepam — Flunitrazépam	300 000
Flurazepam — Flurazépam	5 000 000

Gamma-hydroxybutyric acid (GHB) —
  Acide *gamma*-hydroxybutirique (GHB) —
  Ácido *gamma*-hidroxibutírico (GHB)
	200 000

Glutethimide — Glutéthimide — Glutetimida	1 000
Ketazolam — Kétazolam	400 000
Levamfetamine — Lévamfétamine — Levanfetamina	100
Levomethamphetamine — Lévométhamphétamine — Levometanfetamina	100
Lorazepam — Lorazépam	600 000
Lormetazepam — Lormétazépam	50 000
Mazindol	100 000
Medazepam — Médazépam	500 000
Meprobamate — Méprobamate — Meprobamato	15 000 000
Metamfetamine — Métamfétamine — Metanfetamina	2 000
Methaqualone — Méthaqualone — Metacualona	2 000
Methylphenidate — Méthylphénidate — Metilfenidato	5 000 000
Methylphenobarbital — Méthylphénobarbital — Metilfenobarbital	400 000
Midazolam	500 000
Nitrazepam — Nitrazépam	1 000 000
Nordazepam — Nordazépam	100 000
Oxazepam — Oxazépam	2 000 000
Pemoline — Pémoline — Pemolina	300 000
Pentazocine — Pentazocina	500 000
Pentobarbital	1 000 000
Phencyclidine (PCP) — Fenciclidina (PCP)	1 000
Phenobarbital — Phénobarbital — Fenobarbital	40 000 000

Table V.   Assessments of annual domestic medical and scientific requirements
Tableau V.   Évaluations des besoins annuels médicaux et scientifiques intérieurs
Cuadro V.   Previsiones de las necesidades anuales internas
para fines médicos y científicos

Country (or territory) and substance Pays (ou territoire) et substance País (o territorio) y sustancia	Assessment (grams) Évaluation (en grammes) Previsión (en gramos)
Switzerland — Suisse — Suiza	
(continued — suite — continuación)	
Phentermine — Fentermina	500 000
Prazepam — Prazépam	150 000
Secbutabarbital	100 000
Secobarbital — Sécobarbital	10 000
Temazepam — Témazépam	1 000 000
Tetrazepam — Tétrazépam	100 000
Triazolam	50 000
Zipeprol — Zipéprol	2 000 000
Zolpidem	1 000 000
Syrian Arab Rep. — Rép. arabe syrienne —	
Rep. Árabe Siria	
Alprazolam	35 000
Bromazepam — Bromazépam	35 000
Chlordiazepoxide — Chlordiazépoxide —	
Clordiazepóxido	500 000
Clobazam	60 000
Clonazepam — Clonazépam	10 000
Clorazepate — Clorazépate — Clorazepato	80 000
Diazepam — Diazépam	150 000
Lorazepam — Lorazépam	20 000
Medazepam — Médazépam	20 000
Meprobamate — Méprobamate — Meprobamato	2 000 000
Methylphenidate — Méthylphénidate — Metilfenidato	1 500
Midazolam	55 000
Nitrazepam — Nitrazépam	10 000
Pentazocine — Pentazocina	70 000
Phenobarbital — Phénobarbital — Fenobarbital	2 500 000
Zolpidem	50 000
Tajikistan — Tadjikistan — Tayikistán	
Alprazolam	185
Clonazepam — Clonazépam	300
Diazepam — Diazépam	36 000
Lorazepam — Lorazépam	410
Medazepam — Médazépam	6 100
Meprobamate — Méprobamate — Meprobamato	610
Midazolam	410
Nitrazepam — Nitrazépam	6 100
Oxazepam — Oxazépam	6 100
Phenobarbital — Phénobarbital — Fenobarbital	204 000
Temazepam — Témazépam	400
Tetrazepam — Tétrazépam	300
Triazolam	200
Thailand — Thaïlande — Tailandia	
Alprazolam	100 000
Amfepramone — Amfépramone — Anfepramona	600 000
Amfetamine — Amfétamine — Anfetamina	1
Amobarbital	170 000
Barbital	12 000
Bromazepam — Bromazépam	16 000
Buprenorphine — Buprénorphine — Buprenorfina	400
Butobarbital	300 000
Cathine — Catina	40 000
Chlordiazepoxide — Chlordiazépoxide —	
Clordiazepóxido	500 000
Clobazam	60 000
Clonazepam — Clonazépam	50 000
Clorazepate — Clorazépate — Clorazepato	500 000

Country (or territory) and substance Pays (ou territoire) et substance País (o territorio) y sustancia	Assessment (grams) Évaluation (en grammes) Previsión (en gramos)
Delta-9-tetrahydrocannabinol —	
Delta-9-tétrahydrocannabinol —	
Delta-9-tetrahidrocannabinol	1
Diazepam — Diazépam	5 000 000
Ethyl loflazepate — Loflazépate d'éthyle —	
Loflazepato de etilo	2 500
Etilamfetamine — Étilamfétamine — Etilanfetamina	60 000
Fencamfamin — Fencamfamine — Fencanfamina	1
Flunitrazepam — Flunitrazépam	3 500
Flurazepam — Flurazépam	100 000
Gamma-hydroxybutyric acid (GHB) —	
Acide *gamma*-hydroxybutirique (GHB) —	
Ácido *gamma*-hidroxibutírico (GHB)	20
Lorazepam — Lorazépam	90 000
Lormetazepam — Lormétazépam	1 500
Mazindol	300
Medazepam — Médazépam	7 000
Metamfetamine — Métamfétamine — Metanfetamina	20
Methaqualone — Méthaqualone — Metacualona	1
Methylphenidate — Méthylphénidate — Metilfenidato	13 000
Midazolam	250 000
Nitrazepam — Nitrazépam	7 000
Nordazepam — Nordazépam	1
Pemoline — Pémoline — Pemolina	1
Pentazocine — Pentazocina	30 000
Pentobarbital	100 000
Phencyclidine (PCP) — Fenciclidina (PCP)	1
Phenmetrazine — Phenmétrazine — Fenmetracina	1
Phenobarbital — Phénobarbital — Fenobarbital	5 000 000
Phentermine — Fentermina	2 500 000
Pinazepam — Pinazépam	30 000
Prazepam — Prazépam	40 000
Secobarbital — Sécobarbital	1
Temazepam — Témazépam	80 000
Triazolam	500
The former Yugoslav Rep. of Macedonia —	
L'ex-Rép. yougoslave de Macédoine —	
La ex Rep. Yugoslava de Macedonia	
Alprazolam	6 000
Bromazepam — Bromazépam	260 100
Clorazepate — Clorazépate — Clorazepato	1 500
Diazepam — Diazépam	250 000
Flurazepam — Flurazépam	7 000
Lorazepam — Lorazépam	16 000
Medazepam — Médazépam	17 000
Nitrazepam — Nitrazépam	1 000
Pentazocine — Pentazocina	1 100
Phenobarbital — Phénobarbital — Fenobarbital	260 000
Prazepam — Prazépam	42 000
Timor-Leste	
Diazepam — Diazépam	5 000
Phenobarbital — Phénobarbital — Fenobarbital	1 500
Togo	
Alprazolam	1
Bromazepam — Bromazépam	4 950
Buprenorphine — Buprénorphine — Buprenorfina	9
Chlordiazepoxide — Chlordiazépoxide —	
Clordiazepóxido	90
Clobazam	540

Table V.   Assessments of annual domestic medical and scientific requirements
Tableau V.   Évaluations des besoins annuels médicaux et scientifiques intérieurs
Cuadro V.   Previsiones de las necesidades anuales internas para fines médicos y científicos

Country (or territory) and substance Pays (ou territoire) et substance País (o territorio) y sustancia	Assessment (grams) Évaluation (en grammes) Previsión (en gramos)
Clonazepam — Clonazépam	1 000
Clorazepate — Clorazépate — Clorazepato	7 200
Diazepam — Diazépam	15 000
Lorazepam — Lorazépam	360
Meprobamate — Méprobamate — Meprobamato	2 400
Midazolam	2
Nitrazepam — Nitrazépam	360
Oxazepam — Oxazépam	525
Pentazocine — Pentazocina.................	30
Phenobarbital — Phénobarbital — Fenobarbital	210 000
Prazepam — Prazépam	2 500
Tetrazepam — Tétrazépam.................	2 520
Zolpidem.............................	720
Tonga	
Alprazolam	10
Amfetamine — Amfétamine — Anfetamina	5
Clonazepam — Clonazépam	200
Diazepam — Diazépam.....................	700
Methylphenidate — Méthylphénidate — Metilfenidato ..	40
Midazolam.............................	1 000
Nitrazepam — Nitrazépam	500
Phenobarbital — Phénobarbital — Fenobarbital	3 000
Temazepam — Témazépam	50
Triazolam	3
Trinidad and Tobago — Trinité-et-Tobago — **Trinidad y Tabago**	
Alprazolam	1 000
Amfetamine — Amfétamine — Anfetamina	3
Amobarbital...........................	56
Barbital	56
Bromazepam — Bromazépam.................	1 000
Brotizolam	570
Butalbital	1 155
Butobarbital...........................	825
Cathine — Catina.......................	56
Chlordiazepoxide — Chlordiazépoxide — Clordiazepóxido	1 705
Clobazam	2 000
Clonazepam — Clonazépam	1 000
Clorazepate — Clorazépate — Clorazepato	1 000
Cyclobarbital — Ciclobarbital	56
Diazepam — Diazépam.....................	44 055
Fencamfamin — Fencamfamine — Fencanfamina ...	56
Fenetylline — Fénétylline — Fenetilina	2
Fenproporex	56
Flunitrazepam — Flunitrazépam	60
Flurazepam — Flurazépam	935
Lorazepam — Lorazépam	3 000
Lormetazepam — Lormétazépam	500
Mazindol	99
Mecloqualone — Mécloqualone — Meclocualona	2
Medazepam — Médazépam	56
Meprobamate — Méprobamate — Meprobamato	5 555
Metamfetamine — Métamfétamine — Metanfetamina ..	3
Methaqualone — Méthaqualone — Metacualona.....	2
Methylphenidate — Méthylphénidate — Metilfenidato ..	2 500
Midazolam............................	2 500
Nitrazepam — Nitrazépam.................	220
Oxazepam — Oxazépam....................	56
Pentazocine — Pentazocina	2 000
Pentobarbital	3 355

Country (or territory) and substance Pays (ou territoire) et substance País (o territorio) y sustancia	Assessment (grams) Évaluation (en grammes) Previsión (en gramos)
Phenobarbital — Phénobarbital — Fenobarbital	60 000
Phentermine — Fentermina..................	4 455
Secobarbital — Sécobarbital	2
Temazepam — Témazépam	209
Tetrazepam — Tétrazépam..................	56
Triazolam	143
Vinylbital — Vinilbital	56
Tristan da Cunha — Tristán da Cunha	
Diazepam — Diazépam....................	1 500
Lorazepam — Lorazépam	1
Midazolam............................	5
Tunisia — Tunisie — Túnez	
4-Bromo-2,5-dimethoxyphenyl-ethylamine (2C-B) — 4-bromo-2,5-diméthoxyphényléthylamine (2C-B) — 4-bromo-2,5-dimetoxifeniletilamina (2C-B)	1
Allobarbital — Alobarbital	2
Alprazolam	1 200
Amfepramone — Amfépramone — Anfepramona	2
Amfetamine — Amfétamine — Anfetamina	2
Amineptin — Amineptine — Amineptina...........	2
Aminorex.............................	2
Amobarbital...........................	2
Barbital	2
Benzfetamine — Benzfétamine — Benzfetamina	1
Bromazepam — Bromazépam.................	40 000
Brotizolam............................	1
Buprenorphine — Buprénorphine — Buprenorfina	25
Butalbital.............................	2
Butobarbital...........................	1
Camazepam — Camazépam.................	1
Cathine — Catina.......................	2
Chlordiazepoxide — Chlordiazépoxide — Clordiazepóxido	17 000
Clobazam	60 000
Clonazepam — Clonazépam	2 200
Clorazepate — Clorazépate — Clorazepato	130 000
Clotiazepam — Clotiazépam	1
Cloxazolam	1
Cyclobarbital — Ciclobarbital	2
Delorazepam — Délorazépam	1
Delta-9-tetrahydrocannabinol — *Delta*-9-tétrahydrocannabinol — *Delta*-9-tetrahidrocannabinol	1
Dexamfetamine — Dexamfétamine — Dexanfetamina ..	2
Diazepam — Diazépam.....................	30 000
Estazolam	1
Ethchlorvynol — Etclorvinol	1
Ethinamate — Éthinamate — Etinamato	1
Ethyl loflazepate — Loflazépate d'éthyle — Loflazepato de etilo	1
Etilamfetamine — Étilamfétamine — Etilanfetamina ..	1
Fencamfamin — Fencamfamine — Fencanfamina ..	1
Fenetylline — Fénétylline — Fenetilina	1
Fenproporex	1
Fludiazepam — Fludiazépam	1
Flunitrazepam — Flunitrazépam	2
Flurazepam — Flurazépam	1
Gamma-hydroxybutyric acid (GHB) — Acide *gamma*-hydroxybutirique (GHB) — Ácido *gamma*-hidroxibutírico (GHB)	2
Glutethimide — Glutéthimide — Glutetimida	1

323

Table V. Assessments of annual domestic medical and scientific requirements
Tableau V. Évaluations des besoins annuels médicaux et scientifiques intérieurs
Cuadro V. Previsiones de las necesidades anuales internas para fines médicos y científicos

Country (or territory) and substance / Pays (ou territoire) et substance / País (o territorio) y sustancia	Assessment (grams) / Évaluation (en grammes) / Previsión (en gramos)
Tunisia — Tunisie — Túnez	
(continued — suite — continuación)	
Halazepam — Halazépam	1
Haloxazolam	1
Ketazolam — Kétazolam	1
Lefetamine (SPA) — Léfétamine (SPA) — Lefetamina (SPA)	1
Levamfetamine — Lévamfétamine — Levanfetamina	2
Levomethamphetamine — Lévométhamphétamine — Levometanfetamina	2
Loprazolam	1
Lorazepam — Lorazépam	24 000
Lormetazepam — Lormétazépam	1
Mazindol	1
Mecloqualone — Mécloqualone — Meclocualona	2
Medazepam — Médazépam	1
Mefenorex — Méfénorex	1
Meprobamate — Méprobamate — Meprobamato	3 600 000
Mesocarb — Mésocarbe — Mesocarbo	1
Metamfetamine — Métamfétamine — Metanfetamina	2
Metamfetamine racemate — Racémate de métamfétamine — Racemato de metanfetamina	2
Methaqualone — Méthaqualone — Metacualona	2
Methylphenidate — Méthylphénidate — Metilfenidato	1 000
Methylphenobarbital — Méthylphénobarbital — Metilfenobarbital	2
Methyprylon — Méthyprylone — Metiprilona	1
Midazolam	9 000
Nimetazepam — Nimétazépam	1
Nitrazepam — Nitrazépam	15
Nordazepam — Nordazépam	1
Oxazepam — Oxazépam	2
Oxazolam	1
Pemoline — Pémoline — Pemolina	1
Pentazocine — Pentazocina	2
Pentobarbital	2
Phencyclidine (PCP) — Fenciclidina (PCP)	1
Phendimetrazine — Phendimétrazine — Fendimetracina	1
Phenmetrazine — Phenmétrazine — Fenmetracina	1
Phenobarbital — Phénobarbital — Fenobarbital	1 200 000
Phentermine — Fentermina	1
Pinazepam — Pinazépam	1
Pipradrol	1
Prazepam — Prazépam	140 000
Pyrovalerone — Pyrovalérone — Pirovalerona	1
Secbutabarbital	1
Secobarbital — Sécobarbital	2
Temazepam — Témazépam	2
Tetrazepam — Tétrazépam	140 000
Triazolam	2
Vinylbital — Vinilbital	1
Zipeprol — Zipéprol	1
Zolpidem	20 000
Turkey — Turquie — Turquía	
Allobarbital — Alobarbital	550 000
Alprazolam	38 000
Amfetamine — Amfétamine — Anfetamina	4
Amobarbital	1
Bromazepam — Bromazépam	1
Brotizolam	500
Buprenorphine — Buprénorphine — Buprenorfina	4
Cathine — Catina	1
Chlordiazepoxide — Chlordiazépoxide — Clordiazepóxido	300 000
Clobazam	40
Clonazepam — Clonazépam	35 000
Clorazepate — Clorazépate — Clorazepato	50 000
Delta-9-tetrahydrocannabinol — *Delta*-9-tétrahydrocannabinol — *Delta*-9-tetrahidrocannabinol	20
Diazepam — Diazépam	400 000
Flunitrazepam — Flunitrazépam	1
Lorazepam — Lorazépam	5 000
Medazepam — Médazépam	700 000
Meprobamate — Méprobamate — Meprobamato	5 000 000
Methylphenidate — Méthylphénidate — Metilfenidato	60 000
Midazolam	22 000
Nordazepam — Nordazépam	1
Oxazepam — Oxazépam	1
Pentobarbital	1
Phenobarbital — Phénobarbital — Fenobarbital	2 500 000
Triazolam	2
Zolpidem	1 500
Turkmenistan — Turkménistan — Turkmenistán	
Bromazepam — Bromazépam	1 233
Clonazepam — Clonazépam	81
Diazepam — Diazépam	21 200
Gamma-hydroxybutyric acid (GHB) — Acide *gamma*-hydroxybutirique (GHB) — Ácido *gamma*-hidroxibutírico (GHB)	300 800
Lorazepam — Lorazépam	20
Medazepam — Médazépam	60
Meprobamate — Méprobamate — Meprobamato	11 392
Nimetazepam — Nimétazépam	2 610
Oxazepam — Oxazépam	247
Phenobarbital — Phénobarbital — Fenobarbital	51 780
Turks and Caicos Islands — Îles Turques et Caïques — Islas Turcas y Caicos	
Alprazolam	10
Bromazepam — Bromazépam	4
Chlordiazepoxide — Chlordiazépoxide — Clordiazepóxido	100
Clonazepam — Clonazépam	7
Diazepam — Diazépam	300
Flurazepam — Flurazépam	100
Lorazepam — Lorazépam	250
Methylphenidate — Méthylphénidate — Metilfenidato	100
Midazolam	10
Pentazocine — Pentazocina	20
Phendimetrazine — Phendimétrazine — Fendimetracina	15
Phenobarbital — Phénobarbital — Fenobarbital	700
Temazepam — Témazépam	100
Tuvalu	
Chlordiazepoxide — Chlordiazépoxide — Clordiazepóxido	7
Diazepam — Diazépam	40
Nitrazepam — Nitrazépam	3
Pentazocine — Pentazocina	3
Phenobarbital — Phénobarbital — Fenobarbital	105

Table V. Assessments of annual domestic medical and scientific requirements
Tableau V. Évaluations des besoins annuels médicaux et scientifiques intérieurs
Cuadro V. Previsiones de las necesidades anuales internas para fines médicos y científicos

Country (or territory) and substance Pays (ou territoire) et substance País (o territorio) y sustancia	Assessment (grams) Évaluation (en grammes) Previsión (en gramos)	Country (or territory) and substance Pays (ou territoire) et substance País (o territorio) y sustancia	Assessment (grams) Évaluation (en grammes) Previsión (en gramos)
Uganda — Ouganda		Loprazolam	1 000
Alprazolam	500	Lorazepam — Lorazépam	1 000
Chlordiazepoxide — Chlordiazépoxide —		Lormetazepam — Lormétazépam	200
Clordiazepóxido	1 000	Methylphenidate — Méthylphénidate — Metilfenidato	1 500
Clonazepam — Clonazépam	500	Midazolam	4 000
Diazepam — Diazépam	185 000	Nitrazepam — Nitrazépam	100
Flurazepam — Flurazépam	100	Oxazepam — Oxazépam	200
Lorazepam — Lorazépam	100	Pentazocine — Pentazocina	500
Midazolam	100	Pentobarbital	10 000
Nitrazepam — Nitrazépam	1 000	Phenobarbital — Phénobarbital — Fenobarbital	150 000
Pentazocine — Pentazocina	1 500	Secbutabarbital	100
Phenobarbital — Phénobarbital — Fenobarbital	475 000	Secobarbital — Sécobarbital	100
Triazolam	100	Temazepam — Témazépam	300
Zolpidem	100	Zolpidem	200
Ukraine — Ucrania		**United Kingdom — Royaume-Uni — Reino Unido**	
Alprazolam	600	Allobarbital — Alobarbital	5 000
Bromazepam — Bromazépam	500	Alprazolam	50 000
Brotizolam	1 000	Amfepramone — Amfépramone — Anfepramona	1 000 000
Buprenorphine — Buprénorphine — Buprenorfina	2 271	Amfetamine — Amfétamine — Anfetamina	10 000
Chlordiazepoxide — Chlordiazépoxide —		Amobarbital	2 000 000
Clordiazepóxido	1 000 000	Barbital	5 000 000
Clobazam	10 000	Benzfetamine — Benzfétamine — Benzfetamina	1 000
Clonazepam — Clonazépam	16 500	Bromazepam — Bromazépam	30 000
Cyclobarbital — Ciclobarbital	50 000	Brotizolam	2
Delorazepam — Délorazépam	2 000	Buprenorphine — Buprénorphine — Buprenorfina	110 000
Diazepam — Diazépam	1 086 752	Butalbital	100
Estazolam	460	Butobarbital	250 000
Flunitrazepam — Flunitrazépam	17 000	Cathine — Catina	5
Gamma-hydroxybutyric acid (GHB) —		Chlordiazepoxide — Chlordiazépoxide —	
Acide gamma-hydroxybutirique (GHB) —		Clordiazepóxido	500 000
Ácido gamma-hidroxibutírico (GHB)	10 522 191	Clobazam	200 000
Loprazolam	1 000	Clonazepam — Clonazépam	250 000
Lorazepam — Lorazépam	10 200	Clorazepate — Clorazépate — Clorazepato	50 000
Medazepam — Médazépam	430 000	Cyclobarbital — Ciclobarbital	1
Meprobamate — Méprobamate — Meprobamato	9 000	Delta-9-tetrahydrocannabinol —	
Midazolam	1 000	Delta-9-tétrahydrocannabinol —	
Nitrazepam — Nitrazépam	173 500	Delta-9-tetrahidrocannabinol	3 500
Oxazepam — Oxazépam	870 000	Dexamfetamine — Dexamfétamine — Dexanfetamina	80 000
Pentazocine — Pentazocina	1 000	Diazepam — Diazépam	3 500 000
Phenobarbital — Phénobarbital — Fenobarbital	98 170 000	Ethinamate — Éthinamate — Etinamato	1 000
Temazepam — Témazépam	74 000	Fenproporex	1 000
Tetrazepam — Tétrazépam	1 000	Flunitrazepam — Flunitrazépam	30 000
Triazolam	1 000	Flurazepam — Flurazépam	500 000
Zolpidem	30 000	Gamma-hydroxybutyric acid (GHB) —	
		Acide gamma-hydroxybutirique (GHB) —	
United Arab Emirates — Émirats arabes unis —		Ácido gamma-hidroxibutírico (GHB)	1 600 000
Emiratos Árabes Unidos		Glutethimide — Glutéthimide — Glutetimida	75
Allobarbital — Alobarbital	1 000	Levamfetamine — Lévamfétamine — Levanfetamina	100
Alprazolam	2 000	Levomethamphetamine — Lévométhamphétamine —	
Amfetamine — Amfétamine — Anfetamina	12	Levometanfetamina	400 000
Barbital	1 000	Loprazolam	5 000
Bromazepam — Bromazépam	4 500	Lorazepam — Lorazépam	500 000
Buprenorphine — Buprénorphine — Buprenorfina	200	Lormetazepam — Lormétazépam	10 000
Chlordiazepoxide — Chlordiazépoxide —		Mazindol	8 000
Clordiazepóxido	5 500	Medazepam — Médazépam	1 000
Clobazam	200	Meprobamate — Méprobamate — Meprobamato	1 000 000
Clonazepam — Clonazépam	1 500	Metamfetamine — Métamfétamine — Metanfetamina	50 000
Clorazepate — Clorazépate — Clorazepato	3 200	Metamfetamine racemate —	
Dexamfetamine — Dexamfétamine — Dexanfetamina	3	Racémate de métamfétamine —	
Diazepam — Diazépam	4 500	Racemato de metanfetamina	50
Fludiazepam — Fludiazépam	200	Methaqualone — Méthaqualone — Metacualona	500
Flurazepam — Flurazépam	200	Methylphenidate — Méthylphénidate — Metilfenidato	2 000 000

Table V. Assessments of annual domestic medical and scientific requirements
Tableau V. Évaluations des besoins annuels médicaux et scientifiques intérieurs
Cuadro V. Previsiones de las necesidades anuales internas para fines médicos y científicos

Country (or territory) and substance Pays (ou territoire) et substance País (o territorio) y sustancia	Assessment (grams) Évaluation (en grammes) Previsión (en gramos)
United Kingdom — Royaume-Uni — Reino Unido	
(continued — suite — continuación)	
Methylphenobarbital — Méthylphénobarbital — Metilfenobarbital	100 000
Midazolam	85 000
Nitrazepam — Nitrazépam	1 000 000
Nordazepam — Nordazépam	1
Oxazepam — Oxazépam	2 500 000
Pemoline — Pémoline — Pemolina	1 000
Pentazocine — Pentazocina	125 000
Pentobarbital	4 500 000
Phencyclidine (PCP) — Fenciclidina (PCP)	55
Phendimetrazine — Phendimétrazine — Fendimetracina	25
Phenmetrazine — Phenmétrazine — Fenmetracina	5
Phenobarbital — Phénobarbital — Fenobarbital	21 000 000
Phentermine — Fentermina	500 000
Prazepam — Prazépam	4
Secobarbital — Sécobarbital	3 010 000
Temazepam — Témazépam	4 000 000
Tetrazepam — Tétrazépam	1
Triazolam	200 000
Zolpidem	250 000
United Rep. of Tanzania — Rép.-Unie de Tanzanie — República Unida de Tanzanía	
Alprazolam	1 000
Amfetamine — Amfétamine — Anfetamina	1
Bromazepam — Bromazépam	1 000
Buprenorphine — Buprénorphine — Buprenorfina	1 000
Chlordiazepoxide — Chlordiazépoxide — Clordiazepóxido	1 000
Clonazepam — Clonazépam	240
Dexamfetamine — Dexamfétamine — Dexanfetamina	1
Diazepam — Diazépam	180 000
Glutethimide — Glutéthimide — Glutetimida	1 000
Lorazepam — Lorazépam	400
Metamfetamine — Métamfétamine — Metanfetamina	1
Metamfetamine racemate — Racémate de métamfétamine — Racemato de metanfetamina	1
Midazolam	45
Nitrazepam — Nitrazépam	1 000
Pentazocine — Pentazocina	1 000
Pentobarbital	1 000
Phenobarbital — Phénobarbital — Fenobarbital	2 782 000
Temazepam — Témazépam	240
United States — États-Unis — Estados Unidos	
4-Bromo-2,5-dimethoxyphenyl-ethylamine (2C-B) — 4-bromo-2,5-diméthoxyphényléthylamine (2C-B) — 4-bromo-2,5-dimetoxifeniletilamina (2C-B)	2
Allobarbital — Alobarbital	132
Alprazolam	2 649 000
Amfepramone — Amfépramone — Anfepramona	1 647 846
Amfetamine — Amfétamine — Anfetamina	7 622 433
Amineptin — Amineptine — Amineptina	1
Aminorex	18
Amobarbital	101 000
Barbital	3 790 000
Benzfetamine — Benzfétamine — Benzfetamina	889 000
Bromazepam — Bromazépam	4
Brotizolam	1
Buprenorphine — Buprénorphine — Buprenorfina	415 300
Butalbital	24 469 000
Butobarbital	219 000
Camazepam — Camazépam	1
Cathine — Catina	616 897
Chlordiazepoxide — Chlordiazépoxide — Clordiazepóxido	1 767 000
Clobazam	3 584
Clonazepam — Clonazépam	1 288 000
Clorazepate — Clorazépate — Clorazepato	980 000
Clotiazepam — Clotiazépam	1
Cloxazolam	1
Cyclobarbital — Ciclobarbital	1
Delorazepam — Délorazépam	1
Delta-9-tetrahydrocannabinol — *Delta*-9-tétrahydrocannabinol — *Delta*-9-tetrahidrocannabinol	312 500
Dexamfetamine — Dexamfétamine — Dexanfetamina	7 464 956
Diazepam — Diazépam	8 485 000
Estazolam	21 000
Ethchlorvynol — Etclorvinol	100
Ethinamate — Éthinamate — Etinamato	1
Ethyl loflazepate — Loflazépate d'éthyle — Loflazepato de etilo	1
Etilamfetamine — Étilamfétamine — Etilanfetamina	1
Fencamfamin — Fencamfamine — Fencanfamina	1
Fenetylline — Fénétylline — Fenetilina	1
Fenproporex	1
Fludiazepam — Fludiazépam	1
Flunitrazepam — Flunitrazépam	6
Flurazepam — Flurazépam	683 000
Gamma-hydroxybutyric acid (GHB) — Acide *gamma*-hydroxybutirique (GHB) — Ácido *gamma*-hidroxibutírico (GHB)	8 000 000
Glutethimide — Glutéthimide — Glutetimida	2
Halazepam — Halazépam	5
Haloxazolam	1
Ketazolam — Kétazolam	4
Lefetamine (SPA) — Léfétamine (SPA) — Lefetamina (SPA)	1
Levamfetamine — Lévamfétamine — Levanfetamina	1 010
Levomethamphetamine — Lévométhamphétamine — Levometanfetamina	680 000
Loprazolam	1
Lorazepam — Lorazépam	1 439 000
Lormetazepam — Lormétazépam	5
Mazindol	7
Mecloqualone — Mécloqualone — Meclocualona	1
Medazepam — Médazépam	1
Mefenorex — Méfénorex	1
Meprobamate — Méprobamate — Meprobamato	6 338 371
Mesocarb — Mésocarbe — Mesocarbo	1
Metamfetamine — Métamfétamine — Metanfetamina	2 405 000
Metamfetamine racemate — Racémate de métamfétamine — Racemato de metanfetamina	3 130 000
Methaqualone — Méthaqualone — Metacualona	10
Methylphenidate — Méthylphénidate — Metilfenidato	35 000 000
Methylphenobarbital — Méthylphénobarbital — Metilfenobarbital	363 000
Methyprylon — Méthyprylone — Metiprilona	195
Midazolam	1 382 181
Nimetazepam — Nimétazépam	1

Table V.   Assessments of annual domestic medical and scientific requirements
Tableau V.   Évaluations des besoins annuels médicaux et scientifiques intérieurs
Cuadro V.   Previsiones de las necesidades anuales internas
para fines médicos y científicos

Country (or territory) and substance Pays (ou territoire) et substance País (o territorio) y sustancia	Assessment (grams) Évaluation (en grammes) Previsión (en gramos)
Nitrazepam — Nitrazépam	1 842
Nordazepam — Nordazépam	5
Oxazepam — Oxazépam	1 368 000
Oxazolam	1
Pemoline — Pémoline — Pemolina	232 000
Pentazocine — Pentazocina	1 803 170
Pentobarbital	20 335 000
Phencyclidine (PCP) — Fenciclidina (PCP)	2 021
Phendimetrazine — Phendimétrazine — Fendimetracina	3 500 000
Phenmetrazine — Phenmétrazine — Fenmetracina	2
Phenobarbital — Phénobarbital — Fenobarbital	30 283 000
Phentermine — Fentermina	8 942 000
Pinazepam — Pinazépam	1
Pipradrol	1
Prazepam — Prazépam	3
Pyrovalerone — Pyrovalérone — Pirovalerona	1
Secbutabarbital	5
Secobarbital — Sécobarbital	12 881
Temazepam — Témazépam	7 292 000
Tetrazepam — Tétrazépam	1
Triazolam	115 000
Vinylbital — Vinilbital	1
Zipeprol — Zipéprol	1
Zolpidem	12 005 009
Uruguay	
Alprazolam	150 000
Barbital	3 000
Bromazepam — Bromazépam	300 000
Butalbital	25 000
Chlordiazepoxide — Chlordiazépoxide — Clordiazepóxido	15 000
Clobazam	60 000
Clonazepam — Clonazépam	50 000
Clorazepate — Clorazépate — Clorazepato	500
Cloxazolam	20 000
Diazepam — Diazépam	350 000
Ethyl loflazepate — Loflazépate d'éthyle — Loflazepato de etilo	500
Flunitrazepam — Flunitrazépam	30 000
Ketazolam — Kétazolam	30 000
Lorazepam — Lorazépam	60 000
Mazindol	100
Meprobamate — Méprobamate — Meprobamato	300 000
Methylphenidate — Méthylphénidate — Metilfenidato	15 000
Midazolam	40 000
Nitrazepam — Nitrazépam	500
Oxazepam — Oxazépam	30 000
Pemoline — Pémoline — Pemolina	5 000
Pentobarbital	35 000
Phenobarbital — Phénobarbital — Fenobarbital	450 000
Zolpidem	150 000
Uzbekistan — Ouzbékistan — Uzbekistán	
Allobarbital — Alobarbital	1
Alprazolam	3 600
Amfetamine — Amfétamine — Anfetamina	1
Amobarbital	5 300
Barbital	44 500
Bromazepam — Bromazépam	1 700
Brotizolam	1
Buprenorphine — Buprénorphine — Buprenorfina	452
Butobarbital	7 650
Camazepam — Camazépam	1
Cathine — Catina	1
Chlordiazepoxide — Chlordiazépoxide — Clordiazepóxido	25 350
Clonazepam — Clonazépam	12 200
Clorazepate — Clorazépate — Clorazepato	11 625
Cyclobarbital — Ciclobarbital	36 050
Delorazepam — Délorazépam	1
Delta-9-tetrahydrocannabinol — Delta-9-tétrahydrocannabinol — Delta-9-tetrahidrocannabinol	1
Diazepam — Diazépam	44 770
Estazolam	1
Ethinamate — Éthinamate — Etinamato	1
Fludiazepam — Fludiazépam	1
Flunitrazepam — Flunitrazépam	2 010
Gamma-hydroxybutyric acid (GHB) — Acide gamma-hydroxybutirique (GHB) — Ácido gamma-hidroxibutírico (GHB)	700 000
Ketazolam — Kétazolam	1
Lorazepam — Lorazépam	955
Medazepam — Médazépam	45 100
Meprobamate — Méprobamate — Meprobamato	12 000
Mesocarb — Mésocarbe — Mesocarbo	57 500
Metamfetamine — Métamfétamine — Metanfetamina	1
Methaqualone — Méthaqualone — Metacualona	1
Midazolam	7 300
Nimetazepam — Nimétazépam	1
Nitrazepam — Nitrazépam	42 750
Oxazepam — Oxazépam	57 750
Oxazolam	1
Pentobarbital	1 700
Phenobarbital — Phénobarbital — Fenobarbital	838 700
Temazepam — Témazépam	12 080
Tetrazepam — Tétrazépam	1
Triazolam	180
Zolpidem	1 600
Vanuatu	
Amfepramone — Amfépramone — Anfepramona	500
Bromazepam — Bromazépam	1 000
Buprenorphine — Buprénorphine — Buprenorfina	1
Clonazepam — Clonazépam	1 000
Dexamfetamine — Dexamfétamine — Dexanfetamina	15
Diazepam — Diazépam	4 000
Lorazepam — Lorazépam	2 000
Methylphenidate — Méthylphénidate — Metilfenidato	27
Midazolam	10
Nitrazepam — Nitrazépam	1 500
Oxazepam — Oxazépam	100
Phenobarbital — Phénobarbital — Fenobarbital	8 000
Temazepam — Témazépam	3 000
Zolpidem	100
Venezuela (Bolivarian Rep. of) — Venezuela (Rép. bolivarienne du) — Venezuela (Rep. Bolivariana de)	
Alprazolam	200 000
Amfepramone — Amfépramone — Anfepramona	5 000
Barbital	1 000
Bromazepam — Bromazépam	460 000
Brotizolam	1 000

Table V. Assessments of annual domestic medical and scientific requirements
Tableau V. Évaluations des besoins annuels médicaux et scientifiques intérieurs
Cuadro V. Previsiones de las necesidades anuales internas para fines médicos y científicos

Country (or territory) and substance Pays (ou territoire) et substance País (o territorio) y sustancia	Assessment (grams) Évaluation (en grammes) Previsión (en gramos)
Venezuela (Bolivarian Rep. of) — **Venezuela (Rép. bolivarienne du) —** **Venezuela (Rep. Bolivariana de)**	
(continued — suite — continuación)	
Butobarbital	1 000
Chlordiazepoxide — Chlordiazépoxide — Clordiazepóxido	30 000
Clobazam	150 000
Clonazepam — Clonazépam	90 000
Clorazepate — Clorazépate — Clorazepato	10 000
Diazepam — Diazépam	510 000
Fenproporex	350 000
Fludiazepam — Fludiazépam	50 000
Flurazepam — Flurazépam	50 000
Loprazolam	20 000
Lorazepam — Lorazépam	80 000
Methylphenidate — Méthylphénidate — Metilfenidato	65 000
Methylphenobarbital — Méthylphénobarbital — Metilfenobarbital	1 000
Midazolam	80 000
Oxazepam — Oxazépam	30 000
Pemoline — Pémoline — Pemolina	3 000
Phenobarbital — Phénobarbital — Fenobarbital	10 000 000
Phentermine — Fentermina	70 000
Triazolam	13 000
Zolpidem	103 000
Viet Nam	
Alprazolam	1 000
Bromazepam — Bromazépam	5 000
Buprenorphine — Buprénorphine — Buprenorfina	1 000
Chlordiazepoxide — Chlordiazépoxide — Clordiazepóxido	5 000
Clonazepam — Clonazépam	1 000
Clorazepate — Clorazépate — Clorazepato	3 000
Diazepam — Diazépam	1 000 000
Flunitrazepam — Flunitrazépam	5 000
Lorazepam — Lorazépam	3 000
Meprobamate — Méprobamate — Meprobamato	1 500 000
Midazolam	3 000
Nitrazepam — Nitrazépam	1 000
Pentazocine — Pentazocina	5 000
Pentobarbital	5 000
Phenobarbital — Phénobarbital — Fenobarbital	6 000 000
Temazepam — Témazépam	500
Tetrazepam — Tétrazépam	10 000
Zolpidem	8 000
Wallis and Futuna Islands — Îles-Wallis-et-Futuna — *Islas Wallis y Futuna*	
Alprazolam	4
Bromazepam — Bromazépam	30
Clonazepam — Clonazépam	21
Clorazepate — Clorazépate — Clorazepato	9
Diazepam — Diazépam	13
Meprobamate — Méprobamate — Meprobamato	230
Midazolam	4
Phenobarbital — Phénobarbital — Fenobarbital	173
Tetrazepam — Tétrazépam	330

Country (or territory) and substance Pays (ou territoire) et substance País (o territorio) y sustancia	Assessment (grams) Évaluation (en grammes) Previsión (en gramos)
Yemen — Yémen	
Alprazolam	10 000
Bromazepam — Bromazépam	8 000
Buprenorphine — Buprénorphine — Buprenorfina	500
Chlordiazepoxide — Chlordiazépoxide — Clordiazepóxido	100 000
Clonazepam — Clonazépam	1 500
Diazepam — Diazépam	70 000
Lorazepam — Lorazépam	7 000
Midazolam	3 000
Nitrazepam — Nitrazépam	2 000
Pentazocine — Pentazocina	2 000
Phenobarbital — Phénobarbital — Fenobarbital	50 000
Temazepam — Témazépam	100
Zambia — Zambie	
Alprazolam	2
Amfetamine — Amfétamine — Anfetamina	1
Bromazepam — Bromazépam	5
Buprenorphine — Buprénorphine — Buprenorfina	10
Chlordiazepoxide — Chlordiazépoxide — Clordiazepóxido	5
Clonazepam — Clonazépam	2
Delta-9-tetrahydrocannabinol — *Delta*-9-tétrahydrocannabinol — *Delta*-9-tetrahidrocannabinol	1
Dexamfetamine — Dexamfétamine — Dexanfetamina	1
Diazepam — Diazépam	120 000
Flunitrazepam — Flunitrazépam	1
Lorazepam — Lorazépam	50
Meprobamate — Méprobamate — Meprobamato	20 000
Metamfetamine — Métamfétamine — Metanfetamina	1
Methylphenidate — Méthylphénidate — Metilfenidato	1 000
Midazolam	1
Nitrazepam — Nitrazépam	500
Oxazepam — Oxazépam	20
Pentazocine — Pentazocina	2 000
Phenobarbital — Phénobarbital — Fenobarbital	350 000
Temazepam — Témazépam	30
Zimbabwe	
Amfepramone — Amfépramone — Anfepramona	3 000
Barbital	4 000
Bromazepam — Bromazépam	5 000
Chlordiazepoxide — Chlordiazépoxide — Clordiazepóxido	25 000
Clonazepam — Clonazépam	2 000
Dexamfetamine — Dexamfétamine — Dexanfetamina	100
Diazepam — Diazépam	150 000
Flunitrazepam — Flunitrazépam	2 000
Meprobamate — Méprobamate — Meprobamato	5 450 000
Methylphenidate — Méthylphénidate — Metilfenidato	900
Midazolam	5 000
Nitrazepam — Nitrazépam	30 000
Pentazocine — Pentazocina	2 000
Pentobarbital	40 000
Phencyclidine (PCP) — Fenciclidina (PCP)	1
Phenobarbital — Phénobarbital — Fenobarbital	2 000 000
Secobarbital — Sécobarbital	200
Triazolam	1 000

aAssessment established by the International Narcotics Control Board. — Prévisions établies par l'Organe international de contrôle des stupéfiants. — Previsiones establecidas por la Junta Internacional de Fiscalización de Estupefacientes.

328

Table VI.   Prohibition of and restrictions on export and import pursuant to article 13 of the Convention on Psychotropic Substances of 1971

The Secretary-General has transmitted to all Governments notifications concerning the prohibition of the importation of specific substances in Schedules II, III or IV of the Convention on Psychotropic Substances of 1971 that were received from the countries indicated in the table below. The notifications are presented as follows: notifying countries listed alphabetically, followed by the prohibited substances and dates of notification. The prohibitions are effective, with respect to exporting countries, as of the date of receipt of the Secretary-General's notification.

Upon notification of a prohibition, an exporting country must take measures to ensure that none of the substances specified in the notification are exported to the country or any of the regions in the notifying country. Exports of a prohibited substance may be permitted only when a special import licence has been issued by the notifying country, in accordance with the provisions of article 13 of the 1971 Convention.

Tableau VI.   Interdiction et restrictions à l'exportation et à l'importation conformément à l'article 13 de la Convention de 1971 sur les substances psychotropes

Le Secrétaire général a transmis à tous les gouvernements des notifications reçues des pays énumérés dans le tableau ci-après concernant l'interdiction d'importer certaines substances figurant aux Tableaux II, III ou IV de la Convention de 1971 sur les substances psychotropes. Les notifications sont présentées de la façon suivante: pays ayant fait une notification, classés par ordre alphabétique, suivis des substances interdites et de la date de la notification. Les interdictions prennent effet pour les pays exportateurs à la date de réception de la communication émanant du Secrétaire général.

Au reçu d'une notification d'interdiction, les autorités des pays exportateurs doivent prendre les mesures nécessaires pour s'assurer qu'aucune des substances spécifiées dans ladite notification ne sera exportée vers le pays ayant fait la notification, ou vers une de ses régions. L'exportation d'une substance interdite ne peut être autorisée que si un permis spécial d'importation a été émis par l'autorité compétente du pays ayant fait la notification, conformément aux dispositions de l'article 13 de la Convention de 1971.

Cuadro VI.   Prohibición y restricciones a la exportación e importación de conformidad con el artículo 13 del Convenio sobre Sustancias Sicotrópicas de 1971

El Secretario General ha transmitido a todos los gobiernos notificaciones recibidas de los países, que se indican en el cuadro siguiente, relativas a la prohibición de la importación de determinadas sustancias sicotrópicas de las Listas II, III o IV del Convenio sobre Sustancias Sicotrópicas de 1971. Las notificaciones se indican a continuación de la siguiente forma: países notificantes por orden alfabético seguidos de las sustancias prohibidas y las fechas de notificación. Las prohibiciones surtirán efecto, con respecto a los países exportadores, a partir de la fecha en que éstos reciban la notificación del Secretario General.

Al recibir una notificación de prohibición de importación, las autoridades de los países exportadores deberán tomar las medidas necesarias para asegurar que ninguna de las sustancias especificadas en la mencionada notificación sea exportada al país que ha hecho la notificación ni a ninguna de sus regiones. La exportación de una sustancia prohibida puede ser autorizada solamente si las autoridades competentes del país que ha hecho la notificación emiten un permiso especial de importación con arreglo a las disposiciones del artículo 13 del Convenio de 1971.

Table VI. Prohibition of and restrictions on export and import pursuant to article 13 of the Convention on Psychotropic Substances of 1971

Tableau VI. Interdiction et restrictions à l'exportation et à l'importation conformément à l'article 13 de la Convention de 1971 sur les substances psychotropes

Cuadro VI. Prohibición y restricciones a la exportación e importación de conformidad con el artículo 13 del Convenio sobre Sustancias Sicotrópicas de 1971

Country and prohibited substances Pays et substances interdites País y sustancias prohibidas	Date of notification Date de la communication Fecha de notificación
Argentina — Argentine	
Mecloqualone — Mécloqualone — Meclocualona	15/1/87
Methaqualone — Méthaqualone — Metacualona	24/3/82
Australia — Australie	
Methaqualone — Méthaqualone — Metacualona	8/8/80
Belize — Belice	
Amfetamine — Amfétamine — Anfetamina	9/5/89
Dexamfetamine — Dexamfétamine — Dexanfetamina	
Fenetylline — Fénétylline — Fenetilina	
Levamfetamine — Lévamfétamine — Levanfetamina	
Levomethamphetamine — Lévométhamphétamine — Levometanfetamina	
Mecloqualone — Mécloqualone — Meclocualona	
Metamfetamine — Métamfétamine — Metanfetamina	
Metamfetamine racemate — Racémate de métamfétamine — Racemato de metanfetamina	
Methaqualone — Méthaqualone — Metacualona	
Methylphenidate — Méthylphénidate — Metilfenidato	
Phencyclidine (PCP) — Fenciclidina (PCP)	
Phenmetrazine — Phenmétrazine — Fenmetracina	
Secobarbital — Sécobarbital	
Bulgaria — Bulgarie	
Amfetamine — Amfétamine — Anfetamina	12/8/93
Dexamfetamine — Dexamfétamine — Dexanfetamina	
Fenetylline — Fénétylline — Fenetilina	
Levamfetamine — Lévamfétamine — Levanfetamina	
Metamfetamine — Métamfétamine — Metanfetamina	
Metamfetamine racemate — Racémate de métamfétamine — Racemato de metanfetamina	
Chile — Chili	
Glutethimide — Glutéthimide — Glutetimida	1/7/81
Lefetamine (SPA) — Léfétamine (SPA) — Lefetamina (SPA)	
Mecloqualone — Mécloqualone — Meclocualona	
Methaqualone — Méthaqualone — Metacualona	
Phencyclidine (PCP) — Fenciclidina (PCP)	
Phenmetrazine — Phenmétrazine — Fenmetracina	
Colombia — Colombie	
Methaqualone — Méthaqualone — Metacualona	11/11/81
Gabon — Gabón	
Methaqualone — Méthaqualone — Metacualona	28/7/93

Country and prohibited substances Pays et substances interdites País y sustancias prohibidas	Date of notification Date de la communication Fecha de notificación
Iceland — Islande — Islandia	
Phencyclidine (PCP) — Fenciclidina (PCP)	28/11/79
India — Inde	
Aminorex	30/9/05
Amfepramone — Amfépramone — Anfepramona	30/5/91
Benzfetamine — Benzfétamine — Benzfetamina	
Brotizolam	30/9/05
Camazepam — Camazépam	30/5/91
Clotiazepam — Clotiazépam	
Cloxazolam	
Delorazepam — Délorazépam	
Estazolam	
Ethinamate — Éthinamate — Etinamato	
Ethyl loflazepate — Loflazépate d'éthyle — Loflazepato de etilo	
Fludiazepam — Fludiazépam	
Flunitrazepam — Flunitrazépam	
Haloxazolam	
Ketazolam — Kétazolam	
Lefetamine (SPA) — Léfétamine (SPA) — Lefetamina (SPA)	
Loprazolam	
Lormetazepam — Lormétazépam	
Mazindol	
Mesocarb — Mésocarbe — Mesocarbo	30/9/05
Medazepam — Médazépam	30/5/91
Methaqualone — Méthaqualone — Metacualona	30/4/93
Methyprylon — Méthyprylone — Metiprilona	30/5/91
Oxazolam	
Phendimetrazine — Phendimétrazine — Fendimetracina	
Pinazepam — Pinazépam	
Pipradrol	
Prazepam — Prazépam	
Tetrazepam — Tétrazépam	
Japan — Japon — Japón	
Amfetamine — Amfétamine — Anfetamina	31/1/91
Dexamfetamine — Dexamfétamine — Dexanfetamina	
Levamfetamine — Lévamfétamine — Levanfetamina	
Levomethamphetamine — Lévométhamphétamine — Levometanfetamina	
Metamfetamine — Métamfétamine — Metanfetamina	
Metamfetamine racemate — Racémate de métamfétamine — Racemato de metanfetamina	
Latvia — Lettonie — Letonia	
Amfetamine — Amfétamine — Anfetamina	7/11/95
Cathine — Catina	
Dexamfetamine — Dexamfétamine — Dexanfetamina	

Table VI. Prohibition of and restrictions on export and import pursuant to article 13 of the Convention on Psychotropic Substances of 1971 (continued)

Tableau VI. Interdiction et restrictions à l'exportation et à l'importation conformément à l'article 13 de la Convention de 1971 sur les substances psychotropes (suite)

Cuadro VI. Prohibición y restricciones a la exportación e importación de conformidad con el artículo 13 del Convenio sobre Sustancias Sicotrópicas de 1971 (continuación)

Country and prohibited substances Pays et substances interdites País y sustancias prohibidas	Date of notification Date de la communication Fecha de notificación
Etilamfetamine — Étilamfétamine — Etilanfetamina	
Fenetylline — Fénétylline — Fenetilina	
Fenproporex	
Levamfetamine — Lévamfétamine — Levanfetamina	
Mefenorex — Méfénorex	
Metamfetamine — Métamfétamine — Metanfetamina	
Metamfetamine racemate — Racémate de métamfétamine — Racemato de metanfetamina	
Phentermine — Fentermina	
Lebanon — Liban — Líbano	
Amfetamine — Amfétamine — Anfetamina	16/10/00
Cathine — Catina	

Delta-9-tetrahydrocannabinol —
  Delta-9-tétrahydrocannabinol —
  Delta-9-tetrahidrocannabinol	

Dexamfetamine — Dexamfétamine — Dexanfetamina	
Fenetylline — Fénétylline — Fenetilina	
Levamfetamine — Lévamfétamine — Levanfetamina	
Levomethamphetamine — Lévométhamphétamine — Levometanfetamina	
Mecloqualone — Mécloqualone — Meclocualona	
Metamfetamine — Métamfétamine — Metanfetamina	
Metamfetamine racemate — Racémate de métamfétamine — Racemato de metanfetamina	
Methaqualone — Méthaqualone — Metacualona	
Phencyclidine (PCP) — Fenciclidina (PCP)	
Lithuania — Lituanie — Lituania	
Amfetamine — Amfétamine — Anfetamina	29/8/97
Cathine — Catina	
Dexamfetamine — Dexamfétamine — Dexanfetamina	
Fenetylline — Fénétylline — Fenetilina	
Levamfetamine — Lévamfétamine — Levanfetamina	
Metamfetamine — Métamfétamine — Metanfetamina	
Metamfetamine racemate — Racémate de métamfétamine — Racemato de metanfetamina	
Madagascar	
Methaqualone — Méthaqualone — Metacualona	15/12/78
Nigeria — Nigéria	
Amfetamine — Amfétamine — Anfetamina	27/2/86
Dexamfetamine — Dexamfétamine — Dexanfetamina	
Metamfetamine — Métamfétamine — Metanfetamina	
Methaqualone — Méthaqualone — Metacualona	
Methylphenidate — Méthylphénidate — Metilfenidato	
Pemoline — Pémoline — Pemolina	29/10/90
Phencyclidine (PCP) — Fenciclidina (PCP)	

Country and prohibited substances Pays et substances interdites País y sustancias prohibidas	Date of notification Date de la communication Fecha de notificación
Phenmetrazine — Phenmétrazine — Fenmetracina	
Secobarbital — Sécobarbital	
Pakistan — Pakistán	
Amfepramone — Amfépramone — Anfepramona	6/12/85
Amfetamine — Amfétamine — Anfetamina	
Barbital	
Benzfetamine — Benzfétamine — Benzfetamina	
Camazepam — Camazépam	
Clotiazepam — Clotiazépam	
Cloxazolam	
Cyclobarbital — Ciclobarbital	
Delorazepam — Délorazépam	
Dexamfetamine — Dexamfétamine — Dexanfetamina	
Ethchlorvynol — Etclorvinol	
Ethinamate — Éthinamate — Etinamato	
Ethyl loflazepate — Loflazépate d'éthyle — Loflazepato de etilo	
Flunitrazepam — Flunitrazépam	
Flurazepam — Flurazépam	
Glutethimide — Glutéthimide — Glutetimida	
Halazepam — Halazépam	
Haloxazolam	
Lefetamine (SPA) — Léfétamine (SPA) — Lefetamina (SPA)	
Loprazolam	
Mazindol	
Mecloqualone — Mécloqualone — Meclocualona	
Metamfetamine — Métamfétamine — Metanfetamina	
Methaqualone — Méthaqualone — Metacualona	
Methylphenobarbital — Méthylphénobarbital — Metilfenobarbital	
Methyprylon — Méthyprylone — Metiprilona	
Nordazepam — Nordazépam	
Oxazolam	
Phencyclidine (PCP) — Fenciclidina (PCP)	
Phendimetrazine — Phendimétrazine — Fendimetracina	
Phenmetrazine — Phenmétrazine — Fenmetracina	
Pipradrol	
Secobarbital — Sécobarbital	
Tetrazepam — Tétrazépam	
Russian Federation — Fédération de Russie — Federación de Rusia	
Cathine — Catina	09/11/05
Saudi Arabia — Arabie saoudite — Arabia Saudita	
Fenetylline — Fénétylline — Fenetilina	31/12/87
Methaqualone — Méthaqualone — Metacualona	

Table VI. Prohibition of and restrictions on export and import pursuant to article 13 of the Convention on Psychotropic Substances of 1971 *(concluded)*

Tableau VI. Interdiction et restrictions à l'exportation et à l'importation conformément à l'article 13 de la Convention de 1971 sur les substances psychotropes *(fin)*

Cuadro VI. Prohibición y restricciones a la exportación e importación de conformidad con el artículo 13 del Convenio sobre Sustancias Sicotrópicas de 1971 *(conclusión)*

Country and prohibited substances Pays et substances interdites País y sustancias prohibidas	Date of notification Date de la communication Fecha de notificación
Senegal — Sénégal	
Amfetamine — Amfétamine — Anfetamina	16/5/80
Dexamfetamine — Dexamfétamine — Dexanfetamina	
Mecloqualone — Mécloqualone — Meclocualona	31/1/91
Metamfetamine — Métamfétamine — Metanfetamina	16/5/80
Methaqualone — Méthaqualone — Metacualona	
Methylphenidate — Méthylphénidate — Metilfenidato	
Phencyclidine (PCP) — Fenciclidina (PCP)	
Phenmetrazine — Phenmétrazine — Fenmetracina	
South Africa — Afrique du Sud — Sudáfrica	
Methaqualone — Méthaqualone — Metacualona	15/12/78
Thailand — Thaïlande — Tailandia	
Amfetamine — Amfétamine — Anfetamina	15/8/91
Dexamfetamine — Dexamfétamine — Dexanfetamina	
Fenetylline — Fénétylline — Fenetilina	
Levamfetamine — Lévamfétamine — Levanfetamina	
Levomethamphetamine — Lévométhamphétamine — Levometanfetamina	
Metamfetamine — Métamfétamine — Metanfetamina	
Methylphenidate — Méthylphénidate —Metilfenidato	
Phenmetrazine — Phenmétrazine — Fenmetracina	
Togo	
Amfetamine — Amfétamine — Anfetamina	28/7/93
Ethinamate — Éthinamate — Etinamato	
Lefetamine (SPA) — Léfétamine (SPA) — Lefetamina (SPA)	
Mecloqualone — Mécloqualone — Meclocualona	
Metamfetamine — Métamfétamine — Metanfetamina	
Methylphenidate — Méthylphénidate —Metilfenidato	
Methylphenobarbital — Méthylphénobarbital — Metilfenobarbital	
Methyprylon — Méthyprylone — Metiprilona	
Pemoline — Pémoline — Pemolina	
Phencyclidine (PCP) — Fenciclidina (PCP)	
Pipradrol	
Secobarbital — Sécobarbital	
Turkey — Turquie — Turquía	
Amfepramone — Amfépramone — Anfepramona	30/6/81
Amfetamine — Amfétamine — Anfetamina	
Dexamfetamine — Dexamfétamine — Dexanfetamina	

Country and prohibited substances Pays et substances interdites País y sustancias prohibidas	Date of notification Date de la communication Fecha de notificación
Fenetylline — Fénétylline — Fenetilina	27/9/99
Flunitrazepam — Flunitrazépam	
Metamfetamine — Métamfétamine — Metanfetamina	30/6/81
Metamfetamine racemate — Racémate de métamfétamine — Racemato de metanfetamina	27/9/99
Methaqualone — Méthaqualone — Metacualona	20/8/82
Methylphenidate — Méthylphénidate — Metilfenidato	30/6/81
Pemoline — Pémoline — Pemolina	27/9/99
Phendimetrazine— Phendimétrazine — Fendimetracina	30/6/81
Phenmetrazine —Phenmétrazine — Fenmetracina	
Phentermine — Fentermina	
Pipradrol	
United States — États-Unis — Estados Unidos	
Flunitrazepam — Flunitrazépam	9/10/96
Methaqualone — Méthaqualone — Metacualona	9/9/85
Venezuela (Bolivarian Rep. of) — Venezuela (Rép. bolivarienne du) — Venezuela (Rep. Bolivariana de)	
Amfetamine — Amfétamine — Anfetamina	2/6/92
Dexamfetamine — Dexamfétamine — Dexanfetamina	
Levamfetamine — Lévamfétamine — Levanfetamina	
Levomethamphetamine — Lévométhamphétamine — Levometanfetamina	
Metamfetamine — Métamfétamine — Metanfetamina	
Metamfetamine racemate — Racémate de métamfétamine — Racemato de metanfetamina	
Methaqualone — Méthaqualone — Metacualona	22/5/86
Phenmetrazine — Phenmétrazine — Fenmetracina	2/6/92
Yemen — Yémen	
Amfetamine — Amfétamine — Anfetamina	18/11/80
Ethinamate — Éthinamate — Etinamato	
Lefetamine (SPA) — Léfétamine (SPA) — Lefetamina (SPA)	
Metamfetamine — Métamfétamine — Metanfetamina	
Methaqualone — Méthaqualone — Metacualona	
Methylphenidate — Méthylphénidate —Metilfenidato	
Methylphenobarbital — Méthylphénobarbital — Metilfenobarbital	
Methyprylon — Méthyprylone — Metiprilona	
Phencyclidine (PCP) — Fenciclidina (PCP)	
Phenmetrazine — Phenmétrazine — Fenmetracina	
Pipradrol	

International Narcotics Control Board

The International Narcotics Control Board (INCB) is an independent and quasi-judicial control organ, established by treaty, for monitoring the implementation of the international drug control treaties. It had predecessors under the former drug control treaties as far back as the time of the League of Nations.

Composition

INCB consists of 13 members who are elected by the Economic and Social Council and who serve in their personal capacity, not as government representatives. Three members with medical, pharmacological or pharmaceutical experience are elected from a list of persons nominated by the World Health Organization (WHO) and 10 members are elected from a list of persons nominated by Governments. Members of INCB are persons who, by their competence, impartiality and disinterestedness, command general confidence. The Council, in consultation with INCB, makes all arrangements necessary to ensure the full technical independence of the Board in carrying out its functions. INCB has a secretariat that assists it in the exercise of its treaty-related functions. The INCB secretariat is an administrative entity of the United Nations Office on Drugs and Crime, but it reports solely to the Board on matters of substance. INCB closely collaborates with the Office in the framework of arrangements approved by the Council in its resolution 1991/48. INCB also cooperates with other international bodies concerned with drug control, including not only the Council and its Commission on Narcotic Drugs, but also the relevant specialized agencies of the United Nations, particularly WHO. It also cooperates with bodies outside the United Nations system, especially Interpol and the Customs Cooperation Council (also called the World Customs Organization).

Functions

The functions of INCB are laid down in the following treaties: the Single Convention on Narcotic Drugs of 1961 as amended by the 1972 Protocol; the Convention on Psychotropic Substances of 1971; and the United Nations Convention against Illicit Traffic in Narcotic Drugs and Psychotropic Substances of 1988. Broadly speaking, INCB deals with the following:

(a) As regards the licit manufacture of, trade in and use of drugs, INCB endeavours, in cooperation with Governments, to ensure that adequate supplies of drugs are available for medical and scientific uses and that the diversion of drugs from licit sources to illicit channels does not occur. INCB also monitors Governments' control over chemicals used in the illicit manufacture of drugs and assists them in preventing the diversion of those chemicals into the illicit traffic;

(b) As regards the illicit manufacture of, trafficking in and use of drugs, INCB identifies weaknesses in national and international control systems and contributes to correcting such situations. INCB is also responsible for assessing chemicals used in the illicit manufacture of drugs, in order to determine whether they should be placed under international control.

In the discharge of its responsibilities, INCB:

(a) Administers a system of estimates for narcotic drugs and a voluntary assessment system for psychotropic substances and monitors licit activities involving drugs through a statistical returns system, with a view to assisting Governments in achieving, inter alia, a balance between supply and demand;

(b) Monitors and promotes measures taken by Governments to prevent the diversion of substances frequently used in the illicit manufacture of narcotic drugs and psychotropic substances and assesses such substances to determine whether there is a need for changes in the scope of control of Tables I and II of the 1988 Convention;

(c) Analyses information provided by Governments, United Nations bodies, specialized agencies or other competent international organizations, with a view to ensuring that the provisions of the international drug control treaties are adequately carried out by Governments, and recommends remedial measures;

(d) Maintains a permanent dialogue with Governments to assist them in complying with their obligations under the international drug control treaties and, to that end, recommends, where appropriate, technical or financial assistance to be provided.

INCB is called upon to ask for explanations in the event of apparent violations of the treaties, to propose appropriate remedial measures to Governments that are not fully applying the provisions of the treaties or are encountering difficulties in applying them and, where necessary, to assist Governments in overcoming such difficulties. If, however, INCB notes that the measures necessary to remedy a serious situation have not been taken, it may call the matter to the attention of the parties concerned, the Commission on Narcotic Drugs and the Economic and Social Council. As a last resort, the treaties empower INCB to recommend to parties that they stop importing drugs from a defaulting country, exporting drugs to it or both. In all cases, INCB acts in close cooperation with Governments.

INCB assists national administrations in meeting their obligations under the conventions. To that end, it proposes and participates in regional training seminars and programmes for drug control administrators.

Reports

The international drug control treaties require INCB to prepare an annual report on its work. The annual report contains an analysis of the drug control situation worldwide so that Governments are kept aware of existing and potential situations that may endanger the objectives of the international drug control treaties. INCB draws the attention of Governments to gaps and weaknesses in national control and in treaty compliance; it also makes suggestions and recommendations for improvements at both the national and international levels. The annual report is based on information provided by Governments to INCB, United Nations entities and other organizations. It also uses information provided through other international organizations, such as Interpol and the World Customs Organization, as well as regional organizations.

The annual report of INCB is supplemented by detailed technical reports. They contain data on the licit movement of narcotic drugs and psychotropic substances required for medical and scientific purposes, together with an analysis of those data by INCB. Those data are required for the proper functioning of the system of control over the licit movement of narcotic drugs and psychotropic substances, including their diversion to illicit channels. Moreover, under the provisions of article 12 of the 1988 Convention, INCB reports annually to the Commission on Narcotic Drugs on the implementation of that article. That report, which gives an account of the results of the monitoring of precursors and of the chemicals frequently used in the illicit manufacture of narcotic drugs and psychotropic substances, is also published as a supplement to the annual report.

L'Organe international de contrôle des stupéfiants

L'Organe international de contrôle des stupéfiants (OICS) est un organe de contrôle indépendant et quasi-judiciaire, créé par traité, qui est chargé de surveiller l'application des traités internationaux relatifs au contrôle des drogues. Il a été précédé par d'autres organes qui, du temps de la Société des Nations, déjà œuvraient dans ce domaine en vertu des précédents traités relatifs au contrôle des drogues.

Composition de l'Organe

L'Organe se compose de treize membres élus par le Conseil économique et social, qui siègent à titre personnel et non en qualité de représentants de leur pays. Trois membres ayant l'expérience de la médecine, de la pharmacologie ou de la pharmacie sont choisis sur une liste de personnes désignées par l'Organisation mondiale de la santé (OMS) et dix membres sur une liste de personnes désignées par les gouvernements. Les membres de l'Organe doivent être des personnes qui, par leur compétence, leur impartialité et leur désintéressement, inspirent la confiance générale. Le Conseil prend, en consultation avec l'Organe, toutes les dispositions nécessaires pour assurer la pleine indépendance technique de ce dernier dans l'exercice de ses fonctions. L'Organe a un secrétariat chargé de l'aider dans l'exercice des fonctions qui lui incombent au titre des traités. Ce secrétariat est une unité administrative de l'Office des Nations Unies contre la drogue et le crime, mais, pour les questions de fond, il en réfère exclusivement à l'Organe. Ce dernier collabore étroitement avec l'Office dans le cadre des dispositions approuvées par le Conseil économique et social dans sa résolution 1991/48. L'Organe collabore également avec d'autres organismes internationaux qui s'occupent aussi du contrôle des drogues. Au nombre de ces organismes figurent non seulement le Conseil et sa Commission des stupéfiants, mais aussi les institutions spécialisées des Nations Unies compétentes en la matière, en particulier l'Organisation mondiale de la santé. L'Organe coopère également avec des organismes qui n'appartiennent pas au système des Nations Unies, en particulier Interpol et le Conseil de coopération douanière (également appelé l'Organisation mondiale des douanes).

Fonctions de l'Organe

Les fonctions de l'Organe sont énoncées dans les traités suivants: la Convention unique sur les stupéfiants de 1961, telle que modifiée par le Protocole de 1972; la Convention de 1971 sur les substances psychotropes; et la Convention des Nations Unies contre le trafic illicite de stupéfiants et de substances psychotropes de 1988. En gros, les fonctions de l'Organe sont les suivantes:

a) En ce qui concerne la fabrication, le commerce et l'usage licites des drogues, l'Organe, agissant en coopération avec les gouvernements, s'efforce de faire en sorte que soient disponibles en quantités suffisantes les drogues requises à des fins médicales et scientifiques et que les drogues ne soient pas détournées des sources licites vers les circuits illicites. L'Organe surveille également comment les gouvernements contrôlent les produits chimiques utilisés dans la fabrication illicite des drogues et les aide à prévenir le détournement de ces produits vers le trafic illicite;

b) En ce qui concerne la fabrication, le trafic et l'usage illicites des drogues, l'Organe identifie les lacunes qui existent dans les systèmes de contrôle national et international et contribue à y remédier. Il est également chargé d'évaluer les produits chimiques utilisés dans la fabrication illicite des drogues, afin de déterminer s'il y a lieu de les placer sous contrôle international.

Pour s'acquitter des tâches qui lui sont imparties, l'Organe:

a) Administre un régime d'évaluations pour les stupéfiants et un système volontaire de prévisions pour les substances psychotropes et surveille les activités licites relatives aux drogues, à l'aide d'un système de rapports statistiques, pour aider les gouvernements à réaliser, notamment, un équilibre entre l'offre et la demande;

b) Suit et encourage les mesures prises par les gouvernements pour prévenir le détournement de substances fréquemment utilisées dans la fabrication illicite de stupéfiants et de substances psychotropes, et évalue les substances de ce type afin de déterminer s'il y a lieu de modifier le champ d'application des Tableaux I et II de la Convention de 1988;

c) Analyse les renseignements fournis par les gouvernements, les organes de l'Organisation des Nations Unies, les institutions spécialisées ou d'autres organisations internationales compétentes, afin de veiller à ce que les dispositions des traités internationaux relatifs au contrôle des drogues soient appliquées de façon appropriée par les gouvernements, et recommande, le cas échéant, des mesures correctives;

d) Entretient un dialogue permanent avec les gouvernements pour les aider à s'acquitter de leurs obligations en vertu des traités internationaux relatifs au contrôle des drogues et, à cette fin, recommande, le cas échéant, qu'une assistance technique ou financière leur soit fournie.

L'Organe est appelé à demander des explications en cas de violation apparente des traités, à proposer aux gouvernements qui n'en appliquent pas entièrement les dispositions, ou rencontrent des difficultés à les appliquer, les mesures correctives appropriées et à les aider, le cas échéant, à surmonter ces difficultés. Si, toutefois, l'Organe constate que les mesures propres à remédier à une situation grave n'ont pas été prises, il peut porter le problème à l'attention des parties intéressées, de la Commission des stupéfiants et du Conseil économique et social. En dernier recours, les traités autorisent l'Organe à recommander aux parties d'arrêter l'importation ou l'exportation de drogues, ou les deux, en provenance ou à destination du pays défaillant. Dans toutes circonstances, l'Organe agit en étroite collaboration avec les gouvernements.

L'Organe aide les administrations nationales à s'acquitter de leurs obligations en vertu des conventions. Pour ce faire, il propose des séminaires et des stages de formation régionaux à l'intention des administrateurs chargés du contrôle des drogues et y participe.

Rapports de l'Organe

En vertu des traités internationaux relatifs au contrôle des drogues, l'Organe doit établir un rapport annuel sur ses activités. Ce rapport analyse la situation mondiale en matière de contrôle des drogues et permet ainsi de tenir les autorités nationales informées des problèmes qui se posent aujourd'hui ou risquent de se poser demain et qui sont de nature à compromettre la réalisation des objectifs des traités internationaux relatifs au contrôle des drogues. L'Organe appelle l'attention des États sur les lacunes et les insuffisances constatées dans le domaine du contrôle national et de l'application des traités. En outre, il suggère et recommande des améliorations aux niveaux international et national. Le rapport est fondé sur les renseignements communiqués par les gouvernements à l'Organe international de contrôle des stupéfiants, ainsi qu'aux autres organes et organismes des Nations Unies. Il s'appuie également sur des informations fournies par l'intermédiaire d'autres organisations internationales, telles que l'OIPC/Interpol et l'Organisation mondiale des douanes, ainsi que des organisations régionales.

Le rapport annuel de l'Organe est complété par des rapports techniques détaillés qui présentent des données concernant le mouvement licite des stupéfiants et des substances psychotropes requis à des fins médicales et scientifiques, ainsi que l'analyse par l'Organe de ces données. Ces dernières sont nécessaires au bon fonctionnement des mécanismes de contrôle du mouvement licite des stupéfiants et des substances psychotropes, ainsi qu'à la prévention de leur détournement vers les circuits illicites. De plus, en vertu des dispositions de l'article 12 de la Convention de 1988, l'Organe fait rapport chaque année à la Commission des stupéfiants sur l'application dudit article. Ce rapport, qui fait état des résultats du contrôle des précurseurs et des produits chimiques fréquemment utilisés dans la fabrication illicite de stupéfiants et de substances psychotropes, est également publié comme supplément au rapport annuel.

Junta Internacional de Fiscalización de Estupefacientes

La Junta Internacional de Fiscalización de Estupefacientes (JIFE) es un órgano de fiscalización independiente y cuasi judicial, establecido por un tratado, para la aplicación de los tratados internacionales de fiscalización de drogas. Sus predecesores en virtud de los anteriores tratados de fiscalización de drogas datan de la época de la Sociedad de Naciones.

Composición

La JIFE está constituida por 13 miembros elegidos por el Consejo Económico y Social que desempeñan sus funciones a título personal, y no como representantes de los gobiernos. Tres de sus miembros, con experiencia en campo de la medicina, la farmacología o la farmacia se seleccionan de una lista de candidatos presentada por la Organización Mundial de la Salud (OMS), y los otros diez de una lista de candidatos propuesta por los gobiernos. Los miembros de la JIFE son personas que gozan de la confianza general por su competencia, imparcialidad e independencia. El Consejo, en consulta con la JIFE, lleva a cabo todos los arreglos necesarios para asegurar la plena independencia técnica de la Junta en el desempeño de sus funciones. La JIFE cuenta con una secretaría que la asiste en el ejercicio de las funciones que le corresponden en virtud de los tratados. La secretaría de la JIFE es una entidad administrativa de la Oficina de las Naciones Unidas contra la Droga y el Delito, si bien en cuestiones sustantivas responde únicamente ante la Junta. La JIFE colabora estrechamente con la Oficina en el marco de los acuerdos aprobados por el Consejo en su resolución 1991/48. La JIFE colabora también con otros órganos internacionales relacionados con la fiscalización de drogas, entre los que se incluyen no solo el Consejo y la Comisión de Estupefacientes, sino también los organismos especializados pertinentes de las Naciones Unidas, en particular la OMS. También colabora con órganos que no forman parte del sistema de las Naciones Unidas, en especial con Interpol y con el Consejo de Cooperación Aduanera (también denominado Organización Mundial de Aduanas).

Funciones

Las funciones de la Junta están consagradas en los siguientes tratados: la Convención Única sobre Estupefacientes de 1961, enmendada por el Protocolo de 1972; el Convenio sobre Sustancias Sicotrópicas de 1971; y la Convención de las Naciones Unidas contra el Tráfico Ilícito de Estupefacientes y Sustancias Sicotrópicas de 1988. En términos generales, la Junta se ocupa de lo siguiente:

a) En relación con la fabricación, el comercio y el uso lícitos de drogas, la Junta, en cooperación con los gobiernos, procura asegurar que haya suministros de drogas adecuados para fines médicos y científicos y que no se produzcan desviaciones de drogas de fuentes lícitas a canales ilícitos. La Junta también vigila la fiscalización que aplican los gobiernos a los productos químicos utilizados en la fabricación ilícita de drogas y les presta asistencia para prevenir la desviación de esos productos químicos hacia el tráfico ilícito;

b) En relación con la fabricación, el tráfico y el uso ilícitos de drogas, la Junta determina las deficiencias de los sistemas de fiscalización nacionales e internacionales y contribuye a corregir esas situaciones. La Junta también tiene a su cargo la evaluación de los productos químicos utilizados en la fabricación ilícita de drogas, a fin de determinar si deben ser sometidos a fiscalización internacional.

En cumplimiento de esas obligaciones, la Junta:

a) Administra un sistema de previsiones de las necesidades de estupefacientes y un sistema de presentación voluntaria de previsiones de las necesidades de sustancias sicotrópicas, y supervisa las actividades lícitas con drogas mediante un sistema de información estadística, con miras a ayudar a los gobiernos a lograr, entre otras cosas, un equilibrio entre la oferta y la demanda;

b) Vigila y promueve las medidas tomadas por los gobiernos para impedir la desviación de sustancias utilizadas frecuentemente en la fabricación ilícita de estupefacientes y sustancias sicotrópicas, y evalúa tales sustancias para determinar si es necesario modificar el ámbito de la fiscalización aplicada en virtud de los Cuadros I y II de la Convención de 1988;

c) Analiza la información proporcionada por los gobiernos, los órganos de las Naciones Unidas, los organismos especializados u otras organizaciones internacionales competentes, con miras a velar por que los gobiernos cumplan adecuadamente las disposiciones de los tratados internacionales sobre fiscalización de drogas, y recomienda las medidas correctivas necesarias;

d) Mantiene un diálogo permanente con los gobiernos para ayudarlos a cumplir las obligaciones que les imponen los tratados de fiscalización internacional de drogas y recomienda, cuando procede, que se proporcione asistencia técnica o financiera con esa finalidad.

La Junta debe pedir explicaciones en casos de violaciones aparentes de los tratados, a fin de proponer las medidas correctoras apropiadas a los gobiernos que no estén aplicando plenamente las disposiciones de los tratados, o que tropiecen con dificultades para aplicarlas y, cuando sea necesario, prestar asistencia a los gobiernos para superar esas dificultades. Ahora bien, si la Junta observa que no se han tomado las medidas necesarias para remediar una situación grave, puede señalar la cuestión a la atención de las partes interesadas, la Comisión de Estupefacientes y el Consejo Económico y Social. Los tratados facultan a la Junta, como último recurso, a recomendar a las partes que dejen de importar drogas del país que haya incurrido en falta, o que no exporten drogas a ese país, o ambas cosas. En todos los casos, la Junta actúa en estrecha cooperación con los gobiernos.

La Junta presta asistencia a las administraciones públicas de los países para que cumplan las obligaciones que les corresponden de conformidad con los convenios y convenciones. A ese fin, la Junta propone programas y seminarios de capacitación regional dirigidos a funcionarios de las administraciones que trabajan en la fiscalización de drogas y participa en dichos programas y seminarios.

Informes

Los tratados internacionales de fiscalización de drogas exigen que la JIFE prepare un informe anual sobre la labor que realiza. En el informe anual figura un análisis de la situación mundial de la fiscalización de drogas a fin de que los gobiernos tengan conocimiento de la existencia y las posibles situaciones que pueden poner en peligro los objetivos de los tratados internacionales de fiscalización de drogas. La JIFE señala a la atención de los gobiernos las lagunas y deficiencias que existen en la fiscalización nacional de drogas y en el cumplimiento de los tratados; asimismo hace sugerencias y recomendaciones con el fin de lograr mejoras tanto en el plano nacional como internacional. El informe anual se basa en la información que proporcionan los gobiernos a la JIFE, entidades de las Naciones Unidas y otras organizaciones. También se utiliza información que se obtiene por mediación de otras organizaciones internacionales, como la Interpol y la Organización Mundial de Aduanas, así como de organizaciones regionales.

El informe anual de la JIFE se complementa con informes técnicos detallados en los que figuran datos sobre el movimiento lícito de estupefacientes y sustancias sicotrópicas utilizados para fines médicos y científicos, junto con un análisis que realiza la JIFE de esos datos. Los datos son necesarios para el funcionamiento adecuado del sistema de fiscalización del movimiento lícito de estupefacientes y sustancias sicotrópicas, incluida su desviación a canales ilícitos. Además, de conformidad con lo dispuesto en el artículo 12 de la Convención de 1988, la Junta informa anualmente a la Comisión de Estupefacientes sobre la aplicación de este artículo. Dicho informe, en el que se recogen los resultados de la vigilancia de los precursores y los productos químicos que se utilizan con frecuencia en la fabricación ilícita de estupefacientes y sustancias sicotrópicas, se publica también como complemento al informe anual.